1982

Juvenile
Delinquency

Juvenile Delinquency

Second Edition

Martin R. Haskell
California State University at Long Beach

Lewis Yablonsky
California State University at Northridge

Rand McNally College Publishing Company • Chicago

78 79 80 10 9 8 7 6 5 4 3 2 1

Preface

JUVENILE "MISBEHAVIOR" is a social problem experienced by all members of society, young or old, at some time in their lives. Children generally perceive their socializing agents (parents, teachers, and others) as intruding on their autonomy as people, and adults usually consider the administration of some form of social control over children as a responsibility they must discharge. Most adult-youth conflict and interaction in the arena of "socializing" children is related to normative, perceptual, or value differences, is usually a productive experience, and therefore should not be considered as a social problem. A debatable line, therefore, is drawn between the point where normal misbehavior ends and juvenile delinquency begins.

Part of the demarcation between misbehavior and delinquency was determined by the development of a legal concept formulated around the turn of the century. Historically, the term *juvenile delinquency* came into legal use in the United States in 1899 with the establishment of the first juvenile court, and it was applied to all young people determined by the court to be delinquent. Prior to 1899, most disapproved behavior now labeled "delinquent" was treated as a family or, in some cases, a community discipline problem. Now, some eighty years after the development of the juvenile court concept, a vast array of social machinery has evolved to deal with juvenile deviance—including courts, detention, probation, child welfare programs, psychiatric clinics,

v

and gang and delinquency diversion programs. All of these programs are well intentioned, and most are humanistic; however, many have become so mechanized and bureaucratic that many children have become pawns in an ahuman system. In our analysis we will attempt to deal with all facets of the issue society has labeled as juvenile delinquency.

Because much of the phenomenon of juvenile delinquency is debatable and subjective, we feel it is useful for the students of our book to know something about the authors' perspective on the subject.

We have not restricted ourselves to the role of "armchair sociologists," although we have both been professors of academic sociology and have contemplated and developed theories about crime and delinquency for over twenty-five years. During this period, in addition to our teaching and research activity, we have both worked directly on the "firing line." One has served as head of a delinquency-prevention program with violent gangs, the other as head of an aftercare program, both in New York City. Each has directed psychodrama, role-training, and group psychotherapy sessions with juvenile delinquents, including those on probation and parole, in institutional settings and in the community. The authors have directed many educational programs for probation officers, parole agents, police officers, and others working in the field of corrections. Each has taught classes in criminology and juvenile delinquency in various universities and carried out a variety of juvenile delinquency research projects.

Both authors have had young people who have been labeled "juvenile delinquents" living in our homes at various times, experienced very positive feelings for these young people, and developed close personal relationships with them. This process has in some cases redirected these youngsters into more positive and productive lifestyles. Both have dealt with juvenile delinquents considered very dangerous by most people. All of these young people, the ones with whom we wouldn't hesitate to share our homes and the ones whom we considered dangerous, had been labeled "juvenile delinquents." They represent the extremes on a continuum that includes millions of young people who have been so labeled.

We concur with those in our society who see the need for change in the way we treat young people who violate our laws. Our major goals in this book are to describe juvenile delinquency as it exists in our society, to delineate the various patterns of delinquency, and to describe official and informal treatment approaches. We shall also present and discuss various relevant causal explanations of delinquency, and, finally, we shall present recommendations for changes in the treatment of youths labeled "delinquent."

We gratefully acknowledge our indebtedness to the many sociologists, psychologists, and other writers who have stimulated our thinking and supplied us with data. Donald Hartley, in particular, was most helpful in researching data for several chapters in this book. We are especially grateful to Dr. J. L. Moreno, who greatly influenced our thinking over many years. It was from him that we learned to regard all forms of deviant behavior as symptomatic of problems in interpersonal or intergroup relationships. We are also grateful to Professor Wellman J. Warner for all he contributed to our understanding of sociology and the applied role of the sociologist and for encouraging us to attempt to synthesize the disciplines of sociology, psychology, and law.

Many of the ideas about the criminal justice system advanced by Dr. Alexander B. Smith have been used directly and indirectly in this book, and we are grateful to him for enriching this volume with his perspective. We are also appreciative of the direct and indirect aid afforded us by many other colleagues too numerous to mention.

Lawrence J. Malley, Manager and Editor-in-Chief of Rand McNally College Publishing Company, provided us with editorial aid and spiritual guidance in our trilogy of books on crime and delinquency. Martha M. Urban, editor for the Rand McNally College Publishing Company, assisted us by her meticulous reading and copy editing of the first edition of this book; and Richard Hagle did a fine job of copy editing this second edition. The management of the book's overall production was proficiently handled by David Rust. We are most grateful to all of these people for their invaluable assistance.

We offer a special tribute to our wives, Rochelle Haskell and Donna Yablonsky, for their sympathetic understanding and valuable assistance in the preparation of this volume.

MARTIN R. HASKELL
LEWIS YABLONSKY

Contents

Tables

Figures

Part One

THE JUVENILE DELINQUENT IN SOCIETY

IN CONTEMPORARY LAW, the juvenile delinquent is distinguished from the adult criminal by several factors:

1. In most jurisdictions the cutoff point between delinquency and criminality is marked by age, usually eighteen.

2. Juvenile delinquents are generally considered less responsible for their behavior than adult offenders and hence less culpable.

3. In the handling of a juvenile delinquent, the emphasis is more on the youth's personality and the motivation for his illegal act than on the offense itself. The opposite is usually true of the adult criminal.

4. Treatment of the juvenile delinquent has been directed more toward therapeutic programs than punishment.

5. Although there have been some recent modifications, the judicial process for a juvenile has tended to deemphasize the legal aspects of due process and has been geared to a more informal and personalized court procedure.

This differential treatment of juveniles is not a recent phenomenon. Throughout recorded history we can find evidence of special treatment for young offenders and the recognition that such offenders constitute a special problem. The misbehavior of young people has been regarded as a problem apart from criminality as far back as the Code of Hammurabi in 2270 B.C. This code prescribed specific punishments for children who disowned their parents or ran away from home.[1] The Hebrews divided young people into three age categories—infant, prepubescent, and adolescent—and established increased penalties as offenders advanced to succeeding age groups. Old English law also indicated differential treatment for juvenile offenses by providing less severe punishment for persons under sixteen.[2] The founding of Hospes St. Michael in Rome for the rehabilitation of young people indicates a concern with this problem by the Vatican as early as the seventeenth century.[3]

Industrialization and urbanization, with their accompanying changes in family structure and function, have resulted in increased emphasis on juvenile delinquency. Parents working away from home have not been able to fulfill the socialization function (preparation of their children for life in the society) in the same way as families in prior periods of human history.

The increasingly impersonal relationships that accompany urbanization have produced an increased tendency to resort to formal social control of children. Misbehavior that had been traditionally handled by the family and friends in smaller communities now results in complaints to the police and petitions to courts in large urban areas. The juvenile court has become a significant social and legal instrument for defining and controlling juvenile delinquency.

---

[1] Albert Kocourek and John H. Wigmore, *Source of Ancient and Primitive Law, Evolution of Law: Select Readings on the Origin and Development of Legal Institutions* (Boston: Little, Brown, 1951), vol. 1.

[2] Frederick J. Ludwig, *Youth and the Law* (New York: Foundation Press, 1955).

[3] Paul W. Tappan, *Comparative Survey on Juvenile Delinquency,* Part 1: *North America* (New York: United Nations Department of Social Affairs, Division of Social Welfare, 1952), p. 9.

Chapter

1

The Nature and Extent of Juvenile Delinqency

IT IS DIFFICULT to define juvenile delinquency in terms of deviance from conduct norms because these norms vary from state to state, city to city, and neighborhood to neighborhood. Moreover, whether or not these norms are applied to a particular child may depend on the class position of his parents and the provisions of the law in his community. The community's response is also regulated by the policies of community leaders and law-enforcement officials.

As we have seen, legally a "juvenile delinquent" is a youth who has been so adjudged by a juvenile court. Even so, the behavior that leads to a judgment of juvenile delinquency is vaguely defined by the statutes, and the procedures followed by the various juvenile courts are not uniform. In the final analysis, the legal status of "delinquent" tends to depend more on the attitudes of parents, the police, the community, and the juvenile courts than on any specific illegal behavior of a child.

The difficulty of applying a legal definition to juvenile delinquency is well expressed by Ruth Cavan:

> In defining juvenile delinquency, laws are of little use. Usually laws are specific only in relation to serious adult offenses, such as murder, assault, robbery, burglary, and so forth. Children are delinquent if they

are found guilty in court of breaking any of the federal, state, or local laws designed to control adult behavior. Delinquency statistics, however, indicate that these serious offenses account for only a small proportion of the delinquencies of children. Most of the behavior that gets a child into trouble with the police and courts comes under a much less definite part of the law on juvenile delinquency. Examples are easy to find. The Illinois law defines as delinquent a child who is incorrigible or who is growing up in idleness, one who wanders about the streets in the night time without being on any lawful business, or one who is guilty of indecent or lascivious conduct. Laws in some other states are still more vague. New Mexico rests its definition on the word "habitual." A delinquent child is one who, by habitually refusing to obey the reasonable and lawful commands of his parents or other persons of lawful authority, is deemed to be habitually uncontrolled, habitually disobedient, or habitually wayward; or who habitually is a truant from home or school; or who habitually so deports himself as to injure or endanger the morals, health, or welfare of himself or others. In these laws there is no definition of such words or phrases as incorrigible, habitual, indecent conduct, or in the night time. How much disobedience constitutes incorrigibility? How often may a child perform an act before it is considered habitual?[1]

The attitudes and actions of parents exercise an important influence on whether or not a child is found to be incorrigible, disobedient, or a runaway. One mother may petition a juvenile court, allege that her son doesn't obey her, and have the child declared a juvenile delinquent; another may regard the same behavior as reflecting an independent spirit.

The policies of the police and the attitudes prevailing in the community also influence the action taken. The breaking of store windows on a main street in the course of an encounter of two groups of boys may or may not be classified as delinquency. If the boys are college sophomores horsing around, the incident is likely to be referred to the college for disciplinary action. If the two groups are defined by the police as gangs, the boys are likely to be arrested, taken before a juvenile court, and stigmatized as delinquent.

In a tri-city study in Pennsylvania,[2] Nathan Goldman determined that there were great variations of arrest practices on the part of the police. The status of juvenile delinquent depended on police attitudes, the racial background of the children, and often the time of the day or night the offense was committed. A lower class youth "steals" a car, but a middle class youth is more

---

[1]Ruth Shonle Cavan, "The Concepts of Tolerance and Contraculture as Applied to Delinquency," *Sociological Quarterly* 2(Fall 1961):243.

[2]Nathan Goldman, *The Differential Selection of Juvenile Offenders for Court Appearances* (New York: National Council on Crime and Delinquency, 1963).

likely to be a "borrower" in the view of the police. It is therefore not the behavior alone that results in the label "juvenile delinquent," but the policies of the police, often reflecting attitudes of significant people in the community. A significant factor therefore in the determination of who is delinquent is the element of "labeling." William B. Sanders comments as follows on the process of labeling:

> When we talk about a delinquent, we refer to someone who has been labeled as such by the juvenile justice system. Once a person has been labeled, he is often forced to play the role he has been given even though he may prefer another course. Labeling theory focuses on the *interactive* aspects of deviance in that it takes into account not only the delinquent activity and performer but also the others who come to define the situation and the actor as delinquent.
>
> To understand this theory, it is important to know a little about *symbolic interactionist theory.* First, labeling theory assumes that all reality is grounded in the symbols we use to talk about it, or, as W. I. Thomas (1923) put it, "If men define situations as real, they are real in their consequences." For example, if some juveniles are playing in front of a house when a bird flies against a window and breaks it, then flies away, the juveniles are believed to be responsible for the act, the police may be called, and as a consequence of this definition of the situation the juveniles may be labeled delinquents. Now, we might say that they were falsely accused, but the point is that their innocence of the act does not alter the consequences. They have been defined as delinquents, on the basis of this definition, they are treated as such.[3]

On this issue Joseph W. Rogers and M. D. Buffalo have examined modes of adaptation to a deviant label.[4] In their article they develop two principal indictments about labeling theory. The indictments they develop include: (1) viewing the labelee as overly passive and (2) viewing the labelee in individual rather than in collective analytical units. A position has been taken that labeling stigma has been emphasized to the neglect of systematically delineating "fighting back" techniques. Therefore, a nine-cell typology of adaptations is presented and conceived in terms of tactical and societal relationships considered with a social interaction frame of reference. The alternatives which have been pursued include: (1) acquiescence, (2) repudiation, (3) flight, (4) channeling, (5) evasion, (6) modification, (7) reinterpretation, (8) redefinition, and (9) alteration. The typology is developed as possessing entrances, motion

---

[3]William B. Sanders, *Juvenile Delinquency* (New York: Praeger, 1976), p. 51.
[4]Joseph W. Rogers and M. D. Buffalo, "Fighting Back: Nine Modes of Adaptation to a Deviant Label," *Social Problems* 22,1(October 1974):101–18.

within, and exits. Adaptation is not limited to single cells but is discussed in terms of hypothetical modular paths. The point Rogers and Buffalo make is that labeling is only as potent as the "labelee" allows.

The procedures of the juvenile court also significantly influence the determination of delinquency. The court is more likely to deal unofficially with children whose parents show an interest in them and come to defend them. It *must act officially*, however, in those cases in which parents present petitions charging their children with delinquency.

Another important determinant of delinquency status is the antisocial behavior treated by welfare departments and social work agencies. For example, in Washington, D.C., and New York City, a Central Register of Delinquents is maintained, including the names of all children in the community who are referred to agencies for behavior similar to that which might have brought them to the attention of a court. In analyzing the registration of delinquents in Washington, D.C., Sophia M. Robison found that less than half of all the children registered as delinquents were known to the juvenile court, and that although there was a decided increase in Washington's total child population, the percentage of delinquents *decreased* from 26.8 in 1954 to 19.1 in 1958. The New York City Youth Board Central Register revealed that juvenile court figures account for less than 12 percent of the total number of delinquents.[5]

Two St. Elizabeth Hospital psychiatrists, Drs. Samuel Yochelson and Stanton E. Samenow, corroborate this data in a study of delinquents labeled as mental patients. Each delinquent acknowledged to Yochelson and Samenow that during his life he had committed "literally thousands of crimes."[6] The doctors further assert that "the 'first offender' notion is a mistaken one. The criminal gets away with far more than is ever known by anyone else. By the time he is apprehended, he has more than likely committed hundreds, if not thousands, of offenses."

There are indications that less than half the children *known to have committed* acts classified as delinquent become part of the recorded statistics. Other studies indicate that similar behavior engaged in by middle class children *does not become known* to any agency, public or private. Austin L. Porterfield had students at three colleges in Texas record acts of delinquent behavior they had participated in while attending high school. Forty-three percent reported truancies, and 15 percent reported running away from home. Almost half of the college students admitted to petty thefts in their high school days. Porterfield reports that on the average each student might have been apprehended and charged with delinquency on at least eleven occasions, yet none of them had ever been charged with an offense. Porterfield compared

---

[5]Sophia Robison, *Juvenile Delinquency* (New York: Holt, Rinehart & Winston, 1960), pp. 47–50.
[6] *Washington Star,* August 25, 1976.

these student reports with offenses charged against 2,000 delinquents at the Fort Worth juvenile court. He found that 43 percent of the delinquent boys had been charged as truants and runaways, and 27 percent had been charged with theft.[7]

A comparison of the responses of high school boys in Seattle, Washington, with records of boys from that area committed to state training schools revealed little difference in the type or frequency of delinquent acts.[8]

On the basis of these studies, one may reasonably conclude that a large amount of delinquent behavior engaged in by middle class children goes undetected or is not recorded by enforcement agencies. However, there is considerable evidence to support the conclusion that an even greater amount of lower class delinquency is not reflected in our statistics. Two scholars have noted that

> working class youngsters also commit undetected and unrecorded delinquencies—probably more serious and more frequent. Careful studies of off-the-record delinquency in Passaic, the District of Columbia, and Cambridge-Somerville (Massachusetts) all show a very large amount of unofficial delinquency among lower class youth. One study of 114 underprivileged boys (40 of whom were official court delinquents) conservatively estimated that they had committed a minimum of 6,416 infractions of law in 5 years—only 95 of which became a matter of official complaint.[9]

While it is difficult to develop a definition of juvenile delinquency based on behavior that would be applicable to persons in all parts of the United States or, for that matter, in any state or city, one definition is clear: *a youth is defined as a juvenile delinquent when that status is conferred upon him by a court.*

A child may also become a juvenile delinquency statistic if he is arrested and charged by the police, even if his case is not referred to a court. Arrest data such as these provide the basis for FBI statements about the amount of delinquency in the United States. Yet about half of the children arrested are never referred to a court.[10]

The misbehavior that leads to an arrest and court action is often serious

---

[7]Austin L. Porterfield, *Youth in Trouble* (Fort Worth, Tex.: Leo Potishman Foundation, 1946).

[8]James F. Short, Jr. and F. Ivan Nye, "Extent of Unrecorded Juvenile Delinquency: Tentative Conclusions," *Journal of Criminal Law, Criminology, and Police Science* 49(July–August 1958): 296–302.

[9]H. L. Wilensky and C. N. Lebeaux, *Industrial Society and Social Welfare* (New York: Macmillan, 1958), p. 190. Reprinted with permission of the Macmillan Publishing Co. Copyright 1958 by Russell Sage Foundation.

[10]Federal Bureau of Investigation, U.S. Department of Justice, *Uniform Crime Reports for the United States, 1976* (Washington, D.C.: U.S. Government Printing Office, 1977), p. 220.

enough to constitute a crime if committed by an adult. It is often, however, an offense peculiarly applicable to children. Curfew violation, truancy, incorrigibility, and running away from home are the most common such offenses. Lower and upper age limits of juvenile delinquency are fixed by state and federal law and are not uniform. The federal government and thirty-three states set eighteen as the upper age limit. Seven states set the limit at seventeen, four at sixteen, and two at twenty-one. Offenders below the upper age limit are placed under the jurisdiction of a juvenile court.

When a child (any person below the upper age limit) is alleged to have committed a serious crime (murder, robbery, etc.), criminal courts usually have concurrent jurisdiction with juvenile courts. Prosecuting agencies may have the option of referring to *either* the criminal court or the juvenile court. In some jurisdictions they are required by law to prosecute the child in a criminal court. When this occurs, the criminal court judge may dismiss the case and refer it to a juvenile court. Therefore, when a serious crime is alleged, we cannot predict, by behavior alone, whether the child will be considered a criminal or a juvenile delinquent. The action of a law-enforcement agency is often the determining factor.

The Extent of Official Delinquency

It should be clear from the foregoing analysis that we cannot accurately determine who is a delinquent and who is not and that we therefore are not able to determine the extent of delinquency with any precision. However, despite the many problems involved, there are some official statistics that provide relevant clues to the incidence of delinquency.

The Federal Bureau of Investigation, beginning with its 1964 *Uniform Crime Reports,* has annually presented several tables on arrest rates for persons under eighteen years of age. Their expansion of these statistics with each succeeding year has proved of considerable value to students of juvenile delinquency.

The police maintain two types of statistics based on arrests. One is a count of the number of persons taken into custody for a particular crime; the unit of count is the *person.* The second is a record of the crimes cleared by arrest; the unit of count is the *offense,* without regard to the number of persons who are arrested and charged. A person may be arrested for a robbery, and in the course of the police investigation it is determined that he committed three burglaries as well. *All four offenses* would be considered cleared by arrest.

Persons under eighteen years of age were represented in 41.5 percent of all the arrests for Crime Index offenses. (See Table 1.1.) The arrest rates of persons under eighteen had gone up 144.1 percent between 1960 and 1975.

Since the age group from ten through seventeen constitutes only about 15 percent of the population, the arrest record of this age group is disproportionately high. The clearance data indicate, however, that about 36 percent of the serious crimes are cleared by arrest of persons under eighteen and that this percentage is nearly the same as it was in 1966 and has not changed significantly since 1960. When we consider that arrests of persons under eighteen have gone up 144.1 percent in the fifteen years 1960–75 while the percentage of *offenses cleared by arrest* has remained almost the same, we must conclude that the statistics reflect increased law-enforcement activity directed at persons under eighteen rather than increased criminal activity.[11]

Are persons under the age of eighteen who commit serious crimes juvenile delinquents, or are they young criminals? There is considerable difference of opinion on this subject. Albert K. Cohen implies that offenses committed by children, even when they are legally identical with those committed by adults, have a different meaning for them.

> The common expression "juvenile crime" has unfortunate and misleading connotations. It suggests that we have two kinds of criminals, young and old, but only one kind of crime. It suggests that crime has its meanings and its motives which are much the same for young and old; that the young differ from the old as the apprentice and the master differ at the same trade; that we distinguish the young from the old only because the young are less "set in their ways," less confirmed in the same criminal habits, more amenable to treatment, and more deserving, because of their tender age, of special consideration.
>
> The problem of the relationship between juvenile delinquency and adult crime has many facets. To what extent are the offenses of children and adults distributed among the same legal categories, "burglary," "larceny," "vehicle-taking," and so forth? To what extent, even when the offenses are legally identical, do these acts have the same meaning for children and adults? To what extent are the careers of adult criminals continuations of careers of juvenile delinquency? . . .
>
> What we see when we look at the delinquent subculture (and we must not even assume that this describes *all juvenile crime*) is that it is *nonutilitarian, malicious,* and *negativistic.* [12]

Sociologists have found that there are important differences in *self-concept* between potential delinquents and nondelinquents. The nondelinquents, unlike the potential delinquents, did not ever expect to be taken to

---

[11]FBI, *Uniform Crime Reports, 1972,* p. 111. See also Table 28, p. 122.

[12]Albert K. Cohen, *Delinquent Boys* (New York: Free Press, 1955), pp. 24–25. Copyright 1955 by The Free Press, a Corporation. Reprinted with permission of the Macmillan Publishing Co., Inc.

Table 1.1

Total Arrests of Persons Under 15, Under 18, Under 21, and Under 25 Years of Age, 1976 (10,119 agencies; 1976 estimated population 175,499,000)

Offense Charged	Grand Total All Ages	Number of Persons Arrested				Percentage			
		Under 15	Under 18	Under 21	Under 25	Under 15	Under 18	Under 21	Under 25
TOTAL	**7,912,348**	**665,781**	**1,973,254**	**3,259,174**	**4,490,039**	**8.4**	**24.9**	**41.2**	**56.7**
Criminal homicide:									
(a) Murder and nonnegligent manslaughter	14,113	190	1,302	3,414	6,013	1.3	9.2	24.2	42.6
(b) Manslaughter by negligence	2,650	43	275	808	1,362	1.6	10.4	30.5	51.4
Forcible rape	21,687	915	3,745	7,771	12,403	4.2	17.3	35.8	57.2
Robbery	110,296	10,156	36,990	62,269	83,856	9.2	33.5	56.5	76.0
Aggravated assault	192,753	9,552	32,678	60,837	93,481	5.0	17.0	31.6	48.5
Burglary—breaking or entering	406,821	78,275	209,396	290,597	342,917	19.2	51.5	71.4	84.3
Larceny-theft	928,078	173,535	399,235	560,812	684,610	18.7	43.0	60.4	73.8
Motor vehicle theft	110,708	14,726	58,279	79,266	92,481	13.3	52.6	71.6	83.5
Violent crime[a]	338,849	20,813	74,715	134,291	195,753	6.1	22.0	39.6	57.8
Property crime[b]	1,445,607	266,536	666,910	930,675	1,120,008	18.4	46.1	64.4	77.5
Subtotal for above offenses	1,787,106	287,392	741,900	1,065,774	1,317,123	16.1	41.5	59.6	73.7
Other assaults	354,010	25,907	69,904	121,319	182,743	7.3	19.7	34.3	51.6
Arson	14,534	4,626	7,601	9,443	10,831	31.8	52.3	65.0	74.5
Forgery and counterfeiting	55,791	1,090	6,681	17,171	30,663	2.0	12.0	30.8	55.0
Fraud	161,429	879	4,614	21,724	56,490	.5	2.9	13.5	35.0

Embezzlement	8,218	103	525	1,507	3,456	1.3	6.4	18.3	42.1
Stolen property: buying, receiving, possessing	92,055	8,142	28,940	48,749	64,738	8.8	31.4	53.0	70.3
Vandalism	175,082	60,569	109,712	133,016	148,266	34.6	62.7	76.0	84.7
Weapons: carrying, possessing, etc.	121,722	4,549	19,649	39,689	61,787	3.7	16.1	32.6	50.8
Prostitution and commercialized vice	58,648	205	2,570	17,256	37,208	.3	4.4	29.4	63.4
Sex offenses (except forcible rape and prostitution)	51,776	3,779	9,902	16,782	24,974	7.3	19.1	32.4	48.2
Narcotic drug laws	500,540	15,514	119,522	262,529	381,007	3.1	23.9	52.4	76.1
Gambling	65,437	392	2,547	7,793	14,540	.6	3.9	11.9	22.2
Offenses against family and children	58,249	1,595	4,198	12,569	22,986	2.7	7.2	21.6	39.5
Driving under the influence	837,910	254	17,264	112,871	243,539	c	2.1	13.5	29.1
Liquor laws	302,943	9,679	108,934	206,607	236,547	3.2	36.0	68.2	78.1
Drunkenness	1,071,131	3,866	39,750	144,977	275,510	.4	3.7	13.5	25.7
Disorderly conduct	545,639	35,845	113,898	222,482	323,801	6.6	20.9	40.8	59.3
Vagrancy	32,731	1,741	5,848	11,956	19,025	5.3	17.9	36.5	58.1
All other offenses (except traffic)	1,330,969	107,901	295,952	513,901	757,747	8.1	22.2	38.6	56.9
Suspicion	31,298	2,363	8,213	15,929	21,928	7.6	26.2	50.9	70.1
Curfew and loitering law violations	88,601	24,217	88,601	88,601	88,601	27.3	100.0	100.0	100.0
Runaways	166,529	65,173	166,529	166,529	166,529	39.1	100.0	100.0	100.0

SOURCE: Federal Bureau of Investigation, *Uniform Crime Reports for the United States, 1976* (Washington, D.C.: U.S. Government Printing Office, 1977), Table 33, p. 183.

[a] Violent crime is offenses of murder, forcible rape, robbery and aggravated assault.

[b] Property crime is offenses of burglary, larceny-theft and motor vehicle theft.

[c] Less than one-tenth of 1 percent.

juvenile court or jail.[13] The nondelinquent boys tended to view themselves as good, while the potentially delinquent viewed themselves as bad. Within the potentially delinquent group there were important differences in self-concept found between boys who had previous legal involvement and those who had not had such contact.[14]

In an effort to further understand the relationship between self-concept and delinquency, two Canadian sociologists, James C. Hackler and John L. Hagan, attempted to lower the high delinquency rate among 240 fourteen- and fifteen-year-old Seattle boys.[15] They worked with youths from four urban housing developments through the Opportunities for Youth Project. Most of the boys were encouraged to see themselves as capable and productive (i.e., nondelinquent) either through paid participation in a group work program (gardening in city parks, etc.) or through helping to evaluate teaching machines for use with younger children. One group of boys went through both the work program and the teaching-maching experience while the rest served as nonparticipating controls.

Three years after the one-year project had ended, Hackler and Hagan reviewed police records to see how their protégés had fared. Compared to the controls, they discovered a slight decrease in delinquency among those who had evaluated the teaching machines but a small increase among those involved in the work program. A deeper probe into the boys' individual characteristics revealed that those who were black, less intelligent, and initially rated as "bad" by their teachers, and who thought their mothers, teachers and friends perceived them as "bad" were particularly vulnerable to a negative impact resulting from the work program. The weekly projects did not heal the boys' already severely bruised ego and low self-concept and did not significantly affect their propensity to be delinquent.

A person's self-concept is in large part a reflection of the images others have of him. Thus, if the police, the courts, and the community regard an individual as a delinquent and treat him accordingly, he is likely to think of himself as a delinquent.

Apart from his self-concept, an arrest record often very directly proves to be a serious handicap to a young person—this despite the fact that many of those arrested by the police *are not necessarily guilty and in many cases are not even turned over to courts for prosecution.* Some of the reasons advanced for failure to turn over an offender to a court are: failure of the victim to

---

[13]Walter C. Reckless, Simon Dinitz, and Barbara Kay, "The Self Component in Potential Delinquency and Potential Non-Delinquency," *American Sociological Review* 22(October 1957):566–570.

[14]Reckless, Dinitz, and Kay, "The Self Component," p. 569.

[15]Derived from a summarized report of research by James C. Hackler and John L. Hagan, *Human Behavior* (September 1975).

cooperate in the prosecution; release of the arrested person with a warning; insufficient evidence to support a formal charge; police determination that the arrested person did not commit the offense.[16] Of all juveniles taken into custody by the police in 1976, almost half were handled within the police department and released *without formal charge or referral to any court.* Most of the rest were referred to juvenile courts. (See Table 1.2.)

Data pertaining to the cases referred to juvenile courts, such as the number of cases referred, the reasons for referral, and the dispositions made, were contained in *Juvenile Court Statistics,* published annually by the Children's Bureau of the U.S. Department of Health, Education, and Welfare. The number of juvenile delinquency cases referred to courts was calculated from reports of a national sample of 502 juvenile courts considered representative of the country as a whole. On the basis of these reports, it was estimated that 697,000 delinquency cases were handled by juvenile courts in the United States in 1965. Since the same child may have been referred more than once during the year, the estimated number of *different children* involved in these cases was somewhat lower.[17] The Children's Bureau ceased publishing *Juvenile Court*

Table 1.2

Police Disposition of Juvenile Offenders
Taken into Custody in 1976, in Percentages

Disposition	Percentage
Handled within department and released.	39.0
Referred to juvenile court jurisdiction	53.4
Referred to welfare agency	1.6
Referred to other police agency.	1.7
Referred to criminal or adult court	4.4
Total	100.0

SOURCE: Based on data contained in *Uniform Crime Reports, 1976*, Table 57, p. 220.

---

[16]FBI, *Uniform Crime Reports, 1976.*

[17]*Juvenile Court Statistics, 1966,* Children's Bureau Statistical Series no. 61 (Washington, D.C.: U.S. Government Printing Office, 1967), p. 9.

Statistics in 1966. The task was taken over in 1968 by the Youth Development and Delinquency Prevention Administration, an agency of the Social and Rehabilitative Service of the Department of Health, Education and Welfare, and that agency published its first *Juvenile Court Statistics* in 1970.

Reports from juvenile courts serving nineteen of the thirty largest cities in the country, indicate that over 42 percent of the offenses for which juveniles were referred to court in 1965 were those against property: larceny, auto theft, burglary, robbery, and vandalism. An additional 8.4 percent were offenses against persons: homicide, rape, assault, and sex offenses; and 26.4 percent were offenses applicable to juveniles only: running away, being "ungovernable," truancy, violation of curfew, etc. Over half of the delinquency cases were disposed of "nonjudicially," that is, without the filing of a petition.[18] It should be noted, however, that even in those cases disposed of judicially, there is no indictment, no criminal trial, and *no finding of guilt of a crime.* Although a petition may allege that a youth committed a burglary, the procedure of the juvenile court is flexible enough to permit consideration of matters completely extraneous to the issue of whether or not he did in fact commit the burglary. *The juvenile court cannot convict him of the crime of burglary.* It can merely find him to be a juvenile delinquent. Judicial cases involving approximately one-fourth of the juveniles were dismissed. About half of the judicial cases were disposed of by placing the juvenile on probation.[19]

All of these sources of information about juvenile delinquency have defects. Yet in total, the varied data give many important clues to the nature and extent of juvenile delinquency.

Trends in Juvenile Delinquency

Since a relatively small percentage of the children who engage in misbehavior achieve the status of delinquent or become part of our juvenile delinquency statistics, *a rise in statistics does not necessarily indicate an increase in antisocial behavior.* It often simply reflects changes in family responses to children who do not conform to the expectations of their parents.

The family in the urban industrial society has turned more and more to community resources and public authorities for assistance in performing its traditional functions. People who perceive the law not primarily as an instrument for the punishment of offenders, but rather as a means for the salvation of misbehaving children, tend to relinquish their customary controls over children to juvenile courts.

The rise in statistics may also reflect changes in community policies or

---

[18] *Juvenile Court Statistics, 1971,* Social and Rehabilitative Service Publication no. (SRS)73-03452 (Washington, D.C.: U.S. Government Printing Office, 1972).

[19] *Juvenile Court Statistics, 1966,* p. 10.

police effectiveness. What was formerly "unknown" antisocial behavior may become "known" delinquent behavior owing to increased police activity. More of the known delinquency may be brought to the attention of courts.

On the basis of reports received from juvenile courts, the Children's Bureau from 1930 to 1966 periodically published estimates of the number of juvenile delinquents in the United States. In 1930 the estimate was 200,000 delinquents. By 1950 the estimate was 435,000; by 1956, 450,000; 1963, 601,-000; and by 1965, 697,000 (excluding traffic violations).[20] The trends appear to reflect changes in economic conditions:

1929–1935:	downward (depression)
1938–1944:	upward (World War II)
1946–1948:	downward (post-World War II)
1948–present:	generally upward, with periodic recessions

Peaks in delinquency statistics were reached in 1943 and 1945. Notably, the number of court cases in 1945 was 70 percent above the figure for 1938. At the same time, the number of children ten to seventeen years of age actually decreased slightly. Beginning with the end of the war, juvenile court cases dropped spectacularly from 1945 to 1948. With the onset of the cold war in 1948, an even more spectacular upward trend began, and the child population also began to increase. The increase in delinquency cases cannot, however, be attributed directly to the increase in child population because the ratio was in fact not direct nor were increases in delinquency and child population proportional.

Between 1950 and 1957 the trend in court cases again increased out of proportion to the increase in youth population, for while the number of youths aged ten to seventeen increased 27 percent, the number of court cases increased 115 percent.[21] Juvenile court statistics after this date, as we have previously noted, were reorganized in 1957, so that data after that date are not really comparable with earlier data. Today, court statistics are a far better index of the extent of "official" juvenile delinquency and the use of the courts. (See Figure 1.1.)

Juvenile Court Statistics presents a picture of the frequency with which the courts are used in handling juvenile delinquency. Data are no longer available in the national juvenile court statistical reporting program on the types of offenses for which juveniles are referred to the courts. To examine these, one needs to rely on the data on police arrests of juveniles reported by

[20]*Juvenile Court Statistics, 1966,* p. 12.

[21]Ruth Shonle Cavan, *Juvenile Delinquency* (Philadelphia: Lippincott, 1962), p. 30.

Figure 1.1

Trend in Juvenile Court Delinquency Cases and
Child Population 10 to 17 Years of Age, 1957–71

(Semilogarithmic Scale)

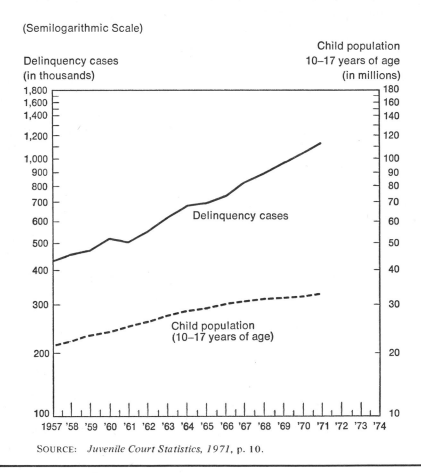

SOURCE: *Juvenile Court Statistics, 1971*, p. 10.

the Federal Bureau of Investigation in its *Uniform Crime Reports.* These
include arrests for nonstatus offenses, which would be crimes if committed by
adults, as well as two juvenile-status offenses (running away and curfew violations). Inasmuch as the police are the major source of referral of delinquency
cases to juvenile courts, the offenses for which juveniles are arrested should
pretty well represent most offenses for which juveniles are referred to court.

In the 1975 edition of *Uniform Crime Reports,* the Federal Bureau of
Investigation reported that arrests of juveniles under eighteen years of age, for

all types of offenses combined, more than doubled (144.1 percent) between 1960 and 1975. For a group of serious offenses selected as being most reliably reported (criminal homicide, forcible rape, burglary, robbery, aggravated assault, larceny, and auto theft), the combined increase between 1960 and 1975 was 144 percent. When offenses against the person (homicide, forcible rape, aggravated assault, and robbery), which are generally accepted as being the most serious crimes, are selected from the reliably reported group, the increase between 1960 and 1975 was 293.4 percent.[22]

As determined from police arrest data, all types of offenses—serious as well as relatively minor—have been increasing, with the most serious ones showing substantially greater proportionate increases. Serious offenses against persons, however, still represent only about 3 percent of all arrests of juveniles.

Since both the *Juvenile Court Statistics* and the *Uniform Crime Reports* reflect only the extent to which juvenile misbehavior comes to the official attention of legal authorities, neither represents precisely the extent or trends of juvenile delinquency. Nevertheless, both indexes have shown a similarity in their delinquency trends over a long period of time extending back to World War II, despite their differences in definitions, units of count, and extent of coverage.

Both show an upward surge during World War II, a decrease immediately afterward, and a steady climb upward since 1949. The *Uniform Crime Reports* depicts a 3 percent increase in juvenile arrests in 1965; the *Juvenile Court Statistics* shows an increase in delinquency cases of 2 percent. Thus, if used carefully and knowledgeably, both series of data can be utilized effectively in estimating official delinquency.

Trends of change in the volume of delinquent offenses have a tendency to be gradual, not abrupt or dramatic. Too often, seeming increases in official delinquency reflect changes more apparent than real. However, socioeconomic cataclysms do generate observable changes in the nature, extent, and volume of delinquent behavior, further manifested in higher official rates. Wars and economic depressions are two such portents of change. During World War II there was a significant increase in delinquency rates, 54 percent for boys and 94 percent for girls.

There are many possible reasons for this wartime increase, perhaps the most salient being the disruption of family life through the employment of mothers and the absence of fathers in the armed forces. In addition, many working parents kept irregular hours because of the introduction of multiple work shifts and extended working hours, which left many children unattended and open to opportunities for misconduct that might not otherwise have occurred.

The war was also responsible for internal migrations and decreases in high school enrollment; many pupils went to work in industry and did not

[22]FBI, *Uniform Crime Reports, 1976,* p. 182.

Table 1.3

Total Arrest Trends, 1960–75
(2,726 agencies; 1975 estimated population 96,429,000[a])

| | Number of Persons Arrested | | | | | | | | |
| | Total All Ages | | | Under 18 Years of Age | | | 18 Years of Age and Over | | |
Offense Charged	1960	1975	Percent Change	1960	1975	Percent Change	1960	1975	Percent Change
TOTAL	3,454,216	4,537,390	+31.4	485,007	1,184,105	+144.1	2,969,209	3,353,285	+12.9
Criminal homicide:									
(a) Murder and nonnegligent manslaughter	4,766	11,083	+132.5	359	1,117	+211.1	4,407	9,966	+126.1
(b) Manslaughter by negligence	1,855	1,509	−18.7	138	207	+50.0	1,717	1,302	−24.2
Forcible rape	7,006	13,976	+99.5	1,247	2,519	+102.0	5,759	11,457	+98.9
Robbery	30,066	96,900	+222.3	7,389	35,099	+375.0	22,677	61,801	+172.5
Aggravated assault	53,213	121,775	+128.8	6,347	21,617	+240.6	46,866	100,158	+113.7
Burglary—breaking or entering	118,703	263,634	+122.1	57,375	136,242	+137.5	61,328	127,392	+107.7
Larceny-theft	201,780	573,555	+184.2	96,610	256,717	+165.7	105,170	316,838	+201.3
Motor vehicle theft	54,354	76,227	+40.2	33,204	41,221	+24.1	21,150	35,006	+65.5
Violent crime[b]	95,051	243,734	+156.4	15,342	60,352	+293.4	79,709	183,382	+130.1
Property crime[c]	374,837	913,416	+143.7	187,189	434,180	+131.9	187,648	479,236	+155.4
Subtotal for above offenses	471,743	1,158,659	+145.6	202,669	494,739	+144.1	269,074	663,920	+146.7

Other assaults	130,639	217,242	+66.2	12,734	43,258	+239.7	117,955	173,984	+47.5
Forgery and counterfeiting	22,639	35,504	+56.4	1,643	4,165	+153.5	21,056	31,339	+48.8
Fraud and embezzlement	34,806	86,812	+149.4	890	3,222	+262.0	33,916	83,590	+146.5
Stolen property; buying, receiving, possessing	9,753	61,769	+533.3	2,658	19,579	+636.6	7,095	42,190	+494.6
Weapons; carrying, possessing, etc.	32,337	84,830	+161.9	6,377	13,639	+113.9	26,010	71,191	+173.7
Prostitution and commercialized vice	25,236	43,358	+71.8	431	2,037	+372.6	24,805	41,321	+66.6
Sex offenses (except forcible rape and prostitution)	43,531	32,893	-24.4	8,758	6,328	-27.7	34,773	26,565	-23.6
Narcotic drug laws	25,857	291,061	+1,025.7	1,458	65,864	+4,417.4	24,399	225,197	+823.0
Gambling	113,039	39,669	-64.9	1,570	1,379	-12.2	111,519	38,290	-65.7
Offenses against family and children	42,635	28,716	-32.7	710	3,326	+368.5	41,975	25,390	-39.5
Driving under the influence	153,726	416,719	+171.1	1,229	7,475	+508.2	152,497	409,244	+168.4
Liquor laws	88,845	126,661	+42.6	16,976	49,528	+191.8	71,869	77,133	+7.3
Drunkenness	1,299,140	695,720	-46.4	13,081	22,078	+68.8	1,286,059	673,642	-47.6
Disorderly conduct	387,286	346,343	-10.6	47,850	65,082	+36.0	339,436	281,261	-17.1
Vagrancy	129,786	23,697	-81.7	8,291	2,972	-64.2	121,495	20,725	-82.9
All other offenses (except traffic)	442,958	847,737	+91.4	157,682	379,434	+140.6	285,276	468,303	+64.2
Suspicion (not included in totals)	122,033	19,142	-84.3	22,820	4,450	-80.5	99,213	14,692	-85.2

SOURCE: FBI, *Uniform Crime Reports, 1975*, p. 182.

a Based on comparable reports from 2,090 cities representing 82,195,000 population and 636 counties representing 14,234,000 population.

b Violent crime is offenses of murder, forcible rape, robbery and aggravated assault.

c Property crime is offenses of burglary, larceny-theft and motor vehicle theft.

return to school. Many teaching staffs were substandard; school terms and days were shortened to enable students to work a full shift after school. Illegal child labor existed, and breakdowns occurred in community relations and services in areas flooded by workers following migrating industries. Inundated with tremendous population influxes, many small cities were unable to provide housing, sanitation, education, and recreation facilities for the immigrants. Trailer parks, overcrowded schools, and unsupervised children proliferated in small cities especially. All of these events and changes undoubtedly influenced the rise in delinquency rates during the war.

While economic conditions and accompanying changes in society seem to exert a broad influence on the nature (offenses) and extent (rate, volume, frequency) of juvenile delinquency, the studies that have thus far attempted to decipher the nature of this relationship have been conflicting and inconclusive.

Major fluctuations in the business cycle—economic depression and prosperity, especially as these conditions affect the economic conditions of families and communities—seem to have far-reaching effects on delinquency trends. The direct relationship between the family and economic fluctuations is clear. The more subtle and indirect effects, however, are more obscure. Certain types of crimes against property increase in periods of depression and extensive unemployment. We might expect certain types of nonutilitarian crimes, crimes for fun and kicks and excitement (joyriding in a borrowed car), during periods of prosperity. Where crimes relative to economic depression could be ameliorative—that is, supplementary of food and income—crimes committed during periods of prosperity seem to reflect the ongoing character of good times.

David Bogen, in an early study of delinquency, examined the relation of juvenile court cases to economic trends in Los Angeles County from 1925 through 1941, certainly a comprehensively eventful era. He arranged a business index of this period of time, juxtaposed with school population and boys' and girls' court cases, and concluded that delinquency cases closely paralleled fluctuations in the business cycle.[23] Harry M. Shulman observed the drop in delinquency rates during periods of economic depression by measuring court statistics during the Great Depression that began in 1929 and found that the rate of court cases for boys dropped from 100 per 100,000 in the year of the stock-market crash to 74 per 100,000 in 1936. The rate for girls also declined appreciably.[24] John O. Reinemann studied the relationship between juvenile delinquency and the business cycle in Philadelphia covering a similar period in history and came to different conclusions. He found that: (1) delinquency is only of average proportions during reasonably high prosperity; (2) delinquency is high during depression periods; (3) delinquency is low in periods of fairly normal economic development when there is neither prosperity nor

---

[23]David Bogen, "Juvenile Delinquency and Economic Trends," *American Sociological Review* 9(April 1944):178–84.

[24]Harry M. Shulman, *Juvenile Delinquency* (New York: Harper & Row, 1961), pp. 56–60.

depression; and (4) delinquency is highest during extreme prosperity.[25] The contradictory findings may be attributed to differences in areas studied, types of cases used, and methods of analysis and reporting; in short, the research designs.

Another factor that at one time in the history of the United States affected the delinquency rate was immigration. Statistics on juvenile delinquency are no longer significantly affected by waves of immigrants coming to the United States. The combined effects of World War I, restrictive immigration legislation in the early 1920s, the depression of the 1930s, and World War II have resulted in a major reduction in the number of immigrants.

In the past, foreign immigrant groups that came to this country generally settled in colonies established and inhabited by members of their own nationalities. The immigrants themselves did not become much of a law-enforcement problem, but their children did constitute a sizable problem. These young people were often torn between the values and traditions of their parents and those of their newly adopted homeland. They were marginal men, under pressure to conform to new norms of behavior and aspiring to values of a new culture yet inhibited by the "right ways" of the old cultures. This adjustment process often led to a loss of effective social control of behavior. They suffered from what Sellin has called "culture conflict."

These first-generation children were neither completely American nor foreign. Their allegiance was in part to both associations and cultures. Being inculcated with the success goals of the dominant majority while to a great extent being deprived of equal opportunity to attain them fostered alienation and animosity. At the same time, these people, adults and children alike, were being judged by the standards of the American society. This in turn produced schism and incongruity between the two groups. In this kind of situation, with few alternatives and little recourse to lawful avenues to success, the children often turned to deviant means of achievement. This explains the high rates of immigrant children's court cases during the first part of this century.

This overall trend has diminished, except for Negroes and Puerto Ricans, who are recent migrants to troubled urban areas. The children of these groups produce high rates of delinquency today as measured by arrest rates and referrals to courts. This is largely a result of urban problems and culture conflict.

In an overview study of delinquency trends following World War II, Negley K. Teeters and David Matza came to the conclusion that "although official statistics perhaps overrate the increase in delinquency rates, there has, nevertheless, been some real increase." They further point out that delinquency rates in the past probably have been at certain times higher than they are today. "This means that unless we adhere to the view that modern times

---

[25]John O. Reincmann, "Juvenile Delinquency in Philadelphia and Economic Trends," *Temple University Law Quarterly* (April 1947).

are decadent and some unspecified era in the past the repository of all things good, there is reason to suppose that delinquency rates were higher in other periods. . . ." In one large metropolitan area they found that delinquency rates were twice as high in World War I as in World War II.[26]

It is apparent that there is a trend toward an increase in delinquency. The evidence indicates, however, that delinquency has been at least as high and as serious in other periods of the history of the United States.

In 1970, the number of juvenile delinquency cases handled by juvenile courts was 1,052,000. Even this figure represented only a fraction of the total number of children dealt with by the juvenile justice system. According to Commissioner Robert J. Gemignani of the Youth Development and Delinquency Prevention Administration, almost four million youths had a police contact in 1970, and two million of those contacts resulted in arrests, half of which were referred to juvenile courts. Of the million referred to juvenile courts, about half were counseled and released with no further action; the other half were dealt with officially through some form of court hearing.[27]

Commissioner Gemignani further estimated that unless more effective strategies were adopted, there would be nearly 1,500,000 juvenile delinquency cases handled by courts in 1977. He advocated a strategy for national adoption to divert young people from the juvenile justice system, "First, by providing prevention programs; and, second, by offering community-based rehabilitation programs as alternatives to placement of delinquent youths in traditional correctional facilities."[28]

The objectives of the Youth Services Systems supported by the Youth Development and Delinquency Prevention Administration are as follows:

1. Provide more socially acceptable and meaningful roles for youth.
2. Divert youth away from the juvenile justice systems into alternate programs.
3. Reduce negative labeling. This involves diverting children from those institutions that apply the labels—courts and correctional institutions.
4. Reduce youth-adult alienation. It is assumed that a reduction in youth-adult alienation would bring about an increased participation by youths in the total community's activities and result in lower rates of official delinquency.[29]

---

[26]Negley K. Teeters and David Matza, "The Extent of Delinquency in the United States," *Journal of Negro Education* 28(Summer 1959):200–218.

[27]Robert J. Gemignani, "Youth Services Systems," *Federal Probation* 36(December 1972):48–53.

[28]Gemignani, "Youth Services Systems," p. 49.

[29]Gemignani, "Youth Services Systems," p. 52.

Conclusion

From all of these observations it should be concluded that the nature and extent of juvenile delinquency is a complex phenomenon. In order to understand "who is the delinquent," there are many broad social issues that require assessment. These include: (1) the definitions of a specific community regarding deviance, (2) the specificity of the law in a particular area, (3) the personality and concept of the juvenile judge in a particular jurisdiction, (4) the specific practices of law enforcement in a given area, and (5) in large measure the definitions of parents about the behavior of their children. Generally speaking, official juvenile delinquency is directly related to the degree to which any given community wants to relate deviant behavior to the socialization process or to the official agencies that define juvenile delinquency.

Chapter
2

The
Juvenile
Court

As RECENTLY as the latter part of the nineteenth century, children were tried for their crimes exclusively in criminal courts in both England and the United States. The age of the child was considered a factor in determining whether or not he should be held responsible for his acts, but in most other respects his treatment resembled that accorded an adult charged with a crime. He was likely to be detained in the same jail as an adult criminal, tried by the same court, and sent to the same correctional facility.

The common law exempted children under seven years of age from responsibility for criminal behavior. A child below the age of seven could not be found guilty of committing a criminal act because of the absence of one essential element: *mens rea,* or criminal intent. But children between the ages of seven and fourteen might be tried and convicted. They were *presumed* to be incapable of formulating an intent to commit a crime, but this presumption could be overcome by evidence to the contrary presented by the prosecution.

Chancery courts, which had their origin in fifteenth-century England, also dealt with problems of children. English common law imposed a duty upon parents to provide support, supervision, and care of their children. It also provided that parents had a right to custody of their children unless they defaulted in their duties. Chancery courts were created by the king, as *parens patriae,* father of his country, to protect children in need of protection. Women and children could not own property in the England of that period. If they were left without support as a result of divorce, abandonment, or death of the husband or father, they were often destitute. The chancery court, a court of equity, assumed the duty of seeing to it that parents, particularly fathers, carried out their obligations to spouses and children. The *welfare of the wife or child* was the sole and fundamental consideration of action by the court.

The courts did not normally deal with cases in which misbehavior of children was alleged. They protected children who would now be referred to as "neglected" or "dependent" and were concerned principally with the administration of property or the ordering of financial support for dependents. They acted *in loco parentis,* in place of the parents, taking whatever steps they deemed necessary to provide for their needs. They acted *on behalf of the child.* In the United States, courts of equity, applying English common law, traditionally have acted to protect the health, morals, and welfare of children where necessary to *prevent* injury to the child.[1]

In 1825, with the establishment of the House of Refuge in New York City, many states began providing correctional facilities for children separate from those dealing with adults. The House of Refuge was restricted to children adjudged offenders by criminal courts. By 1960 there were sixteen such specialized institutions in the United States. They had been established at the insistence of reformers who objected to having children confined with adult criminals in jails and penitentiaries and subjected to potentially harmful associations and influences.

In 1841, largely owing to the efforts of John Augustus, a Boston shoemaker who helped children in trouble, probation was first tried as a method of treating offenders outside of a correctional institution and under the supervision of a criminal court. In 1869, Massachusetts officially established probation for children and provided for the supervision of juvenile delinquents.

By the end of the nineteenth century, as the states provided specialized treatment for children in training schools, the criminal courts began to sentence children to these schools instead of to prison and to place children on probation for minor offenses. Persons interested in social reform actively sought the establishment of a specialized court for children organized around objectives significantly different from those of the criminal courts. They wanted a court that would understand the child, diagnose his problems, and provide treatment that would restore him to a constructive role in the community. The *welfare of the child* was considered more important than the question of guilt or innocence of an offense. It is these purposes that led the reformers

---

[1] Negley K. Teeters and John O. Reinemann, *The Challenge of Delinquency* (New York: Prentice-Hall, 1950).

to seek the establishment of the juvenile court and that continue to motivate its proponents today.[2]

The first statute defining *delinquent child* and creating a juvenile court to deal with dependent, neglected, and delinquent children was enacted in Illinois in 1899. The court established by this statute began operation in Cook County (Chicago) in June of that year. The Latin phrase *parens patriae* best summarizes the legal and social philosophy upon which its policies were based. The establishment of the juvenile court thus came as a logical sequel to the creation and expansion of separate correctional facilities for children and the introduction of probation as a method of treatment.

The Children's Bureau was created thirteen years after the first juvenile court and under the leadership of social workers exercised an important influence over the development of juvenile courts throughout the United States. By 1945, every state had passed laws providing for the differential treatment of juvenile delinquents.[3]

The juvenile court is *not* a criminal court, nor is it a chancery court, although as far as children are concerned it performs the functions of both. It is a *statutory court,* whose powers are provided for and limited by statute, and whose procedures are fixed by the judges of the court when they are not fixed by law.

Juvenile court statutes do not necessarily create specialized courts completely independent of the criminal or civil court system. In forty states, authority over juveniles rests wholly or in part in courts that are primarily engaged in some other function. Usually the judge who presides over a juvenile court spends most of his time as judge of a criminal court. In a few states and several large cities, there are completely differentiated juvenile courts. In most states, however, a child may be referred to either a juvenile court or a criminal court if he is charged with a serious offense. In twenty-two states the criminal courts have exclusive jurisdiction over homicides and other specified offenses. However, all states have statutes providing for juvenile courts, either specifying or permitting procedures that differ from those required in criminal courts. When a judge normally assigned to a criminal court sits as a juvenile court

---

[2]For a discussion of the assumption of these obligations by the juvenile courts, see Orman W. Ketcham, "The Unfulfilled Promise of the American Juvenile Court," in *Justice for the Child,* ed. Margaret K. Rosenheim (New York: Free Press, Macmillan, 1962), pp. 22–43; and H. H. Lou, *Juvenile Courts in the United States* (Chapel Hill: University of North Carolina Press, 1927), pp. 1–25.

[3]For a detailed discussion of the criminal law applicable to children, see Frederick B. Sussman, *Law of Juvenile Delinquency: The Laws of the Forty-Eight States* (New York: Oceana Publications, 1950); Paul W. Tappan, *Comparative Survey on Juvenile Delinquency,* Part I: *North America* (New York: United Nations Department of Social Affairs, Division of Social Welfare, 1952); and Robert G. Caldwell, "The Juvenile Court: Its Development and Some Major Problems," *Journal of Criminal Law, Criminology, and Police Science* 51(January–February 1961):493–511.

judge on a particular day of the week, that court *becomes a juvenile court for that day,* and the procedures followed are those legally prescribed for the juvenile court.

The Police Role and Juvenile Arrest

Children are brought into the processes of a juvenile court through what is known as a petition. A petition may be initiated by a parent or another adult; however, in most cases it is presented by a police officer. Children are often arrested by a regular police officer; however, in some police departments officers with special training in handling juveniles, variously known as "youth squads," or "juvenile officers," are assigned to delinquency work. A study by McKeachern and Bauzer concluded that the number of petitions requested for juvenile court varies according to the investigating policemen. They found that policemen handle three out of four apprehended delinquents without reference to court or probation officers.[4] The fact that three out of four cases are handled by police outside of the juvenile court gives the police considerable control over behavior defined as juvenile delinquency.

A study by Malcolm Klein, Susan Rosensweig, and Ronald Bates found juvenile arrest procedures vague and ambiguous.[5] The three researchers investigated the uniformity of juvenile arrest definitions and operations with three major issues current in criminology underlying their study: (1) translating legislative intent into efficient and just administrative or operational activities, (2) the problem of developing adequate information systems for criminal justice, and (3) reporting and making decisions on the current status and progress of agencies and programs. An empirical documentation of the disparate meanings that the common concept of juvenile arrest has to the various levels of people concerned was attempted. The collected data from forty-nine separate police departments in a large metropolitan county which included rural, suburban, and urban areas. Generally the stations were asked to report their arrest statistics to the state and federal government as well as to their local agencies. They found ambiguous guidelines and differential reporting forms in various police stations. There were different sets of criteria and statistics, making uniformity hard to achieve. Structured interviews with forty-five chiefs of police revealed less than 50 percent agreement that "booking" was the critical point in determining arrest. Booking does not correspond to the legal definition of either arrest or recording procedures. The chiefs' lack

---

[4]A. McKeachern and R. Bauzer, "Factors Related to Disposition in Juvenile Police Contacts," *Juvenile Gangs in Context,* ed. Malcolm V. Klein and Barbara G. Meyerhoff (Englewood Cliffs, N.J.: Prentice-Hall, 1967), pp. 148–60.

[5]Malcolm W. Klein, Susan Labin Rosensweig, and Ronald Bates, "The Ambiguous Juvenile Arrest," *Criminology* 13,1(May 1975):78–89.

of knowledge and interest in this issue seemed to indicate a general tendency for juvenile officers and bureaus to be relatively independent even in highly structured departments. One hundred and thirty juvenile officers and their supervisors filled out questionnaires, and seventy-seven juvenile officers, one in every station in the county, participated in a structured interview. Consistent with the chiefs' lack of clarity was the variation among juvenile officers in different and in the same departments. To some, an "arrest" was a field contact; to others it was bringing a suspect to the station, while for others it was considered a formal arrest. The authors can confirm similar findings based on their work with the police in New York.

In many cases police may handle juveniles outside of the police station court in a judicious way by talking to their parents or by reprimanding or advising the child; however, there is evidence to support the viewpoint that police contact with juveniles, especially in high-delinquency areas, is less than ideal.

In one analysis Barbara Tomson and Edna R. Fielder characterize police behavior vis-à-vis juveniles as "police press" and describe the interaction regarding juveniles as follows.[6]

Tomson and Fielder observe that in "high-delinquency areas" police are continually harassing youth who look delinquent, and therefore they note that police are considered enemies in lower class neighborhoods. The gang delinquent interprets the effect of this police attitude on his life in a way that results in a vicious circle: the delinquent becomes more of a "cop hater" and moves deeper into delinquency, and this causes the policeman to become more of a "delinquent hater."

Based on their analysis of the situation, Tomson and Fielder concluded that when the police apprehend a delinquent, they usually have several choices of action, and the choice they make varies among police departments. They delineate five alternatives open to the police: outright release, release and submission of a field interrogation report, official reprimand and release to parents or guardian, petition to the juvenile court, or arrest and confinement in juvenile hall. Treatment of the minor offender (who comprises 90 percent of the violations) depends on the youth's personal characteristics: group affiliation (Is he a gang member?), age, race, grooming, dress, and—most important —demeanor. Tomson and Fielder note a high correlation between cooperative demeanor (exhibited by contriteness, respectfulness, and fearfulness) and police leniency.

Constant police harassment of youths who match the delinquent stereotype results in much negative contact between such youths and the police. As the frequency of contacts increases, the process becomes routine, and youth

---

[6]Barbara Tomson and Edna R. Fielder, "Gangs: A Response to the Urban World," in *Gang Delinquency,* ed. Desmond S. Cartwright, Barbara Tomson, and Hersey Schwartz (Monterey, Calif.: Brooks/Cole, 1975), pp. 149–50.

lose their fear of police. They become indifferent and hostile—attitudes the police will interpret as characteristic of a hardened criminal—and the police will treat them severely, reinforcing the youth's hostilities. (In another study Piliavin and Briar conclude that the official delinquent is the result of the policeman's judgment made on the basis of the offender's image rather than on the basis of his offense.)

Negative attitudes between police and juveniles have long-term effects not only in determining the rate of juvenile delinquency but also in forming attitudes conducive to gang delinquency. Tomson and Fielder note that

> The juvenile delinquent's increasing indifference toward the police re-
> sults in his increasing contempt for the policeman's legitimate role. Once
> the delinquent begins to withdraw legitimacy, he no longer recognizes
> the right of the police to control him or the validity of the laws the police
> enforce.
>
> The policeman in a lower class neighborhood has more roles,
> flexibility, and importance than his counterpart in a middle class neigh-
> borhood. He appears in crisis situations, including ambulance calls or
> family fights. He has a more flexible role because inhabitants of lower
> class neighborhoods are not used to complaining about the police, in
> contrast to middle class neighborhoods.
>
> The policeman's importance as an agent of social control increases
> as traditional means of social control break down during slum develop-
> ment, yet he is always viewed with suspicion and distance. Even if he
> should become a parent substitute or role model, the relationship will be
> a formal secondary one rather than an informal primary one.[7]

Tomson and Fielder further note that the alienation of the police by motorization (auto rather than foot patrol), race, home area, and aggressive preventive patrols increases community distrust and suspicion of police: "The alienation of the police from the community can heighten a delinquent's tendency to withdraw attributions of legitimacy from the law." Some of these negative emotions about law and law enforcement are no doubt projected by juveniles onto the juvenile court and its procedures.

Juvenile Court Procedures

As we have noted, the juvenile court was from the outset intended to be primarily rehabilitative and operated in the interest of the child. It did not convict a person before it of a crime, but found him or her to be a "juvenile

---

[7]Tomson and Fielder, "Gangs," p. 150.

delinquent," a "dependent" child, or a "neglected" child in need of care and further official attention. The ideal was "individualized justice."

A typical juvenile court act provided for state control as a substitute for parental control and an informal proceeding instead of a trial. In 1920 a Children's Bureau publication listed the following as essential characteristics of the juvenile court:

1. Separate hearings for children's cases.
2. Informal or chancery procedure.
3. Regular probation service.
4. Separate detention of children.
5. Special court and probation records.
6. Provision for mental and physical examination.[8]

The procedures followed by the juvenile courts were borrowed from criminal courts, civil courts, administrative boards and agencies, and social agencies. The type of court and its organizational structure largely determined procedure. The following organizational forms developed:

1. *Independent specialized courts with jurisdiction over children.* These courts were organized on a citywide, countywide, or statewide basis. Probation services were usually supplied by the court or by the city, county, or state in which the court operated. This type of specialized juvenile court developed in California, New York, Illinois, and other states containing large urban centers. Statewide courts were established in Connecticut and Rhode Island, states occupying small areas with high population density.

2. *Family courts with jurisdiction over specialized offenses and relationships and over specified types of family conflict.* These courts, located largely in urban centers, provide services to children similar to those available in specialized juvenile courts. These services are furnished by persons attached to the court or are provided by independent agencies under contract to the court.

3. *Juvenile and domestic-relations courts.* These are either independent courts or parts of courts with more general jurisdiction. Such courts are often found in urban centers. Services generally available in juvenile courts are provided by personnel attached to these courts or by independent agencies working with them.

4. *Juvenile courts as sections or parts of courts with more general jurisdiction.* A county court, for example, may have a juvenile part or division, with one of its judges sitting as a juvenile court judge one or more days a week. Circuit courts, probate courts, and courts of common pleas may also have juvenile parts or divisions, with one or more judges designated to serve on

---

[8]Evelina Belden, *Courts in the United States Hearing Children's Cases,* U.S. Children's Bureau Publication no 65 (Washington, D.C.: U.S. Government Printing Office, 1920), pp. 7–10.

specified occasions as juvenile court judge. At times the duty of juvenile court judge is rotated, each of the members of the court taking a turn. Services generally available in juvenile courts are provided by personnel attached to the courts or by independent agencies.[9]

In 1973 the specialized juvenile court with a full-time judge existed in less than a hundred jurisdictions. In nearly three thousand counties the juvenile court was a branch of another court, whose objectives frequently differed from those of the juvenile court. Furthermore, although the provision of probation services is considered an essential function of the juvenile court, more than half the counties in the United States in 1952 failed to provide probation services of any kind.[10] Only 16 percent of the 2,034 courts from which information was obtained met the three basic criteria set forth by the Children's Bureau in 1920: separate hearings, regular probation services, and special court and probation records.[11]

Official cases in the juvenile court (designated as well as specialized) are initiated by *petition.* If a child has been arrested by the police, the petitioner may be the police officer, the victim, or a representative of a prosecuting agency. The petition is similar to a complaint against a criminal in that it alleges a wrongdoing on the part of the child and requests the court to take action. It differs, however, in that it purports to be *on behalf of the named child,* not against him. The intake officer, usually a probation officer, schedules the case for a court hearing. If the child is in court under arrest when the petition is filed, he is arraigned. This means he is told the nature of the charge, that he has the right to secure witnesses, and that he has a right to counsel.

After arraignment, the case is usually adjourned in order to permit the probation officer to conduct a *social investigation.* While awaiting the hearing, the child is normally permitted to return to his home unless in the opinion of the court he *(a)* might harm himself, *(b)* might endanger others in the community, *(c)* is likely to run away, or *(d)* has violated probation.

Whether the child is released to his parents or placed in a detention facility, frequently a local jail, depends on the policy of the court. The social investigation, usually required by law, elicits information about the family living conditions, neighborhood, school relationships, working conditions, health, and any other information that the probation officer can secure from the child himself or from any other source. The investigator may refer to any source or interview any person about the child without the knowledge or consent of the child or of his family. Prior to 1961, the report of the social investigation was usually given to the judge *before* the hearing, and the probation officer was generally permitted to testify with respect to it at the hearing.

---

[9]Frederick Killian, "The Juvenile Court as an Institution," *Annals of the American Academy of Political and Social Science* 261(January 1949):90–91.

[10]Herbert A. Bloch and Frank T. Flynn, *Delinquency* (New York: Random House, 1956), p. 315.

[11]Belden, *Courts in the United States Hearing Children's Cases,* p. 10.

The hearing is likely to be held in a private room from which all except parents and witnesses are excluded. The proceeding is informal. Very few children are represented by lawyers. Some judges demand proof that the child committed the offense with which he was charged in the petition before considering the case and exclude irrelevant, immaterial, and hearsay evidence. These judges are in the minority. In most juvenile courts the emphasis is on *social* rather than *legal* evidence because it is claimed that in the juvenile court the child is not charged with a crime and that a finding of juvenile delinquency does not constitute conviction of a crime.

The procedure followed in a juvenile court may be distinguished from that of a criminal court by the following:

1. The hearing is *private*. Only interested persons are present.
2. The hearing is *informal*. The proceeding resembles a conference called to bring forth facts rather than an adversary proceeding in which an attempt is made to prove that someone is guilty of some offense.
3. Juries are not used.
4. The report of a social investigation is often available to the court before the hearing.
5. It is virtually assumed that the child committed the act that brought him to the attention of the authorities. The emphasis is on *why* he did it. In a criminal trial the accused is presumed innocent, and his guilt must be established beyond a reasonable doubt by legal and competent evidence.
6. The disposition, in theory at least, provides for treatment rather than punishment.[12]

At the conclusion of the hearing the case may be disposed in any of the following ways:

1. The case may be dismissed. This amounts to a finding of "not guilty."
2. The child may be placed under the supervision of a probation officer.
3. The child may be removed from his home and placed in a foster home.
4. The child may be sent to a residential treatment center for emotionally disturbed children.
5. The child may be sent to a camp or other minimum-security correctional institution.
6. The child may be sent to a state training school.

---

[12]Paul W. Tappan and Ivan Nicolle, "Juvenile Delinquents and Their Treatment," *Annals of the American Academy of Political and Social Science* 399(January 1962):157–70.

Unofficial cases generally do not require a formal complaint or petition calling for a court hearing and official action. They are not entered on the court calendar, but are usually adjusted by the judge, referee, probation officer, or other court officer. The term *unofficial* refers to alleged but not proved cases of delinquency, to cases in which the probation officer feels that social casework rather than legal action is needed, and to cases that come before the court in which the nature of the delinquency is too trivial to demand court action. Whether a case is handled officially or unofficially may depend more on community or court policy than on the behavior of the child or his needs. In some states and jurisdictions, most cases are handled officially, while in others most cases are handled unofficially. Such variations are related to the philosophy and policy of the community and the individual judge and to the facilities available for handling the number of cases referred.

In 1965 most juvenile cases were dismissed; approximately one-fifth of the children were placed on probation; 9 percent were put under informal supervision; and only 8.5 percent were committed to institutions. Of the official cases, about half were disposed of by probation, and more than one-fifth were dismissed. Less than one-fifth of the children officially brought before the courts were committed to institutions for formal correction. Of the unofficial cases, nearly half (49.1 percent) were dismissed, while in 16.1 percent the children were placed under informal supervision.[13]

Whether dealing with the child officially or unofficially, the juvenile court tends to treat the youth as if he were maladjusted or presented some kind of problem. This tendency often obscures the differences between the delinquent and the dependent or neglected child. The purpose is not to make a judicial determination as to whether the child committed an act for which he should be held; it is aimed, in theory at least, at finding out the causes of his misbehavior and providing corrective treatment.

The Juvenile Court and Due Process

The juvenile court has been considered to be a tribunal of civil jurisprudence acting *on behalf of children.* For that reason the constitutional rights normally guaranteed to persons accused of crimes have not been deemed applicable to children brought before it.

As recently as 1955 the U.S. Supreme Court held in the Holmes case that "since juvenile courts are not criminal courts, the constitutional rights granted to persons accused of crime are not applicable to the children brought before them."[14] The position of the Court was that the state was not seeking to punish

---

[13] *Juvenile Court Statistics, 1966,* Children's Bureau Statistical Series no. 61 (Washington, D.C.: U.S. Government Printing Office, 1967), p. 13.

[14] *In re Holmes,* 109A, 2d 523 (1955), cert. denied 348 U.S. 973. For discussion, see Paul W. Tappan, *Crime, Justice, and Correction* (New York: McGraw-Hill, 1960), pp. 390–92.

Holmes, the defendant, as an offender but to salvage him and safeguard his adolescence.

Holmes, a boy of eighteen, was arrested in a stolen car operated by another boy. He was sent to state training school by the municipal court of Philadelphia, acting pursuant to Pennsylvania's juvenile court act. His lawyer, on appeal, contended (1) that Holmes had not been represented by counsel; (2) that he had not been informed of the specific charges against him; (3) that he was not advised of his rights at his trial, particularly of his right to refuse to testify; (4) that testimony admitted into evidence at his trial was incompetent and inadmissible; and (5) that the competent evidence presented at the trial did not link Holmes with any illegal acts.

The reviewing court ruled that all of these objections were irrelevant; in other words, that the court was not required to accord the accused rights that every person charged with a crime is guaranteed by the Constitution.

Holmes's attorneys appealed the case to the Supreme Court on the grounds that the protections of the Fourteenth Amendment against deprivation of liberty without due process had been violated. *The Court refused to hear the case.* Yet, if the juvenile court was created to protect the child and act on his behalf, it seems unreasonable to many that the child is accorded *less,* not more, consideration than is granted an adult charged with crime in a criminal court. While it is true that the child is not convicted of a crime by a juvenile court, the status of juvenile delinquent, if conferred upon him, not only serves to stigmatize him but often deprives him of liberty for a long period.

In summarizing his opposition to juvenile court practice, Tappan says:

> It has been popular practice thus to rationalize the abandonment, partial or complete, of even the most basic conceptions of due process of law: a specific charge; confrontation by one's adverse witnesses; right to counsel and appeal; rejection of prejudicial, irrelevant, and hearsay testimony; adjudication only upon proof or upon a plea of guilt. The presumption is commonly adopted that since the state has determined to protect and save its wards, it will do no injury to them through its diverse officials, so that these children need no due process protections against injury. Several exposures to court; a jail remand of days, weeks, or even months; and a long period in a correctional school with young thieves, muggers, and murderers—these can do no conceivable harm if the state's purpose be beneficent and the procedure be "chancery"! Children are adjudicated in this way every day without visible manifestations of due process. They are incarcerated. They become adult criminals, too, in thankless disregard of the state's good intentions as *parens patriae.* [15]

---

[15]From *Juvenile Delinquency* by Paul W. Tappan, p. 205. Copyright 1949 by McGraw-Hill Book Company. Used with permission of McGraw-Hill Book Company.

The 1959 edition of the Standard Juvenile Court Act represented an effort to provide more precision in procedure and greater protection of the rights and status of children and their families. The Children's Bureau preferred to differentiate between two parts of the hearing: *(a)* the findings as to the allegations in the petition, the trial portion in which the judge decides whether or not the child committed the acts alleged, and *(b)* the disposition, the portion of the proceeding on which the judge bases his determination of the appropriate treatment.[16] But in general it supported the Standard Act.

By 1966 the Children's Bureau modified its earlier position and sought to combine its essential philosophy for handling children's cases, "individualized justice," with the recognition of the need to protect the legal and constitutional rights of parents and children. The court was still to be a "legal tribunal where law and science, especially the science of medicine and those sciences which deal with human behavior, such as biology, sociology, and psychology, work side by side,"[17] and its purpose was still to be remedial and, to a degree, preventive rather than punitive.

It was recommended that for a court to become a fully effective and fair tribunal operating for the general welfare, there must be:

1. A judge and a staff identified with and capable of carrying out a nonpunitive and individualized service.
2. Sufficient facilities available in the court and community to ensure:
    (a) That the dispositions of the court are based on the best available knowledge of the needs of the child.
    (b) That the child, if he needs care and treatment, receives these through facilities adapted to his needs and from persons properly qualified and empowered to give them.
    (c) That the community receives adequate protection.
3. Procedures designed to ensure:
    (a) That each child and his situation are considered individually.
    (b) That the legal and constitutional rights of both parents and child and those of the community are duly considered and protected.[18]

The typical juvenile court act provides for state control as a substitute for parental control and an informal proceeding instead of a trial by a criminal

---

[16]"Standard Juvenile Court Act," *National Probation and Parole Association Journal* 5(October 1959):329–91.

[17]William H. Sheridan, *Standards for Juvenile and Family Courts,* Children's Bureau Publication no. 437 (Washington, D.C.: U.S. Government Printing Office, 1966), pp. 1–7.

[18]Sheridan, *Standards for Juvenile and Family Courts,* p. 2.

court. Because the state undertakes to provide for the child's welfare and does not subject him to trial, the child is deemed not to be entitled to due process. As we have previously noted, the courts have so held. The child brought before a juvenile court has thus been denied trial by jury, protection against self-incrimination, open hearings, proof beyond a reasonable doubt, the right to counsel, protection against hearsay evidence and other evidence ordinarily inadmissible, and the right to release on bail.[19]

On May 15, 1967, the Supreme Court for the first time considered the constitutional rights of children in juvenile courts. In writing the majority opinion of the Court in the *Gault* case, Justice Abe Fortas said: "Neither the Fourteenth Amendment nor the Bill of Rights is for adults only. Under our Constitution, the condition of being a boy does not justify a kangaroo court."[20] Although the decision does not give to juveniles all of the protections accorded adults charged with crimes, the disenchantment with the juvenile court was explicit and the trend of opinions predictable.

It is interesting to note that the Gault boy had been given what amounted to an indeterminate sentence by an Arizona juvenile court for allegedly having made obscene phone calls to a woman neighbor—this at a time when there are tremendous intergenerational differences in defining obscenity. Gault was, in effect, sentenced to detention for using four-letter words originally stigmatized as obscene because they were part of the language of an inferior people, the Anglo-Saxons, who refused to or were unable to learn the "respectable" language of their conquerors, the Normans. The extremely high-handed action taken by the Arizona judge made it clear to many, including the justices of the Supreme Court, that the time had come to stop such abuses. After a hearing in which a fifteen-year-old boy was not advised of his rights, was not permitted to cross-examine the only witness against him, and was not represented by counsel, the judge committed him as a juvenile delinquent to the state industrial school "for the period of his minority (six years) unless sooner discharged by due process of law." The judge defined *juvenile delinquent* as one who was habitually involved in immoral matters. The only evidence of any past immoral behavior on the part of young Gault was a referral made two years earlier alleging that he had stolen a baseball glove and lied to the police department about it. *No petition or hearing apparently resulted from this "referral."*

The penalty for violation by an adult of the section of the Arizona Criminal Code that the fifteen-year-old Gault boy allegedly violated was a fine of $5 to $50, or imprisonment for not more than two months.[21] Under Arizona

---

[19]Ketcham, "The Unfulfilled Promise of the American Juvenile Court," p. 25.

[20]*In re Gault,* 387 U.S. 1 (1967).

[21]Alan Neigher, "The Gault Decision: Due Process and the Juvenile Courts," *Federal Probation* 31(December 1967):13. This article contains an excellent analysis of the *Gault* case and the constitutional rights of children after the Supreme Court decision.

law a juvenile does not even have the right to appeal a decision of the juvenile court.

Gault's lawyers failed in their attempts to get the appellate courts of Arizona to review the findings of the juvenile court judge. The appeal to the U.S. Supreme Court was based on violations of Gault's rights, of which the following were basic:

1. The right to notice of the charges against him.
2. The right to counsel.
3. The right to face witnesses against him and to cross-examine them.
4. The right to refuse to answer questions that might tend to incriminate him.
5. The right to a transcript of the proceedings.
6. The right to appellate review.

The Court reversed the action of the Arizona court on all of these grounds. With respect to Arizona's claim that the juvenile proceeding was not a criminal proceeding, the Court said, "For this purpose, at least, commitment is a deprivation of liberty. It is incarceration against one's will, whether it is called 'criminal' or 'civil.' And our Constitution guarantees that no person shall be compelled to be a witness against himself when he is threatened with deprivation of his liberty."

In Part II of the decision in the *Gault* case the Supreme Court discussed the history of the juvenile court and specialized treatment accorded children. The *parens patriae* doctrine and the way in which it is applied by the juvenile courts was attacked in far stronger terms than those used by Professor Tappan in the 1950s. The Court noted that the early reformers meant to provide "substitute parents" in establishing specialized courts and treatment for children, but these turned out to be, in effect, procedures for sending juveniles to what are in fact correctional institutions in which they are confined with other juveniles sent to these institutions for offenses ranging in seriousness from minor juvenile delinquencies to serious crimes. Although the Court did not require that children be granted all the rights that persons charged with crime are guaranteed, a reading of the *Gault* decision leads to the conclusion that the Court may very well move in that direction.

One of the effects of the *Gault* decision was the appearance of lawyers in the juvenile court representing the accused. Before *Gault* only 4 percent of our major cities indicated that more than 50 percent of juveniles were represented in delinquency cases. In 1974, a survey of judges in sixty-eight of our largest cities revealed that nearly two-thirds of them reported the presence of defense counsel in 75 percent of the cases involving a felony or serious crime. In nearly half of the cities, over 75 percent of the juveniles charged with less serious crimes, not felonies, were represented by counsel. Even in PINS (person in need of supervision—under the New York Family Court Act, a child who has misbehaved repeatedly but not criminally) and neglect cases, nearly half of the cities reported that over 75 percent of the juveniles were represented by counsel.[22]

This increased activity of defense lawyers in the juvenile court has led to increased use of prosecutors who are lawyers. In 1974 in more than half of the cities in the survey, attorney-prosecutors appear for the state in more than 75 percent of the adjudication hearings. Even for nonfelonies, the less serious cases, almost half the cities reported use of prosecutors in 75 percent of the cases. More than a third of the PINS cases were prosecuted by lawyers.[23] Thus, one important impact of the *Gault* decision is to turn the juvenile court adjudication hearing into an adversary proceeding.

The following seven general principles for juvenile court prosecution are advanced in the guidelines set by the Boston Juvenile Court:

1. Advocacy of the state's interest in juvenile court includes concern for community protection together with promotion of the best interests of the juvenile.

2. In balancing the demands of community protection with his responsibilities as *parens patriae,* the juvenile prosecutor should consider the circumstances of each particular case.

3. As advocate, the juvenile prosecutor should act to ensure proper preparation and presentation of the state's case at all stages and should also participate in efforts to advance legitimate law enforcement and child welfare goals.

4. Certain punitive objectives (e.g., retribution) are inappropriate elements of juvenile prosecution.

5. The juvenile prosecutor should seek to encourage early diversion of appropriate cases and to impose the least restrictive alternatives possible; the prosecutor should proceed only on legally sufficient complaints or petitions even where a need for treatment is indicated.

6. The juvenile prosecutor shares responsibility for ensuring that pre- and post-disposition rehabilitative programs are carried out and that services and facilities for treatment and detention meet proper standards.

7. The juvenile prosecutor has a duty to promote justice by insisting on fair and lawful procedures.

---

[22]M. Marvin Finkelstein et al., *Prosecution in the Juvenile Courts* (Washington, D.C.: Department of Justice, Law Enforcement Assistance Administration, December, 1973), p. 16.

[23]Finkelstein, *Prosecution in the Juvenile Courts,* pp. 17–18.

The Juvenile Court Judge

Despite the *Gault* decision, the juvenile courts still hold broad powers over children. These powers include the right to depart from legal procedures established for criminal courts and to deny to children and their parents privileges normally accorded defendants in civil courts.

The juvenile court may, for example, consider evidence that would be inadmissible in both criminal and civil courts. There can be no doubt that at times these powers have been exercised in a high-handed manner and that rights of appeal from abuses are inadequate. The justification offered for this vast delegation of power over children is that it is essential if the court is to determine how best to rehabilitate the child and how to provide adequate care for him. The justice function of the court has been subordinated to what may be regarded as a social welfare function. Persons in tune with the original objectives of the juvenile court recognized the need for specially qualified judges and professional social workers to assist them.

According to the standards suggested by the United States Department of Health, Education, and Welfare, if a juvenile court is to become fully effective and a fair tribunal operating for the general welfare, it must have the following:

1. A judge and a staff identified with and capable of carrying out a nonpunitive and individualized service.
2. Sufficient facilities available in the court and the community to ensure:
   (a) That the dispositions of the court are based on the best available knowledge of the needs of the child.
   (b) That the child, if he needs care and treatment, receives these through facilities adapted to his needs and from persons properly qualified and empowered to give them.
   (c) That the community receives adequate protection.
3. Procedures designed to ensure:
   (a) That each child and his situation are considered individually.
   (b) That the legal and constitutional rights of both parents and child and those of the community are duly considered and protected.[24]

In many jurisdictions the juvenile court judge is expected to perform a judicial function and to administer a probation program and treatment program including diagnostic and rehabilitation services. He has the following duties and responsibilities:

---

[24]U.S. Department of Health, Education, and Welfare, *Standards for Juvenile and Family Courts* (Washington, D.C.: U.S. Government Printing Office, 1966), p. 2.

1. To conduct a judicial proceeding in a fair and equitable manner. If the proceeding is perceived to be arbitrary and unfair by the children who appear before him, he may be contributing to disrespect for law and, in a very real sense, to the future delinquencies of children.
2. To decide, after a fair hearing, whether or not the child before him committed the offense alleged in the petition. He has traditionally had the power to make a finding of delinquency if he has determined that the child committed some infraction other than the one alleged. However, since the *Gault* case this practice might be subject to challenge.
3. To protect society. He must determine whether or not allowing the child to remain in the community would be dangerous to society or to the child.
4. To determine whether or not the child will remain with his family or be taken from the family and:
   (a) Placed in a foster home.
   (b) Sent to a private treatment center.
   (c) Sent to a correctional institution.
5. To decide what measures will be taken to rehabilitate the child.
6. If he decides to place a child in an institution, he must determine the one most appropriate to the needs of the child and the protection of society.
7. In addition to the foregoing, the judge is generally charged with overall supervision of probation and treatment personnel attached to his court.

For a judge to be fully qualified to perform these functions, the standards for juvenile courts specify that the individual should have been admitted to the bar in the state where the person serves and have had some experience in the practice of law. A judge should also be:

1. Deeply concerned about the rights of people.
2. Keenly interested in the problems of children and families.
3. Sufficiently aware of the contributions of modern psychology, psychiatry, and social work that he can give due weight to the findings of these sciences and professions.
4. Able to evaluate evidence and situations objectively and to make dispositions uninfluenced by personal concepts of child care.
5. Eager to learn.
6. A good administrator, able to delegate administrative responsibility (applicable when administrative judge).
7. Able to conduct hearings in a kindly manner and to talk to children

and adults sympathetically and on their level of understanding without loss of the essential dignity of the court.[25]

The guidelines set down by the National Probation and Parole Association additionally require that the juvenile court judge have a working knowledge of social casework, child psychology, the elements of psychiatry, and the
other behavioral sciences.[26]

In recent years judges are becoming increasingly aware of the need to
deal with children in the context of the family. In an article on this subject,
Thomas F. Johnson points out that the child's family should be brought
together whenever possible, to discuss the child and his behavior, along with
their feelings about those problems with the judge.[27] Johnson found that a
large number of families of children in trouble were not organized in how to
function as a group. These were families with high incidences of suicide or drug
addiction. He concluded that "If juveniles are to be helped to stay out of
trouble, there must be some form of intervention with their families. By doing
so they can help him keep clear of the law in the future."

For a judge to administer the juvenile court in accordance with the
philosophy underlying it, he must indeed possess most of the qualifications
enumerated above. Legal training is certainly necessary if he is to preside over
a court and provide justice. In order to decide wisely on the type of treatment
a child requires he must know a great deal about child psychology and psychiatry. Even when psychological and psychiatric advisers are available to
him, he has to be able to evaluate their written reports properly. The training
required to do this is not usually provided in law schools.

As we have seen, a juvenile court investigation is usually initiated when
a complaint is made about a child by either police, parents, teachers, or social
workers. These complaints are generally screened by the probation officer of
the court, a person appointed by the juvenile court judge. In recent years the
qualifications of probation officers have been raised considerably, but even at
the present time less than half have had any training in social work, psychology, or guidance. The usual practice has been for a probation officer to
gather information about the child and his family before any hearing in order
to help the judge understand the case and decide what to do about it. This
information is usually concentrated on the child's background and not related
to the offense with which he has been charged. It is gathered from police
records, school records, records maintained by social work agencies, comments from community members, parents' opinions, the opinions of neighbors,

---

[25] *Standards for Juvenile and Family Courts,* pp. 103–4.

[26] *Guides for Juvenile Court Judges* (New York: National Probation and Parole Association, 1957),
p. 125.

[27] Thomas F. Johnson, "The Juvenile Offender and His Family," *The National Council of Juvenile
Court Judges* (February 1975):34–38.

and the reputation of the child in the community. The probation officer's report also incorporates the results of intelligence tests, school achievement tests, a medical examination, a psychiatric evaluation, and any other data available to him, and his recommendation for treatment and disposition. If the judge is to evaluate these recommendations and reports properly, he must understand the assumptions underlying them. Training in the behavioral sciences would appear to be essential. The requirements to be an adequate juvenile court judge are great. Despite this, the methods of selection of juvenile court judges are varied indeed.

Some juvenile court judges are elected by the people. Others are appointed by mayors or governors, with or without the recommendations of local bar associations. Bar associations base their recommendations on the legal qualifications of the candidate and his reputation as a person of good character.

Appointments may be for life but are generally for a period ranging from two to ten years. Qualifications enumerated in statutes and administrative regulations are vague. They refer to character, personality, tact, patience, common sense, and understanding of the problems of families and children. In reality, a good many juvenile court judges are political appointees, selected for the job largely as a reward for political services rendered to the mayor or governor appointing them.

Since the judge is presumed to act in the best interests of the child and since the procedures of the juvenile court depend largely on the ways in which he interprets the law and applies it in each case, the way in which the juvenile court judge views his role is important to the outcome of any case. In an effort to evaluate the role perceptions and role behaviors of juvenile court judges, two experienced graduate students in a school of social work observed 219 sessions presided over by fifteen judges in a large-city juvenile court over a period of eight months. During this time, cases involving 325 children charged with offenses ranging from truancy to murder were heard by the court. The students found that no two of the judges conceived of their role in exactly the same way. On the basis of their observations, the students were able to identify five more or less distinct roles performed by the judges: parent, counselor, chancellor, lawyer, and antagonist.

The parent-judge appeared to take the role of a parent, to respond to the situation as a parent, and to be concerned mainly with obedience.

The counselor-judge appeared to emphasize the unique individuality of each child. He insisted upon seeing the complete history of the child prior to the hearing and considered psychiatric, psychological, and other evaluations of experts available to him.

The chancellor-judge appeared to balance the child's rights with those of the parents and the community. He saw himself as an arbitrator and tried to reach an accommodation among all concerned.

The lawyer-judge was primarily concerned with the legal aspects of the case. He behaved very much like a judge in an adult court and used the law as a tool.

The antagonist-judge reacted personally to each situation and appeared hostile to the child before him. There were three such judges out of the fifteen observed.

Each of these categories of judges displayed its own distinctive attitudes toward lawyers, toward probation officers, toward social workers, and toward the confidentiality of the hearings.[28]

Warren Dunham has also observed important differences in the ways in which juvenile court judges conduct their hearings. Some are rigid, others flexible; some authoritarian, others permissive; some dictatorial, others democratic. Whether the court tends to be the authoritarian-legalistic type, the permissive–social agency type, or something in between depends in large part on the self-image of the judge and whether he views the court as primarily a legal or a social agency. Dunham notes that those judges attached to courts other than juvenile courts appear more closely to approximate the legalistic image. Full-time juvenile court judges with completely independent organizations tend to adhere to the social-agency image, which requires the judge to understand the child, to diagnose his difficulty, to treat his condition, and to fit him into the community.

The evolution of the social agency image and its development at the expense of the juvenile court's more legalistic role are attributed by Dunham to five influences:

1. The aggressive social work orientation of the United States Children's Bureau.
2. The broadening jurisdiction of the juvenile courts over all matters of a legal nature involving children.
3. The gradual professionalization of social work.
4. Various court decisions that have permitted the juvenile courts to make major departures from legal procedures followed in adult courts.
5. The growing prospect of treatment because of the increased acceptance by social workers of psychoanalytic theory and techniques.[29]

The Children's Bureau and persons with social work orientation emphasize the need for improvement in the training of judges. The assumption is that judges adequately prepared to deal with social issues could perform effectively

---

[28]Sophia M. Robison, *Juvenile Delinquency* (New York: Holt, Rinehart and Winston, 1960), pp. 251–67.

[29]A. Warren Dunham, "The Juvenile Court: Contradictory Orientations in Processing Offenders," *Law and Contemporary Problems* 23(Summer 1958):508–27.

as juvenile court judges and properly carry out the philosophy of the juvenile court.

A recent survey of juvenile court judges in the United States revealed that *half of all juvenile court judges have no undergraduate degree;* a fifth have received no college education at all; a fifth are not members of the bar. Almost three-quarters devote less than a quarter of their time to juvenile and family matters, and judicial hearings often turn out to be little more than attenuated interviews lasting from ten to fifteen minutes. In a similar vein, more than four-fifths of the juvenile court judges polled in a recent survey reported no psychologist or psychiatrist available to them on a regular basis.[30]

From the point of view of members of the legal profession, the problem is not simply one of requiring better training for judges. Lawyers prefer a government of law, which does not depend on the infallibility of an individual. No matter how well qualified judges may become either in the law or in the social sciences, they are still people. Strict procedural requirements, with rights of appeal, serve to protect an adult charged with crime from arbitrary or authoritarian actions by a judge. Permitting the judge of any court to disregard the constitutional rights of a person before him, whether that person is an adult or a child, appears to set a dangerous precedent.

The juvenile court judge often acts on the advice of psychologists, social workers, and psychiatrists. Under what conditions are we prepared to allow psychologists, psychiatrists, and social workers to interfere with the life of a child "for his own good"? Are these disciplines so well established that they can accurately predict what will be in the best interests of the child? These questions have been raised by the Supreme Court in the *Gault* case. Apparently the Court is inclined to the view that the constitutional rights of the child should be paramount and that the child should be given the same protections of the law as those guaranteed to an adult charged with a crime. The lawyer-judge is certainly best qualified to apply rules of evidence, conduct a fair hearing, and make a determination as to the guilt or innocence of the accused.

Once such a determination is made, we in no way violate the constitutional rights of a child or the legal protections to which he is entitled when we assign the tasks of treatment and disposition to persons best qualified to choose among those available. Regardless of the amount of training in psychology, psychiatry, social work, and the behavioral sciences that we give the lawyer-judge, he cannot become as well qualified for these tasks as a team of specialists in these disciplines. A treatment tribunal that included psychologists, psychiatrists, social workers, and educators would be far better qualified to determine disposition and treatment. We can legitimately and lawfully

---

[30] *The Challenge of Crime in a Free Society: A Report by the President's Commission on Law Enforcement and Administration of Justice* (Washington, D.C.: U.S. Government Printing Office, 1967), p. 80.

assign these functions to such a treatment tribunal only after a fair trial, with all constitutional guarantees and protections, has been accorded the accused, adult or child.

Trends in Juvenile Court Practices

The practices and procedures followed by the juvenile court of Arizona and so strongly condemned by the U.S. Supreme Court in the *Gault* case are still in effect in varying degrees in most states of the Union. The juvenile court laws in California and New York most closely approximate the requirements of the *Gault* decision.

The juvenile court in California is given a combination of the functions of the chancery court and what amounts to a criminal court for children. A child may be brought before it pursuant to a petition alleging *neglect* of the child by his parents or guardians, *dependence* of the child upon society as a result of the inability or unwillingness of others to look after him, or *delinquent behavior* attributed to him. The delinquent behavior may vary from very serious acts that would be considered crimes if committed by an adult to such minor breaches of discipline as violation of curfew regulations. The following account illustrates the diversity of the cases coming before a juvenile court and dealt with by the juvenile justice system.

Bobby was 9 when he was arrested for shoplifting. As they always do with first offenders, Los Angeles police spoke sternly to him and released him. Three months later, Bobby had graduated to burglary, and was released with a warning. Bobby's sixteenth arrest—he was 12 years old by then—earned him his first jail term, two years at a California Youth Authority Camp, from which he escaped four times. A few days after his release, at age 14, he killed a man. He has been charged with 26 crimes, including murder. But now that he has turned 18, he is, so far as the law is concerned, no longer a juvenile. He is a free man.

Mark's mother was a junkie and he was born in 1965 with heroin withdrawal symptoms. He spent his first six years in a foster home before being returned to his mother, whom he did not know. When she went to work, she regularly tied Mark to a bed. A year later, she told New York juvenile authorities that he was disruptive and uncontrollable, and Mark was institutionalized. Last year he was in court, charged with fighting with his peers and being difficult to control. He is 10 years old.

Bobby and Mark are both products of the American system of juvenile justice. One has compiled an awesome criminal record; the other has never committed a crime. Yet they both have juvenile records, and they have been confined in institutions for about the same time. Both are poisoned products of one of the starkest shortcomings of American justice: how to cope with children who fall into trouble with the law. "The system has failed," says veteran Detroit Judge James H. Lincoln. "We do no more than clean the boil without treating the disease."[31]

The following provisions of the Welfare and Institutions Code of California grant jurisdiction over children in the above categories to the juvenile courts:

600. *Persons within jurisdiction of court.* Any person under the age of 21 years who comes within any of the following descriptions is within the jurisdiction of the juvenile court, which may adjudge such person to be a dependent child of the court:

   (a) Who is in need of proper and effective parental care or control and has no parent or guardian, or has no parent or guardian willing to exercise or capable of exercising such care or control, or has no parent or guardian actually exercising such care or control.

   (b) Who is destitute, or who is not provided with the necessities of life, or who is not provided with a home or suitable place of abode, or whose home is an unfit place for him by reason of neglect, cruelty, or depravity of either of his parents, or of his guardian or other person in whose custody or care he is.

   (c) Who is physically dangerous to the public because of a mental or physical deficiency, disorder, or abnormality.

601. Any person under the age of 21 years who persistently or habitually refuses to obey the reasonable and proper orders or directions of his parents, guardian, custodian, or school authorities, or who is beyond the control of such person, or any person who is a habitual truant from school within the meaning of any law of this State, or who from any cause is in danger of leading an idle, dissolute, lewd, or immoral life, is within the jurisdiction of the juvenile court, which may adjudge such person to be a ward of the court.

602. Any person under the age of 21 years who violates any law of this State or of the United States or any ordinance of any city or county of this State defining crime or who, after having been found by the juvenile court to be a person described by Section 601, fails to obey any lawful order of the juvenile court, is within the jurisdiction of the juvenile court, which may adjudge such person to be a ward of the court.[32]

---

[31]"Children and the Law," *Newsweek,* September 8, 1975, p. 66. Copyright 1975 by Newsweek, Inc. All rights reserved. Reprinted by permission.

[32]*California Laws Relating to Youthful Offenders* (Sacramento: California Department of Youth Authority, January 1968), pp. 18–19.

The rights of minors before the juvenile court are enumerated as follows:

627.5 *Rights of minor.* In any case where a minor is taken before a probation officer pursuant to the provisions of Section 626 and it is alleged that such minor is a person described in Section 601 or 602, the probation officer shall immediately advise the minor and his parents or guardian that anything the minor says can be used against him and shall advise them of the minor's constitutional rights, including his right to remain silent, his right to have counsel present during any interrogation, and his right to have counsel appointed if he is unable to afford counsel. If the minor or his parent or guardian requests counsel, the probation officer shall notify the judge of the juvenile court of such request and counsel for the minor shall be appointed. . . . [33]

Aside from the fact that the California law provides for closed hearings, a child before the court pursuant to Section 602 of the Welfare and Institutions Code is given most of the rights accorded a person charged with a crime, both before the court hearing and in the course of it. In addition to the right to counsel and the privilege against self-incrimination, a minor has the right to confront and cross-examine witnesses.[34] Furthermore, California law distinguishes between the treatment that may be accorded neglected and dependent children, on the one hand, and delinquent children, on the other.

Dispositions provided by the law are as follows:

725. *Disposition by court.* After receiving and considering the evidence on the proper disposition of the case, the court may enter judgment as follows:
    (a) If the court has found that the minor is a person described by Sections 601 or 602, it may, without adjudging such minor a ward of the court, place the minor on probation, under the supervision of the probation officer, for a period not to exceed six months.
    (b) If the court has found that the minor is a person described by Sections 601 or 602, it may order and adjudge the minor to be a ward of the court.
    (c) If the court has found that the minor is a person described by Section 600, it may order and adjudge the minor to be a dependent child of the court.[35]

---

[33] *California Laws Relating to Youthful Offenders,* p. 24.
[34] *California Laws Relating to Youthful Offenders,* pp. 30–32.
[35] *California Laws Relating to Youthful Offenders,* p. 34.

The California statute does not employ the term *juvenile delinquent* in referring to a child before the court. Children brought before the court pursuant to Section 600 of the Welfare and Institutions Code, whether neglected or dependent, are adjudged to be *dependent children.* Children brought before the court pursuant to Section 601 for behavior that causes them to become discipline problems that families and/or schools believe to be serious enough for court action may be adjudged *wards of the court.* Children who are accused of violating laws are brought before the court pursuant to Section 602 of the code. So are those who fail to obey orders imposed upon them by the juvenile court pursuant to Section 601. They, too, may be adjudged wards of the court.

Although not referred to as delinquents, both categories of juveniles brought before the juvenile courts under the provisions of Section 601 and 602 are treated in the same way as juvenile delinquents in other states. They may be placed on probation, kept in detention, sent to county juvenile homes, ranches, or camps, or referred to the California Youth Authority, which may place them in state correctional institutions for juveniles.

Whether a child is judged to be a dependent child or a ward of the court, he is supervised by a probation officer of the court. In many ways all such children on probation come to be regarded as wards of the court. California, in keeping with the recommendation of the Standard Juvenile Court Act, has avoided the delinquency tag and thus offers some protection to the child who has committed a serious delinquent act. It may, however, be doing a disservice to the nondelinquent child, the "dependent" or "neglected" child, and to the child who is a discipline problem and is under court supervision pursuant to Section 601 of the code. The term *ward of the court* may in time be equated with *juvenile delinquent,* a term that is already equated in the minds of many with *young criminal.* Avoiding the use of the terms *delinquent* and *neglected* does not eliminate the categories; it merely avoids naming them.[36]

The New York Family Court Act applies the term *juvenile delinquent* only to a child between the ages of seven and sixteen who has committed an act that would constitute a crime if it were done by an adult. Juvenile delinquent, thus used, is almost synonymous with young criminal. A child who has misbehaved repeatedly but not criminally is called a person in need of supervision (PINS):

(a) "Juvenile delinquent" means a person over 7 and less than 16 years of age who does any act which, if done by an adult, would constitute a crime.

(b) "Person in need of supervision" means a male less than 16 years of age and a female less than 18 years of age who is an habitual truant

---

[36]Sol Rubin, *Crime and Delinquency* (New York: Oceana Publications, 1958), pp. 51–52.

or who is incorrigible, ungovernable, or habitually disobedient and beyond the lawful control of parent or other lawful authority.[37]

Among the reasons given by the New York Joint Legislative Committee on Court Reorganization for differentiating the above categories was the desire to avoid stigma. *Juvenile delinquent* is now a term of disapproval. The judges of the Children's Court and the Domestic Relations Court were of course aware of this and were aware also that government officials and private employers often learn of adjudication of delinquency. Some judges were therefore reluctant to make such an adjudication in the absence of conduct violating the penal law. In some cases, however, they felt compelled to do so when they concluded that supervision was necessary for the proper development of the child. The committee had been asked to avoid the need for an adjudication of delinquency in those circumstances by the expedient of not using that term or any similar term in describing any of the occasions for the exercise of the court's jurisdiction. But the practical result of this proposal, the committee feared, would be continued indiscriminate grouping of all children within the court's jurisdiction as delinquents, no matter what other term was used. The committee therefore proposed that the category of juvenile delinquency be redefined and the new category of person in need of supervision added. Though there was no certainty about these judgments, the committee expected that this pattern would reduce the instances of stigma and at the same time permit the court to use appropriate resources in dealing with persons in need of supervision.[38]

Another reason for differentiating the two categories was the desire to define different police and court powers for the two types of cases. The police, for example, may take an alleged juvenile delinquent into custody without court order under provisions of law similar to those giving them the right to take an alleged criminal into custody. It was the intention of the committee to limit the powers of the police in the case of a person in need of supervision. A person alleged to be a juvenile delinquent may be kept in detention pending court proceedings, while a person alleged to be in need of supervision may not. Furthermore, under the provisions of the original New York Family Court Act (1963), a juvenile delinquent could be committed by a court to a state correctional institution. A person in need of supervision might be placed in a residential treatment center or other facility dealing with nondelinquent children, but cannot be placed by a court in a state correctional institution.[39]

The rights of an accused to be advised of the nature of the offense of which he is charged and the time and place of its alleged commission, essential

---

[37]New York Family Court Act (1963), sec. 712.

[38]New York Joint Legislative Committee on Court Reorganization, *The Family Court Act* (1962), pt. 2,p. 7.

[39]*The Family Court Act,* (1962) pp. 7–8.

if an accused is to prepare to defend himself properly, are protected by the New York Family Court Act. The act requires that in a juvenile delinquency case, the petition must specify the act that, if done by an adult, would constitute a crime and the time and place of its commission; a petition alleging a person to be in need of supervision must set forth specific acts on which the allegations of habitual truancy, incorrigibility, habitual disobedience, or ungovernability are based, and the time and place of their occurrence.[40]

The New York Family Court Act not only guarantees the right to counsel, but also makes provision for children to be represented by appointed legal guardians. It has been apparent for a long time that for a court to give a twelve-year-old child the right to cross-examine adverse witnesses is meaningless unless he has an attorney to represent him. The New York Family Court Act recognized this obvious fact in stating: "Counsel is often indispensable to a practical realization of due process of law and may be helpful in making reasoned determinations of fact and proper orders of disposition."[41]

The New York law provides for separate hearings on adjudication (determination of guilt or innocence) and disposition (sentencing). The rules for the admission of evidence are not unlike those prescribed for the criminal courts. Only evidence that is competent, material, and relevant may be admitted in the adjudicatory (fact-finding) hearing, while evidence that is material and relevant may be admitted during a dispositional hearing. Statements made by an accused to intake officers or others at conferences held to determine whether or not a petition was to be filed are not admissible at adjudicatory hearings. Thus, protection against self-incrimination has been extended to children.[42]

New York has gone further than California in the extent to which it distinguishes between juvenile delinquents and dependent and neglected children. It thus appears to recognize the extent to which the general public equates *juvenile delinquent* with *young criminal* and makes it clear that a dependent or neglected child has not committed a criminal act.

Will people nevertheless set a stigma on a child labeled "PINS," a person in need of supervision? It appears likely that a child requiring action by a court will be stigmatized in some way by that fact alone.

The juvenile court systems in Japan and France are somewhat similar to those in the United States. The Scandinavian countries have no juvenile courts, nor has the Soviet Union. In these countries, a juvenile court experience is considered traumatic for very young children, and too light a treatment for older offenders.

In Sweden a child welfare council performs the functions of a juvenile court and represents a diversion from a juvenile justice system. The council consists of five members: a person trained in law, if available; a pastor of the

---

[40]New York Family Court Act (1963), secs. 731 and 732.

[41]New York Family Court Act (1963), sec. 241. See also sec. 249.

[42]New York Family Court Act (1963), secs. 742–46.

Lutheran State Church; a public school teacher; and at least two others chosen for their special interest in the care of children and youth. Members are elected by the communal council for a four-year term and serve without pay or for nominal fees. In 1956 there were 1,037 such child welfare councils. Each has child welfare consultants and child care assistants who do most of the work with children. All children under fifteen years of age who present discipline problems or violate laws are referred to a child welfare council. *None can be sent to a court.* Youths fifteen to eighteen and those eighteen to twenty-one years of age may be diverted from courts to welfare councils at the discretion of the public prosecutor. All children coming before the child welfare council are treated as welfare problems and are not stigmatized in any way. For children under fifteen, a system of diversion from courts has been established. For older youth, there is a dual system that permits diversion at the option of the prosecutor. The result is that children may be treated without any stigma for children's offenses, while older adolescents may be tried by courts for serious offenses. If they are tried by courts, they are given the same privileges and rights accorded adults.[43]

Norway and Denmark have child welfare councils similar to the ones in Sweden with minor differences in procedure.

In an effort to remove neglected, dependent, and problem children from the jurisdiction of courts and correctional treatment, the British in 1965 announced a completely new approach to the treatment of child delinquents:

> The Government's plan for abolishing the juvenile courts, and treating child delinquents as in need of care rather than punishment, will be published before the end of this month.
>
> After protracted and sometimes acrimonious inter-ministerial disputes, a White Paper setting out details of a projected Bill was approved by the Cabinet just before the recess and is now with the printers.
>
> The Government intends to set up a family service under Home Office auspices. It will incorporate and develop most of the functions of existing central and local government departments relating to children and families with children. It will work closely with voluntary agencies concerned with family problems.
>
> Each local authority will be required to set up its own family service committee with a chief officer who would have the same status as the chief medical officer and the director of education.
>
> The penal element in the treatment of children will be eliminated and the term *approved school* abolished. Existing educational establishments will be renamed and redirected toward dealing with different types of problem children.

---

[43]Ola Nyquist, "How Sweden Handles Its Juvenile and Youth Offenders," *Federal Probation* 20(March 1956):36–42.

Although it is understood that the White Paper will not mention the vexed question of the age of criminal responsibility, it will provide that children of school age who commit offenses will no longer be charged by the police and taken to court.

Instead the police will report the matter to the family service and social workers will discuss with the parents what should be done. If there is any dispute, either because the child denies committing the offense or because the family service and the parents disagree on the treatment, the matter will go to a family court. There will be no question of forcibly separating a child from its family without the full processes of the law.

Nearly 90 percent of the cases at present coming before juvenile courts will, it is expected, be settled without the whole paraphernalia of judicial proceedings. The family court will still be composed of magistrates named by the Lord Chancellor. It will deal not only with a small proportion of delinquents whose cases cannot be solved by the social workers, but also with other family matters, such as maintenance, illegitimacy and adoption.[44]

While the Children and Young Persons Bill enacted by Parliament in June 1969 did not abolish juvenile courts, it established procedures intended to reduce substantially the number of children brought before them. It provided that a child between the ages of ten and fourteen charged with an offense be referred to a juvenile court only if deemed in need of care, protection, and control. The commission of an offense would, of itself, not warrant bringing him before the court. It further provided that children between the ages of fourteen and seventeen could be prosecuted only on the authority of a summons or warrant issued by a juvenile court magistrate. Furthermore, police are required before seeking such a warrant to consult the children's department, to consider all available information, and to dispose of cases informally, without any court intervention, if this is appropriate. The safeguards of judicial procedures remain for those who maintain their innocence or claim duress.

The National Probation and Parole Association, the National Council of Juvenile Court Judges, and the Children's Bureau have developed a new standard Family Court Act, which recommends the establishment of family courts that would perform the same functions as the British family courts. They would be given jurisdiction over all types of cases involving children or families when laws have been violated and legal action is deemed necessary. When a child is accused of a crime, the court would be required to provide him with all of the safeguards included in due process of law. It appears to be the intent of this act to provide a child under the age of eighteen as much protection as an adult charged with a crime.

---

[44] *The Observer* (London), August 8, 1965, p. 1.

The American juvenile court system is in a state of rapid change. The rationale for this change is indicated by the following comment in a Supreme Court decision: "There is evidence, in fact, that there may be grounds for concern that the child receives the worst of both worlds; that he gets neither the protection accorded to adults nor the solicitous care and regenerative treatment postulated for children."[45]

A particular category of child brought into court (both juvenile and adult) is most clearly not accorded the "solicitous care and regenerative treatment" mentioned if his problem requires special attention. These are children who are brought into court and juvenile detention for no reason other than the fact that they were the victim of the behavior of a criminal adult. Child-battering parents, abandonment, or child molestation are cases in point. In such cases the juvenile court and the judge have a special responsibility to the child. In this regard child psychiatrist Dr. Edward H. Weiss in collaboration with several other doctors drew up recommendations to help standardize acute medical and psychiatric care for assault victims.[46] Their list included private rooms for questioning and examining young victims, special comfort from nurses to make the experience less frightening, and instruction for parents to let them know what to expect and to help them give emotional support and avoid making the child feel guilty because of their own guilt.

According to Dr. Weiss, in addition to needing emotional support themselves, parents need to be able to give extra love and attention during the crisis. "Children may develop fears of night, of strange men and of going out alone, and they might show such regressive phenomena as an inability to concentrate in school." This is a transitory stage, Weiss reassures, and it is important for parents not to panic or convey their own anxiety. It is also important to encourage such children to talk about their feelings and to correct their distortions, emphasizing that the victims are not guilty of wrongdoings and that not all adults are like the sick one(s) who violated them.

This type of support, along with psychiatric treatment when necessary, goes a long way toward helping the child deal with the bad experience; but it is not enough, says Dr. Weiss—"we need also to change our legal procedure. The Sixth Amendment guarantees any accused the right to be confronted by his or her accuser, even if that accuser is a five-year-old child. Children in this country must therefore face their assailant in a public trial, if so demanded, where they will be cross-examined; and some have even had to accompany police in a search for the attacker." Weiss's suggested alternatives would be either to employ videotaping or to follow the European model: a private trial, without cross-examination, in the judge's chambers. Juvenile court judges have to be aware of the fact that such children in court should not become "double victims," victims of an adult offender and then victims of the administration

---

[45]*Kent* v. *U.S.,* 383 U.S. 541 (1966).

[46]Dr. Edward Weiss reports on this issue in *Human Behavior* (April 1976).

of justice. Children who are victims in the context described require special treatment in the juvenile court.

The Juvenile Court Movement and the Social Structure

In some measure the administration of law in the juvenile court movement—if it continues on its present course—can significantly affect not only justice, but the overall social structure as well. Both social scientists and lawyers specializing in jurisprudence thus have a great obligation.

Loosely defined legal procedure tends grossly to increase the power of the state over the individual. (This is certainly evidenced in the juvenile court.) Richard R. Korn and Lloyd W. McCorkle make this point in a discussion of the shift from accusatory or adversary judicial procedure to inquisitorial methods. They argue that in the adversary form of judicial process (standard U.S. procedure in criminal cases), the role of the state is severely limited:

> The government merely supplies an impartial referee who decides the issue, awards the victorious "adversary," and determines the penalty or forfeit of the loser. This form of proceeding is in sharp contrast to that in which the State supplies not only a referee but a government prosecutor, who supplants the private accuser. The process in which the State initiates and presses the accusation is called "inquisitorial" (from the Latin word meaning "seek into"), and places enormously greater power in the hands of the political authorities.
>
> The political and social consequences flowing from the use of one or the other of these basic methods are far-reaching. Historically, a shift from accusatory to inquisitorial proceedings has almost invariably paralleled—has, in fact, been one of the principal instruments of—a shift toward more autocratic systems of government.[47]

It may seem an exaggeration to describe the tone of the juvenile court as *inquisitorial,* yet the term accurately reflects many aspects of this form of judicial procedure. The juvenile court tends to hold secret hearings, there is greater emphasis on the individual's personal characteristics than on his offense, the accused has a limited legal defense, and hearsay evidence is not only admitted in court but vigorously sought after. Although this mode of justice is currently restricted to the socialized courts, if it becomes more widespread in judicial practice it could have a broad impact on the overall social system.

---

[47]From *Criminology and Penology* by Richard R. Korn and Lloyd W. McCorkle, p. 382. Copyright 1959 by Holt, Rinehart and Winston, Inc. Reprinted by permission of Holt, Rinehart and Winston, Inc.

Juvenile Justice in the 1970s

In December 1971, the California Supreme Court ruled that police questioning of a juvenile arrested for a crime must cease when he asks to see one of his parents. The court's opinion extended the U.S. Supreme Court's decision given in 1966 in the case of *Miranda* v. *Arizona,* which required that police questioning of an adult taken into custody be halted if he indicates that he wants to remain silent or consult an attorney. The *Miranda* ruling was based on the privilege against self-incrimination provided by the Fifth Amendment to the U.S. Constitution. The California Supreme Court extended that privilege to children.

With respect to the rights of minors, California law as applied in 1973 provides:

1. That a juvenile be advised of his constitutional rights to remain silent, and to refuse to answer any question that might incriminate him when he is first apprehended by a police officer.
2. That he be advised of his right to an attorney by the arresting officer.
3. That he again be advised of his constitutional rights by a probation officer on his first contact with a juvenile court or probation.
4. That an attorney must be appointed to represent him if he or his family cannot afford to pay for counsel.
5. That the family and attorney of a juvenile are entitled to adequate notice of the proceedings and of the nature of charges against him.
6. That he is entitled to subpoena witnesses at state expense.
7. That he is entitled to a full record of the proceedings at his hearing with a free transcript of the proceedings.
8. That he has a right to appeal the decision of the juvenile court.

He does not have any of the following rights that are accorded an adult in a criminal trial:

1. The right to be released on bail pending disposition of his case.
2. The right to a trial by jury.
3. The right to a public trial at which reporters and other interested persons may be present.
4. While an adult must be found guilty "beyond a reasonable doubt," a juvenile may be found delinquent based on a "preponderance of evidence." The latter involves far less proof of guilt.

In the 1970s, particularly after the Supreme Court action in the *Gault* case, most states have adopted the practice followed in California and New York of having two hearings, one to adjudicate the facts and the other for disposition. At the adjudicatory hearing the juvenile court applies the rules of evidence and generally accords the juvenile due process. At the disposition hearing there are no limitations on evidence the judge may consider. Obviously, a child not represented by counsel is unable to adequately avail himself of the rights and privileges the law accords him. He is not qualified to cross-examine witnesses, present his own case in an effective manner, or evaluate the evidence for or against him. He may not know, for example, which portion of the evidence presented against him is inadmissible. In effect, then, to protect the child and to provide him with a fair trial, he must be provided with counsel.

In one study made to determine the effect of the 1961 California Juvenile Court Law, which provided due process as later set forth in the *Gault* case, it was found that children represented by counsel fared far better than those who were not so represented. Dismissals and informal probation were ordered nearly three times as often when counsel was present as when no counsel was present. With no attorney representing them, children were more likely to be placed away from home. Also it was found that private attorneys were more successful than public defenders in obtaining home placement.[48]

Another study analyzed the role of the public defender representing juveniles in the juvenile court of a large midwestern city, which the authors called "Metro." In 1966, the juvenile court in Metro handled 11,636 delinquency cases, of which 25 percent were adjusted administratively without referral to courts. Of the remaining 8,920 cases, only 345, some 4 percent, were handled by the public defender. The average client was a fourteen-and-one-half-year-old Negro male who was charged with a serious offense. An analysis of individual cases showed that the public defender:

1. Rarely appeared at detention hearings.
2. Made oral rather than written motions and made no motions at all in 83 percent of the cases.
3. Had no continuances (postponements) in one-third of his cases.
4. Held only one conference with his client prior to court appearance in almost half of his cases.
5. Had no witnesses in over one-half of his cases.

Because the rule of reasonable doubt did not apply, prosecutors won juvenile cases with minimal evidence.[49]

Leonard Edwards, a deputy public defender in Santa Clara County, California, pointed out that the county had three deputy public defenders, each assigned to from thirty to sixty cases weekly. He expressed the view that

---

[48]Edwin H. Lemont, "Legislating Change in the Juvenile Court," *Wisconsin Law Review* no. 2(1967), pp. 421–48.

[49]Anthony Platt, Howard Schechter, and Phyllis Tiffany, "In Defense of Youth: A Case Study of the Public Defender in Juvenile Court," *Indiana Law Journal* 43(1968):619–40.

juveniles did not receive the legal protections accorded adults nor the special care and treatment postulated for children.[50] Generally, he stated his position as follows:

1. The formal legal process should be used only as a last resort.
2. The range of conduct considered delinquent should be limited.
3. Alternatives to the institutions and out-of-home placements should be developed and utilized, and
4. The cases involving more serious offenders should include adjudicatory procedures consistent with basic principles of due process. . . .

There should be few if any arrests for truancy, curfew violations, or for being beyond control of one's parents or school authorities. Runaway cases should not result in arrests unless the child needs protection. Citations should be issued for petty law violators giving them notice of their appointment with the investigating authorities.[51]

In other words, juvenile behavior that would not constitute criminal behavior if committed by an adult should not come before the juvenile court at all. This would include children called "persons in need of supervision" in New York, or violators of Section 601 of the Welfare Code of California.

Edwards also expresses the view that the child, to be adequately protected, should be represented by counsel not only at his jurisdictional hearing but also at his detention and disposition hearings.[52] If these recommendations were followed, only those juveniles charged with crimes would come before a juvenile court; these children would be accorded all of the rights and privileges given an adult in a criminal court.

Diversion

The movement to deal with a wide variety of deviant behavior without referral to courts or other establishment agencies is referred to as *diversion.* Diversion for juveniles has come to mean providing an alternative to the juvenile justice system, most particularly the juvenile court. Prior to or immediately following an arrest, the young person is "diverted" to an agency or activity providing services designed to prevent delinquent behavior. School counseling, family counseling, occupational training, or some other service or therapy may be provided. In 1970 the Sacramento Probation Department established a diversion project designed to keep children out of juvenile hall, keep the family problem out of court, and still offer counseling to the family. After two years of an experiment with Section 601 cases, it was determined

---

[50]Leonard Edwards, "The Rights of Children," *Federal Probation* 37(June 1973):34–41.

[51]Edwards, "The Rights of Children," p. 35.

[52]Edwards, "The Rights of Children," pp. 36–38.

that "diversion" of such cases was effective. The number of court petitions, the number of informal probations, the number of days spent in detention, and the cost of handling were all less for project than for control cases. Recidivism was also less. Based on these findings, Sacramento County adopted the program as its basic method for dealing with 601 cases. In April 1972 the county initiated a new experiment to determine whether the 601 diversion approach could be successfully applied to 602 cases, those involving some more serious offenses. The procedures followed and results obtained are described as follows:[53]

Project Operation.   The 601 diversion project began handling cases on October 26, 1970. For purposes of the experiment the project handles cases on four days of the week with the regular intake unit handling the other three days. Days are rotated monthly.

On project days when a referral on a 601 matter is received—whether from the police, the schools, the parents, or whomever—the project staff arranges a family session to discuss the problem. Every effort is made to insure that this session is held as soon as possible and most are held within the first hour or two after referral. Through the use of family counseling techniques the project counselor seeks to develop the idea that the problem is one that should be addressed by the family as a whole. Locking up the youth as a method of solving problems is discouraged and a return home with a commitment by all to try to work through the problem is encouraged. If the underlying emotions are too strong to permit the youth's return home immediately, an attempt is made to locate an alternative place for the youth to stay temporarily. This is a voluntary procedure which requires the consent of both the parents and the youth.

Families are encouraged to return for a second discussion with the counselor and, depending upon the nature of the problem, for a third, fourth, or fifth session. Normally, the maximum number of sessions is five. Sessions rarely last less than one hour and often go as long as two or two and one-half hours. First sessions take place when the problem arises. Since the project staff remains on duty until 2:00 A.M., a few begin after midnight. Crisis line service after project closing hours is handled through referral by the probation department switchboard to the home of the probation counselor. This service has not been used a great deal, but its availability is important in conveying the counselor's concern to the family.

Staff.   The unit staff consists of a supervisor and six deputy probation officers. The unit supervisor has approximately ten years' experience and his assistant

---

[53]Roger Baron and Floyd Feeney, *Juvenile Diversion Through Family Counseling* (Washington, D.C.: Office of Technology Transfer, National Institute of Law Enforcement and Criminal Justice, Law Enforcement Assistance Administration, 1976), pp. 1–19.

seven years' experience. The deputies range from no experience in a probation setting to approximately four years of experience. There are three male and three female deputies. The three deputies without probation experience all have some previous experience in a social service agency.

Training.   The techniques of crisis intervention and family crisis counseling are crucial to the concept of the project. Normally these are techniques employed by therapists who have undergone long periods of training. Moreover, the application of these techniques at the intake point of probation presents some novel and difficult questions. The training portion of the project is therefore one of its most crucial aspects. Project training involves two phases: initial training and ongoing training.

Initial training was conducted during a one-week period. This included demonstrations of actual family counseling by a number of different therapists, intensive discussion, and role-playing of the kinds of problems that counselors were expected to face.

The ongoing portion of the training is built around weekly consultations with the project psychiatrists and with the project psychologist.

In these sessions the project counselors have opportunities to observe, discuss, and work with the project consultants. Other training sessions have focused on the role that other agencies play in helping to deal with family situations.

Cases Handled.   The project does not handle all 601 cases. Out-of-county and out-of-state cases, cases in which the juvenile already has a case pending in court or a warrant outstanding, cases involving youths who are in court placement, and cases involving youths who are already on probation for serious criminal offenses were excluded from project coverage because of administrative and other problems involved in their handling. Some citation and other noncustody referrals are also excluded from the project as not requiring handling as intensive as that of the project. For the first nine project months about 40 percent of all 601 referrals were excluded from the project for these reasons.

Results.   Results of the project to date are highly promising. During its first nine months the project handled 803 referrals involving opportunities for diversion but filed only 18 petitions. Court processing was thus necessary in only 2.2 percent of these referrals as opposed to 30.4 percent in a three-month preproject period and 21.3 percent of the referrals handled in the normal manner in the control group.

Available data concerning repeat offenses indicate that the project group is doing better than either the preproject sample or the control group. Young people handled during the first four months of the project were followed up for a period of seven months after initial handling to determine the number of repeat offenses. At the end of this period, 45.5 percent of the control group

Referrals and Petitions—First Nine Project Months

	No. of Referrals	No. of Petitions	Percent
Preproject period*	362	110	30.4
Control cases	558	119	21.3
Project cases	803	18	2.2

*July 1 to September 30, 1970

had been rebooked for either a 601 or 602 offense while the comparable figure for the project group was 35.0 percent. This represents an improvement of over 23 percent in the rate of repeat offenses.

Perhaps even more significant is that for repeat offenses involving criminal conduct (section 602), the improvement was even greater. For this category the repeat rate for the control group was 23.4 percent and 15.3 percent for the project group. This is a drop in the rate of repeated offenses of 34.6 percent.

Data concerning overnight detention indicate that project youths initially require overnight detention in less than 10 percent of the cases while the figure for control cases is over 60 percent. The control group spent an average of 5.3 nights in detention per youth while the project group had an average of 0.1 nights in detention per youth as a result of initial handling.

Cost of Service.   Original projections for the project indicated that crisis counseling could be performed within the cost allocations required for more traditional service, assuming that complete case costs including intake, court, and supervision were included within the totals for traditional service. Based on the project's record to date in diverting cases out of juvenile court and in reducing juvenile hall detention and recidivism, a comparison of project and control costs indicates that diversion is less expensive than the more traditional procedures. The average total cost, for example, for project handling of a case not including repeat bookings was $29 as compared with an average cost of $222 for control cases. If the cost of repeat bookings is included, the average

Percent of Juveniles Rebooked Within Seven Months
(Cases initially handled October 26, 1970, to February 28, 1971)

	601 or 602	602 Only
Preproject period	48.6	27.0
Control cases	45.5	23.4
Project cases	35.0	15.3

project cost cost per project case is $170 and the average control group cost $405.[54]

Based on the 601 project's first year in which over five hundred cases were handled by the project staff and compared with a control group of regular intake cases, the evaluation indicated that:

1. The number of court petitions was reduced by over 80 percent.
2. Overnight detention was reduced more than 50 percent.
3. The number of youths involved in repeat offenses of any kind was reduced by more than 14 percent.
4. The number of youths subsequently becoming involved in criminal behavior was reduced by 25 percent.
5. The cost of the new techniques was less than half the cost of the previous procedures.

The results concerning recidivism are particularly impressive. The whole delinquency literature shows less than twenty projects with some proven record of accomplishment in recidivism reduction. Most programs are not evaluated at all. Of those which have been, by far the most frequent finding is that of no improvement or change. The Sacramento approach on the other hand shows a clear record of improvement for a large number of cases.

The objectives of the 602 project are essentially the same as those of the 601 project. The accomplishments—based on available data—are for the most part even better:

1. Court petitions were reduced by over 99 percent.
2. The number of youths committing new criminal acts was reduced over 50 percent.
3. The number of youths involved in any type of repeat behavior was reduced over 40 percent.
4. The cost comparisons developed for the 601 project are essentially valid for the 602 concept as well.

In the first two years of the 602 project, out of 982 cases only 6 resulted in petitions to the juvenile court whereas 62 petitions were filed in six months involving members of the control group.[55]

The Expansion of Children's Rights in the Courts

The rights of children seem to be expanding. According to one report, some of these rights include: a full hearing before a child can be committed by his parents to a mental institution; the opportunity to present evidence in foster-

[54]Baron and Feeney, *Juvenile Diversion Through Family Counseling,* pp. 8–16.

[55]Baron and Feeney, *Juvenile Diversion Through Family Counseling,* p. 18.

care proceedings; and in one case, where a child flunked kindergarten, the decision was found to be unconstitutional. In an article on child rights, Peter B. Sandman, director of the Youth Law Center in San Francisco, commented: "There's been an explosion in children's rights. Children's rights had been neglected for many years. Now they're part of the whole civil rights movement . . . and the courts have become more sympathetic."[56]

Samuel C. McKnight, a lawyer in the quoted article, cites a number of juvenile cases whose outcome, he asserts, results in harm to the people who are supposedly intended to become the beneficiaries of the legal encounter. McKnight makes his debatable point by referring to several cases of this type:

In 1975, the Louisiana Supreme Court ruled that school principals and instructors—like police—must abide by the Fourth Amendment's prohibition against unreasonable search and seizure. The court held illegal a gymnasium teacher's search for marijuana in a student's locker.

The same year, the Supreme Court held that students could not be suspended from school unless they had received a notice of the charges and an explanation of the evidence against them and unless they had been given an opportunity to present their side.

In April 1976, a three-judge federal district court in New York ruled that before foster children could be transferred from a foster home, they were entitled to their own representation at a hearing at which all parties—biological parents, foster parents, and children—could present "relevant information." The State of New York, warning that the decision amounted to a "wholesale judicialization" of the foster-care process, appealed to the Supreme Court, and the justices agreed to hear the case later this term.

In June 1976, the Supreme Court struck down a Missouri law requiring that unmarried minors must have parental consent to obtain abortions.

In an unprecedented federal district court case in Philadelphia, the mother of a boy who had been denied entrance to the first grade because he had not satisfactorily completed kindergarten charged denial of due process and equal protection of the law and won the case.

Perhaps the most significant children's rights case of the Supreme Court's term involves an appeal of a federal district court ruling in Philadelphia establishing new procedural guarantees for minors whose parents seek to commit them to mental institutions. The district court held that because parents "at times may be acting against the interest of their children," minors were entitled to notice, hearings, counsel, and other procedural rights before commitment. The case, now under Supreme Court review, is being watched closely by both sides as an important test of the competing principles of children's rights and parents' rights. (In 1975, the Court ruled that adults could not be committed involuntarily without fair hearings.) Sandman, of the San Francisco Youth Law Center, contends that the decision on commitment

of children to mental institutions could be a culmination of the whole movement. He reasons that "in the past we've pressed the rights of children against
the state, society and the educational system. Now we have a case in which
rights of children are being weighed against parental rights. . . . And in some
ways, that's the hardest kind of case."

The Court's decision is likely to have widespread effects. According to
the National Institute of Mental Health, more than twenty-five thousand
persons under age eighteen are admitted annually to mental institutions.

The suit, a class action, was filed in behalf of all children alleged to be
mentally ill and committed to Pennsylvania mental health institutions. (Since
the suit was filed, the state has changed its procedures to provide for certain
procedural rights to minors, including a hearing and free counsel, but the suit
and the issues it raised remain before the Court.)

Lawyers for the juveniles involved charged that the children had been
denied their constitutional rights when they were committed involuntarily and
that parents did not have an absolute right to deprive their children of liberty.

Paul Piersma, director of the National Juvenile Law Center in St. Louis,
is an advocate for increasing children's rights. He states the position that "An
amazingly high percentage of parents seems to want to dump their kids into
institutions; and we've found that kids aren't helped all that much by institutions."

On the other side, lawyers, opposing the district court's ruling say that
the elaborate procedures it requires for the hospitalization of disturbed children amount to an "overdose of due process" based on the erroneous assumption that courts are better equipped than parents to decide what is best for the
children. The procedures, they fear, will make it much more difficult—even
impossible—to obtain care for children who need it.

McKnight, representing the Michigan Association of Emotionally Disturbed Children, which is opposing the ruling because of its potential impact
on Michigan and other states, warned that the "lower court ruling invites
'strangers' to usurp the custody and control of parents over their sick children."

The juvenile court is the basic arbitrator of many of the rights of children. Increasingly it appears in the late seventies that many of these arbitra-
tions are moving into the United States Supreme Court. In a persuasive book
on the subject of children's rights appropriately titled *Birthrights,* Dr. Richard
Garson makes a case for granting children *full* rights related to their destiny.
One significant question of many raised by this trend as we approach the 1980s
is: should children be granted the same legal rights as those accorded adults
—and at the same time not be held as accountable for their deviant behavior
as adults? Time may provide an answer to this question and others as we
observe the effects of increasing the rights of children over their parents and
other adults in society. One clear conclusion seems in order at this time: the
legal power of children appears to be growing.

Some Attributes of the Juvenile Delinquent

ANTISOCIAL BEHAVIOR that results in the status of delinquent correlates highly with certain sociological and psychological factors. The following profiles typifying the boys and girls committed to the California Youth Authority for the first time provide some guidelines to the understanding of the "average" juvenile delinquent. The delinquent behavior pattern depicted in these California Youth Authority profiles is very similar to the pattern revealed by the juvenile court statistics of the entire United States and by comparable studies of delinquents in Illinois, New York, Massachusetts, and other states.

Profiles of Delinquent Behavior

A California Youth Authority Male in 1975

His Home Environment:

1. Forty-three percent came from neighborhoods which were below average economically, 50 percent came from average neighborhoods, and 7 percent from above average neighborhoods.
2. Thirty-two percent lived in neighborhoods with a high level of delin-

quency, and 37 percent in moderately delinquent neighborhoods. Only 6 percent lived in neighborhoods considered nondelinquent.

3. A significant proportion (37 percent) came from homes where all or part of the family income came from public assistance.

His Family:

1. Thirty percent came from unbroken homes. One natural parent was present in an additional 59 percent of the homes.
2. One-half of the wards had at least one parent or one brother or sister who had a delinquent or criminal record.
3. Only 3 percent were married at the time of commitment, and 6 percent had children.

His Delinquent Behavior:

1. Sixty-eight percent had five or more delinquent contacts prior to commitment to the Youth Authority. Fifty-seven percent had been previously committed to a local or state facility.
2. The major problem area for 43 percent was undesirable peer influences.

His Employment/Schooling:

1. Of those in the labor force, 13 percent were employed full time while two-thirds were unemployed.
2. Twenty percent were last enrolled in the ninth grade or below. Fifty-three percent had reached the eleventh grade when they were first committed, and 10 percent had graduated from High School.[1]

A California Youth Authority Female in 1975

Her Home Environment:

1. Forty-five percent came from neighborhoods which were below average economically, 45 percent came from average neighborhoods, and 10 percent from above average neighborhoods.
2. Twenty-nine percent lived in neighborhoods with a high level of delinquency and 41 percent in moderately delinquent neighborhoods. Only 7 percent lived in neighborhoods considered nondelinquent.

[1]*Annual Statistical Report, California Youth Authority,* 1975 (Sacramento: California Department of Youth Authority, 1976).

3. A significant proportion (37 percent) came from homes where all or part of the family income came from public assistance.

Her Family:

1. Twenty-three percent came from unbroken homes. One natural parent was present in an additional 68 percent of the homes.
2. Over one-half of the wards had at least one parent or one brother or sister who had a delinquent or criminal record.
3. Eight percent were married at the time of commitment and 19 percent had children.

Her Delinquent Behavior:

1. Fifty-four percent had five or more delinquent contacts prior to commitment to the Youth Authority. Forty-three percent had been previously committed to a local or state facility.
2. The major problem area for 40 percent was mental or emotional problems.

Her Employment/Schooling:

1. Of those in the labor force, 6 percent were employed full time while 85 percent were unemployed.
2. Twenty-one percent were last enrolled in the ninth grade or below. Fifty-two percent had reached the eleventh grade, and 6 percent had graduated from High School.[2]

Statistical Highlights

1. First Commitments: In 1965 the Youth Authority received 6,190 first commitments, the highest in its history. This total decreased each year until 1972, when only 2,728 first commitments were received. During 1975 there were 3,404 first commitments to the Youth Authority, 1,829 from the juvenile courts and 1,575 from the adult courts. This is the third consecutive year since 1972 that the total of first commitments has been higher than that of the previous year. It is anticipated that this trend of increasing commitments will continue, at least for the immediate future.

2. Area of First Commitments: Sixty-two percent of all first commitments to the Youth Authority during 1975 were from the Southern California area,

[2] *Annual Statistical Report, California Youth Authority.*

with 21 percent from the San Francisco Bay area, and the balance of 17 percent from the remaining counties. These percentages parallel the total youth population of these areas. Los Angeles County supplied approximately 34 percent of all commitments, while San Diego County was second highest with 9 percent followed by San Francisco and Alameda counties with approximately 5 percent each.

3. Court of First Commitments: During 1975, 54 percent of all commitments were from the juvenile courts and 46 percent from the adult courts. This is in contrast to the 75 percent committed by the juvenile courts and 25 percent by the adult courts in 1965. The Probation Subsidy program has had its greatest effect in curtailing juvenile court commitments, as shown by the shift in the proportions of juvenile court/criminal court cases committed over the past several years. A trend recently, however, has been for an increasing proportion of juvenile court cases being committed to the Youth Authority.

4. Age of First Commitments: The mean age of first commitments to the Youth Authority during 1975 was 17.5 years, with a mean of 16.2 years for juvenile court cases and 19.0 years for criminal court cases. The mean age of juvenile court commitments has increased from 15.5 years in 1965 to 16.2 years in 1975. The mean age of criminal court commitments has remained about the same over this time period.

5. First Commitment Offenses: For the first time in Youth Authority history, robbery ranked as the most common commitment offense, followed by burglary and then assault and battery a distant third. Together the violent-type offenses of homicide, robbery, and assault accounted for 42 percent of all commitments, with property-type offenses accounting for 39 percent. This is in contrast to 15 percent violent-type offenses and 40 percent property-type offenses in 1965.

6. Length of Stay: The mean length of stay of wards in Youth Authority institutions has increased from 9.4 months in 1965 to 12.7 months in 1975. The major factors contributing to changes in institutional length of stay are the increasing proportions of wards committed for violent-type offenses and to changes in Youth Authority Board policy regarding time setting for this group.

7. Long-Term Trends: Institutional population in the Youth Authority has increased from approximately 4,200 in 1960 to a high of 6,700 in 1964 and then back down to 4,100 in 1973. Current Institutional population as of the end of 1975 was 4,758. Youth Authority parole population over the same period increased from 10,000 in 1960 to a high of over 15,000 in 1966 and then back to the current figure of slightly under 8,000 at the end of 1975. Youth Authority institutional population is expected to continue to increase in line with the increasing first commitments. Parole population, on the other hand, will continue to decline for another year or so at which point it will stabilize and begin an upward trend.[3]

Age and Juvenile Delinquency

Of the 7,912,348 arrests in 1976, youths under eighteen years of age constituted 24.9 percent of the total. They accounted for close to half of all arrests for burglary, larceny, and auto theft. While these offenses are categorized as "serious" crimes by the FBI, all of them are property offenses that do not involve the use of weapons, violence, or force. Table 3.1 presents the total number of arrests made in 1976 together with the percentage distribution by age. The percentage of children arrested increases progressively from ages ten through sixteen and then declines each year from seventeen through twenty. The lower arrest rates of very young children undoubtedly reflect the tendency of adults to deal with childhood deviance on an informal basis. Nevertheless, there were 73,223 children ten years of age and under arrested in 1976.

The sixteen-, seventeen-, and eighteen-year olds are arrested more frequently than persons of any other age category. The cultural role of a person sixteen, seventeen or eighteen years old is particularly unclear in our society. He has attained a high degree of physical maturity and yet is denied any significant economic or social role. This is especially true of the male in a poverty area. He has most of the social, sexual, and material wants of a man, yet without money he is deprived of a legal means of satisfying these wants. He has only two alternatives: he can either continue in school and suppress or repress his desires or drop out of school and attempt to find employment or some other way of obtaining money. Unemployment, especially among sixteen- and seventeen-year-olds who enter the labor market before completing high school, helps to explain the age distribution of arrests for delinquency. Youths tend to quit high school partly because of lack of interest in education but also because they feel the need to earn money to obtain the material things to which they aspire. Lack of the education and skills necessary to obtain worthwhile employment results in further frustration. Most fail to obtain employment they consider acceptable; many do not achieve steady employment of any kind. Thus, unemployed and without money, these young people find themselves on the streets with nothing to do. These are the boys who are likely to engage in delinquent activity, particularly property offenses.

Many had some experiences at delinquency when they were thirteen and

---

[3]*Annual Statistical Report, California Youth Authority.*

Table 3.1

Total Arrests by Age, 1976
(10,119 agencies; 1976 estimated population 175,499,000)

Offense Charged	Grand Total All Ages	Ages Under 15	Ages Under 18	Ages 18 and Over	Age 10 and Under	11-12	13-14	15	16	17	18	19	20	21
TOTAL	7,912,348	665,781	1,973,254	5,939,094	73,223	148,112	444,446	392,526	465,308	449,639	469,471	429,657	386,792	355,572
Percent distribution[a]	100.0	8.4	24.9	75.1	.9	1.9	5.6	5.0	5.9	5.7	5.9	5.4	4.9	4.5
Criminal homicide:														
(a) Murder and nonnegligent manslaughter	14,113	190	1,302	12,811	12	30	148	197	416	499	692	755	665	690
(b) Manslaughter by negligence	2,650	43	275	2,375	8	7	28	26	91	115	173	192	168	159
Forcible rape	21,687	915	3,745	17,942	57	158	700	685	1,019	1,126	1,343	1,389	1,294	1,330
Robbery	110,296	10,156	36,990	73,306	539	2,034	7,583	7,532	9,631	9,671	9,696	8,480	7,103	6,482
Aggravated assault	192,753	9,552	32,678	160,075	947	2,151	6,454	6,149	8,145	8,832	9,437	9,593	9,129	8,854
Burglary—breaking or entering	406,821	78,275	209,396	197,425	8,374	18,162	51,739	43,147	46,860	41,114	34,954	26,019	20,228	16,463
Larceny-theft	928,078	173,535	399,235	528,843	21,019	46,553	105,963	73,124	80,558	72,018	65,566	52,634	43,377	36,757
Motor vehicle theft	110,708	14,726	58,279	52,429	371	1,703	12,652	14,857	16,107	12,589	9,179	6,755	5,053	4,240
Violent crime[b]	338,849	20,813	74,715	264,134	1,555	4,373	14,885	14,563	19,211	20,128	21,168	20,217	18,191	17,356
Percent distribution[a]	100.0	6.1	22.0	78.0	.5	1.3	4.4	4.3	5.7	5.9	6.2	6.0	5.4	5.1
Property crime[c]	1,445,607	266,536	666,910	778,697	29,764	66,418	170,354	131,128	143,525	125,721	109,699	85,408	68,658	57,460
Percent distribution[a]	100.0	18.4	46.1	53.9	2.1	4.6	11.8	9.1	9.9	8.7	7.6	5.9	4.7	4.0
Subtotal for above offenses	1,787,106	287,392	741,900	1,045,206	31,327	70,798	185,267	145,717	162,827	145,964	131,040	105,817	87,017	74,975
Percent distribution[a]	100.0	16.1	41.5	58.5	1.8	4.0	10.4	8.2	9.1	8.2	7.3	5.9	4.9	4.2
Other assaults	354,010	25,907	69,904	284,106	3,044	6,356	16,507	12,924	15,320	15,753	17,187	17,130	17,098	16,668
Arson	14,534	4,626	7,601	6,933	1,372	1,190	2,064	1,172	974	829	712	634	496	405

Offense													
Forgery and counterfeiting	55,791	1,090	6,681	49,110	39	167	884	1,085	1,961	2,545	3,405	3,497	3,588	3,654
Fraud	161,429	879	4,614	156,815	82	160	637	683	1,288	1,764	4,122	5,843	7,145	8,418
Embezzlement	8,218	103	525	7,693	3	24	76	58	138	226	274	309	399	447
Stolen property: buying, receiving, possessing	92,055	8,142	28,940	63,115	565	1,681	5,896	5,685	7,472	7,641	7,664	6,578	5,567	4,838
Vandalism	175,082	60,569	109,712	65,370	12,441	17,130	30,998	18,105	16,897	14,141	9,925	7,451	5,928	4,793
Weapons: carrying, possessing, etc.	121,722	4,549	19,649	102,073	297	824	3,428	3,780	5,245	6,075	7,159	6,639	6,242	6,262
Prostitution and commercialized vice	58,648	205	2,570	56,078	10	21	174	301	661	1,403	3,996	5,291	5,399	5,972
Sex offenses (except forcible rape and prostitution)	51,776	3,779	9,902	41,874	445	808	2,526	1,904	2,074	2,145	2,196	2,355	2,329	2,266
Narcotic drug laws	500,540	15,514	119,522	381,018	244	1,330	13,940	22,135	36,677	45,196	52,053	48,457	42,497	36,550
Gambling	65,437	392	2,547	62,890	16	40	336	470	722	963	1,724	1,742	1,780	1,710
Offenses against family and children	58,249	1,595	4,198	54,051	753	212	630	624	936	1,043	2,925	2,770	2,676	2,683
Driving under the influence	837,910	254	17,264	820,646	50	32	172	697	4,768	11,545	28,842	33,007	33,758	35,488
Liquor laws	302,943	9,679	108,934	194,009	271	773	8,635	16,891	34,883	47,481	42,383	32,196	23,094	9,974
Drunkenness	1,071,131	3,866	39,750	1,031,381	240	392	3,234	5,780	11,197	18,907	35,793	35,328	34,106	37,914
Disorderly conduct	545,639	35,845	113,893	431,741	3,996	8,274	23,575	20,815	26,909	30,329	39,075	36,474	33,035	30,759
Vagrancy	32,731	1,741	5,848	26,883	99	303	1,339	1,326	1,249	1,532	2,245	2,039	1,824	2,225
All other offenses (except traffic)	1,330,969	107,901	295,952	1,035,017	13,179	23,048	71,674	63,036	63,402	61,613	73,630	73,715	70,604	67,735
Suspicion	31,298	2,363	8,213	23,085	233	492	1,638	1,639	2,012	2,199	3,121	2,385	2,210	1,836
Curfew and loitering law violations	88,601	24,217	88,601	—	968	4,184	19,065	21,265	28,991	14,128	—	—	—	—
Runaways	166,529	65,173	166,529	—	3,549	9,873	51,751	46,434	38,705	16,217	—	—	—	—

SOURCE: Federal Bureau of Investigation, *Uniform Crime Reports for the United States, 1976* (Washington, D.C.: U.S. Government Printing Office, 1977), Table 32.

[a] Because of rounding, the percentages may not add to total.

[b] Violent crime is offenses of murder, forcible rape, robbery, and aggravated assault.

[c] Property crime is offenses of burglary, larceny, and auto theft.

fourteen, as indicated by the high arrest rates at these ages. While at school they were occupied part of the time. Once they have dropped out of school, their need for money not satisfied legitimately, they may and frequently do turn to delinquency and criminality. The largest number and percentage of school dropouts appear to coincide with the minimum age at which children can legally leave school. This fact tends to confirm a relationship between dropping out of school, unemployment, and delinquency.[4] The estimated effect of unemployment on delinquency was found by one researcher to be uniformly positive. A 1 percent increase in unemployment is associated on the average with an increase of approximately 0.15 percent in the rate of delinquency.[5]

The relationship between age and juvenile delinquency is more than a statistical association. Also involved are the *cultural roles of the individual at different age levels.* Offenses associated with the cultural role of the child, for example, include rock-throwing and vandalism. This sort of behavior usually decreases through adolescence. Offenses involving daring and aggression tend to increase in middle adolescence for males, then to decrease in later adolescence as the youth's anxiety about supermasculine identity lessens.

Cavan has noted that child and adolescent offense patterns parallel social situations and roles. Offenses of young children are mostly limited to the home, the immediate neighborhood, the school, and a few local institutions accessible to a small child. Adolescents tend to use brute strength or crude weapons, whereas the sophisticated adult criminal depends more on skill and psychological manipulation of victims. Young offenders often combine play with their offenses, while the adult criminal is serious and methodical. Young offenders usually do not plan their escapades, but seize upon good opportunities for committing offenses (theft), while the adult offender carefully plans his crimes. Further, the needs satisfied by antisocial behavior differ with age: very few adults are arrested for auto theft that is intended to be simply a joyride, and adolescents rarely engage in fraud and gambling.[6]

Sex and Juvenile Delinquency

Juvenile delinquency is essentially a problem of boys. Juvenile court statistics indicate that boys are referred to court four times as often as girls. Moreover, boys are arrested, charged in court, and committed to correctional institutions more often than girls.

Delinquency is predominantly a boy's problem for much the same reasons that crime is a man's problem. As previously indicated, any person's total

---

[4]Belton M. Fleisher, *The Economics of Delinquency* (Chicago: Quadrangle Books, 1966), pp. 83–84.

[5]Fleisher, *The Economics of Delinquency,* p. 68.

[6]Ruth Shonle Cavan, *Juvenile Delinquency* (Philadelphia: Lippincott, 1962), p. 141.

life organization is determined to a significant extent by the particular subculture in which he or she lives. Thus, male and female role expectations and behavior are strongly influenced by the larger cultural environment and by one's subcultural identifications. Since men are expected to be aggressive, males are more likely to be delinquent than females, who are expected to adopt a more passive role. Despite this, the arrest rate of females is increasing. This may be a consequence of the narrowing of the difference between male and female cultural roles in recent years. The economic and social roles available to women in our society tend ever more closely to approximate those available to men. This is particularly true in the big cities. It is no longer unusual for a woman to work outside the home, to be a principal breadwinner, and to share equally with the male members of the household in the decision-making processes affecting all members. A young girl brought up in such a home, identifying with her mother, tends to consider herself as important as male members of the family, believes herself capable of doing almost anything they can do, and feels free to engage in most of the activities that they are involved in— including delinquency.

In some measure because of these developing attitudes, statistics reveal that between 1960 and 1976 the general crime and delinquency rate for females rose more than six times faster than for males. The most significant increases were in burglary, armed robbery, and possession of a deadly weapon. The increase is over 600 percent in females under eighteen years of age. To some extent these figures may be magnified by a changing attitude toward females. Whereas once, many females, especially those under eighteen, may not have been formally subjected to the judicial system, they may now be victims of "overkill" in terms of arrest and court decisions by the developing attitude toward women: "You want to be equal. Okay, we will not show you any special courtesy because you are a female."

In an interview for *People* magazine in response to the question, "How big a part does women's liberation play in female criminality?" Criminologist Dr. Freda Adler replied,

> The dramatic rise cannot be directly attributed to one factor. The feminist connection is that women are taking on more of the behavior of men. This also means taking on the stress, strain and frustration that males have traditionally dealt with. Many of these women, unskilled and untrained, may turn in desperation to crime. There was a time when a female confined her criminal acts to prostitution and shoplifting. Now she is committing armed robbery, auto theft, and burglary, traditionally male crimes, so that we see a definite change in both the dimension and form of female criminality."[7]

---

[7]Freda Adler, "In Her Own Words," *People,* October 13, 1975, pp. 20–22.

Women now seem to be gravitating toward the center of the action in crime and delinquency. While this, of course, is not a positive outgrowth of the women's movement, it does nevertheless show that women's self-concepts are more nearly approaching that of men's equals than in the past. The general attitudes inherent in the women's liberation attitude tend to filter down to adolescent girls—and no doubt are part of the causal backdrop to increased female delinquent behavior.

In a report recently published by the National Institute of Mental Health, Dr. Rita James Simon, professor of Sociology at the University of Illinois, referred to statistics that show that the percentage of women arrested for crimes of violence has fluctuated between 10 and 13 percent for the past twenty years.[8] Her analysis of female criminality concludes that the increase is not from violence but comes from property offenses such as forgery, fraud, and embezzlement. James notes that the picture for property offenses is markedly different between the ratio of men to women in crime. For example, in 1953, one in every twelve persons arrested for a property crime was a woman, and in 1973, one in every five property crimes was committed by a woman. In her report, Dr. Simon comments: "It is reasonable to assume that the women's movement has had some effect on the psyche, the consciousness and the self perceptions of many women in American society. But the extent to which it has motivated those women to act outside the law in order to gain financial rewards, vengeance, or power is still too early to assess." Dr. Simon further states that her major hypothesis is that increased participation in the labor force in recent years has given women more opportunities to commit larceny, fraud, embezzlement, and other financial and white collar crimes. "If the present trends continue, in 20 years women will probably be involved in white collar crimes in a proportion commensurate with their representation in the society. The fact that female arrests have increased for these offenses and not for all offenses is consistent both with the opportunity theory and with the presence of a sizable women's movement."

In another study of self-reporting by boys and girls by Peter C. Kratcoski and John E. Kratcoski, it was revealed that girls are becoming more involved in delinquent activities formerly the province of boys.[9] The researchers studied eleventh and twelfth graders in three high schools, including college preparatory, vocational, and general education students. The students were given a self-reported delinquency questionnaire listing illegal acts and asking which had been committed and background questions. Of twenty-five illegal acts males continue to be more aggressive, but in regard to minor delinquent behavior the study revealed few male-female differences, especially for popular

[8]Rita James Simon, "The Contemporary Woman and Crime," *National Institute of Health Publication* (Washington, D. C.: U. S. Government Printing Office, September 1975), p. 46.

[9]Peter C. Kratcoski and John E. Kratcoski, "Changing Patterns in the Delinquent Activities of Boys and Girls: A Self-Reported Delinquency Analysis," *Adolescence* 10 (Spring 1975):563–607.

activities such as drug use. They concluded that the closeness of the male-female ratio in delinquency "may derive from changing female roles, or from increasing willingness of police to punish illegal acts committed by females, causing more to be reported."

These patterns are clearly revealed in the most recent juvenile court statistics.

Not only are girls being arrested more frequently for crimes previously exclusive to boys, but the percentage increases are higher than those for boys. The largest percentage increase in arrests of children under eighteen from 1960 to 1972 was for alleged violations of narcotic drug laws. While the number of arrests for narcotics offenses has continued to increase for boys, the number of arrests for girls under eighteen has declined since 1970. The reasons for this are unclear.

For females under eighteen years of age, the largest percentage increase in arrests of children under eighteen from 1970 to 1975 was for offenses against family and children. Arrests for boys increased 386.8 percent; of girls, 586.9 percent. (This does not include forcible rape, which rose 4800 percent between 1970 and 1975.) These tremendous changes would appear to reflect the increased use of violence among juveniles. This also reflects, in part, a change in law-enforcement policy, tending to take control of family problems away from the family.

As Table 3.2 clearly indicates, the arrest rates of girls for all sorts of delinquent behavior are indeed increasing. Moreover, arrests of girls for burglary, larceny, and auto theft have been increasing far more rapidly than have arrests of boys for these offenses. The total number of arrests of females under eighteen for burglary increased 62.9 percent from 1970 to 1975, while the increase in arrests of males under eighteen for the same offense was 42.1 percent. During the same period the arrest rate of girls under eighteen for auto theft increased by 12.5 percent, while the arrest rate for boys under eighteen for that offense decreased 19.6 percent. Larceny arrests of girls increased 37.9 percent during this period; of boys 20.0 percent.

This trend is especially reflected in drug abuse, which has increasingly become a unisex activity. In this regard, J. S. Rosenberg, S. V. Kasl, and R. M. Berberian, in a study of male-female adolescent drug use, found a rising rate of female drug use.[10] In the study, sex differences in preferred illicit drugs and trends in use over time were identified for a large sample of junior and senior high school students. Current use and lifetime prevalence were anonymously reported by two comparable samples one year apart. Between survey years the number of females who "ever used" a drug increased significantly for nine out of eleven drug categories, while the number of males increased in only three categories. They found that "current usage remained fairly stable

---

[10]J. S. Rosenberg, S. W. Kasl, and R. M. Berberian, "Sex Differences in Adolescent Drug Use: Recent Trends," *Addictive Diseases* 36 (January 1974):146.

Table 3.2

Total Arrest Trends by Sex for Persons Under 18, 1970–75
(4,217 agencies; 1975 estimated population 130,678,000)

| | Males | | | | | | Females | | | | | |
| | Total | | | Under 18 | | | Total | | | Under 18 | | |
Offense Charged	1970	1975	Percent Change	1970	1975	Percent Change	1970	1975	Percent Change	1970	1975	Percent Change
TOTAL	4,858,934	4,945,313	+1.8	1,133,092	1,283,786	+13.3	827,793	993,182	+20.0	311,039	350,982	+12.8
Criminal homicide:												
(a) Murder and nonnegligent manslaughter	9,077	11,196	+23.3	933	1,170	+25.4	1,711	2,020	+18.1	84	131	+56.0
(b) Manslaughter by negligence	2,174	1,741	−19.9	179	200	+11.7	274	232	−15.3	22	39	+77.3
Forcible rape	13,176	17,524	+33.0	2,686	3,140	+16.9	6	165	+2,650.0	1	49	+4,800.0
Robbery	70,432	105,279	+49.5	23,656	36,916	+56.1	4,672	7,993	+71.1	1,823	3,001	+64.6
Aggravated assault	96,181	131,881	+37.1	15,574	23,867	+53.2	14,125	20,877	+47.8	2,554	4,593	+79.8
Burglary—breaking or entering	234,839	329,682	+40.4	123,512	175,537	+42.1	11,448	18,630	+62.7	5,858	9,545	+62.9
Larceny—theft	394,336	520,579	+32.0	208,028	249,615	+20.0	158,784	250,180	+57.6	74,776	103,100	+37.9
Motor vehicle theft	105,736	88,714	−16.1	60,603	48,724	−19.6	5,622	6,503	+15.7	3,388	3,813	+12.5
Violent crime*	188,866	265,880	+40.8	42,849	65,093	+51.9	20,514	31,055	+51.4	4,462	7,774	+74.2
Property crime†	734,911	938,975	+27.8	392,143	473,876	+20.8	175,854	275,313	+56.6	84,022	116,458	+38.6
Subtotal for above offenses	925,951	1,206,596	+30.3	435,171	539,169	+23.9	196,642	306,600	+55.9	88,506	124,271	+40.4
Other assaults	219,402	240,587	+9.7	36,147	46,083	+27.5	33,038	39,784	+20.4	9,151	12,755	+39.4
Arson	7,536	9,868	+30.9	4,617	5,483	+18.8	798	1,327	+66.3	382	599	+56.8
Forgery and counterfeiting	30,689	31,649	+3.1	3,148	3,892	+23.6	9,627	13,183	+36.9	1,143	1,599	+39.9

Fraud	47,710	72,648	+52.3	1,798	2,817	+56.7	17,817	38,106	+113.9	633	1,034	+63.3
Embezzlement	5,793	5,429	−6.3	253	434	+71.5	1,917	2,676	+39.6	88	123	+39.8
Stolen property; buying, receiving, possessing	50,803	72,459	+42.7	15,455	24,612	+59.2	5,281	8,827	+67.1	1,227	2,297	+87.2
Vandalism	89,024	125,502	+40.8	65,733	82,565	+25.6	7,511	11,198	+49.1	4,798	6,763	+41.0
Weapons; carrying, possessing, etc.	81,624	97,506	+19.5	13,854	16,748	+20.9	5,929	8,692	+46.6	591	1,122	+89.8
Prostitution and commercialized vice	7,995	12,125	+51.7	305	539	+76.7	34,998	34,985	—	749	1,678	+123.8
Sex offenses (except forcible rape and prostitution)	36,942	38,393	+3.9	7,060	7,674	+8.7	5,332	3,381	−36.6	1,894	973	−48.6
Narcotic drug laws	249,883	334,528	+33.9	53,158	73,403	+47.5	47,608	54,982	+15.5	15,555	15,472	−.5
Gambling	67,308	40,036	−40.4	1,358	1,471	+8.3	5,812	3,841	−33.9	54	82	+51.9
Offenses against family and children	44,004	29,939	−32.0	515	2,507	+386.8	4,362	4,424	+1.4	245	1,683	+586.9
Driving under the influence	340,873	509,723	+49.5	3,850	9,707	+152.1	24,394	45,879	+88.1	199	771	+287.4
Liquor laws	171,355	158,145	−7.7	55,282	59,539	+7.7	25,684	27,319	+6.4	11,978	15,612	+30.3
Drunkenness	1,279,657	802,854	−37.3	30,523	25,818	−15.4	97,049	61,949	−36.2	4,592	3,982	−13.3
Disorderly conduct	383,254	345,798	−9.8	87,483	75,094	−14.2	75,241	96,511	+28.3	19,237	16,190	−15.8
Vagrancy	75,481	25,820	−65.8	9,459	3,702	−60.9	18,979	5,644	−70.3	1,653	650	−60.7
All other offenses (except traffic)	595,739	651,222	+9.3	160,012	162,933	+1.8	112,011	123,582	+10.3	50,601	43,036	−15.0
Suspicion (not included in totals)	53,890	20,676	−61.6	14,214	5,358	−62.3	8,668	3,414	−60.6	2,935	893	−69.6
Curfew and loitering law violations	75,419	74,485	−1.2	75,419	74,485	−1.2	20,277	18,508	−8.7	20,277	18,508	−8.7
Runaways	72,492	60,711	−17.1	72,492	60,111	−17.1	77,486	81,784	+5.5	77,486	81,784	+5.5

SOURCE: FBI, *Uniform Crime Reports, 1975*, p. 185.

*Violent crime is offenses of murder, forcible rape, robbery and aggravated assault.

†Property crime is offenses of burglary, larceny-theft and motor vehicle theft.

for both sexes." Although the females' overall use is more similar to the males' in survey year two than in year one, the data suggested preferences for certain drugs by sex: (1) more males than females have either "ever used" or are current users of alcohol, marijuana, hashish, glue, and heroin; (2) more females were current users of amphetamines and barbiturates.

Despite such reported increases in drug use by females, larceny, theft, robbery, and other property offenses are still more characteristic of boys than of girls. It is for these offenses, and for mischief, destruction of property, truancy, and traffic violations, that boys are brought before juvenile courts. The type of offenses with which boys are charged tends to be overt, aggressive in form, and harmful to others. Girls, on the other hand, are brought to court principally on the basis of petitions alleging incorrigible behavior, running away, petty larceny, and sex offenses.

The sex ratio of male adult criminals to female adult criminals is approximately 6 to 1; this is much larger than the juvenile delinquency ratio of 3.6 boys to 1 girl. It is therefore assumed that boy offenders are more likely to continue into adult criminality than are girl offenders.

John P. Clark and Edward W. Haurek, in a study of age and sex roles of adolescents, agree that the disproportionate ratio of male and female offenders is largely a reflection of the more docile and dependent role traditionally played by girls and women in our society.[11] They question, however, the magnitude of the reported sex ratios. Differential treatment of the sexes in reporting, enforcement, and court handling may account in large part for the higher official male offense rates.

This view is seriously challenged by Meda Chesney-Lind and other researchers who maintain that the evidence indicates discrimination against females by our juvenile justice system. In a study of the Honolulu Juvenile Court, Chesney-Lind found:

1. The great majority of females referred to the court were charged with running away from home, incorrigibility, curfew violations, and other conduct which would not be criminal if committed by adults. Very few boys were charged with these offenses. Furthermore, the results of self-report studies indicated that the percentages of girls and boys engaging in these types of behavior were about the same.

2. Females were far more likely than males to be given physical examinations. Seventy to 80 percent of the females were examined as opposed to 12 to 18 percent of the males. Furthermore, girls were given gynecological examinations even if they were referred to the court for offenses not related to sexual behavior, such as burglary or larceny.

3. While females constituted 17 to 20 percent of the children before the

---

[11]John P. Clark and Edward W. Haurek, "Age and Sex Roles of Adolescents and Their Involvement in Misconduct: A Reappraisal," *Sociology and Social Research* 50 (July 1966): 495–508.

court, 30 percent of them were kept in detention and on the average spent three times as long in detention as were males.

4. Whereas 25 percent of the males referred to the court were immediately released, only 10 percent of the females were. Also females were twice as likely to be sent to a state training school as were males.[12]

After reviewing studies of females involved with juvenile justice in other parts of the United States, Chesney-Lind concluded that the juvenile court was harsher with girls than with boys: girls were six times more likely than boys to appear before a juvenile court judge on their first offense. They were also more likely to be placed on probation or other supervision after only one offense. Girls are more likely to be incarcerated for minor offenses even before trial than are boys, and the commitments of girls to institutions are for longer periods of time.[13]

Ethnicity, Race, and Juvenile Delinquency

Most persons who migrated from Europe to the United States in the latter part of the nineteenth century and the first quarter of the twentieth century came in search of economic opportunities. By and large they migrated from rural areas in eastern and southern Europe, with well-developed languages and cultures differing from those of the American majority. Immigration laws and practices excluded people with serious diseases or histories of criminality. Generally, the immigrant was poor, uneducated, honest, and willing and able to work. In the United States he tended to settle in areas inhabited by members of his ethnic group because in these areas he found people who understood his language and his ways. Furthermore, his initial migration was usually encouraged by relatives or friends in the United States, and his first residence was in or near the homes of these relatives or friends. This sort of migration pattern resulted in the establishment and expansion of self-segregated populations of Polish, Italian, Jewish, and other ethnic groups in the big cities.

Although the cultures of these ethnic groups differed from that of the dominant American society, these people were not delinquent or criminal, nor did they approve of violation of American laws. Yet, as we have seen, official data on crime and delinquency show that the children of these immigrants had the highest rates of criminality and delinquency.

Before 1930, over 50 percent of the delinquency cases were American-born children of foreign-born parents. Since that time their numbers and rate have continually decreased but, of course, so has most of the immigration. The

---

[12]Meda Chesney-Lind, "Judicial Enforcement of the Female Sex Role," *Issues in Criminology* 8 (Fall 1973):51–69.

[13]Meda Chesney-Lind, "Juvenile Delinquency—The Sexualization of Female Crime," *Psychology Today* 8 (July 1974):43–46.

most recent immigrants to the urban slum areas are Negroes, Puerto Ricans, Mexicans, and to a lesser degree poor whites from Southern mountain states. Children of these more recent migrants to urban areas now constitute an overwhelming proportion of delinquency cases. Arrest rates and court statistics reveal that the highest rates of juvenile delinquency in America today appear among Negroes, Puerto Ricans, Mexican-Americans, and other Latin Americans.

There are many explanations offered for the fact that the most recent groups to migrate to urban centers always have the highest delinquency rates. Historically, such minority groups have been restricted or excluded from full participation in the social and economic life of American society. With the exception of the American Negro, minority groups speak a foreign language, are socialized in a society with a culture different from the dominant one, and are regarded as foreigners by members of the dominant society. The societal reaction to them as persons with different languages and cultural backgrounds makes it exceedingly difficult for minority group members to make the "necessary" adjustments to prepare them for the middle class status. They find it difficult to obtain employment other than unskilled labor, partly because of lack of formal education, partly because of discrimination. They are often frustrated in their search for avenues of assimilation because they find greater obstacles in their paths than did immigrants from Europe in past generations.

In Table 3.3 we can observe that Indian, Chinese, and Japanese youths under eighteen have low delinquency rates. This may be accounted for by strong intrafamilial and community organizations that tend to control children's misbehavior.

In a study to examine the validity of official statistics, Chambliss and Nagasawa compared delinquency statistics with responses to questionnaires regarding delinquent behavior. The subjects were white, black, and Japanese boys enrolled at a high school in the central, lower class, *high*-delinquency area of a metropolis. Questionnaires were administered to 226 male students, 201 of whom responded. Self-reported delinquency derived from these responses were compared with official statistics. According to the official statistics, the black students had a far higher rate than did the white and Japanese students. The self-reported rates indicated a fairly similar involvement in delinquency for all three groups.

The researchers attributed the differences in official rates to:

1. Bias of the official agencies.
2. Visibility of the offenses.
3. Demeanor of the youth when confronted with adult authority.

They concluded that their data supported the argument that official statistics may tell us a good deal about the activities of agencies responsible for generating statistics but very little about the distribution of delinquent activities. The official rates, they felt, provided a complete distortion of the actual incidence of delinquent behavior.[14]

The Negro and Juvenile Delinquency

Negroes constitute approximately 12 percent of the total population of the United States, yet in 1976 they constituted 22 percent of all persons arrested under eighteen years of age and approximately 25 percent of all adult arrests. Their arrests for Crime Index offenses constitute over half of the total number of arrests. Negro arrest rates for crime as well as delinquency continue to exceed those of other minority groups—Puerto Ricans, Mexican-Americans, Chinese, Japanese, and American Indians.[15]

More Negro youths are committed to institutional care than white youths. This may be due to the juvenile courts' philosophy of earlier state intervention in the case of youths living under conditions of severe poverty, accompanied by family disorganization. Action is taken regarding Negroes more often and for less serious offenses than more favored groups. Like the immigrants of earlier periods, Negroes today are restricted to depressed and obsolescent residential areas, which manifest more forms of social disorganization than most other areas. Vice, crime, and social disorder become traditional in such ghetto areas, owing to selective negative forces. In many instances Negroes move into slum areas abandoned by the poor immigrant groups that preceded them. Delinquent groups and patterns of behavior are present and are rapidly transmitted to the new arrivals.

A veiled, castelike system accounts in part for the differences between white and Negro delinquency rates. A subordinate socioeconomic position or lifestyle, with its bitter implications of economic deprivation, overcrowded and substandard housing, and inadequate education, has a tremendous negative impact on the self-concepts and personalities of developing children. These factors and others already noted produce a disproportionately high rate of delinquency among Negro children.

It has often been alleged that achievement motivation is a significant factor contributing to the delinquency of black adolescents. A study by Frank H. Farley and Trevor Sewell explored this issue.[16] The study was concerned

---

[14]William J. Chambliss and Richard H. Nagasawa, "On the Validity of Official Statistics: A Comparative Study of White, Black and Japanese High School Boys," *Journal of Research in Crime and Delinquency* 6 (January 1969):71–77.

[15]Joseph H. Douglass, "The Extent and Characteristics of Juvenile Delinquency Among Negroes in the United States," *Journal of Negro Education* 28 (Summer 1959):214–29.

[16]Frank H. Farley and Trevor Sewell, "Attribution and Achievement Motivation Differences Between Delinquent and Non-Delinquent Black Adolescents," *Adolescence* 22 (Fall 1975): 391–97.

Table 3.3

Total Arrests by Race for Persons Under 18, 1976
(10,058 agencies; 1976 estimated population 173,488,000)

Offense Charged	Arrests Under 18							Percent Distribution[a]						
	Total	White	Negro	Indian	Chinese	Japanese	All Others	Total	White	Negro	Indian	Chinese	Japanese	All Others
TOTAL	1,848,625	1,407,153	406,231	15,748	612	1,047	17,834	100.0	76.1	22.0	0.9	b	0.1	1.0
Criminal homicide:														
(a) Murder and nonnegligent manslaughter	1,163	520	620	8	—	2	13	100.0	44.7	53.3	.7	—	.2	1.1
(b) Manslaughter by negligence	268	224	39	2	—	—	3	100.0	83.6	14.6	.7	—	—	1.1
Forcible rape	3,376	1,490	1,796	35	—	5	50	100.0	44.1	53.2	1.0	—	.1	1.5
Robbery	28,269	9,728	17,929	136	8	19	449	100.0	34.4	63.4	.5	—	.1	1.6
Aggravated assault	28,816	16,533	11,775	252	12	3	241	100.0	57.4	40.9	.9	—	b	.8
Burglary—breaking or entering	196,612	140,472	52,508	1,365	45	161	2,061	100.0	71.4	26.7	.7	—	.1	1.0
Larceny-theft	383,295	264,101	110,568	2,788	232	417	5,189	100.0	68.9	28.8	.7	0.1	.1	1.4
Motor vehicle theft	53,402	40,357	11,516	620	21	26	862	100.0	75.6	21.6	1.2	—	—	1.6
Violent crime[c]	61,624	28,271	32,120	431	20	29	753	100.0	45.9	52.1	.7	—	—	1.2
Property crime[d]	633,309	444,930	174,592	4,773	298	604	8,112	100.0	70.3	27.6	.8	—	.1	1.3
Subtotal for above offenses	695,201	473,425	206,751	5,206	318	633	8,868	100.0	68.1	29.7	.7	—	.1	1.3
Other assaults	64,842	40,790	22,775	416	24	31	806	100.0	62.9	35.1	.6	—	—	1.2
Arson	7,229	5,983	1,161	30	2	1	52	100.0	82.8	16.1	.4	—	—	.7
Forgery and counterfeiting	6,457	5,130	1,245	48	1	1	32	100.0	79.4	19.3	.7	—	—	.5
Fraud	4,386	3,330	1,009	21	1	1	24	100.0	75.9	23.0	.5	—	—	.5

Embezzlement	507	401	99	3	—	—	4	100.0	79.1	19.5	.6	—	—	.8
Stolen property: buying, receiving, possessing	26,963	18,679	7,872	138	7	10	257	100.0	69.3	29.2	.5	—	—	1.0
Vandalism	103,528	88,730	13,603	479	19	36	661	100.0	85.7	13.1	.5	—	—	.6
Weapons: carrying, possessing, etc.	18,508	12,904	5,306	124	2	7	165	100.0	69.7	28.7	.7	—	—	.9
Prostitution and commercialized vice	2,405	984	1,371	13	—	1	36	100.0	40.9	57.0	.5	—	—	1.5
Sex offenses (except forcible rape and prostitution)	9,273	6,518	2,625	42	2	7	79	100.0	70.3	28.3	.5	—	—	.9
Narcotic drug laws	114,613	99,492	13,756	629	31	53	652	100.0	86.8	12.0	.5	—	—	.6
Gambling	2,346	1,053	1,194	4	3	1	86	100.0	45.1	50.9	.2	.1	—	3.7
Offenses against family and children	4,162	3,053	1,054	35	—	2	18	100.0	73.4	25.3	.8	—	—	.4
Driving under the influence	16,986	16,023	576	237	2	7	141	100.0	94.3	3.4	1.4	—	—	.8
Liquor laws	107,260	101,948	3,162	1,538	20	25	567	100.0	95.0	2.9	1.4	—	—	.5
Drunkenness	39,321	35,702	2,520	911	9	7	172	100.0	90.8	6.4	2.3	—	—	.4
Disorderly conduct	108,041	83,257	23,416	786	22	11	549	100.0	77.1	21.7	.7	—	—	.5
Vagrancy	4,312	3,113	1,042	36	2	—	119	100.0	72.2	24.2	.8	—	—	2.8
All other offenses (except traffic)	252,418	195,058	52,628	2,199	58	114	2,361	100.0	77.3	20.8	.9	—	—	.9
Suspicion	7,943	5,943	1,893	54	1	1	51	100.0	74.8	23.8	.7	—	—	.6
Curfew and loitering law violations	87,856	61,829	24,294	1,055	31	40	607	100.0	70.4	27.7	1.2	—	—	.7
Runaways	164,068	143,803	16,879	1,744	57	58	1,527	100.0	87.6	10.3	1.1	—	—	.9

SOURCE: FBI, *Uniform Crime Reports, 1976*, Table 35, p. 186.
a Because of rounding, the percentages may not add to total.
b Less than one-tenth of one percent.
c Violent crime is offenses of murder, forcible rape, robbery, and aggravated assault.
d Property crime is offenses of burglary, larceny, and auto theft.

with two major characteristics that might be expected to differentiate black delinquent from black nondelinquent adolescents—achievement motivation and locus of control. It was expected that delinquents would be lower in need-for-achievement and more external in perceived locus of control than nondelinquents. A matched sample of black inner-city delinquent adolescents ($N = 27$) was compared with black inner-city nondelinquent adolescents ($N = 28$). No significant differences in locus of control or achievement motivation were obtained between the delinquents and nondelinquents. Farley and Sewell concluded that achievement motivation may not be importantly involved in delinquency among black adolescents.

Differential treatment by the police may account for the high Negro delinquency rates, according to Piliavin and Briar. Their assessment was based on nine months of observation of juvenile officers in the police department of a large industrial city of 450,000. Through observation and interviews with the police, they concluded that the police exercised wide discretion in dealing with juvenile offenders. Police dispositions recorded for sixty-six youths whose encounters with police were observed during the study indicated that the demeanor of the youth was the prime factor, other than previous arrest, for making a disposition. Police estimated that 50 to 60 percent of first-offense dispositions were based on demeanor. Officers acknowledged that the differential arrest rate between Negro and white boys was often due to the uncooperative demeanor exhibited by blacks. The way the Negro youth looked, talked, walked, and conducted himself was an important factor in influencing his arrest.[17]

Personality Characteristics of the Juvenile Delinquent

Personality refers to the totality of an individual's physical, temperamental, emotional, and intellectual makeup. It does not involve commitment to an ethical position. The term is ethically neutral. Character is personality plus the ingredients of ethical, religious, or other ideals or goals that typically dictate an individual's conduct. A person may have a "good" or "bad" character depending upon the extent to which his actions conform with accepted normative expectations.[18]

Many classification systems have been developed to delineate the different types of delinquent personality. The California Youth Authority, after administering a series of tests and correlating a variety of measurements, classifies delinquents according to three major "interpersonal maturity levels":

---

[17]Irving Piliavin and Scott Briar, "Police Encounters with Juveniles," *American Journal of Sociology* 70 (September 1964):206–14.

[18]Sheldon Glueck and Eleanor Glueck, *Delinquents in the Making: Paths to Prevention* (New York: Harper, 1952), p. 139.

Maturity Level 2 (I_2).   The individual whose interpersonal understanding and behavior are integrated at this level demands that the world take care of him. He sees others primarily as givers or withholders and has no conception of interpersonal refinement beyond this level. He is unable to explain, understand, or predict the behavior or reaction of others. He is not interested in anything outside himself except as a source of supply. He behaves impulsively, unaware of the effects of his behavior on others.

Maturity Level 3 (I_3).   The individual who operates at this level is attempting to manipulate his environment in order to get what he wants. In contrast to the person at level 2, he is at least aware that his own behavior has something to do with whether or not he gets what he wants. He still does not differentiate among people, however, except to the extent that they can or cannot be useful to him. He sees people only as objects to be manipulated. He will either conform to the rules of those who seem to have the power at the moment ("If you can't lick them, join them") or engage in the type of maneuvering characteristic of the confidence man ("Make a sucker out of him before he makes a sucker out of you"). He tends to deny having any disturbed feelings or strong emotional involvement in his relationships with others.

Maturity Level 4 (I_4).   An individual whose understanding and behavior are integrated at this level has internalized a set of standards by which he judges his and others' behavior. He is aware of the influence of others on him and their expectations of him. To a certain extent, he is aware of the effects of his own behavior on others. He wants to be like the people he admires. He may feel guilty about not measuring up to his internalized standards. If so, conflict produced by feelings of inadequacy and guilt may be internalized, with consequent neurotic symptoms, or acted out in antisocial behavior. If he feels no such guilt, he may feel conflict over values. Or, without conflict, he may admire and identify with delinquent models, internalizing their delinquent values.[19]

The three major types of delinquents are divided into subtypes, each given a code name:

Maturity Level	Code Name	Delinquent Subtype
I_2	Aa	Unsocialized, aggressive
	Ap	Unsocialized, passive
I_3	Cfm	Conformist, immature
	Cfc	Conformist, cultural
	Mp	Manipulator

---

[19]John E. Riggs, William Underwood, and Marguerite Q. Warren, *Interpersonal Maturity Level Classification: Juvenile,* C. T. P. research report no. 4 (Sacramento: California Department of Youth Authority, February 1964), pp. 1–2.

Maturity Level	Code Name	Delinquent Subtype
I_4	Na	Neurotic, acting-out
	Nx	Neurotic, anxious
	Ci	Cultural identifier
	Se	Situational emotional reaction

Lester E. Hewitt and Richard L. Jenkins, psychiatrists specializing in child guidance, studied the case records of 500 children referred to the Michigan Child Guidance Institute and developed another typology of personality structure. Of the 500 cases, 305, or 61 percent, were not classified as maladjusted and were presumably "normal." The remaining 195, 39 percent of the total, were divided into three categories: *overinhibited, unsocialized aggressive, and socialized delinquent.* Children showing at least three of the traits associated with a syndrome were placed in that category.

The Overinhibited Child.   Traits associated with this syndrome are seclusiveness, shyness, apathy, worry, sensitiveness, and submissiveness. The overinhibited child feels inferior, frequently has physical complaints, and is prone to neurotic illness. Seventy-three children, 14.6 percent of the total, were found to be in this category.

The Unsocialized Aggressive Child.   Traits associated with this syndrome are assaultive tendencies, cruelty, defiance of authority, malicious mischief, and inadequate guilt feelings. This child is characterized by gross failure of conscience or inhibitions and has a low frustration tolerance. His family history indicates parental rejection, and this is believed to be a predisposing factor for this type of personality. Fifty-two children, 10.4 percent of the total, were found to be in this category.

The Socialized Delinquent Child.   The socialized delinquent associates with bad companions, engages in gang activities, steals furtively and in company with others, is habitually truant from school, runs away from home, and stays out late at night. This type of boy makes an excellent adjustment to a gang and can do well in the armed forces. Parental negligence and exposure to delinquent behavior patterns are predisposing factors for this type of personality. Seventy children, 14 percent of the total, were found to be in this category.[20]

As we have already noted, differences in personal self-concept have also

---

[20]Richard L. Jenkins and Lester E. Hewitt, "Types of Personality Structure Encountered in Child Guidance Clinics," *American Journal of Orthopsychiatry* 14 (January 1944):84–94. See also Richard L. Jenkins, "Motivation and Frustration in Delinquency," *American Journal of Orthopsychiatry* 27 (January 1957):528–37.

been used to differentiate the delinquent from the nondelinquent.[21] Researchers suggest that one of the preconditions of law-abiding or delinquent behavior is to be found in the concept of self and others acquired in primary group relationships. "Good" boys, for example, are those who are insulated against delinquency, and this is an ongoing process reflecting an interrealization of nondelinquent values and conformity to the expectations of significant others. Whether or not the insulated boys remain good depends on their ability to maintain their present self-images in the face of various situational pressures. This concept of self may work negatively. To attribute certain abstract characteristics and predictions of delinquency to certain individuals or groups could possibly influence these persons to accept the ascribed roles, a self-fulfilling prophecy. Applying labels and epithets such as "juvenile delinquent" and "young criminal" does not help anyone to think well of himself. Active, aggressive, impetuous, sometimes violent and irrational behavior does not automatically mean that a child is a junior public enemy. Equating healthy defiance with delinquency may encourage a child to think of himself as a delinquent.

In this regard, delinquent attitudes and self-esteem are often correlates of delinquent behavior. Spencer Rathus and Larry J. Siegal studied this in a comparison of eighty-six junior and high school "nondelinquent students" compared to a sample of sixty-three male probationers.[22] The relationships between the delinquents' and nondelinquents' attitudes towards the criminal justice system and their self-esteem were studied. It was assumed that those achieving rewards within the system were more likely to both possess high self-esteem and value those persons and institutions that function to maintain the social order. It was predicted that this relationship would be positive. Although individual correlations tended to be small, it was possible to infer that the justice system was considered decidedly negatively by delinquents. This finding was consistent with the subcultural hypothesis that "self-esteem for many delinquents is largely dependent upon the derogation of those who serve in reciprocal role relationships—more particularly, the criminal justice personnel who participate in the process of labeling them as bad, wrong, and incompetent in meeting their needs according to conventional modes of conduct."

John J. Conger and Wilbur C. Miller matched delinquents and nondelinquents and measured their personality development from early childhood through adolescence. They found that distinct personality and behavior characteristics tend to emerge at an early age, evidence some shifts in emphasis, and become more completely and increasingly differentiated in later school

[21]Walter C. Reckless, Simon Dinitz, and Ellen Murray, "Self-Concept as an Insulator Against Delinquency," *American Sociological Review* 21 (December 1956):744–46.
[22]Spencer Rathus and Larry J. Siegal, "Delinquent Attitudes and Self-Esteem," *Adolescence* 7 (August 1973):265–76.

years. If there are early indications of future delinquency, as the authors claim, one must turn to the family and siblings, as the primary agents in affecting personality development, in seeking answers. The family is the first socializing vehicle and is important in shaping the expression of drives. It thus directly influences personality development. By choosing the place of residence, it influences peer associations and school contacts and indirectly selects these other important socializing agencies. Thus, according to Conger and Miller, both directly and indirectly the family exerts an important influence on the development of personality and delinquency.[23]

Although many children develop a low self-concept from their family interaction and are socialized into illegal attitudes because of such negative impacts, researchers into delinquency are increasingly aware of children who overcome many personal difficulties and rise above delinquent behavior. Two recent researchers, Dr. Norman Garmezy, his associate Dr. Vernon Devine, and some researchers at the University of Minnesota are beginning to study a group of children they call "invulnerables" for want of a better term. According to Garmezy,

> "These are children who have come through. They are the ones who have not just survived but have flourished, despite a variety of genetic, psychological and sociological disadvantages." They offer as an example Todd, who is eleven and lives with an alcoholic father who sometimes works as a handyman but is usually unemployed. Todd's mother died when he was three, and he lives in an environment of poverty and unrelieved grimness. By all our usual laws of child development, he should be well on his way to juvenile delinquency.
>
> Instead, he is cheerful, bright, does well in school, is a natural leader, and is much loved by his friends—as well as by school officials. And there are other Todds, we are learning, everywhere: not just in the barrio, ghettos and inner cities, but in suburbia as well.[24]

Garmezy, Devine, et al. spent about two years discussing issues, parameters, and theories on "invulnerables" and another year locating a group of "invulnerables" to study. They did this by going into the Minneapolis schools and telling principals and social workers that they were looking for children who "when you learned about their background gave you much concern; yet now, when you see them in the halls, you look at them with pleasure." It was an unusual request for school officials, but it was successful. The researchers concluded that out of nearly 400 "candidates," about 10 percent turned out to be invulnerables.

---

[23]John J. Conger and Wilbur C. Miller, *Personality, Social Class, and Delinquency* (New York: Wiley, 1966).

[24]As reported by Eleanor Hoover in *Human Behavior* (April 1976).

The full analysis of what makes them invulnerables has yet to come, but Devine suspects the presence of a role model somewhere who provides a positive image for the youngsters. According to Garmezy, "Invulnerables try to find solutions, rather than blame; they test reality, rather than retreat before it; and they learn to make something out of very little. They bounce back. They have a real recovery ability. We don't know why yet, but they do."

The pursuit of the reason why invulnerables overcome great social obstacles to become positive citizens is an area of valuable research. In the process it should be kept in mind that some of the invulnerables located and studied in their teen years may explode into delinquency at a later age. Despite some of the problems inherent in this research, it is valuable to bear in mind that in the process of researching the many attributes and socialization factors that produce a delinquent we should not overlook the insights into delinquency that might be obtained by studying the other side of the coin, children and adults who do not become delinquent or criminal.

Chapter
4

The
Family
and
Delinquency

Our Earth is degenerate ... children no longer obey their parents.
(Carved in stone 6000 years ago by an Egyptian priest)

THE SOCIAL CONFIGURATION that usually exerts the most profound influence on every human being is his family. Dislocation in a youth's family, the absence of the family's potentially positive effects, or any severe disturbance in one or both parents can produce devastating negative impacts—certainly including juvenile delinquency. The fundamental meaning of the family to a person is cogently expressed by Robert Bierstedt:

> Of all of the groups that affect the lives of individuals in society none touches them so intimately or so continuously as does the family. From the moment of birth, when young parents gaze with adoration upon their very own creation, to the moment of death, when sons and daughters are summoned to the bedside of a passing patriarch, the family exerts a constant influence. The family is the first social group we encounter in our inchoate experience, and it is the group with which, in one form or another, we shall have the most enduring relationship. Every one of us, with statistically small exceptions, grows up in a family and

every one of us, too, with perhaps a few more exceptions, will be a member of a family for the larger part of his life.

The family almost without question, is the most important of any of the groups that human experience offers. Other groups we join for longer or shorter periods of time, for the satisfaction of this interest or that. The family, on the contrary, is with us always. Or rather more precisely, we are with it, an identifiable member of some family and an essential unit in its organization. It is the family, in addition, that gives us our principal identity and even our very name, which is the label of this identity, in the larger society of which we are a part.[1]

The family is therefore an important determinant of whether or not a child will become delinquent. The family, as the basic agent of socialization, determines a child's socioeconomic class, and its structure and process is vital in the personality formation of the individual. All of these factors—socialization, class, and dynamics—impinge on the development of either a law-abiding or a delinquent child. These factors are inextricably bound together and will therefore be discussed in their gestalt, as they pertain to the family and delinquency.

Despite its importance, the decision of which family to be born into is the most important decision that the individual will never be able to make. The family into which an individual is born is obviously a condition over which he has no control. In this sense, his destiny has, significantly, already been determined.

This event has determined the social class he will initially, at least, move in, along with the values, advantages, and disadvantages of the class. His class membership will most probably control his economic position, which in turn will select his neighborhood, his friends, his school, the church he will attend, as well as the kind and quality of other community agencies and resources that will be available.

His family's economic resources will also be related to his physical development and the efficiency of biological functioning in terms of dietary standards and access to quality medical care.

His birthright will also set some limits on his intelligence, will probably provide some basic emotional makeup, and will give him a physical appearance that may work to his advantage or disadvantage in a culture where a certain "look" is considered superior.

A child has no control over the actual structure of the family: whether one, two, or no parents are available, and whether or not grandparents are present. The child's family composition of siblings is also not within the purview of his control.

---

[1]From *The Social Order* by Robert Bierstedt. Copyright 1957 by McGraw-Hill Book Company. Used with permission of McGraw-Hill Book Company.

A child also has limited, if any, control over his family's emotional dynamics. His parents may be neurotic, schizophrenic, or alcoholic. The parents may be physically abusive or rejecting. The child may become the family "scapegoat" and, thus, the symptomatic carrier of a family pathology that stems not from the youth's personal inclinations but from the family's structural problems.

Psychologist Eric Bermann has given a cogent description of this problem. In an article adapted from his book *Scapegoat,*[2] he tells how an eight-year-old boy's personal problems and subsequent delinquent behavior resulted from an effort to repress the family's basic problem.

In the course of the year, I discovered the family's central and well-concealed secret: Roscoe's father had been for years in precarious health with a heart condition and was now literally on the brink of death. Open heart surgery was his only hope; without it doctors gave him but a few months to live.

Despite the explosive meaning of these circumstances, and despite the fact that he could die at any time, the family never talked about his condition or their own future. Yet the effect of the knowledge was hardly lost on them; it created an unbearable tension that normal defense mechanisms could not withstand. New defensive measures were required to contain the tension which threatened routine functioning and to reestablish the family's stability.

With each succeeding visit I began to understand further the depth of the family's trouble. Their terror and the desperation of the "tactics" for avoiding overt recognition of an ever present death-fear became apparent. Small moments and casual comments that earlier had seemed inconsequential now exploded with new force and meaning. It became increasingly clear that in the face of their overwhelming dread, this family of seven had—in collusive but entirely nonconscious and unspoken fashion—selected an "expendable member" to serve as the scapegoat.

A middle-American family frightened by death to the breaking point, and desperately trying to maintain its balance, was driven routinely to victimize one of its weakest members—namely a child, Roscoe.

The "reign of terror" instituted against Roscoe amounted to an intensive psychological effort by the entire family. First they worked to demoralize him and strip him of his self-hood and then to convince him that he was potentially a malevolent force—one that could be held accountable for destroying the family or the father.

The family demoralized Roscoe in quiet ways. They simply

---

[2]Eric Bermann, *Scapegoat: The Impact of Death-Fear on an American Family* (Ann Arbor: University of Michigan Press, 1973).

stopped reacting to him on his own terms. When he walked into a room, no one acknowledged his presence; it was as if he was not there. At the dinner table while the family shared the events of the day, nobody inquired how Roscoe's day had gone. According to my observations, fully 40 percent of his attempts to talk with other persons were ignored.

In still other situations his brother was allowed to take credit and gain recognition for skills that were obviously Roscoe's. Roscoe came to have the status of an outsider in his own home. Denied his individuality, he submitted to the demoralization with sadness. In one important regard his parents were correct. Roscoe was "no trouble" at home. He was quiet, conforming and dispirited. It was outside the home that he struck back. . . .

Today's child is the inevitable repository for the accumulated frustrations, projections and displacements of the parents. His crucial function has become that of freeing them psychically so that they might carry on their jobs and family activity effectively without confronting each other with their antagonisms. Once trained and molded in the scapegoat role, the child becomes indispensable to his family. He provides a center for their grievances in a highly efficient and automatic fashion, and, as whipping boy, stabilizes the social system of the family.

Lacking retaliatory power, children have little choice but to suffer the consequences. They often do endeavor to fight back, but such attempts are likely to land them in the courts or in settings for emotionally disturbed children.[3]

Roscoe's delinquent behavior between the ages of eight and fifteen was looked upon by society as his personal problem, when in fact his behavior was a function of his family's structural problems. As the "scapegoat," he was arrested over five times, and his delinquent career was fostered by his further deviant socialization in juvenile detention. It is important to understand a child's family and his socialization process to understand his delinquent behavior.

Socialization refers to the process by which a newcomer learns to participate effectively in social groups and to acquire new skills, a process that continues throughout life. This lifelong process may be divided into two stages.

The first stage occurs between conception and approximately five years of age, when the primary socializing agent is the family. During this time the child must learn and master a number of activities if later development is to proceed without difficulty. He must master basic motor control and then advance to more complicated skills. He must learn breath control, if language and communication are to develop. The child must develop and understand

---

[3]Berman, *Scapegoat,* pp. 83–84.

basic concepts about himself, other people, and the world around him. He must learn that things have names and that events occur together. He must understand a cognitive, aesthetic, and moral value system. Later in the process, he must learn to relate to other people and to the world on a personal basis.

The second stage of the socialization process occurs from the time the child engages in group interaction until his death. Throughout his lifetime he is constantly forming, evaluating, and refining methods of group interaction to satisfy his needs.

Familization corresponds to the first stage of this socialization process. It is the process by which family members reactively and proactively develop a universe of meaning relevant to the family.

The family plays the central role in the socialization process. The transfer of responsibility from nuclear family to societal institutions, such as the school and the peer group, does not usually occur until the child is five or six years of age, roughly coinciding with what many people call the "formative years." Even after other institutions start "taking over," the family still plays a continuing role, and its attitudes toward other institutions may condition the child's relation to such institutions. Hiram and Ruth Grogan discuss the family's influence on delinquency in a study of family tension.[4] The authors stress that in families disorganized by unresolved and recurring internal conflicts, the process of socialization, of teaching the child by precept and example the multitude of attitudes, values, and behavioral patterns is extremely difficult. The family that is beset with chronic conflict and tensions labors under a handicap at meeting its socialization responsibilities effectively. The focal point of the article is that such a family, "the criminogenic family," produces an inadequately socialized child, one who is ill prepared to face and accept values, standards, and codes of conduct that are law-abiding. The article focuses on: (a) personality development; (b) intrafamily conflict; (c) parent-child conflict; and (d) effects on family tension.

The child's personality develops within the limits imposed by the child's biological nature, his physical setting and sociocultural environment, and his family. The Grogans assert that family disruption lowers the child's resistance to withstand the pressures of his aggressive tendencies in the presence of frustrations, thereby increasing the child's receptivity to delinquency. Thus one of the basic themes of the Grogans is that a "criminogenic family" is a family in which significant conflict and tension disrupt the atmosphere conducive to the wholesome personality development of the child by interfering with his socialization patterns of learning. As an inadequately socialized child grows older, the Grogans assert, he may turn away from his family and seek comfort in a clique, or gang, where he eagerly accepts all the antisocial or delinquent values of the group.

---

[4]Hiram Grogan and Ruth Grogan, "The Criminogenic Family: Does Chronic Tension Trigger Delinquency?" *Crime and Delinquency* 14 (January 1971):220–25.

Dr. Raymond R. Crowe of the Department of Psychiatry at the University of Iowa's College of Medicine, carried out a study to determine whether or not any genetic basis for antisocial behavior emerged from the family.[5] Dr. Crowe studied two groups of adoptees—one that included forty-six children of convicted female felons (90 percent) and misdemeanants (10 percent) and the control group made up of forty-six adoptees specially chosen to parallel the other group demographically.

The offspring of mothers with criminal records had more marks against them socially than did the controls. Seven of them were arrested as adults—all seven had been convicted at least once—some having multiple arrests and convictions. Three were considered felons, and six had spent time locked up either as an adult or as a juvenile—one as both. Only one of control group had been arrested and convicted. In the experimental sample, eight subjects had been treated psychiatrically—seven as inpatients and one as an outpatient—while only one control spent time inside a psychiatric facility and only one was an outpatient. Six of the hospitalized subjects had been sent there by the courts, and seven of the eight were treated for antisocial behavior. Although both controls had been treated for antisocial behavior, neither had been sent by the courts, and neither had arrest records. This clearly revealed that more of the subjects had antisocial personalities than the controls. Dr. Crowe asserts that

> The unique finding in the present study is that the unfavorable environmental influences were associated with the development of antisocial personality in the probands but not in the controls, although the groups were comparable with respect to their exposure to these influences. The evidence at this time points to the importance of both genetic and environmental influences in the development of antisocial personality. Further study is definitely needed before assigning primary importance to heredity as a factor in delinquent behavior.

An increasingly common mode of adaptation to a negative family's influence is for a child to run away. Becoming a runaway in our society automatically places a child in a delinquent position. A conservative estimate is that over 500,000 children run away from home each year in the United States.

In one study by psychiatrists Donald N. Haupt and David R. Offord, they examined the case history of ninety-two runaway children (average age, thirteen).[6] They were immediately struck by the severity of the "social dislocation" that seemed common to such children's lives. Over half had been in at

---

[5] *Human Behavior* (May 1975).
[6] *Human Behavior* (April 1973).

least one foster home, and on the average they had experienced more than four guardianship changes. But their troubles were not limited to being passed around from one set of disappointed parents to the next. Haupt and Offord attempted to come up with a measure for the total problems each child had known, and they developed a "hardship score" based on such factors as: number of changes of guardianship, parental physical abuse, and poverty in their early life situation. Runaways scored much higher on the "hardship score" when compared to a matched sample of nonrunaways.

Another researcher, Christine Chapman, made a more extensive study of runaways.[7] The central issue to which Chapman addressed herself is what the presence of runaways in such vast numbers revealed about American society. She reported that although most eventually return home—at least for a time—the act is a statement of severance between child and parent, and the tie will never be the same again. Chapman reports how one mother whose returned daughter insisted on and was granted her own rules of behavior commented, "It is the most frightening thing in the world for parents to feel if they say or do the wrong thing the child will run away. Beth held running away over us like a weapon."

Her research revealed that most, but nowhere near all, runaways come from homes in which family life has broken down in some way: "parents don't get along; children feel pressured to behave in ways they feel they cannot, or where they don't feel protected. Sometimes the children are physically beaten, but more often parent and child no longer communicate successfully."

Chapman was intrigued by the parental response to their runaways.

When I talked to the parents, they surprised me with their innocence. They were victims too—of their own belief in absolutes. Many had held dear to one way of raising children, one idea about the nature of children. They felt society erupting around them, but the fortress of the family would withstand the turbulence, they reassured each other. For their parenthood they had followed the custom of the country. The worst of it was they could not explain themselves. They were as inarticulate as children. They expected understanding without making the effort to be clear. Love, they had thought, was enough. Tradition would carry the day. The responsibility of parents for children was to be matched by the loyalty of children for parents. No matter how the world turned, they believed children and parents would stay close and comforting. They watched the indecisiveness of the schools, the confusion of the law, the inability of government to govern honestly, and they still believed that the family was immutable![8]

---

[7]Christine Chapman, *America's Runaways* (New York: William Morrow, 1976).

[8]Chapman, *America's Runaways,* p. 273.

What runaways do when they leave home is detailed in the following article.

NEW YORK (AP)—One of them was 11 years old the first time she tried to commit suicide by taking a drug overdose. Another was 13 when she ran away from home to escape beatings administered by her drunken mother. The third was 15 when she started selling drugs and her body to support the narcotics habit of her 25-year-old lover.

The three young women were witnesses Tuesday at a hearing of the State Assembly's Standing Committee on Child Care. It was the second of three sessions examining runaways and juvenile prostitutes and how law enforcement and social agencies deal with them.

The three young women—two of Irish and Spanish background and the third a black—testified about running away from unhappy homes and living in parks and building hallways and taking up dope and prostitution after falling in with older men.

"A frightened girl on her own makes easy pickings for the experienced pimp or any older protective figure," Dr. Mitchell S. Rosenthal, a child psychiatrist, said in introducing the witnesses, evidently New Yorkers, although information about where they grew up was not disclosed.

All three are currently enrolled in Phoenix House, a long-term rehabilitation residence program that Rosenthal helped found. He said out-patient care was inadequate for such women because that type of treatment didn't remove them from the environment in which their problems developed.

A majority of the nation's estimated one million runaways a year are female, he said, and most of them flee from homes that "cannot provide the physical or emotional security young people need."

Diana Williams, 21, said she ran away from home at age 13.

"Mother used to drink a lot," she said. "Every time my mother got drunk she would beat me . . . I had no place to go. I stayed in hallways and in parks with older people. . . . I met a friend. He started me prostituting when I was 17. He was 42. He had me in the streets every day. I had to bring in a certain amount of money. If not, he would beat me. He had the drugs I needed."

Rose Cruz, 17, told the lawmakers that she found herself in the midst of "a lot of family problems," and both parents beat her. She escaped to the park, smoking pot and drinking with friends, she said.

"At 15 I met Billy, who was 10 years older, and he let me stay in his apartment. Billy got fired from his job, so I thought I had to have a job to pay the bills. I started selling drugs. Then I started selling my body. Billy was a drug addict."

She said she served nine months in the Manhattan Rehabilitation Center, where she said drug-trafficking was rampant and some of the staff members frequently appeared to be "high."

Nancy Owens, 16, said she first tried to kill herself at age 11 by taking a drug overdose. Her parents were alcoholics, she said, and she tried suicide again during the next three years before she was committed to a mental institution, from which she escaped. At 14, living with a man of 33, she began hustling, she said.

"I needed it for drugs and the only time I prostituted was when I absolutely needed the money—once or twice a week. Otherwise I would steal or go to the welfare and lie," she said.[9]

In still another context, another researcher notes how "the criminal sins of parents are visited on children." Dr. Phyllis Magrab, director of the Child Development Center of Georgetown University in Washington, D.C., researched the impact of "the Washington Merry-Go-Round" on the children of people in the limelight. According to Dr. Magrab,

> The sad fact is that the gossip, innuendo, and rumor that help keep the Washington merry-go-round spinning come home to roost most heavily not on their subjects but on their children. Children don't have the experience or the systems that adults have to deal with this kind of thing. They just don't have the coping mechanisms. Most children form a strongly positive image of their parents. Stress begins when this image is contradicted by another, and the more contradictory the images are, the greater the stress. After a while, the child's actions will begin to reflect the stress according to his personality. If he is naturally aggressive, he might find himself constantly fighting. He could develop vicious feelings toward his parents—the cause of his troubled emotions—or turn to antisocial, delinquent behavior. If the child is withdrawn, he will probably find it harder and harder to face his classmates. He might start using drugs, have eating problems and sleeping problems at home. At the very extreme, such a child could turn suicidal. Older children have to cope with peer pressure, but younger children, with their sense of being at the center of the world, could begin to think the conflict was in some way their fault.[10]

Family Influence on Roles and Norms

Since it is through the socialization process that the individual acquires a culture, one might anticipate that everyone socialized in a society would conform strictly to the rules he is taught. We know, however, that it does not

---

[9] *Long Beach* (Calif.) *Press-Telegram,* Dec. 1, 1976.

[10] Gordon Chaplin, "Watergate and the Children of Scandal," *Washington Post,* October 10, 1976.

work out that way. All of us deviate from some of the rules. Some deviate to such a degree that society takes action against them. We do not have universal conformity for some or all of the following reasons:

1. There are differences among individuals accounted for by heredity. People differ from birth.
2. There are differences in rules supported by socializing agencies. The family may emphasize different sets of rules than do the school or peer groups.
3. There are differences in values, attitudes, and life experiences within each category of socializing agents. Family, school, peer group—each has its own values, born of its own experience.

In the course of his socialization, the child learns his *roles:* what is expected of him by his parents and other adults, by his siblings and other peers, and by his school and other institutions of the society. He also learns the *norms* or rules of behavior defined by the socializing agencies and comes to accept their standards of behavior. Knowing his roles helps him to determine what he is supposed to do in a given situation. Knowing the norms helps him select a right way of doing it. When the norms of the three major socializing agencies reinforce each other, his choice of appropriate behavior is relatively simple. It is when they are in conflict that complications arise.

Recent research reveals the changing functions of the family and the increasing influence of other socializing agencies, particularly the peer group. In the predominantly rural society of a century ago, the individual was introduced to virtually all of his adult roles in the family. The farm family was a producing as well as a consuming unit. From childhood on, the individual was exposed to the occupational roles that he would be required to perform as an adult. The community was small enough so that by the time he was a youth he knew most of the people in it, their roles (what he could expect them to do), and the behavior expected of him toward everyone else. He was, in effect, socialized in the gestalt of a family and a coherent community.

In twentieth-century America, the family is largely a consuming unit and not a cohesive producing unit. Many of its functions have undergone major modifications. Parents simply do not have the necessary training and are not sufficiently familiar with the social and career requirements confronting their children to teach them what they need to know. The child is therefore trained for the performance of occupational and community roles outside the family. The family exerts an influence on the child's acceptance and success in school roles, however. It is in his family that he is motivated to attend school and is prepared for acceptance of school regulations. A child brought up in a middle class family goes to school better prepared for success than one brought up in a lower class family. The value placed on education by his parents is a decided advantage to him.

The family also influences the friendship associations of the child, first by selecting the neighborhood he grows up in and then by influencing the choice of friends invited to the home. Failure in school roles frequently leads to delinquency. Failure in friendship roles may be even more damaging. The child may never learn to relate compassionately to others and become a sociopath. Success in family, school, and friendship roles during childhood may be expected to result in success in family, occupational, and community roles in adulthood. (Figure 4.1 depicts the patterning of these social roles.)

As the United States changed from a predominantly rural, agricultural society to one that is overwhelmingly urban and industrial, the family became far less effective as a socializing agency. It could still prepare the child for family roles, but it lacked the capability to prepare him for occupational and community roles. The incomplete family, characterized by the absence of one parent, has an additional handicap. A one-parent family, whether as a result of divorce, desertion, or death, usually consists of a mother and children living together. The mother often finds it difficult to provide sustenance and guidance, and the absence of a father leaves the male children without an adult male model. Children born out of wedlock and brought up by their mothers are in much the same position. Whether or not being a member of such a household causes serious emotional disturbances in the child, it adversely affects his socialization.

In summary, therefore, the family may contribute to delinquency in the following ways:

1. In choice of neighborhood. Voluntarily or involuntarily, parents pick the location of the home. Locating the home in a high-delinquency area makes it more likely that the child's early associations will be with children adhering to a delinquent subculture.
2. In failing to influence the friendship patterns of the child. Maintaining an interest in his associations and rewarding the choice of nondelinquent playmates is believed to influence the child in a nondelinquent direction.
3. In failing to prepare the child adequately for a successful school experience.
4. In failing to influence the child in favor of nondelinquent clubs, play groups, and other interest groups.

The way in which the child will relate to other socializing agencies is influenced by his family but not totally determined by it. Where the family fails, therefore, other socializing agencies take on increasing importance.

Figure 4.1

The Patterning of Social Roles

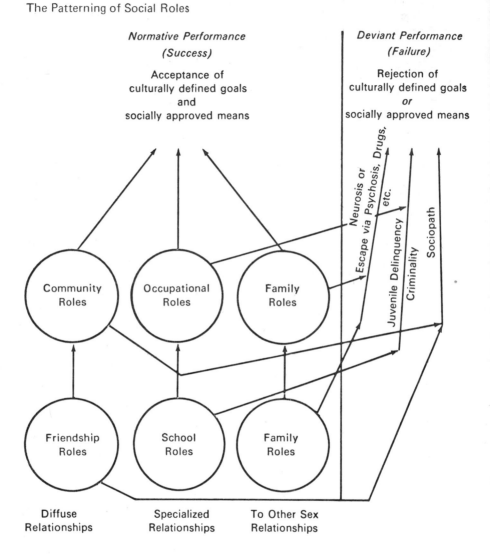

Circles represent problem areas, lines represent movement.

If through inadequacies in role performance or other deficiency the individual fails in a problem area, he moves toward rejection of the culturally defined goals or toward the use of deviant means.

Failure in one problem area contributes to failure in the other two.

Failure in a problem area as a child (lower level) contributes to failure in that problem area as an adult.

Erikson's Eight Stages of Development, and Juvenile Delinquency

Before determining more specifically where family structure and dynamics break down to produce delinquency, we will focus more precisely on the problems that a child has to solve, with or without the help of the family, if a healthy adult personality is to be achieved in terms of Erik Erikson's conception of the socialization process.[11]

Erikson states that there are eight developmental stages in the life of every individual which, if properly handled, will produce the following: trust instead of mistrust, autonomy instead of shame and doubt, initiative instead of guilt, industry instead of inferiority, identity instead of role diffusion, intimacy instead of isolation, generativity instead of stagnation, and ego integrity instead of despair.

The "sense of trust" develops in the first year of life and is simply built upon rewarding experiences and satisfaction of basic needs in the family. The baby's feelings of hunger are anticipated or closely followed by food; feelings of uneasiness or anxiety will soon be assuaged by the comfort and warmth of being held closely and securely. Not only will the baby learn to trust others, he will learn to trust himself when the reach for an object is eventually followed by its grasp. He will learn to trust the world when objects that disappear, like mother's face, consistently and invariably reappear. This sense of trust in others, in oneself, and in the world may well be the most important element in a healthy personality that is not delinquency prone.

According to Erikson, the "sense of autonomy" primarily starts developing when the child is twelve to fifteen months old. For the next couple of years, he will be trying to assert that he has a mind and a will of his own. If all goes well, he will get the feeling that he is an independent and separate human being who nevertheless can still depend on the help of his parents and others in certain situations. This stage is decisive for the proper balance between love and hate, giving and receiving, and expressing and controlling his feelings. If the child is successful, he will be able to maintain proper self-control without any loss of self-esteem. If unsuccessful, he will have doubts about himself and others and feelings of shyness and shame. Donald R. Peterson and Wesley Becker, speaking from a more classical psychoanalytic framework, tend to support Erikson's concepts when they state that the four basic childhood needs up to this point are: (1) the security and backing of two present parents; (2) parental love and understanding; (3) an optimum period of gratification for infantile sexual desires; and (4) opportunities to express hostilities, antagonisms, and aggressiveness, so that the child can learn what these feelings are like and how to deal with them. Peterson and Becker list three fears that

---

[11]Erik H. Erikson, *Childhood and Society,* 2d ed. (New York: Norton, 1963), pp. 247–74.

children in this age group are subject to: (1) fear of being deserted, (2) fear of not being loved, and (3) fear of being mutilated.[12]

A "sense of initiative" is developed, according to Erikson, in the fourth and fifth years. This is a period of experimentation and imagination, or play and fantasy, when the child wants to find out what it can "do." With the arrival of "conscience," the child wants to know the limits of how far he can go without being inhibited by "pangs of guilt." The superego, the censor, says Erikson, must allow the young boy or girl the freedom to "move." A "self-imposed" denial of this freedom often results in a rigid and constricted personality accompanied by resentment, bitterness, and a vindictive attitude against the world. If this occurs, a child would be more prone to be delinquent.

The "sense of industry" begins at around the sixth year and extends over the next five or six years. The slow acquisition of skills and knowledge go on during this period. A child learns fair play and cooperation and the "rules" for becoming a social creature in the larger society. The positive outcome is a sense of duty and personal accomplishment, as opposed to feelings of inadequacy and inferiority.

A "sense of identity" begins roughly with the onset of adolescence, a period of physiological changes and rapid physical growth. The central question to be answered during this period is, "Who am I?" The adolescent is trying to find out who he is, whether he is a child or an adult, whether he is capable of becoming a husband and father, or wife and mother, how he will make a living, and whether he will be a success in life or a failure. Hopefully, the child will develop an ego identity and an occupational identity that will provide hope and confidence in himself and the future. Some adolescents, according to Erikson, can't seem to "get hold of themselves" or "find themselves"; they don't seem to know who they are or what their place in life really is and are thus more disposed towards delinquent behavior.

Erikson postulates that a sense of intimacy can come only after a sense of personal identity has been established. The individual must have sufficient mastery over mind and body and sufficient ego strength to take the risks involved in personal relationships, close friendships, sexual intimacy, and love. The avoidance of such relationships and experiences due to the fear of ego loss may result in excessive introspection, self-absorption, and a deep sense of isolation and loneliness. Again, this sense of alienation can make a youth more vulnerable to delinquency.

The "sense of generativity" is an adult development; it is the "parental sense" and is characterized by an interest in producing and caring for one's own children, an interest in producing and guiding the next generation.

---

[12]Donald R. Peterson and Wesley C. Becker, "Family Interaction in Delinquency," in *Juvenile Delinquency: Research and Theory,* ed. Herbert C. Quay (Princeton, N.J.: Van Nostrand, 1965), pp. 36–99.

The "sense of integrity" is the fruit of the seven earlier stages. The meaning of this stage is explicitly defined by Erikson:

> Only in him who in some way has taken care of things and people and has adapted himself to the triumphs and disappointments adherent to being, the originator of others or the generator of products and ideas —only in him may gradually ripen the fruit of these seven stages. . . .
> Each individual, to become a mature adult, must to a sufficient degree develop all the ego qualities mentioned, so that a wise Indian, a true gentleman, and a mature peasant share and recognize in one another the final stage of integrity. . . .[13]

In summary, it can be inferred from Erikson's stages of development that breakdowns within the frame of the family at any point could lead toward delinquent behavior. The effective socialization of the child is, therefore, the best insulation from delinquency.

Parent-Child Interactions

An important aspect of the socialization process and an insulator to delinquency is the *quality* and process of interaction between parent and child. Robert G. Andry carried out an in-depth study of delinquency and parental pathology.[14] Basically, Andry explored the quality of parental affection and love as it related to youths who become delinquent and nondelinquent. His findings were summarized as follows:

> Delinquents and nondelinquents were radically differentiated in their feelings as to the adequacy of the affective roles of the parents.
> 1. Delinquents tended to feel that their mother loved them most, whereas nondelinquents tended to feel loved by both parents—thus the differentiating feature here was the inadequate love given by the father among delinquents.
> 2. This last statement was reinforced in that delinquents tended to feel that their father should love them more, whereas nondelinquents felt that neither parent should love them more. . . .
> 3. Delinquent boys tended to feel that their parents (but especially their fathers) were embarrassed to show open affection for them, whereas nondelinquents did not feel this.

---

[13]Erikson, *Childhood and Society,* pp. 268–69.
[14]Robert G. Andry, *Delinquency and Parental Pathology,* rev. ed. (London: Staples Press, 1971).

4. There was a tendency for delinquents, in contrast to nondelinquents, to feel embarrassment at showing open love for their parents— implying a causal link between parents' inability to show open love and that of the child.

5. There was a tendency for delinquents to feel parental hostility towards them (in terms of "nagging"), whereas nondelinquents did not feel this.

6. There was a tendency for delinquents to feel that they had their mothers' ways rather than their fathers' ways, whereas nondelinquents tended to feel they had both parents' ways or their fathers' ways—thus indicating delinquents tend less to identify with their fathers than do nondelinquents.[15]

Briefly, Andry's results indicate that delinquent boys receive less strong and open love from their parents than do nondelinquents, and it is the father's affective role that is (consistently) less satisfactory than the mother's among delinquents, in contrast to a sense of satisfaction with both parents among nondelinquents.

Andry's last point places doubt on the theory that "maternal deprivation" is necessarily the primary determinant of delinquency, at least as far as delinquents who do not come from broken homes are concerned. Very briefly, one can conclude from this study that delinquent boys (suffering neither from mental defects or diseases nor from broken homes) tend to perceive greater defects in their fathers' roles than in their mothers' roles, whereas nondelinquents tend to perceive the roles of both parents as being adequate. Thus, according to Andry's research, the prime differentiating feature between delinquents and nondelinquents, as far as parental role-playing is concerned, is the delinquents' negative perception of their fathers' role.[16]

In another study on "affective ties to parents," Eric Linden and James C. Hackler concluded that delinquents may have the same beliefs as do conventional adolescents, but contact with deviant peers might make delinquency involvement more likely among those who have only weak ties to their families.[17]

A study by F. Ivan Nye and his associates of 605 cases involved combinations of parent-child relationships that ranged from mutual acceptance to mutual rejection.[18] Between these extremes were gradations ranging from either the father's or mother's accepting or rejecting a child, or the reverse, to

---

[15] Andry, *Delinquency and Parental Pathology,* pp. 40–41.

[16] Robert G. Andry, "Faulty Paternal and Maternal-Child Relationships, Affection and Delinquency," *British Journal of Delinquency* 1 (1950):34–48.

[17] Eric Linden and James C. Hackler, "Affective Ties and Delinquency," *Pacific Sociological Review* 16 (January 1973):27–46.

[18] F. Ivan Nye, *Family Relationships and Delinquent Behavior* (New York: Wiley, 1958).

the child's accepting or rejecting either or both of the parents. The children were rank ordered in terms of "delinquent" behavior, from "most delinquent" to "least delinquent." Of the 292 cases of mother-child mutual acceptance, only 14 percent of the children were in the "most delinquent" group, whereas 86 percent were in the "least delinquent" group. Of the 313 cases of mutual mother-child rejection, 48 percent of the children were in the "most delinquent" group, and 52 percent were in the "least delinquent" group. Between these extremes, the percentages of delinquency varied in proportion to the degrees of either acceptance or rejection.

The combinations of father-child acceptance and rejection had similar effects on the children. The data indicated that rejection of the child by the parents closely related to delinquent behavior; acceptance between parent and child was correlated with less chance of juvenile delinquency.

A significant relationship was found between delinquent behavior and the attitudes of boys and girls toward their parents. More emphasis is placed on rejection of parents by children than the rejection of children by their parents.

Sheldon and Eleanor T. Glueck, in comparing an officially delinquent and a nondelinquent group, made an extensive analysis of the relation between boys and their parents as possible factors in delinquency.[19] They studied affectional relations, emotional ties, acceptability for emulation, parental concern for the welfare of their children, and the boys' estimate of parents' concern. They did not attempt to measure or estimate how much of the hostility was the cause or product of delinquency, but their data indicated that there was considerably more hostility and less affection between parents and boys in the delinquency sample than in the nondelinquency group.

More of the boys in the delinquent than in the nondelinquent group regarded their father as unacceptable of emulation. Parents of delinquents seemed to be less concerned about the welfare of their children than were parents of nondelinquents. When the boys sensed this lack of parental concern for their future, it only added to the difficulty.

William and Joan McCord, in reexamining the cases of the Cambridge-Sommerville Youth Study, stressed various phases of the relation of the family structure to crime.[20] Their data cover a variety of aspects, but some of the main findings dealt with the effects of parents' personality traits as role models; the relative effects of loving, overprotective, and nonloving relations, interpreted of both father and mother; parental discipline (consistent, erratically love oriented, erratically harsh, lax); and the son's position in the family. The McCords found that maternal love is the most important socializing force.

---

[19]Sheldon Glueck and Eleanor T. Glueck, *Unravelling Juvenile Delinquency* (New York: Commonwealth Fund, 1950), chap. 11.

[20]William McCord and Joan McCord, *Origins of Crime* (New York: Columbia University Press, 1959), chap. 5.

Paternal warmth is generally effective as a substitute for maternal love, but if behavior of the parents is deviant, rejection is likely to cause delinquency. In a parallel study Harriett Wilson found that nonloving, inferior parents were a social handicap and contributed to delinquency.[21] Wilson determined in a study of fifty-six families that juvenile delinquency correlated significantly with "social handicaps" and parental criminal record.

In *Cultural Factors in Delinquency,* Gibbens and Ahrenfeldt[22] note that indirect learning plays an important part in the origins of delinquency. Conflict between parents who are demonstrating opposing ideas or a parental pattern of "Don't do as I do; do as I say" may indirectly teach lessons that were completely opposite of what was intended. This form of indirect learning by observing negative parental role models was recognized as an important factor in causing delinquency.

In a study by James F. Alexander twenty-two "normal" and twenty "delinquent" families were videotape recorded in a discussion of the "resolution-of-differences" tasks.[23] The interaction data generally supported the hypotheses generated by systems theory and prior small-group research that abnormal families would express high rates of system disintegrating while normal families would express more system-integrating or supportive communications.

As has been noted in considerable research, disturbed family relations play a very important role in the causes of delinquency. In an investigation of high-delinquency areas in New York City, Craig and Glick found three factors to be related to increased likelihood of delinquency in boys: (1) careless or inadequate supervision by the mother or mother substitute, (2) erratic or overstrict discipline, and (3) lack of cohesiveness of the family unit.[24]

Bandura and Walters came up with somewhat similar findings in a study of twenty-six delinquent boys and an equal number of nondelinquents from the same social class and IQ range.[25] Both the boys and their parents were interviewed and rated for a variety of psychological variables. The parents of the delinquents were found to be more rejecting and less affectionate than those of the nondelinquents. It is Bandura and Walters' opinion that the boys' relations with their fathers constitute a more important factor in development than their relationships with their mothers. They noted that the fathers of

---

[21]Harriett Wilson, "Juvenile Delinquency, Parental Criminality and Social Handicap," *British Journal of Criminology* 24 (July 1975):241–50.

[22]T. C. N. Gibbens and R. H. Ahrenfeldt, eds., *Cultural Factors in Delinquency* (London: Tavistock Publications, 1966), p. 95.

[23]James F. Alexander, "Defensive and Supportive Communication in Normal and Deviant Families," *Journal of Consulting and Clinical Psychology* 14 (April 1973):223–31.

[24]M. M. Craig and S. J. Glick, *Crime and Delinquency* (New York: New York City Youth Board, 1963), pp. 231–32.

[25]Albert Bandura and R. H. Walters, *Adolescent Aggression* (New York: Ronald Press, 1959), pp. 153–55.

delinquent boys were prone to ridicule them when they made a mistake and that there was an atmosphere of ill will between father and son. Somewhat similarly, it has been found that the number of criminal convictions was higher among boys whose fathers were rated "cruel" or "neglecting" than among those rated "passive" or "warm." The likelihood of delinquency was also increased if the child was disciplined in an erratic fashion or left undisciplined. A higher number of convictions was also found when the mother was rated as "nonloving" than when she was rated as loving and used consistent discipline.[26]

Discipline is another interrelated part of family relationships that affects delinquency. In their 1950 study, Sheldon and Eleanor Glueck found that in most cases of delinquents where the disciplinary attitudes and practices of the fathers of the boys were known: 4.1 percent of the fathers were found to use sound discipline; 26.7 percent fair; and 69.3 percent unsound. The Gluecks defined discipline practices as follows:

Sound—consistent and firm control of the boy by the parent, but not so strict as to arouse fear and antagonism;

Fair—control which is indefinite: sometimes strict, sometimes lax;

Unsound—extremely lax or extremely rigid control by the parents, which on the one hand gives the boy unrestrained freedom of action and on the other restricts him to the point of rebellion.[27]

Of the delinquent cases in which the disciplinary practices of the mothers were known, 2.5 percent were considered sound, 27.4 percent fair, and 70.1 percent unsound. Discipline practice is therefore a crucial interaction pattern in the development of delinquent behavior patterns.

Consistency and persistence in discipline are needed if controls are to be adequately internalized into a youth's personality. Situations, and appropriate methods of dealing with them, must recur regularly enough to let the child develop concepts of conduct and be able to distinguish suitable and unsuitable responses.

McCord and McCord, in their study of parental influences on a group of children, found that passive and ineffectual fathers, who might be expected to provide an inadequate role model for the sons and who have frequently been blamed in recent years for delinquency in their children, did not produce many delinquents when the mother role was efficiently carried out. Passive and ineffectual mothers, however, frequently had delinquent children. This study indicated that the major part of early consistent teaching depends on the mother. Criminal fathers can therefore be insulated from having a negative impact on their child—if the mother role is adequately performed.[28]

---

[26]Bandura and Walters, *Adolescent Aggression.*

[27]Glueck and Glueck, *Unravelling Juvenile Delinquency.*

[28]McCord and McCord, *Origins of Crime.*

This also suggests that a "criminal" parent may not transmit delinquent values. On this theme, Travis Hirschi, in *Causes of Delinquency*, states:

> It seems clear, then, that the lower-class parent, even if he is himself committing criminal acts, does not necessarily publicize this fact to his children. Since he is as likely to express allegiance to the substantive norms of conventional society as is the middle-class parent, he operates to foster obedience to a system of norms to which he himself may not conform.[29]

J. L. Moreno, founder of sociometry and group psychotherapy, has aptly pointed out that a negative relationship between parents, or their deviant relationship to the larger society, does not necessarily negatively affect their proper socialization of their child. Parents can often blockade their negative influence from their children. Although this is true, the chances for delinquency in a child are obviously less when the parents function as effective role models.

Family Structure, "Broken Homes," and Juvenile Delinquency

Broken homes, a child's family position, and family size have been the subjects of considerable research in the crime and delinquency field.

In 1950, there were 40.5 million children living in homes containing both a father and a mother, and 4.1 million children living in broken homes. According to the U.S. Census Bureau, in 1970 there were 7.6 million minors (under eighteen years of age) growing up without one or both parents.

In 1960, one of every four black families was headed by a woman who was divorced, separated from her husband, or abandoned. In 1972, almost one out of every three black families was without a father, compared with one in ten for whites.

With the increase in such patterns as divorces (in 1976 one in every three marriages ended in divorce), separations and working mothers, children are increasingly being entrusted to single parents, daycare centers, neighbors, and the television. (One estimate is that 34 percent of wives with preschool age children are now working.) Child-rearing patterns have, thus, undergone drastic changes. In an article on this issue Sandra Pesmen notes that "Although fewer babies are being born now, there are more and more very young children with working mothers than ever before."[30]

---

[29]Travis Hirschi, *Causes of Delinquency* (Berkeley: University of California Press, 1969), p. 341.

[30]Sandra Pesmen, "The Search for a Mother Substitute," *Chicago Daily News,* September 19, 1976, p. 12.

All of the mothers we interviewed agreed that the biggest problems they face are:

> Finding good care for their infants.
> Dealing with worry and guilt feelings.
> Lack of emotional support from relatives, and friends and husbands.
> Physical and mental exhaustion caused by trying to do two full-time jobs at once.

Although six million preschool age children have working mothers, only one-sixth of these children can be accommodated in the licensed preschools.[31] Many welfare-supported women with too many children in too few rooms have taken in neighbor's children to supplement their income. The result is more overcrowding, less supervision, and less effective socialization of children.

All these forces have resulted in a growing number of "latchkey" children—children who return home to empty houses to await the return of their parents. Many feel that this has created an "emotional vacuum," where children grow up without any values or goals.

The result is increasing runaways, teenage suicides, juvenile delinquency, teenage parenthood, and, ultimately, a series of unhappy marriages and divorces. In addition, this syndrome is no longer confined to low-income families. Cornell University social psychologist Urie Bronfenbrenner notes: "In terms of such characteristics as the proportion of working mothers, number of adults in the home, single-parent families, or children born out of wedlock, the middle-class family of today increasingly resembles the low-income family of the early 1960s."[32]

As the trend toward "surrogate" parenting increases, child-rearing, or the lack of it, becomes more and more a social problem. The pattern regenerates itself. Charles F. Geiger of the Catholic Social Services of Detroit points out: "Each generation seems to be getting less nurturing and support from within the family. Babies are just not given the intimate attention they need. . . . And these children grow up to become parents who don't nurture their own infants. All of these various forces of broken homes, divorce, and latchkey children contribute to the delinquency problem."[33]

There have been numerous studies of broken homes. One study by I. J. Gordon indicates that 30 to 60 percent of the juveniles who are regarded as delinquents by law-enforcement agencies come from broken homes.[34] However, when such studies are controlled for other variables, such as age, sex, type of offense, and quality of single parent–child relationship, the conclusion is

---

[31]"As Parents' Influence Fades, Who's Raising the Children?", *U.S. News and World Report,* October 27, 1975, p. 83.

[32] *U.S. News and World Report,* November 27, 1975.

[33] *U.S. News and World Report,* November 27, 1975.

[34]I. J. Gordon, *Human Development: Birth to Adolescence* (New York: Harper & Row, 1962).

reached that it is not the removal of one parent per se that can be correlated with delinquency, but some other aspect of the family. Koutrelakos has made this point, indicating that the child between three and six years of age is most adversely affected by the loss of a parent.[35]

In one classic study of the problem, Shaw and McKay studied several thousand boys from broken homes.[36] They used a sample of delinquent boys who appeared in the Cook County Juvenile Court in 1929 and a like number of boys, matched for age, race, and nationality, from twenty-nine Chicago public schools. They found that 42.5 percent of the delinquent boys and 36.1 percent of the nondelinquent (school) boys came from broken homes, which when expressed in ratio is 1.18 to 1.0. Although Shaw and McKay found that the difference between the rates in the delinquent and the control groups furnished an inadequate basis for the conclusion that the broken home is an important factor in delinquency, they point out that this does not mean that the family is of no significance in behavior problems. The actual separation of parents through divorce or desertion may not be as important in the life of the child as the tensions and emotional conflicts that resulted in the breakdown of family relationships.

In a later significant study, Maude A. Merrill studied 300 delinquents who were consecutive cases in a California juvenile court and compared them with a similar number of nondelinquents matched for age, sex, and home neighborhood with respect to several environmental factors that made up the social frame of reference.[37] Information was obtained regarding the structure of the home, economic status and parental occupations, home relations and family controls, companionships and the use of leisure. There were about four times as many boys as girls in the experimental group, and the average age was fifteen years. Merrill found that 50.7 percent of the delinquents came from broken homes (divorced, divorced and remarried, separated, deserted, mother dead, father dead, both parents dead, father dead but mother remarried, mother dead but father remarried). In the delinquent group, fewer children came from homes that were rated satisfactory or excellent; there was also less affection, poorer discipline, less fondness for parents, more children, and more brothers with delinquent records.

The Gluecks in their study made an elaborate analysis of home conditions, the setting and quality of family life, and the degree of stability or instability of the families of their sample of 500 delinquents.[38] In the life span of the boys from birth to the time of inclusion in the study, 302 (60.4 percent)

[35]James Koutrelakos, "Perceived Parental Values and Demographic Variables as Related to Maladjustment," *Perceptual and Motor Skills* 32(1971):151–58.

[36]Clifford R. Shaw and Henry D. McKay, *Juvenile Delinquency and Urban Areas* (Chicago: University of Chicago Press, 1942).

[37]Maude A. Merrill, *Problems of Child Delinquency* (Boston: Houghton Mifflin, 1947) 1947).

[38]Glueck and Glueck, *Unravelling Juvenile Delinquency.*

of the delinquents compared with only 171 (34.2 percent) of the nondelinquents had experienced broken homes.

On the basis of a study of 44,448 juvenile offenders, of whom 24,811 were first offenders, Thomas P. Monahan found that over a five-year period the proportion of broken homes among Negro male offenders was considerably greater than among whites and that female offenders in each group were more often from broken homes than were males in each class.[39] Twenty-two percent of the white and 49 percent of the Negro male first offenders were from incomplete families, that is, children living with one parent only.

Monahan's review of other research and his own study led him to conclude that there is a definite relationship between the "socially broken home" and delinquency. The psychological broken home, one in which the parents are constantly bickering, is also believed to influence delinquency. However, we have no way of knowing how many children live in psychologically broken homes. We do know that husband and wife often engage in a war of nerves for long periods prior to a divorce and that during those periods of time the home, while socially intact, is psychologically broken. In any case, most children from socially broken homes are not delinquent.

Not all children in a family are affected in the same way. There is evidence that most brothers and sisters of delinquent children are not delinquent. In one study by William C. Kvaraceus, 761 delinquents were found to be members of 687 families.[40] Despite the fact that the average delinquent had four brothers and sisters, nine out of ten were the only juvenile members of their families with delinquency contacts. Less than 9 percent of the families had two children with delinquency contacts, and about 1 percent had three such children.

In an effort to determine the effects of paternal absence on male children, McCord, McCord, and Thurber compared children whose fathers were absent with children from intact families for feminine identification, anxiety, and antisocial behavior.[41] They observed no significant differences in homosexuality or dependency. In fact, the boys whose fathers were absent tended to be *more* aggressive than those from intact families. They found *no support* for the theory that paternal absence leads to abnormal fears.

Although there was a relatively high rate of criminality among children whose fathers were absent, they found little support for the theory that paternal absence leads to delinquent or criminal activities. The proportion of gang delinquents whose parents quarreled but remained together was significantly

[39]Thomas P. Monahan, "Family Status and the Delinquent Child: A Reappraisal and Some New Findings," *Social Forces* 35(March 1957):250–58.

[40]William C. Kvaraceus, *Juvenile Delinquency and the School* (Yonkers, N.Y.: World Book Co., 1945), pp. 78–79.

[41]Joan McCord, William McCord, and Emily Thurber, "Some Effects of Paternal Absence on Male Children," *Journal of Abnormal and Social Psychology* 64(May 1962):361–69.

higher than the proportion of those whose fathers were absent. The relationship between juvenile delinquency and paternal absence appears to be largely a result of the general instability of broken homes rather than of paternal absence in itself.

In the study cited earlier, Nye and his colleagues obtained responses to questions about deviant behavior tabulated from anonymous self-administered questionnaires.[42] Recognizing that there are disproportionate numbers of delinquent children from broken homes in reformatories and training schools, they used noninstitutionalized school groups to verify their data about the forms and extent of deviant behavior and the possible relation of the family to the various types of behavior patterns. They also made comparisons between training-school boys and boys in the high schools. Most of the high school students (3,128) in three small towns (population from 10,000 to 30,000) filled out a questionnaire. Elaborate scaling techniques were used to ascertain the differences in background conditions of the "most delinquent" group (about one-third of the total) and the "least delinquent" group (the remaining two-thirds).

While the Nye study was not a random sample, did not include high school populations from metropolitan areas or from rural communities, and contained few nonwhites and children of foreign-born parents, the method of study enabled the investigators to obtain extensive data on unrecorded delinquency of a fairly large sample. The data derived from institutionalized delinquents were used for comparative purposes, and the family structure in relation to delinquency was analyzed. Socioeconomic status, other structural aspects (size, composition, affiliations outside the family, ethnic background), legally and psychologically broken homes, employed mothers, and spatial mobility were also studied carefully. Nye found that proportionately more of the state training-school boys (48.1 percent) came from broken homes than did the "most delinquent" boys in the high schools (23.6 percent). In the high school group (both boys and girls), fewer of the "most delinquent" lived with their original parents than did the "least delinquent," more came from broken homes (mother and stepfather, father and stepmother, mother only, father only, adopted and other), and more came from unhappy homes. Except for the institutionalized cases, according to Nye, "unhappiness in a home was more significantly related to delinquency than a structurally broken home."[43]

An aspect of family structure that has received a great deal of attention, especially from psychiatrists, is the temporary or permanent removal of the mother from the home. The British psychiatrist Dr. John Bowlby has especially stressed the importance of the maternal relationship, particularly for the younger child: "It is this complex, rich, and rewarding relationship with the mother in the early years, varied in countless ways by relations with the father

---

[42]Nye, *Family Relationships and Delinquent Behavior.*
[43]Nye, *Family Relationships and Delinquent Behavior,* p. 48.

and the siblings, that child psychiatrists and many others now believe to underly the development of character and of mental health."[44]

Bowlby asserts that considerable damage is done to the child by the mother's absence, the amount of damage varying with the age of the child when the absence occurs, the length of the absence, and the quality of the substitute care that is provided. Bowlby related this maternal deprivation to delinquency. In a 1946 study of a group of delinquents, he found significantly more maternal deprivation among the delinquents than among a control group from a child guidance center. He concluded that "on the basis of this varied evidence it appears that there is a very strong case indeed for believing that prolonged separation of a child from his mother (or mother-substitute) during the first five years of life stands foremost among the causes of delinquent character development and persistent misbehavior."[45]

A later study by Roland J. Chilton and Gerald E. Markle emphasizes the continuing effects of family disruption on the problem of delinquency.[46] They summarized their findings as follows:

> Employing seriousness of offense as a measure of delinquency, we re-examine the relationship between delinquency referal and family disruption. Information from the Juvenile and Country Courts of Florida for the first four months of 1969 provided us with uniform delinquency data for 8,944 children. We compare the family situations of 5,376 of these children with the situations of children in the U.S. population in 1968. The analysis suggests (1) that children charged with delinquency live in disrupted families substantially more often than children in the general population, (2) that children referred for more serious delinquency are more likely to come from incomplete families than juveniles charged with minor offenses, and (3) that family income is a more important factor for understanding the relationship between delinquency referral and family situation than age, sex, or urban-rural residence, but that it may not be more important than race. . . .[47]

In conclusion, Chilton and Markle note:

> . . . our study provides added empirical support for the conclusions of earlier investigators who have suggested that proportionately more children who come into contact with police agencies and with juvenile courts on delinquency charges live in disrupted families than do children

---

[44]John Bowlby, *Maternal Care and Mental Health* (Geneva: World Health Organization, 1951), p. 11.

[45]Bowlby, *Maternal Care and Mental Health.*

[46]Roland J. Chilton and Gerald E. Markle, "Family Disruption, Delinquent Conduct and the Effect of Subclassification," *American Sociological Review 27* (February 1972):93–99.

[47]Chilton and Markle, "Family Disruption, Delinquent Conduct and the Effect of Subclassification," p. 93.

in the general population. In addition, the study suggests that children charged with more serious misconduct more often come from incomplete families than children charged with less serious delinquency.[48]

Before concluding our analysis of the relation between broken homes and juvenile delinquency, we must note that most research into family influences on delinquency are derived from studies of boys. There is evidence, however, that similar forces influence female delinquency. Ashley Weeks suggested that the differential impact of the broken home by sex disappeared when one controlled for type of offense.[49] Most girls are arrested for incorrigibility, running away, and sex offenses, while most boys are arrested for vandalism, theft, and assault. (Weeks also concluded that a broken family due to the death of a parent was less consequential than divorce.)

An interesting study, dealing exclusively with girls, was carried out by K. M. Koller and reported in the *British Journal of Psychiatry*.[50] Koller explored the question of parental loss, deprivation, and delinquency by examining early adverse experiences related to female delinquency in particular and to behavior disturbances in general.

Out of a group of 160 girls at a training school, 121 were chosen at random. The girls were between the ages of sixteen and seventeen and were designated as belonging to the "unskilled, partly skilled occupations." The girls were committed to the training school for a number of reasons: 44 percent were reported as being exposed to moral danger, 39 percent were uncontrollable, and 12 percent were admitted because of stealing, drugs, and pregnancy. Another group of 101 unmarried girls was chosen randomly from the general population. They were of similar socioeconomic status and age as the delinquent girls.

The following summary of Koller's findings is of significance in understanding both male and female delinquency as related to family impacts. Of the "delinquent" subjects, 61.5 percent experienced parental loss. Most common was the absence of the father or of both parents. Eighty percent of the delinquent subjects who experienced parental deprivation came from broken homes. The delinquent girls came from large families with younger-than-average parents. The intermediate female children were most likely to be affected. It is apparent from these conclusions that the absence of a parental figure can have severe effects on a juvenile of either sex, and result in delinquency.

---

[48]Chilton and Markle, "Family Disruption, Delinquent Conduct and the Effect of Subclassification," p. 98.

[49]Ashley Weeks, "Male and Female Broken Home Rates," *American Sociological Review* 5(1940): 601–9.

[50]K. M. Koller, "Parental Deprivation, Family Background, and Female Delinquency," *British Journal of Psychiatry* 118(March 1971):319–27.

In another study into the relationship of female delinquency to broken homes, Susan K. Datesman and Frank R. Scarpitti came to some interesting conclusions.[51] In their study of 1,103 adjudicated delinquents, they found that when type of offense was controlled, a higher proportion of broken homes among female delinquents resulted in a greater involvement in "morals" offenses. They further determined that black males arrested for property and person offenses were more likely to come from broken homes than black females. They generally concluded that there appeared to be no unique relationship between broken homes and female delinquency, except for family-related offenses.

It may also be concluded from the variety of research cited that it is not the absence of a parent per se that is associated with delinquency, but rather the kind of relationship that exists between children and remaining parent. A warm, stable single parent has a much better chance of raising a nondelinquent child than do two parents who are in conflict. Nevertheless, there is very powerful evidence that there is a direct causal nexus between broken homes and delinquency. Table 4.1 summarizes this theme in terms of several of the significant studies we have discussed here. The major findings of these well-

Table 4.1

Incidence of Broken Homes Among Delinquents
and Nondelinquents

| Investigator | Sex | From Broken Homes | | | |
| | | Delinquents | | Controls | |
		N	%	N	%
Burt, 1929	Both	197	57.9	400	25.7
Weeks and Smith, 1939	Boys	330	41.4	2,119	26.7
Shaw and McKay, 1942	Boys	1,675	42.5	7,378	36.1
Gardner and Goldman, 1945	Men	500	58.6	200	32.0
Merrill, 1947	Both	300	50.7	300	26.0
Glueck and Glueck, 1950	Boys	500	60.4	500	32.4
Nye, 1958	Boys	368	23.6	792	17.6
Koller, 1971	Girls	121	61.5	101	12.9

---

[51]Susan K. Datesman and Frank R. Scarpitti, "Female Delinquency and Broken Homes," *Criminology* 13 (May 1975):33–56.

controlled studies show that the direction of the differences is the same in all comparisons. Broken homes are one one-half to two times more frequent among delinquents than among nondelinquents.

Family Size and Ordinal Position in the Family

The ordinal position that a child occupies in a family has a great effect on his eventual personality and the possibility of his being delinquent. The following assertions are based on a variety of research findings. The first child is born to inexperienced parents and is sometimes called the "trial baby." The child lives the first years of his life as an only child and relates entirely to his parents. He relates easily to adults and is likely to incorporate adult values more rapidly than are later children.

As the size of a family grows, a child is subjected to a number of different relationships: the relationship between the parents, each parent's relationship to the children, the children's relationship to the parents, the relationship among the children, and a particular child's relationship with his siblings. By increasing the number of family members, the number of interpersonal relations is increased. Thus each child's world is different from the world of his siblings. This helps explain the unique personalities that develop in a family and why one child may become delinquent while other members of the family are law-abiding.

The first child, who is more apt to enter the family at a time of greater financial stress, has only five possible interpersonal relationships—between parents, each parent to child, and child to each parent. I. J. Gordon points out that the first child tends to be anxiety prone, will give up in the face of difficulty, and handles feelings through withdrawal.[52]

The second child arrives into a ready-made family with six interpersonal relations—between parents, each parent to child, child to each parent, and child to older sibling. He can approach his sibling as a peer and model. The second child tends to be more peer oriented and more sociable. He seeks more physical affection from his parents and will try to get their attention by approved or unapproved means.

Martin M. Chemers has noted that later-born children are raised in a more complex social environment.[53] The last-born child, for instance, has parents who are by now experienced in child-raising. He has two or more older sibs who function in the capacity of peers and models for imitation and identification. He is more socially oriented and responsive than his sibs, feels secure and adequate in his world, and shows strong desires to establish his own identity.

---

[52]Gordon, *Human Development,* p. 43.

[53]Martin M. Chemers, "Relationship Between Birth Order and Leadership Style," *Journal of Social Psychology* 80(1970):243–44.

Lees and Newson studied the differences among delinquents that might be caused by sibling position and found that intermediaries—sibs with younger and older siblings—were significantly overrepresented in the delinquent populations studied.[54] The Gluecks in their research found that 60 percent of the delinquents studied were intermediate children, while only 47.8 percent of their nondelinquent control group were. Ivan Nye found that both the youngest sibs and the intermediaries were overrepresented in the "very delinquent" group.

These conclusions tend to explain the overrepresentation of the middle children in delinquency populations. Middle children seem to have the greatest need for attention and affection and are the very ones who are less apt to get it. The parents are apt to "realistically" devote most of their parental time to the youngest child because of his physical and emotional immaturity, while the older sib may claim some "right" by virtue of his age for special attention and consideration.

Nye has speculated that intermediaries get "squeezed out" of the family into gangs because the parents give their attention to younger and older sibs. Although this tendency may exist in some families, one can find many cases of conforming intermediaries in families with both older and younger delinquent sibs.

Researchers have also found some relationship between delinquency and family size. The studies of both Nye and the Gluecks have indicated that delinquents are more apt to come from large families. It is quite possible that parental controls and the familization process is "spread too thin" in large families. A. J. Reiss found that a greater proportion of delinquents from large families had poor superego controls.[55] Again, however, the significant variable is not family size per se, but other pressures characteristic of many large families: poverty and poor educational, economic, and social opportunities.

Family Dynamics

A considerable amount of research indicates that internal family dynamics are more closely related to social deviance in general and delinquency in particular than are structural elements of the family. It is probably not surprising that gross physical and emotional abuse and outright rejection are closely related to delinquent conduct. It has nevertheless been somewhat difficult to assess this area because of the understandable legal and social attitudes regarding the sanctity and privacy of the home. Public behavior is visible and to some extent

---

[54]J. P. Lees and L. J. Newson, "Family or Sibship Position and Some Aspects of Juvenile Delinquency," *British Journal of Delinquency* 5(1954):46–65.

[55]A. J. Reiss, "Social Correlates of Psychological Types of Delinquency," *American Sociological Review* 17(1952):710–80.

controllable, but what goes on behind the closed doors of homes is largely invisible and beyond control.

The most usual case to come to public attention is either the gross physical abuse case, referred to as the "battered child syndrome," or outright parental abandonment. Short of this extreme physical abuse, which usually results in hospitalization, or of actual abandonment, the reality is that families can subject their children to severe physical and emotional abuse (particularly the latter) for years without public or research detection.

In an article aptly titled "The Family As a Cradle of Violence," Suzanne K. Steinmetz and Murray A. Straus state:

> ... It would be hard to find a group or institution in American society in which violence is more of an everyday occurrence than it is within the family. Family members physically abuse each other far more often than do nonrelated individuals. Starting with slaps and going on to torture and murder, the family provides a prime setting for every degree of physical violence. So universal is the phenomenon that it is probable that some form of violence will occur in almost every family.
>
> The most universal type of physical violence is corporal punishment by parents. Studies in England and the United States show that between 84 and 97 percent of all parents use physical punishment at some point in their child's life. Moreover, such use of physical force to maintain parental authority is not confined to early childhood. Data on students in three different regions of the United States show that half of the parents sampled either used or threatened their high school seniors with physical punishment.
>
> Of course, physical punishment differs significantly from other violence. But it is violence nonetheless. Despite its good intentions, it has some of the same consequences as other forms of violence. Research shows that parents who use physical punishment to control the aggressiveness of their children probably increase rather than decrease their child's aggressive tendencies. Violence begets violence, however peaceful and altruistic the motivation.
>
> The violent tendencies thus reinforced may well be turned against the parents, as in the case of Lizzie Borden. Although most intrafamily violence is less bloody than that attributed to Lizzie, some family abuse does go as far as ax murder. Examination of relationships between murderer and victim proves that the largest single category of victim is that of family member or relative.
>
> The magnitude of family violence became particularly obvious during the summer heat wave of 1972. Page 1 of the July 22, 1972 *New York Times* carried an article describing the increase in murders during the previous few days of extreme heat in New York City and summariz-

ing the statistics for murder in New York during the previous six months. Page 2 held an article totalling deaths in Northern Ireland during three and a half years of disturbances. About as many people were murdered by their relatives in one six-month period in New York City as had been killed in three and a half years of political upheaval in Northern Ireland. . . .

A survey conducted for the National Commission of the Causes and Prevention of Violence deals with what violence people would approve. These data show that one out of four men and one out of six women approve of slapping a wife under certain conditions. As for a wife slapping a husband, 26 percent of the men and 19 percent of the women approve.

. . . Richard Gelles of the University of New Hampshire, who has done a series of in-depth case studies of a sample of 80 families, found that about 56 percent of the couples have used physical force on each other at some time.

In a second study, freshman college students responded to a series of questions about conflicts which occurred in their senior year in high school, and to further questions about how these conflicts were handled. Included in the conflict resolution section were questions on whether or not the parties to the disputes had ever hit, pushed, shoved, thrown things or kicked each other in the course of a quarrel.

The results show that during that one year 62 percent of the high school seniors had used physical force on a brother or sister and 16 percent of their parents had used physical force on each other. Since these figures are for a single year, the percentage who had *ever* used violence is probably much greater.[56]

In most juvenile institutions it is usually apparent that delinquent, emotionally disturbed, or schizophrenic teenagers have been subjected to abusive treatment and family pathology from the time of birth. Many times the admission to the institution is occasioned by some bizarre, retaliatory act the teenager had perpetrated against himself or family members. Even when instances of gross abuse come to "public" attention, there is no guarantee of appropriate intervention.

One of the authors studied a case of felonious child abuse involving parental delinquency that was adjudicated in the Los Angeles Superior Court in 1969.[57] The case concerned a child who would be inclined in later years

---

[56]Suzanne K. Steinmetz and Murray A. Straus, "The Family as Cradle of Violence," *Society* 10(September 1973):50–51. This article was adapted from the introduction to *Violence in the Family,* by Suzanne K. Steinmetz and Murray A. Straus. Copyright © 1974 by Dodd, Mead & Company, Inc. Reprinted by permission of Dodd, Mead & Company, Inc.

[57]*People* v. *Stephenson and Tymick,* Los Angeles Superior Court, June 1969.

toward delinquent status. The child's parents were arrested in August 1969 after they brought their three-year-old son, the third born of six children, the oldest of whom was five, to a hospital for treatment of multiple bruises, lacerations, and burns.

An investigation by the probation department verified that the defendants had approached a community agency in March of 1969 with the explicit statement that they were having trouble controlling the victim, could not discipline him, and wanted help with him. Up to the time of the parents' arrest, one social agency had made a home call and promised to help the family. It was later learned that the caseworker had gone on vacation and nothing was done about the case. The agency later blamed its lack of follow-up on "personnel changes" and "this is just a case of a file being misplaced." Another agency made a home call at the family's request, but it was noted that the victim "seemed normal to our worker and even went to the potty for the worker." Several clinic appointments were made for the mother but she did not go because she could not locate a babysitter for her other small children, including a five-month-old baby. The agency offered no help with this problem. Even subsequent to their conviction, the family had great difficulty finding an agency that would help them. The evaluation in the probation officer's presentence report helps to understand the problem.

Although defendant is responsible for the highly charged crime of abusing a child, it nevertheless would appear that society, through its social agencies, must also share in this responsibility. Had the defendant behaved humanely, the child would not have been abused. In mitigation, however, had social agencies responded differently, the possibility also exists that the child would not have been abused. On March 11, 1969, the defendant initially approached an agency admitting that he did not know how to cope [with the child] and requesting assistance. The "interested parties" section documents some of his attempts to manipulate his way through the segmented, autonomous and specialized system of welfare and health services which have been constructed by society to assist families with the kind of problem defendant was presenting. It is no easy task for a sophisticated, middle-class citizen to get a timely response from this bureaucratic network; it is especially difficult for someone of defendant's (lower class) background. Even subsequent to defendant's conviction, it would appear that defendant's present involvement with a psychiatric setting has been largely the result of his own persistence.

The largely "invisible" problem, therefore, of family pathology is complicated by the inability of society to make an appropriate response when it becomes visible and apparent.

Another bizarre child-abuse case occurred in June 1973 and involved parents who were religious zealots. The parents claimed that their diabetic ten-year-old child was "cured" by the Lord and no longer needed his life-giving medicine. They withheld the medicine and within a week the child was dead. On their way to jail, the parents informed the press that their child was blessed and would rise like Jesus in a week.

It is relatively easy to measure structural elements such as size of family and whether or not the home is broken, but it is much more difficult to identify most instances of child abuse unless they are as extreme as the cases here described. As a consequence, most of the delinquency studies in this area have relied on self-reporting questionnaires given to delinquents. Some caution must therefore be used in evaluating the findings of these studies. As an example, it is possible that delinquent and conforming boys would report the same discipline technique quite differently. It is also quite possible that a particular way of treating a child did not cause the child's delinquency but was the result of the child's becoming delinquent and was engaged in only "after" the child became delinquent. Studies in such areas have nevertheless been quite valuable, and they help to explain family dynamics and delinquency. Thus despite these research problems, the quality of parent-child relationships as measured by "discipline techniques" has received considerable attention.

Discipline is generally characterized by three variables: consistency, intensity, and quality. *Consistency* pertains to the predictability of the discipline and takes into account the circumstances in which the offense occurred. Discipline that is consistent, rational, and based on explanation is more likely to produce adequate internal controls. *Intensity* is related to the severity and rationality of the punishment. Discipline based on explanation and understanding between parents and child rather than strict, punitive punishment is more likely to produce internalized control from the child. *Quality* is related to the type of punishment, such as physical punishment, love withdrawal, nagging, or explanation. Nagging and love withdrawal will produce control by the child based on a fear of losing parental affection, not on an internalized set of standards of behavior. According to Peterson and Becker, "If one endorses the common assumption that capacities for internal control are complexly but closely related to previously imposed external restraints, then parental discipline assumes focal significance as a factor in delinquency."[58]

The Gluecks reported in their 1950 study that lax and inconsistent techniques of discipline were associated with a higher percentage of delinquents than were very strict techniques. Firm but kindly disciplinary measures were found to be associated much more frequently with nondelinquents. The Gluecks also found that physical punishment as a disciplinary method was used more frequently by parents of delinquents than by parents of nondelinquents, who reasoned with their children.

[58]Peterson and Becker, "Family Interaction in Delinquency."

McCord and McCord concluded in their studies that consistency was more important than the kind of discipline. They reported that consistent love-oriented or punitive discipline by both parents significantly reduced delinquency. Nye, based on his research, reported that 49 percent of both male and female delinquents who reported that their mothers "very often" failed to carry out threats of punishment were found in the "most delinquent" category. This compared to 30 percent of the boys and 22 percent of the girls who reported that their mother "never failed" to implement her threats. The overall relationship is significant for girls but not boys. Nye did show that of the children in his study who considered their father's discipline "always fair," only 30 percent of the boys and 20 percent of the girls fell into his "most delinquent" group. On the other hand, 55 percent of the boys and 44 percent of the girls who felt their father was "unfair" fell into the "most delinquent" group. Slocum and Stone have also reported a significant relationship between fairness of parental discipline and conforming male and female children.[59] In summary, most of these studies have demonstrated a strong correlation between consistency and fairness of discipline and conforming behavior of children and the opposite approach more likely to be associated with juvenile delinquency.

Another family variable of considerable importance is the "quality" of marriage existing in the home. The Gluecks found that 31.2 percent of their delinquents came from homes with poor marital relationships compared with 14.9 percent of the nondelinquent population. In addition, they found that strong family cohesiveness characterized 61.8 percent of the nondelinquent homes but was found in only 16 percent of the delinquent homes. Nye found that 46 percent of the boys and 49 percent of the girls from "unhappy" homes were in his "most delinquent" group compared with 23 percent of the boys and 22 percent of the girls who reported being from "completely happy" homes.

Slocum and Stone report that 52 percent of the "most delinquent" boys in their study described their families as noncooperative compared with 16 percent of the boys from the conformist group. Lester Jaffe also found a correlation between disagreement within the family and a high score on a delinquency-proneness scale.[60]

Based on specific case histories and the general results of comprehensive studies by other researchers, the Grogans, in their study of "criminogenic families," concluded that excessive conflict and tension in a family interfere with the personality development of a child, with accompanying disruption of his social development.[61] These factors often cause such children to seek social

---

[59]Walter Slocum and Carol L. Stone, "Family Culture Patterns and Delinquent-Type Behavior," *Marriage and Family Living* 25(1963):202–8.

[60]Lester D. Jaffe, "Delinquency Proneness and Family Anomie," *Journal of Criminal Law, Criminology and Police Science* 54(1963):146–54.

[61]Grogan and Grogan, "Criminogenic Family."

values in a peer group rather than the family environment. The Grogans further concluded that, in a significant number of cases, this seems to be a major contributory factor to the occurrence of criminal or delinquent behavior. All of these studies clearly relate delinquency to family variables such as family disagreement and tension.

Lack of affection and rejection also occupy an important casual role in the findings of the Gluecks, Andry, Nye, Slocum and Stone, and McCord and McCord. In another study, Kirson Weinberg says about the parents of delinquents: "Indifference or hostility hindered their children from acquiring positive attitudes towards authority."[62]

In some cases, especially for the violent delinquent, the family influence on the child's behavior is not complex. There are situations where the most dreadful act by a child contains a high level of rationality—in the context of family provocations. The following case from a book by Dr. Muriel Gardiner is a classic, and even though the child's behavior is homicidal, it has a degree of rationality.[63]

"Get that cat out of here, you good-for-nothing son of a bitch," exploded Harry, obviously pleased to have someone on whom to vent his anger.

"I won't let her bother you; I'll keep her in my room," pleaded Tom.

"The hell you will!" cried his uncle, seizing the kitten. And, before Tom's unbelieving eyes, he wrung her neck.

Tom, in a flood of tears, carried the warm little body into his room. He tried in vain to revive it. At last, still weeping, Tom lay down on his bed, stroking and caressing the only thing he had ever loved. . . .

"What's all this mumbo-jumbo?" Harry cried angrily, looking at the patch of earth and the little homemade cross.

"Please, Uncle Harry," implored Tom in terror, "please don't do anything. I just made a little grave for my cat, that's all."

With one great kick, Harry splintered the cross, then stamped on the soft earth of the grave. Turning, he slapped Tom's face with the back of his hand, and strode into the house.

Tom went into the furnace room. He picked up one of his uncle's guns, and, pausing only to make sure it was loaded, went upstairs to where Harry, Bertha, and Catherine were sitting at the breakfast table. Tom raised the gun, and carefully shot his uncle, then his aunt, then Catherine.

---

[62]S. Kirson Weinberg, "Sociological Processes and Factors in Juvenile Delinquency," in *Juvenile Delinquency,* ed. Joseph S. Roucek (New York: Philosophical Library, 1958), pp. 126–27.
[63]Muriel Gardiner, *The Deadly Innocents* (New York: Basic Books, 1976), p. 108.

The studies of Bandura and Walters are also relevant to this theme.[64] When they compared a group of aggressive delinquents and their families with a group of nondelinquents and their families, they found a higher proportion of the parents of the aggressive boys had denied them an opportunity to express their feelings of dependency; rejection, defined in terms of punishment of the boys' striving for gratification of dependency needs, was significantly higher for boys in the delinquent group. It was also concluded that boys whose dependency needs had not been met were less apt to internalize parental standards and values.

If one can assume that parental values generally support conventional behavior and that affectionate parent-child relationships promote such internalization, then affectional parent-child relationships can serve to insulate the child against delinquency. The opposite, however, can also no doubt be assumed. One of the authors recalls the case of a fifteen-year-old delinquent boy in juvenile hall talking to his father on visiting day. The father put his arm around the boy when they met, and both father and son continued to relate to each other in a very affectionate and friendly manner. The entire conversation was nevertheless restricted to the father's relating his latest physical altercations to the boy. He told his son how he had assaulted a neighbor when the latter had requested that he move his car because it was partially blocking the driveway. The boy's eyes glowed as his father related his *macho* adventures in great detail. It is of interest that the boy was in juvenile hall for gang activity related to an assault he had committed on a boy who was then in critical condition in the hospital.

Another incident recalled by one of the authors on visiting day was the case of a fifteen-year-old girl incarcerated for "promiscuity." The father greeted his daughter with a "french kiss" that, if portrayed in a film, would be X-rated. He obviously had sexual feelings for his daughter that were probably unconscious and never acted out. However, from the girl's point of view, it appeared that the sexual stimulation of her father was reciprocated on a host of neighborhood boys, and this was why she was in custody.

In Shaw's interesting study of jackrollers, he stated that some neighborhoods encourage crime: "Stealing in the neighborhood was a common practice among children and approved by the parents."[65] Walter Miller has also expressed the opinion that the parents of many lower class children express values that are conducive to delinquency.[66] To the extent that this view is representative, then, even affectionate parent-child relationships can sometimes result in the internalization of delinquent values if the parent encourages this behavior. Thus a double message is often given the child on deviance.

---

[64]Bandura and Walters, *Adolescent Aggression.*

[65]C. R. Shaw, *The Jack-Roller* (Chicago, University of Chicago Press, 1930), p. 54.

[66]Walter B. Miller, "Lower Class Culture as a Generating Milieu of Gang Delinquency," *Journal of Social Issues* 14, no. 3 (1958):5–19.

Sykes and Matza assert: "There is a strong likelihood that the family of the delinquent will agree with respectable society that delinquency is wrong, even though the family may be engaged in a variety of illegal activities."[67]

It may be that certain families tolerate or even encourage the commission of certain offenses but not others. There is also no doubt that many parents covertly encourage their children to commit criminal acts. We are particularly thinking of drug offenses. Parents who depend on drugs, whether they get them illegally or are able to get them legally, are setting an example that many children no doubt follow. The classic case is the portrait of a parent with a martini in his hand bitterly admonishing his child about the abuse of drugs.

A number of psychiatrists have concentrated their attention on the tendency of some families to encourage delinquency in their children. Adelaide Johnson believes that middle class parents foster delinquency in their children by projecting their own problems onto the children, suggesting that the resulting delinquent behavior satisfies unconscious needs of the parents.[68] Ruth S. Eissler also holds this view that the child is the victim of family pathology.[69] David Abrahamsen essentially believes that all delinquents are emotionally disturbed and are produced by tensions and conflicts within the family.[70] Nathan Ackerman essentially holds the view that disturbed individuals almost always come from disturbed families:

> Parents displace onto their children anxieties and hostile urges which belong to their disturbed relations with their own parents and with wider society. Being preoccupied with their own needs, they do not make adequate emotional room for their children's needs. They react to the children's needs as if exorbitant and menacing. They do not love fully or freely. What they give to their children means to them that much less for themselves. Out of a sense of guilt they try to pacify their children, overindulge them inappropriately in material things, and accord them disproportionate power within the home. Out of their own insecurity, doubt, and impotence, parents find themselves governed by their own children. The absence of confidence and natural pleasure in parenthood is expressed in attitudes of rejection, cruelty, overindulgence, anxious overprotection, inconsistent and inappropriate discipline. . . . Precisely because control patterns are weak, erratic and undependable, there is an

---

[67]Gresham M. Sykes and David Matza, "Techniques of Neutralization: Theory of Delinquency," *American Sociological Review* 22 (1957):665.

[68]Adelaide M. Johnson, "Sanctions for Super Ego Lacunae of Adolescents," in *Searchlights on Delinquency,* ed. K. R. Eissler et al. (New York: International Universities Press, 1949), pp. 225–46.

[69]Ruth S. Eissler, "Scapegoats of Society," in *Searchlights on Delinquency,* ed. K. R. Eissler et al. (New York: International Universities Press, 1949), pp. 288–305.

[70]David Abrahamsen, *The Psychology of Crime* (New York: Columbia University Press, 1960).

exaggerated concern with issues of control and discipline. There is a
failure to understand that matters of control and discipline cannot be
mediated apart from the related issues of basic security, satisfaction, and
unity ... the instability of the family favors implementation of such
pathological defenses against anxiety as substitution of aggression for
anxiety, scapegoating, magic doing and undoing, projection, isolation,
and the tendency to externalize conflict, i.e., to act out. Episodically,
these families may turn "delinquent."[71]

Ackerman, in this appraisal, summarizes many of the family dynamics
that correlate well with the production of delinquency.

A special case that illustrates many of the structural and dynamic aspects
of the family that we have found to be associated with delinquency is seen in
some transplanted Mexican-American families. In Mexico, the man takes
great pride in being the head of the family, in being the provider and protector
of his family, while his wife takes care of the home. The concept of *machismo*
or *macho* (pride, manliness, masculinity) is a crucial one in family dynamics
and male personal identity. The husband's ability to maintain his *macho,* as
head and chief provider of the family, preserves the paternalistic Mexican
family. When the family moves north to the border, however, it is not unusual
for the family and the children to suffer in the new socioeconomic environment.

A "man" is one who takes care of his family, and one who takes care
of his family works at a job in which he can have some pride and which pays
him sufficient income to meet his family's needs. The sad plight of many
Mexican-Americans in the United States, however, involves a situation where
the man of the house frequently does not have the kind of skills or the
educational requirements demanded by a technical, specialized economy. His
inability to compete is rapidly translated into inability to support his family,
which entails loss of self-respect and of his role as "man" of the house. The
family must nevertheless survive and consequently may end up on public
assistance, a situation the man may find humiliating. The problem may be
exacerbated when his wife, of necessity, seeks and finds employment. This
accelerates the corrosion of paternalistic traditions. Marital discord, desertion,
and divorce frequently follow. When the man is still physically in the house,
he is apt to try to regain his *machismo* through essentially dysfunctional
techniques such as drinking, fighting, and bragging about past exploits. This
condition often negatively affects the son and too often leads to delinquency.

The adolescent Mexican-American boy watches the father, whom he
once held in great esteem, become humiliated and destroyed. He also wants

---

[71]Nathan W. Ackerman, *The Psychodynamics of Family Life: Diagnosis and Treatment of Family
Relationships* (New York: Basic Books, 1958), pp. 117–18. Copyright 1958 by Nathan W. Ackerman, Basic Books, Inc., Publishers, New York.

to live up to the traditional *macho* role but is confused by family conflict, male-female role reversals, and the "gringo" society that has belittled his father and discriminated against his people. Since he is neither Mexican nor American, he rejects the values of both and attempts to create new values, often within the vehicle of a gang. The only old value he brings with him is *machismo*. However, this old value has acquired a new meaning one that has violence built into it. *Machismo* thus often becomes a hostile, ultramasculine, exquisitely sensitive feeling that can explode into senseless violence over an imagined "bad look" or an unknowing "insult." It is associated almost exclusively with rather primitive notions of physical and emotional toughness.

Octavio Paz asserts that the "pachuco" sees manliness as never cracking, never breaking down or backing down. Only cowards "open up."[72]

The violent gang often becomes a surrogate family for a Mexican youth. It is a vehicle for the Mexican-American youth to prove his *macho* both to himself and his peer group. It is also understandable that many Mexican-American gangs are leaderless entities since if you have leaders, you have to have "followers" and an "inferior" role contradictory to the whole notion of *machismo*.

One aspect of the Chicano gang member's alienation from both the Mexican and the American cultures is his development of a private language, referred to as "the other language," or *caló*. This youth becomes trilingual: he speaks Spanish at home, English in school, and *caló* on the streets with his peers. *Caló* is neither Mexican nor English. It is a bastardized form of both, being equally unintelligible to his Mexican parents and to his Anglo enemies. It has been described as a "snarl language," which implies an uncompromising attitude of anger, sarcasm, cynicism, and undifferentiated rebellion. This private language confers upon the speaker a sense of uniqueness and identity. It becomes a powerful organizing force in his life because this is the language of the gang, the only group that has any meaning in his life. The gang becomes in effect a peculiar surrogate family that in many ways replaces his family of orientation. This pattern we have described is obviously not the unique dynamics of the Mexican family. Any family that is transplanted can experience the complex dynamics described here. Such complex cultural and family forces produce the problems of delinquency for many youths from other social, ethnic, and religious backgrounds.

The family, through its genetic, psychological, and sociological contribution to its children, occupies a dominant role in theories of delinquency. If we can represent "the reason" for an individual's becoming delinquent as a puzzle with all of the pieces put together, there is no doubt that each such puzzle for each delinquent will contain many pieces representing different aspects of the family.

---

[72]Octavio Paz, *The Labyrinth of Solitude: Life and Thought in Mexico* (New York: Grove Press, 1961).

Chapter
5

The
School
and
Delinquency

Then said a teacher, Speak to us of Teaching.

And he said:

No man can reveal to you aught but that which already lies half asleep in the dawning of your knowledge.

The teacher who walks in the shadow of the temple, among his followers, gives not of his wisdom but rather of his faith and his loving-ness.

If he is indeed wise he does not bid you enter the house of his wisdom, but rather leads you to the threshold of your own mind.

KAHLIL GIBRAN, *The Prophet*

ONCE UPON A TIME the rural family assumed almost total responsibility for the socialization of its young. The farm lad of eight or nine would stretch his legs to keep pace with his father as they plowed the field and gathered its crops. This lad had only to follow—literally—in his father's footsteps until the day when he would look back and see the strain on his own son's face as the latter tried to match his stride. The complexities of an occupational identity were reduced to the simplicity of a footprint in the field. The ABCs, learned by the glow of a kerosene lamp as Mom read from the family bible, were about as useful as the shadows hiding in the corners of the room. At Mom's insistence, and given good weather, slow periods on the farm might be interrupted by the kids walking over the hills to a one-room school for a couple of weeks to be with the schoolmaster, who was usually depicted as part devil, part teacher, and part preacher. But when harvest came, the schoolhouse became just part of the landscape as the kids got back to more important things.

In this *gemeinschaft* setting, the family, usually by direct example, educated the children and taught them whatever they needed to know in preparation for adult roles on a continuing and consistent twenty-four-hour-a-day basis. In an important sense, the family into which one was born was one's destiny. It attempted to meet all of the educational needs of the young—religious, ethical, occupational, academic. There were few if any other resources or alternatives of significance.

The alternatives came, however. With the concentration of capital and industrialization, the family members were recruited to run the mammoth machines of production. Cities sprang up around the industrial centers, and the boy no longer followed the plow but watched the lunch pail come and go. The concept of marriage as a "partnership" arrived with World War II, and the mother also joined the labor force, leaving no more time for bible reading. The home and the family had rather suddenly become something that opened for business at five or so in the evening and closed down at seven or so in the morning. The family reflected the specialization in industry by itself becoming specialized. The educational and developmental functions that used to take place at home during the day had to be contracted out. The public schools got the contract and, in many respects, became the daytime family. This, however, introduces the crucial question: Precisely which functions formerly performed by the rural family were to become the responsibility of the public school system? Were they to provide moral and religious instruction? Were they to administer to the emotional needs of students? Were they only to prepare them for an occupational role or were they also to produce more well-rounded citizens? Were they simply to teach the ABCs? It is our contention that many pressures toward delinquency exist because of no common answer to these questions.

Whatever the goals of the schools, a condition that complicates the educational system is the growing problem of juvenile delinquency. One indicator of this increasing problem is the fact that a nationwide Gallup Poll conducted in 1975 revealed that delinquency has become one of the top ten problems in American schools. Lack of discipline retained its traditional place in these surveys as the number one problem, while "drinking" (use of alcohol) —for the first time—was mentioned by enough correspondents to establish a new category, although it was not one of the top ten.

Below, in order of frequency, is the list of the top ten problems of the public schools, as viewed by the public in 1975:

1. Lack of discipline
2. Integration/segregation/busing
3. Lack of proper financial support
4. Difficulty of getting "good" teachers
5. Size of school/classes
6. Use of drugs
7. Poor curriculum
8. Crime/vandalism/stealing
9. Lack of proper facilities
10. Pupil's lack of interest.[1]

Function of the Schools

Over a hundred years ago Horace Mann expressed the optimistic notion that education was the "great equalizer of the conditions of men—the balance wheel of the social machinery." Since all men were equally educable, education could provide the poorest child with an equal chance to share in the good life. Mann and his votaries believed that the public school system not only made democracy workable but also guaranteed its prosperity. The "seven cardinal principles of secondary education," formulated in 1918, stressed health, command of the fundamental processes, worthy home membership, vocational preparation, civic education, leisure-time activities, and ethical character as the goals of secondary education. The same objectives appeared in the statements of the Educational Policies Commission from the 1930s onward, especially in *Education for All American Youth* in 1944.[2] These rather exalted conceptions of education are still with us. Based on position statements by the Educational Policies Commission of the National Education Association and other authoritative sources, Schafer and Polk summarize their view regarding the responsibilities of the public schools.

> We assume that all children and youth must be given those skills, attitudes, and values that will enable them to perform adult activities and meet adult obligations. Public education must ensure the maximum development of general knowledge, intellectual competence, psychological stability, social skills, and social awareness so that each new genera-

---

[1]"Results of the 1975 Annual Gallup Poll Towards Education," *The American Teacher* (January 1976).
[2]Educational Policies Commission, *Education for All American Youth* (Washington, D.C.: National Education Association, 1944).

tion will be enlightened, individually strong, yet socially and civically responsible.[3]

So one can see that the role assigned to the public schools far exceeds teaching the ABCs: the school's responsibility also ranges over the psychological and social well-being of its charges. The fact that the school may receive a new student from a dysfunctional or deprived family in no way mitigates the school's responsibility. Robert MacIvar stressed this point at the completion of his five-year juvenile delinquency study in New York:

> The school's function is to educate and where the family and the community fail to promote the social adjustment and the psychological development necessary to prepare the young to receive the education the school offers, it must step in to provide it with the area of its capacity.[4]

The school is usually the first institution entrusted with the care of a child away from the protective cloak of his family. As a socializing agency it trains the child to accept rules laid down by strangers and enforced impersonally. At school he learns to read and write and acquires intellectual skills. He also learns to compete with his peers in intellectual and athletic endeavors under the watchful eye of professionals who promulgate and enforce regulations.

As indicated, in predominantly rural and folk societies, children learned to act like adults by observing the behavior of adult members of their families. Occupational roles were learned in the family, a productive as well as a consuming unit. With urbanization and industrialization the schools became more complex, and course content began to include skills related to adult careers. For middle class children in particular, the school years have become a preparatory phase for professional or business education.

The child is expected by his parents and by society to succeed in life. Neither the family nor the school defines for him what success means in his particular case, what he has to do to achieve it, and how his education will help toward that end. Where the child in the predominantly rural society attained social maturity as soon as he reached biological maturity, the youth in contemporary urban society may find social maturity indefinitely postponed, with no sure way of attaining it. The family frequently cannot and does not socialize the child in adult occupational and community roles. The assumption is that the school will take over this function. Indeed, most of the child's development, physical, personality, and academic, is assumed to rest with the

[3]W. E. Schafer and Kenneth Polk, "Delinquency and the Schools," in *Task Force Report: Juvenile Delinquency and Youth Crime* (Washington, D.C.: U.S. Government Printing Office, 1967), p. 224.

[4]Robert M. MacIvar, *Final Report: Juvenile Delinquency Evaluation Projects* (New York: The City of New York, 1962).

school. The school, however, does not have the resources, personnel, or curriculum to perform these functions adequately. Lower class children, particularly the dropouts and delinquents, have no well-defined occupational goals and see no connection between what they learn in school and what they will do when they leave it.

Although we have not limited the goal of the schools to the "teaching" of subject matter, Friedenberg has said that this is "simply an accidental by-product which may or may not occur; the real goal of education is something very different."[5] He sees the school system as a sort of screening agency which puts its stamp of approval on its graduates. This "Good Housekeeping seal of approval" is the school system's most important function because it guarantees to future employers and to society that the student so stamped is sufficiently square, naive, and uncreative that he will fit very nicely into the conventional world. He has sufficient lack of character that he will not be upset by the unethical practices of the business world; he has sufficient lack of ability that he will not be able to perform the "official" goals of an agency yet will have enough ability to perform the covert and real goals, which may simply be keeping the internal operation running. The schools thus perform a very clever and valuable service because they can assure society that the candidate has the hidden qualities that society and employers cannot publicly advertise for or admit they value. Friedenberg mentions the examples of social workers who understand the dynamics of social stratification and group work but, more importantly, are not capable of organizing the poor into an effective political action group, of police officers who "know" the rights of citizens but do not permit this knowledge to interfere with their conception of "doing their job", of teachers who feel a personal or an official commitment to teach their students but would not let this inhibit their more important covert role of controlling the children.

Teaching the children and providing them with real skills is not the point, and employers understand that the credential is in no way a statement regarding ability. Employers understand and accept that they will have to train the graduate. But what the school has assured them of by conferring the degree is that this person is "trainable": he will be very content advertising a service he cannot provide, or selling a product that has obsolescence built into it, or convincing consumers that they "need" a product that has no functional value. He will not make any particular distinctions between manufacturing gasoline or napalm, bow and arrows or bazookas, baby cribs or bombs. They will not be controlled by their own values for the very excellent reason that they have none; they will be controlled by the values previously built into whatever role they assume in society. If the credential-holder subsequently achieves some

[5]Edgar Z. Friedenberg, "Status and Role in Education," in *Crisis in American Institutions,* ed. Jerome H. Skolnick and Elliott Currie (Boston: Little, Brown, 1970), p. 226. This article first appeared in *The Humanist,* September/October 1968 and is reprinted by permission.

position of power in society, the school further guarantees that he will use it to maintain the status quo. Friedenberg states this case:

> Wide acceptance of the value-positions conveyed by the school mystique keeps our social institutions going and reduces conflict; it stabilizes our society. But this is just another way of saying that the schools support the status quo, and, particularly, that the restriction of opportunity to those who come to terms with it virtually ensures that our society, in all its echelons, will be led by people who cannot conceive of better social arrangements or despair of even getting them adopted, and with good reason. This seems to me the final irony—the school, by controlling access to status on terms that perpetuate the characteristics of mass society, while serving simultaneously as the registrar and guarantor of competence, holds competence in escrow. And it does not release it until competence has demonstrated, over a period of years and under a variety of provocations, that its bearer has other qualities that make him unlikely or even unable to direct his competence toward major social change. By placing the school in control of the only legitimate channel to status and power, we virtually ensure that those who gain status and power will use them to perpetuate our difficulties rather to create new and radical solutions.[6]

An additional beauty of this arrangement is that not only is mass society happy, content, and unthreatened, but the credential-holder is also well pleased.

> Those who accept it [the school] well enough to emerge after 16 years with a favorable credential can usually be trusted to have sufficiently conventional goals, motives, and anxieties to find the larger social system into which they are released rewarding. To those who have learned to endure and even have fun in a small trap, the big trap built to a similar plan but on a much more lavish scale and with much richer bait looks like freedom. It offers, in any case, all they are likely to have learned to desire or even imagine. "T.V. dinner by the pool! Aren't you glad you finished school?"[7]

One can see, then, that the disadvantaged minority children, with perhaps a natural predilection for social change and the "feeling" that things are not as they should be for them, have great difficulty becoming "certified" by the school system. It is of interest, however, that some of them are able to become certified nowadays. More interesting, however, is how well they

---

[6]Friedenberg, "Status and Role in Education," p. 225.
[7]Friedenberg, "Status and Role in Education," p. 224.

learned their lessons and how well they reflect mass society. Many a black defendant without certification who has found himself standing before a black judge or black probation officer can testify to this. Those few minority members who have become certified take it quite seriously and seem to understand their "true" function much better than certified whites.

Jonathan Kozol has a similar conception of the school as an agency of social control that utilizes punitive techniques to keep minority children in their place in society. Those few minorities who do "get ahead" do so in spite of the school system, not because of it.[8]

What exists in many instances, therefore, is a dysfunctional, perhaps single-parent family that does not meet the emotional needs of the children and a school system that cannot meet the emotional needs of the children. Who, then, will meet these emotional needs? Where can the child go to find comfort and support? Since the adult world has made no answer, the youth culture has provided its own answer. It is called "the Egyptian Kings," "the Jesters," "the West Side Dragons," "the Balkans," "the Vultures" "the Crips": It is called the gang.

As we mentioned earlier, many executives tend to surround themselves with subordinates who are not argumentative and rebellious because the executives do not have the interpersonal competence to deal with dissent. They prefer the quiet, the passive, the obedient. It is no secret that the public school system in this country is a middle class system manned by middle class teachers who, we might add, feel most comfortable with middle class students who generally react in a predictable, "intelligent," understandable fashion. If the students do get upset, they are likely to suppress the feeling in respectable middle class fashion and not embarrass anyone. They have self-control. Even under stress they are apt to retain this control and intellectualize their complaints in quite good anti-Ciceronian prose. These are the teachable students, and they are the proper subjects of the educational process. They will go on to college and become lawyers and doctors, politicians and soldiers, and really quite respectable people. Some may even join a Watergate Gang. Whatever they do, they at least will do it with some class. Some will no doubt become teachers, and remembering how conforming and well treated they had been, will not be able to understand some of the loud-mouthed, vulgar, dull students who will slouch in their classrooms. Many middle class teachers are openly rejecting of lower class students simply because they are perceived as "different."

The teacher is the key person upon whom the educational system depends. His behavior and his attitudes, once he closes the door to the classroom, determine whether learning, indifference to learning, or rejection of learning takes place. Although some teachers, through prejudice and fear, consciously reject youth who are different, most teachers who

[8]Jonathan Kozol, *Death at an Early Age* (Boston: Houghton Mifflin, 1967).

reject children do so unconsciously, registering distaste and rejection by the nuances and subtleties of their behavior. Refuge behind the classroom walls is not possible if true school-community relationships are to be built.[9]

School Problems and Delinquency

One form of rejection comes out through the attitude that lower class children, particularly those from minority groups, are simply slow, dull, and intellectually inferior. A New York study concluded that "the major reason why an increasing number of central Harlem pupils fall behind in their grade level is that substandard performance is expected of them."[10] This attitude of middle class teachers was recently reinforced when Berkeley psychologist Arthur Jensen made public his contention that whites as a group were intellectually superior to blacks as a group by virtue of superior genes. Whites were allegedly 15 IQ points higher on the average than blacks, and Jensen preferred to explain this difference on the basis of heredity, not environment. Of course many middle class teachers "knew this all along." A stormy controversy started when Harvard psychologist Richard Herrnstein agreed with Jensen that IQ was largely inheritable but went on to explain the 15-point differential between blacks and whites in terms of environmental disadvantages and advantages. Geneticist Theodosius Dobzhansky nevertheless points out in his book *Genetic Diversity and Human Equality* that this focus on IQ may not be all that important anyway. The concept of IQ is a rather narrow one, and quite obviously many other traits are crucial relative to success or failure. A panhandler with an IQ of 180 is still a panhandler.

There is no doubt that white supremacists and educators looking for an excuse for failure will continue to hold the view of white intellectual superiority and project this into curriculum and classroom. With many "well-meaning" teachers, the prejudice comes out in a condescending and embarrassing way. Frank Reissman notes: "The specific forms of patronization are manifold: The tendency to talk down to the deprived child, to speak his language, to imitate slang and speech inflections; the assumption that these children are lacking intellectual curiosity and conceptual abilities; the lowering of academic standards and the failure to set high goals for the deprived; the too quick taken for granted attitude they are not interested in learning."[11] The projection of these kinds of attitudes provides the children with a "license for failure." It is quickly communicated to them that they really are not expected to succeed;

[9]Robert S. Fisk, "Task of Educational Administration," in *Administrative Behavior in Education,* eds. R. F. Campbell and R. T. Gregg (New York: Harper, 1957), p. 211.

[10]Kenneth Clark, *Dark Ghetto: Dilemmas of Social Power* (New York: Harper & Row, 1965), p. 139.

[11]Frank Reissman, *The Culturally Deprived Child* (New York: Harper & Row, 1962), p. 22.

there really is not much point in trying because they can't make it anyway. Davidson and Lang have pointed up the connections between belief in limited potential and educational failure:

> It is therefore likely that a lower class child, especially if he is not doing well in school, will have a negative perception of his teacher's feelings toward him. These negative perceptions will in turn tend to lower his efforts to achieve in school and/or increase the probability that he will aggravate the negative attitude of his teachers toward him, which in turn will affect his self-confidence and so on.[12]

Expect failure from the children and the children will give you failure. Ravitz quite rightly makes an issue of this self-fulfilling prophecy in the education of culturally deprived children.

> Not infrequently teachers, counselors, principals assigned to the depressed area schools have been people without any real concern for these children and with the common stereotype of them as children of low ability. As a result of this low estimate of potential, the self-fulfilling prophecy went into effect. The children were not encouraged to learn very much; the teacher expended little energy on anything but maintaining order and bemoaning her lot; as a consequence, the children fulfilled the lowest expectations, which in turn enforced the original assumption to prove that the teacher was right.[13]

In fact, the school system doesn't know whether deprived children can be "educated" or not—they have never tried it. These damaging attitudes projected by the middle class school onto lower class children is compounded by the fact that an irrelevant and fairy-tale world is presented to the deprived children through the use of essentially middle class–oriented instructional materials. When the ghetto child walks into the school system, he walks into a middle class world that may literally shock him. He may be so awed by the mammoth physical facilities and have so little experience in such middle class settings that he never does find his way around. He may stumble into the right classroom but immediately decide that it is the wrong room for him when confronted with subtle or overt rejection by teacher and middle class students. His feeling that he is not really wanted here, that he is somehow out of place, will not be changed by the textbook illustration of the ruddy-faced grandfather

---

[12]Helen H. Davidson and Gerhard Lang, "Children's Perceptions of Their Teachers' Feelings Toward Them Related to Self-Perception, School Achievement and Behavior," *Journal of Experimental Education* 29(December 1960):114.

[13]Mel Ravitz, "The Role of the School in the Urban Setting," in *Education in Depressed Areas,* ed. A. Harry Passow (New York: Teachers College Press, 1963), p. 19.

giving the golden-haired girl in the party dress a piggyback ride in front of the fireplace in the spacious living room, with mom and dad holding hands and smiling in the background. The ghetto child's psychological survival may partially hang on the fact that he cannot read the dialogue beneath the picture. He nevertheless knows that he is in a strange world where he does not really belong and is not really wanted. He may have to fall back on, and even exaggerate, "lower class" patterns of behavior, which are the only acts familiar to him, thus eliciting even more overt forms of rejection from this educational prison to which he has been sentenced until the age of sixteen. Ralph Tyler has summed up this situation:

> The fact that writers of textbooks and teachers have come from a fairly restricted middle-class environment may account to a great extent for the limiting of content of elementary school reading materials and of the books used in other subjects to those aspects of life which are largely middle class in character. Elementary school books do not deal with homes as they are known by a large percentage of American children. The books in use treat of business, industry, politics, and the professions usually in the terms of the white-collar participants rather than in terms of that which would be most understandable to a large fraction of the children.[14]

Instead of presenting experiences that would tend to foster identification with the school, experiences of alienation are concatenated page after page, book after book. Schafer and Polk in their excellent work recorded the response of a former delinquent to educational materials in the public school:

> It wasn't interesting to me, I liked the science books but I didn't dig that other stuff. Dick and Jane went up the hill to fetch a pail of water and all that crap. Mary had a little lamb. Spot jumped over the fence. See Spot jump over the fence. I mean I got this stuff in the seventh grade too. I got a little book no bigger than that. I opened it up. Dick and Jane was in the house. Mom and dad was going to the market. Spot was outside playing with the ball with Sally. I say, ain't this the cutest little story. And I took the book one day and shoved it straight back to the teacher and said I ain't going to read that stuff.[15]

These kinds of materials are insulting to the good intelligence of many culturally and economically deprived children. It is difficult enough to understand

---

[14]Ralph W. Tyler, "Can Intelligence Tests be Used to Predict Educability?" in *Intelligence and Cultural Differences: A Study of Cultural Learning and Problem-Solving,* ed. Kenneth Eells et al. (Chicago: University of Chicago Press, 1951), p. 45.

[15]Schafer and Polk, "Delinquency and the Schools," p. 238.

how middle class children tolerate them: apparently such materials don't contrast as sharply with the middle class child's real-world experiences as they do with the "project" child's world. Even for middle class children, however, these kinds of books and materials do not prepare them for the real world. The school presents them with a make-believe world that does not even introduce, much less wrestle with, the real problems in the world. What about Vietnam, and recession, and police brutality, and unemployment, and capital punishment, and prejudice, and parenthood, and love, and mental illness, and poverty, and conspicuous consumption, and growing old, and marriage, and life and death? What about education? There is no wonder that middle class students are shocked and confused and overwhelmed when they leave college and report for their first job at a probation department or public social service agency and are confronted by the fact that nothing they learned seemed to have anything to do with the realities of the work world.

William Kvaraceus has also stressed the infantilism of the school world:

> Since the high school is careful to skirt and detour around real-life problems and controversial issues regarding race relations, alcoholism, materialism, religion, politics, collectivism, consumer competency, it involves the learner in a type of artificially contrived busy work and shadowboxing that either dulls the adolescent into a stupor or drives him in his resentment out of school to avert aggression and resentment. In protecting youths from real-life problems, the school enters into a tragic conspiracy of irresponsible retreat from reality. The perversion of the high school curriculum to neutral and petty purposes emasculates the school program and disintegrates the ego.[16]

The goal of the middle class school system seems to be the perpetuation of the middle class lifestyle for middle class students, particularly the college-bound students. We will not discuss here how successful they are at achieving this limited class goal. The doors are open to lower class children, but the tone is set by many teachers who expect them to either knock the door down on the way in or not be able to find the handle. The school then responds in a fashion that shows the way out much more clearly than it showed in the way in. Middle class teachers are largely rational, intellectual beings who have been "trained" by rational, intellectual beings to go underground with their feelings and emotions. Any student (or others) who respond with an emotional outburst is quickly put down for not being reasonable or rational, for "losing control." Many middle class teachers are not competent in the management of those aspects of interpersonal relationship that involve emotion and feeling: they intellectualize their conflicts. This is essentially a middle class style, which

---

[16]William C. Kvaraceus and Walter B. Miller, *Delinquent Behavior* (Washington, D.C.: National Education Association, 1959), vol. 1, *Culture and the Individual,* p. 83. Copyright 1959 by the National Education Association of the United States. Reprinted with permission.

is significantly reinforced by immersing oneself in middle class values and surrounding oneself with middle class people who are essentially the same. Difference cannot be tolerated, particularly the real and fantasized violent kind of acting-out difference attributed to the lower classes. The lower classes consequently get left out, run out, and pushed out of this rejecting, unreal, irrelevant, middle class setting. Their anger provides the fuel that runs many delinquent and deviant subcultures.

In an article by John P. DeCecco and Arlene K. Richards, some of these issues are analyzed.[17] The article was based on the findings of an eighteen-month study conducted by the Senate Subcommittee on Juvenile Delinquency and on interviews conducted by the authors, of eighty-five hundred people, eight thousand of whom were students in more than sixty junior and senior high schools. The conclusion was that there was a serious problem of conflict and anger in most public school systems. They noted that the most popular strategy for dealing with problems of vandalism, serious assaults, and robbery broke down into two patterns of response: avoidance and force. The authors felt that a better pattern of response to the problems would be group interaction between students and faculty.

Schooling and the Delinquent Child

The child going to school from a poor family encounters many special difficulties, some attributable to his early experiences in the family, others resulting from deficiencies in the school system. The fact that almost every delinquent has a record of poor achievement, truancy, or both suggests a serious failure of the school to meet his needs. As Kvaraceus points out:

> Literature in the field of juvenile delinquency reveals, on the whole, rather unsatisfactory school adjustments for most children who fall into difficulty with the law. Retardation is usually high, low school achievement and poor marks predominate, truancy is frequent, dislike for school and teachers is the rule rather than the exception, and early school leaving is very often the delinquent's own solution of an unsatisfactory situation.[18]

Kvaraceus found that in a sample of 761 children being handled by the Children's Bureau of Passaic, New Jersey, very few went on to finish high school, 52 percent never completed junior high school, and 7 percent left even

---

[17]John P. DeCecco and Arlene K. Richard "Civil War in the High Schools," *Psychology Today* (November 1975):51–56, 120.

[18]William C. Kvaraceus, *Juvenile Delinquency and the School* (Yonkers, N.Y.: World Book Co. 1945), p. 135.

before completion of seventh grade. Their school grades were so low that marks of excellent, very good, and good had to be combined in one group before Kvaraceus could work with them statistically. The truancy rate of the delinquents was found to be 34 percent, as compared with 6.8 for the general population of schoolchildren.

Kvaraceus asserts that these factors cause the child to feel inferior and often frustrated. A child who is kept back a grade is usually the biggest and oldest child in his class. Since he cannot show his superiority academically, he often finds some other way to establish high status. The pattern is usually one frowned on by both teachers and parents.

William S. Amoss found evidence that further supports the relationship between low school performance and delinquency.[19] He selected seventy-six male and fifty-two female grade school students by using the criterion that the child had a "demonstrated need for supervision by the juvenile court." He then matched them to "normal" kids, scanning the school records of each, taking into account factors such as age, race, changes in family residence, intelligence, the number of parents at home and the kinds of ratings they had compiled in social attitudes and work habits.

The records of the group with the eyes of the court upon them were different than those of the less troublesome youngsters. Delinquent girls had more unstable home conditions and were older than their academic peers, while the boys with bad reports had low grade point averages and poor attitudes and work habits.

Possibly, delinquent girls got the same grades and department ratings as their nondelinquent sisters because these ratings are usually made by female teachers. Amoss suggests that there may be "a psychological conflict for the male delinquent with female standards of behavior in the classroom." Since the unstable home conditions of the girls usually meant an absent father, they could be having problems with "psychosexual development." As far as their comparatively advanced age was concerned, Amoss speculated that the delinquent girls might have been seeking older peers outside of school by whom they were negatively influenced.

The delinquent pattern for boys as a group seems to be more concretely connected to school matters; however, clues that point toward delinquency can be found in the school records of both sexes.

In another study, researchers found a link between juvenile delinquency and learning disabilities. In most cases juvenile delinquents had a history of poor performance in reading, writing, and verbal communication, in their predelinquent behavior. The study concluded that the learning-disabled child and juvenile delinquent had similar characteristics—"both develop a negative self-concept and low frustration tolerance."[20]

---

[19]As quoted in a report on William S. Amoss in *Human Behavior* (March 1976).
[20]Gary H. Bachara and Chris W. Love, "A Diagnostic Team Approach for Juvenile Delinquents with Learning Disabilities," *Juvenile Justice* 12 (February 1975):46.

In research focusing on reading as a predictor of delinquency, Thomas J. Taglianetti observed that the problem of reading failure affects about one-third of our nation's students.[21] The subjects of the study were 1,200 elementary school children (tested at normal intelligence) and 200 former residents of juvenile detention facilities. Among the delinquents Taglianetti found that failure to read caused "general school failure, and constituted a possible contributing basis for delinquency."

For the delinquent, then, "school and the process of learning may be an extension of the distortion he finds everywhere else. The normal school may emphasize his difference from the 'in group' or become a battlefield for home-originated hostility."[22] The learning process may seem unreal to him either because of his personal problems or because he sees no relation between what he learns in school and life as he knows it in his home and community.

The result has been cogently stated by Milton L. Barron: "The insistence of schools in teaching children subjects in which they cannot succeed often damages self-confidence, leads to rejection by teachers and classmates, and makes them vulnerable to neurotic and delinquent behavior."[23] Children start to wonder why they are in school and what good it is actually doing them. When they do not get good marks, they are made to feel like failures, when actually they may have other, nonacademic assets worth development.

Other negative factors often operating in the schools include textbooks too difficult for use or understanding by children from underprivileged families and areas, teachers excessively permissive or excessively rigid in control or inconsistent in discipline, and careless gossip among teachers about children who have been in trouble or whose families are in difficulty.[24]

The question arises whether or not it is advisable to require a child to go to school until he is sixteen years old. If a boy is doing poorly in school, does not wish to continue, and is physically able and anxious to get a job, should we compel him to stay in school? If we do, perhaps the school curriculum should be adapted to his perceived needs.

Several school programs have been developed to help prepare young people for occupational roles. One is the New York School to Employment Program for boys fifteen years of age and over who show signs of being able to succeed in a job despite poor school records. The boys go through a modified school program, attending regular and select classes in the morning and then working at jobs in the afternoon, for which they can receive school credit. The Detroit Job Up-Grading, designed for boys sixteen to twenty, attempts to get

---

[21]Thomas J. Taglianetti, "Reading Failure: A Predictor of Delinquency," *Crime Prevention Review* 2(April 1975):24–30.

[22]Benneta B. Washington, *Youth in Conflict* (Chicago: Science Research Associates, 1963), p. 27.

[23]Milton L. Barron, *The Juvenile in Delinquent Society* (New York: Knopf, 1960), p. 177.

[24]Bernice Milburn Moore, "The Schools and the Problems of Delinquency: Research Studies and Findings," *Crime and Delinquency* 7(March 1961):201–12.

high school dropouts back in school long enough to train for a job and get placed in one. Counseling continues for six months after the end of the course. The Chicago Double E (Education and Employment) Program is designed for dropouts selected by counselors. After a preemployment session, the boys start to work in a department store that sponsors the program along with the Chicago Board of Education. They attend classes concurrently with their jobs. With a working knowledge of the operations of such a store, they can get jobs upon completion of school. Other companies are also becoming interested in this type of program.

This idea of school-to-employment adjustment is summed up by James B. Conant:

> *I submit that in a heavily urbanized and industrialized free society the educational experiences of youth should fit their subsequent employment.* There should be a smooth transition from full-time schooling to a full-time job, whether that transition be after grade ten or after graduation from high school, college, or university.[25]

The schools should not just propel delinquents or problem children out their front doors; they should make efforts to help them. School is the first testing ground away from the protective atmosphere of the family. The school should be able to detect early misbehavior and to help the child while he is still young and more receptive to treatment than he will be later. There is no better place to detect negative behavior than the school, and it should be able to serve a very useful purpose in preventing delinquency. There are several failures in the school system that are believed to contribute to delinquency. These include:

1. *Providing frustrating experiences.* If the child experiences failure at school every day, he not only learns little, but becomes frustrated and unhappy. Curricula that do not provide a reasonable opportunity for *every* child to experience success in some areas may therefore be said to contribute to delinquency.

2. *Failing to maintain interest.* Teaching without in some way relating the subject matter to the needs and aspirations of the student leaves him uninvolved. There is little or no effort in most schools to develop curricula specifically of interest to the students.

3. *Failing to provide a feeling of satisfaction among children.* To many lower class children, school is a prison. They find little or no activity designed to give them pleasure. They are seldom asked what they would really like to learn and then given the opportunity to do so.

4. *Failing to provide satisfying personal relationships between students*

---

[25]James B. Conant, *Slums and Suburbs* (New York: McGraw-Hill, 1961), p. 41.

and teachers. Many classes are too large and impersonal to permit any warm relationships to develop. A child who fails to develop warm relationships with parents and relatives is unlikely to find such relationships in the impersonal school.[26]

The child is required each day to spend more of his waking hours in school than in any other place, with the possible exception of his home. In his first few years at school, the child is likely to be assigned to one teacher, who becomes, in effect, a parent substitute. Under these conditions he may very well spend more time under the teacher's direction than under parental supervision, especially if his mother is employed outside the home. Thus, whatever the reason for his leaving school, the child who does not adjust and drops out is deprived of the socializing influence of an adult who could influence his conformity to the law. The absence of such influence makes it more likely that he will become a delinquent.[27] That delinquency and school adjustment are related is evidenced by the fact that approximately 61 percent of the delinquents between the ages of eight and seventeen are not in school.[28]

Children who find the school traumatic tend to stay away. Repeated truancy may become defined as delinquency. In any case, children are more likely to learn and engage in delinquent behavior on the streets then they would if they stayed in school. As a result of frequent absences, the child falls behind in his work. Most delinquents are about two years behind others of their age in their schoolwork, particularly in reading. Retardation makes further attendance at school even more difficult, and many such children drop out of school entirely. The school dropout is less likely to secure employment and more likely to engage in delinquent behavior than youth who remain in school. Thus, by failing to involve the child in the school program, the school contributes to delinquency via truancy and retardation.[29]

Several experimental programs have indicated that those not able to benefit by existing kinds of education can be motivated to stay in school. The Godwin School in Boston, Massachusetts, adjusted its curriculum to meet the needs of boys sent there because they had been unmanageable or had been repeated truants. Of six thousand such boys sent there over twenty years, 84 percent were living normal lives as responsible citizens.[30] All-day neighborhood schools in New York City with club programs and emphasis on warm

---

[26]For a detailed analysis of these issues, see Bernice Milburn Moore, *Juvenile Delinquency* (Washington, D.C.: National Education Association, 1958); and William C. Kvaraceus and William E. Ulrich, *Delinquent Behavior: Principles and Practices* (Washington, D.C.: National Education Association, 1959).

[27]Bruce Balow, "Delinquency and School Failure," *Social Problems* 9(June 1961):15.

[28]Moore, "The Schools and Problems of Delinquency," p. 202.

[29]Moore, *Juvenile Delinquency,* pp. 56–59.

[30]Moore, *Juvenile Delinquency,* p. 59.

personal relationships also reported lack of truancy, a minimum of vandalism, and reduced delinquency rates.[31]

The School Dropout

The term *dropout* has generally been used to describe a person who leaves school without completing his educational program and has thus been applied to children who dropped out of elementary school, high school, and college.

We have already noted that the lower class child is subjected to many frustrating experiences at school and that this often results in mass truancy. These experiences contribute not only to his failure at school but also to the development of a self-image of failure in life. School responsibility terminates when the student leaves school, whether or not he has graduated. The child of a poor family who drops out of school is not likely to get much help in finding employment or in obtaining additional training for an occupational career. According to a United States census report, 4,039,000 persons between fourteen and twenty-four dropped out of school during the twelve months prior to October 1970.[32] Furthermore, the Census Bureau reported in 1971 that 9.5 percent of all white youth and 10.8 percent of all Negro youth aged sixteen and seventeen were not enrolled in school.[33]

In an article on truancy, Claire Berman describes the problem in New York City.

The 15-year-old boy pointed to his signature "Dune 1"—an artfully spray-painted nom de graffitti in bold, 4-foot letters on the concrete wall of a school playground, "Everybody knows my name," he said proudly, "I painted it all over the city."

His proclamation notwithstanding, Dune 1 is a nobody to a city school system that lost track of him more than two years ago. He is one of possibly 90,000 youngsters listed by the Board of Education as long-term absentees—and frequently referred to as "ghosts."

Instead of going to school, they crowd department stores, the Port Authority bus terminal, the Bronx Zoo, Central Park, Coney Island. They wander the hallways of other schools. They join gangs. They spend hours on the subways, their transistor radios blaring. Many like Dune

---

[31]Adele Franklin, "The All-Day Neighborhood Schools," *Annals of the American Academy of Political and Social Science* 322(March 1959):62–68.

[32]U.S. Bureau of the Census, "School Enrollment: October 1970," *Current Population Reports,* series P-20, no. 222 (Washington, D.C.: U.S. Government Printing Office, 1971), p. 26.

[33]U.S. Bureau of the Census, "Social and Economic Characteristics of Students: October 1971," *Current Population Reports,* series P-20, no. 241 (Washington, D.C.: U.S. Government Printing Office, 1972), p. 4, table F.

1 have learned to decorate the trains, using cans of spray paint "lifted" from the shelves of local stores. They commit petty crimes and some of them get into trouble—known to the law if not the schools.[34]

While many young people who drop out of school remain unemployed indefinitely, others accept employment commensurate with their abilities, and many of these advance to skilled-labor jobs after a few years of occupational training and experience. While there is considerable evidence that a large percentage of delinquents and criminals dropped out of school, we have no clear idea what percentage of school dropouts become delinquent or criminal. We do know that many of the dropouts from the larger society, those who as a result of some failure in the socialization process do not adapt to the normative economic and political systems, use drugs and adopt a way of life that has become identified with a counterculture.

In most cases the middle class dropout has dropped out *voluntarily;* the lower class dropout has done so *involuntarily* because for the most part he is denied access to significant status positions in the society. The middle class dropout has access to a variety of relevant roles in the society, but because he is severely disillusioned with the society, he turns his back on its usual success goals and patterns.

The middle class dropout appears to be cynical and passive, whereas the lower class dropout appears to be frustrated and angry. The differential use of drugs by the two types of dropouts has been described this way:

> Some traditional delinquents are so frustrated by not being able to achieve success that they retreat. In a sense, the old-style drug-addict delinquents took drugs (and many still do) to console themselves about their lack of achievement of the goals of society. The drug reverie is in part an escape from the addict's failure to succeed American style. This is in direct contrast with the [middle class] psychedelic-drug addicts, who are trying to scramble their circuits to eliminate from their consciousness both the total social game-playing scene (the paths to achievement) and the goals of American society.[35]

Labeling Juvenile Delinquency in School

Labeling students should be done cautiously, particularly so when the labels are negative ones. The dangers can be seen simply by looking up the term, or label *juvenile delinquent* in the *Dictionary of Education:* "... Any child or

---

[34]Clair Berman, "The 90,000 Ghosts Who Haunt the Schools," *New York Times,* November 14, 1976.

[35]Lewis Yablonsky, *The Hippie Trip* (Indianapolis: Pegasus, 1968), p. 318.

youth whose conduct deviates sufficiently from normal social usage to warrant his being considered a menace to himself, to his future interests, or to society itself."[36] This calls for a judgment, and suppose this judgment takes place in the middle class school setting where the conduct of the lower class child is apt to "deviate" significantly from that of the middle classes just on the basis of class and cultural differences. Are all of these deviations going to be labeled "delinquent"? The authors suggest that "difference" superimposed on a background of expected middle class behavior frequently gets labeled "delinquent" or if not "delinquent" then "unacceptable," or "bad," or perhaps simply "young gentlemen just don't conduct themselves like that here."

One of the authors recalls a young high school teacher who had in one of her classes a "very rebellious and recalcitrant boy" whom she wanted suspended. The boy appeared in her class one Monday morning boasting the stubble of a beard. The teacher became incensed and asked the boy to leave the class and not return until he was "clean shaven and respectable looking." The boy took offense to this and essentially told the teacher that his beard was none of her business. The teacher continued to refer to him as a "disrespectful troublemaker," and the incident culminated in a scene that disrupted the class for the rest of the period. When discussing this situation later, the teacher could only say that she simply "can't stand beards and thinks that they are disgusting." So the teacher's opinion that beards were disgusting was publicly translated into "this student is rebellious, recalcitrant, disrespectful, a troublemaker, dirty, and not respectable looking." It is difficult to know what feelings of embarrassment, rage, frustration, and impugned masculinity this young man experienced.

These kinds of episodes have most probably given rise to the notion that deviant behavior does not refer to some intrinsic quality of a specific act but rather is external to the act; it is a property "conferred" upon some form of behavior by observers. Howard Becker states the case in even stronger terms:

> Social groups create deviance by making the rules whose infraction constitutes deviance, and by applying these rules to particular people and labeling them outsiders. From this point of view, deviance is not a quality of the act the person commits, but rather a consequence of the application by others of rules and sanctions to an "offender." The deviant is one to whom that label has successfully been applied; deviant behavior is behavior that people so label.[37]

Although there is no doubt deviant behavior is behavior that people so label, most of us want to say that there are certain kinds of behavior that are

---

[36] Carter V. Good, ed., *Dictionary of Education,* 3rd ed. (New York: McGraw-Hill, 1973).

[37] Howard S. Becker, *Outsiders: Studies in the Sociology of Deviance* (New York: Free Press, 1963), p. 9.

intrinsically deviant. It nevertheless appears that much of what Becker is saying is applicable to the school system. Cavan has similarly conceptualized delinquency as a matter of "public tolerance, intolerance, or outright condemnation."[38] Backing up the public school system is a middle class system that demands conformity to middle class modes of dressing, looking, speaking, and behaving. One of the ways it attempts to induce conformity is through the labeling process, through the induction of guilt and the manipulation of the child's need to be loved and to belong. As Fromm says, control is no longer maintained through overt authority but through anonymous authority masquerading as the best interest of the child.

> While the teacher of the past said to Johnny, "You must do this. If you don't, I'll punish you"; today's teacher says, "I'm sure you'll 'like' to do this." Here, the sanction for disobedience is not corporal punishment, but the suffering face of the parent (or teacher), or what is worse, conveying the feeling of not being "adjusted," of not acting as the crowd acts. Overt authority used physical force; anonymous authority employs psychic manipulation.[39]

So in the attempt to induce "respectable" middle class behavior and to control "difficult" behavior, many students will be mislabeled as bad or troublemakers on the basis of traits, qualities, and characteristics that really do not refer to any genuinely "bad" act. The labeling process may actually be only a function of the teacher's conscious and unconscious attitudes towards class and race. The danger of the labeling process is that the kind of label and the manner in which it is applied will determine (1) the kind of self-image the student develops, (2) the kind of response to the person who applies the label and to the system that person represents, and (3) the kind of reputation the student might get and the responses of others to that reputation.

Walter Reckless has found that one of the important variables determining an adolescent's commitment to delinquency is his self-image. Delinquents whom Reckless has examined consistently held a bad self-image as opposed to the improved self-images of nondelinquents.[40] In accordance with Cooley's "looking-glass self,"[41] the boy is apt to start seeing himself as others see him and begin acting accordingly or to increase his slightly deviant behavior to where it fits or exceeds his developing poor self-image. If this evaluative process goes on publicly, which it most probably does, the impact on the youth

---

[38]Ruth Shonle Cavan, *Juvenile Delinquency* (Philadelphia: Lippincott, 1969), p. 28.

[39]Erich Fromm in the introduction of A. S. Neill, *Summerhill* (New York: Hart, 1960), p. x.

[40]Walter C. Reckless, *The Crime Problem* (New York: Appleton-Century-Crofts, 1960).

[41]Richard Dewey, "Charles Horton Cooley: Pioneer in Psychosociology," in *An Introduction to the History of Sociology,* ed. Harry Elmer Barnes (Chicago: University of Chicago Press, 1948).

can be psychologically as well as educationally devastating. It may not take many such public shamings to turn the youth totally against teachers, schools, authority, and respectable society, particularly if he already has the strong sense of injustice that many lower class boys have. It is also quite possible that a boy's alleged bad reputation can be reduced to one bad interaction with one teacher (such as the boy with the beard in a former example). Yet that one teacher, facilitated by the "will to believe" manifested by the other teachers, can spread that reputation throughout the school during one break in the faculty lunchroom. In the student's other classes and in upper grades, teachers will be more apt to react to his "rep" than to him. This kind of boy may soon decide that he just can't adjust to the school setting and drop out and try to find a job.

Our position is certainly not that students do not break rules and even commit crimes on campus. But again, the reaction of the school personnel is crucial to the future course the student might take.

> One of the factors affecting the chances that misconduct in the school will be reduced or will be repeated and extended to include misbehavior in the community is the character and effect of the school's sanctioning system. On one hand, the school can prevent behavior problems from re-occuring by imposing firm sanctions, while at the same time involving the student in the legitimate system, rewarding him for conforming behavior, and developing academic and social competencies. On the other hand, the school can inadvertently push the student toward illegitimate commitments by imposing overly-punitive sanctions in a degrading way; by locking the individual out of the legitimate system through such mechanisms as expulsion, suspension, withdrawal of extra-curricular privileges, and placement in a special classroom for the "emotionally disturbed."[42]

A prime difficulty, of course, is that many students enter the school already labeled "white, nicely dressed, middle class, intellectually superior, business or college bound, my kind of student"; "black, funny looking, dull, lower class, poor child"; "brown, sullen, unattractive lower class type, definitely not one of us," etc. Children walk into the school system having already been evaluated and divided and labeled by society at large. The school system then consciously and unconsciously decides which children are worth saving and which are not, which are educable and which are not, which shall pursue the American dream and which shall become victims of that dream. Once the labels are applied and the categories established, there may be very little the children can do other than play out the role they have been assigned.

---

[42]Schafer and Polk, "Delinquency and the Schools," p. 234.

School's Role in Combating Delinquency

Martin Deutsch sees the school as a sort of secondary line of defense in combating juvenile delinquency. He has stated that "when the home is a proportionately less effective socializing force, the school must become a proportionately more effective one."[43] It appears, then, that the public school system is that institution to which society has assigned the primary role of providing children with the kinds of skills and values that will enable them to assume productive and responsible adult roles. This responsibility is not limited to motivated middle class children or to "bright" children; its referent is "all children." It must meet the children at whatever emotional, cultural, and intellectual level they happen to be and then create and implement whatever kinds of programs they need to achieve their potential for a full, fruitful adult life. As former Secretary of Health, Education, and Welfare John Gardner once said, "What we want is a system in which youngsters at every level of ability are stretched to their best possible performance and get the maximum education of which they are capable."[44]

All of this seems to assume that to the extent the public school system meets this awesome responsibility, it avoids juvenile delinquency and social deviance; to the extent that it fails, it encourages or provides pressure toward delinquency.

The student whose most difficult problem may be her relationship in a dysfunctional and multiproblem family may, in addition to being a student, be a daughter, or a surrogate mother, or even an unwed mother. Because of personality factors and family dynamics, her primary identification may be with the role of "daughter" or "mother," not with the role of "student." If a conflict should arise between these roles and she communicates the conflict to a teacher or school official, she is probably not going to be impressed by some intellectual argument that is geared solely to the role of student and ignores her intrafamilial turmoil. The teacher/administrator, trapped in an objective intellectual role, may not be able to respond beyond some conception like, "This is an institution of learning, not a counseling center; there is nothing I can do about your problem." There is no doubt that nothing can be done about the problem if it has a high emotional content, but it is being treated as though it were a totally objective problem, requiring only a rational response.

If a student communicates a problem to a teacher about, say, a parental conflict or a feeling that he can't "keep up," there must be some attempt to handle the student's frustration or anger. It may even be that the teacher is

---

[43]Martin Deutsch, "Minority Group and Class Status as Related to School and Personality Factors in Scholastic Achievement," Monograph no. 2 (Ithaca, N.Y.: Society for Applied Anthropology, 1960).

[44]Eli Ginzberg, ed., *The Nation's Children* (New York: Columbia University Press, 1960), vol. 2, *Development and Education,* p. 237.

unable to "solve" the problem: perhaps the means to a solution is not available in the institutional framework. But this is precisely the point where teacher skills (interpersonal skills) should come into play in terms of working with the student's feelings of hopelessness or anxiety. To belabor the point, if the student comes to the teacher because of a problem that is not really solvable in the school setting, then perhaps the rational position is valid. However, if the student comes to the teacher because of his need to be understood by an adult, a need to express feelings of anger and rejection, then to treat these subjective feelings and needs in an objective way is at best untenable and at worst sadistic and cruel. A great deal may be done in the way of helping (allowing) the student to express his feelings, of giving him the impression that his feelings and he are a matter of teacher/administrator concern. This is not asking that every teacher be a professional counselor, but it is asking that every teacher be a sensitive human being with some insight into the "higher level" needs of people and with some degree of interpersonal skill in meeting these needs.[45]

The teacher/administrator, who has nevertheless become the victim of a *gesellschaft* society[46] and finds himself interpersonally incompetent and affectively deprived, cannot perceive nor respond supportively to the emotional needs of others. He can only retreat behind some rigid and unsatisfactory comment such as, "Kids just don't respect adults like they did in my day" or "nothing can be done about it and that's that."

One extensive project carried out by two researchers, Gertrude Moskowitz and John L. Hayman, provides some insights for improving teacher-student relations in delinquency-prone inner-city schools.[47] Moskowitz and Hayman noted that new teachers tended to use the formula "Start out tough —you can always ease up later when you've got them under control." They found that this was the traditional advice for a new teacher beginning a career in an inner-city school. When attempts to follow that homily trigger student backlash, the teacher often discovers just how tough such a job can be. This may be part of the reason high percentages of the novice teachers assigned to ghetto schools fail to last out their first years in the profession. The best teachers in inner-city schools seem to know better.

Moskowitz and Hayman employed observers in classrooms at three inner-city junior high schools in Philadelphia. Teachers there were observed during their first contacts with their classes and during the four weeks that followed. The best teachers (defined as those students said they liked and learned most from) were found to have a style quite different from that of

---

[45]Abraham H. Maslow, "A Theory of Motivation," in *New Knowledge in Human Values,* ed. A. H. Maslow (New York: Harper, 1959), p. 127.

[46]Ferdinand Tönnies, *Community and Society (Gemeinschaft und Gesellschaft)*, trans. Charles P. Loomis (London: Routledge and Kegal Paul, 1955).

[47]*Human Behavior* (September 1974).

novices. On the first day, the best teachers generally dealt more with student feelings, explained their expectations and standards, and began orienting their students to the subject matter of the course. They also joked more.

New teachers apparently saw little funny about their situation. They tended to use the first day on such routine matters as calling the roll as assigning seats. From that time on, misbehavior in class increased. Their students were increasingly out of order over the weeks to follow. Compared to the best teachers the novices spent more time criticizing their pupils and less time praising them. The amount of time the novices spent talking was lower than that for the best teachers, which might seem at first a boon to student participation. For the new teachers, however, this was largely because they were finding it increasingly difficult to get a word in edgewise. Moskowitz and Hayman noted, based on the anecdotal reports of their observers, that "the new teachers' failure to lecture more than the others does not appear to be part of their teaching style but seems related to the fact that there was so much disorder they were unable a good part of the time to deal with content or to be heard at all."

Order seems the crucial element. The best teachers generally took no nonsense from the start, criticizing before interruptions got off the ground. But they joked and praised more than the new teachers in addition to disapproving, and their pupils seemed more eager to respond to questions they felt they could answer. Although the new teachers criticized more overall, they seemed to allow much disorder to go unnoticed initially, the observers reported, "as though it would go away by itself if not acknowledged." Soon their classes were beyond control.

Generally, new teachers who tried to start out tough seemed to create problems by attempting to force their students into an untenable routine. Their worst disciplinary problems usually took place when students were working at their seats on an assignment while the teachers busied themselves with administrative matters. First-year teachers introduced little new work in the weeks following their initial meeting with their classes. They reviewed and drilled more. Only one time was a new teacher seen using an audiovisual aid.

The best teachers used a variety of such aids. They did not raise their voices when disciplining and sometimes joked when being critical. Yet the amount ot time when their classes were out of order remained low. They combated student boredom and restlessness with timely topics, discussions, and open-ended questions. They also smiled more. In brief, the more effective teachers expressed their feelings and enabled the students to express their emotions.

The foregoing study dealt implicitly with the basic issue in the schools —to what degree do teachers deal with course material and to what degree do they deal with emotional issues that become manifest in the form of misbehavior?

Generally speaking, people with low interpersonal competency usually cannot deal with themselves or others on a "feeling level." Getting in touch with one's own feelings or permitting others to attempt to express feelings is taboo. Since feelings must be suppressed, neither the individual nor others are allowed to "own" their feelings. The guiding principle here is "self-control": there really are no problems that can't be solved "if you will only sit down, get control of yourself (i.e., stop feeling), and discuss this thing rationally." Friedenberg commented on this subject:

> There is first an anxious and sometimes brutal intolerance of deep feelings between persons, of emotional commitment to others. This permeates school routines; love and loyalty are violations of its code and are severely punished. In some ways this is evident—the school forbids any kind of physical expression of affection at the same time that it maintains and supports a teasing attitude toward sexual attraction; its erotic ethos is basically that of a key club with unpaid bunnies. Love between members of the same sex, though a real and valid aspect of adolescent growth, is of course even more brutally punished, and hippiness, which refuses to limit itself by considerations of gender at all, is perhaps most condemned. Calm, gentle, long-haired boys arouse genuinely pathological hatred in physical education teachers.[48]

The following dialogue was taken from a psychodrama session with a school counselor who was role-playing an interaction she had the prior day with one of her students who was having family problems.

COUNSELOR: What did you and your mother do last night?

STUDENT: Do you like me?

COUNSELOR: That wasn't the question.

STUDENT: I know, but do you like me?

COUNSELOR: You're always changing the subject; we're talking about you and your mother.

STUDENT: I didn't see my mother last night, she went out. Do you like me?

COUNSELOR: She didn't stay out all night did she? Didn't you talk to her before you went to bed?

STUDENT: No. (Girl starts crying.)

COUNSELOR: You're changing the subject again. You're going to have to decide if you want to cry or talk. We can't talk while you're crying. You want me to help you don't you?

---

[48]Friedenberg, "Status and Role in Education," pp. 225–26.

The counselor in this case was really a likable person who worked hard, was instrumental in arranging group rap sessions at her school, and took her job seriously. She really wanted to help her student, but she could not express (own) her own feelings toward the girl, nor could she allow the girl to express (own) her feelings. The counselor never did answer the question, "Do you like me?" When the psychodrama director asked her if she did in fact like the girl, she answered, "I don't know, I never really thought about it." When this point was pursued, the counselor defended her refusal to answer the girl's question by arguing that she thought it was important for the girl to talk about her relationship with her mother because that was the girl's "problem." She believed that the girl "was being resistant." Her role as counselor was to "keep the girl on the problem relationship with her mother because that's what has to be worked through."

The counselor was a very bright person and was probably quite good at helping students solve curriculum conflicts and problems that could be "thought through." Since rational decision-making was her area of competency, she had to keep herself and her counselee out of blatantly emotional areas. All of the dynamics of the case presented are not known, but a seductive hypothesis is that the girl had a great need to find out if she was "likable" and had a great need to identify with another adult female. This case is also an example of unrecognized emotional content blocking an understanding of the problem and actually interferring with the counselor's intellectual abilities. Argyris makes this point with the example of some engineering executives who had developed strong attachments to certain technical issues.

> During discussions held to resolve technical rational issues, the emotional involvements tended to block understanding. Since the men did not tend to deal with emotions, their inhibiting effects were never explored. On the contrary, they were covered up by technical, rational arguments. Since these arguments were attempts by people to defend their self or attack others', there was a tendency for the rationality of the arguments to be weak. This in turn troubled the receiver of the argument, who tended to attack obvious rational flaws immediately. The attack tended to increase the degree of threat experienced by the first person, and he became even more defensive. Similar impacts upon rational decision making were also discovered in areas such as investment decisions, purchasing policies, quality control standards, product design, and marketing planning.[49]

One suspects that the same kind of denial of feeling and rational coverup goes on in the school's dealings with lower class behavior, in curriculum design and

---

[49]Chris Argyris, "Interpersonal Competence and Organizational Effectiveness," in *Interpersonal Dynamics,* ed. Warren G. Bennis, Edgar H. Schein, David E. Berlew, and Fred L. Steele (Homewood, Ill.: Dorsey Press, 1964).

teaching techniques, and in a great many of the "objective, rational" problem areas involved in operating a school. This might help explain the tenacity with which some schools cling to archaic curriculums, teaching methods, classification systems, discipline, etc.

Lower class children are more committed to the "act" than to the "word." They have different coping styles. The intellectualizing, internalizing, neurotic, middle class style is not theirs. They tend to react on a motor level, to "act out" their conflicts. They tend to live closer to their emotions and to feel more, perhaps because their experiences with daily poverty, crime, abuse, and violence make them feel more. They tend to be more emotional "out front." This emotionality is a part of them, a big part of who they are. This is the part that the middle class school wants no part of. This is the part that triggers the "feelings" in the middle class teacher. This is the part that has to go. So rather than respect this emotionality, work with it, channel its creative energy, reward it, the school administration puts the lid on; then one afternoon right after lunch it blows. Community psychiatrists have finally come to realize that they have to develop different techniques for nonverbal lower class patients. So must the school system.

One way to maintain the values of objectivity and rationality is to reject (consciously and unconsciously) ideas and values whose exploration would tend to uncover suppressed feelings. This defensive system is apt to also exclude certain ideas and values that are perceived as threatening. As the willingness to be open and entertain new ideas decreases, willingness to experiment will decrease, and the fear of risk-taking will increase. As reluctance to engage in risk-taking increases, experimentation and the range of openness decrease, resulting in decreased tendencies to take risks. We now have a closed circuit, which may account for many irrelevant, archaic, inflexible elements of the public school system. If the school system is not flexible enough to develop new, relevant curricula taught by new, realistic methods, children will continue to discard education as a means to success goals and will pursue other means up to and including delinquency. As Stinchcombe has put it:

> . . . Rebellion . . . occurs when future status is not closely related to present performance. When a student realizes he has not achieved status increment from improved current performance, current performance loses meaning. The student becomes hedonistic because he does not visualize achievement of long run goals through current self-constraint. He reacts negatively to a conformity that offers nothing concrete. He claims autonomy from adults because their authority does not promise a satisfactory future.[50]

The public school system is that institution which has "officially" picked up the tab for the almost total educational role formerly assumed by the family.

---

[50]Arthur L. Stinchcombe, *Rebellion in a High School* (Chicago: Quadrangle Books, 1964), p. 5.

The goals that have been assigned to it include the academic, occupational, moral, psychological, and social development of youth to the point where they can assume responsible, fruitful, adult roles. Assuming essential innate equality in man, education has traditionally been construed as the "great equalizer," overriding and canceling out accidental disadvantages such as poverty and class status. It is the "means" by which all persons in a democratic system can participate in private and community life to the maximum of their potential. In fact, however, the public school system has become a predominately middle class medium through which middle class children can be funneled toward college and materialistic success. It has almost totally failed to meet the needs of the disadvantaged class that requires it the most. These children, ridiculed, misunderstood, presented with foreign and irrelevant materials, are rejected in a thousand ways and pressured out of the system. Being ill-prepared for life and the world of satisfying work, being angry and frustrated at the system that does not want them, they drift toward an alternative avenue available in society: delinquency and adult criminal careers.

Another characteristic of the school system is its task orientation and commitment to objectivity and rationality, with the corollary of suppressed feelings and emotionality. Many teachers and administrators tend to be emotionally rigid, defensive, uncreative people who lack the ability to deal with the emotional aspects of intellectual material, their own lives, or the lives of students. The resulting intolerant, impersonal school system alienates both middle class and lower class children, forcing them to give up the American dream and attempt to find some meaning outside the legitimate system.

It is not our intent here to generalize about all school teachers and administrators. There are many creative and open people who have gone into teaching with a willingness and ability to meet children wherever their emotional needs happen to be. Many of these people, however, are pressured out of the system because they are "troublemakers"; those who manage to stay feel their frustration and sense of futility build as the system daily undermines their attempts to create a human experience with and for the children.

The shift toward an urbanized and technocratic society, combined with a stripping of the family's traditional socializing and educational functions, has created a situation that is best expressed by the principle, society has created more positions of responsibility than it has responsible people to fill them. Let it be said, however, that this principle does not apply just to the school system, but it takes in many institutions and agencies in society.

Erich Fromm, in his foreword to *Summerhill,* states that the public school system is only as good as the society in which it functions:

> Our economic system must create men who fit its needs; men who cooperate smoothly; men who "want" to consume more and more. Our system must create men whose tastes are standardized, men who can be easily influenced, men whose needs can be anticipated. Our system needs

men who "feel" free and independent but are nevertheless willing to do what is expected of them, men who will fit into the social machine without friction, who can be guided without force, who can be led without leaders, and who can be directed without any aim except the one to "make good."[51]

Many youths rebel against educational systems that attempt to make them into robopaths, and one form of their rebellion is delinquency. In addition, blacks, Chicanos, and other ethnic minorities deeply resent the school system's imposition of white, middle class values. Although it goes against the grain of many "subject matter only" schools, there is a need for greater humanism and for a concern with the emotional problems of the student. The harnessing of these forces would have a potent effect on making schools more resonant with the needs of children and adolescents and a more vital force in deterring delinquency. Before we can offer a possible solution to this described pattern of dehumanization in the schools, we must examine in greater depth the broader societal context of the problem.

Dehumanization in the Schools

The general problem of dehumanization often found in the school derives from the larger social context. The products of this system have been identified by one of the authors as robopaths.[52] The term *robopath,* simply defined, relates to the pathology of robot behavior.

Educating Robopaths

In addition to parents as socializing agents, educational institutions exert a powerful influence on the emergence of robopaths. There is considerable evidence that many educational systems have become social machines that complement robopath-producing families.

Many schools (at all levels) are large, bureaucratic, ahuman teaching machines that place no emphasis on people relating to people. In some cases, actual mechanical teaching machines have replaced human beings in interaction. In other cases, the teachers are as mechanistic in their approach as the machines. As Charles E. Silberman (among many other observers) suggests in his book *Crisis in the Classroom,* routine, order, and discipline have become more important than humanistic education, and teachers are more concerned with routine and order than education.

In fact, youngsters who display spontaneity are referred to by human teaching machines as "hyperactives." In many cases the normal and healthy

---

[51]Fromm, introduction to *Summerhill,* p. xi.

[52]Lewis Yablonsky, *Robopaths: People as Machines* (Baltimore: Penguin Books, 1972), pp. 40–41.

exuberance of childhood is viewed as an emotional problem. Increasingly, in many schools around the country, such children who "act out" too much are sedated with various kinds of drugs—to calm them down. These drugs are, of course, legally administered by the "system." Later in life, in their teenage years, when these same young people take drugs outside of the established order in a kind of self-administered therapy for changing their emotional state, they may be arrested and labeled "criminal." The point is that spontaneity is suspect and is too often placed under rigid controls by a social-machine educational system.

One of the social philosophers who envisioned these problems was J. L. Moreno, who in the mid-1920s attempted to develop an innovative "impromptu school" that would counterattack the educational social-machine impact of overconformity. His rationale was:

> Children are endowed with the gift of spontaneous expression up to the age of five, while they are still in an unconscious creative state, unhampered by the laws and customs laid down by a long succession of preceding generations. After that they fall heir to accepted methods of expression; they become imitative, turn into automatons and in a large measure are deprived of natural outlets of volitional creation. . . .
>
> Until a certain age all children's learning is spontaneously acquired. . . . Soon, however, the adult begins to introduce into the child's world subjects unrelated to its needs. The little victim from then on is pressed by many adult sophistries into learning poems, lessons, facts, songs, and so on, all of which remain like a foreign substance in an organism. The child begins to accept as superior that which is taught him and to distrust his own creative life. So very early in the life of the individual there is a tendency to mar and divert creative impulses. . . .
>
> Here the impromptu comes to the rescue. It offers a school of training which can be practiced in the small or large group or within the family circle itself. The impromptu method concerns itself with mental and emotional states. We do things and learn things because we are in certain states—states of fear, of love, of excitement, aspiration, etc. These states may be directly affected through stimulation and control of imagination and emotion. When the impromptu instructor recognizes the pupil to be lacking in a certain state, e.g., courage, joy, etc., he places him in a specific situation in which the lacking state will be emphasized. The pupil "plays" that situation, dramatizing the state impromptu. In other words, if lacking in courage, he "plays" courage until he learns to be courageous.[53]

---

[53]J. L. Moreno, M.D., *Theatre of Spontaneity* (Beacon, N.Y.: Beacon House, 1947), pp. 105–6.

In summary, the "natural" press of socialization by parents, friends, and school in machine societies often tends to make children grow into robopathic adults. Many children, however, are able to incorporate the rules, roles, expectations, and aspirations of the society into their personality and maintain their spontaneous, creative, and compassionate abilities and capacities. Children caught in the press of a heavy social-machine society do not become self-actualized in the Maslow sense; they tend to become robopathic role-players and thus help perpetuate the social-machine system. Another fallout of this behavior is a disposition to violence from frustration and the child's limited compassion.

Robopathic students are members of an impersonal school system in which they are treated impersonally; the net result is often a feeling of alienation. Durkheim,[54] Merton,[55] Cloward and Ohlin,[56] and others have documented the destructive effects of this lack of integration into society and significant groups. Tönnies[57] and a long line of successors have stressed the impersonalization that accompanies the complexities of city life.

What is happening in the schools must be viewed against the conceptual background of alienation and robopathology. Teachers and administrators must be cogently aware of the cost in morale of a bureaucratic, impersonal approach to campus problems, especially in high schools. It appears that a caste system has developed in schools, with a we-they differentiation of students and their teachers/administrators. Administration has become the "enemy" who issues orders from "above" but is silent on communications from "below." The effect of this breakdown in communications is to render the students impotent; they are victims in a system over which they have no control. The importance of "feelings of efficacy"[58] in schizophrenia has certainly been well documented but is no doubt generalizable to all people, including students. We like to feel that we have some part in determining the conditions of our life. Even if indeterminism is an illusion, it is a grand illusion that most of us have a need to maintain.

In 1965, a conference of adolescents met in California to discuss problems of youth concerning schools. Unanimous recommendations were: (1) students be given more responsibility in student affairs, (2) students be involved in setting school standards and rules through youth councils, (3) school and youth organizations be encouraged to involve students more actively in problems concerning the community. Every effort should therefore be made

---

[54]Emile Durkheim, *Le Suicide,* Paris, 1897.

[55]R. K. Merton, *Social Theory and Social Structure* (Glencoe, Ill.: Free Press, 1957).

[56]Richard A. Cloward and Lloyd E. Ohlin, *Delinquency and Opportunity* (New York: Free Press of Glencoe, 1960).

[57]Tönnies, *Community and Society.*

[58]Lewis Yablonsky, *The Violent Gang* (New York: Macmillan, 1962).

to involve students in decision-making, particularly in decisions that affect their lives in important ways. If this is not accomplished, if the communication block remains intact, students will continue to act out more dramatic ways of communicating.

Many pressures toward delinquency derive from a conflict regarding the goals of the public school system. Although society has said that the schools have the multiple goals of responding positively to the academic, occupational, emotional, and social needs of students, especially of culturally deprived children, it is our thesis that many of these goals do not get implemented at the classroom level. The goals that are not realized are precisely those that require warmth, understanding, insight (into self as well as others), patience—in short, those that require good interpersonal skills. Robopathic, impersonal school systems do not have the kind of personnel that responds to the emotional needs of children. Many of them are rigid, anxiety-ridden people who can barely handle their own "emotional" lives. They consequently retreat into an intellectual area where they feel more comfortable and more competent—the straight teaching of academic materials.

Friedenberg has some thoughts regarding the function of the school's impersonal treatment of children.

> For lower status, or otherwise "culturally deprived" youth, the schools' insistence on impersonality is anathema. Murray and Rosalie Wax, in a continuing series of published studies of the effect of imposing formal education on the Oglala Sioux, have made it clear that this issue is the focus of a complete educational stalemate. Sioux children will not adopt American competitive folkways and refuse to respond to the teacher at all; adolescents sit in third grade year after year in derisive silence rather than meet the teacher's terms. Similar difficulties, as the Waxes point out, arise in encounters between lower-status urban youth and the schools; and one wonders why so common and serious a source of educational frustration has not resulted in a more flexible response to the children. But in the allocation of status and role the frustration is functional; it ensures that youngsters, whether Indian, Negro or just unusually autonomous, who refuse to be depersonalized will get bad credentials that will stigmatize them as lazy or slow learners, keeping them down without involving the school in a disagreeable overt conflict about values.[59]

An associate of the author's had the experience of teaching a class in juvenile delinquency to elementary, junior high, and high school teachers. Their attitude, he recalls, consistently expressed the belief that the role of the teacher was to "teach" academic subject matter. When confronted with the

---

[59]Friedenberg, "Status and Role in Education," p. 226.

notion that emotional and family problems might interfere with learning, the general response was, "That's not our problem. We can't do anything about that." It is quite possible that they couldn't. Stated very simply, people and teachers do what they can. Most teachers have sufficient formal education to teach formal education. They do not have sufficient interpersonal skills and adequacy of personality to become "involved" with the problems of children, unless the problems are strictly academic, and perhaps not even then.

A former student who now teaches in the Los Angeles school system told this story to one of the authors: Turrell, a third grader at an elementary school, was slow in his math ability. Nevertheless he was in a higher math class where most of the children were at their grade level in ability. Through the first few months of the term Turrell would constantly ask for help, complaining that he did not understand. His frustration continued to grow because, due to lack of time, he was not given the help he needed. Very shortly Turrell became a discipline problem and stopped asking questions. He showed up late for class, attended less and less, and had a much different attitude. The teacher, in turn showing her frustration to Turrell's behavior, announced to the class, "Just ignore Turrell, he's just plain ignorant." We know that's what Turrell was before the teacher's remark. What was he afterwards?

The "task" that the impersonal school system feels comfortable in attempting is "teaching," retreating into an objective, unambiguous world of books and blocks and work plans and schedules. As Glasser has noted, the importance of personal contact in teaching has been receiving less attention as the emphasis on methods, objective testing, and classification of students has increased. The prevailing attitudes is to "remain objective and detached, don't get involved"; but teaching *should* be personal. Treating children as objects rather than people who desperately need involvement only compounds the problem.[60]

Glasser developed his reality-therapy approach more fully in his book *Schools Without Failure.*[61] In this book Glasser notes that most schools in the central areas of cities process children for failure because their educational programs are "irrelevant and do not provide methods for effectively involving children in the educational process." Children react to this failure with withdrawal and, often, delinquent behavior. Glasser's central thesis is that "if a child, no matter what his background, can succeed in school he has an excellant chance for success in life." He asserts that teachers should in effect become reality therapists—"offer friendship understanding, and get involved with helping children overcome their emotional problems." To accomplish this he recommends that every subject taught should be related to something the child acts out in his day-to-day life inside and outside of school.

[60]William Glasser, *Reality Therapy* (New York: Harper & Row, 1965), p. 165.

[61]William Glasser, *Schools Without Failure* (New York: Harper & Row, 1968).

In the same context psychodrama, related to both curriculum and personal problems, is a method that can involve children more effectively than most discussion techniques. Psychodrama relevantly applied in the classroom situation can counterattack the conditions that produce the emotional problems that emerge later in life.

Toward a New Approach: Psychodrama and Group Methods in the Classroom

Psychodrama has been utilized at every level of the educational system —from kindergarten to the postgraduate seminar.[62] The sessions have not only been related to subject matter but to current social events, "character development," and preventing delinquency. Not everyone is an advocate of psychodrama in the classroom, and the practice is of sufficient social-political importance to agitate (an archdelinquent) former Vice-President Spiro T. Agnew. In a speech in 1971 delivered to the Illinois Agricultural Association he commented:

> Perhaps you have heard of the so-called "psycho-dramas" that children of all ages are forced to act out in the classroom. Listen to this account that I read recently in a newspaper: ". . . teachers frequently ask them (the pupils) to act out such things as obtaining an abortion, inter-racial dating, smoking marijuana—and how their parents would react. Parents find even more objectionable "psychodramas' in which children act out actual incidents from the home, something which parents consider a clear invasion of their privacy. There have also been 'talk-ins' where two or three children will go to the school counselor and answer highly personal questions, such as: 'What does your father wear when he shaves?' or 'Do you love your parents?' One child was assigned an essay on the subject, 'Why do I hate my mother more than my father?' " Character that was once molded in the home is now more often the product of the classroom. . . .

The debate over teacher's dealing with a child's emotional state in class —beyond the curriculum—is still a controversial issue in many school systems, but despite this, the application of role-playing that relates to emotional and deviance problems has become an established practice in the classroom. Psychodrama is utilized in the classroom for both the child's emotional growth and for curriculum purposes on subject matter. In connection with transmit-

---

[62]The following analysis on psychodrama as a theory-methodology for humanizing the school situation and preventing delinquency is derived from Lewis Yablonsky, *Psychodrama: Resolving Emotional Problems Through Role Playing* (New York: Basic Books, 1976).

ting information, many teachers use a wide array of role-playing techniques to involve delinquency-prone children into learning more effectively.

Many teachers have role-playing sessions where children (after being informed on a subject) psychodramatically assume the role of an inanimate or animate object they are studying. To understand the subject or role on a deeper level a child may become a tree or an animal or assume the role of police officer, judge, lawyer, or attendance officer. (In this latter context a child playing the role of his attendance officer invariably asks himself, "Why do you play hookey?" This often produces a meaningful discussion of why kids do not attend school.) We would suggest that the literature and the characters be acted out in a free style that facilitates the student's development of spontaneity and gives him a broad range for interpretation. For example, consider the possibilities of the "To Be Or Not To Be" scene from Hamlet. In a session one of the authors ran with high school–age students, it kicked off an exciting and useful examination of the social problems, implications of suicide, violence, and homicide. It was noted that the youths most prone to this behavior were the students most involved in the sessions.

History can be made exciting and interesting through role-playing that goes beyond the surface into emotional issues. Portraits of significant periods and episodes in history tend to personally and emotionally stimulate student involvement. For example, in examining patriotic emotions, it might be useful in lieu of saluting the flag to have a different child, each day, role-play "the flag" and talk about such issues as how he (as the flag) came into existence and what he stands for. Dialogue with the "student-flag" should, of course, be encouraged. This type of psychodramatic interaction would breathe some life into a role ritual that no longer has much meaning for most children. It fosters a discussion by many delinquency-prone children into the meaning and values of laws and the Constitution.

In a deeper historical context, a student can play George Washington, Abraham Lincoln, John F. Kennedy, or Richard Nixon and present each former president's speeches. Have students (black and white) play blacks of that era and militants of today as the audience to the speech. Properly done, this type of session will veer into a psychodrama on contemporary race relations between students, racial militancy and the role of deviant presidents and politicians, and reveal some of the emotions young people have about these issues.

On a more direct emotional level, psychodrama sessions in the classroom can encompass such subjects as dating, meeting new people, envying others, not having lots of clothes (or the right clothes), getting low grades, being embarrassed to speak in front of the class, getting high grades on tests, making a mistake in front of the class, being complimented, having money stolen, cheating on tests, gossiping, running for school office, taking drugs, "sexual promiscuity," vandalism, losing in a contest, being absent from school fre-

quently, losing one's possessions, forgetting things, not completing assignments, and fair and unfair discipline by teachers.

The psychodrama sessions can utilize the following order of action:

1. Have students select and discuss a problem as a warmup.
2. Assign roles according to the problem situation.
3. Enact a specific situation or situation involving tensions and conflict.
4. Analyze patterns of conflict which appear in the role-playing.
5. Replay for better relationships and improved role performance.

One inner-city teacher's report on her role-playing in the classroom
reveals the broad range of subjects covered and the practice involved.

> With the younger pre-school children my "games" are painless
> "let's pretend" although I do like to ask the children the whys of the
> profession they choose and also to try to have the significant others
> present (i.e., doctors, and nurses, football players and spectators or
> coaches, teachers and, of course, students). In all these role-playing
> experiences I feel the children are being creative, however with the
> primary grade children I go one step further. Instead of just "playing"
> roles I have them reverse roles. One that seems to be the favorite is that
> boys are girls and girls are boys, or children from different ethnic or
> racial groups reverse roles. When the children are finished at playing
> each other I ask them to share what it *felt* like. I like to know if they
> would like to always be a boy (girl), black (white), parent (child) teacher
> (student), or if they were glad it was a game. Most indicate they like their
> real role.
>
> It was really helpful to use this technique in disciplinary action. If
> a child is really making a lot of disturbance or is hurting another child
> I use role reversal with the child and myself or let the two children do
> it. Of course this involves a short explanation of the theory and method,
> but I try to let them confront each other as soon as possible in role-
> playing after the fight.
>
> I have often thought that when I am having a particular crabby day
> it would be good for me to let one of the children reverse roles with me,
> but my courage has not permitted this as yet. If by using these techniques
> I am able to encourage the humanness in my children then the rewards
> are self evident.

The potential of the use of psychodrama in schools among those children
who are having learning and social problems is illustrated by a group psychodrama experiment conducted in a New York school with a class of eighteen
so-called maladjusted delinquent boys. Of the eighteen boys, ten were con-

firmed truants, and most had been involved in petty theft or vandalism. All of the boys were aggressive, and many were prone to acting-out violence. All of the boys were performing well below standards in school, were discouraged easily in school, and then either cut school, lost their tempers, fought, or stole. All of the boys in the study tended to be disruptive and undisciplined in school. Whenever they ran up against a situation they could not handle, they became antagonistic and quarrelsome, sulked, walked around the room, and generally interfered with other children who were working.

In applying psychodrama to their learning situations, it was not merely a matter of getting a selfish boy to play a generous role or a cowardly child a heroic role, although this appeared to have value, but rather to present the children with situations in their daily lives which trouble them and to which they responded inadequately. It was recognized that positive change in these boys could not be achieved in just one session. As a consequence of many psychodrama sessions, there were improved social responses in the various situations these boys confronted daily in their home, family, and school life. In five weeks some remarkable changes were noted in the behavior of most of the boys. By the end of the school term they showed better attitudes, developed improved relationships with classmates, had greater self-discipline, and class attendance and work all showed a marked improvement.

Using psychodrama with problem children in school is much more effective if the children's parents can be involved. In this regard, as part of a delinquency prevention program one of the authors ran in New York, he introduced this approach with positive results.

The project took place at P.S. 93 in Manhattan—a school located in an urban area beset by the many complex and extreme problems of contemporary society. We first selected the parents we would work with on the basis of having teachers select the top twenty most difficult problems children in the entire school. The determination of who these students were was simply handled by having the principal and a panel of ten teachers list their "top twenty troublemakers." There was a remarkable consensus—interestingly—in identifying these students, and most of these students had been to juvenile court. The principal then invited the parents to "become part of a group exploring children's problems in school."

The group met one night a week for a six-month period. Most of the parents (fathers and mothers) attended regularly. We moved into role-playing situations about disciplining children, good and bad teachers, and a range of personal-family problems. A report was written at the end of the program that summarized the following "therapeutic effects":

    1. Parents felt free to "blast" the school within the group. Some catharsis was observed as well as some understanding about the fact that they were in many cases projecting onto the school their own limitations as parents.

2. Parents seemed to benefit from the knowledge that other parents had problems similar to theirs.

3. Parents found they could help each other to understand and resolve conflict situations by acting out and discussing their experiences in the group. They agreed that more dimensions of a problem were brought to light in the role-playing than in their discussions. Moreover, the discussion parts of the session were more dynamic after role-playing.

4. Many recommendations and suggestions about methods and techniques for positively dealing with their children emerged in the group as a result of the role-playing, and the group gave its support to these parents who wanted to try them out.

5. The group established parent behavior norms. Permissive and punitive disciplinary approaches were acted out with the extremes tending to give way to more moderate approaches.

The authors have often used psychodrama in their college classrooms. It is a valuable tool for having students understand delinquency on a more personal and profound level. For example, after exploring a concept, such as "the violent sociopath," in a delinquency course, we would have a student come forward and play the role. The class would ask the "student sociopath" a variety of interesting and self-revealing questions. In exploring crime causation we often get a student who is courageous enough to admit to a delinquent act from his past as a protagonist. In one session, at the height of "an act of burglary as a teenager," we had a student protagonist freeze in the moment of the role and soliloquize his motivations. We then had other volunteer students double with his soliloquy. It is interesting to note that almost a third of the students in classes where this type of psychodrama was presented come forward one-by-one and soliloquize a parallel act—and their motivations. The process seems to make the subject more interesting, but more important, it provides an opportunity for a student to personally and emotionally identify with the subject.

As professors of sociology over the past twenty-five years, we have both taught courses on the subject of psychodrama, crime, and delinquency almost every semester. The course always involves actual sessions with students. The discussion of sociological concepts is invariably enriched by a psychodrama session. For example, it seems arid to present a lecture on role theory without actually involving students in some scene in their life that related to communication, empathy, or the socialization process. When all of these concepts are taught, various psychodramatic techniques seem to be intrinsic vehicles to help the student to understand basic concepts. In exploring role theory, for example, the Charles Horton Cooley concept of the "looking-glass self" or the G. H. Mead theory of empathy or "taking" the role of the other is actualized and explicated when a student psychodramatically reverses roles, doubles, or becomes an auxiliary ego. The method is especially helpful to students who plan to become teachers, work in the field of delinquency prevention, or in a juvenile institutional setting.

In brief, the use of a range of psychodramatic concepts and group methods in education at all levels helps to resolve regular and complex educational problems, can serve as an aid to transmitting standard educational material, and can enliven the day-to-day procedures of the classroom so that it becomes a more attractive and enjoyable human situation. These goals are basic directions required for counterattacking the forces that produce delinquency in the educational system.[63]

[63]For a fuller discussion of the psychodrama theory and method as applied to delinquency control in education, see Martin Haskell, *Socioanalysis* (Long Beach, California: Role Training Associates, 1976) and Lewis Yablonsky, *Psychodrama* (New York: Basic Books, 1976).

Chapter
6

Juvenile
Gang
Patterns

A PHENOMENON THAT has received considerable attention and study by social scientists is the youth gang. Since the turn of the century, gangs of various kinds have been part of the American social scene. In some respects city youth gangs may be viewed as an overt barometer of deeper social forces in society. The "gang problem" in urban ghettos has been cyclical. Violent gangs were very prevalent in the post–World War II era, became less visible in the sixties, and then resurfaced with a vengeance in the seventies.

Based on a study funded by the Federal Law Enforcement Assistance Administration, Dr. Walter Miller of the Harvard Law School's Center for a Criminal Justice reported:

> Youth gang violence is more lethal today than ever before. Violence and other illegal activities by members of youth gangs and groups in the United States of the 1970's represents a crime problem of the first magnitude which shows little prospect of early abatement. The schools are a major arena for gang activity in all six gang-problem cities. Problems currently appeared to be most widespread and/or serious in Los Angeles, Philadelphia and Chicago. The shooting and killing of teachers by gang

members was reported for Chicago and Philadelphia, and of nongang students in Chicago and Los Angeles.[1]

Miller has concluded that the composition of youth gangs has not changed significantly in the seventies. Gang members tend to be males between the ages of twelve and twenty-one, living predominantly in low-income ghettos. If anything, according to Miller, the weaponry of gangs has escalated:

> The prevalence, use, quality and sophistication of weaponry in the gangs of the 1970's far surpasses anything known in the past. Murder by firearms or other weapons, the central and most dangerous form of gang-member violence, in all probability stands today at the highest level it has reached in the history of the nation.[2]

Apart from weaponry and increased violence, there is evidence that in recent years the age level of gang members has gone down to encompass younger and younger children in urban ghettos. Desmond S. Cartwright, Barbara Tomson, and Hershey Schwartz report:

> Some cities saw substantial decreases in gang fighting during the 1960s, with as much as 40 percent fewer conflict incidents reported. This decrease may have been due only to a change to less visible activities, but, in any case, there has been a resurgence in gang activity in the 1970s. Youth-gang violence has flared up in Chicago, New York, Los Angeles, and Philadelphia; 700 gangs are said to "retain their identity" in Chicago alone. In Philadelphia, 160 killings in four years have been attributed to street gangs. Recent reports from Los Angeles, Boston, San Francisco, and rural Montana indicate that many violent gangs of 8-to-12-year-olds are creating "mousepack mayhem."[3]

Another pattern of gang activity is a growing shift from pedestrian violent activity to a mechanized form of assault and murder from a passing automobile. This is illustrated by a growing number of homicides that take the following prototypical form where an individual, often a nongang member is shot from a passing car.

> A 16-year old gang member released back into the community after serving a 90-day evaluation sentence for the killing of a high school student, was shot to death himself Friday night in South-Central Los Angeles, police reported.

---

[1]Walter Miller, *Los Angeles Times,* May 14, 1976.

[2]Miller, *Los Angeles Times,* May 14, 1976.

[3]Desmond S. Cartwright, Barbara Tomson and Hershey Schwartz, *Gang Delinquency* (Monterey, Calif.: Brooks/Cole, 1975), p. vii.

Howard Morrison, identified as a member of the 109th St. Crips gang, was shot in the head as he and two others stood on the balcony of an apartment building at 113 E. 109th St. where they were attending a party.

Shots fired from a passing car also wounded Adrian Rogers, 20, in the left arm and grazed the chin of Trevin Fuller, 14.[4]

Another general pattern of increasing concern related to violent gangs is the manner in which the mayhem has moved out of the ghetto and into the larger community. The old saw "we only kill each other," first stated by Benjamin (Bugsy) Siegal, a chief of one of the earliest and deadliest gangs, New York's Murder, Inc., is no longer as true today as it was in the past. Gang violence increasingly has been transplanted to the suburbs and downtown areas of our major cities. A prototypical example of this phenomenon is the rash of gang violence in downtown areas that has plagued many large cities, in particular Detroit.

Police Chief Philip G. Tannian has been given an ultimatum—he calls it a "challenge"—to bring Detroit's youth gang violence under control or be replaced. Sunday's violence began at a concert at Cobo Hall in downtown Detroit by two rock groups—the Average White Band and Kool and the Gang. It later spilled over into the area around the hall. Just as the concert was getting started, said Thomas Moss, a deputy police chief, a group of about 80 youths, belonging to two of the city's black gangs, stormed the stage and threw chairs about. Some in the audience were robbed and beaten, Moss said, as gang members blocked exits to prevent patrons from leaving.[5]

One constant in gang structure is that there has always been a variety of juvenile gangs available to youths growing up in urban areas. Some comprise youths in a close, friendly association, as in athletic clubs. At the other extreme are delinquent and violent gangs. Gangs of this type are extremely negative socializing agents that train youths into delinquent and violent patterns of behavior.

This negative pattern is illustrated by a homicidal assault by the Egyptian Kings, a particularly extremist violent gang, on two boys in a New York City park. Here is a description[6] of the assault given by some of the gang members and by one of the victims, Roger McShane, who, although badly

---

[4]*Los Angeles Times,* January 19, 1975.

[5]*Los Angeles Times,* August 19, 1976.

[6]Derived in part from Lewis Yablonsky, *The Violent Gang,* rev. ed. (Baltimore: Penguin Books, 1970).

stabbed, survived the attack. The other boy, Michael Farmer, who was a polio victim, was killed.

McSHANE: It was ten-thirty when we entered the park. We saw couples on the benches, in the back of the pool, and they all stared at us, and I guess they must'ave saw the gang there—I don't think they were fifty or sixty feet away. When we reached the front of the stairs, we looked up and there was two of their gang members on top of the stairs. They were two smaller ones, and they had garrison belts wrapped around their hands. They didn't say nothin' to us, they looked kind of scared.

FIRST EGYPTIAN KING: I was scared. I knew they were gonna jump 'em an everythin', and I was scared. When they were comin' up, they all were separatin' and everythin' like that.

McSHANE: I saw the main body of the gang slowly walk out of the bushes, on my right. I turned around fast, to see what Michael was going to do, and this kid came runnin' at me with the belts. Then I ran, myself, and told Michael to run.

SECOND EGYPTIAN KING: He couldn't run anyway, 'cause we were all around him. So then I said, "You're a Jester," and he said, "Yeah," and I punched him in the face. And then somebody hit him with a bat over the head. And then I kept punchin' him. Some of them were too scared to do anything. They were just standin' there, lookin'.

THIRD EGYPTIAN KING: I was watchin' him. I didn't wanna hit him, at first. Then I kicked him twice. He was laying' on the ground, lookin' up at us. I kicked him on the jaw, or someplace; then I kicked him in the stomach. That was the least I could do, was kick 'im.

FOURTH EGYPTIAN KING: I was aimin' to hit him, but didn't get a chance to hit him. There were so many guys on him—I got scared when I saw the knife go into the guy, and I ran right there. After everybody ran, this guy stayed, and started hittin' him with a machete.

FIRST EGYPTIAN KING: Somebody yelled out, "Grab him. He's a Jester." So then they grabbed him. Magician grabbed him, he turned around and stabbed him in the back. I was . . . I was stunned. I couldn't do nothin'. And then Magician—he went like that and he pulled . . . he had a switchblade and he said, "You're gonna hit him with that bat or I'll stab you," So I just hit him lightly with the bat.

SECOND EGYPTIAN KING: Magician stabbed him and the guy, he . . . like hunched over. He's standin' up and I knock him down. Then he was down on the ground, everybody was kickin' him, stompin' him, punchin' him, stabbin' him, so he tried to get back up and I knock him down again. Then the guy stabbed him in the back with a bread knife.

THIRD EGYPTIAN KING: I just went like that, and I stabbed him with the bread knife. You know, I was drunk, so I just stabbed him. (*Laughs*) He was screamin' like a dog. He was screamin' there. And then I took the knife out and I told the other guys to run. So I ran and then the rest of the guys ran with me. They wanted to stay there and keep on doin' it.

FOURTH EGYPTIAN KING: The guy that stabbed him in the back with the bread knife, he told me that when he took the knife out o' his back, he said, "Thank you."

McSHANE: They got up fast right after they stabbed me. And I just lay there on my stomach and there was five of them as they walked away. And as they walked away . . . this other big kid came down with a machete or some large knife of some sort, and he wanted to stab me too with it. And they told him, "No, come on. We got him. We messed him up already. Come on." And they took off up the hill and they all walked up the hill and right after that they all of 'em turned their heads and looked back at me. I got up and staggered into the street to get a cab. And I got in a taxi and asked him to take me to the Medical Center and get my friend and I blacked out.

The coroner's report reveals the intensity of the violence:

> I found a fifteen-year-old white boy, five feet and a half inches in length, scale weight 138 pounds, the face showing an ecchymosis . . . [a]hemorrhage beneath the skin. . . . You would compare it to a black-and-blue mark.
>
> There was an ecchymosis of the outer aspect of the right eye, with a superimposed superficial abrasion. . . . There was an incised wound . . . one made with a very sharp implement . . . situated over the bridge of the nose and [extending] . . . over the right eyebrow.

He had found wounds and abrasions on the knuckles and hands, the doctor said, which seemed to indicate that Michael Farmer had raised his hands to protect himself against the blows being rained upon him. The doctor had also found an incised wound beneath the left armpit, but that one had not penetrated deeper than the epidermis. A wound on the right thigh had been deeper: "It measured one and a half inches in length with a gap that was slightly less than three-quarters of an inch . . . a gaping wound with sharp edges. . . ."

On the left side was another penetrating stab wound, lower and more deadly. This one "went through the entire back into the pleural cavity" and "severed a vein and a nerve." This wound, four inches deep, had caused Farmer's death.

A Brief History of Gangs in America

The violent gang such as the Egyptian Kings is a comparatively recent phenomenon. Earlier gangs used violence, but they were more cohesive than are contemporary gangs, and there was more camaraderie among their members.

Significant sociological appraisals of gangs first appear in the early writings (1920 to 1940) of sociologists associated with what was termed the *Chicago school.* This group, which included such pioneers as Frederic M. Thrasher, Frank Tannenbaum, Clifford R. Shaw, Henry D. McKay, and William F. Whyte, relied heavily on firsthand research data collected directly from the boys in the gangs. In general, their assessments of the problem of gang causation were tied to theories of the slum community and the disorganized "interstitial" area. Ganging and delinquent activity were considered essentially a result of what Edwin H. Sutherland later termed *differential association.*

The Chicago School and Gangs

During the late twenties and the depression era of the thirties, a group of sociologists at the University of Chicago focused upon various social problems that they attributed to urban social disorganization. Thrasher, Shaw, and McKay, in particular, instituted several delinquency research projects that produced data that remain the backbone of many current conceptions of delinquency and gangs. Their research and writing were heavily based upon case-history material and personal documents obtained from offenders both in institutions and in the open community.

Thrasher's Gangs.   Frederic M. Thrasher may be credited with the first extensive sociological study of gangs. His findings were presented in a classic volume appropriately called *The Gang.* On the basis of his study of 1,313 cases, he defined the gang as "an interstitial group originally formed spontaneously and then integrated through conflict," and characterized by "meeting face to face, milling, movement through space as a unit, conflict, and planning." The result of this behavior is the development of a "tradition, unreflective internal structure, *esprit de corps,* solidarity, morale, group awareness, and attachment to a local territory."[7] Thrasher's definition has been the basis for most current conceptions of the gang.[8]

The Chicago Area Project.   The Chicago Area Project, instituted in the early thirties and currently operating out of the Juvenile Division of the Illinois

---

[7]Frederic M. Thrasher, *The Gang* (Chicago: University of Chicago Press, 1926). © 1926, 1954 by The University of Chicago. Reprinted by permission.

[8]Currently some of the most widely used college textbooks on criminology base their discussions of gangs on Thrasher's appraisal.

Department of Corrections, has contributed some of the most significant theories, research, and correction programs that have evolved in the field of American criminology. Early in its career the project was described by its originators as a program that sought to discover by demonstration and measurement a procedure for the treatment of delinquents and the prevention of delinquency in those Chicago neighborhoods that sent disproportionately large numbers of boys to the Cook County Juvenile Court. Residents of the neighborhoods were encouraged to aid in planning and operating the program. An effort was made to effect changes in the social environment of the neighborhoods by providing residents with facilities and professional guidance for the development of their own programs of child welfare.[9]

Clifford Shaw and Henry McKay were the prime movers of the Chicago Project. Their work over several decades, with the aid of many able assistants, revealed a conception of delinquency that remains currently of major significance. Their basic working assumptions were that delinquency was normal in the slum ("interstitial") neighborhood, that most offenses (about 95 percent) were committed in association with others in gangs, and that most boys were trained into criminal careers by other offenders in the neighborhood; in short, that the average offender evolved in the normal course of events as a product of his social training.

In the early stages of the delinquent's development, according to Shaw and McKay, robbery was a playful act in a kind of game:

> When we were shoplifting we always made a game of it. For example, we might gamble on who could steal the most caps in a day, or who could steal caps from the largest number of stores in a day, or who could steal in the presence of a detective and then get away. We were always daring each other that way and thinking up new schemes. This was the best part of the game. I would go into a store to steal a cap, by trying one on and when the clerk was not watching walk out of the store leaving the old cap. With the new cap on my head I would go into another store, do the same thing as in other store, getting a new hat and leaving the one I had taken from the other place. I might do this all day and have one hat at night. It was the fun I wanted, not the hat. I kept this up for months and then began to sell the things to a man on the west side. It was at this time that I began to steal for gain. . . .[10]

---

[9]Ernest W. Burgess, Joseph D. Lohman, and Clifford R. Shaw, "The Chicago Area Project," in *N.P.P.A. Yearbook* (Washington, D.C.: National Probation and Parole Association, 1937), pp. 8–28. See also Anthony C. Sorrentino, "Chicago Area Project After 25 Years," *Federal Probation* 23 (June 1959):40–43.

[10]Clifford R. Shaw and Henry D. McKay, "Social Factors in Juvenile Delinquency," in *Report on the Causes of Crime,* National Commission on Law Observance and Enforcement report no. 13 (Washington, D.C.: U.S. Government Printing Office, 1931).

After the initial gang play activity, stealing would become a more serious business. In the late thirties Tannenbaum described the gang boy's graduation to more serious crimes. The youth went from shoplifting to rolling bums. Then came pickpocketing, car stealing, holdups, and sometimes murder. All of these activities were carried out in company with other members of the gang. It was a collective enterprise that had the approval of the group. The play group became the criminal gang by slow differentiation and habituation.[11]

Delinquent-trained youths tend to become further pulled into the gang as they begin to conflict with some elements of the community. The gang seems to develop almost according to the Toynbee scheme of "challenge and response." Its increased cohesion is a function of the response it meets in the community. According to Thrasher, it does not become a gang until it begins to "excite disapproval and opposition." The opposition could come from another gang or from any adult representatives of the community; the cops begin to "shag" it (chase it), or some representative of the community steps in and tries to break it up. This is the real beginning of the gang, for now it begins to draw itself more closely together as it becomes a conflict group.[12]

Tannenbaum broadens Thrasher's conception of delinquent gang formation to include the youth's conflict with additional elements of the "out-group" law-abiding community. These forces, he contends, help to sharpen the gang youth's delinquent self-conception. In his conflict with the community there develop two opposing definitions of the situation. For the young delinquent it may be a form of play, adventure, excitement, interest, mischief, fun. "Breaking windows, annoying people, running around porches, climbing over roofs, stealing from pushcarts, playing truant—all are items of play, adventure, excitement."[13] To the community, however, these activities take on a form of "nuisance, evil, delinquency, with the demand for control, admonition, chastisement, punishment, police court, truant school."[14] The conflict arises out of a divergence of values. As the problem develops, the situation gradually becomes redefined and the community attitude demands suppression. Under these conditions of conflict, the gang becomes more developed and cohesive. The delinquent gang wins out against more socially acceptable forces not because of its inherent attraction but because the positive sociocultural forces that might train a youth into socially acceptable behavior patterns are weak.

The Chicago school gave heavy weight to family disorganization in the production of the delinquent. It saw the disorganized family as a family whose potential positive social force did not fulfill its function.

---

[11]Frank Tannenbaum, *Crime and the Community* (New York: Columbia University Press, 1939).

[12]Thrasher, *The Gang*, p. 30.

[13]Tannenbaum, *Crime and the Community*, pp. 9–10.

[14]Tannenbaum, *Crime and the Community*, pp. 9–10.

"Street Corner Society."   The Chicago school spurred other studies of street gangs. A major participant-observation study by William Whyte[15] tended to confirm many of the speculations of the earlier Chicago studies. Whyte moved into the Italian neighborhood of a large Eastern city near Boston, which he called "Cornerville." He learned Italian and hung out with the "Norton Street Gang," the focus of his study. For three years he participated in the activities of the gang, developed friendly relations with the leaders, and, with their cooperation, studied the group's structure.

A central fact about the Norton Street Gang was that it was a product of the Depression. Most of the members were in their twenties and normally would have been working if jobs had been available. The gang, according to Whyte, emerged because the boys could accomplish more together than separately. The gang gave its members a feeling of solidarity or belonging. They participated in constructive activities, engaged in athletics, helped each other financially (when they could), and discussed mutual problems. The Norton Street Gang was a cooperative group, beneficial to its members.

This pattern of essentially constructive interaction is in considerable contrast to the mutual hostility, aggression, and violence found among contemporary violent gangs. In addition to a high degree of cooperative action and esprit de corps, Whyte found permanence and cohesion in the corner gangs he studied:

> The corner-gang structure arises out of the habitual association of the members over a long period of time. The nuclei of most gangs can be traced back to early boyhood, when living close together provided the first opportunities for social contacts.... The gangs grew up on the corner and remained there with remarkable persistence from early boyhood until the members reached their late twenties or early thirties.
>
> The stable composition of the group and the lack of social assurance on the part of its members contribute toward producing a very high rate of social interaction within the group. The group structure is a product of these interactions.
>
> Out of such interaction, there arises a system of mutual obligations which is fundamental to group cohesion.[16]

Whyte's comments on gang leadership further support an image of the Norton Street Gang as a constructive organization:

---

[15]William F. Whyte, *Street Corner Society* (Chicago: University of Chicago Press, 1955). Whyte's analysis of criminal influence and politics was also a major contribution of this book; however, this theme is not discussed here in any detail, since the focus is on youth gangs.

[16]Whyte, *Street Corner Society*, p. 255.

The leader is the man who acts when the situation requires action. He is more resourceful than his followers. Past events have shown that his ideas were right. In this sense "right" simply means satisfactory to the members. He is the most independent in judgment. While his followers are undecided as to a course of action or upon the character of a newcomer, the leader makes up his mind.

When he gives his word to one of the boys, he keeps it. The followers look to him for advice and encouragement, and he receives more of their confidence than any other man.

The leader is respected for his fair-mindedness. . . .[17]

Not only did Whyte's studies support the earlier images of the Chicago school; they also fostered conceptions of the gangs dealt with in the postwar era of the forties and fifties.

Youth Board "Bopping Gangs"

About 1946 New York City was struck by the emergence of violent youth gangs that committed a number of seemingly senseless and vicious homicides. Workers were sent into the streets to deal with them in a special project that became known as the "detached-worker program." The mayor later developed a permanent social agency called the New York City Youth Board to carry out work along these lines with the gangs. In a series of manuals and books based on its work, the Youth Board developed a concept of the gang that has become an accepted diagnostic image for many similar programs in urban areas throughout the country:

The gangs with which we worked were surprisingly well organized, on both a formal and informal level. Each club was divided into several divisions, usually on the basis of age. These divisions were called the Tiny Tims, Kids, Cubs, Midgets, Juniors, and Seniors. Nine- to 13-year-old boys usually belonged to the Tiny Tims, while young men over 20 were members of the Seniors division. These divisions regarded themselves as autonomous groups; at the same time they had a strong feeling of kinship with each other. As the boys grew older they "graduated" from one division to another—a feeding process which insured the continued life of each club. The divisions were in a hierarchical relationship to each other, the older groups having more power, status, and influence than the younger groups. . . .

Each division had its own officers including a president, vice-president, war counsellor, and "light-up" man. The gang president played a central role in coordinating the group's activities, in exerting discipline,

---

[17]Whyte, *Street Corner Society,* p. 256.

and in determining club goals. In addition, he frequently represented his group in its dealings with other clubs. The war counsellor contacted enemy gangs with whom fights were to take place; he arranged the time and place for these "rumbles" and the weapons to be used. He also planned strategy and tactics.[18]

The Youth Board seemed to accept fully the stories of gang organization and leadership operation presented to them by gang members. An appraisal of Youth Board publications reveals their conceptual view. According to the Youth Board, the gangs with which they worked generally possessed the following characteristics: (1) their behavior was "normal" for youths; (2) the gangs had a high degree of cohesion, esprit de corps, and organization; (3) gang size or membership was measurable; (4) the gang's role patterns were clearly defined; (5) gangs possessed a consistent set of norms and expectations clearly understood by all members; (6) they had a group of clearly defined leaders who were respected by gang members, distinctly specified, and vested with a direct flow of authority; and (7) they had a coherent organization for gang warfare. The Youth Board's image of the modern "bopping gang" was apparently greatly influenced by the earlier work of Thrasher, Shaw, McKay, and Whyte.

Gang Theory and Research in the Fifties and Sixties

More recent research has added additional perspectives to our understanding of the structure and process of gangs. Two studies, one by Albert Cohen and the other by Richard Cloward and Lloyd Ohlin, are seminal works not only with regard to gang theory but also with regard to a more general theory of juvenile delinquency. These studies will be discussed briefly here in terms of their perspective on gangs and then more fully in chapters 11 and 12, which deal with the causes of crime and delinquency.

Value Conflicts

Cohen, in his book *Delinquent Boys,* emphasizes that gang youths have a different value system than do youths in the general population.[19] However, gang members are negatively judged by middle class values in schools and in other settings. This, Cohen asserts, leads to a "status frustration" that is acted out in a "nonutilitarian, negativistic" fashion through the vehicle of the gang. In Cohen's context, the gang is a subculture for striking back at an unjust social system.

---

[18] *Working with Teenage Gangs: A Report on the Central Harlem Street Clubs Project* (New York: Welfare Council of New York City, 1950).

[19] Albert K. Cohen, *Delinquent Boys: The Culture of the Gang* (New York: Macmillan, 1955).

Carl Werthman and Irving Piliavin noted this subcultural conflict, in this case between gang members and the police, as representatives of middle class American society:

From the front seat of a moving patrol car, street life in a typical Negro ghetto is perceived as an uninterrupted sequence of suspicious scenes. Every well-dressed man or woman standing aimlessly on the street during hours when most people are at work is carefully scrutinized for signs of an illegal source of income; every boy wearing boots, black pants, long hair, and a club jacket is viewed as potentially responsible for some item on the list of muggings, broken windows, and petty thefts that still remain to be cleared; and every hostile glance directed at the passing patrolman is read as a sign of possible guilt.

The residents of these neighborhoods regard this kind of surveillance as the deepest of insults. As soon as a patrolman begins to interrogate, the suspect can easily see that his moral identity is being challenged because of his dress, his hair style, his skin color, and his presence in the ghetto itself.

Negro gang members are constantly singled out for interrogation by the police, and the boys develop their own techniques of retaliation. They taunt the police with jibes and threaten their authority with gestures of insolence, as if daring the police to become bigots and bullies in order to defend their honor. Moreover, these techniques of retaliation often do succeed in provoking this response. When suspect after suspect becomes hostile and surly, the police begin to see themselves as representing the law among a people that lack proper respect for it. They, too, begin to feel maligned, and they soon become defensively cynical and aggressively moralistic. From the point of view of a patrolman, night sticks are only used upon sufficient provocation, and arrests are only made with just cause.[20]

Gang Subcultures and Urbanism

Irving Spergel explores three different styles of delinquency in three different lower class areas of a large Eastern city.[21] He recorded his data as a field worker in New York City. Spergel's study is based on firsthand field study interviews and is liberally sprinkled with the verbatim responses of gang youths.

Spergel's fundamental assumption is that delinquent subcultures are

[20]Carl Werthman and Irving Piliavin, "Gang Members and the Police," in *The Police,* ed. David J. Bordua (New York: Wiley, 1967), p. 46.

[21]Irving Spergel, *Racketville, Slumtown, Haulburg: An Exploratory Study of Delinquent Subcultures* (Chicago: University of Chicago Press, 1964).

created and thrive under the impetus of socially unacceptable opportunities available to youths for achieving acceptable, culturally induced success goals. he found three major types of such delinquent youth subcultures: one characterized by racket activities, another by violence and conflict, and a third by theft. These patterns depend on the interaction of conventional and criminal opportunities. Drug addiction in these neighborhoods, Spergel states, develops "mainly as a variant and transitional pattern for older adolescents and young adults, many of whom have been participants in the major delinquent-youth subcultures."[22]

It is readily apparent that Spergel's working hypotheses are derived from the Cloward and Ohlin schema in *Delinquency and Opportunity.*[23] One departure from the Cloward and Ohlin system is to further subdivide their category of criminal subculture into two different subcultures: racket and theft. The study also deviates in another major respect from the Cloward-Ohlin formulation. Spergel states the following about Cloward and Ohlin's retreatist subculture of addiction:

> The patterns of retreatists, or drug-users, have not been regarded as sufficiently distinct to comprise a special delinquent subculture. The delinquent behavior, norms, and values of drug-users and drug addicts were found to be more like than unlike the respective modes of the delinquents in each of the three types of lower class neighborhoods. Therefore, the drug-use delinquent pattern is viewed as a variant or subcategory of each of the three forms of delinquent subcultures. It was observed to be primarily a late-teenage and young-adult phenomenon.[24]

Despite this departure, Spergel closely adheres to the Cloward and Ohlin notion that "when legitimate or conventional means of achieving common success-goals are not available, delinquency or crime may become an alternate way of reaching them." Spergel further points out that even criminal careers may not be equally available to youths in different lower class neighborhoods. Possession of special skills, a minimal store of criminal knowledge, appropriate attitudes, and access to a complex criminal organization or to "connections" may be essential for the achievement of success by criminal means.

A later analysis by Barbara Tomson and Edna R. Fielder tends to support Spergel's general assumption that gang membership is often a response to the urban scene.[25] Their research dealt with the gang member's response

---

[22]Spergel, *Racketville, Slumtown, Haulburg,* p. xv.

[23]Richard A. Cloward and Lloyd E. Ohlin, *Delinquency and Opportunity: A Theory of Delinquent Gangs* (New York: Free Press, 1960).

[24]Spergel, *Racketville, Slumtown, Haulburg,* pp. xii–xiii.

[25]Barbara Tomson and Edna R. Fielder, "Gangs: A Response to the Urban World," in *Gang Delinquency,* ed. Barbara Tomson and Edna Fielder (Monterey, Calif.: Brooks/Cole, 1975), p. 83.

to the urban structure, the political structure, and the mass media—institutions in which they are unlikely to have formalized individual contacts. In this context, gangs provide a positive identity for their individual members.

1. The urban setting in which gangs thrive produces varied pressures: the need to deal successfully with strangers, the need to deal with a money-based economy, loneliness, and lack of privacy. The delinquent responds to these pressures by identifying with the gang, which offers him symbols of identity, activities, and helps him obtain money, companionship, and friends.

2. The purpose of the political machinery is to provide services and resolve conflicts for members of the society. Delinquents assess the political situation correctly by concluding that they do not belong to society and are not wanted. They can, however, identify with and be understood by a gang.

3. Mass media teaches slum-dwelling youngsters by default. Possessions are emphasized in the mass media, and filmed aggression has a longer-lasting influence on delinquents than on other members of society. The delinquent's response is to agree with the mass media's use of aggression; gang members successfully use aggression to get what they want.

Aleatory Nature of Gangs

In Chicago during the late fifties and early sixties, James F. Short, Jr., carried out extensive research into gangs. Among the conclusions of his varied studies was that aleatory (or chance) elements play a considerable part in gang behavior. Gang activities, whether for fun or profit, usually involve a degree of risk. Most of the time these activities are engaged in without serious consequences, but sometimes something happens and the outcome is calamitous. Writing with Fred L. Strodtbeck, Short discusses the implication of these aleatory risks, particularly in relation to the gang's seemingly hedonistic impulses:

> . . . our use of the term *aleatory* did not restrict it to events which are independent of the actions of the persons involved. It was incidentally true that the events in question were not, for this stratum, punished by society. However, we now wish to be beyond this feature and direct the argument to instances of serious aggression in which the outcome is not desired either by the boys or the community, and for which serious consequence, like imprisonment, may result from the response by the larger society. We do not say that all cases of serious aggression result from action with such an aleatory element, but that, etiologically, those which do should be distinguished from cases in which serious injury is the clear intent of the actor.

Specifically, it is our hypothesis that much of what has previously been described as short-run hedonism, may, under closer scrutiny, be revealed to be a rational balancing, from the actor's perspective, of the near certainty of *immediate* loss of status in the group against the remote possibility of punishment by the larger society *if* the most serious outcome eventuates. Viewed in this way, one does not hold that punishable behavior occurs because the youngsters are blind to the possibility of unfortunate consequences.[26]

In a later study based on Short's Chicago research, Short, Rivera, and Tennyson[27] attempted to apply certain aspects of Cloward and Ohlin's opportunity-structure paradigm in a study of delinquent gangs in Chicago. Negro and white lower class gang boys were compared with lower class nongang boys from the same neighborhood, and with middle class boys of the same race. They found that the ranking of the six race-by-class-by-gang-status groups on official delinquency rates corresponded more closely to ranking on perceptions of legitimate opportunities than to ranking on perceptions of illegitimate opportunities, which is consistent with the assumption that illegitimate opportunities intervene after legitimate opportunities have been appraised and found wanting. Gang members, lower class boys, and Negro youth perceived legitimate opportunities to be less available than did nongang boys, middle class boys, and white youth. Differences in perceptions of illegitimate opportunities were in the reverse direction, as expected.

Another series of significant studies was carried out by Malcolm Klein and associates over a five-year period (1962–67) of field research with Negro and Mexican-American gangs in Los Angeles.[28] The report was primarily an exposition of observations and speculations for the purpose of updating delinquency studies. A detached worker was assigned to all the gangs under observation.

Based on the findings, Klein concluded that leadership is not a position, as many have theorized, but is rather a collection of functions. Leadership varies with the activity, such as fighting, athletics, girls, etc. Most leaders are not sociopaths. The leaders are often difficult to pick out except by the reactions of other members. Age is an influence in leadership. Structure and function are part of the same phenomenon. Leadership is often "hesitant." Many leaders are ambivalent and will back away from leadership in a crucial situation.

---

[26]Fred L. Strodtbeck and James F. Short, Jr., "Aleatory Risks Versus Short-Run Hedonism in Explanation of Gang Behavior," *Social Problems* 12 (Fall 1964):128–29. Reprinted with permission of the authors and the Society for the Study of Social Problems.

[27]James F. Short, Jr., Ramon Rivera, and Ray A. Tennyson, "Perceived Opportunities, Gang Membership, and Delinquency," *American Sociological Review* 30 (February 1965):56–67.

[28]Malcolm W. Klein, "Impressions of Juvenile Gang Members," *Adolescence* 3 (Spring 1968): 53–76.

Also, according to Klein's findings, gang boys portray a caricature of adolescence. They behave and react in excess, and they definitely overplay roles. Gang boys have little confidence in themselves and are insecure with respect to their own abilities and social relationships. These feelings of inadequacy often result in a dependence on the peer group and, consequently, on arrest-provoking behavior. Adolescents float together as they reject and are rejected by their community. Thus the gang is a cluster of youths held together by their individual incapacities rather than common goals or interests. It serves a need satisfaction and leads to delinquency only secondarily.

Short, in a later study, attempted to reexamine his earlier study of gangs in Chicago in the sixties.[29] In his more recent research Short attempted to utilize as subjects the same gang members and detached social workers with whom he had worked in his research in the 1960s. He determined that the changes attributed to gang behavior in the past decade are more a product of the attitude of legitimate society toward gangs than the gangs themselves. Despite attempts on the part of detached social workers to involve youth in civil rights and other political issues, the gangs participated as more or less "innocent bystanders." They did not get involved in the political ideologies but merely responded to the pressures placed on them from outside. According to Short, the supergangs that emerged in the 1960s as a result of community support were not independent and were not capable of understanding or integrating into a political framework. Some of the surface political activities undertaken by these groups were simply reactions to police harassment and the actions of the GIU (Gang Intelligence Unit). Finally, attempts on the part of legitimate society to involve youth gangs in business and other endeavors, in some cases, actually caused an increase in criminal behavior due to the inability of these groups to appropriate funds and pursue legitimate activities. Short concluded that "what changed, more than the behavior of youngsters, most of whom still meet on corners to pass the time away, was the behavior of adults, particularly the agents and agencies of 'respectable society'."

Many former gang members who were recruited during the seventies for gang-prevention programs of the type Short alludes to, performed admirably and effectively. There were many cases, however, where an ex-gang member exploited the system or, in gang parlance, "blew his cool." One example of this was the case of a former Los Angeles gang member who, while serving in a city-sponsored project, shot a member of a "rival gang."[30]

A gang member serving as coordinator for a city-sponsored project to combat gang violence is facing assault charges for an alleged shotgun

---

[29]James F. Short, Jr., "Youth, Gangs and Society: Micro- and Macrosociological Processes," *Sociological Quarterly* 36 (Winter 1974):3–19.

[30]William Farr, "Official in Gang Project Facing Assault Charges," *Los Angeles Times,* January 4, 1977.

attack on rival gang members at the project's headquarters, the district attorney's office disclosed Monday.

Bennie R. Simpson, 22, the No. 2 man in a city-financed program called Project Longtable and a member of the so-called Crips gang, was charged with five counts of assault with a deadly weapon stemming from an Oct. 18 incident at the project's Broadway and 46th St. headquarters.

Five other young men affiliated with the Crips and Project Longtable were named as codefendants with Simpson in a 13-count criminal indictment filed last week by Dep. Dist. Atty. Richard Jenkins.

Jenkins said the Oct. 18 confrontation reportedly occurred when members of the Brims, another South-Central Los Angeles gang, came to the project's offices seeking funds to finance a funeral for Jimmy Celestin, a 19-year-old Brim gunned down two days earlier by assailants on bicycles.

As the Brims departed from the unsuccessful negotiations, they reportedly were attacked with shotguns and wooden clubs.

Four other felony charges were filed against Simpson for alleged efforts to shake down nongang youths for money and guns last July. Two counts of extortion, one count of attempted extortion and one count of kidnaping were charged against Simpson in connection with these alleged events.

In one of the alleged extortion incidents, Simpson and others reportedly abducted a youth in his own car, forced him to sign over the pink slip.

Toward a Definition of Gangs

Emile Durkheim exhorts the sociologist to "emancipate himself from the fallacious ideas that dominate the mind of the layman; he must throw off, once and for all, the yoke of these empirical categories which from long continued habit have become tyrannical."[31]

Not only is a freedom from preconception urged; Durkheim's second canon is the necessity of being explicit:

> Every scientific investigation is directed toward a limited class of phenomena, included in the same definition. The first step of the sociologist, then, ought to be to define the things he treats, in order that his subject matter may be known. This is the first and most indispensable condition of all proofs and verifications. A theory, indeed, can be

---

[31]Emile Durkheim, *The Rules of Sociological Method,* 8th ed. (Glencoe, Ill.: Free Press, 1950), p. 32.

checked only if we know how to recognize the facts of which it is intended to give an account.[32]

A Classification of Gangs

Three types of gangs appear most persistently in "gang neighborhoods": (1) social gangs, (2) delinquent gangs, and (3) violent gangs. Although these prototypes seldom appear in pure form, the structure and behavior of the ideal type may be described: the *social gang* is a social group comprised of tough youths who band together because they find their individual goals of a socially constructive nature can most adequately be achieved through a gang pattern; the *delinquent gang* is characterized by delinquent patterns of activity, such as stealing or assault, with material profit as the essential objective; the *violent gang* is characterized by sociopathic themes of spontaneous prestige-seeking violence, with psychic gratification (kicks) as the goal. There are, of course, youths who belong to more than one type of gang during their gang careers, and some youths belong to several simultaneously. (See Figure 6.1)

Social Gangs.   The social gang is a relatively permanent organization that centers around a specific location, such as a candy store or clubhouse. All members are intimately known to one another and there is a strong sense of comradeship. Members are the in-group; all others are outsiders. Members may wear club jackets or sweaters with insignia that identify them to the external community.

Activities are socially dominated and require a high degree of responsible social interaction in the group: organized athletics, personal discussions, dances, and other socially acceptable activities characteristic of youths. Membership is not based upon self-protection (as in the violent gang) or on athletic prowess (as on an athletic team) but upon feelings of mutual attraction. Cohesiveness is based on the feeling that through the group the individual can lead a fuller life. Members are willing to submerge individualistic interests to group activities. Leadership is based upon popularity and constructive leadership qualities and generally operates informally. The leader is apt to be the idealized group member.

This type of gang seldom participates in delinquent behavior, gang warfare, or petty thievery except under unusual circumstances. Members may become involved in minor gang clashes, but only under pressure. The social gang has considerable permanence. Its members often grow up together on the same block and develop permanent lifelong friendships that continue when they leave the "corner" and move into adult life patterns.

The social gang is closely associated with and acts in accordance with the values of the larger society. It draws its membership from the most emotionally stable and socially effective youths in the neighborhood—those most

---

[32]Durkheim, *The Rules of Sociological Method,* pp. 34–35.

Figure 6.1

Gang Patterns of Slum Youths

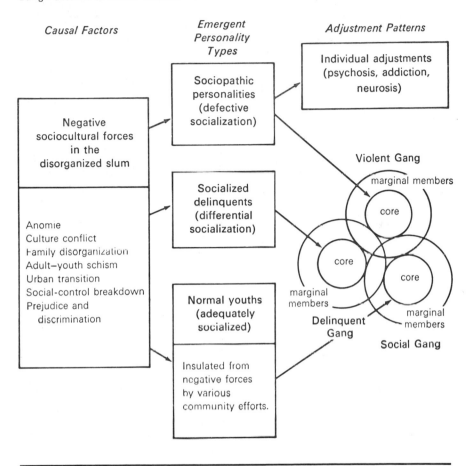

closely influenced by and involved with the norms and values of the more inclusive society. Thus, of all gang types, the social gang is the one least dissociated from the overall society.

Delinquent Gangs.   The delinquent gang is primarily organized to carry out various illegal acts. The social interaction of the members is a secondary factor. Prominent among the delinquent gang's activities are burglary, petty thievery, mugging, assault for profit—not simply kicks—and other illegal acts directed at "raising bread." It is generally a tight clique, a small mobile gang that can steal and escape with minimum risk. It would lose its cohesive quality and the intimate cooperation required for success in illegal ventures if it became too large. Membership is not easily achieved and must generally be approved by all gang members.

The delinquent gang has a tight primary-group structure. The members know each other and rely heavily upon each other for cooperation in their illegal enterprises. The group has some duration and lasting structure. This usually continues in action until interrupted by arrest or imprisonment. Members lost in this way are usually replaced. The leader is usually the most effective thief, the best organizer and planner of delinquent activities.

Often members of these cliques also participate in the activities of violent or social gangs, but such participation is only a sideline; their basic allegiance is to the delinquent gang, with its opportunities to act out their impulses for fun and profit.

With some exceptions, delinquent gang members are emotionally stable youths. Their delinquency is more likely to result from being socialized in delinquent behavior patterns than from emotional disturbance. The emotionally disturbed delinquent is more likely to steal or assault on his own in a bizarre way. He does not usually have the social ability required to belong to the organized delinquent gang.

In summary, the delinquent gang is comprised of a cohesive group of emotionally stable youths trained into illegal patterns of behavior. Violence may be employed as a means toward the end of acquiring material and financial rewards, but it is rarely an end in itself since the activities of the gang are profit oriented. The delinquent gang accepts the materialistic success goals of the society but rejects the normative ways of achievement.

Although the criminal gangs studied by the Chicago school are similar in structure to the current delinquent gangs, there are some differences. Chief among them is the lack of a criminal hierarchy in which the young offender may rise. The delinquent gang member is restricted to present-oriented delinquent "success." The only criminal future he may look forward to is the possibility of learning a good criminal trade (safecracker, policy number-writer). Generally, however, the delinquent gang member from a disorganized slum does not concern himself with the future. He accepts his later criminal life as it develops without any significant planning.

Violent Gangs.   In contrast with the other gang types, the violent gang is primarily organized for emotional gratification, and violence is the theme around which all activities center. Sports, social, even delinquent activities are side issues to its primary assaultive pattern. The violent gang's organization and membership are constantly shifting in accord with the emotional needs of its members. Membership size is exaggerated as a psychological weapon for influencing other gangs and for self-aggrandizement. Small arsenals of weapons are discussed and, whenever possible, accumulated. These caches include switchblades and hunting knives, homemade zip guns, standard guns, pipes, blackjacks, and discarded World War II bayonets and machetes. The violent gang is thus essentially organized around gang-war activities, although occasionally certain youths will form delinquent cliques or subgroups within the overall violent gang.

Membership characteristics are unclear in the violent gang's structure. Leaders are characterized by megalomania, a strong need to control, and an emotionally distorted picture of the gang's organization. The image of the leader is often exaggerated and glorified by gang members to enhance their own self-concepts. Strong power drives in the violent gang are demonstrated by attempts to control territory. Territorial disputes are constant sources of conflict between gangs.

Because of the unclarified nature of its structure, the violent gang has a chameleonlike quality. Its organization shifts with the needs of its members and is always in a state of flux. Conflicts with other groups go on constantly either in discussion or in actuality. Other gangs are allies one day and enemies the next, according to the whims of disturbed gang members and leaders.

A considerable amount of the gang boys' time is spent "sounding," a pattern of needling, ridiculing, or fighting with other members; consequently a great deal of their social participation is of a negative nature. The underlying theme of these street-corner sounding sessions is an attempt to prove oneself and to disprove and disparage others. Verbal and physical attack and defense are almost constant. In most discussions the underlying theme is one of hostility and aggression.

The expression of violence by the group appears to be more acceptable than individual violent behavior. The consensus factor of the group seems to permit a wider range of "legitimate" abnormal behavior. A disturbed youth may therefore cloak his pathology in the group image, which simultaneously aggrandizes him and lends him anonymity.

Many gang leaders appear to be involved in an attempt to redefine earlier years when they were disturbed, insecure, and unhappy. At this later period in their lives (approximately between the ages of eighteen and twenty-five), they act out the powerful role they could not achieve when they were younger.

Gang warfare usually has no clear purpose or consensus of definition for all participants. For many gang members it is an opportunity to channel personal aggressions and hostilities. Many gang wars originate over trivia. Territory, a "bad look," an exaggerated argument over a girl, or a nasty remark may stir up a large collection of youths into gang warfare. Such surface provocations give disturbed youths a *cause célèbre* and a banner under which they can vent hostilities related to other issues. The gang members' emotions are fanned through interaction and produce a group contagion. What starts out as a "bad look" from one youth toward another can thus develop into a major battle. Each youth who becomes involved can project into the battle whatever angers or hostilities he has toward school, his family, the neighborhood, the Man, or any other problems he may be living through at the time.

An important facet of the mass gang war is the negotiation and manipulation of alliances and affiliations as demonstrations of strength. Many agreements and contracts are made in the process of putting on the rumble. These are generally pseudobargains, which mobilize the gang members to flex muscles they are unsure they have.

At the actual gang-war event, most youths on hand have little or no idea why they are there or what they are expected to do, except to assault someone. Leaders, gang members, citizens, and sometimes the police and the press are caught up in the fallout of gang-war hysteria. Although violent gang members may not be clear about their motives or their gang's organization, the gang war çan result in homicide—a very clear situation indeed. In fact, the confused nature of the gang and its fantasies helps to make it a highly destructive instrument of violence.

Thus gang violence results from a set of interrelated circumstances:

1. Varied negative sociocultural dislocations exist in the disorganized, rapidly changing urban slum area.

2. These dislocations produce dysfunctional gaps in the socialization process that would ordinarily train the child for normative social roles.

3. Children not adequately socialized may develop asocial or sociopathic personalities.

4. The resulting sociopathic personalities are essentially characterized by (*a*) a lack of social conscience; (*b*) a limited ability to relate, identify, or empathize with others except for egocentric objectives; and (*c*) impulsive, aggressive, and socially destructive behavior when impulsive, immediate needs are not satisfied.

5. Because of his personality deficiencies, the sociopathic individual cannot relate adequately to more socially demanding groups (including delinquent and social gangs).

6. Individualized emotional outbursts are more stigmatized, are considered more bizarre, and to some extent are more unrewarding than group pathological expressions. In the context of the violent gang, such individualistic expression becomes socially "legitimate."

7. The malleable nature of the violent gang makes it a compatible and legitimate vehicle for adjusting the emotional needs of the sociopathic youth, who cannot relate adequately in more demanding social groups.

The Pseudocommunity of the Violent Gang

Normal groups are constellations of roles defining prescribed ways in which members may interact effectively and harmoniously. The normal group may be viewed partially as a projected model for behavior toward the accomplishment of the mutually agreed-upon goals of its members. A dominant characteristic of such a group is the fact that most members are in consensual agreement about the important norms and reciprocal expectations that regulate and determine each group member's behavior. Thus essential elements in a normal group are its members' agreement upon and ability to fulfill certain prescribed norms or standards of behavior.

According to Norman Cameron, a group makes certain demands upon the individual, and in the normative pattern of life the individual gives of himself to group demands. This the normal individual finds satisfying. On the daily level of group interaction, relevant "others" validate the individual's group participation at a minimal level of social expectation. However, "under certain circumstances individuals with socially inadequate development fail progressively to maintain such a level, with the result that they become socially disarticulated and very often have to be set aside from the rest of their community to live under artificially simplified conditions."[33] The violent gang serves the sociopathic youth as a "simplified" refuge from the more demanding community.

The person who requires this forced or voluntary dissociation from the general community has sociopathic characteristics. His essential limitation is his inability to take the role of another, except for egocentric purposes. He lacks a social conscience. To oversimplify, this type of individual tends to become paranoid and to have interchangeable delusions of persecution and excessive grandeur. These emotions result from an essentially correct assessment of his personal and social disability—a disability developed in a vacuum of effective socializing agents and processes. The paranoid's reactions of delusion and persecution are useful in enabling him to fool himself into believing that he is powerful and at the same time to blame his social disability upon a world that unfairly persecutes him. Both paranoid devices (grandeur and persecution) tend temporarily to relieve his already battered ineffectual self of blame for his problems.

The delusional process is at first internal and on the level of personal thought; however, in time it tends to become projected onto and involved with the surrounding community. According to Cameron:

> The paranoid person, because of poorly developed role-taking ability, which may have been derived from defective social learning in earlier life, faces his real or fancied slights and discriminations without adequate give-and-take in his communication with others and without competence in the social interpretation of motives and intentions.[34]

This type of person, whose role-taking skills are impaired, lacks the ability adequately to assess the "other" in interaction. He begins to take

---

[33]Norman Cameron, "The Paranoid Pseudo-Community," *American Journal of Sociology* 49 (July 1943):32–38.

[34]Cameron, "The Paranoid Pseudo-Community," p. 33.

everything the wrong way, and because of his inability to think as others do, he becomes increasingly alienated and dissociated from the real world. His delusional fantasies become hardened, and he begins to see and experience things not consensually validated or similarly felt by others. As Cameron specifies, he "becomes prejudiced with regard to his social environment." His responses tend first to select reactions from his surroundings that fit into his personal interpretation and then to reshape in retrospect things that seemed innocent enough when they occurred, until they support the trend of his suspicions. Because of his already incipient disturbance, and particularly if the individual is evolving in a defective socializing community (for example, the disorganized slum), he is unable to get relevant responses from others to counteract a developing reaction formation that finally hardens into what Cameron has termed a *paranoid pseudocommunity.*

As he begins attributing to others the attitudes he has toward himself, he unintentionally organizes these others into a functional community, a group unified in its supposed reactions, attitudes, and plans with respect to him. In this way he organizes individuals, some of whom are actual persons and some only inferred or imagined, into a whole that satisfies for the time being his immediate need for explanation but which brings no reassurance with it and usually serves to increase his tensions. The community he forms not only fails to correspond to any organization shared by others but actually contradicts the consensus. More than this, these others do not actually perform the actions or maintain the attitudes he ascribes to them; they are united in no common undertaking against him. What he takes to be a functional community is only a pseudocommunity created by his own unskilled attempts at interpretation, anticipation, and validation of social behavior.

This pseudocommunity of attitude and intent that he succeeds in thus setting up organizes his own responses still further in the direction they have been taking; and these responses in turn lead to greater and greater systematization of his surroundings. The pseudocommunity grows until it seems to constitute so grave a threat to the individual's integrity or to his life that, often after clumsy attempts to get at the root of things indirectly, he bursts into directly defensive or vengeful activity. This brings out into the open a whole system of organized responses to a supposed functional community of detractors or persecutors which he has been rehearsing in private. The real community, which cannot share in his attitudes and reactions, counters his actions with forcible restraint or retaliation.[35]

The real community's response and retaliation only serve to strengthen the individual's suspicions and distorted interpretations. He sees this as further evidence of the unfair discrimination to which he is being subjected. "The

---

[35]Cameron, "The Paranoid Pseudo-Community," p. 35.

reactions of the real community in now uniting against him are precisely those which he has been anticipating on the basis of his delusional beliefs."[36] The pseudocommunity calcifies, becomes more articulate and real to him. He begins after a while to live in his delusional realm almost to the exclusion of other social alternatives.

The processes through which an individual becomes enmeshed in a paranoid pseudocommunity closely parallel the processes that hook a sociopathic youth into the violent gang. The sociopathic youth growing up in the disorganized slum has a personality syndrome that easily interlocks with the paranoid pseudocommunity of the violent gang.

Development of a Pseudocommunity

The pseudocommunity processes as they apply to the violent gang show the following sequential pattern of development:

1. *Defective socialization.* The socialization vacuum of the disorganized slum, with its many inconsistencies, produces sociopathic youths with limited social conscience or ability to relate. This asocial milieu is fertile for negative conditioning.

2. *Alienation and dissociation.* Owing to their sociopathic tendencies, these youths are further disconnected and alienated from the more consensually real and constructive community. Their negative feelings of "difference," social ineffectiveness, and rejection become reinforced and hardened by the disorganized and callous world to which they are exposed.

3. *Paranoid reactions.* Two paranoid patterns, delusions of grandeur and delusions of persecution, emerge in reaction to the world around the defectively socialized youth. These patterns become functional in shifting the responsibility from himself to others and take the pressure off an already weak and suffering self. Gang leadership, control of "large divisions," being part of a "vast gang army," and a reputation for violence give the depressed youth some illusionary ego strength. Indications of persecution—enemy gangs, getting kicked out of school, and so on—are seized upon and enable the sociopathic youth to shift the responsibility from himself to society. His prejudice toward the community hardens, and he selectively perceives the outside world's behavior to fit his emotional needs.

4. *The pseudocommunity of the violent gang.* For this type of youth, the violent gang becomes a convenient pseudocommunity, one that is functional in at least temporarily alleviating his personal inadequacies and problems. The structure of the violent gang, with its flexibility of size, power roles, and delusionary possibilities, makes it a most convenient and socially acceptable escape hatch for the sociopathic youth.

---

[36]Cameron, "The Paranoid Pseudo-Community," p. 35.

The "Legitimate" Quality of Violent-Gang Structure

The worship of the hoodlum as a hero and the acceptance of violent gang behavior as normal by the larger society help to harden the gang's arteries. Most pathological behavior is stigmatized and/or sympathized with; not so the activities of the violent gang. The general community response of intrigue, and in some fashion covert aggrandizement, reinforces the violent gang as a most desirable, stigma-free pseudocommunity for the sociopathic youth. The community's almost positive response to this pattern of pathology may be partially accounted for by a traditional American worship of aggressive, adventuresome, two-gun heroes who go it alone, unencumbered by social restraints or conscience.[37]

Another possible explanation of the seeming public acceptance of the violent gang syndrome may be found in an assumption that pathological behavior is restricted to individuals; that is, if one individual commits a bizarre act, he is considered disturbed, but the same act committed by fifty youths together achieves a sort of legitimacy that gives the individual a degree of immunity to the stigma of pathology. The appraisal of collective behavior patterns gives some clue to this element of group legitimization and sanction for bizarre and pathological group action. Lang and Lang make this point in a discussion of crowds. They comment that certain aspects of a group situation help to make pathological acts and emotions acceptable.

> The principle that expressions of impulses and sentiments are validated by the social support they attract extends to collective expressions generally. The mere fact that an idea is held by a multitude of people tends to give it credence.
>
> The feeling of being anonymous sets further limits to the sentiment of responsibility. The individual in the crowd or mass is often unrecognized; hence, there is a partial loss of critical self-control and the inhibitions it places on precipitate action. There is less incentive to adhere to normative standards when it appears to the individual that his behavior is not likely to provoke sanctions against him personally. . . . Each person sees himself acting as part of a larger collectivity which, by inference, shares his motives and sentiments and thereby sanctions the collective action. In this sense the crowd is an excuse for people all going crazy together.[38]

---

[37]To some extent the competitive, aggressive salesman, unencumbered by conscience, serves as a positive role model. Other sociopathic heroes include many mass media leading men, such as Marlon Brando as the motorcycle gang leader in *The Wild One,* George Raft as the archetypical hood, Warren Beatty as Clyde Barrow. See Lewis Yablonsky, *George Raft* (New York: McGraw-Hill, 1974). In the criminal tradition, John Dillinger, Al Capone, and Frank Costello have served as idealized figures for many youths. (Costello was once mobbed by a crowd of autograph-hunting hero worshipers of all ages when he was released from prison.)

[38]Kurt Lang and Gladys Engel Lang, *Collective Dynamics* (New York: Crowell, 1961), p.35.

When all the boys in a violent gang go crazy together, their behavior tends, at least in the public view, to have greater rationality. Gang legitimacy therefore partially derives from the fact that group behavior, however irrational, is generally not considered truly bizarre. Although society may disapprove, the gang remains as a rational social group in the public mind. Thus, public agencies give recognition to the violent gang and try to redirect it as an entity. (In "detached street gang worker" projects, for example, the violent gang is viewed as a legitimate, nonpathological entity suffering only from misguided efforts that need to be redirected into "constructive channels.")

Another clue to the legitimation of gang violence may lie in its uncomfortable closeness to the behavior of the overall society. The warfare of the violent gang and its paramilitary structure are bizarre replicas of current structures of international violence. In the social context of the current international scene, violent gang machinations do not appear too pathological. Although many gang adjustments require closer examination, the violent gang interestingly caricatures many patterns of the larger world. The gang president (even if he doesn't really lead), drafting new soldiers (even if they are not really members), forging grand alliances (even if its members do not fully cooperate), and attending summit peace meetings (even if they are only for propaganda and solve nothing), bears a striking resemblance to men whose names are internationally known.

The gang thus emerges as a desirable pseudocommunity reaction for many sociopathic youths. Various degrees of membership participation meet the individual's momentary emotional needs. The gang leader and the core gang member are more closely identified with the violent-gang paranoid pseudocommunity than are more marginal members. Of considerable significance is the fact that the nature of the violent gang's pathological membership produces an unusual pattern of group structuring quite different from the structure usually found in normal groups.

The Violent Gang as a Near-Group

The organization of human collectives may be viewed as a continuum of organization factors. At one extreme, an organized, cohesive collection of persons interacting around shared functions and goals for some period of time forms a normal group. At the other extreme of human organization, a loose collection of individuals, generally characterized by anonymity and spontaneous leadership, motivated and ruled by momentary emotions, forms a mob or crowd. Although the term *mob* fits a youth riot and *group* fits a cohesive delinquent gang, neither group nor mob seems especially appropriate to describe violent gang structure.

Groups that emerge midway on a continuum of organization are distorted in one direction or the other by most perceivers. It appears as though there is a psychological (autistic) need to consolidate one's view of the world.

Violent gangs, therefore, despite considerable evidence to the contrary, are often mistakenly perceived by observers as cohesive groups, and in some youth riots no organization is seen despite the fact that in most cases a degree of organization exists.

Because no existing group conceptions seem suitable for describing the violent gang, it may be referred to as a near-group.[39] The near-group stands midway on the continuum from mob to group. (See Figure 6.2) It is differentiated from other collectivities that are temporarily midway because it has some degree of permanence or homeostasis. A cohesive group may be partially disorganized for a period of time, but it is in a state of becoming either organized or disorganized. The violent gang as a near-group consistently maintains its state of partial organization.

The violent gang as an ideal-type near-group structure includes most of the following characteristics:

1. Participants in the violent gang near-group are generally sociopathic personalities. The most sociopathic are core participants or leaders.
2. To these individuals the near-group gang is a compensatory para-

Figure 6.2

Collective Structures

---

[39]One of the authors carried out extensive research during a five-year period in New York City (1953–58) from which he developed a theory of gangs based on group structure. The theory was originally presented in an article by Lewis Yablonsky, "The Delinquent Gang as a Near Group," *Social Problems* 7 (Fall 1959):108–17, and was later expanded into the book *The Violent Gang* (New York: Macmillan, 1962; rev. ed., Penguin, 1970). Since that time, numbers of researchers have confirmed the near-group concept. In 1966 and 1973, the author again studied several gangs and concluded that the original thesis of the near-group continues to be a valid system for understanding violent gang structure and process.

noid pseudocommunity, which serves as a more socially desirable adjustment pattern than other pathological syndromes available in the community.

3. Individualized roles are defined to fit the emotional needs of the participants.
4. The definition of membership is diffuse and varies for each participant.
5. Behavior is essentially emotion motivated within loosely defined boundaries.
6. Group cohesiveness decreases as one moves from the center of the collectivity to the periphery.
7. Membership requires only limited responsibility and social ability.
8. Leadership is self-appointed and sociopathic.
9. There is a limited consensus among participants in the collectivity as to its functions or goals.
10. There is a shifting and personalized stratification system.
11. Membership is in flux.
12. Fantasy membership is included in the size of the collective.
13. There is a limited consensus of normative expectations for behavior.
14. Norms and behavior patterns are often in conflict with the inclusive social system's prescriptions.
15. Interaction within the collectivity and toward the outer community is hostile and aggressive, with spontaneous outbursts of violence to achieve impulsively felt goals.

Validation of Near-Group Theory

After the appearance of near-group theory in 1959, Howard and Barbara Myerhoff[40] and other researchers carried out extensive empirical and theoretical research into the near-group thesis. These later findings affirmed the validity of the concept for illuminating the structure of many cases of lower class and middle class gangs. Myerhoff and Myerhoff summarize these findings:

The sociological literature about gangs contains at least two sharply conflicting descriptions of the extent of gang structure and the nature of their values. In the most prevalent view, the gang is seen as a kind of primary group, highly structured, relatively permanent and au-

---

[40]Howard L. Myerhoff and Barbara G. Myerhoff, "Field Observations of Middle-Class Gangs," *Social Forces* 42 (March 1964):328–36.

tonomous, possessing a well-developed delinquent subculture which is transmitted to new members. . . .

Cohen has identified the primary needs met by the gang as those of resolving status frustration for lower class boys, and providing an expression of masculine identification for middle-class boys. Parsons has also emphasized the achievement of sexual identity as a problem dealt with by delinquent behavior. Cloward and Ohlin, following Merton's conception, have specified the discrepancy between aspirations toward success goals and opportunities for achieving them as the problem giving rise to gang behavior. Kvaraceus and Miller have stressed the inherent conflict between lower and middle-class values and the delinquent's predisposition to the former in explaining gang behavior. Eisenstadt and Bloch and Niederhoffer have pointed to the gang as a collective response to the adolescent's striving toward the attainment of adulthood and the frustrations attendant on the transition from one age status to another. These authors identify different components of the gang subculture according to their interpretation of its function, but implicit or explicit in all these positions is the view of the gang as an integrated and relatively cohesive group.

A strikingly different interpretation of the structure of gangs describes them as informal, short lived, secondary groups without a clear-cut, stable delinquent structure. Lewis Yablonsky has suggested a conceptualization of the gang as a "near-group," specifying the following definitive characteristics: diffuse role definitions, limited cohesion, impermanence, minimal consensus on norms, shifting membership, emotionally disturbed leaders, and limited definition of membership expectations. On a continuum of the extent of social organization, Yablonsky locates the gang midway between the mob at one end and the group at the other.[41]

The authors go on to explicate near-group theory, noting some views on the theory:

James F. Short, Jr. objects to Yablonsky's description of the gang as a near-group on the grounds that he has overstated the case, but agrees, nevertheless, that gangs do not have "the stability of membership, the tightly knit organization and rigid hierarchical structure which is sometimes attributed to them." Most of the groups he has observed have the kind of shifting membership which Yablonsky described.[42]

---

[41]Myerhoff and Myerhoff, "Field Observations of Middle-Class Gangs," pp. 328–29.
[42]Myerhoff and Myerhoff, "Field Observations of Middle-Class Gangs," p. 329.

The Myerhoffs expand on this in a footnote:

> In a recent article Pfautz raised the question of whether Yablon-sky's "near-group" concept is necessary. He suggests that Yablonsky's findings could be more productively recast into the theoretical traditions of collective behavior in general and social movements in particular. Certainly, Pfautz's point that this would widen the theoretical relevance of Yablonsky's findings is well taken. There are two reasons for the authors' preference for the near-group concept rather than a collective behavior orientation: first, in immediate concern with indicating the point by point similarity between these observations and those reported by Yablonsky, regardless of the conceptual framework he uses in describing them, and second, the authors' feeling that in view of the fragmented and discontinuous state of the literature on the subject, it is at present more important to compare and relate studies of adolescent collective deviant activities to one another than to more general sociological issues and concepts.[43]

They then present another conceptualization:

> The supervisor of a large, long-lived detached worker program in Los Angeles, with many years of gang experience there and in Harlem, has given a description much like that of Yablonsky. He observed that delinquent gangs seldom act as a corporate group and that most of their antisocial activities are committed in groups of two's or three's, or by a single person. He found communication between members to be meager and sporadic, reflecting the same limitations in social abilities that Yablonsky identified. . . .[44]

In summary, the Myerhoffs note: "There is a coincidence of opinion based on three sets of observations (Yablonsky's, the supervisor of a detached worker program in Los Angeles, and those reported in this paper) suggesting that the common conception of the gang as a highly organized primary group is not always accurate. . . ."[45] Regarding the gangs they studied and their appraisal of gang literature, the Myerhoffs concluded that "the groups described here manifest all but one of the characteristics (disturbed leadership) described by Yablonsky as those of a near-group."[46]

---

[43]Myerhoff and Myerhoff, "Field Observations of Middle-Class Gangs," p. 329.

[44]Myerhoff and Myerhoff, "Field Observations of Middle-Class Gangs," pp. 329–30.

[45]Myerhoff and Myerhoff, "Field Observations of Middle-Class Gangs," p. 335.

[46]Myerhoff and Myerhoff, "Field Observations of Middle-Class Gangs," p. 335.

The Violent Gang and Minority Youths

In the modern disorganized slum, the violent gang has been for many minority group youths their only source of identity, status, and emotional satisfaction. Ill-trained to participate with any degree of success in the dominant white middle class world of rigid ideas, community centers, and adult demands, they construct their own community. They set goals that are achievable; they build an empire, partly real and partly fantasy, that helps them live through the confusion of adolescence.

For youngsters growing up in places like the Watts barrio, Chicago's South Side, the East Bronx, or Harlem, the schools, community centers, and government projects are foreign domains with values and expectations they do not understand. The demands of scheduled activities, forms, dues, and middle class skills can be all but incomprehensible to a youth who has grown up in the ghetto.

The demands for performance and responsibility in the violent gang, however, are readily adapted to the personal needs of these youths. Usually the criteria for membership are vague. In many gangs, a youth can say he belongs one day and quit the next without necessarily telling any other gang member. Some boys say that the gang is organized for protection and that one role of a gang member is to fight. For others, the standard violent gang still provides the company that misery seeks. Among the "sanctioned" opportunities the gang provides a youth in his confused search for "success" are robbery and intimidation. Other ways to Nirvana include alcohol, drug addiction, and kicks based on assault and violence. If only in caricature, he can become a "success" and at the same time strike back at society.

In the violent gang, a ghetto youth can become president or war lord, control vast domains, and generally act out a powerful even though sometimes fantasized success image. The boys can mutually expand their shared and highly valued success by reinforcing each other's fantasies of power. The unwritten contractual agreement is "Don't call my bluff and I won't call yours"; "I'll support your big-man gang image if you'll support mine." This lends prestige to all involved in the charade. Aside from real addiction, common among deprived minority group youths, the violent gang can serve as a social narcotic.

In most respects Chicano, black and Puerto Rican gangs parallel each other. In one study into the social context in which gang violence occurs in a Mexican-American community, Ruth Horowitz and Gary Schwartz studied the norms of Mexican-American gangs.[47] Based on their research, they conclude that gang violence arises in situations where one party impugns the honor of his adversary. This sort of conduct violates the norms of interpersonal

---

[47]Ruth Horowitz and Gary Schwartz, "Honor, Normative Ambiguity and Gang Violence," *American Sociological Review* 39 (April 1974):238–51.

etiquette and constitutes a violation of "personal space." Horowitz and Schwartz focused on the normative processes whereby acts and complex structures of action "were built, elaborated and transformed into violence."

The exploits and involvement of an effective barrio gang worker, Leo Cortez, provides other insights into the dynamics of Chicano gangs, a permanent configuration that has become a fixed part of Los Angeles culture and history.[48]

East L.A. Gangs: Youth Worker Struggles for Peace in Barrio

The night before, a youth with a sawed-off shotgun had shot a middle-aged mother who was picnicking with several small children in an East Lost Angeles park. And now, although the woman's sons and their friends were probably plotting a bloody gang revenge at this very minute, Leo Cortez found himself sitting inside a small county office while assorted law officers and social workers drank coffee, ate doughnuts and wondered what to do about the youth gang problem in East Los Angeles. At times such as these, Leo Cortez, 37, a county youth worker and one-time gang member, wonders why he isn't out on the streets working with those he understands so well.

So well, in fact, that many residents of that small 8.36-square-mile enclave known as unincorporated East Los Angeles, population about 140,000, are convinced that Leo Cortez has probably averted more gang wars and saved more lives than all the sheriff's deputies combined. . . .

Cortez drove directly to County-USC General Hospital where he made his way through the maze of corridors to her room, a crowded ward on the ninth floor.

Momentarily, he stood at the bedside, silently surveying the damage.

Her bruised body was riddled with at least 50 shotgun pellets, two of them only a fraction away from her right eye.

Gently, he touched her shoulder, and, once her dazed eyes focused, she smiled, almost brightly.

But her thoughts were confused, her mind as baffled as a child's.

Because she was an East Los Angeles mother, she understood gangs. Her two sons belonged to one of the roughest gangs in the area. And, she whispered, with weary acceptance, "they only try to kill each other. . . ."

So, why her?

Cortez only shrugged, perhaps thinking of the long day ahead, a day of shuttling back and forth among half a dozen barrios, trying to keep the peace.

And as she read his mind, the woman's clouded eyes momentarily cleared, filled with sudden, sharp alarm.

---

[48]Bella Stumbo, "East L.A. Gangs: Youth Worker Struggles for Peace in Barrio," *Los Angeles Times,* September 19, 1976. Copyright, 1976, *Los Angeles Times.* Reprinted by permission.

"Leo," she said, her voice beseeching, as she raised a battered arm toward him. "The boys . . . Don't let them go for revenge? Make them stay home?"

[Cortez meets with the gang.]

"Man, tonight we'll go down there and kill a couple of those vatos (bad dudes)," declared one skinny youth of 14. The only problem was that, though they all suspected the assailant had come from one particular rival gang, nobody was sure.

"But I tell you something!" shouted another boy of 18 whose nickname was "Little Boy" and whose eyes were glazed over by something much stronger than liquor.

"When we go, we'll be cool. We won't go around shooting women and kids. We'll kill the vato who did it."

Patiently, in soft Spanish, Cortez urged them all to leave the park. Getting arrested wouldn't help anything. Better yet, why not visit the hospital?

With surprising passivity, like small, uncertain children, most quickly agreed.

Even Little Boy, who was reeling so badly he could hardly walk.

And so Cortez gave him a lift home, not knowing, when he let the boy out that in two days Little Boy would be dead himself—shot to death by youths from another barrio. . . .

Leo Cortez seems to know not only the names of almost every youth in East Los Angeles but also the names of their friends and their enemies.

He also knows which kids are hard-core murderers, which ones can be influenced to kill, which ones never

could, and, finally, which youths are "locos"—crazy enough to be altogether unpredictable.

Whatever he doesn't already know, his grapevine apparently tells him. Indeed, it sometimes appears that Leo Cortez knows about most gang crimes before they even happen —in time to head them off.

So when he cruised into a strange barrio, "just to see what's happening," it seemed likely that Cortez at least suspected which gang was to blame for the shooting. Perhaps he even knew the identity of the assailant.

"What most people don't understand is that the kids out here, the gang members, don't consider themselves criminals," Cortez said.

"Here, even when they kill, national standards just don't apply. Because, here, a gang member regards himself as a soldier, you understand? Even if he's only patrolling a few square blocks. No matter how small his turf is, he still regards himself as a patriot . . . protecting his homeland. Because that's all he's got, all he's ever had. . . .

East Lost Angeles Sheriff's Administrative Lt. Hayden Finley, who calls the entire area "a damned war zone," documented the increasing violence. In 1975, he said, a total of 333 "gang-related incidents," including 17 murders, were reported—compared to 319 "incidents," including 13 murders, during only the first six months of 1976.

And, he said, "those are only the reported crimes. The actual figures are probably much higher, because most people are too afraid of retaliation out here to report anything to us."

Even so, to local workers like Leo Cortez, the statistical increase in crimes isn't nearly so frightening as the changing nature of those crimes.

"Sometimes it really scares me," said Cortez, "because too many kids nowadays aren't following any of the old rules."

In the old days, Cortez added almost sadly, gang members made certain that when they went on a retaliatory raid, they hit their enemy.

But, now, he said, they often are sloppy, or heedless, simply speeding by an enemy house at night and spraying it with bullets, regardless of who's inside.

Likewise, Cortez continued, there was a time when small children weren't allowed to even associate with gang members.

"But now I see little kids, 10 or 12 years old, wandering around with guns . . . and, now, too, even 8-year-old kids are sniffing glue, paint, Angel Dust (an animal tranquilizer) . . . and even doing hard stuff."

"Actually," Cortez concluded, "I think that's why there's more violence here now . . . the drugs. In the old days, we never fried our brains like that . . . they've got no future, nothing but their barrio and their 'home-boys.' So, they can only prove their manhood by standing up and getting killed, or killing. . . ."

Violent Gangs in the Seventies: A Summary

For a time during the sixties and early seventies there was a diminution of violent gang activities. This decrease in violence is difficult to account for. Perhaps it occurred because of a sense of hope that positive social change might take place and perhaps because potential violent gang members were involved in the then-vibrant civil rights movement. But as apathy and despair reappeared in the ghetto, violent gangs reemerged as vehicles for venting anger and frustration.

The symptom of violent gangs is often an overt reflection of deeper disorders in a society. The violent gang can be a counterattack against the overall society and ultimately lead to a positive revolutionary change in the system. Historically, many total societies have been changed by politically oriented violent gangs.

The resurgent violent gangs of the seventies do not have any clear-cut political characteristics. Our observations indicate that the new violent urban gangs are very similar to the gangs researched mainly in the fifties. This genre of violent gang was for thousands of young people living under the oppression of the American urban ghetto a viable alternative way of life. The violence had a seemingly senseless quality. It was not turned against any oppressor or the society at large. The pattern fits the model "we only kill each other."

Gang forms, as described in the 1960s, were modified. Violence was used as a vehicle for social change. For example, during the Watts riots, black gangs that had previously fought each other joined forces against their common enemy—Whitey. Many ghetto youngsters who, in the fifties, would almost automatically join a "senseless" violent gang became members of quasi-political militant groups like the Black Panthers or the Brown Berets. Their violence was no longer senseless: it appeared to have purpose.

The extravagant faith in these varied minority group militant organizations has clearly diminished. Intensive leadership battles, ego trips, selling-out to impotent bureaucratic programs seem to have taken their toll, and many of these organizations have become unattractive or defunct. As these vehicles for social change diminish, the despair, alienation, and hopelessness of many young people are now being rechanneled into structures that parallel the violent gangs of the fifties.

The "new" gangs of the seventies are structurally the same as the 1950 model with an added superficial patina of "doing-good and helping the community," as illustrated by various gangs in New York and Chicago. Beneath this social work surface is the same senseless violent gang of hopeless youth trapped in a society that holds out limited opportunity for human achievement to these young people.

A sense of despair and alienation produces this type of violent gang. For an individual who sees little hope or opportunity for achievement in the overall society, the violent gang becomes an acceptable substitute. In it, the youth has identity and an extravagant hope for "stardom" in a success and power-oriented society. With one stroke of a knife or bullet from a gun, the individual can achieve status among his peers and, in a perverted way, in the larger society.

The youth most susceptible to violent gang membership emerges from a social milieu that trains him inadequately for assuming constructive social roles. In fact, the defective socialization process to which he is subjected fosters a lack of humanistic feelings. At hardly any point is he trained to have feelings of compassion or responsibility for other people.

In a technological society that values machines over people there are large pockets of deprived people who become egocentric, hedonistic, frustrated, and consequently, violent. Violent gangs become a standard cultural form when there are thousands of young people with limited compassion. In a machine system people are dehumanized and unable to experience the pain of the violence they may inflict on others since they have a limited ability to identify or emphathize with others. They are capable, therefore, of committing spontaneous acts of "senseless" violence without feeling concern or guilt. The classic sociopathic comment of a gang member who had killed another boy aptly describes this pattern of feeling: "What was I thinking about when I stabbed him? Man, are you crazy? I was thinking about whether to do it again!"

The selection of violence by gang youths is not difficult to understand. Violent behavior requires limited training, personal ability, or even physical strength. (As one gang boy stated, "A knife or a gun makes you ten feet tall.") Because violence is a demonstration of easily achieved power, it becomes the paramount value of the gang. Violence requires characteristics that gang boys have in quantity: limited social ability and training, considerable resentment and aggression, and a motivation to retaliate against others and the system. Violence serves as a quick and sure means for upward social mobility within the violent gang and, to some extent, in the overall society.

The very fact that it is "senseless" rather than "rational" violence that appeals to the gang boy tells us a great deal about the meaning of violence to him. It is an easy, quick, almost magical way of achieving power and prestige. In a single act of unpremeditated intensity, he establishes a sense of his own identity and impresses this existence on others. No special ability is required to commit this brand of violence—not even a plan—and the guilt connected with it is minimized by the gang code of approval, especially if the violence fulfills the gang's idealized standards of a swift, sudden, and senseless outbreak.

An aspect of senseless violence is related to a concept we would term *existential validation,* the validation of one's existence. This basically involves the individual's sense of alienation from human feeling or meaning. People increasingly have a more limited awareness of their personal human value in a vast, technological, dehumanized society. Many people feel a social death. Extremist violence is one way of establishing identity and experiencing some feeling of existence.

Most people have a sense of identity and existence in their everyday activities. They do not require intense emotional excitement to know they are alive, that they exist. In contrast, many people, including the sociopath, do need such arousal; indeed, their sense of being ahuman and unfeeling requires increasingly heavier dosages of bizarre and extreme behavior to validate the fact that they really exist. Extreme violent behavior is one pattern that gives the sociopath a glimmer of feeling. Existential validation through violence (or other extremist bizarre behavior involving, say, sex or drugs) gives the socially dead person some feeling. As one gang killer reported, "When I stabbed him once, it felt good. I did it again and again because it made me feel alive for the first time in my life."

Violence is not exclusively the prestige symbol of the gang. The larger society covertly approves of, or is at least intrigued by, the outrageous as depicted in literature, television, movies, and other mass media. On the surface most members of society condemn violence; however, on a covert level there is a tendency to aggrandize and give recognition to violent people. The sociopathic personality who commits intense acts of violence is the "hero" of many plays and stories portrayed in the contemporary mass media.

The reemergence in the 1970s of "senseless" violent gangs is an indicator of the deep despair and alienation experienced by many minority and ghetto youths. This phenomenon is strong evidence that many significant social dislocations persist in American society.

Social
Class
and
Delinquency

AN EXAMINATION OF DELINQUENCY statistics published by federal and state governments reveals no data whatsoever on social class. The *Uniform Crime Reports,* which contain our most complete delinquency data, make no reference to social class, nor do the Juvenile Court Statistics. Yet most newspaper and journal articles on juvenile delinquency create the impression that it is largely a lower class phenomenon. Most comprehensive studies in the social class tradition have dealt with a more or less well-defined portion of the lower class, such as delinquent gangs, violent gangs, and delinquent subcultures found in lower class neighborhoods. While none of the sociologists directing such studies or drawing conclusions from them has implied that all lower class children are involved in illegal behavior, the thrust of their work appears to justify the conclusion that illegal behavior on the part of young people occurs primarily in lower class neighborhoods and involves children of lower class parents.[1]

Furthermore, over the years studies attempting to find differences between delinquents and nondelinquents have compared institutionalized delinquents with children who have not been adjudicated delinquent. The

---

[1]John P. Clark and Eugene P. Wenninger, "Socio-economic Class and Area as Correlates of Illegal Behavior Among Juveniles," *American Sociological Review* 27(December 1962):826–34.

assumption seemed to be that those children who had not been judged delinquent by a court had not engaged in delinquent behavior. The vast majority of the children found to be delinquent by courts were from the most economically deprived segments of our population. In Massachusetts, for example, 90 percent of the children committed to the corrections department each year (up to 1973) came from families receiving some form of welfare.[2] Conclusions based upon such studies, if generalized beyond the populations compared, have been criticized by sociologists who maintain that many of the "nondelinquent" children have violated legal norms without being caught or at least without being adjudicated delinquent. Various studies in which anonymous questionnaires were utilized indicated that middle class children were involved in delinquent behavior similar to that of the adjudicated delinquents. Some of these studies will be discussed later in this chapter. To better understand the use of such terms as *lower class* and *middle class,* we shall proceed to a general discussion of social class.

The Meaning of Social Class

While Karl Marx was not the first social philosopher to employ the term *class,* his writings on the subject are predominant in over half the world and exert an influence on psychologists and sociologists in the United States. Marx defined classes in terms of their relationship to ownership of land and capital. There were the bourgeoisie, who owned capital and property, and the proletariat, who did not possess capital or property. The latter class was a working class whose members depended on their labor. According to Marx, there are three basic classes: wage laborers or workers, owners of capital, and landlords. By virtue of their position in the economic order and their relationship to property, members of each class share common experiences, economic and political interests, and ways of life. Class conflict, according to Marx, arises when proletarian class consciousness emerges because of the common difficulties experienced by the members of the working class.[3]

Lenin, leader of the Russian Revolution and a Marxist, defined classes more precisely in terms of their relationship to the means of production. According to Lenin, classes are human groups, one of which can appropriate for itself the products and labor of another because of its position in a given economic system. Not only are property rights involved, but also the individual's right to decide his own destiny. Without control of the means of production, the working class is alienated.[4]

---

[2]Yitzhak Bakal, "The Massachusetts Experience," *Delinquency Prevention Reporter,* April 1973, p. 1.

[3]Karl Marx, *Capital,* trans. Ernest Untermann from 1st German ed. (Chicago: Kerr, 1909), vol. 3, p. 1031.

[4]Louis Soubise, *Le Marxisme Après Marx* (Paris: Aubrier Montaigne, 1967), p. 22.

In the United States there was and is no large class-conscious proletariat. Indeed it has been contended by many that the United States is essentially a classless society. A survey by George Gallup in 1939 showed that 88 percent of the people place themselves in the middle class while only 6 percent considered themselves in the upper class and 6 percent in the lower class.[5] A *Fortune* survey taken in 1940 showed 79.2 percent identifying themselves as middle class, 7.6 percent as upper class, and 7.9 percent as lower class.[6]

The idea of the United States as largely "middle class" is still held by a large majority of American people. The following article typifies this view.

A Society That Would Baffle Marx

Jimmy Carter isn't the only one who has difficulty defining "middle income." He's just lucky he didn't say "middle class" instead.

Sociologists and economists, who like to try to fit us into convenient categories as a way of seeming to be scientific, have had some recent go-rounds with classifying us again. But almost no one in the United States likes to think of himself as belonging to a class. It rubs against the grain of our individuality. And it divides us into layers in ways we have traditionally opposed.

If compelled to label ourselves by class, however, most of us pick "middle class." (In a recent survey, 82 per cent of Americans interviewed put themselves in the middle class category and the pollsters who questioned them concurred with the valuation.)

But the middle class category blurs at both ends and fuzzes in between. Is middle class the same as middle income? If so, then the truck driver who makes $14,500 with the waitress wife who clears $6,500 is obviously middle class. But how do you classify the graduate student-teaching assistant couple who make do on her fellowship and his $3,500 stipend? Or the scientist whose income slipped to $10,700 when he retired?

Robert L. Heilbroner, professor of economics at the New School for Social Research, sticks to the income-only definition of "middle class" in an article in the October issue of Atlantic. He considers all who have a family income between $15,000 and $32,000 to be middle class. (Heilbroner's "poor" are those with a family income less than $6,500 a year; his "working class" get up to $15,000; and he calls those in the $32–$100,000 bracket "upper class" and people still richer "rich.")

Irving Kristol, professor of urban values at New York University, picks about the same cutoff sum for poverty, figuring it should be half of the median family income. This is about $12,500—as President Ford's staffers have pointedly reminded Carter.

But Kristol notes in the Wall

---

[5]George H. Gallup and S. F. Rae, *The Pulse of Democracy* (New York: Simon and Schuster, 1940).

[6]"The People of the U.S.: A Self-Portrait," *Fortune*, February 1940, p. 21.

Street Journal that a family of four on welfare in New York City now gets between $7,000 and $7,500 in cash and benefits, and that therefore by the income-only definition, there should be no more "poor" in the nation's largest city.

Income, then, doesn't work as a way to define class. But neither does social life, family background, manners, food, or life styles. For how would you classify the son of a corporation executive who was graduated from a top college but is now making sandals and writing poetry in the Colorado mountains? Or the classical musician who is on unemployment compensation almost as often as he is working?

Education no longer divides us neatly along class lines. Our colleges actively recruit among the poor and the minorities, and there is no class reason why the children of every one of us may not aspire to at least one degree.

Clothes don't identify us classwise, any more. Blue jeans are an inexpensive universal. Whatever high fashion there may be is quickly available in on-the-rack copies for those who care. And if there is any imitating of one income level by another, it's because trends are working up from the less affluent, as with T-shirts, jump suits, work boots, and tank tops.

Occupation used to be a handy tool for sociologists intent on dividing us up into their own neat boxes. But today, the farmer may well be a college graduate with a bigger investment in land and equipment than most of us will ever own. The plumber may run his own business and belong to the tennis club. And many of the offspring of the affluent seem intent on achieving downward mobility in the guise of doing their own thing.

The point is there is no point in trying to fit us all into tidy classifications, even if it makes it possible for sociologists and economists to publish rather than to perish. We are truly close to becoming a classless society, where we are not typed from birth by the socio-economic characteristics of the group into which we are born. And for that we should rejoice.[7]

Most scholars studying social class in the United States define the term in one of three different ways, and their approach to the study of social class is closely related to their definition of the term.

Anthropologists W. Lloyd Warner and Paul S. Lunt, who conducted an extensive study of a New England city which they called Yankee City, defined *class* as follows:

> By *class* is meant two or more orders of people who are believed to be, and are accordingly ranked by the members of the community, in socially superior and inferior positions. Members of a class tend to marry

---

[7]Joan Beck, "A Society That Would Baffle Marx," *Long Beach* (Calif.) *Press-Telegram,* September 29, 1976. Reprinted, courtesy of the Chicago Tribune.

within their own order, but the values of the society permit marriage up and down. A class system also provides that children are born into the same status as their parents. A class society distributes rights and privileges, duties and obligations, unequally among its inferior and superior grades. A system of classes, unlike a system of castes, provides by its own values for movement up and down the social ladder. In common parlance, this is social climbing or, in technical terms, social mobility.[8]

In their studies of social class, Warner and associates employed a *reputational approach*. Their interviewers asked people to evaluate others in their community and rank them on a class scale. The interviewers were also instructed to find out from their informants what criteria were used in making these rankings. This method is effective only in relatively small communities where most people know each other. In the Yankee City study, the researchers also obtained considerable objective data by observing the interviewers. Based on the data gathered in Yankee City, the researchers concluded that there were six classes, which are distributed as follows:

    1.44 percent were upper upper
    1.56 percent were lower upper
  10.22 percent were upper middle
  28.12 percent were lower middle
  32.60 percent were upper lower
  25.22 percent were lower lower

Crime and delinquency were found largely in the lower classes. The two upper classes accounted for less than three-quarters of 1 percent of those arrested; the two middle classes, for about 10 percent; and the two lower classes, for approximately 90 percent of the crime in Yankee City.

All of the causes for arrest in the top three classes (upper upper, lower upper, and upper middle) were petty ones. Some were for driving and parking offenses. One grew out of a quarrel over a dog, and there were other minor offenses. The crimes in the two lower classes ranged from the most serious, such as rape and theft, to the least serious, such as drunkenness and improper driving of automobiles.

Eleven percent of the lower lower class and 3 percent of the upper lower class had records of arrest. One percent of the lower middle class had their names on the police records and less than 1 percent of the lower upper and the upper middle classes were recorded. About a third of the lower lower class was on welfare. Most were poor. Yet the evaluations of lower lower class members by others did not emphasize poverty. The evaluations did contain

---

[8]W. Lloyd Warner and Paul S. Lunt, *The Social Life of a Modern Community* (New Haven, Conn.: Yale University Press, 1941), p. 82.

many references to immorality and lack of worth. It is evident from a reading of the study that the application of the term *lower class* had a derogatory connotation.

Sociologists, in their studies of social class, tend to define social class as a stratum in society. They use an *objective approach,* employing such criteria as income, occupation, residence, and education. The occupational status of the father or guardian, for example, may be used to define the class level of a family. Erickson and Empey, in their study of delinquency and class position, developed an occupational prestige scale to determine occupational status.[9]

Richard Centers, the psychologist who contributed most to research in the area of social class, contends that classes are improperly and confusingly identified with social strata. Stratification is something objective and derives primarily from the economic system prevalent in a given society. The process of getting a living imposes functions, statuses, and roles on people. Social and economic categories based on occupation, income, education, and similar objective criteria are properly called strata. He distinguishes between strata and classes as follows:

> *But these strata, as some have seen, are not necessarily classes.* Classes are psychosocial groupings, something that is essentially subjective in character, dependent upon class consciousness (i.e., a feeling of group membership), and class lines of cleavage may or may not conform to what seem to social scientists to be logical lines of cleavage in the objective or stratification sense.
>
> Class, as distinguished from stratum, can well be regarded as a *psychological* phenomenon in the fullest sense of the term. That is, a man's class is a part of his ego, *a feeling on his part of belongingness to something;* an *identification* with something larger than himself.[10]

Centers advances an interest group theory of social classes in the following terms:

> *This theory implies that a person's status and role with respect to the economic processes of society impose upon him certain attitudes, values and interests relating to his role and status in the political and economic sphere. It holds, further, that the status and role of the individual in relation to the means of production and exchange of goods and services give rise in him to a consciousness of membership in some social class which shares those attitudes, values and interests.*[11]

---

[9]Maynard L. Erickson and LaMar T. Empey, "Class Position, Peers, and Delinquency," *Sociology and Social Research* 49(April 1965):271.

[10]Richard Centers, *The Psychology of Social Classes* (Princeton, N.J.: Princeton University Press), p. 27.

[11]Centers, *The Psychology of Social Classes,* pp. 28–29.

In his research, Centers used a *subjective approach* to social class. A representative sample consisting of 1,100 adult males was asked in which class each placed himself and what criteria he considered applicable to that class. The four classes mentioned were upper, middle, working, and lower. Other questions related to political identification, voting behavior, religion, education, opportunity, and satisfaction. Over half, 51 percent, identified with the working class, 43 percent with the middle class, 3 percent with the upper class, and 1 percent with the lower class (2 percent either didn't know or wouldn't say).[12] When manual workers were asked to what class they belonged, 79 percent identified with the working and lower classes.[13]

The term *lower class* was in a sense a stigmatizing term. Regarding its use in this context, Centers has this to say:

> "What puts a person in the lower class?" Here people again give answers in terms of both criteria and causes. The most obvious answer is "being poor," and it is by a considerable margin the most frequent one received. Poor education or lack of education is next. A surprisingly large proportion of people appear to think of the lower class as a rather despicable group. Poor character and low morals, drink, crime, lack of ability, low intelligence, shiftlessness, laziness, lack of ambition or motivation, menial labor, etc. all indicate the disesteem in which this group is held. The middle and working classes differ little in their responses on the whole. For both of them the term lower class frequently connotes a despised or déclassé group. The lower class itself is scarcely present in sufficient number to defend itself, but those that are present say poverty and lack of education are either the factors that put them there or are the signs by which they distinguish themselves from others.[14]

Apparently those interviewed had no hesitancy about identifying themselves as working class, but very few were willing to call themselves lower class.

Most research in delinquency, including the subsequent studies cited in this chapter, employ the objective approach, which in effect equates stratum with class. It must be clearly understood, therefore, that the term *lower class* refers specifically to the economic criteria employed and in no way implies inferiority in any other respect. We much prefer the term *working class;* however, since many of the children are from families without employment, perhaps this term, too, is inaccurate. In any event, it should be clear that the researchers are referring to persons in the lower economic stratum—i.e., poor people—as lower class without regard to any subjective evaluation of the persons so labeled. (The relevance of "subjective identifications" of people in poverty areas to delinquency will be discussed later in this chapter.)

---

[12]Centers, *The Psychology of Social Classes,* pp. 76–77.
[13]Centers, *The Psychology of Social Classes,* p. 85.
[14]Centers, *The Psychology of Social Classes,* pp. 95–96.

Some Explanations of Lower Class Delinquency

William A. Bonger, a Dutch sociologist, offered a Marxist explanation that applied to crime and delinquency committed by rich people as well as poor but that is particularly applicable to criminal and delinquent behavior of underprivileged workers and the unemployed.[15] Bonger's theoretical position leads to the conclusion that it is the members of the working class and the unemployed who become disproportionately involved in crime because of the economic demands of the capitalist system. This view of society is referred to as *economic determinism.* Describing man's potential as both altruistic and selfish, Bonger concludes that capitalism stimulates the selfish side of man. People produce for profit rather than for personal consumption and this fact results in, among other things, intense competition between capital and labor for the fruits of labor. Employers try to purchase labor at the lowest possible price; workers try to sell their labor for the highest possible price.

This "selfish *egoistic* competition fostered by the capitalist system," according to Bonger, transforms the entrepreneur or businessman into a "parasite" who lives without working, feels no moral obligation to his fellow man, and regards workers as things to serve and entertain him. Crime is by his definition an expression of human selfishness. This selfishness and social irresponsibility causes unemployment, lack of education, and other disabilities of the poor that lead to the commission of crime. The unplanned economic system breaks down frequently because factories overproduce and are closed. Working people underconsume because the total amount they receive in wages is less than the total retail price of commodities. The result is unemployment, increased poverty, greater inequality, and greater resentment—all causes of crime and delinquency. We then have three classes: the idle rich, the dependent idle poor, and the working class.

Competition for the sale of human labor may be unscrupulous, and it arouses intense emotions of hostility. The great inequalities produced by capitalism stimulate jealousy and hatred in the less privileged classes. Members of the working class experience deprivation, and retaliate with crimes of vengeance against those who exploit them. This sort of conflict, Bonger feels, is a cultural value fostered by capitalism.

Quinney presents a contemporary Marxist view of crime control in the American society. He maintains that, since 1 percent of the population owns 40 percent of the nation's wealth and nearly all power in the American society is concentrated in the hands of a few large corporations, government and business are inseparable. As a capitalist society the United States has two major classes, one which owns and controls, and a working class. Professionals, small businessmen, office workers and cultural workmen may cut across

---

[15]William A. Bonger, *Criminality and Economic Conditions,* trans. Henry P. Horton (Boston: Little, Brown, 1916).

class lines. However, the ruling class owns and controls the means of production and through its economic power uses the state to dominate the society. The dominant class is the ruling class. Quinney summarizes his position with respect to crime control as follows:[16]

1. American society is based on an advanced capitalist economy.
2. The state is organized to serve the interests of the dominant economic class, the capitalist ruling class.
3. Criminal law is an instrument of the state and ruling class to maintain and perpetuate the existing social and economic order.
4. Crime control in capitalist society is accomplished through a variety of institutions and agencies established and administered by a governmental elite, representing ruling class interests, for the purpose of establishing domestic order.
5. The contradictions of advanced capitalism—the disjunction between existence and essence—require that the subordinate classes remain oppressed by whatever means necessary, especially through the coercion and violence of the legal system.
6. Only with the collapse of capitalist society and the creation of a new society, based on socialist principles, will there be a solution to the crime problem.

Applying Bonger's or Quinney's thinking to present conditions, we would conclude that they would expect the poor people on welfare, the unemployed, and the workers who consider themselves exploited to share values favorable to the commission of crimes against the more privileged and against the economic and political establishment that is controlled by the wealthy. The underprivileged classes, having little or no voice in their destiny, would be expected to be alienated, hostile, and favorable to retaliatory activities which would be defined as crimes. In encouraging unrestrained "egoism," "self-interest," or "rugged individualism," a capitalist society inspires attacks on the social organization by those who consider themselves disadvantaged. We should, therefore, anticipate that underprivileged working class people and dependent poor people would have high delinquency rates. Such high delinquency rates might well be interpreted as incipient class consciousness and the early stages of class conflict.

In the United States, it is in the slum areas of the city, areas inhabited by the lower socioeconomic classes, that we find the highest rates of juvenile delinquency—the highest arrest rates of young people, the largest number of court referrals, and the largest number of recidivists (repeaters). From these

---

[16]Richard Quinney, "Crime Control in Capitalist Society," in *The Criminologist: Crime and the Criminal,* ed. Charles E. Reasons (Pacific Palisades, Cal.: Goodyear Publishing Co., 1974), pp. 136–43.

areas come a large majority of the young people who find themselves in correctional institutions.[17] In 1971, for example, 64 percent of the total number of delinquency cases disposed of by juvenile courts involved youths from urban areas, while rural areas accounted for 7 percent. Some rural areas, in terms of occupational, income, and educational data, would be considered lower class, yet the rates of delinquency in these areas are insignificant when compared with those in the cities.[18]

The Juvenile Delinquency Project of the National Education Association, headed by William C. Kvaraceus and Walter B. Miller, published a report that enumerated the components of the lower class culture, contrasted it with the middle class culture, and described the ways in which the lower class culture contributes to the delinquency of lower class children. The conclusion reached appears to reject personal pathology as a principal cause of delinquency in favor of the life situation and values associated with lower class status in America. It estimates that *"the preponderant proportion of our delinquent population consists essentially of normal lower class youngsters."*[19]

The concerns, values, and characteristic patterns of behavior of the lower socioeconomic class are the products of a well-formed cultural system. It is estimated that between 40 and 60 percent of the total population of the United States share or are significantly influenced by the major outlines of the lower class cultural system. Many youngsters growing up in these areas are "normally delinquent" if they conform to their culture.[20]

Behavior of those in a given cultural system is said to be motivated by a set of "focal concerns"—concerns that receive special emphasis within that culture. In lower class society, the following concerns are dominant: trouble, toughness, smartness, excitement, fate, autonomy.

Trouble. A boy or girl may be accorded recognition or prestige by being successfully involved (in trouble) with the authorities (police or school) or for avoiding such involvement (staying out of trouble).

Toughness. Physical prowess, "masculinity," endurance, athletic ability, and strength rank high in the concerns of lower class adolescents, as is evident in

---

[17]Clifford R. Shaw and Henry D. McKay, *Juvenile Delinquency and Urban Areas* (Chicago: University of Chicago Press, 1942). Data indicate a preponderance of delinquency in the slum areas of Chicago and twenty-one other large cities in the United States during the 1920s and 1930s. More recent juvenile court statistics show very little change in the geographic distribution of delinquency.

[18]*Juvenile Court Statistics, 1971,* Social and Rehabilitative Service Publication no. (SRS)73-03452 (Washington, D.C.: U.S. Government Printing Office, 1972), p. 8.

[19]William C. Kvaraceus and Walter B. Miller, *Delinquent Behavior* (Washington, D.C.: National Education Association, 1959), vol. 1, *Culture and the Individual,* pp. 55–75.

[20]Kvaraceus and Miller, *Delinquent Behavior,* p. 63.

the kinds of heroes they select—tough guy, gangster, tough cop, combat infantryman, "hard" teacher. Boys in the streets boast of acts that indicate toughness and belittle those who appear soft.

Smartness.   Skill in duping and outsmarting the other guy is admired, as well as the ability to avoid being duped by others. The con man is the hero and model. The victim of a con man is seen as a sucker or fool.

Excitement.   The search for thrills and stimulation is a major concern when life is often monotonous and drab.

Fate.   Drinking, gambling, and fighting are popular as sources of excitement. Lady Luck is a reigning goddess of lower class society. Success is attributed to good luck, failure to bad luck. Gambling is viewed as a way of testing one's luck.

Autonomy.   Lower class adolescents say in no uncertain terms that no one is going to boss them. Yet they frequently seek out, through norm-violating behavior, situations in which they will be told what to do, when to do it, how to do it, and whether it is right when done.

How does the cultural milieu contribute to the lower class youngster's involvement in delinquent behavior? There are three processes: (1) Engaging in certain cultural practices that comprise essential elements of the total life pattern of lower class culture automatically violates certain legal norms. (2) In certain instances when alternative avenues to valued objectives are available, the law-violating route frequently entails a relatively smaller investment of energy and effort than the law-abiding one. (3) The *demanded* response to certain situations recurrently engendered within lower class culture may call for the commission of illegal acts. *The lower class youngster who engages in a long and recurrent series of delinquent acts that are sanctioned by his peer group is acting so as to achieve prestige within this reference system.*

Albert K. Cohen, on the other hand, sees the delinquency of the working class boy as a form of rebellion against the middle class and its values. He describes the delinquent subculture as "nonutilitarian, malicious and negativistic." In addition to such obviously nonutilitarian delinquent acts as vandalism, Cohen contends that even stealing by those involved in the delinquent subculture is nonutilitarian. He says of this:

> In homelier language, stealing "for the hell of it" and apart from considerations of gain and profit is a valued activity to which attaches glory, prowess and profound satisfaction. There is no accounting in rational and utilitarian terms for the effort expended and the danger run in stealing things which are often discarded, destroyed or casually given

away. A group of boys enters a store where each takes a hat, a ball or a light bulb. They then move on to another store where these things are covertly exchanged for like articles. Then they move on to other stores to continue the game indefinitely. They steal a basket of peaches, desultorily munch on a few of them and leave the rest to spoil. They steal clothes they cannot wear and toys they will not use. Unquestionably, most delinquents are from the more "needy" and "underprivileged" classes, and unquestionably many things are stolen because they are intrinsically valued. However, a humane and compassionate regard for their economic disabilities should not blind us to the fact that stealing is not merely an alternative means to the acquisition of objects otherwise difficult of attainment.[21]

Cohen then concludes that other activities of the delinquent are even less motivated by rational, utilitarian considerations. He notes that there is a kind of *malice* apparent, an enjoyment in the discomfiture of others, a delight in the defiance of taboos.

While Kvaraceus and Miller regard the activities of lower class delinquents as derived from and related to the focal concerns of the adults in their class, Cohen sees the acts of adherents to the delinquent subculture as essentially *negativistic.* He sees an element of active spite in their flouting of rules, defiance of teachers, and misbehavior in school. It is, as Cohen sees it, a revolt against the middle class and its values by the working class boys. He puts it this way:

All this suggests also the intention of our term *negativistic.* The delinquent subculture is not only a set of rules, a design for living which is different from or indifferent to or even in conflict with the norms of the "respectable" adult society. It would appear at least plausible that it is defined by its "negative polarity" to those norms. That is, the delinquent subculture takes its norms from the larger culture but turns them upside down. The delinquent's conduct is right, by the standards of his subculture, precisely *because* it is wrong by the norms of the larger culture.[22]

Other characteristics of the delinquent subculture noted by Cohen include: *versatility,* demonstrated by a lack of specialization; *short-run hedonism,* evidenced by a lack of planning and absence of long-range goals; and *group autonomy,* expressed through intolerance of restraint except from the informal

---

[21]Albert K. Cohen, *Delinquent Boys* (New York: Free Press, 1955), p. 26. Copyright 1955 by The Free Press, a Corporation. Reprinted with permission of the Macmillan Publishing Co., Inc.

[22]Cohen, *Delinquent Boys,* p. 28.

pressures within the delinquent group. Relations with other groups, he feels, tend to be indifferent, hostile, or rebellious.[23]

The "carriers" of the delinquent subculture, according to Cohen, are working class boys. He concludes that juvenile delinquency in general, and the delinquent subculture in particular, are overwhelmingly concentrated in the male, working class sector of the juvenile population. Acknowledging that police and court biases may account in part for the correlation between juvenile delinquency and social class, Cohen nevertheless concludes, and almost all statistical analyses of juvenile delinquency agree, that delinquency *in general* is predominantly a working class phenomenon. His review of "self-reporting" studies that indicate considerable middle class delinquent behavior does not lead him to modify this conclusion.[24] As Cohen sees it, working class children are evaluated in accordance with middle class standards set by middle class teachers, social workers, ministers, adults managing settlement houses, etc. Working class children must come to terms with these norms, which are a tempered version of the Protestant ethic that requires one to strive, by dint of rational, ascetic, self-disciplined, and independent activity, *to achieve* in worldly affairs. *Success* is a sign of the exercise of moral qualities. The middle class norms emphasize control of violence and aggression, respect for property, and constructive use of leisure time.[25]

The working class boy sees himself not likely to succeed in school, at work, or anywhere else that middle class norms are applied. He sees himself at the bottom of the heap. He therefore joins with others like himself in rejecting the middle class culture and developing a subculture that opposes it. Delinquency, then, becomes, in a sense, a rebellion against the middle class, a form of class conflict. Frustrated by the fact that his socialization in the working class handicaps him for success in the middle class status system, he rebels against it and finds a solution in delinquency.[26]

Studies Employing Self-Reporting Questionnaires

The explanations offered by Kvaraceus and Miller and by Cohen assume that delinquency is largely a lower class urban phenomenon. Although this assumption is supported by most available statistics, there is a considerable body of research that indicates little or no difference in magnitude between lower class delinquent behavior and middle class delinquent behavior. Since the delinquencies of middle class children, according to some researchers, are not accurately reflected in official statistics, they have developed other instruments

[23]Cohen, *Delinquent Boys*, pp. 28–32.
[24]Cohen, *Delinquent Boys*, pp. 36–44.
[25]Cohen, *Delinquent Boys*, pp. 84–97.
[26]Cohen, *Delinquent Boys*, pp. 121–37.

for obtaining data. One such instrument is a questionnaire in which young people are asked to report instances of delinquent behavior. Another is the in-depth interview in which similar information is elicited.

Relationship of Status and Delinquency

In one study in which data were obtained through the use of anonymous questionnaires, Nye, Short, and Olson attempted to answer the question, Does delinquent behavior occur differentially by socioeconomic status?[27] The researchers rejected studies of delinquent behavior based on court records, police files, records maintained by correctional institutions, and other official sources. Such studies, they maintained, may be adequate for an examination of *official delinquency* but are unreliable as an index of *delinquent behavior* in the general population. The distinction between the concepts "official delinquency" and "delinquent behavior" was considered important by the researchers. Essentially, the difference is that delinquent behavior is behavior violating legal norms; it becomes official delinquency only when it results in action by official authority such as police and courts. Official delinquency thus represents a *reaction of society* to delinquent behavior.

In general, when sociologists refer to people as members of the lower, middle, or upper classes, they base their differentiations on the economic status of the child's family. The occupation of the head of the family, family income, educational attainments, or some combination of the three are generally used as criteria for placing a child in a particular class. In other words, *the class position of the family is ascribed to the child.* In this study, the father's occupation was used to place the child in one of four status groupings: (1) unskilled or semiskilled labor, (2) skilled labor and craftsmen, (3) white collar workers and small businessmen, and (4) professionals and large businessmen.

The sample for this study was drawn from two sources—selected high schools in several Western and Midwestern communities. The Western sample involved 2,350 boys and girls attending high school in three cities whose population ranged from ten to twenty-five thousand. The Midwestern sample was collected from questionnaires soliciting comparable data from 250 boys and 265 girls in grades nine through twelve in high schools in three communities with populations of under twenty-five hundred. No samples were taken from large cities or from large non-Caucasian groups. The young people in the sample were not classified as delinquent nor were any of the subjects school dropouts.

Delinquent behavior was measured by means of an anonymous delinquency checklist and by a delinquency scale constructed from it. The list was designed to include a broad sampling of juvenile misconduct, although it did

---

[27] F. Ivan Nye, James F. Short, Jr., and Virgil J. Olson, "Socioeconomic Status and Delinquent Behavior," *American Journal of Sociology* 63(January 1958):381–89.

not include the more serious types of delinquency such as rape, breaking and entering, armed robbery, etc.

Five statistical tests were applied to the data to determine significant differences in delinquent behavior by socioeconomic status. One test (chi-square test) showed the following differences to be significant: in the Western sample, "heterosexual relations" were committed most frequently by lower class boys, and "purposely damaging or destroying property" was committed most frequently by upper class boys and girls; in the Midwestern sample, "taking a car without permission" and "skipping school" were admitted most often by lower class boys, and "running away from home" was reported most frequently by upper class girls.

In all, 756 differences were tested for, and 33 were found to be significant. That is, 33 significant differences were found in the proportion of acts committed by a particular socioeconomic category. The two middle status groups had the highest proportion of delinquency in 4 instances; the upper status group in 13 instances; and the lower status group in 16 instances. From this the researchers concluded that either middle class delinquent behavior is underreported or middle class parents are more effective in socializing their children and controlling their behavior.

A Retest

Following essentially the same procedure as that used by Nye, Short, and Olson, Ronald Akers did a retest to determine differences in delinquent behavior by socioeconomic status.[28] The setting for Akers's 1961 investigation was a northeastern Ohio community of about 275,000 population. The subjects were all the ninth-grade boys and girls in three junior high schools who were present on the days the questionnaires were administered. The total number responding to the questionnaires was 992. Of these, 156 were excluded because of insufficient information, leaving a total of 429 boys and 407 girls to be used in the main analysis. The mean age was 14.9 years.

The father's occupation was used as an indicator of socioeconomic status, and the North-Hatt Occupational Prestige Scale was employed to rank the occupations into one of four categories. The questionnaires were passed out without advance notice in each of the three schools by classroom teachers after an orientation session with the researcher and principal (in two schools) or according to written instructions (in one school).

No significant differences were found when the responses of boys and girls for each socioeconomic status were combined. It is further evident from the results that no significant differences were found for either boys or girls. Mean delinquent behavior scores were computed for each socioeconomic

[28]Ronald I. Akers, "Socioeconomic Status and Delinquent Behavior: A Retest," *Journal of Research in Crime and Delinquency* 10(January 1964):38–46.

status, separately for boys and girls, and compared for differences. The highest mean score for both boys and girls was found in the lowest socioeconomic status. Further comparison showed a negative correlation between socioeconomic status and delinquent behavior for boys; a U-shaped pattern was found for girls. The differences were not significant, however.

Akers concluded that his results were, on the whole, in agreement with those of Nye, Short, and Olson. The main value of the retest, then, lies not in any positive contribution to theory as such but in the support it gives to the question raised by the Nye study; that is, can delinquent behavior be considered a function of lower class living, since the findings indicate no significant differences in delinquent behavior among socioeconomic strata?

A more recent study by Delos H. Kelly further affirms the foregoing conclusions.[29] Kelly's self-reported delinquency data was obtained from 173 seniors (both males and females) attending two high schools in western New York State. His analysis indicated data strongly supportive of the recent trends noted, namely that track position or "school status"—one's location in the reward structure of the school—is a far more important predictor of juvenile delinquency than the student's social class background. The "school status" theory approach underscores the need to consider not only where a student comes from in the societal class system but also his status in the school system.

In a later study in the Pacific Northwest on the social class issue, Delos H. Kelly teamed up with William T. Pink.[30] The relationship between status origins and delinquency was examined by use of a range of status-origin indicators together with self-report and official measures of delinquency. Data were drawn from an ongoing longitudinal investigation of adolescents in a county in the Pacific Northwest. A random sample was drawn of 309 male sophomores attending high school. Social class origins were determined by: (1) A. B. Hollingshead's Index of Social Position combined with an Oregon Supplement to classify the father's occupation, (2) the father's educational level, (3) the mother's educational level, and (4) an index combining the three preceding measures. Three separate groups of dependent variables were selected: *(a)* self-reports on involvement in rebellious activities, e.g., drinking with friends; *(b)* hypothetical situations involving conflicting demands between peers and adult authorities, e.g. peers vs. police, *(c)* actual involvement in youth rebellion and delinquency e.g., "drink beer"; and *(d)* actual involvement in the juvenile justice system based on court records. Levels of association were computed for each status level using the four indicators and eight rebellion items. With few exceptions all four measures of status origins offered extremely low predictive utility vis-à-vis delinquent involvement. Kelly and Pink con-

---

[29]Delos H. Kelly, "Status Origins, Track Positions, and Delinquent Involvements: A Self-Report Analysis," *Sociological Quarterly* 16(Spring 1975): 264–71.

[30]Delos H. Kelly and William T. Pink, "Status Origins. Youth Rebellion, and Delinquency: A Reexamination of the Class Issue," *Journal of Youth and Adolescence* 4(December 1975):339–47.

cluded that future efforts might instead be directed at unraveling more fruitful indicators of delinquency. They recommended examining the structure, process, and implications of differential status allocation. They concluded that tracking the student's status within the educational system was a more productive approach to predicting delinquency than simply examining the youth's social class background in the society.

Sex, Class, and Delinquency

In another study comparing delinquent behavior of boys and girls in different socioeconomic strata, Voss also obtained self-reported data.[31] The subjects of the study were 620 students in a public intermediate school. Attention was focused primarily on the information provided by 284 male respondents. The data were gathered in Honolulu, a metropolitan center in which the majority of the population is Oriental. Anonymous questionnaires were administered to a 15.5 percent random sample of seventh-grade students. The researcher recorded on a chart the number of times a youth had committed a particular act and the minimum frequency required for the youth to be classified delinquent. Children were placed in four classes based on the socioeconomic position of the father. The four strata were (1) unskilled and semiskilled labor, (2) skilled labor and craftsmen, (3) white collar workers and small businessmen, and (4) professionals and large businessmen.

The data were subjected to three tests in an attempt to locate significant differences in the incidence of delinquent behavior. In the first test the distribution of most and least delinquent groups of boys and girls by socioeconomic status was tested. The girls in the various status levels were found not to differ significantly. However, for boys, socioeconomic status was found to be significantly related to incidence of delinquent behavior. Boys in the two upper social strata reported more extensive involvement in delinquent activity than did boys in the other two groups. The reported delinquent activity by groups was: Group 1, 29.2 percent; Group 2, 29.9 percent; Group 3, 52.4 percent; and Group 4, 40.0 percent. The second test included only those boys who had reported at least three serious delinquent acts. A slightly larger percentage of the boys in the two higher status levels reported at least three serious delinquent acts, but the difference was not significant. The third test, which was designed to determine differences in specific delinquent acts, was conducted under the assumption that the types of delinquent behavior reported might differ by status level. Of the eighteen categories tested, only one significant relationship was observed. The number of those who "purposely damaged or destroyed property" was reported to be higher in the two upper strata.

The researcher concluded that the incidence of admitted illegal behavior

[31]Harwin L. Voss, "Socioeconomic Status and Reported Delinquent Behavior," *Social Problems* 13(Winter 1966):314–24.

of lower status children did not differ significantly from those of middle and upper status children. The fact that boys in the two higher strata reported more property destruction appeared to conflict with Cohen's position. If vandalism is part of the delinquent subculture, as Cohen says it is, one would expect vandalism by the lower class children to be more frequent.

Class, Peer Pressure, and Delinquency

Erickson and Empey used self-reported data in an attempt to find more significant aspects concerning the who and where of juvenile delinquency as related to class position and peers.[32] They were concerned primarily with studying the child's relationship to peers. They noted that explanations of delinquency are often based on the assumption that the child's class position and his exposure or lack of exposure to educational and other socializing activities are directly related to delinquent behavior. Because lower class children lack the "successes and satisfactions" of the upper and middle class children, it is believed they are more frequently inclined to become delinquent.

One theory suggested by the authors is that "a low-class child joins with delinquent peers and participates in delinquent activities because these things represent an alternative means for acquiring many of the social and emotional satisfactions that other children obtain from conventional sources." If their theory is accurate, the study should indicate that (1) delinquency is more indicative of the lower class than of the middle or upper classes, (2) peer relations are more predictive of delinquent or nondelinquent behavior than is lower class position, and (3) children from the lower class are more apt to associate with and have a commitment to delinquents than are children from middle or upper classes.

In testing the validity of these hypotheses, the authors used a sample of white males, aged fifteen to seventeen, selected at random from a county population of 110,000 in Utah. Racial minorities were excluded since they did not represent a numerically significant portion of the population in Utah. Two hundred boys were selected, at random, from groups of boys who had been in prison, boys who had been to court once, boys who were on probation, and boys who had never been to court. The occupation of the guardian or father was used as the basis for defining class level. The lower class included holders of unskilled or semiskilled jobs; the middle class included skilled and white collar workers and small businessmen; the upper class encompassed most of the professional occupations, corporate positions, and scientists and artists.

In relation to twenty-two various delinquent acts (which were grouped into three categories: petty thefts, and common delinquency such as illegal

---

[32]Erickson and Empey, "Class Position, Peers and Delinquency," pp. 268–82.

drinking, fighting, truancy, etc.), each subject was interviewed personally and asked: (1) had he ever committed such an offense, (2) if so, how many times, and (3) if so, how often had he been caught, arrested, or brought into court. More serious crimes such as narcotics, arson, etc., were eliminated because they did not play a significant or frequent role in the lives of the youth in the sample.

Erickson and Empey found no significant correlation between class position and delinquency. A slight difference between the classes was explained by a lower amount of delinquency in the upper class rather than a high degree of occurrence in the lower class. The study also indicated that there was much correlation of responses between the lower and middle classes. In studying the association with delinquents, results showed that those boys already delinquent were more apt to associate with other delinquents, although this did not necessarily infer identification with the group. All classes responded negatively to "informing on a peer" or "ratting." The authors concluded from their results that social class position is less predictive of delinquency than is association and identification with delinquent peers.

Erickson and Empey summarize their findings as follows:

1. There was a slight but statistically reliable relationship between social class and delinquency. However, when variance was traced, it was discovered that the correlation was significant more because upper class respondents differed from the other two than because low class respondents differed from the other two. Middle and low class did not differ significantly from each other.

2. The same pattern characterized the relationship of social class to delinquent associates. The upper class group was significantly less inclined than the other two to have delinquent associates. Middle and low class respondents did not differ.

3. The pattern was confirmed even more in the analysis of respondent commitment to peer expectations. Upper class respondents were significantly less committed than others to the expectations of their peers, delinquent or nondelinquent. But, in addition, there was some suggestion that it was the middle rather than the low class group which had the greatest commitment of all.

The data would definitely not support the notion that peer standards have more importance for the low than the middle class juvenile. In fact, these findings might lead one to hypothesize that because they are departing perhaps even further from the expectations of their parents than low class children, middle class offenders have greater need for peer support than low class offenders.

4. Delinquent associates and peer commitment variables proved to be far more predictive of delinquent behavior than did social class. As

a part of an overall pattern, it strongly implied the need to examine more carefully the role of peers, as contrasted to class, in attempting to understand delinquency.[33]

Social Class, Community, and Delinquency

Most self-reported delinquency studies have drawn their samples from small cities and from Caucasian populations. It may very well be that in the small community the differences in behavioral patterns of adolescents in the various social strata are not very pronounced. There appears, however, to be a world of difference in behavioral patterns, performance in school, and style of life when boys who live in urban slums are compared with boys of any social class who live in small cities and suburban areas. Most researchers have indicated an awareness of these differences.

Clark and Wenninger used self-administered questionnaires in a study of differences in delinquent behavior exhibited by members of different social classes in four types of communities.[34] A total of 1,154 students drawn from the sixth through twelfth grades of the public school systems of four different types of communities were the subjects. The students responded to a self-administered, anonymous questionnaire given in groups of from twenty to forty students by the senior researcher, John P. Clark.

Considerable precautions were taken to insure reliability and validity of responses. The students who were chosen came from four types of communities: (1) rural farm (farms and very small villages), (2) lower class urban (ghetto-type area of a large metropolis), (3) industrial city (diffuse, autonomous small industrial city), and (4) upper class urban (wealthy suburb of large city). An inventory of thirty-eight offenses was assembled from delinquency scales, legal statutes, and *FBI Uniform Crime Reports.* No sex offenses were included. Respondents were asked if they had committed any of the listed offenses within the past year and the number of times they had committed each.

In order to determine whether significant differences existed in the incidence of illegal behavior among the various types of communities, a two-step procedure was followed. First, each community was assigned a rank for each offense on the basis of the percentage of respondents admitting commission of that offense. The resultant numerical total provided a very crude overall measure of the relative degree to which the same population from each community had been involved in illegal behavior during the past year. Second, the communities were arranged in the order given above and the significance of

---

[33]Erickson and Empey, "Class Position, Peers and Delinquency," p. 281.

[34]Clark and Wenninger, "Socio-economic Class and Area as Correlates of Illegal Behavior Among Juveniles."

the differences between adjacent pairs was determined. Only comparisons involving either industrial city or lower urban versus upper urban or rural farm resulted in any significant differences.

The findings showed that juveniles from the lower urban community reported significantly more illegal behavior than did the juveniles from the upper urban community and that the two lower class urban communities—lower urban and industrial city—were quite similar in their high rates of delinquency while the lower class rural community was similar to the upper class urban community in having a much lower rate. On most of the offenses, youths from the lower urban and industrial city communities reported no significant differences. Rural farm youngsters were more prone to commit unsophisticated acts of deviance consonant with rural life. The greatest difference between rates of illegal conduct occurred between the lower urban and upper urban communities. The researchers failed to detect any significant differences in illegal behavior rates among the social classes of rural and small urban areas. However, significant differences were found, both in quantity and quality of illegal acts, among communities consisting of one predominant socioeconomic class. The lower class areas had higher delinquency rates, particularly for the more serious offenses.

Clark and Wenninger feel that their research suggests some interesting relationships:

1. The pattern of illegal behavior within small communities or "status areas" of a large metropolitan center is determined by the predominant class of that area.

2. Although juveniles in all communities admit participation in a variety of offenses, serious offenses are more likely to be committed by lower class urban youth.

3. Present explanations that rely heavily on socioeconomic class as an all-determining factor should be further specified to include data relative to the type of community involved.

Another interesting factor related to social class, community, and delinquency is the perception of "the majority" toward who is the delinquent. The white majority tends to take it for granted that minority group youngsters are more likely to be delinquent, and they are not as "alarmed" by minority youth delinquency as they are by the delinquent acts of white majority children. A recent study by psychologists Edward Dietiker and Edlynn Nau supports this perception.[35]

The researchers presented three short profiles like the following to sixty-four white mothers from a local PTA.

---

[35]*Human Behavior* (September 1976).

Nine-year-old Jimmy has a personality disorder: he is shy and anxious, plays alone and his teacher says he is afraid to give a book report in class. Randy, too, is a loner who suffers from a conduct disorder: he seems to have been "born angry," swearing at everybody, fighting at the slightest provocation, and hellbent on destruction. Gary can be just as destructive, but, as a social delinquent, he carries out his antisocial acts as a member of a gang known for its truancy, shoplifting and vandalism.

The sixty-four white mothers read the short profiles on three such boys and then rate the severity of their behavior problem on a scale from one to seven. Some of the children were described as white, some black, and some Chicano. A control group of sixteen mothers was given no information about the ethnicity of the three boys they evaluated.

Dietiker and Nau's hypothesis was confirmed. The white mothers tended to underestimate the severity of all three disorders when rating black or Chicano boys as compared with the "problem child" who was described as white. White mothers were most alarmed about deviant behavior when they knew for a fact that the child in question was white rather than a member of a minority group. Furthermore, the mothers in the control group made no distinctions as to the severity of the three types of disorders, while there were significant differences in each case where ethnicity was known The findings for white mothers seem to suggest that what they consider "sick or deviant in their own is somehow to be expected from the children of other ethnic groups."

Another study—of police officers—by Marcia Garrett and James F. Short tends to support the Dietiker and Nau hypotheses that there are differential perceptions of lower class delinquents by members of the community.[36] The Garrett and Short study dealt with police attitudes towards delinquents. Data was analyzed to determine police images of delinquency: their estimates of the delinquent involvement of boys from different social class backgrounds and their predictions, on the basis of first official contacts, of individual boys subsequently repeating. Data were collected in three cities. Ninety-three unstructured interviews of police were conducted; also questionnaires were administered to 453 officers. Officers' predictions about future delinquency were tested over a six-year followup period. Police in widely different settings base their judgments on "street" experience and similar theories of delinquency causation linking social class background, parental neglect, and delinquent behavior. Police perceived lower class minority group boys as more likely to be involved in delinquent conduct than boys with "higher" family and social

[36]Marcia Garrett and James F. Short, "Social Class and Delinquency: Predictions and Outcomes of Police-Juvenile Encounters," *Social Problems* 22(February 1975):368–83.

class backgrounds. The officers' predictions for individual boys prove to be inaccurate when measured by official contact records over the six-year period.

Hidden Delinquency

While there have been few studies focusing on the differences in types of delinquency committed by children of different social classes, a study by Empey and Erickson into "hidden delinquency" indicated that important differences do exist.[37] The subjects of the study were 180 white male youths, ages fifteen to seventeen, living in Utah. Fifty of the boys were high school students who had never been to court, 30 had been to court once, 50 were on probation, and 50 were incarcerated offenders. The boys in each of the four categories were selected at random from the respective population of which they were a part.

The method of study was to interview personally each of the 180 boys, questioning him about twenty-two different offenses which were defined in detail. The respondent was asked if he had ever committed the offense; how many times; if he had ever been caught, arrested, or brought to court for that offense; and if so, how many times. Court records were checked, and it was determined that the respondents were truthful about the offenses. Social status was determined by the occupation of the father. Of the three status levels, 29 percent of the boys were in the lower, 55 percent in the middle, and 16 percent in the upper category.

A tremendous number (in the thousands) of violations were reported. Virtually all respondents had committed not one but a variety of offenses, and 90 percent of these offenses were undetected and unacted upon. In regard to the amount or number of delinquent acts committed, the data provided little support for the notion that there are status differences. Respondents on one status level were neither more nor less delinquent than respondents on another status level (two kinds of statistical analysis were used to provide a better comparison). However, there were some hints that there were some differences among status levels with respect to *kinds* of delinquency, especially among the minority of respondents who have been the most delinquent. Of the upper status delinquents, the major offense was "defying parents." Middle status delinquency was highest in areas of general traffic violations, theft and forgery, *defying authority,* property violations, and armed robbery. Low status delinquents were high on the following offenses: driving without a license, stealing (over $50.00), auto theft, buying alcohol, using narcotics, skipping school, fighting, and assault. The above differences for all three levels held up among incarcerated offenders as well as those not officially defined as delinquent.

---

[37]LaMar T. Empey and Maynard L. Erickson, "Hidden Delinquency and Social Status," *Social Forces* 44(June 1966):546–54.

Class Status and Serious Delinquency

Another study by Reiss and Rhodes indicated more serious delinquencies committed by lower status boys even when based on self-reported delinquencies.[38] In their study involving 9,238 white boys, twelve years old and over, registered in one of the public, private, or parochial junior or senior high schools of Davidson County, Tennessee, during the 1957 school year, Reiss and Rhodes divided the boys into three status groups defined according to the occupation of the head of the household:

1. *Low status:* children of laborers, including farm laborers, operatives, kindred workers, service workers (except protective service workers), peddlers, and door-to-door salesmen.
2. *Middle status:* all craftsmen, foremen, clerical and kindred workers, managers and proprietors of small businesses, sales workers of wholesale and retail stores, and technicians allied to professional services.
3. *High status:* all managers, officials, proprietors, and professional and semiprofessional workers not included in the middle-status category, and sales workers in finance, insurance, and real estate.

Delinquency rates were based on a combined total of official and unofficial cases known to the juvenile court. The researchers concluded that there was no simple relationship between ascribed social status and delinquency. Their data led them to the conclusions that:

1. There is more frequent and serious delinquent deviation in the lower than in the middle strata when the self-reports of delinquent deviation by boys are examined. This is true for all classes of deviation: career- and peer-oriented delinquents, nonconforming isolates, and conforming nonachievers.

2. *The career-oriented delinquent is found only among lower class boys.*

3. Peer-oriented delinquency is the most common form of delinquent organization at both status levels.

4. The major type of lower status boy is a conforming nonachiever, while the conforming achiever is the major type in the middle class.

5. Conformers are more likely to be isolates than are nonconformers. The lone delinquent is infrequent in a population of boys. If it is assumed that in many lower class areas the pressures of groups are toward nonconforming activities, then at least in these communities isolation from the group may be the price of social conformity. Conforming isolates are more frequent in blue collar than in white collar strata. There is much more support for group-organized conventional behavior in middle class areas.

---

[38] Albert J. Reiss, Jr., and Albert Lewis Rhodes, "The Distribution of Juvenile Delinquency in the Social Class Structure," *American Sociological Review* 26(October 1961):720–32.

Limitations of Self-Reporting

If we accept the studies based on self-reporting as valid, we must conclude that there is no substantial difference between the amount of delinquent behavior committed by lower class boys and by middle class boys. Several reasons for doubting the findings of self-report studies with respect to the relationship between social class and delinquency have been suggested by Hirschi: (1) The self-report measure of delinquency is invalid for this purpose. (2) The samples used in these studies deal only with a restricted class range. (3) The measures of socioeconomic status are invalid. (4) The effects of socioeconomic status are suppressed by the effects of some third variable. (5) Contrary to their assertions, some of the "no-difference" self-report studies do show a relation between socioeconomic status and delinquency.[39]

Furthermore, the acts reported by middle class youths, although technically illegal, may not be truly comparable with offenses charged against lower class youths. For example, a fourteen-year-old middle class boy, a subject in one self-report study, took a can of beer from his mother's refrigerator without permission and drank it. He reported himself guilty of two delinquent acts, stealing, and illegal use of a drug or intoxicant. This offense can hardly be considered comparable with stealing a bicycle and selling it to buy drugs, acts for which a lower class boy may be found delinquent by a court. On some anonymous questionnaires the two respondents would be checking the same boxes. Furthermore, middle class youths might be considered more likely to exaggerate their "admitted" delinquencies in order to assert their masculinity. It is necessary to take this possibility into consideration when discussing middle class delinquency. Certainly, the self-image of the youth exerts an influence on his responses to such questionnaires.

In the context of these issues, Fannin and Clinard found important differences in the conception of self as a male held by lower and middle class delinquents.[40] Random samples of lower and middle class white delinquents committed to a training school in a Midwestern state were the subjects of their study. The boys, sixteen and seventeen years of age, were from urban areas with a population of at least 300,000. Each boy was given a class rank on the basis of his father's or his guardian's level of education and occupation. The most crucial information was elicited through in-depth interviews and the administration of self-conception scales. Official records were used to determine class affiliation and reported delinquent histories. Operationally, self-conception as a male was defined by the relative intensity of specific traits that the delinquent felt characterized him when he was placed, verbally, in varying situations that made him explicitly aware of his sex status. A list of fifteen traits

---

[39]Travis Hirschi, *Causes of Delinquency* (Berkeley: University of California Press, 1969), p. 70.

[40]Leon F. Fannin and Marshall B. Clinard, "Differences in the Conception of Self as a Male among Lower and Middle-Class Delinquents," *Social Problems* 13(Fall 1965):205–14.

was administered three times. The subjects were asked to rank the traits contained in each list according to how they felt the traits actually described them as males (actual self); how they would like to be as males (ideal self); and, last, how they felt other people in general believed them to be as males.

Lower class boys felt themselves to be (actual self) tougher, more powerful, fierce, fearless, and dangerous than middle class boys. Middle class delinquents conceived of themselves as being more loyal, clever, smart, smooth, and bad. Lower class boys would like to be (ideal self) tougher, harder, and more violent than middle class boys, while the latter would like to be more loyal, lucky, and firm. Generally speaking, lower class delinquents felt themselves to be "tough guys," while middle class delinquents felt themselves to be "loyal and daring comrades."

The vast majority of lower class delinquents, 84 percent, had committed at least one robbery or assault, compared with 28 percent of middle class boys. Lower class delinquents also fought singly and in groups significantly more often than middle class delinquents. Lower class boys also carried weapons more frequently than middle class boys did. Fannin and Clinard concluded that a significant proportion of offenses involving physical violence may be committed by delinquents who stress certain "masculine" traits in their self-conceptions, and this helps to channel and legitimize their violence.

Some Explanations of Middle Class Delinquency

Although there is ample evidence that the vast majority of young people adjudicated delinquents by our juvenile courts are from working class families, there are many whose families are middle class. If we take into consideration research indicating more favorable treatment of middle class children by the police and the courts, we must conclude that there are probably far more middle class delinquents than the statistics indicate. Furthermore, the self-report studies suggest that the incidence of delinquent behavior among middle class boys may be as great as that among lower or working class boys. Since we would expect middle class parents to provide socialization strongly favoring conformity to the law and since middle class children have few, if any, economic needs not satisfied by their parents, how can we account for what is claimed to be a large and growing amount of delinquent behavior among middle class youth? Some efforts to account for this phenomenon will be presented in the next section.

Kvaraceus and Miller, who related lower class delinquency to such focal concerns of the lower class as trouble, toughness, smartness, and autonomy, consider middle class delinquency in relation to the focal concerns of the middle class. They note that middle class concerns are centered around:

1. Achievement through directed work effort
2. Deferment of immediate pleasures and gains for future goals
3. Responsibility
4. Maintenance of the solidarity of the nuclear family
5. Child-rearing
6. Accumulation of material goods and maintenance of property
7. Education
8. Formal organization
9. Cleanliness
10. Ambition

Kvaraceus and Miller feel that orientation toward these concerns deters middle class children from delinquency and that the legal codes support the middle class focal concerns.[41]

The middle class tradition exerts pressure on children to postpone gratification. Self-denial and impulse control is encouraged. The increase in middle class delinquency may be attributed, in part, to a weakening of this tradition. Installment buying and buying on impulse, which have in the past been part of the lower class culture, have spread to the middle class and weakened the idea that success is achieved through deferred gratification, self-discipline, and hard work.

Kvaraceus and Miller have also noted the tendency of lower class fads and culture to influence middle class youth through a process of diffusion of the lower class culture. They also feel that when serious delinquency occurs in middle class groups, it may be a portent of pathological behavior since it is conduct counter to the definitions of significant reference group. They point out that "the middle-class youngster who engages in norm-violating behavior may often be viewed more usefully as a 'behavior problem' than as a 'delinquent'."[42]

Albert K. Cohen, who sees the delinquent subculture as representing the working class boy's rebellion against the middle class and its values, also offers an explanation for middle class delinquency.[43] He describes middle class standards in much the same way as Kvaraceus and Miller describe middle class focal concerns. Cohen recognizes that the circumstances that give rise to the delinquent subculture may be found in families considered middle class by purely economic criteria. Families that are middle class in terms of income and occupation are usually middle class in terms of culture. However, some families that are middle class in economic terms and live in middle class neighborhoods may be working class in terms of the experiences they provide their

[41]Kvaraceus and Miller, *Delinquent Behavior,* vol. 1, pp. 77–86.

[42]Kvaraceus and Miller, *Delinquent Behavior,* p. 86.

[43]Cohen, *Delinquent Boys,* pp. 88–102.

children. For example, a worker brought up in a working class area and hostile to middle class values may increase his income to middle class levels and may even be promoted to a middle class occupational level without changing his attitudes toward middle class values. He may move into a suburban middle class area, resent tax increases, vote Republican, and object to welfare programs in conformity with his new interests and his middle class neighbors. His children, however, may be rejected by their middle class neighbors and may never develop any loyalty to the middle class "focal" concerns with which their middle class peers have been indoctrinated.

While recognizing the above as a possible explanation of middle class delinquency, Cohen tends, as do Kvaraceus and Miller, to view middle class delinquency in terms of personal pathology. He discusses Talcott Parsons's view that in our society mother has the dominant role in socialization. According to this view, the father is preoccupied with his occupational role and is away from the home most of the time. Because of this, as Parsons notes, the child, particularly the middle class suburban child, is likely to perceive his mother as the principal exemplar of morality, source of discipline, and object of identification.[44] The middle class delinquent knows it is shameful for a boy to be like a woman and feels constrained to rebel against impulses that suggest femininity and to exaggerate behavior that connotes masculinity. "Goodness" represents femininity and "badness" masculinity. Hence, middle class delinquency may be a form of masculine protest.

Cohen also notes that society fails to give the middle class boy a meaningful occupational role, and it prolongs his dependence by requiring many years of schooling. These latter considerations, added to sex-role anxieties and masculine protest, Cohen concludes, may provide a basis for boys who share these problems to come together and create a delinquent subculture. Thus, while the working class delinquent subculture represents a revolt against the middle class, the middle class delinquent subculture represents a revolt against "femininity" and dependence.[45]

A study by D. Frease, K. Polk, and F. L. Richmond, concluded that Albert Cohen's delinquency theory was vulnerable to demonstrations of similar qualities, as well as similar quantities of delinquency between middle and working class groups.[46] In their analyses of questionnaire data from a high school male population, no significant differences in incidence of delinquency emerged between classes. They further concluded that no significant differences obtain between classes of delinquents on items tapping the peer or subcultural dimensions Cohen considers particularly characteristic of working

---

[44]Talcott Parsons, "Certain Primary Sources and Patterns of Aggression in the Social Structure of the Western World," *Psychiatry* 10(May 1947):167–81.

[45]Cohen, *Delinquent Boys,* pp. 157–69.

[46]D. Frease, K. Polk, and F. L. Richmond, "Social Class, School Experience, and Delinquency," *Criminology* 44(December 1974):84–96.

class delinquency. And, lastly, they found that delinquency was shown to be related to academic performance, regardless of class.

Ralph England raises the following objections to Parsons's explanation of middle class delinquency, which Cohen adopted:

> A number of objections to this theory can be raised. (*a*) In the process of "protesting masculinity" why is the trait of adult male responsibility shunned while other presumed traits of the male (loud, aggressive, rambunctious behavior) are adopted? (*b*) One can imagine middle-class boys who live in dormitory suburbs and large cities having some difficulty picturing their fathers' occupational roles, but this may not be true in smaller cities and in towns where the fathers' places of work are more readily accessible for visits, and where their roles are less likely to be obscured by employment in bureaucratic organizations. (*c*) How can the participation of girls in the youth culture be explained by Parsons' theory? (*d*) Are mothers' roles especially ubiquitous in communities where commuting time for the father is not so great that he cannot be with his family meaningfully except on weekends? "Catching the 7:05" each morning before the children are up and returning in the evening shortly before their bedtime is a pattern found only in our largest cities. (*e*) Is it to be assumed that the seeming increases in middle-class delinquency since the Second World War is the result of a postwar increase in sons' difficulties in identifying with their fathers' roles, in the absence of basic postwar changes in our society's occupation structure?[47]

England sees the emergence of a teenage culture as a result of increased communication among teenagers since World War II. He feels the following conditions have influenced the emergence of a teenage culture:

> 1. The enlargement of a market for teenage goods and services. The wide distribution of such teenage items as rock and roll movies, records, portable phonographs, motor scooters, unusual clothing, and other popular items is contributing to the growth of a nationally shared but age-restricted material culture.
>
> 2. Increased reliance on canned material in radio broadcasting has brought into prominence the disc jockey who caters to teenagers.
>
> 3. Television programming of teen dance shows and the promulgation by TV of a particular image of teenage life.

---

[47]Ralph W. England, Jr., "A Theory of Middle-Class Juvenile Delinquency," *Journal of Criminal Law, Criminology, and Police Science* 50(March–April 1960):536. Reprinted by special permission of the Journal of Criminal Law, Criminology and Police Science. Copyright © 1960 by Northwestern University School of Law, Vol. 50, No. 6.

4. The growth of teenage magazines with emphasis on hedonistic values, play, and diversion, and not on preparation for responsible adulthood.

5. Public attention given to juvenile problems.[48]

As a result, according to England, a complex of attitudes and values is evolving that tends to control and motivate teenagers in ways consistent with their role as a youthful group having leisure, relatively ample spending money, and few responsibilities. England is, of course, describing middle class youth, and he sees an emerging culture with increasing institutionalization of immature and irresponsible hedonism. If the teenager's urgent need for status affirmation is met by the teenage culture, it becomes necessary for the adolescent to reject adult influences that threaten it and accept those that give it support. Hard work, thrift, study, and self-denial are values running counter to the short-run hedonism of the teenage culture.

Among the ways in which this teenage culture gives rise to delinquency are:

1. Driving privileges are abused by playing "chicken," drag racing, speeding, and in other ways using a car as a plaything. Also, "borrowing" cars without permission for joyrides.

2. Competitive spirit is applied to fights, car chases, and vandalism as games.

3. Sex and love are redefined as ends in themselves.

4. Alcoholic beverages are used for the hedonistic purpose of intoxication. Drinking parties are held in automobiles, parks, and motels to avoid adult interference.[49]

Thus, middle class delinquency is largely attributed to the hedonistic pursuits emphasized by the teenage culture and its preoccupation with play.

Scott and Vaz maintain that the bulk of middle class delinquency occurs in the course of *customary, nondelinquent* activities and falls within the limits of adolescent group norms.[50] They note that under changing social and economic conditions, the patriarchally controlled family gave way to a more "democratic" family unit in which children shared in the decision-making process. The family atmosphere became more permissive and achievement goals more difficult to inculcate. The school, too, has become more permissive. As a result, the adolescent role has become vague, and the distinction between right and wrong soft-pedaled. The adolescent is left to define for himself what

[48]England, "A Theory of Middle-Class Juvenile Delinquency," pp. 537–38.

[49]England, "A Theory of Middle-Class Juvenile Delinquency," p. 539.

[50]Joseph W. Scott and Edmund W. Vaz, "A Perspective on Middle-Class Delinquency," *Canadian Journal of Economics and Political Science* 29(August 1963):324–35.

is "right" conduct. Peer-group relationships substitute for ambiguous family relationships and influence the teenager. Conformity to peer-group norms is required and these oppose scholastic effort. Teenage participation is rewarded since even his parents want him to obtain this sort of social approval. A middle class youth culture similar to the teenage culture described by England has developed, and the middle class youth cannot jeopardize his status in his peer group. Joyriding, drunkenness, and sexual intercourse are variations of conduct patterns that are acceptable. Scott and Vaz describe the process as follows:

> In the course of legitimate, everyday activities and relationships within the middle-class youth culture, "veiled competition" for status leads to varying efforts at innovation. Such innovation covers a wide range of exploratory acts and is likely to be tentative, uncertain, and ambiguous. Yet because there is "mutual exploration and joint elaboration" of behavior among adolescents, such small, almost unobtrusive, acts gradually lead to unanticipated elaboration beyond the limits of legitimacy—into the realm of delinquency and the illegitimate. But since each succeeding exploratory act is so small an increment to the previously acceptable pattern, at no stage in the process need the behavior be perceived as "delinquent." Once these patterns develop and are socially rewarded, they generate their own morality, norms, standards, and rewards, It is in this manner that delinquent behavior gradually emerges from socially acceptable, nondelinquent, activities among adolescents within the middle-class youth culture.[51]

Just as England attributed middle class delinquency to the hedonistic emphasis of the teenage culture and its preoccupation with play, Scott and Vaz attribute it to the need to conform to a middle class youth culture, with its prominent, culturally esteemed patterns. Delinquent behavior of the middle class youth, according to this view, can best be understood through knowledge of the structure and content of the *legitimate* youth culture.

Conclusions and Implications

The distinction between strata and social classes is an important one. Persons in the lower strata may be socially and economically mobile. A person in a lower stratum who is upwardly mobile may commit delinquencies and crimes when frustrated by the denial of employment or other opportunity. However, if he accepts the system and aspires to upward mobility within the system, affording him opportunities for success should result in conforming rather than delinquent behavior on his part. We would expect this to occur even if

---

[51]Scott and Vaz, "A Perspective on Middle-Class Delinquency," pp. 329–30.

he joins with others to form a delinquent gang. If he is an "egoist," "selfish," a "rugged individualist," he will be primarily concerned with his own welfare, his own road upward. With respect to such persons, a class-conflict theory or interest-group theory explaining their delinquency is inapplicable. Ralf Dahrendorf, in explaining why there is no socialism in the United States, points out that it is still possible to escape the spell of the capitalist economy or at least the narrow cycle of wage labor.[52] The possibility of both vertical and horizontal mobility exists. A large number of potential or actual members of suppressed classes have the possibility to rise socially and economically. People can move from one social position to another as individuals without class action. Delinquent acts on the part of such persons are individual acts for selfish reasons. Conformity can be obtained when vehicles leading to the aspired roles and positions are provided.

If, on the other hand, a person identifies with an underprivileged class and acts in concert with others who so identify themselves, we have an interest group in conflict with the establishment. Such an individual will not be seeking upward mobility for himself as a person, but for his group or class. Persons who feel they have been deprived of life chances at success, and develop a class consciousness, commit offenses that are aggressions against the oppressive society. Their objective position in the stratified order is not sufficient to categorize them. Identification with a social class is a subjective matter. Richard Centers found, for example, that although 70 percent of the people objectively determined to be white collar workers, professionals, and businessmen identified themselves with the *middle class,* approximately 30 percent identified themselves as *working class.* What is even more important, those who identified themselves as middle class tended to be conservative, while about a fourth of those who identified themselves as working class tended to be radical, and some 30 percent took an intermediate position between radical and conservative.[53] This would lead us to hypothesize that many of the middle stratum boys who engage in delinquent behavior may be from families that identify as working class and are less committed to support of the establishment than their middle class neighbors.

On the basis of the variety of research cited here and other data known to the authors, we would summarize the relationship between delinquency and class as follows:

1. The vast majority of adjudicated juvenile delinquents in the United States are from the lower strata of society.

2. Since in the American society children are socialized to be "selfish," "egoistic," and "individualistic," they will take available roads toward upward mobility. If denied access and frustrated in their movement, such children may

---

[52]Ralf Dahrendorf, *Conflict After Class,* the Third Noel Buxton Lecture of the University of Essex, March 2, 1967 (London: Longmans, for the University of Essex, 1967), pp. 8–9.

[53]Centers, *The Psychology of Social Classes,* pp. 128–35.

be moved to engage in delinquent behavior to accomplish the goals held forth by the society.

3. When upward mobility is denied over a long period of time to large numbers of young people, they may begin to identify themselves as belonging to an underprivileged group or social class which has been unfairly oppressed. The Black Power and Brown Power movements of the late 1960s, although on the surface seeking racial identities, were, in effect, tendencies in the direction of class consciousness, motivated to obtain a power base through solidarity of "brothers and sisters."

4. As consciousness of class begins to develop, the motivation for delinquent action shifts from individual goals to group goals, and the established order becomes the enemy. A good deal of the nonutilitarian, malicious, negativistic, and aggressive action described by Cohen may therefore be directed at the oppressive establishment.

5. Society may deal with actions of social classes directed at its established order by physical suppression or by making some concessions to the disaffected classes. Severe suppression has been moderately successful in Fascist countries. Where this occurs, solidary action or group conflict becomes, at least for a time, impossible. Conflict may then be converted into individual delinquent actions and, in some cases, violent acts of terrorism.[54] Therefore it is apparent that the complex forces of status oppression and injustice can account for a significant amount of juvenile delinquency.

---

[54]Dahrendorf, *Conflict After Class,* pp. 18–21.

Part Two

SIGNIFICANT PROBLEM AREAS IN JUVENILE DELINQUENCY

IN PART ONE we described the nature and extent of juvenile delinquency, the juvenile court, and some attributes of young people who are adjudicated delinquent. We then discussed the relation between the principal socializing agencies—family, school, and peer groups—and delinquency. In this discussion delinquency was viewed as representing a failure in the socialization process to achieve conforming behavior in those youths labeled "delinquent." In the chapters on juvenile gang patterns and social class and delinquency, we noted that a substantial percentage, perhaps a majority of those labeled "delinquent," had been socialized into a delinquent subculture with a delinquent value system. We also noted that some of the members, and particularly the leaders of violent gangs, were sociopaths.

In Chapter 8, we shall attempt to distinguish the socialized delinquent from the sociopathic delinquent and describe in detail the sociopathic delinquent and ways of treating him. In Chapter 9, we shall deal with the relationship between violence of adults in society and violent behavior on the part of children. Vandalism, as a form of violent behavior, will be discussed, as will the effect of violence in the media, particularly television, on the behavior of children. In Chapter 10, we shall deal with drug abuse, both as a way of acquiring the status of delinquent and as a factor in other forms of delinquent behavior. We shall also closely examine the symbiotic relationship between adult narcotic use and drug abuse by young people.

Chapter
8

Socialized and Sociopathic Delinquents

JUVENILES WHO VIOLATE the law manifest a variety of personality characteristics. Most research indicates that delinquents are no more emotionally disturbed than the general population. However, they may appear to be more emotionally disturbed than most law-abiding youngsters because they are more often subject to the close analysis of social workers, psychologists, and psychiatrists, who tend to perceive their delinquency in terms of neurosis and psychosis.

In seeking to understand the personalities of criminals and delinquents, Dr. Manfried Guttmacher, a psychiatrist affiliated with the Baltimore courts, grouped the delinquents whom he examined into five categories. The categories and their distributions are as follows:

1. *The normal delinquent:* the antisocial individual who has identified with the asocial elements in our society and generally with morally and socially defective parental figures. According to Guttmacher, this group constitutes *75 to 80 percent of delinquents.*

2. *The accidental or occasional delinquent:* the individual with an essentially healthy superego who has become overwhelmed by a special set of circumstances. This, Guttmacher contends, is a very small group.

3. *The organically or constitutionally predisposed delinquent:* a disparate group comprised of numerous subgroups (the intellectually defective, the post-

245

encephalitic, the epileptic, the senile deteriorative, the posttraumatic, etc.) and representing a small portion of the total number of criminals and delinquents. According to Guttmacher, the vast majority of persons with these maladies are noncriminal.

4. *The psychopathic or sociopathic delinquent:* the individual who is not psychotic (insane), but who indulges in irrational antisocial behavior, probably resulting from hidden unconscious neurotic conflicts. This is a complex group that, in Guttmacher's view, comprises 10 to 15 percent of the criminal population.

5. *The psychotic delinquent:* an individual whose criminal behavior is a symptom of his psychosis. He suffers from one of the major mental disorders. According to Guttmacher, who is psychoanalytically oriented:

> These insanities are marked by regressive behavior in which the ego is overwhelmed by primitive aggressive drives. These may be directed against himself or against others. As bizarre and as unintelligible as much of insane behavior appears to be, it has an economic utility for the individual. Were we wise enough, its meaning and significance could in every instance be deciphered. Only one and a half to two percent of criminals are definitely psychotic.[1]

There are three aspects of the relationship between emotional disorder and delinquency that we feel are important to summarize before beginning our more comprehensive discussion of personality and delinquency.

1. An assumption upon which most psychotherapy in the field of juvenile delinquency is based is that delinquent behavior is a symptom of some underlying emotional disturbance or disorder. There is no doubt that some delinquent acts are committed by emotionally disturbed youths and that some "normal" youths commit delinquent acts when under great emotional strain. However, in our view, emotional disturbance does not explain the predominant proportion of delinquent behavior. Most youths who commit delinquent acts are no more "emotionally disturbed" than other youths in the general population.

2. Behavior considered symptomatic of emotional disturbance is likely to receive more attention when exhibited by one charged with or convicted of an act of juvenile delinquency than when displayed by conforming youth. This tendency results from the widely held belief that juvenile delinquents are in fact emotionally disturbed people.

3. "Normal" delinquent behavior may result in emotional disorder.

---

[1] Manfried S. Guttmacher, "The Psychiatric Approach to Crime and Correction." Reprinted, with permission, from a symposium, "Crime and Correction," appearing in *Law and Contemporary Problems* (vol. 23, no. 4, Autumn 1958), published by the Duke University School of Law, Durham, N.C. Copyright, 1958–59, by Duke University.

What is suggested here is that an individual who has become delinquent may develop an induced emotional disturbance as a result of juvenile detention, long-term incarceration, or the variety of abnormal social forces involved in the administration of juvenile justice.

From our overall analysis of characteristics of delinquents, we support the conclusion that the "personalities" of delinquents do not differ significantly from those of other people. Some delinquents certainly exhibit traits that lead professionals properly to classify them as mental defectives, psychotics, neurotics, and sociopaths, but most delinquents do not have these characteristics.

Aspects of the Socialized Delinquent

As indicated, a significant number of delinquents, probably a substantial majority, are no more "emotionally disturbed" than the general population. What sets them apart is the status of delinquent conferred upon them by a juvenile court after findings that they had violated provisions of the law. Many of these youths have been socialized or trained into systems of values, role definitions, and subcultures favoring delinquent behavior.

The Classical Pattern of Delinquency

A classic example of this pattern may be seen in the "criminal tribes" that were of national concern to the government of India during the 1920s and 1930s. These tribes clearly socialized their children into delinquent activities. At early ages the children were role-trained to commit acts of burglary, to operate confidence games, and, if they were girls, to become prostitutes. The training or socialization was methodically carried out by parents and tribal elders. The tradition of crime as a means of earning a living was passed on from generation to generation as a "normal" pattern of behavior. There was no moral stigma associated with a life of crime, and children growing up in this subculture had no guilt or conflict about commiting delinquent acts. This was what they were supposed to do. The "deviants" in the criminal tribes of India were, paradoxically, the few youths who did not adhere to the values and behavior of the dominant criminal ethos.

Young people growing up in urban slums in Western societies are often confronted with a similar type of socialization. Although the pull toward delinquency is not so overwhelmingly strong or persuasive as in the Indian criminal tribes, it is seductive. When their peers hold delinquent norms, when the neighborhood hero is a "successful" criminal or racketeer, youths may seek to emulate these patterns. Becoming a juvenile delinquent for many youths growing up in this social context is therefore more a matter of conformity than of deviance.

Donald R. Cressey makes the point that the Cosa Nostra, that is, organized crime, is a most attractive potential field of endeavor for young poor youths growing up in urban ghettos.[2] Cressey asserts that the Cosa Nostra feeds on the urban poor. Of the thousands of people involved in organized crime, the "street men" or street-level commission agents are visible manifestations of a seductive criminal lifestyle, and they exert a primary influence on juvenile delinquency. The agents of organized crime have high status in their neighborhoods and are the idols of young ghetto residents; they are the men who have "made it. In the eyes of many urban youths, the "image of success is that of a hustler who promotes his interests by using others."

Cressey takes the position that the cooperation of organized criminals influences the general delinquency rate in the inner city in three ways. First, they demonstrate to the young people that crime does pay. Second, according to Cressey, the presence of organized crime exhibits the corruption evident in law-enforcement and political organizations. This makes it more difficult for parents to teach their children to achieve in the world by "hard honest labor in service to their family, country, and God." Third, organized crime, through the numbers rackets, prostitution, gambling, and drugs, appreciably affects and lowers the economic status of the people in the community; thus the people have less to lose if convicted of crime. Delinquency is therefore more attractive to lower class youth. Cressey summarizes his observations into three dimensions: (1) *attraction,* (2) *corruption,* and (3) *contamination.*

Attraction.   Because of these forces, according to Cressey, slum boys grow up in an economic and social environment that makes some participation in organized crime attractive, natural, and relatively painless. Cressey cites Irving Spergel, who, in his studies of juvenile delinquents in three different neighborhoods in Chicago, concluded that developing specific skills is less necessary than learning the point of view or attitudes conducive to the development of organized crime.

In response to Spergel's question to delinquents. "What is the job of the adult in your neighborhood whom you would want to be like?" eight out of ten responded by naming some aspect of organized crime. Spergel's "Racketville" delinquents believed that connections are the most important quality in getting ahead. "Seven out of ten chose education as the least important factor" in getting ahead.

Corruption.   Organized crime, in its alliances with politicians and law-enforcement officials, helps, as Cressey sees it, "to break down the respect for law and order. How can a boy learn to respect authority when that authority figure is known to be on the payroll of criminals?"

---

[2]Donald R. Cressey. "Organized Crime and Inner City Youth," *Crime and Delinquency* 16(April 1970):129–38.

Contamination.   Cressey asserts that because the areas of low socioeconomic status are the areas of high delinquency and crime in American cities, it must be concluded that in some areas lawlessness has become traditional. He reasons that in poverty areas the values, social pressures, and norms favorable to crime are strong and constant. The persons responsible for enforcing these moral systems and concepts are organized criminals. Cressey quotes Dr. Martin Luther King, who once stated, "Organized crime flourishes in the ghetto as 'permissive crime' because no one cares particularly about ghetto crime."

Cressey concludes his observations by stating: "Keeping vice out of affluent areas while allowing it to flourish in the ghettos, together with corruption that supports the practice, [contributes to] the traditions of delinquency and crime characterizing our inner city areas. In these areas opposition to crime and delinquency is weak because the city is poor, mobile and heterogeneous and people can't act effectively to solve their problems."[3] Cressey asserts that most people living in low-income or poverty areas are either delinquent or criminals because they are isolated from law-abiding behavior patterns and are in close, continuing contact with criminal influences "that affect forces favorable to delinquency." Cressey believes that the "incidence of inner city delinquency may be reduced by eliminating the behavior patterns spread by organized criminals or by expanding these anticriminal behavior patterns that keep inner city youth out of trouble."

The Making of a Socialized Delinquent

Cressey's general viewpoint is articulated in the case of one young man who grew up and was essentially socialized by the "criminal forces in the inner city" cited by Cressey. Lewis Yablonsky became closely acquainted with John during the process of researching Synanon, the anticriminal social organization. After a lifetime of delinquent activities in the inner city, John came to Synanon when he was around twenty years old and was successfully resocialized by the "anticriminal behavior patterns" at work in Synanon. John later organized his own successful "anticriminal society," known as Delancey Street, in San Francisco.

John grew up in a delinquent subculture on the West Side of Manhattan. His neighborhood socialized him into a delinquent–drug addict style of life. The process "naturally" involved the development of a delinquent mask or image for survival. John, exhausted with his way of life, arrived at Synanon to attempt to change his lifestyle. His childhood and teenage years had effectively trained him for an adult life of crime; however, Synanon was successful

---

[3]Cressey, "Organized Crime and Inner City Youth," p. 137.

in tearing away the delinquent mask that had evolved and retrained him for a law-abiding posture toward life.

John was first institutionalized at the age of five by his parents. He doesn't remember the reason. From then on, however, he felt extreme hatred for his parents, especially his father. In the institution, he "always felt a need to protect the underdog in a fight." He had several fights each day and found the "home" he was in a "house of horror." He was in what he called his "juvenile jail" for four years and learned all about crime from the older boys.

When he left the institution at about the age of nine, he began running with various young kid gangs in New York on the West Side. They were involved in petty theft and destructive acts. He remembered learning to hate his father more and more. "I always stayed out late, and when he would get me at home, he would beat me up pretty badly. Then he would actually sentence me, like a judge. For example, he would give me 'sixty days in the bedroom.' I began my jail time early."

During most of his early life, John worshiped gangsters and criminals. He wanted to be like them. In his neighborhood there were many to imitate. A criminal he especially admired was Trigger Burke, who, according to John, "killed a few wrong guys and went to the hot seat at Sing Sing without a whimper."

When John was twelve, he took his first fix of heroin in the course of his delinquent-training apprenticeship to the mob. "I use to run dope and deliver heroin for some of the big pushers in the neighborhood. One day, I delivered a package of heroin to some older guy, and out of curiosity I asked him for a little. He fixed me, and that was it. I began using from then on. It's hard to describe my first feelings about heroin. The best way I can describe it is that it's like being under the covers where it's nice and warm on a cold day. Of course, now I don't recommend it to anyone except as a mercy killing."

John continued to run the streets, used drugs whenever he could, and received more training for a life of crime. "In my neighborhood, when I was twelve or thirteen, I was considered a 'cute kid.' The whores liked me, and once in a while, for a gag, they would turn a trick with me. I admired the standup guy gangsters. They were my idols. I had two heroes at that time, the head of the Mafia, Frank Costello, and General MacArthur."

John, in his teenage years, was a thin, baby-faced young fellow. His pale, ascetic face had an almost religious quality. In his neighborhood on the Upper West Side of Manhattan, he became known by some of his peers as "Whitey the Priest."

He received this nickname from an addict who was kicking a habit. As John relates it:

> Once, when I was in detention in jail, some Spanish guy who was kicking a bad habit came to for a minute. He saw me and began to scream hysterically in Spanish that I was a priest. Later on, it was picked up by

other people who knew me around the city. Some of the whores on Columbus Avenue would even "confess" to me as Whitey the Priest. First I made sure they gave me a good fix of heroin, or money for a fix, and then I would actually listen to their "confession"! They weren't kidding; they were dead serious. After the "confession" took place, usually in some hallway or in a bar, after they poured out their tragic story, I would lay a concept on them. Something like "into each life some rain must fall." I'd bless them and cut out.

I took my first big fall at fourteen. I was sent to the reformatory at Otisville. I hated everyone there and wanted to kill the director and some of the guards. I was always fighting and spent a lot of time in the hole [solitary confinement]. This gave me a chance to think and plot different ways to kill the guards and the man who ran the joint.

At age sixteen, John was transferred from Otisville to another reformatory for older boys. From then on he spent time in various institutions. These included several trips to Rikers Island Penitentiary, Lexington for a "winder" ("You wind in and out"), Riverside Hospital for youthful addicts, and various New York City jails.

John always considered himself to be a "standup guy" (a criminal with ethics) and had set his personal goal at becoming a professional criminal. At one point, he tried to learn how to be a safecracker from an old-timer. "Somehow I wasn't very good. I did go on a few capers. But it wasn't right for me. Whenever I was out of jail, which wasn't too often, I would just use drugs and steal. I became a baby-faced stall for some cannons [pickpockets]. The stall sets up the mark, and the cannon picks his pocket. I made a fair living in this business. I use to like to pick pockets in museums. In fact, I don't know why, but I spent a lot of time walking around museums." (Certain works of art tend to mesmerize the pickpocket's victim and render him oblivious to having his pocket picked.)

In lengthy discussions with John, Yablonsky never determined that the young man had any significant neurotic, psychotic, or sociopathic personality traits. It appeared that his delinquent lifestyle resulted from the "straight line" learning of delinquent behavior in a neighborhood social milieu that stressed delinquency as a correct and logical way of life.

The individual socialized in a delinquent subculture acquires skills useful in crime and values and attitudes that make a delinquent career attractive. He learns to commit burglaries, thefts, and other property offenses as skills, and engages in them to earn his livelihood. He desires a career that involves professional crime. In later life, young delinquents like John usually develop into what Edwin H. Sutherland has defined as "the professional criminal."

Edwin H. Sutherland's conception of the professional criminal parallels the sociological model of socialized delinquents. Sutherland's classic theory of "differential association," grossly oversimplified, states that delinquents learn to become delinquent from association with other offenders.[4] They are trained into delinquent patterns at an early age. Sutherland's "professional thief" is the role that the socialized delinquent will achieve if he becomes a specialist in a particular criminal activity. According to Sutherland:

> Professional thieves make a regular business of theft. They use techniques which have been developed over a period of centuries and transmitted to them through traditions and personal association. They have codes of behavior, esprit de corps, and consensus. They have a high status among other thieves and in the political and criminal underworld in general. They have differential association in the sense that they associate with each other and not, on the same basis, with outsiders, and also in the sense that they select their colleagues.
>
> Because of this differential association they develop a common language or argot that is relatively unknown to those not in the profession, and they have organization. A thief is a professional when he has these six characteristics: regular work at theft, technical skill, consensus, status, differential association, and organization.
>
> Professional thieves have their group ways of behavior for the principal situations that confront them in their criminal activities. Consequently professional theft is a behavior system and a sociological entity.[5]

This model image of the professional criminal characterizes him as resourceful, well-trained, and effective, a member of a profession (albeit illegal) with certain ethics and values that dictate his conduct. In criminal jargon, the professional thief has class. He would not "rat on his buddies," and even certain victims were proscribed. Assault and violence were used as means to an end, not as ends in themselves. Here is a personal report of a "socialized delinquent" and his on-the-job training for the purpose of becoming a professional criminal:

> When I was sixteen or seventeen I used to hang around a pool hall in our neighborhood a lot. I got so I could shoot pool pretty good and once in a while I would make a couple of bucks. But there were older guys there who were really doing good. They had good reputations in the neighborhood and they always had money, cars, and broads. Me and some kids my age were doing a lot of petty stealing at this time, cars and things from cars, but we didn't know how to make any real money. What

---

[4]Edwin H. Sutherland and Donald R. Cressey, *Criminology,* 8th ed., 1970. By permission of the publishers, J. B. Lippincott Company.

[5]Sutherland and Cressey, *Criminology,* p. 213.

we wanted to do is get in with the older guys so we could learn something and make some real money.

One day, I remember, I had just got out of jail for some petty beef and one of the older thieves; a guy that was supposed to be one of the slickest safe men around, came over to me and talked to me for awhile. This made me feel pretty good. Later one of his friends asked me if I wanted to help him carry a safe out of some office. We worked half a night on that safe and never did get it out of the place. But from then on I was in with the older bunch. Every once in a while one of them would get me to do some little job for him, like "standing-point" [lookout] or driving a car or something like that; and once in a while when they had snatched a safe, I would get to help them open it. I was learning pretty fast.

By the time I was nineteen or twenty, me and a couple of my buddies had real solid names [reputations] with the older thieves. We were beating a lot of places on our own and we handled ourselves pretty well. But we were still willing to learn more. We used to sit around some coffee shop half the night or ride around in a car listening to a couple of the old hoodlums cut up different scores [crimes]. We would talk about different scores other guys had pulled or scores we had pulled, and we would also talk about how you were supposed to act in other situations; how to spend your money, how to act when you got arrested. We discussed different trials we knew about, we even talked about San Quentin and Folsom and prisons in other states, because usually the older thieves had done time before. We talked about how much time each beef carried, how much time the parole board would give you for each beef. I guess we talked about everything that had anything to do with stealing. Of course we didn't talk about it all the time. Lots of the time we just shot the bull like anyone else. But by the time I was twenty-one I had a pretty good education in crime.[6]

The Sociopathic Delinquent

For a number of years the catchall label "psychopathic" was applied by psychiatrists to all persons whose behavior deviated markedly from the normal, yet who could not be properly categorized as neurotic or psychotic. It included people with schizoid traits, with cyclothymic or paranoid tendencies, sexual deviates of all types, as well as those with antisocial disorders, gross inadequacies of character, and numerous other difficulties. Psychiatrists dealing with persons convicted of crimes included in this category everyone convicted of an offense, from the less serious to the most heinous, if the offender

---

[6]Statement made to Lewis Yablonsky.

could not be classified as either psychotic or neurotic. Such persons, it seemed, could not be considered by the psychiatrists to be "normal." Beginning with the 1930s and continuing through the 1960s, scientific articles appeared in professional journals and books regarding the nature, causes, and treatment of psychopathy. This research led to a rejection of the belief that psychopathy was a hereditary, innate lack of "moral sense." Increasingly, research gave support to the belief that psychopathy was developed in interactions with others, first in the family, and then with peers.[7]

The term *psychopathic personality* was discarded, and in the present nomenclature most of the deviant behaviors previously grouped under that label are now included as personality disorders. Among these are the sociopath and the psychopath. Dr. Hervey Cleckley, the psychiatrist who has contributed much to the clarification of the psychiatric terminology in this area, defines sociopath as follows: "This term refers to chronically antisocial individuals who are always in trouble, profiting neither from experience nor punishment, and maintaining no real loyalties to any person, group, or code. They are frequently callous and hedonistic, showing marked emotional immaturity, with lack of responsibility, lack of judgment, and an ability to rationalize their behavior so that it appears warranted, reasonable, and justified."[8]

McCord and McCord define *psychopath* as *"an asocial, aggressive, highly impulsive person, who feels little or no guilt and is unable to form lasting bonds of affection with other human beings."*[9] The McCords' statement reflects Cleckley's view.[10]

It is apparent from the above discussion that the term *sociopath* and *psychopath* may be used interchangeably. We prefer the term *sociopath* in our analysis because it more aptly implies social origins. We recognize, however, that other writers use the term *psychopath* to describe the same pattern.

According to all available research, the proportion of sociopaths or psychopaths in our criminal population approximates 15 percent. It is the 15 percent of the criminal population that is sociopathic that we shall now try to describe.

The patterns of the *socialized delinquent,* who is a relatively well-trained type of offender, differs considerably from those of the *sociopathic offender.* Contrast John's and Gary's postures described above with the following comments made by a sociopathic youth who was involved in a brutal gang homicide:

---

[7]Hervey M. Cleckley, "Psychopathic States," in *American Handbook of Psychiatry,* ed. Silvano Arieti (New York: Basic Books, 1959), pp. 567–88.

[8]Cleckley, "Psychopathic States," p. 568.

[9]William McCord and Joan McCord, *The Psychopath* (Princeton, N.J.: Van Nostrand, 1964), p. 3.

[10]Cleckley, "Psychopathic States," p. 568.

Momentarily, I started thinking about it inside; I have my mind made up I'm not going to be in no gang. Then I go on inside. Something comes up, then here all my friends coming to me. Like I said before, I'm intelligent and so forth. They be coming to me—then they talk to me about what they gonna do, like kill this guy! Like, "Man, I just gotta go with you." Myself, I don't want to go, but when they start talkin' about what they gonna do, I say, "So, he isn't gonna take over my rep, I ain't gonna let him be known more than me." And I go ahead, just for selfishness. . . .[11]

The senseless "other-directed" violence of such sociopathic offenders is perpetrated for ego status—for "kicks" or "thrills." The kicks involve a type of emotional euphoria that the sociopathic delinquent maintains "makes me feel good." He does it for "selfishness." The goals of the deliquent are self-oriented in a primary fashion, with material gain as a secondary consideration. The socialized delinquent would not place himself in jeopardy for this type of "senseless" gang-violence offense. He uses violence as an instrument for material gain, not for an emotional charge, to validate his existence.

A study by Mark Whitehill, Sandra DeMyer-Gapin, and Thomas F. Scott, of eight boys they identified as "sociopathic" concluded that hedonistic and thrill-seeking behavior may be an attempt to get the kicks most people get in less extreme ways.

To see if young antisocial children ("sociopaths") need more stimulation than either normal or neurotic peers, Whitehill, DeMyer-Gapin, and Scott went to a treatment center for disturbed children and asked the staff to identify eight boys who were difficult to control and not easily influenced by disapproval or discipline. Since neurotics are supposed to be on the other end of the responsiveness and stimulus-seeking scale, they also picked out a group of eight neurotic boys (i.e., easily intimidated by authority and quick to learn from discipline). Both groups were compared to seven "normal" boys from a nearby elementary school. The mean age of the entire sample was 11.5 years.

All boys individually viewed a monotonous sequence of 103 slides picturing the concrete facades of a modern building. The youngsters were told they could either watch the slides as they automatically clicked by in the projector (at twenty-second intervals) or they could switch the slides at their own pace. The boys were also informed that they could leave at any time. The experimenter, who did not know to which group each boy had been assigned, recorded the elapsed time between the slides.

Whitehill, DeMyer-Gapin and Scott concluded:

---

[11]Lewis Yablonsky, *The Violent Gang,* rev. ed. (Baltimore: Penguin Books, 1971), p. 256.

While all three groups started out with similar viewing times, both the normal and antisocial groups tended to get tired of waiting for their slides to change and soon reduced their viewing times substantially. But it took the overly obstreperous boys significantly less time to start flipping the switch themselves. During the last 50 slides, the antisocial boys spent almost 20 seconds less per slide than the normal kids, and the neurotics took at least 20 seconds more per slide than the normals. The neurotics were more likely to wait patiently for the projector to advance the slides.[12]

This is evidence, the researchers contend, that sociopathic-type preadolescents do go to greater lengths to seek stimulation. Violence is often used in a "rational" way as an instrument in the delinquent activities of the socialized delinquent. The violence of a sociopathic offender, on the other hand, is characterized by the following: (1) there is no evidence of prior contact or interaction between the assailant and his victim; (2) the violent act often occurs in an unpremeditated, generally spontaneous and impulsive manner; (3) in some cases (particularly, for example, in gang assault) there is a degree of prior buildup to the act; however, the final consequence (often homicide) is not really anticipated; (4) the violent assailant (or violent gang) has indicated by prior behavior or personality factors a potentiality for the commission of violence; (5) the offender's expressed reaction to the violent behavior is usually lacking in regret and otherwise inappropriate to the act he has committed.

Characteristics of Ideal Type

The ideal type of sociopathic delinquent has a persistent pattern of deviant behavior characterized by an almost total disregard for the rights and feelings of others. A listing of his overt personality and behavior traits would include most, if not all, of the following factors: (*a*) limited social conscience; (*b*) egocentrism dominating most interaction, "instrumental manipulation" of others for self-advantage (rather than affective relating); (*c*) inability to forego immediate pleasure for future goals; (*d*) a habit of pathological lying to achieve personal advantage.

The dominant theme of the sociopathic offender is what has varyingly been called "moral imbecility" or "character disorder." This type of offender may know "right" from "wrong," but a dominating theme of his behavior is that he lacks any coherent discretionary ability. In brief, the distinction between right and wrong doesn't really matter to the sociopath. He has a moral or character disorder.

Paul Tappan describes the sociopath as follows: "He has a condition of psychological abnormality in which there is neither the overt appearance of

---

[12] *Human Behavior* (August 1976).

psychosis or neurosis, but there is a chronic abnormal response to the environment."[13]

Harrison Gough's description further reveals the type of delinquent who may be termed *sociopathic.* According to Gough, he is "the kind of person who seems insensitive to social demands, who refuses to or cannot cooperate, who is untrustworthy, impulsive, and improvident, who shows poor judgment and shallow emotionality, and who seems unable to appreciate the reactions of others to his behavior."[14]

A basic personality defect of the sociopath is a limited social conscience toward almost all others to whom he relates. This characteristic is most apparent in the sociopathic offender's limited feelings of any real sympathy for his victims or regret for the harm he does them. Albert Rabin succinctly describes the trait of defective social conscience apparent in the sociopathic personality:

> There are two major related aspects to this notion of defective conscience. . . . The first aspect is represented in the inability . . . to apply the \moral standards of society to his behavior; he cheats, lies, steals, does not keep promises, and so on. He has not absorbed the "thou shalts" and the "thou shalt nots" of his society and cultural milieu. The second aspect is that of absence of guilt. Guilt is an important part of any well-developed conscience. When a normal person violates the moral code he feels guilty; he feels unhappy and blames himself for the transgression. . . . Guilt is an unknown experience for the personality with no superego. There is none of this automatic self-punishment that goes along with the commission of immoral and unethical acts. The psychopath (sociopath) continues to behave irresponsibly, untruthfully, insincerely, and antisocially without a shred of shame, remorse, or guilt. He may sometimes express regret and remorse for the actions and crimes which he may have perpetrated; however, these are usually mere words, spoken for the effect, but not really and sincerely felt.[15]

The more adequate social self is developed from a consistent pattern of interaction with another person in a normative socialization process. The other person is usually a parent or some other adequate adult role model from whom a youth can learn social feelings of compassion and sympathy. The proper adult role models necessary for adequate socialization are absent from the social environmental of many youths growing up in a disorganized slum.

---

[13]Paul W. Tappan, *Crime, Justice and Correction* (New York: McGraw-Hill, 1960), p. 137.

[14]Harrison G. Gough, "A Sociological Theory of Psychopathy," *American Journal of Sociology* 53(March 1948):365.

[15]Albert I. Rabin, "Psychopathic (Sociopathic) Personalities." From *Legal and Criminal Psychology,* ed. Hans Toch. Copyright © 1961 by Holt, Rinehart and Winston, Inc. Reprinted by permission of Holt, Rinehart and Winston, Inc.

⌐There is some evidence that the basic ingredient missing in the sociopathic delinquent's socialization is a "loving parent." Based on their extensive analysis of the literature, the McCords state: "Because the rejected child does not love his parents and they do not love him, no identification takes place. Nor does the rejected child fear the loss of love—a love which he never had —when he violates moral restrictions. Without love, the socializing agent, the psychopath remains asocial."[16]

Significance of Parent-Child Relations

Megargee and Golden carried out research into this element of causation related to the sociopath. They based their research on the following reasoning:

> ... It would appear the psychopathic offender has a significantly poorer relation with his parents than does either the nondelinquent or the normal (subcultural) delinquent. It is this poor parent-child relation that has been blamed for the psychopath's failure in identification and introjection of normal social values.
>
> The purpose of the present study was to partially test these formulations by comparing the parental attitudes of psychopathic and subcultural offenders and a nondelinquent group of comparable socioeconomic status. A measure of "attitudes toward parents" was chosen because it was felt that this variable could be measured more reliably and validly than could "identification with parents," at least in the settings in which the study was to be carried out. Moreover, attitudes toward parents should show the same pattern of relation as a measure of identification in this case.
>
> On the basis of the literature reviewed above it was hypothesized:
>
> (1) Psychopathic delinquents' attitudes toward *(a)* their mothers and *(b)* their fathers would be significantly more negative than those of nondelinquents.
> (2) Psychopathic delinquents' attitudes toward *(a)* their mothers and *(b)* their fathers would be significantly more negative than those of subcultural delinquents.
> (3) There would be no noteworthy difference in the subcultural delinquents' and nondelinquents' attitudes toward *(a)* their mothers and *(b)* their fathers.[17]

Using various psychological inventories, they cross-compared a sample

---

[16]McCord and McCord, *The Psychopath,* pp. 16–17.

[17]These excerpts from "Parental Attitudes of Psychopathic and Subcultural Delinquents," by Edwin I. Megargee and Roy E. Golden are reprinted from *Criminology,* vol. 10, no. 4(February 1973), pp. 427–39 by permission of the Publisher, Sage Publications, Inc.

of identified sociopaths from a federal correctional institution and a matched control group of students attending a technical trade school. Both institutions were located in Tallahassee, Florida. The correctional institution's final sample of thirty-one was divided into two groups of "subcultural delinquents" (Sample 17) and "psychopathic delinquents" (Sample 14). (The subcultural delinquents would parallel our described socialized delinquents.)

The delinquent groups (both psychopathic and socialized) were contrasted with the nondelinquents with regard to parental relationships. On the basis of their research, Megargee and Golden came to the following conclusion:

> ... the nondelinquents expressed the most favorable attitudes toward both their parents, and the psychopathic delinquents the most negative. For these two groups there was little difference between the ratings for the mother and the father. The subcultural delinquents displayed a different pattern, however; their attitude toward mother was as favorable as that of the nondelinquent group, but their attitude toward father was as negative as that of the psychopathic sample. ...
>
> The data ... highlight the important role played by the mother. While the attitude toward the father was the crucial variable separating the delinquents from the nondelinquents, it was the attitude toward the mother than differentiated the subcultural from the psychopathic delinquents. One might speculate that it is this positive relationship with the mother that permits the subcultural delinquent to appear well adjusted and capable of loyalty to his group and adherence to a code of values, albeit a socially deviant code.
>
> Finally, the data gave further evidence of the value of dividing delinquents into homogeneous subgroups. The fact that the psychopathic and subcultural groups differed from the nondelinquents in unique ways indicated the likelihood of different etiologies, reinforcing the belief that different treatment strategies would be most effective for these two groups.[18]

The notion of adequate self-emergence through constructive social interaction with others, especially parents, is grounded in the theoretical works of Charles Horton Cooley and later developed by J. L. Moreno and George H. Mead. As Mead developed the theme: "The self arises in conduct when the individual becomes a social object in experience to himself. This takes place when the individual assumes the attitude or uses the gesture which another individual would use and responds to it himself." Through socialization, the

---

[18]Megargee and Golden, "Parental Attitudes of Psychopathic and Subcultural Delinquents," pp. 433–37.

child gradually becomes a social being. "The self thus has its origin in communication and in taking the role of the other."[19]

Harry Stack Sullivan saw the self as being made up of "reflected appraisals." The child lacks equipment and experience necessary for a careful and unclouded evaluation of himself. The only guides he has are those of the significant adults or others who take care of him and treat him with compassion. The child thus experiences and appraises himself in accordance with the reactions of parents and others close to him. By facial expressions, gestures, words, and deeds, they convey to him the attitudes they hold toward him, their regard for him or lack of it. A set of positive sympathetic responses, necessary for adequate self-growth, is generally absent in the development of the youth who becomes a sociopath.[20]

Thus the sociopathic delinquent produced by the socialization process characteristic of the disorganized slum tends to be self-involved, exploitative, and disposed toward violent outbursts. This sociopathic individual lacks "social ability," or the ability adequately to assess the role expectations of others. He is characteristically unable to experience the pain of the violence he may inflict on another since he does not have the ability to identify or empathize with others. He is thus capable of committing spontaneous acts of "senseless" violence without feeling concern or guilt.

A classic sociopathic comment of a gang boy who stabbed another boy with a bread knife aptly describes this pattern of feeling: "What was I thinking about when I did it? Man, are you crazy? I was thinking about whether to do it again!"

William and Joan McCord validate this view of the sociopath. They define him as asocial. His conduct, they assert, often brings him into conflict with society. He is driven by primitive desires and an exaggerated craving for excitement. In his self-centered search for pleasure, he ignores the restrictions of the culture.

The sociopath is highly impulsive. He is a youth for whom the moment is a segment of time detached from all others. His actions are unplanned, guided by his whims. The sociopath is aggressive. He has learned few socialized ways of coping with frustration. He feels little if any guilt. He can commit the most appalling acts, yet view them without remorse. The sociopath has a warped capacity for love. His emotional relationships, when they exist, are meager, fleeting, and designed to satisfy his own desires. According to the McCords, these last two traits, guiltlessness and lovelessness, conspicuously mark the psychopath as different from other men.[21]

---

[19]George H. Mead, *Mind, Self and Society* (Chicago: University of Chicago Press, 1934), p. 236.

[20]Harry Stack Sullivan, *Conceptions of Modern Psychiatry* (Washington, D.C.: William Alanson White Psychiatric Foundation, 1947).

[21]McCord and McCord, *The Psychopath*.

Criteria for Viewing Psychopathology

In his aptly titled book, *The Mask of Sanity,* Hervey M. Cleckley developed a comprehensive criteria for viewing the psychopathic personality, as he termed it. His categorical observations, some of which are interchangeable, can be summarized in the following factors:

1. *Unexplained failure.* Despite an average or superior intelligence, the psychopathic individual fails in constructive activities.

2. *Undisturbed technical intelligence.* He has the ability, in most respects, to reason intelligently. He is not usually disturbed (as in a psychosis) by delusions or hallucinations.

3. *Absence of neurotic anxiety.* He does not usually have the anxiety characteristic of the psychoneurotic.

4. *Persistent and inadequately motivated antisocial behavior.* The psychopath generally follows a course of behavior that is antisocial and self-defeating.

5. *Irresponsibility.* The psychopath, after making substantial gains personally and often financially, will for no predictable reason abruptly throw his gains away in an irresponsible manner. He cannot be counted on in any way.

6. *Peculiar inability to distinguish between truth and falsehood.* The psychopath's disregard for truth is remarkable. He seems confident and at ease when making a solemn promise he will never keep. He will lie recklessly to extricate himself from an accusation of obvious misconduct. He will coolly maintain his indefensible position, often to the point where logical men will begin to doubt their accusation. His lies are often unnecessary and grandiose.

7. *Inability to accept blame.* He never gracefully accepts any blame for his outrageous behavior. If the facts become incontrovertible, even for him, he will present extravagant plans for restitution that he never plans to fulfill. Despite all this, there is no real evidence of remorse beyond the moment at hand.

8. *Failure to learn by experience.* There is no evidence that the psychopath ever learns from his continuing negative experiences. He compulsively repeats his failures.

9. *Incapacity for love.* Though he often manifests the overt signs of affection and love, there is no indication that he actually experiences these emotions in any real sense. He cannot and does not form enduring relationships. Despite surface indications of love and compassion, the psychopath is usually callous and destructive to others.

10. *Inappropriate or fantastic reactions to alcohol.* Unlike most alcoholics, the psychopath under the influence of even a modest amount of alcohol may become extremely irrational and destructive.

11. *Lack of insight.* The psychopath has limited insight and is appar-

ently not introspective. He seldom sees himself as others do. This is one of the reasons why rehabilitation generally fails with this type of personality.

12. *Shallow and impersonal responses to sexual life.* The sexual life of both male and female psychopaths is generally promiscuous and for the most part emotionally unfulfilling. Their sexual partner is viewed as an object, rather than a person with feelings.

13. *Suicide rarely carried out.* The psychopath, or sociopath, often threatens suicide but rarely carries it out. The lack of real guilt or shame about his behavior does not produce a true motivation for suicide. The threat is used for egocentric immediate personal advantage.

14. *Persistent pattern of self-defeat.* One of the remarkable features of the psychopath is his consistent pattern of self-defeat. It is one of his few predictable behavioral characteristics.[22]

Applying Cleckley's criteria, we can distinguish the sociopath from the psychotic, a person whose reasoning is disturbed by delusions and hallucinations, and from the neurotic, a person who suffers from an excess of anxiety and guilt. We can also distinguish the sociopath from a "normal" career or socialized delinquent, who has the ability to be compassionate toward other people.

A Sociopathic Sexual Pattern:
The Case of Violent Gang Youths

In discussing the sexual behavior of the sociopath or psychopath, Cleckley comments: "To the psychopath sex is an itch that is to be scratched." For the sociopathic member of a violent gang, sexual interaction does not involve a human association; it supplies hedonistic gratification, and he seeks it whenever the opportunity arises, without any compassion or consideration for the impact on his sexual partner. Practically no emotional relatedness, beyond the physical or fantasy manipulation of another, is apparent in the sociopath's sexual activity.[23]

Sociopathic gang boys tend toward two extreme patterns of sexual behavior: *(a)* the "gang bang" and *(b)* an overt disdain for girls, with homosexual overtones. Each pattern almost rules out the possibility of a warm empathic human relationship between a male and a female.

In the "gang bang" pattern a female is "lined up," and often as many as fifteen or twenty boys will indulge in some form of sexual act with her. The female sexual victim is often a mental defective or severely disturbed girl, who

---

[22]These psychopathic characteristics are derived from Hervey M. Cleckley, *The Mask of Sanity* (St. Louis: Mosby, 1950).

[23]The material on sociopathic sexual patterns is derived from Yablonsky, *The Violent Gang,* pp. 195–205.

is sometimes violated by forceful rape. The sexual situation may occur on a single occasion, or the acts may occur serially over several days.

Another sociopathic mode of sexual behavior by violent gang members entails disdain and exploitation of girls. In this pattern girls are viewed as objects to be manipulated or used for rep-making and ego gratification. The girl becomes a target for hostility and physical brutality, which when reported back to the gang confers prestige on the violator. "Why waste your time with broads?"; "You can't trust 'em"; "I belted her a few times"—these are common expressions that reflect the sociopathic view of women.

Both of these patterns almost prohibit a loving heterosexual relationship. There may be some playful interaction around sexual intercourse, but for the sociopathic youth, a close, warm relationship with a girl entailing mutual responsibility and empathy is rare.

Fear of responsibility and emotional isolation from females make the gang a kind of homosexual community. Constant condemnation of any member of another gang as a "faggot" (homosexual) or by saying, "He eats it," may be viewed as a projection of felt internal homosexual problems. Many sociopathic gang youths manifest homosexual attitudes in their ridicule and exploitation of females, and in their closer feelings toward members of their male peer group.

There is evidence of homosexual experimentation among violent gang boys. This is not usually overtly carried out by gang members among themselves; however, it is common for them to become the passive recipients of such homosexual relations as fellatio with adult homosexuals outside of their gang. A ritual that often recurs involving sex and violence was described by one youth this way: "After this queer bastard blew us [he laughed], we beat the hell out of him—but good." Some initially passive homosexual gang youths become overt active homosexuals when they are older.

Contrary to the popular images created by the film *West Side Story* and other glamorized fictional versions of violent gang activity, the sociopathic gang youth maintains a type of "homosexual" relationship system in the gang that reflects his personality. The youth who attempts a compassionate relationship with a girl is generally a marginal member of the gang, and he is invariably ridiculed by the core sociopathic gang members, who see girls only as simple sexual "tricks" or as objects for exploitation.

The tendency to manipulate others for egocentric gratification is thus an apparent trait of the sociopathic youth in his sexual activity. This pattern is simply an extension of his exploitative approach to all others in the larger society.

In summary, we would conclude that the defective socialization process operative in the disorganized slum produces sociopathic delinquents with characteristically limited social feelings, identity, and compassion for others. Such delinquents manifest sociopathic personalities that reflect some if not all of the following characteristics: *(a)* a defective social conscience marked by limited feelings of guilt for destructive acts against others, *(b)* limited feelings of compassion or empathy for others, *(c)* the acting out of behavior dominated by egocentricity and self-seeking goals, and *(d)* the manipulation of others for immediate self-gratification (for example exploitative modes of sexual behavior) without any moral concern or responsibility.

The sociopathic delinquent finds that delinquent behavior provides a vehicle for achieving gratification consistent with his disordered personality, ability, and needs.

A Classic Sociopath: The Case of José

The emergence of the sociopathic delinquent personality is an enigma that has not been fully clarified. Yet there are patterns that recur consistently enough to enable us to identify them as probable causes of the development of the sociopathic personality. As noted earlier, one is the lack of a proper parental role model of love or compassion. By love we mean the ability to involve oneself with another human being without egocentric designs. Most sociopaths have grown up in a predatory, exploitative, and manipulative social situation. Love and compassion are generally foreign to their lifestyle.

The evolution of a sociopath may be seen in the case of a boy we shall call José Perez, who was known to one of the authors for several years during his five-year study of sociopathic gang youths in New York City.[24] José had brutally participated in the stabbing and killing of another youth, and was convicted of homicide.

José migrated from Puerto Rico to New York City with his family when he was eight years old. José's first remembered reaction to New York City was to the cold and dirt. "It's always summer in Puerto Rico," he explained. Although he had lived in a run-down slum called La Perla in San Juan, it was heaven to him compared to the slum he now lived in on Manhattan's Upper West Side. José could step out of his shack on the island into sunlight and ocean breezes and the friendly greetings of his neighbors. In New York City he would leave his tenement to enter a cold world of hostile or indifferent strangers.

On the island José was somebody. He had an identity. Although they were poor, the Perez family had honor and dignity appropriate to their Spanish background. The Perez name meant something, and José sought to live up to it. His family and friends identified him as an individual; he had a position in the community, even though he was still a child. Everyone in the huddle of poor shacks where he lived knew everyone else; they all had some concern for one another.

---

[24]See Yablonsky, *The Violent Gang.*

In New York he was shocked to discover that he was considered "different." The first time he was cursed at school as a "dirty spick" he became severely upset and angry. In time, under a steady barrage of this sort of prejudice, this reaction slowly changed to some acceptance of inferiority mingled with constant anger. His response became aggressive. He retaliated; finally he began to attack other children without provocation *in anticipation* of their insults.

"Outsiders"—whites and some blacks—were not his only antagonists. He was often picked on by other Puerto Ricans who had lived longer in New York City. To them he was a foreigner, a "tiger."[25] He embarrassed them because he was a Puerto Rican greenhorn and reflected negatively on earlier arrivals who had become assimilated. Other Puerto Ricans suffering from self-hatred as a result of their lowered status, took out their resentment on someone they needed to feel was even more inferior than they.

José had a good school record in Puerto Rico, but in New York he hated school and became a habitual truant. His despised identity as a "spick" was accentuated by his inability to speak English. The teacher tried but, overwhelmed by a large number of students with various problems, she was of limited help. Her students' personal problems, combined with their language difficulties, made teaching specific subject matter almost impossible.

The one available school guidance counselor (for some thousand students) tried to talk to José, but by this time José was considered a "serious" behavior problem. His hatred for school became more intense each time he played hookey. Going back to school seemed increasingly difficult if not impossible. He spent his days at the movies, when he could raise the price of a ticket by petty thievery, or simply sat and daydreamed. He felt weak, inferior, and alone. His favorite cartoon hero was Mighty Mouse. This was his comment about his cartoon hero:

"You know he's a mouse—he's dressed up like Superman. He's got little pants—they're red. The shirt is yellow. You know, and then he helps out the mouse. Every time the cats try to get the mouse, Mighty Mouse comes and helps the mouse, just like Superman. He's stronger than he acts. Nothing can hurt him."

He alternated now between fantasy and direct acts of violence—increasingly delivered to undeserving and often unsuspecting victims. Lectures and threats to have him sent to a reformatory meant little to José. He already knew from a friend that the state reformatory was "all filled up, and they ain't going to send you there for just playing hookey." Roaming the streets produced other delinquent activities: petty thievery and vandalism. These, plus a developed pattern of purse snatching, with greater emphasis on violence than on financial

---

[25]The *Marine Tiger* was one of the ships that carried many Puerto Ricans to New York City early in the Puerto Rican migration. The name was shortened and applied to all newly arrived greenhorns.

gain, helped provide the necessary background for his sentence to the reformatory.

Yet it was not so much what happened to José that caused his unfeeling, asocial behavior to grow; it was what was not happening. In his world there was a dearth of law-abiding youths and adults from whom he could learn any social feeling toward another person. To José, people became things you manipulated to get what you wanted. He discovered that "being nice" was often useful, but only if it helped get what you wanted. When caught stealing, he learned that "sometimes if you hung your head down right and looked pitiful, you could avoid punishment."

There were few people in José's world who ever considered another person's feelings of welfare unless they expected to get something in return. Everything José saw was a con game. The two most successful types of behavior were manipulation and violence. When one didn't work, the other would. José found violence and the threat of violence most effective. As his rep for sudden unexpected violence grew, others responded by complying with his egocentric needs.

José "naturally" learned to manipulate others and to use violence "properly." He never learned to feel affection for anyone, not even the other members of his family. No one ever taught him to express or set any example by displaying such human feelings. In the hostile and asocial world that surrounded him, he learned the most effective adaptation, and his sociopathic personality became more developed with each day's experience.

José's family was of little help to him in New York. His family's rules, language, and appearance were considered old-fashioned and inappropriate. Also, his parents and older brothers were busy battling their own enemies in the cold city. His family was generally not available to his needs for humanism and compassion. He sometimes dreamed with fondness about distant pleasant evenings of the past in Puerto Rico with his family. They used to go to a park near their home in the evenings. Mostly the children would play and the adults would sit around and discuss the day's events. At these times children and adults talked easily with each other. In these old days, now gone, José had the opportunity to discuss his personal troubles with his parents and older brothers. It was even pleasant to be criticized, since it gave José a secure feeling to know someone was concerned. In the park not only his own parents, but relatives and other adults also took an interest in children. One man took the boys swimming; a group of older men from a social club formed a baseball league for the younger boys. José belonged to a community.

All of this changed in New York. His father, an unskilled laborer, found it hard to get a job that paid a living wage. (Some labor unions connected with organized crime made special contracts with employers to provide employees at the lowest minimum wage, selling out the workers.) José's father earned a modest amount when he worked. He was often unemployed. During these periods, quarrels and conflict developed between his parents, and his father became less and less the man of the house—the role he clearly occupied in Puerto Rico. Beset with their own overwhelming problems, José's parents sometimes unfairly attacked their children, who increasingly became a burden to them.

There was no one for José to talk to about his feelings. His father began to drink excessively to escape from immediate realities and a sense of inadequacy he could not face. The more he drank, the more violent he became. In his seemingly senseless rages, he beat José's mother and often attacked José for no apparent reason. Senseless violence surrounded José and he became indifferent to his family. About his father José said, "I'll ask him to take me boat-riding, fishing, or someplace like that, ball game. He'll say no. He don't go no place. The only place where he goes, he goes to the bar. And from the bar, he goes home. Sleep, that's about all he do. I don't talk to my parents a lot of times. I don't hardly talk to them—there's nothing to talk about. There's nothing to discuss about. They can't help me."

Family trouble was compounded by the need for José's mother to take a menial job to help support the family. This removed her further from the home. Rents were exorbitant. The family was barred from moving into certain neighborhoods where Puerto Ricans were not welcome. In any case, their erratic income was insufficient for a steady monthly rental in a more stable neighborhood. The family of six continued to live in a rat- and roach-infested two-room hotel apartment they had moved into originally on a temporary basis. They shared kitchen facilities and an outside toilet with eight other families and paid a rental of over $25 a week. Close quarters intensified the family conflict. José increasingly resolved his problems outside the home.

At one time José became friendly with Juan, an older youth from the neighborhood who took an interest in him and attempted to help him. Juan was a leader in a social gang called the Braves. This group was well organized, participated in sports, ran dances, and belonged to the local community center. The Braves were tough, but they did not go in for "bopping" (gang wars) or other violent activity. Although most members of the Braves engaged in occasional fights and petty thievery, they stayed clear of mass rumbles and participated in more socially accepted activities. Juan tried to get José into the Braves, but José was voted down because the Braves felt he was a "wise punk" and they didn't want him around. He was "too wild, too crazy," and they rejected him flat. He lacked the social ability to be a member.

Then José met a violent gang leader called Loco. As his name implies, Loco was thought to be a little crazy, and this did not displease him. His reputation for sudden violence with a knife or a zip gun made him greatly feared. As part of his usual gang-leader activity, Loco was organizing a West Side Dragons division. José was accepted without question and was appointed a war counselor after Loco saw him stab a younger boy on a dare.

José and other Dragons enjoyed the exciting stories Loco told about Dragon gang divisions throughout Manhattan. José learned, and he began to make brother-gang pacts of his own. Also, as a war counselor for the West Side Dragons, he had what seemed like a good excuse to commit acts of violence every night. His sudden temper and quick use of a blade increased his rep. With Loco he organized a brother-gang pact with another gang on the Upper West Side called the Egyptian Kings. Although José was not acceptable to the Braves, he became an outstanding member of the violent Egyptian Kings gang. The Kings did not really give José a feeling of belonging or provide a comfortable way of life, but the violent gang resolved his anxieties and troubles in the same way alcohol "resolves" problems for the alcoholic and drugs "help" the drug addict: it served to destroy him further.

The Kings provided a vehicle for expressing much of the hatred, disillusionment, and aggression that existed in José. The group also was compatible with the acompassionate, unfeeling, and manipulative sociopathic personality he had developed. Violence was expressed at the right opportunity, or opportunities were created. Also, the gang helped minimize feelings of guilt and anxiety about violence at the increasingly rare times such feelings existed in José.

Any limited concern he had with feelings of worthlessness were diminished by the recognition that there were others like himself. All the Kings were "down cats." "Everyone puts you down" and "Get your kicks now—make it today" were his slogans. "Sounding on people" and "putting them down" were central King activities, and José became an expert.

The violent gang gave José a feeling of power. He was a core member and accepted the mutually supported gang fantasy that he was now "a leader." In the position of war counselor he enjoyed the gang's violence. He found it gratifying and exciting to strike out at others for whom he had no feeling. Violence was a useful instrument for him, and he was well trained for this activity. Quick, senseless violence gave him a "rep." Success, prestige, and fame were achievable through the quick, unexpected stroke of a knife.

On the night José went to Highbridge Park in the Bronx, the trip was just another gang fight. It had all the usual elements of gang activity—mostly talk about violence, about "what we're going to do," "getting even," "being a big shot." Afterward, José's comments that "They called me a dirty spick" and "We fought for territory" were rationales. All of José's social deficiencies converged the night he plunged a bread knife into another boy's back. As another Egyptian King reported, "José's stabbed him in the back with the bread knife and when he took the knife out of his back, he said thank you." Perhaps José was "thanking" his victim for the only gratifying emotions he was now able to feel. José, through the proper set of negative social forces, had emerged as a classic sociopath personality. In the alienated milieu of his brutal urban neighborhood he was not alone. He was not capable of "relating" to others without compassion, and in a paradoxical way he now "belonged" to the ahuman forces of his bizarre sociopathic world, the urban ghetto.

Treatment of the Sociopath

Despite the number of sociopaths in our prisons, estimated to be between 10 and 15 percent of the incarcerated population in the United States, little progress has been made in providing treatment for such persons. This is partly due to the fact that most experts in the field of corrections consider the sociopath untreatable. Furthermore, professionals treating the sociopath, in or out of prison, have not demonstrated a great success.

Hervey Cleckley notes that, in spite of the fact that psychoanalysts have reported a few successes in the treatment of patients regarded as psychopaths, a review of analytic treatment of the psychopathic personality leads to the conclusion that the treatment has proven a failure. He notes further that "all other methods available today have been similarly disappointing in well-defined adult cases of this disorder with which I am directly acquainted.[26] He suggests setting up facilities specifically designed to deal with problems of the psychopath and points out that our large state and federal psychiatric institutions are organized for psychotic patients and are not well adapted to handle the psychopath. Cleckley states further, "Even if no really curative treatment should be discovered, despite organized efforts over the years in institutions specifically adapted to the problems of the psychopath, a great deal might be accomplished through careful supervision and control of destructive activities that today seem to run virtually unchecked."[27]

Cleckley offered this suggestion in 1959. As of 1973 no such institution for the treatment of psychopaths exists in the United States. In Great Britain in 1960, pursuant to the Mental Health Act of 1959, the Welsh Psychopathic Hospital was organized combining milieu therapy with psychiatric treatment.

A Hospital for Psychopaths

In Wales, as in England, the Mental Health Act of 1959 defines psychopaths in terms of a persistent lifetime disorder, serious irresponsibility or aggression, and a doctor prepared to treat them. Whether a diagnosis of psychopathy is applied in Wales depends very much on chance factors, such as whether a deviant child is channeled early into mental health or penal pathways and, later, the parental social class and type of doctor, if any, to which the young person is referred. In Wales, psychopaths are diagnosed and placed into three categories. The first category includes those for whom admission to a hospital for treatment seems unnecessary. They are labeled "psychopathic avoidable," considered harmless, and treated in the community. The second group needs admission and can be persuaded to accept this—often against a background of more severe court measures. Some enter informally.

---

[26]Cleckley, "Psychopathic States," pp. 585–86.

[27]Cleckley "Psychopathic States," p. 586.

For most, however, this Welsh unit requires court conviction and a hospital order with a diagnosis of psychopathic so that the patient sees justice done and, being *impulsive* and *affectionless,* cannot change his mind. The third group is comprised of those unsuitable for admission. This may be because they are English (and their families are not available for help), severely psychopathic (highly aggressive, impulsive, and affectionless), and thus, at outset, more safely forwarded to closed English hospitals, appropriately labeled "criminal," and imprisoned. The characteristics of an individual that lead to a diagnosis of psychopath in Wales are similar to those described by Dr. Cleckley, the McCords, and others in the United States.[28]

The treatment at the Welsh Psychopathic Hospital consists of training with real-life situations—farm, forest, and estate work—continuously used for nursing and medical psychotherapy under trained psychiatric nurses and a consultant psychiatrist. Inmates are taken shopping by bus each week, and most either go home or go camping at Christmas, Easter, and summer holiday times. Discipline depends primarily on interpersonal relationships, fortified by loss of money, privileges, and weekend or home leave. Escapes occur when discipline is unfair. Aftercare involves hostels or residential hotels, and local social worker and psychiatric surveillance.

Over the period 1962 to 1967, the three-year conviction rate has been 49 percent. While in the hospital, the psychopathic patient is given some psychiatric treatment, but the emphasis is on occupational training. He is allowed out on furloughs, and relationships with families are maintained. On aftercare a social worker supervises him and helps with his family and community relationships.[29]

Do psychopaths improve sufficiently so that they can be safely returned to the community? Michael Craft says that they can. According to him, "Follow-up studies, even among extreme examples of psychopathy from English special hospitals, show that between 10 and 20 percent of the patients are improved and return to the community each year." He finds the Danish figures better, and he attributes this to the admission of a greater proportion of psychopaths from the community. Furthermore, he reports that among the most severe English psychopaths there is between 60 and 75 percent improvement rate over a ten-year period.[30]

In an attempt to study the effect of the milieu therapy provided at Wiltwyck, a school for emotionally disturbed delinquent boys, the McCords administered a number of personality tests and questionnaires and obtained behavioral ratings of children admitted to Wiltwyck in 1954. The children were retested in 1955, providing before and after measures of change. They

---

[28]Michael Craft, "The Moral Responsibility for Welsh Psychopaths," in *The Mentally Abnormal Offender,* ed. A. V. S. Rueck and Ruth Porter (Boston: Little, Brown, 1968), pp. 91–106.

[29]Craft, "Moral Responsibility for Welsh Psychopaths," pp. 92–93.

[30]Craft, "Moral Responsibility for Welsh Psychopaths," p. 91.

found that milieu therapy had a decisively positive effect on the psychopathic children. Their level of internalized guilt increased, their view of authority became less fearful and punitive, and their aggression subsided. Their control of impulsivity and destructiveness also increased. In most important aspects —aggression, guilt, view of authority—the psychopathic boys closely approached the scores of the "normal" suburban children after a year at Wiltwyck.

The McCords concluded that Wiltwyck provided an effective instrument for the treatment of psychopathy and that boys treated there need not become sociopathic adults. The warm supportive environment could serve to satisfy the childrens' dependency needs, which had been frustrated by their families. The consistency, nonpunitiveness, and social controls of the Wiltwyck staff could provide the prerequisites for the establishment of a conscience.[31]

Harrison Gough has expressed the belief that psychodrama is uniquely beneficial for the psychopath. Because the psychopath is seriously deficient in his ability to relate to other people, role-playing might help in showing him the feelings of others. Prison psychologists in San Quentin Penitentiary used psychodrama in addition to regular group discussion in a permissive atmosphere.[32]

Raymond J. Corsini, who has reported on the successful use of psychodrama with psychopaths at San Quentin, described in detail a psychodrama session with Don, a young inmate of the state correctional school for boys who had been diagnosed by a psychiatrist as a "primary psychopath, with no apparent conception of right or wrong."[33] In explaining why psychodrama was successful in changing this boy's behavior patterns and personality, he stated:

> In summary, it can be said that some people are impervious to certain kinds of symbols. There are, for example, nonreaders who just cannot comprehend written language. Some of these can be taught to read by motor procedure rather than by the ordinary visual procedures. It may well be that much the same is true with that class of people who appear deaf to reason and logic, who are labelled "psychopaths." In the treatment of such cases, actional procedures such as psychodrama do appear effective. . . .[34]

The therapeutic milieu provided by Synanon has also been credited with producing positive changes in the young sociopath. The constant self-assess-

---

[31]McCord and McCord, *The Psychopath,* pp. 138–65.

[32]McCord and McCord, *The Psychopath,* p. 104.

[33]Raymond Corsini, "Psychodrama with a Psychopath," *Group Psychotherapy* 11(March 1958): 33–39.

[34]Corsini, "Psychodrama with a Psychopath," p. 39.

ment required in the individual's daily life and in the Synanon sessions fosters self-identity and empathy. The individual's self-estimation is under constant assessment and attack by others who are sensitive and concerned about him, since he is significant to their own existence. The process provides the opportunity for the individual almost literally *to see himself as others do*. He is also compelled as part of this process to develop the ability to identify with and understand others. A side consequence of these processes is the development of self-growth, social ability, communicative powers, and empathic ability. The sociopathic behavior pattern is reversed and often corrected.

Chapter
9

The
Juvenile
in a
Violent
Society

ALBERT CAMUS, in *The Rebel,* his philosophical essay on the meanings of rebellion and revolution, had this to say about the contemporary violence that engulfs all citizens and has its special effect on juveniles:

> The poets themselves, confronted with the murder of their fellow men, proudly declare that their hands are clean. The whole world absent-mindedly turns its back on these crimes; the victims have reached the extremity of their disgrace: they are a bore. In ancient times the blood of murder at least produced a religious horror and in this way sanctified the value of life. The real condemnation of the period we live in is, on the contrary, that it leads us to think that it is not bloodthirsty enough. Blood is no longer visible; it does not bespatter the faces of our pharisees visibly enough. This is the extreme of nihilism; blind and savage murder becomes an oasis, and the imbecile criminal seems positively refreshing in comparison with our highly intelligent executioners.[1]

---

[1]Albert Camus, *The Rebel,* trans. Anthony Bower (New York: Knopf, 1954), pp. 279–80.© 1954, Alfred A. Knopf, Inc. Reprinted by permission.

There are still types of "senseless" violence and homicide that produce emotional reactions in the mass mind. The highly intelligent and socially ingrained executions of war, starvation, pollution, and unnecessary disease no longer seem to stir the general population beyond a murmur of tacit recognition. These phenomena are almost unreal since they are mainly experienced secondhand on television, in the newspapers, or on the movie screen. This blurring of reality is most evident in today's children. For many of them, the violence shown in a real-war report on the TV news is not too different from the fictionalized war of a dramatic program.

The fact that some children can still be appalled by some violence is encouraging. A writer for the *Los Angeles Times,* Bella Stumbo, reported in a series of articles a montage of fifth-grade children's responses to the contemporary issues of violence. The following random commentaries by ten- and eleven-year-old boys and girls reflects the violence that engulfs their existence:

"Some guys'll push you around just to show how tough they are. But I know kung fu. I been takin' it for five years. So if a guy hits me, he's dead. He'll turn real green, or else be real wounded."

"I wish my dad had a gun. Where I live people are getting robbed all the time, and somebody even stole my grandmother's TV."

"Sometimes me and my girl friend carry stuff at night, like a shoe or stick. I'd take my knife 'cept I'd probably be scared to use it."

"I've been asked to get in cars by old guys four or five times . . . ughh."

"One time I got beat up real bad. Some guys in a gang did it. I was all bloody and everything. They just started pickin' on me for no reason. So now when I see a bunch of guys walkin' down the street, I run to the other side and duck down."

"I got a pocket knife and I'd use it, too, so nobody better ever try to grab me."

"You shouldn't trust anybody except people your mother knows." . . .

"I always carry some kinda weapon when I go out. Like a bat or a stick, or I wear a belt with a big buckle. I was gonna get a bullwhip, but I don't know how to use it."

"I always wear my dad's steel-tipped shoes when I go empty the garbage at night," said another boy. "They're too big, but it's better than nothing."

"Adults are worse," said a boy, "because children aren't assassins. Like a boy might say he wants to kill another boy, but he wouldn't do it. Adults do it. Especially the crazy ones in bars and with wine and stuff.

Like, when you're a kid, you play with toy guns and say 'bang bang.' But when you are an adult, you get a real gun and shoot for real . . . I guess adults think they shouldn't play with toys anymore . . . the adult does all the violent things that boys do, but he does them for real. Especially when he is a soldier."[2]

That some children can still be emotionally moved by murder is in a strange way a positive commentary on modern society, for it indicates that the ultimate violence of homicide has not yet become a fully acceptable dimension of the human condition.

Some literary observers, like Camus, allege that violence and murder have become normative behavior patterns. For example, in a 1970 film, *Hard Contract* (written and directed by S. Lee Pogostin; distributed by 20th Century-Fox), a hired killer—the story never discloses his employer—sits casually in a theater munching a candy bar. He is calmly watching a newsreel portraying the war in Africa and showing the bloated dying bodies of starving Biafran children. A news commentator on the screen is unemotionally speculating on the predictable death of thousands of Biafran children, future victims of seemingly uncontrollable war and starvation. In the midst of this impersonal human holocaust, the man in the audience leans over and quietly kills his victim-of-the-month. The audience (and we are all in reality part of this audience) is confronted with the question: Which is more horrible—the inexorable murders on the screen or the murder in the theater? Is one more real than the other? The total film message suggests that we have broken through the sound barrier into the humanization (and acceptance) of violence. The film implies that the general public is no longer horrified by violence. It has become an integral part of the new human condition.

Another film "Taxi Driver" (1976) dramatizes the all-too-current condition of loneliness and senseless violence. In it, the taxi driver is a being who moves through the alienated crowd: jostled, brushed, ignored or abused, hassled, or pandered to, but who is somehow utterly untouched by any of it because of his own secret world of fantasy and his inability to communicate with his fellow humans—in short, a lonely man, aching to be noticed, recognized and loved, but unable to attain it.

Paul Schrader, the writer, makes his protagonist a Manhattan cabbie because he feels he is a prime example of a man who moves, works, walks, and talks and yet somehow is invisible to the eyes of his fellow men. He is not really a human being in the mind of his customers; he is part of the mechanics of the automobile, an inanimate thing like the steering wheel or the ash trays or the headlights. Dark confidences are freely discussed by his passengers within

---

[2]Bella Stumbo, "Violence and Youth," *Los Angeles Times,* November 22, 1973, Copyright, 1973, Los Angeles Times. Reprinted by permission.

his hearing, obscenities are performed in the back of his cab within the scope of his rear-view mirror. He is acknowledged briefly when the passenger enters the taxi and then consigned to limbo, to nonexistence, that is, until, at the end of the film, when he goes on a brutal "senseless" mass murder spree, claiming at least five lives.

This brand of dehumanized violence is validated further by a commentary report in the *Los Angeles Times* between two young teenagers arrested for a brutal, senseless murder:

> "Hey man, why did we kill that dude?"
> He shifted uncomfortably in the hard, straightback chair as he asked the question; his eyes searched the floor, as if he expected the answer to somehow appear on the scuffed tiles.
> His partner, older and more streetwise, replied without hesitation:
> "Hell man, we killed him to make an example outa him. That was real cool, the way the blood came outa his mouth and that gargling sound he made."
> "He just laid there and jerked."
> ... There was no simple motive for the crime: not robbery, nor the heat of combat, not even revenge.
> To them, murder was a means of gaining stature on the streets, a human life could be traded as easily as a bubble gum card.
> Even the most hardened police officers—listening to this recently recorded conversation—are horrified by the nonchalance with which today's adolescents assault and kill.
> "I can't think of a time when we've had in this city, 14- and 15-year old kids who were such cold-blooded killers," said Asst. Los Angeles Police Chief Daryl Gates.
> "But, we have them: absolutely cold-blooded killers who think nothing about just killing somebody."[3]

Not all juvenile homicide is violence by strangers against strangers. Often these killings are kept all in the family. One bizarre case of this kind reveals something about the type of crime after which neighbors often comment: "He was a nice quiet kid. I never thought he could hurt a fly." A prototypical case of this pattern is that of a young man who killed his parents and then committed suicide.

> Four days before Gregg Sanders, 15, of Mountainside, N.J., killed his parents with an ax and then threw himself to his death from a water

---

[3] *Los Angeles Times,* January 14, 1973.

tower, he was reprimanded by his history teacher. He was worried about it.

The teacher had threatened the boy with a demerit because he had been talking in class, which meant that a letter would be sent home to Gregg's parents. This had never happened before.

In fact, the tall, good-looking sophomore had been regarded as something of a model student. He had earned good grades, but he was not seen by his classmates as an overly aggressive striver. Instead, they saw him as a humorous boy who joked and teased good-naturedly and who enjoyed sports. His teachers liked him too and his neighbors thought him thoughtful and courteous.

And yet in dozens of interviews with his friends, his teachers, his physician and law-enforcement officials that were conducted after the suicide-murders, another picture of Gregg emerged—that of an adolescent tormented by unattained and secret aspirations, who sought solace in a secret room and in secret dreams. . . .

On Tuesday, Jan. 14, the day Gregg killed his parents and himself, Paul Gleason, Gregg's German teacher, recalled that during class discussion he had asked Gregg what he had been doing the night before.

"I read Shirer's 'The Rise and Fall of the Third Reich,' " the boy answered. [In a secret room in his attic there were a mattress, a lamp, books, empty liquor bottles and canteens of water. There were also a number of Nazi emblems and insignia.] "It was the fifth time."

The teacher asked whether Gregg meant it was the fifth time he had started the 1,245-page book.

"No, it's the fifth time I am reading it through," Gregg replied.

Gleason was intrigued. "Most students Gregg's age have no knowledge of the Nazi period," the teacher said. "I asked him what he thought of Hitler."

Gleason recalled that Gregg thought a while and then replied, "He was a genius; unfortunately he was insane. . . ."

Psychiatrists who have been apprised of the case agree that the secret room, the feelings of pressure and the allure of Hitler signify something profound, but what it is they cannot say. From the evidence at hand they cannot even agree whether Gregg was insane or not. . . .

In an attempt to understand the forces that led to the Sanders family tragedy, Dr. W. Hugh Missildine, professor of psychiatry at Ohio State University, speculated that Gregg could well have been tormented by a conflict between "his tremendous rebellion at the perfectionistic attitudes of his parents and a tremendous desire to please them."

"This boy seemed to keep both his rebellion and self-belittlement under wraps in equal portions, until it built up with great pressure and he could not cope with it anymore.

"But as to what really happened and why, I suppose we will never know."[4]

Murders of this type seem to be happening among younger and younger children. In an article on child homicides (children under eleven who kill), Henry de Young describes several prototypical examples.

A young Cleveland woman, babysitting with her four-month-old niece, rushed to investigate the child's frantic screams. She passed her two-year-old son running from the bedroom, saying, "Hit the baby, Mommy! Baby bad girl!" The infant died a short while later, bludgeoned by the boy with a heavy metal toy.

Two boys on Long Island, aged six and eight, were discovered to have brutally beaten to death a younger child. The boys were taking karate lessons at the time.

A New York infant was found dead in her crib by her mother. Autopsy revealed that the child, amazingly, had drowned. An investigation by the medical examiner's office determined that a three-year-old brother had dragged the baby to the bathroom, drowned it in the toilet and returned the body to the crib.[5]

De Young partially explains the phenomenon by referring to part of the framework of violence:

For the young child, however, there are other factors at work. First of all, and perhaps most relevant, there is television which contributes immensely to the "unreality" of death and the generally low value ascribed to human life. Every night of the week, children may see as many as two dozen shootings, hangings, knifings, poisonings, assaults with clubs and automobiles and countless other forms of mayhem. Furthermore, such assaults on life are rarely depicted as wrong, or even objectionable; they're perpetrated, often as not, by the good guys—police officers, cowboys and cowgirls, private eyes, cartoon characters—against the bad guys, or those who are perceived to be bad. To further confuse the young and undiscriminating mind, the victims of this senseless violence never seem to be really dead: an actor who "dies" on "The Rookies" at 7:30 P.M. is often magically resurrected to appear, unharmed and little the worse off for his ordeal, an hour later on "S.W.A.T." Dying in TV-land is also a nice, clean way of departing this life. There's rarely any blood, and never an honest depiction of what violent death is really like.

---

[4]Michael T. Kaufman, "Boy's Mind A Secret Room," *New York Times,* February 1, 1975. Copyright 1975 by the New York Times Company. Reprinted by permission.

[5]Henry de Young, "Homicide (Children's Division)," *Human Behavior* (February 1976). Copyright 1976 Human Behavior. Reprinted by permission.

"If every kid under 10 could see what a gunshot does to people in real life," observes a Chicago police officer, "I have little doubt that our homicide rate would be cut in half. It's an ugly sight."[6]

Another dimension of the violent society that encapsules juveniles is the proliferation of guns and the senseless way in which weaponry has become a part of the home, like kitchen utensils. Consider the following motiveless homicide which never would have happened if a gun were not available:

Nine-year-old Marie Barcroft thought it was play when a 3-year-old threatened her and her father with a .357-magnum pistol. Then she watched in horror as the youngster turned and killed her 7-year-old friend.

"It was just the awfullest thing I ever saw," the young south Baltimore girl said after her friend's death Sunday.

"Jeffrey just stood there for a moment with a big hole in his stomach and blood all over the place. Then he fell over."

The victim, Jeffrey Krausch, was shot once in the chest from point-blank range, police said. He was pronounced dead at South Baltimore General Hospital shortly after 2 P.M.

Police would not disclose the name of the child who shot Jeffrey.

The father of the 3-year-old is a security guard, and neighbors said they had seen the gun in his car on previous occasions.[7]

On the gross availability of guns, Art Seidenbaum made the following insightful, poignant, and accurate commentary.

The environment of armed camp is where we live, uneasily.

Last week was a magnificent example of the city as bedlam, of urban terror on the ground and in the air as four disturbed individuals in four parts of town held the larger community as hostage.

First there was the young man who flew a near-Kamikaze mission over Seal Beach, with a shotgun as his hand luggage. He was upset, say the reports, because of an irreconcilable difference with his girlfriend over theological matters.

So he stole a plane, made several low passes over innocent residential targets and almost smacked into a pursuing police helicopter. A neighborhood had to be evacuated during the raid. The gun-toting pilot had talked of suicide. He had also mentioned doing something reminiscent of what Charles Whitman did several years ago from the University of Texas tower: firing at will—at people, at random.

Accidentally, no one was killed.

Then came the man who climbed the roof to shoot at downtown Los

---

[6]de Young, "Homicide (Children's Division)."

[7]Los Angeles Times, July 27, 1976.

Angeles. His tower was the top of an old hotel. His weapon was a semi-automatic rifle, newly bought in Hollywood. His stated motive was to set an example for society by strafing it.

"I never intended to shoot anyone," the police said he said after arrest. What he wanted to prove was how easy it is for anybody to buy a gun, take the high ground and use a town for target practice.

He proved it. He fired more than one dozen shots before surrendering. One bank employee, attracted by the commotion, went to his office window and was almost hit by a bullet.

Accidentally, no one was killed.

Meanwhile, in South San Gabriel, a man with a pistol barricaded himself in his own house and held his three children as hostages against sheriff's deputies.

He was a veteran. He was having marital problems. He had been drinking. He had threatened his wife with a .38-caliber revolver. He also happened to have an M-1 carbine and a store of ammunition in the house.

The siege lasted more than 15 hours. The man's stepfather and stepbrother finally subdued him as the sheriff's special weapons team kept vigil outside.

Fortunately, no one was killed or injured.

Finally, a Westminster man with a rifle started another siege situation. He held his mother hostage. He caused a neighborhood evacuation. He'd gone through a divorce and psychiatric treatment. He surrendered.

Happily, no one was injured, no one was killed.

All the men last week were armed. All of them were prepared to turn their upsets inside-out and fire at the world. All of them were young. All of them were eventually captured.

Not one of them was a criminal in the common sense. They didn't want to rob, rape or collect ransom. Their acts may have been more or less premeditated, but none of them had grand designs to steal. Not one of them was in it for the money.

Each of them was endangering life because of his own inability to cope with life.

The persuasive people who argue against gun control are constantly telling us that guns don't kill people, people kill people. A nice phrase.

The not-so-nice reality is that people with guns kill more people than people without guns. Less catchy, but true.

The gun is the perfect device for transforming an anonymous, unhappy human being into a mass murderer everyone will recognize.

The gun is what allows an assassin to become more than just another face in the crowd.

The gun is what gives a psychotic person authority, allowing a self-described victim to reverse the misery and turn the people out there—on the street, in their homes—into the victims.

The gun is one wretched person's anguish pointed at all the rest of us.

Los Angeles was lucky last week: no mass shootouts. But this city, like every city, remains loaded. The deadliest urban problem in America is the precise weapon in the hand of an unbalanced brain.

We are, all of us, under the gun.

And only the politicians—or mass outrage—can take last week's luck and use it as a lesson for disarmament at home.[8]

American society has always had a large amount of this brand of violence, popularly called "senseless violence." Notable in American history are the following cases: the assassinations of John F. Kennedy, Martin Luther King, and Robert Kennedy; the serial killing of eight student nurses by Richard Speck in Chicago; the mass killing of nine people in a home in Victorville, California; the brutal ritualistic murders of Charles Manson's "family"; the murder of over twenty-five migrant farm workers by Juan Corona; and the brutal homicides of over twenty-eight teenagers over a three-year period in Houston, Texas, by Wayne Henley, David Brooks, and Dean Corll. These last grisly murders were described by Brooks in his statement to the police:

> *In all, I guess there were between 25 and 30 boys killed, and they were buried in three different places. I was present and helped bury many of them but not all of them. . . . On the first one at Sam Rayburn [Reservoir] I helped bury him, and then the next one we took to Sam Rayburn. When we got there, Dean and Wayne found that the first one had come to the surface and either a foot or a hand was above the ground. When they buried this one the second time, they put some type of rock sheet on top of him to keep him down.*
> —David Owen Brooks, in his statement to Texas police.

To the people of Pasadena, Texas, a modest industrial suburb of Houston, Dean Allen Corll was a clean-cut, quiet neighbor who kept pretty much to himself. He seemed to be a "nice, polite man who loved to be around kids," one acquaintance recalled. Last week stunned residents of Pasadena had a different view of the 33-year-old bachelor electrician who had been their neighbor since June. After an all-night party in Corll's two-bedroom frame cottage, he was shot to death with his own gun by 17-year old Elmer Wayne Henley.

Henley told police that Corll had turned on him and two other youths, threatening to sexually molest and kill them. Instead, Henley said, he had managed to kill Corll in self-defense. He then recounted to Houston police an incredible tale of horror, homosexual sadism and mass

---

[8]Art Seidenbaum, "We're All Under the Gun," *Los Angeles Times,* December 10, 1976. Copyright, 1976, *Los Angeles Times.* Reprinted by permission.

murder in which he, Corll and a third accomplice, David Owen Brooks, 18, had taken part during the past three years.[9]

Is violence—more explicitly, homicide—now more accepted? Has the audience to seemingly senseless official and unofficial violence become as ahuman as the killers? It is of value to examine these possibilities in the context of what is "logical" and what is "senseless" violence in the larger society, since it is this crucible of social forces that molds or causes juvenile violence.

Legal, Sanctioned, and Rational Violence

War is the ultimate violent activity undertaken by a society that is considered legal, rational, and sanctioned. Under some circumstances this pattern of violence is justified by virtually all segments of the society, especially when the country is the victim of what is defined as an unprovoked attack. In general, wars are considered justified by the dominant groups in the society when the nation is committed to them in an effort to defend the status quo of its social structure. When law-enforcement officials engage in violent activities, they justify their actions as necessary for the maintenance of "law and order," which they tend to equate with the maintenance of the status quo of the social and political structure. In many situations, violent actions by the nation (war) and by law-enforcement officials are forces militating against social change. Violent efforts to maintain present (or idealized versions of former) standards of morality, national boundaries, or spheres of influence and to resist ethical or moral shifts, are regarded as legal, sanctioned, and rational by large segments of our society.[10]

The process of war requires the direct and indirect brutalization of young people—who must necessarily fight the wars. Youngsters must be conditioned and motivated to join the armed forces, where they are systematically trained to kill. War is therefore a pattern of behavior that is glamorized and aggrandized for young people. Often this preparation for violence has the fallout of pushing young people closer to a violent edge of behavior outside of the armed services. Many gang patterns are crude imitations of society's larger and more sophisticated patterns of institutionalized violence.

In Chapter 4 we cited an article by Suzanne Steinmetz and Murray

---

[9] *Time,* August 20, 1973, p. 24. Reprinted by permission from TIME, The Weekly Newsmagazine; Copyright Time Inc.

[10] This viewpoint is further substantiated by a federal investigation that became known as the Walker Report: *Rights in Conflict: A Report Submitted by Daniel Walker, Director of the Chicago Study Team, to the National Commission on the Causes and Prevention of Violence* (New York: Signet, 1969).

Straus in which they describe how we tend to automatically accept family violence in the United States.[11] The article cites the high degree of aggression that "normally" takes place in most American families. On a broader cross-cultural base, the field of anthropology reveals many other examples of legal, sanctioned, and rational violence in other societies. Among certain Eskimo tribes, homicide was a perfectly legal and rational way of freeing the tribe of the burden of the aged when food was difficult to find. A classic case of this homicidal pattern in the family is described by E. M. Weyer:

> A hunter living on the Diomede Islands related to the writer how he killed his own father, at the latter's request. The old Eskimo was failing, he could no longer contribute what he thought should be his share as a member of the group; so he asked his son, then a lad about twelve years old, to sharpen the big hunting knife. Then he indicated the vulnerable spot over his heart where his son should stab him. The boy plunged the knife deep, but the stroke failed to take effect. The old father suggested with dignity and resignation, "Try it a little higher, my son." The second stab was effective and the patriarch passed into the realm of the ancestral shades.[12]

Other examples of this broader base of violence include institutionalized infanticide and a harsh violent approach to "the control of delinquency." Peter Freuchen cites another case of juvenile violence in Eskimo society:

> The boy's debut in terrorism had taken place at Cape York where he collected a load of rotten birds' eggs and hid them high up on a hillside. Then one day he became loudly hysterical and shouted: "A ship! A ship! A big ship is coming!" Magic words, of course, to natives who were seldom visited by outsiders.
> They all hurried up on the hillside to get a look at the boat. Meanwhile the boy crouched behind a rock, and when his friends were close enough he jumped out and pelted them with his peculiarly offensive cache. This naturally reflected upon Kullabak's house, and she had tried to apologize, but being a lone woman, without a husband, there was not much she could say to reestablish herself.
> So she asked Mayark to help her get rid of the boy, and Mayark took him up onto the glacier and pushed him down in a crevasse. That, by all rights, should have been the end of him. Kullabak went into

---

[11]Suzanne K. Steinmetz and Murray A. Straus, "The Family as a Cradle of Violence," *Society* 10 (September 1973):50–56.

[12]E. M. Weyer. *The Eskimos* (New Haven: Yale University Press, 1932).

traditional mourning, but her mourning was pretty effectively interrupted when the boy came walking into the house. By some miracle he had escaped death in the fall, and had followed the crevasse to its portal near the sea.

After that no one dared touch him, and the boy played all manner of tricks to revenge himself. He was a big, strapping youngster, but he had no hunting gear of his own and had to borrow what he wanted from the hunters while they slept. One day, while Mayark was away on a hunting trip, he went to Mayark's house and told his wife that he had followed Mayark some distance and that when they had parted, Mayark had told him that he might stay in his house and take all a husband's privileges. Mayark's wife was an obedient, loving wife, and not until her husband returned home did she realize that she had been tricked. All the villagers had the laugh on Mayark.

The boy also helped himself from various caches and never took the trouble to close them. His mother was at her wits' end, and finally decided that if she wanted to save the honor of her house she must do something desperate. One night while he was asleep with his head protruding beyond the end of the ledge, she made a sealskin-line noose, slipped it over his head and pulled it tight.

Thus ended the criminal pranks of one young man, and his mother was highly honored for her good deed. Now she was remarried, and her great, booming voice was always an asset at parties.[13]

Until relatively recently, the violence of juveniles was generally directed at other juveniles. It took the form of individual fights, gang fights, and vandalism. In the middle 1970s, considerable violence by juveniles has been directed at adults. In one eighteen-month study of 757 school districts, a substantial increase in violent behavior in high schools was discovered. Assaults on teachers in the schools had increased by 77.4 percent between 1970 and 1973. During the same period, assaults on other students was up by 85.3 percent, and robberies were up 36.7 percent. The violence was not limited to slum areas and inner city schools. It occurred in middle class schools as well. During the one year period, approximately $500 million was spent by schools to repair damage to buildings and grounds resulting from vandalism.[14] Violence directed at old people had also increased sharply according to the following article.

---

[13]Peter Freuchen, *Arctic Adventure: My Life in the Frozen North* (New York: Farrar & Rinehart, 1935), pp. 123–24. Copyright 1935, 1962 by Peter Freuchen. Reprinted by permission of Harold Matson Co., Inc.

[14]John P. Dececco, and Arlene K. Richards, "Civil War in the High Schools," *Psychology Today,* November 1975, pp. 51–56 and 120.

'Crib Jobs'

The victims are old people, often very old. Hattie Erwin, who is 103, was inching down a Brooklyn street with the aid of her walker when she was knocked to the ground and robbed of her groceries—worth no more than $2. The assailants are the young—sometimes the very young. It was a 7-year-old boy who accosted Esther Hornick, 68, in her Bronx apartment building, poked her repeatedly with a sharpened broom handle and demanded money—terrifying her so much that now, she says, "I'm afraid of my own shadow." This latest refinement of inner-city life is forcing its victims to live in a state of semi-siege. In some cases, it is more than they can take. After two assaults in less than two months, a New York couple in their 70s recently laid out their best clothes on their bed, wrote a note saying, "We don't want to live in fear any more"—and committed suicide.

In street slang, crimes against the elderly are often called "crib jobs," because they are like taking candy from a baby. They are flaring up in the decaying, racially mixed neighborhoods of urban areas across the nation, and a recent Louis Harris survey showed that fear of a criminal attack is now the major concern of the elderly. Some police officials believe that the recent burst of headlines about attacks on the elderly reflects not so much a real increase as a sudden media interest. But none deny that the youthful criminals who stalk the aged are becoming more sadistic, or that the elderly need more protec-

tion. In several cities, the police and community service groups have begun a number of programs—ranging from escort services to karate lessons—to save the aged from their tormentors.

It often seems a losing battle. Although some elderly victims do testify against their attackers, a far larger number are afraid to do so—or even to notify police for fear that their assailants will retaliate. Some New York City officials speculate that for every victim who reports a crime, as many as 30 keep silent. Since many of those who prey on the aged are young, they are usually given only brief detention sentences—if that—and are soon back on the streets. In addition, prosecutors in New York, for example, are barred from revealing a suspect's juvenile arrest record and judges thus have no idea whether they are facing a first-offender or a long-time criminal.

67 Arrests: In one such case, Ronald Timmons, 20, who had been arrested and charged with beating and robbing an 82-year-old New York woman, was released on $500 bail; the law prevented the judge from being told that Timmons had a record of 67 previous arrests—including one charge of murdering a 92-year-old man. Timmons promptly moved on to Baltimore, where FBI agents arrested him on bail-jumping charges last week.

The elderly are a young criminal's ideal victims. "They're weak and vulnerable," explained Mark Forrester, a San Francisco social worker. "They always have some money with them and are usually too shaken by the attack to remember things clearly." But what outrages police is that the young assailants are not content with simple purse-snatches or apartment break-ins; instead, they seem to enjoy hurting their victims. In Seattle, police reported that violent street crime against the elderly has increased by 18 per cent this year. In New York, two 16-year-old step-brothers allegedly tried to rape a 75-year-old woman after robbing her (her screams brought help and the youths fled). In Detroit, an 80-year-old woman was jumped in a supermarket parking lot by three youths. When she clung to her purse, they shot her in the face. And the New York couple who committed suicide, Hans Kable, 78, and his wife, Emma, 76, were driven to it by young thugs who repeatedly stabbed Emma Kable in the face with a kitchen fork, demanding money that she did not have.

Those who survive are increasingly reclusive. "We find some of them almost starved to death," said New York City detective Donald Gaffney. "They're afraid to leave their apartment after a robbery and won't even go to the supermarket." Some band together for protection, moving in huddled groups and gathering in social clubs—but they are the courageous minority.

Many of the elderly are simply too poor to move to safer neighborhoods, despite their fears. Others are unwilling to abandon the homes that mean

so much to them. "I have my memories in this apartment," said Clara Engelmann, 64, a Bronx resident. "My children were both married here and so was my younger sister." Then, thinking of the youths who have robbed her twice, she snapped: "I wouldn't give the apartment to them, it's too good for them. No! I'm not moving."

Counseling and Karate: Cities have tried to combat the spate of crimes against the elderly in a variety of ways. Young policemen "aged" with make-up shuffle along Seattle's streets, posing as decoys for young hoodlums. Chicago, Los Angeles and New York have obtained $750,000 in Federal funds for self-help and victim-assistance programs. Six young San Francisco men, trained in social counseling as well as karate, provide a federally funded escort service to take the aged on their necessary errands; to date, they have logged 2,700 crime-free trips. Police in Charleston, W. Va., run "Operation Good Morning"; if elderly residents fail to telephone each day, the police check to be sure they are all right.

Police say that they arrest a relatively high number of those who victimize the elderly, and that the attackers often show shame and contrition after their crimes. But that doesn't put an end to the attacks— and as the elderly victims themselves diagnose it, the best thing the police could do would be to put more beat men on the street to protect them.[15]

---

[15]Richard Steele with bureau reports, " 'Crib Jobs'," *Newsweek,* November 29, 1976, p. 39.

The Duet Frame of Violence

A considerable amount of violence by juveniles has an interactional quality where the aggressor in violence winds up as the ultimate victim. A child who comes home crying about being hit or beaten up may have a perceptive parent raise the question, "What did you do to provoke being hit?" Generally, the victim of violence is often a participant in his own injury. The pattern was first analyzed in Hans von Hentig's now classic work, *The Criminal and His Victim.* [16] The concept has been more recently developed by Marvin Wolfgang and has pertinence in the analysis of juvenile violence.

Marvin Wolfgang terms the pattern *victim-precipitated homicide.* On the basis of his research into over 588 consecutive homicides committed in Philadelphia from January 1948 to December 31, 1952, Wolfgang concluded that 150 cases, or 26 percent, were what he calls victim-precipitated homicide. Wolfgang explains the concept this way:

> In many crimes, especially in criminal homicide, the victim is often a major contributor to the criminal act. Except in cases in which the victim is an innocent bystander and is killed in lieu of an intended victim, or in cases in which a pure accident is involved, the victim may be one of the major precipitating causes of his own demise.
>
> Various theories of social interaction, particularly in social psychology, have established the framework for the present discussion. In criminological literature, however, probably von Hentig, in *The Criminal and His Victim,* provided the most useful theoretical base for analysis of the victim-offender relationship. In Chapter XII, entitled "The Contribution of the Victim to the Genesis of Crime," the author discusses this "duet frame of crime" and suggests that homicide is particularly amenable to analysis. In *Penal Philosophy,* Tarde frequently attacks the "legislative mistake" of concentrating too much on premeditation and paying too little attention to motives, which indicate an important interrelationship between victim and offender. And in one of his satirical essays, "On Murder Considered as One of the Fine Arts," Thomas De Quincey shows cognizance of the idea that sometimes the victim is a would-be murderer. Garofalo, too, noted that the victim may provoke another individual into attack, and though the provocation be slight, if perceived by an egoistic attacker it may be sufficient to result in homicide.
>
> The role of the victim is characterized by his having been the first in the homicide drama to use physical force directed against his subse-

---

[16]Hans von Hentig, *The Criminal and His Victim* (New Haven: Yale University Press, 1948), pp. 383–85.

quent slayer. The victim-precipitated cases are those in which the victim was the first to show and use a deadly weapon, to strike a blow in an altercation—in short, the first to commence the interplay or resort to physical violence.[17]

Von Hentig and Wolfgang's interactional hypothesis has been developed further in an analysis by Dr. David Abrahamsen.

> The relationship between criminal and victim is much more complicated than the law would care to acknowledge. The criminal and his victim work on each other unconsciously. We can say that as the criminal shapes the victim, the victim also shapes the criminal. While the law looks upon this relationship from an objective, nonemotional viewpoint, the psychological attitude of the participants is quite different. The law differentiates distinctly between the attacker and the victim. But their relationship may be, and often is, quite close, so that their roles are reversed and the victim becomes the determining person, while the victimizer in the end becomes his own victim. . . .
>
> Trapped and helpless, and beset by inner conflicts, the murderer encounters his victim, who also is full of conflicts. Through the foreplay—comparable to foreplay preceding sexual intercourse—and interplay between attacker and victim, intentions and motivations may be spelled out, because the protagonists do not understand themselves. Instead they act out what they harbor in their mind. There is a victimizer and a victim; and the border between them during the victimization is as blurred as their self-image. Intertwined with each other, they represent on every level of the conscious and unconscious mind a stream of fluid and transitory emotions than can hardly be deciphered.[18]

The pattern of victim-precipitated violence is often acted out by youths who have a chip on their shoulder. Such youths, by their demeanor, provoke violence. For example, it might be impossible to ascertain the victim proneness of the twenty-eight or so youths killed by the mass slayer in Houston, Texas, yet we can speculate with a degree of rationality that a number of them placed themselves in jeopardy by joining gangs, or attending the "sex parties" reputedly run by the killer and his cohorts. Many youths, therefore, are partial participants in being victimized by placing themselves in a position to be assaulted as co-conspirators in their own assaults or deaths.

---

[17]Marvin E. Wolfgang,"Victim-Precipitated Criminal Homicide," *Journal of Criminal Law, Criminology, and Police Science* 48(June 1957):1.

[18]David Abrahamsen, *The Murdering Mind* (New York: Harper & Row, 1973), p. 35.

"Senseless" Violence

Most patterns of violence described so far have, on closer inspection, a cloak of rationality and sanction in the social conditions, issues, and situations that surround their expression. The concept of "senseless violence" refers to violent action that does not flow from any readily comprehensible social conditions or issues. It is a direct expression of an individual's psychic disorder at a given time in his life.

Legal, sanctioned, rational violence, such as war or police violence, constitutes acts propelled by a fundamental desire to maintain the norms and equilibrium of the social structure. War is generally seen by its proponents as an effort to defend or restore the social structure, and violence in law enforcement is justified as an effort to maintain the legal structure. The violence that flows from these circumstances is comprehensible even if there is disagreement about its use. The defense of one's honor as a gang reaction or the unauthorized illegal use of force to defend certain values is also understandable within the framework of societal norms.

Psychiatrists attribute many acts of senseless violence to a psychotic condition. They describe this condition as a type of emotional breakdown that causes an individual to have hallucinations and to fantasize that people are out to get him, and he assaults or kills them before they can harm him. A considerable proportion of incidents of senseless violence by juveniles, however, may best be accounted for by the previously described psychopathic or sociopathic personality, that is, the individual with limited social conscience who has no real compassion for others.

An aspect of the sociopath's breakthrough into violence may be termed *existential validation.* When a person feels constantly alienated from other human beings, he begins to lose the sense of his own humanity and requires increasingly heavier dosages of bizarre and extreme behavior to validate the fact that he really exists. The extreme behavior gives him a glimmer of feeling when nothing else does. As one gang killer commented to one of the authors, "When I stabbed him once, I did it again and again, because it really made me feel alive for the first time in my life."[19]

The noted playwright Arthur Miller, drawing upon a study he made of juveniles in a tough area in New York, described the pattern of "senseless violence" as stemming from boredom:

> The boredom of the delinquent is remarkable mainly because it is so little compensated for, as it may be among the middle classes and the rich who can fly down to the Caribbean or to Europe, or refurnish the house, or

---

[19]This concept is detailed in Lewis Yablonsky's *The Violent Gang,* rev. ed. (Baltimore: Penguin, 1971).

have an affair, or at least go shopping. The delinquent is stuck with his boredom, stuck inside it, stuck to it, until for two or three minutes he "lives"; he goes on a raid around the corner and feels the thrill of risking his skin or his life as he smashes a bottle filled with gasoline on some other kid's head. In a sense, it is his trip to Miami. It makes his day. It is his shopping tour. It gives him something to talk about for a week. It is *life*. Standing around with nothing coming up is as close to dying as you can get. Unless one grasps the power of boredom, the threat of it to one's existence, it is impossible to "place" the delinquent as a member of the human race.[20]

In brief, there are two dominant patterns of delinquency-related violence. One involves, in a sense, an institutional sheath. Violence here is a secondary act that is instrumental to or a by-product of other delinquent activity (e.g., gang retaliation or robbery). The other pattern is primary, raw, senseless violence that emanates from a young person's sociopathic condition.

The Sociocultural Climate of Violence in Contemporary Society

It would be logical to speculate that a youth growing up in a nonviolent social system would be less inclined to be violent than a youth growing up in a climate of violence. War, parental aggression (overt and covert), institutionalized violence by political leaders, mass media presentations of violence—all are factors that produce a violent environment.

More specifically, the violence proneness of adults in a society affects the degree of violence committed by young people in the same society. Obviously, in a nonviolent social system most people would not ordinarily commit acts of aggression. The opposite would also hold true. Within the climate of Nazi Germany, for example, it would be expected that youth growing up in this milieu would be more amenable to violent behavior. A general hypothesis that would be affirmed by most people is that a person (young or old) in Nazi Germany would be more likely to follow orders and commit aggressive acts than would the average individual in American society. Here we are essentially concerned not with the acting out of violence but with the predisposition proneness of Americans to commit acts of aggression. Information on this theme would provide some clues to the violence of young people that often stems from the "violent characteristics" of their adult role models in American society.

One set of experiments that fits into this category was the research of

---

[20]Arthur Miller, "The Bored and the Violent," *Harper's Magazine,* November 1962, p. 51.

psychologist Stanley Milgram at Yale University in the early sixties, and that appears to be a continuing pattern in the seventies.[21] In his studies Milgram was concerned with the conditions under which people would be obedient or disobedient to authority. In his overall project, which extended over a period of several years, almost a thousand individuals were subjects of his research. He investigated a variety of experimental settings and variable modifications. The results, however, were frighteningly uniform. On the basis of his research, Milgram concluded that a majority of "good people," who in their everyday lives were responsible and decent, could be made to perform "callous and severe" acts on other people when they were placed in situations that had the "trappings of authority."

The "harsh acts" included giving electric shocks to another individual who might have just died of a heart attack. The following detailed description of one of Milgram's projects more clearly illustrates the general research approach that was used.

The subjects in this prototype example of the Milgram experiments on obedience were a random sample of New Haven adult males who came to Milgram's Yale Research Center in response to a newspaper advertisement. They were paid by the hour and individually brought to a laboratory and introduced to their partners who were, in reality, members of the research team. Each subject was told that he was going to participate in a learning experiment with his partner. One of them was to be the "teacher" and the other the "learner." It was contrived that the subject always wound up as the teacher, and the research assistant always became the learner. The subject was then told, incorrectly, that the research was being conducted to determine the effects of punishment on learning.

The subject, now the teacher, witnessed the standard procedure by which the learner (in reality a member of the research staff) was strapped into a chair that apparently had electrical connections. The subject was then taken into another room and told to ask the learner certain questions from a questionnaire he was given. The teacher was told to administer electric shocks every time the learner gave a wrong answer. (In some cases, before the learner was strapped into his *electric chair*, he would comment, "Take it easy on me, I have a heart condition.")

In the room with the teacher was another member of the research team who served as an authority figure and as a provocateur. He was present to make sure that the subject administered the proper shocks for incorrect answers.

The subject was told by the authority figure to give progressively stronger shocks to the learner when the latter's answers were incorrect. In front of the subject was an elaborate electric board that, as far as the subject knew, con-

[21]Stanley Milgram, "Some Conditions of Obedience and Disobedience to Authority," *Human Relations* 18 (1965):57–76.

trolled shock levels from 15 to 450 volts in 15-volt gradations. The last two switches were ominously labeled XXX.

The researcher in the room would admonish the subject to increase the shock for each incorrect answer. In a short time the subject was repeatedly, as far as he knew, giving shocks of up to 450 volts to another person in the next room. The "victim" would often dramatically pound the wall and shout "Stop it, you're killing me!" Some subjects balked at continuing but proceeded on the orders of the authority figure, who would simply say, "Continue the experiment."

At a certain point the "victim," after pounding on the wall, would "play dead," or act as if he passed out and make no sound. The researcher in the room would instruct the subject to count "no response" as an incorrect answer. He would then order him to continue to shock an apparently inert or dead body with heavy electric shocks.

In several cases, when the subject refused to act out his robopathic behavior of continuing to shock the victim because "Christ, I don't hear him anymore, maybe I killed him! You know he said he had a bad heart," the researcher would say, "Go on with the experiment." The authoritative voice of the Yale researcher caused more than half of the subjects to continue to robopathically shock what might very well have been a dead body!

In a part of the experiment, some subjects refused to go on. The researcher would tell the subject to continue, and say, "Go ahead, I'll be responsible for what happens to the 'learner'." When this was done, the subject would usually say, "O.K., I'll continue. Remember you're responsible, not me!"

One of Milgram's experiments, conducted with forty subjects, is typical of those overall experiments carried out with almost one thousand people. All forty subjects complied by shocking their "victims" with up to 300 volts. Fourteen stopped at that point or at slightly higher levels. But the majority —twenty-six subjects—continued to administer increasingly severe shocks until they reached 450 volts. This was beyond the switch marked *Danger: Severe Shock.* Thus 65 percent of this representative sample of "good people," paid a few dollars an hour, conformed to the dictates of an experimental authority situation to the point that they supposedly inflicted severe pain or possible death on another human being.

Essentially the research validated the assumption that people would conform to the dictates of people in authority even when they knew they were inflicting severe harm on another person up to and beyond homicide. Authority, in a legitimate social context, thus produced obedience and conformity to ahuman goals—even in America.

It would be difficult to measure the degree of violent components in an individual and perhaps even more difficult to estimate the number of such individuals in a society. (A wild speculation, in accord with the Milgram experiment, would be: more than half of the population.) Perhaps even more difficult is the measurement of the number of what Jules Feiffer calls "little murders," which people "just doing their job" inflict on others in everyday life.

Several issues are blatantly clear. The majority of people tend to support illegal and immoral wars and their concomitant killings. Common people do sanction many little murders and big murders, especially if the perpetrators are legitimately acting within the proper formal societal contexts. This climate of violence surrounds the socialization of young people—and helps to account for the acceleration of "senseless violence" in juveniles.

Another reason for the developing climate of violence that effects violence in juveniles is the growing alienation of people in a machinelike social system. One observer of the scene, Lynn B. Iglitzin, comments:

> By far the most potent source of violence is the ubiquity of feelings of alienation and anomie which plague so many human beings in modern society. Feelings of normlessness and meaninglessness, of estrangement from one's self and from others are the generally accepted characteristics of alienation. The alienated person is out of touch with himself and with other persons; he is at the mercy of his technological creations, a "thing" dependent on unknown powerful forces.[22]

R. D. Laing, the British psychoanalyst, defines alienation in his poignant description of the human condition, particularly of the white European and North American, as a sense of "being at an end: of being only half alive in the fibrillating heartland of a senescent civilization."[23] This pervasive condition of estrangement from ourselves and from the human community provides a setting in which people have perpetrated incredible acts of violence upon each other and have been able to rationalize such behavior as "normality." According to psychiatrists such as Laing and Erich Fromm, it has become "normal" to be alienated, and the more one thus behaves like everyone else—that is, treating others as commodities rather than as human beings—the more one is taken to be sane. It is Laing's belief that those who are considered sick in an alienated world might be the healthiest of all. Laing conceptualizes that "the condition of alienation, of being asleep, of being unconscious, of being out of one's mind, is the condition of the normal man."[24] As support for this premise, he notes that "normal men have killed perhaps 100,000,000 of their fellow normal men in the last fifty years."[25]

In brief, the described "climate of violence" in society is a necessary

[22]Lynne B. Iglitzin, *Violent Conflict in American Society* (San Francisco: Chandler, 1972), p. 97.

[23]R. D. Laing, *The Politics of Experience* (New York: Pantheon Books, 1967), p. xiii.

[24]Laing, *The Politics of Experience,* p. 12.

[25]Laing, *The Politics of Experience,* p. 12.

ingredient to violent behavior on the part of juvenile delinquents. Charles Manson's family, the Houston killers, the violent gangs are not dropped into our society from outer space. These individuals grow up under conditions that can effect the most prone youths to commit acts of violence.

An outstanding example of this behavior may be found in the violence, going beyond the parameters of war, that was perpetrated by soldiers socialized in American society. During the Vietnam war soldiers in the first platoon of Charlie Company, First Battalion, Twentieth Infantry of the United States Army swept into the Vietnamese hamlet of My Lai. They left in their wake hundreds of dead civilians, including women and children. Several small children with bullet-punctured diapers were later photographed lying dead in the dust.

The perpetrators of this horrendous act, later legally defined as a war crime, were not necessarily psychotics or psychopaths but a representative sample of typical American young men, most of whom had been involuntarily drafted into the army. One of the American soldiers who participated in the killings that day later commented in a television interview:

> You know when I think of somebody who would shoot up women and children, I think of a real nut, a real maniac, a real psycho; somebody who has just completely lost control and doesn't have any idea of what he's doing. That's what I figured. That's what I thought a nut was. Then I found out [at My Lai] that an act like, you know, murder for no reason, that could be done by just about anybody.

The young men at My Lai were apparently not too different from the typical Americans in the Milgram experiments who, under orders, shocked people (from their perception) to their death. Nor were they apparently very different from the good citizens who passively play their spectator role of watching people being murdered, as did the thirty-nine people who felt no obligation to intervene in the public stabbing to death of Kitty Genovese in New York.

The rationalization or self-justification for attacks (small or large) on humanity are generally found in the context of the system. Eichmann's classic comment about "only doing his job" has been echoed by other killers who collectively comprise the climate of violence to which delinquent youths conform. Lt. William Calley, in accounting for his personal and indirect killings at My Lai, including his shooting to death of a wounded baby that was attempting to crawl out of a ditch, stated:

> I had tremendous amounts of adrenalin flowing through my body. . . . There was a strong anxiety, I think, that always goes along in situations like that. I was ordered to go in there and destroy the enemy. That was my job on that day. . . . I did not sit down and think in terms

of men, women and children. They were all classified the same, and that was the classification that we dealt with—just as enemy soldiers. I felt then, and I still do, that I acted as I was directed, and I carried out the orders that I was given, and I do not feel wrong in doing so. . . .[26]

A national poll at the time of Calley's conviction revealed that about 75 percent of the population disagreed with the decision that he was a law violator. The common theme expressed was that Calley was "acting under orders." The majority apparently believes that attrocities within the proper normative social framework are not deviant and therefore are not true atrocities.

As often occurs in the case of people who are projected into the spotlight, there was a retrospective "case history" examination of Lt. Calley's growing-up process. The evidence did not reveal any spectacular traumas of an abnormal family or unusual life experiences. Calley was brought up in an average American family, went to standard schools, and lived in typical American communities. Lt. Calley was obviously not a deviant, weirdo, hippie, Commie, pinko revolutionary freak. Perhaps his high school principal summed it up best when he complimented Calley's behavior in high school: "Rusty was not brilliant but he did what he was told."

"Undercontrolled" and "Overcontrolled" Aggressive Types

In the terminology of Edwin Megargee, Calley would be typed as an "undercontrolled aggressive."[27] This categorization described by Megargee is applicable to many violent juvenile offenders.

> Assaultive offenders may be divided into two categories, depending on the way they handle their aggressive impulses. One has a good deal of overt aggression, and relatively little control. He may be called the *undercontrolled aggressive type.* The other has high, uncompromising, brittle controls. He may be called the *chronically overcontrolled* type.
>
> Few if any chronically overcontrolled people should be found among a group of "mildly aggressive offenders." The outbreaks of the chronically overcontrolled are all-or-none phenomena. When they occur, they are extreme. "Mildly" or "moderately" aggressive offenders should therefore be almost exclusively of the undercontrolled type.
>
> "Extremely assaultive offenders," on the other hand, should con-

---

[26]Tom Tiede, *Calley: Soldier or Killer?* (New York: Pinnacle Books, 1971), pp. 38–40.

[27]Edwin Megargee, "Assault with Intent to Kill," *Transaction* 2 (September/October 1965): 27–31. Copyright © 1965 by Transaction, Inc. Published by permission.

tain *both* overcontrolled and undercontrolled types: the undercontrolled lash out when the opportunity and the provocation are strong enough; the overcontrolled strike when the pressures can no longer be borne, even if the immediate provocation is no more serious than others that preceded it.

If true, thesc hypotheses show what seems a paradox: those guilty of the lesser aggressive crimes have the *more* aggressive personalities; and those guilty of the most violent crimes include a far higher percentage of *less* aggressive people.[28]

Megargee cites two typical cases of overcontrolled aggressive types:

A Missouri high school boy, known to be quiet, well-behaved, and always obedient to a stern father, suddenly murders both father and mother with a hunting gun, picks up a girl friend at school, and rides off in the family car. When arrested by the police in another state, he is as calm and meek as ever. . . .

In Colorado a teenager is accused of raping and murdering two girls. His father is incredulous: "When he was in school the other kids would run over him and he would never fight back."[29]

Megargee further explored his concept of the overcontrolled aggressive type in an institutional setting. Megargee conducted an intensive study of juvenile delinquents to test his concept that the "overcontrolled youth" is potentially more dangerous than the undercontrolled.

. . . The writer conducted an intensive study of four groups of juvenile delinquents (seventy-six boys), detained in the Alameda County, California, Juvenile Hall. The "extremely assaultive" group included two cases of homicide, an attempted murder, five assaults with a deadly weapon, and one particularly brutal beating. The boys in the second group, considered "moderately assaultive," were charged primarily with beatings or gang fights.

Two other groups of boys were set up as "contrasts." One was called the "incorrigible" group. They had been detained for defiance, unmanageability, or unruliness at home; it was felt they would be strong on verbal aggressiveness. The last contrast group was made of "property offenders"—thieves and burglars. None of the "contrast" boys had any record of assaults; they were, however, carefully matched with the "aggressives" on race, background, and number of sentences.

During detention each of the seventy-six boys was observed closely

---

[28]Megargee, "Assault with Intent to Kill," pp. 28–29.

[29]Megargee, "Assault with Intent to Kill," p. 28.

by counselors. They were also interviewed and given a battery of tests by Probation Department psychologists.

What did we find?

Under direct observation, the extremely assaultive (EA) group was rated by every criterion as being the least aggressive and most cooperative and controlled.

We hypothesized that if the EA was really more passive and overcontrolled, he was also more likely to be a first offender, to have committed the crime without help or confederates, and to have been, prior to the crime, a social conformist—which could be measured from school conduct and attendance records. We found this to be true. Over 70 percent of the EA's were first offenders, compared with less than 30 percent of the moderate assaultives (MA's). Two-thirds of the EA's were alone with their victims when the crimes were committed, compared with less than one-fifth of the MA's. The EA's had considerably better school attendance and somewhat better school conduct records. In fact, the only two boys in the entire sample who were reported to have "outstanding" attendance records were the two killers. . . .

Results of the interviews and psychological tests were less clearcut, but nevertheless they were all in the predicted direction.

As a whole, therefore, our hypotheses were confirmed. We can state with some confidence that there are two kinds of assaultive offenders, the overcontrolled and the undercontrolled. While the undercontrolled will commit both extreme and moderate assaults, the overcontrolled person will almost invariably commit extreme assaults."[30]

The various studies cited indicate that young people who are too severely restrained by extreme discipline and social controls may erupt if the proper social conditions emerge. It is often apparent in school situations that *some* "model students" who overconform are capable of acting out severe violence when the external restraints that control their behavior are removed. Some aggression and violence felt by such young people growing up in a climate of violence is displaced onto property in acts of vandalism.

Vandalism as Violence

Most of the literature on violence relates to illegal acts of violence that have been sieved through the police, the courts, and the administration of justice. It is apparent that there is a tremendous amount of youthful violence and

[30]Megargee, "Assault with Intent to Kill," p. 30.

aggressive acting out that never falls within the framework of the legal system and, therefore, remains generally unexamined by research, often because the "victim" of the violent or atrocious act is not another human being—but property. The victim of an assault is obviously more capable of reporting an offender, whereas in an assault on property the offender is less apt to be caught.

British criminologist Stanley Cohen, in an article written for the mass media, maintained that most people view vandalism as "mindless, random action." Cohen, however, concluded after careful study that there are "clusters and motives" around various forms of vandalism. According to Cohen:

> Vandalism—the illegal and deliberate destruction or defacement of property—is one of the most complex and misunderstood forms of human behavior.
>
> Even deciding what is and what is not vandalism is not as simple as it might appear. The same action—destruction of property—might be labeled differently according to circumstances and might not always be considered a crime. Some groups are given a sort of collective license to commit vandalism. Much routine property damage (such as graffiti) becomes accepted or condoned, and there are forms of official vandalism such as the destruction of buildings of architectural merit in the name of urban "renewal."
>
> From the outset, the words "wanton," "senseless," "malicious" and so on used by social scientists, the mass media and the public to describe vandalism have obscured any real attempt to understand what such behavior is all about.
>
> In property-oriented societies such as ours, it is incomprehensible that someone could destroy property without any apparent gain. Theft is easy to understand in straightforward economic terms; even personal violence usually seems intelligible. But for most people the only way to make sense of vandalism is to assume that it does not make sense—that it is mindless, random action.
>
> Research in England and America suggests that there are clear clusters of meanings and motives around the various forms of vandalism. There is:
>
> —Acquisitive vandalism: Damage to acquire money or property: breaking open telephone coin boxes, stealing material from construction sites.
>
> —Tactical vandalism: Damage as a conscious tactic used to advance some other end: breaking a window to be arrested and get a bed in prison, jamming a machine in a factory to gain a rest period.
>
> —Ideological vandalism: Similar to some tactical vandalism, but carried out to further an explicit ideological cause or to deliver a message: breaking embassy windows during a demonstration, chalking slogans on walls.

—Vindictive vandalism: Damage done to gain revenge: Breaking windows of a school to settle a grudge against a teacher.

—Play vandalism: Damage done as part of a game: who can break the most windows of a house, who can shoot out the most street lamps.

—Malicious vandalism: Damage as an expression of rage or frustration, often directed at symbolic middle class property. It is this type that has the vicious and apparently senseless facade that many find so difficult to understand.[31]

A central proposition of Cohen's analysis is that vandalism—or, restated, violence against property—is more apt to flourish against an anonymous enemy—"them."

This study is supported by the observations of one of the authors when he directed a delinquency-prevention program for several years on the Upper West Side of Manhattan. The program was partially sponsored by Columbia University.

The vast gray edifices of Columbia were adjacent to a highly deprived ghetto that contained violence of all types. Many young people, bored, deprived, and full of hostility, would target Columbia as a victim of their frustrations and ventilate their aggression by breaking expensive windows and generally vandalizing the property. One youth told the author how he always felt better after he destroyed something at Columbia. To him, the anonymous gray buildings were inhabited by enemies who, he felt, "took care of rich kids —not me."

The author, over a period of years, set up a delinquency-prevention program that helped provide access for several hundred poor, minority youngsters to facilities in Columbia. The gymnasium, swimming pool, and baseball fields were opened up for use by neighborhood youths under controlled conditions. The results—unsurprisingly—were that vandalism in and on the buildings was sharply reduced. The cold, anonymous "them" became part of the juveniles' real community, and they saw no point in destroying property that, in part, now belonged to the youngsters in the neighborhood. The program broke down their formerly aggressive "we-they" stance.

Another recent research project by Richard A. Berk and Howard E. Aldrich confirms that vandalism against property by youths is often a displaced act of aggression against a particular person or class of people.[32] They conclude:

---

[31]Stanley Cohen, "Vandalism," *Los Angeles Times,* October 5, 1973. See also Stanley Cohen, "The Politics of Vandalism," *The Nation,* November 11, 1968, pp. 497–500; "The Future of Vandalism," *The Nation,* August 13, 1973, pp. 110–13; and chapters by Stanley Cohen in *Vandalism,* ed. Colin Ward (London: Architectural Press, 1973).

[32]Richard A. Berk and Howard E. Aldrich, "Patterns of Vandalism During Civil Disorders as an Indicator of Selection of Targets," *American Sociological Review* 37(October 1972):533–47.

. . . patterns of attack during civil disorders strongly imply choices by some rioters. Civil disorders cannot accurately be described as "irrational" or "mindless" destruction. We are not arguing that the overall events were planned, but rather that individual participants appear to have been selecting many of their targets. . . . Apparently some believe consumer goods are distributed unfairly, label the villains and take collective action against them.[33]

Another facet of vandalism is its relationship to a youth's participation in a peer group. Andrew L. Wade makes the point that vandalism is one means of producing group solidarity among alienated youngsters. Wade thus views aggressive juvenile vandalism as a "social act."

In this study juvenile vandalism has been analyzed by viewing it as a social act. Because each behavioral act has a career and is built up in a succession of responses, using this approach has the advantage of bringing into focus the social processes growing out of group interaction. It also emphasizes the definitions held by the actor of himself and of the behavioral act; the two are found to be functionally interrelated.

Within such a framework vandalism is revealed to be spontaneous behavior and the outgrowth of the social situations in which group interaction takes place. There is an observable movement as a result of this interaction. The initial inertia begins to give way as a series of successive interactional responses change the emotional climate of the social situation. Each interactive response builds upon the preceding until a focus develops and a solidary relationship results among the participants.

The act of vandalism functions as a means of ensuring group solidarity. Conformity to the peer group occurs because involvement tends to satisfy the adolescent's need dispositions for status, recognition, and response. Identification with societal property norms becomes subordinate to the demands of the peer group. The adolescent will thus participate in acts of property destruction in order not to appear "chicken." In other words, he can through his involvement maintain a satisfying self-definition and avoid becoming a marginal member of the group. Even though he may recognize the act to be "wrong" or "delinquent," he finds some comfort through the guilt-assuaging rationalizations present in the subculture of the peer group.

Further research is needed in this important area of changing self-definitions. The preceding study pointed out that these redefinitions have a definite relationship to the situational context. The arrest experience is only one such context within which this redefinition takes place.

---

[33]Berk and Aldrich, "Patterns of Vandalism During Civil Disorders," p. 545.

Obviously, there are other significant situations effecting such change. It may occur at the time the participant is involved in a social act, such as, for example, when the boy is with a group on the verge or in the process of committing vandalism.

How easily the redefinition of self takes place may have a real relationship to the ease with which positive changes in treatment programs can be actuated. It may also have an important bearing on efforts to formulate a typology of deviants when one of the important elements in the classification is the development within the behavior system of the individual's self-concept.[34]

In another context Wade comes closer to the violence hypothesis of vandalism when he states:

> Some property destruction appears to function for the adolescent as a protest against his ill-defined social role and ambiguous status in the social structure. Other meanings are more specific. If a boy has suffered frustration, he may express his resentment by a revengeful act of destruction:
>
> "Well, he accused us of stealing some stuff out of his joint. He didn't come right out and say it was us, but the way he talked he made it sound like it, particularly us. We were kidding him about an old rifle he had in there, about ninety years old. And he wanted $15 for it, and the stock on it was all cracked up and everything. And we kept kidding his mother—she's in there [the store] with him—and we kept kidding her. And old Gay [the store owner] himself came over there and started raising the devil, blowing off steam and everything. We didn't like it too well. We left and came back later. I told him [his companion], 'Let's go down and break those windows.' He said, 'Okay,' and we went down there and picked up some rocks along the way. We got down there and stood in front of the place till there weren't any cars very close to us, and we threw the rocks and ran."[35]

In another case Wade uses an example that describes the previously cited theme of vandalism as displaced aggression towards a person:

> "We went over to this one girl's house we didn't like. We threw rotten eggs all over the porch, inside the door—everywhere. Boy, did it

---

[34]Andrew L. Wade, "Social Processes in the Act of Vandalism," in *Criminal Behavior Systems,* ed. Marshall B. Clinard and Richard Quinney (New York: Holt, Rinehart and Winston, 1967), pp. 168–82.

[35]Wade, "Social Processes in the Act of Vandalism," pp. 177–78.

stink around there! We went by the next day and said, 'What happened?' The windows on the second floor were all up, the house and the lawn all covered. She said, 'You know what happened.' 'Prove it,' I said. Boy, did it stink! About 300 eggs we used. That place was an odorous mess! After that [the night of the vandalism] we retired to a friendly drugstore, had a couple of malts; went home to bed. Terrific!"

Whatever guilt may be felt is usually neutralized by the convenient rationalizations motivating the behavior. Such rationalizations may or may not represent the "real" reason: they do reconcile the conflict between legal norms and the acts of vandalism: *Prejudice* is one source of these rationalizations. Both the majority and the minority groups engaging in such behavior find justification for it in prejudice. As an example:

"The neighborhood was old and filled with all kinds of people.... Mexicans and niggers came and everything changed. Niggers and an Indian family lived next door to us and we fought them all the time because we didn't like niggers. The boys would break their windows, holler in their doors, and throw tin cans into their house...."

The minority's justification for vandalism is usually interpreted as a protest against the prejudice and discrimination shown toward it by the majority group. For example, testimony before the Senate subcommittee investigating juvenile delinquency revealed that in Denver three or four significant gangs which were identified by the police as causing a great deal of vandalism were Spanish-American boys. A study of vandalism in that city some time ago tended to substantiate this view. The investigating committee found a similar situation when it met in Boston. It has also been maintained that much of the vandalism participated in by the Puerto Rican youth of New York is due to ethnic prejudice shown them by the majority group.

The act is also justified under the rationalization that "they had it coming to them." The boy insists that what he has done is justifiable in the light of the circumstances. For example, the damage committed is regarded as a form of rightful *retaliation* or punishment:

"I know of some friends of mine who went over to school and we decided to break some of Mr. X's windows for the simple reason that we absolutely despise this teacher. There were about four or five of us."

"Many windows are broken in our school. In one room in particular in which one unpopular teacher holds classes, about twenty-five panes a year have to be replaced. The vandals believe that this is a way to 'get back at' a teacher."[36]

---

[36]Wade, "Social Processes in the Act of Vandalism," pp. 181–82.

Socialization into Violence

In the search for the causes of various patterns of violent behavior, many studies reveal a correlation between brutal parents and violent children. In brief, the use of harsh discipline to socialize children may be a significant factor in producing violent people. A cross-cultural study by psychiatrist Leopold Bellak and psychologist Maxine Antell suggests that cruelty to children appears to be linked to the socialization of latent violent offenders.[37]

Bellak and Antell note that "the Nazis who goosestepped their way across Europe in the 1940s may have begun their training as toddlers on the playgrounds of Germany, and the child-rearing practices that produced Hitler's war criminals may still be raising violence." According to Bellak and Antell, who analyzed their biographies, nearly all of the Nazi leaders were cruelly mistreated as children. As he was wandering through playgrounds in Frankfurt and on the banks of the Main River, Dr. Bellak was struck by the violence both in the play of the children and in the handling of children by their parents. Over a period of several hours, he saw children throw knives dangerously close to one another, pelt one another with rocks, and twist each other's arms. On a similar stroll through playgrounds in Copenhagen, the psychiatrist did not see a single aggressive act. These observations motivated his systematic comparison of aggressive behavior on the playgrounds of different nations.

Two German, two Italian, and two Danish psychologists were asked to choose playgrounds in similar neighborhoods in their respective countries. Each team observed six different groups of children at play. They were not told the nature of the study, they were only told that they were to record everything that took place. The transcripts were then sent to two American graduate students, who also were in the dark about the hypothesis being tested but were asked to score the severity and number of violent acts racked up by the children and parents in each account. In Italy and Denmark, they found not a single act of aggression by parents against children, but in Germany the adults hit a score of 73. In turn, German children were rated significantly more aggressive toward one another than were Italian or Danish children.

The notion that German culture is *kinderfeindlich* (hostile to children) is widely accepted even by Germans themselves, according to Dr. Bellak and Antell. A recent poll in West Germany found that 60 percent of the parents believe in "beating, not slapping or spanking, but beating their children," quotes Dr. Bellak. He also quotes Munich psychologist Rolf Luckert as saying, "We beat our children dumb in this nation." Adult aggressive outlets, including auto accidents, suicides, and self-inflicted injuries and homicides, occurred

---

[37] *Human Behavior* (March 1975).

at much higher rates in Frankfurt than in Florence or Copenhagen, Dr. Bellak notes, perhaps further supporting the notion that people who are abused as children are more likely to abuse others and themselves as adults. Bellak and Antell comment: "The fact seems to be that German treatment of children, as still practiced today and consistent with what is known of past German attitudes toward child rearing, is strongly correlated with cruelty exhibited by these children and likely to be related to behavior of adult Germans in everyday life."[38]

Rather than reproaching only the Germans for their violent child-rearing practices, the researchers question whether parents in other countries are also guilty of such aggression. "Are there certain ethnic or social groups in the United States, for instance, whose methods of discipline and harsh handling of their children are creating people who as adults will be easily prone to express hatred, aggression and prejudiced attitudes toward others or toward other groups?"

Inasmuch as their study describes an apparent relationship between the aggression that an individual endures and the aggression that the person will mete out, Dr. Bellak and Antell suggest that "both Germans and other national groups might do well to examine their practice of child rearing in the light of these findings."

In the context of harsh socialization and its disastrous impacts on increased violence is the growing problem of what has become known as child battering. The problem is basic, since child batterers produce violent progeny.

Dr. Frederic Wertham calls child battering "the maltreatment syndrome" and considers it one of the basic problems of our time:

> The syndrome itself, in all its aspects, is a most important symptom of our time. It is a link in the documentation of my thesis that the spirit of violence is rampant in our society. It is a matter not only of the occurrence of these heartless cruelties against defenseless children, but of the inadequacy of the steps taken so far to prevent them. Physicians, legislators, and child-care agencies have taken up the question belatedly. Even now no proper solution has been found. This is one of those forms of violence which society calls "incredible" and is unequipped to deal with. Why, in an orderly society, should this be such a baffling medical, social, and legal problem?[39]

Another researcher in the field, Dr. Vincent Fontana (a medical doctor specializing in pediatrics), has concluded that child abuse is a more widespread practice than we are willing to admit.

According to Dr. Fontana: "It is a myth that in this nation we love our

---

[38] *Human Behavior* (March 1975).

[39] Frederic Wertham, *A Sign for Cain* (New York: Macmillan, 1966), p. 5.

children." He estimates that each year at least 700 American children are killed by their parents or parent surrogates. Dr. Fontana maintains "that some ten thousand are severely battered every year; 50,000 to 75,000 are sexually abused; 100,000 are emotionally neglected; and another 100,000 are physically, morally, and educationally neglected."[40] The tragic stories behind this appalling statistics are related by Dr. Fontana in his book and his profiles of James Earl Ray, Arthur Bremer, and other convicted criminals illustrate the fate of some of yesterday's battered children—who survived to visit their revenge upon society.

Many child-battering cases end up in murder. An extensive study by social worker David Kaplun and psychiatrist Robert Reich reveals many interesting and significant dynamics of the relationship of child abuse to murder.[41]

Kaplun and Reich studied the records of the chief medical examiner in New York City and found, in a one-year period, 140 cases of apparent homicide of children under the age of fifteen. They reviewed the postmortem reports and police inquiries for the 112 victims who could be identified. They also examined the case reports of the city's public assistance and child welfare agencies for sixty-six of the victims' families.

Poverty seemed to be a strong factor in the child murderer's background. Seventy percent of the victims' families lived in areas of extreme poverty. Many of the murderers in these families were involved in alcoholism, narcotics use, criminal activity, or assault other than child abuse. Most of the victims were infants; over half were under a year old.

According to Kaplun and Reich's study, the murderers usually killed out of rage—beating and kicking the child to death. One mother of three, estranged from her husband, was described by her social worker as "a sweet-tempered, affectionate young woman overburdened with home responsibilities." A short time later her three-year-old son was hospitalized with bruises, burns, and a leg fracture caused, said the mother, by a fall from a crib against a hot radiator. Because the mother was so attentive and affectionate toward her child, the hospital and social worker decided she was not to blame. A year later the boy was killed. The mother again attributed his injuries to an accident, an accident that police investigation disclosed could not have happened. She was not charged, but her two other children were taken from her.

Some mothers did not murder a child themselves but gave aid and opportunity for their lover to commit the crime. A woman's lover rarely killed his own children but murdered the sons of the lover or spouse who preceded him. The biological father was the killer in only 10 percent of the cases.

---

[40]Vincent Fontana, *Somewhere a Child is Crying* (Macmillan, 1973), p. 1.

[41]David Kaplun and Robert Reich, "Child Battering and Murder," *American Journal of Psychiatry* 133, 7 (September 1975):87–99.

After the murders, surviving brothers and sisters or children born later remained in the parents' care in forty-six of the cases. In 32 percent of these, abuse or neglect of the children was reported. Kaplun and Reich found that because of a lack of evidence that would hold up in court, there were few murder convictions. A suspect was not even arrested in twenty to sixty public welfare cases. When the alleged assailants did go to trial, they traded guilty pleas for short sentences on reduced charges. There was only one first-degree murder conviction.

The Kaplun and Reich study points out the perilous state of many children, especially since the figures do not include deaths listed—even though some may actually be cases of murder—as accidental. These deaths outnumber murders four to one.

Even when parents are loving and affectionate in their child-raising activity, external forces of violence can intrude on the socialization process. One such force is the impact of war. Unquestionably, war is a brutalizing force in its impact on children. We have few studies on the effects of war on children; however, some work has been carried out on the issue by a sociologist, Rona Fields.[42]

Following a summer of violence in 1972, children in Derry and Belfast were tested. The Derry children's stories were longer, more complex, and more active in their import. Most carried the theme "if something bad happens, take action against it, even if you can't win." Yet the children still seemed obsessed with tales of shootings and killings. Since several of the children's own fathers had been interned or tortured, such preoccupation was not surprising. Stories told by the older Belfast children were even more strongly characterized by helplessness, death, and destruction than had been the case in 1971.

By the 1973 testing time, the boys in the sample had been interrogated five to eleven times each. One fourteen-year-old boy from the original sample had been beaten to death by soldiers. Several of the Protestant boys had joined gangs, and several of the Catholic boys were already members of the IRA. The dominant theme of their stories seemed to be that one must either acquiesce to or unsuccessfully fight the world's malevolence.

In January 1974, the last series of tests was carried out. Another of the boys previously tested had been shot but had recovered and had been sentenced to Borstal. Others had been shot, beaten, crippled, or orphaned and were involved in junior UDA and IRA gangs. The pervasive theme now was a vigilante thesis. They saw the world as chaotic and unjust and believed one must overcome respect for life and property for the sake of "the cause." They seemed obsessed now with a personal passion for law and order.

The pattern is clear, Fields believes:

---

[42] *Human Behavior* (May 1976).

Young children, feeling helpless, surrounded by death and destruction, experiencing unjust arrests and beatings, finally develop a personal obsession to establish justice and order by the only means they have learned —killing and bombing.

Once the military and political contest is resolved, there remains the need for massive efforts at rehabilitation. Without that, the children of Northern Ireland—those who survive physically, those who do not emigrate—will be militaristic automatons, incapable of participating in their own destiny.[43]

The Mass Media and Juvenile Violence

The children of war and brutal parents are apt to react directly to the reality of their violent world. In another context children in our technological society are constantly battered by the effects of violence in the mass media. Children see a lot of violence on television. A recent Nielsen survey reports that preschoolers watch an average of fifty-four hours of television a week. And according to the "Violence Profile" of the Annenberg Institute of Communications, children's programs contain violence as standard content.

Two psychologists, Ronald S. Drabman and Margaret Hanratty Thomas, studied the relationship between television violence and violence in real life.[44] They specifically analyzed to what extent exposure to televised aggression makes the children more tolerant to the real thing.

One of their experiments involved forty fifth-graders from a white lower middle class parochial school. Each child watched either a fifteen-minute segment from a television detective series that contained several shootings and other acts of violence or a fifteen-minute segment of a baseball game. Then the experimenter said he had to leave for a while and asked each child to keep an eye on two kindergartners playing nearby. The child was told that the toddlers were being filmed by a camera and could be watched on the television screen. If anything went wrong, the fifth-grader was to get help. Actually, what the child saw was a staged videotaped sequence in which the kindergartners became more and more unruly, screaming and fighting until they apparently knocked over the camera and the monitor went blank. The researchers were interested in how long it would take the fifth-grader to seek help after seeing this real-life violence.

The children who had watched the detective show took much longer to respond than did the baseball watchers. Five children in the aggressive-film

---

[43]*Human Behavior* (May 1976).
[44]Ronald S. Drabman and Margaret Hanratty Thomas, "Television Violence" *Pediatrics* 57, 3(September 1975):36–43.

group (two boys and three girls) never went for help at all, as opposed to only one girl in the control group.

In another experiment Drabman and Thomas studied third- and fourth-graders. Half of the children saw a violent Hopalong Cassidy film on a movie screen, while the rest saw no film at all. Fifty-eight percent of the control children ran to get help *before* the kindergartners began slugging it out. It took a lot more aggression to stir the children who had seen the film; 83 percent of them waited until the kindergartners physically battled before they sought help.

Thomas and Drabman suggested two possible reasons for the apathy of the test group. Perhaps violence on television teaches children that aggression is a way of life, not to be taken seriously. Or perhaps real-life aggression simply seems bland when compared to the vicious violence on TV.

There is insufficient research to conclude firmly that media violence does or does not cause violent behavior in children. Despite the inconclusiveness of the evidence, however, occasionally events occur that produce simplistic cause-effect observations. For example, on October 10, 1973, the film *Fuzz* was aired over network television. In the film, teenage boys are shown setting fire to skid-row bums along Boston's waterfront. Two nights later, a woman was burned to death by a group of young blacks in Boston. The woman, Evelyn Wagler, a Swiss divorcee, had moved to Boston only five days earlier and was living in a small commune in the city's Roxbury ghetto with another white and four black women. While she was on her way home from a job-hunting trip, her car ran out of gasoline in the center of Roxbury's business district. Returning to her car with a two-gallon refill can from a service station, the young woman was forced into a trash-filled backyard along Blue Hill Avenue by six black teenagers, beaten and ordered to douse herself with the fuel. After the terrified victim complied, one of them set her afire with a match. Before dying five hours later, she told the police that three of her assailants had been part of a black group that had called her a "honky" the previous day and warned her that whites were unwelcome in Roxbury. Thus a combination of racism and perhaps TV influence may have caused this atrocious homicide. The cause-effect nexus is obviously more complex than it appears.

There are, of course, other aspects to the issue of violence in films and television as they relate to actual violence by juveniles. In many ways the violence in mass media is only a carbon copy of reality. Violence is, after all, an intrinsic part of the American way of life, and the media should accord it realistic representation. On this theme journalist Ralph Gleason makes some perceptive observations:

> Oddly enough, discussions of violence in both TV and film seems to me usually to bypass consideration of the fact that the world in which we live today is so violent that it would be almost literally impossible to make a relevant film without violence. Of course, one could make a film

of ideas with all the content being conversational. I don't mean that kind of film. I mean that really to show what currents flow beneath the surface of our world it is impossible not to touch upon violence. It is all around us. And it is not only the violence of blood letting. There is the violence of that logging camp picture with the terrible scars in the middle of the redwood forest; there is the violence of the new strip mining in the Appalachians, the violence of the traffic in the street, the violence of the jet stream pollution. Is it less violent because it spreads its harm in lazy patterns in the sky and is not audible?

The response of direct physical action to a problem, the response of instant violent retaliation to a wrong (or imagined wrong), law or no law, is what is attractive in a world so complex we cannot get to the nub of any problem. I doubt that the alternative of reason and rationality is ever going to be that attractive, certainly not as long as the motivations of self-interest and greed and the lust for power enable strong men to obfuscate the issues and appeal to the baser instincts. On the other hand, it might just be that exorcising our violence by way of the cinema is a degree better than the Roman circus. And a degree of difference is at least slightly better than no difference at all.[45]

One paradoxical question is therefore raised regarding the mass media's impact on delinquency: How does the mass media influence delinquency, especially violence?

There have been a number of studies that attempt to ascertain the impact of media on juvenile delinquency. Several studies do provide some answers, albeit inconclusive ones, to this basic question, and lift the issue somewhat out of the realm of moral judgments and random speculations. Of course these studies cannot sort out the effects of "the climate of violence" variable on children that no doubt compounds the mass media influence.

Beginning in 1969, the Surgeon General's Scientific Advisory Committee on Television and Social Behavior subsidized twenty-three independent research projects to study (*a*) the characteristics of television program content; (*b*) the characteristics of the audience (Who watches what? for how long?); and (*c*) the potential impact of televised violence on the attitudes, values, and behavior of the viewers. The advisory committee received sixty reports and papers before the end of 1971 and published a summary report[46] and five

---

[45]Ralph Gleason, "Violence Is All Around Us," *San Francisco Chronicle and Examiner*, January 9, 1973, © 1972, Chronicle Publishing Co.

[46]*Television and Growing Up: The Impact of Televised Violence*, Report to the Surgeon General, U.S. Public Health Service, from the Surgeon General's Scientific Advisory Committee on Television and Social Behavior, HEW Publication no. HSM72-9090 (Washington, D.C.: U.S. Government Printing Office, 1972).

volumes of research reports[47] in 1972. Following is a summary of some of this mass of data, combined with the authors' observations.

Television program content includes an enormous amount of violence. Programs designed for children contained by far the most violence. One researcher is quoted as concluding "of all 95 cartoon plays analyzed during the three annual study periods, only two in 1967 and one each in 1968 and 1969 did not contain violence."[48] In this study violent episodes occurred at the rate of five per play or eight episodes per hour, with eight out of ten plays containing some form of violence. Another study reported that during the 1971 season, *71 percent of all* segments had at least one instance of human violence and three out of ten dramatic segments were saturated with violence. About 70 percent of all leading characters studied were involved in some violence, and the odds were two to one in favor of the leading character being a killer, and seven to one that the killer would not be killed in return. Children are the heaviest viewers and they prefer the type of cartoons and situation comedies described.

Another aspect of violence on television is that killing someone is an approved method of solving problems. What does the hero do when he encounters the villain? He draws a weapon and kills him. No action is taken against him. This may very well influence the young viewer into seeking similar solutions to his problems. He can be a hero and resolve his problems by killing somebody.

One study involved the relationship between TV violence and aggression in children.[49] The study examined the TV habits of a large group of children over a ten-year period. The subjects were 427 teenagers of an original group of 875 children who had participated in a study of third-grade children in 1960. The original 875 constituted the entire third-grade population of a semirural county in New York. The 427 subjects were those of the 875 who could be located and interviewed ten years later. The third-grade children were rated on their aggressiveness by their peers, and their preferences for violent television were obtained. All programs mentioned were rated either violent or nonviolent.

In the followup ten years later, each subject reported his four favorite TV programs, and these were categorized as violent or nonviolent. The subjects were also rated by their peers using the same aggression criteria as in the 1960 study. Two hundred eleven of the subjects were male and 216 were female, the modal age being nineteen at the end of the study. The males scored higher on aggression than the females, and those females scoring higher than other females were significantly more masculine in interests and attitudes.

[47] *Television and Social Behavior,* 5 vols. (Washington, D.C.: U.S. Government Printing Office, 1972).

[48] *Television Violence and Social Behavior,* vol. 1, *Media Content and Control.*

[49] *Television Violence and Social Behavior,* vol. 3, *Television and Adolescent Aggressiveness.*

There was a high correlation between a boy's television preferences in the third grade and peer-rated aggression. Also there was a significant relation between a boy's preferences for violent TV programs in the third grade and aggression ten years later. An analysis of the findings in this study led to the conclusion that watching violent television programs in early years influenced aggressive behavior later on. The effect of television violence on aggression was found to be relatively independent of other factors and explained a larger portion of the variance than did IQ, social status, mobility, aspirations, religious practices, ethnicity, and parental disharmony. More than any other factor, watching violent TV shows at age nine influenced aggressive behavior at age nineteen.

A number of other studies pointed to the conclusion that viewing televised violence caused the viewer to become more aggressive. The advisory committee indicated in general that "there is a convergence of the fairly substantial experimental evidence for *short-run* causation of aggression by viewing violence on the screen and the much less certain evidence from field studies that extensive violence viewing precedes some *long-run* manifestations of aggressive behavior."[50]

Another study that attempted to discover the impact of media violence on people was carried out by psychologist Leonard Berkowitz at the University of Wisconsin. The results of Berkowitz's research were summarized as follows:

> Aristotle wrote that watching drama could "accomplish a purgation of . . . emotions," and apologists for the excessive violence in some movies and television shows have taken this concept of catharsis to mean that the physical violence portrayed can be good for the psyche. There hasn't been any scientific evidence to the contrary—until now. . . .
>
> For his experiments, Berkowitz used student volunteers and told them he was simply interested in physiological responses to a variety of stimuli. He even took blood-pressure readings to strengthen his camouflage. In reality, he was after something quite different.
>
> Each experiment involved two subjects, one of them actually Berkowitz's assistant. The first task presented was an intelligence test. Berkowitz's conspirator always finished first, whereupon he would lean over to the subject and with a sly smile make a remark such as, "You're certainly taking a long time with that." This was usually enough for the subject to develop a dislike for his coworker.
>
> Then both subjects were shown a seven-minute film sequence taken from the movie *Champion,* in which Kirk Douglas is reduced to a bloody, battered mess. The last test involved the floor plan for a house, which the conspirator had supposedly drawn up. The subject was to

---

[50] *Television Violence and Social Control,* vol. 4, *Television in Day-to-Day Life: Patterns of Use.*

indicate his degree of disapproval of the plan by pressing a button that he was told would administer electric shocks to his coworker.

In this way, Berkowitz attempted to create a situation mirroring real life when someone nursing some new anger happens to attend a movie depicting physical violence. Soon afterward, he is given the opportunity to vent his feelings. The test results were illuminating.

In the cases where Berkowitz's conspirator refrained from making any insulting remarks during the intelligence test, or when peaceful travel scenes were used instead of the fight sequence, he received fewer shocks during the floor-plan experiment. But he felt a veritable barrage when the subjects were treated to the full course of insults and the violent boxing sequence.

The research also showed that so-called "justified aggression" triggers the greatest violence. In briefing his subjects on the overall plot of the movie, Berkowitz told some that Douglas was an "unprincipled scoundrel." Others were told he was about to go straight. Those who watched what they believed was the bad guy getting beaten almost always delivered more shocks. In other words, Berkowitz writes: "If it was all right for the movie villain to be injured aggressively . . . then perhaps it was all right for them to attack the villain in their own lives."

Still, Berkowitz does not believe movies can make a delinquent out of a model teen-ager. "The effect of filmed violence is temporary," he said in an interview last week. "But by the same token, a normal average citizen who is angry about something and then sees a case of justified aggression is more likely to attack, apparently because what he has seen has weakened his normal inhibitions against committing aggression."[51]

Another noteworthy study that focuses more precisely on the effects of TV violence on children was carried out by psychologist Albert Bandura. For Bandura, the basic issue was what happens to a child who watches violence on television. Bandura reported as follows:

We designed a series of experiments to test the extent to which children will copy aggressive patterns of behavior, when these patterns are shown by adult models in three different situations: in real life, on film and as cartoon characters on film.

The first group observed real-life adults. An experimenter brought the children, one by one, into a test room. In one corner, the child found a set of play materials; in another corner, he saw an adult sitting quietly with a set of tinker toys, a large inflated plastic Bobo doll and a mallet. Soon after the child started to play with his toys, the adult model began

---

[51]"Pictures of Violence," *Newsweek,* February 24, 1964, p. 91. Copyright 1964 by Newsweek, Inc.

attacking the Bobo doll in ways that children rarely would. For example, the adult sat on the doll and punched it repeated in the nose, pummeled its head with the mallet, tossed it up in the air aggressively and kicked it around the room while saying things like "Sock him in the nose!" "Hit him down!" "Throw him in the air!" "Kick him!"

The second group of children saw a movie of the adult model beating up the Bobo doll. The third group watched a movie—projected through a television console—in which the adult attacking the doll was costumed as a cartoon cat. Children in the fourth group did not see any aggressive models; they served as a control group. This gave a basis of standard behavior to compare with the actions of the groups who were exposed to the aggressive models.[52]

At the end of ten minutes, each child was taken to an "observation room" where the youngster was watched through a one-way mirror. The child had access to "aggressive toys" and "nonagressive toys" for a twenty-minute period. According to a team of psychologists-observers, those youngsters who had previously been exposed to the aggressive model showed almost twice as much aggression in the observation room as did the children in the control group.

From this Bandura reached two important conclusions about the effect of the aggressive models on a child:

1. The experience tends to reduce the child's inhibitions against acting in a violent, aggressive manner.

2. The experience helps to shape the form of the child's aggressive behavior. Most of the children from the first three groups sat on the Bobo doll and punched its nose, beat it on the head with a mallet, tossed it into the air and kicked it around the room. And they used the familiar hostile remarks, "Hit him down!" "Kick him!" and so forth. This kind of conduct was rare among the children in the control group.[53]

Bandura's findings led him to a third, and highly significant, conclusion. He noticed that a person who behaved violently on film is as influential as one who behaves violently in real life. The children were not too interested in imitating the cartoon character, but many children copied precisely the actions of both real-life and film models. From these observations, Bandura concluded that televised models are influential sources of social behavior whose impact on personality development can no longer be ignored. He points out that as audiovisual technology improves, television will become even more influential.

---

[52]Albert Bandura, "What TV Violence Can Do to Your Child," *Look,* October 22, 1963, pp. 46, 48.

[53]Bandura, "What TV Violence Can Do to Your Child," p. 48.

In another study on the relation between movies and violence, Dr. Richard Walters at the University of Toronto asked a group of adult men and adolescent boys to assist in a study of the effects of punishment on learning.[54] The subjects could give an electric shock to a "learner" each time he made a mistake on a test. Subjects were permitted to vary the length and intensity of the shock. Before beginning the test, each participant received a few shocks to become familiar with the various levels of pain.

The "learner" then made intentional mistakes, and Dr. Walters measured the length and strength of the shocks he was given. (Unknown to the participants, the electrodes were disconnected, and the learner felt no pain.)

In the second step of the study, half the subjects were shown the switchblade knife scene from the film *Rebel Without a Cause,* while the other half were shown a short film about picture making. All then repeated the shock-administration test.

Those subjects who had seen the picture-making film administered relatively weak shocks. Those who had seen *Rebel* gave longer, more powerful shocks, which would have caused considerable pain if the electrodes had been connected. Moreover, this latter group exhibited a pronounced increase in aggressiveness and hostility on an objective personality test.

The data presented on the relation between viewing violence on television and increased aggressive behavior on the part of children, although not conclusive, does indicate that the mass media have their effect on increasing violence in juveniles. Individuals, particularly very young boys, who watch great stars perform violent "hero" roles are likely to consider violence as an approved way of asserting masculinity and of solving problems. We do not, of course, recommend or support any form of censorship. However, parents of young children should be alerted to the possible dangers of their watching such films.

George Gerbner, a professor of communications, assessed an effort to curb the negative effects of violence on children by what, from 1974 to 1977, became known as "the family hour."[55] Gerbner notes that the concept of a "family viewing" period arose in late 1974. It was a result of congressional prodding. Somebody had to do something to follow up the conclusion former Surgeon General Jesse L. Steinfeld reached, on the basis of extensive investigations, before the Pastore Senate Subcommittee. "It is clear to me," Steinfeld said, "that the causal relationship between televised violence and antisocial behavior is sufficient to warrant appropriate and remedial action."

The concept was eventually expressed as an addition to the Code of the National Association of Broadcasters: "Entertainment programming inappropriate for viewing by a general family audience should not be broadcast during

[54]Cited in Bandura, "What TV Violence Can Do to Your Child," p. 52.

[55]George Gerbner, "Assessing Television's Try for a Non-Combat Hour," *Human Behavior* (November 1976):43–49.

the first hour of network entertainment programming in prime time and in the immediately preceding hour." The rule, riddled with exceptions and embroiled in controversy, went into effect in late 1975. Gerbner concludes:

> Our results to date show that violence in video (as in any storytelling) demonstrates how power works in society: who can—and who cannot—get away with what. Experience in the world of TV drama teaches regular viewers many of their assumptions about the relative risks in life. When you see a fight on television, you do not call the police or an ambulance; you absorb and confirm a sense of relative powers, and risks.
>
> Obviously, a few points' difference on the Violence Index does not necessarily transform the structure of symbolic action. In fact, our measures of the structure, called Risk Ratios, proved to be remarkably stable over the years. For example, for every violent male, there were 1.19 male victims. For every violent female, there were 1.32 female victims; for every young woman, there were 1.67 young women victims. Old, poor and black women mostly appeared as victims. Clearly, the structure of dramatic action on television is rooted in—and thus perpetuates—the pecking order of society. A change in the rate of victimization may be even more significant than a dip in the Violence Index.
>
> The Family Hour should be seen as a gesture of recognition by both broadcasters and the FCC of the growing citizen and congressional concern about the video's power and accountability.[56]

Most research, including the family-hour effort, results in debatable conclusions about the effects of television violence on aggressive behavior. A comprehensive study by two psychology professors, Robert M. Kaplan and Robert D. Singer, concluded that there was no justification for censorship of television programming because of the violence it portrays.[57]

Kaplan and Singer reviewed more than 120 studies of television violence and concluded that "the accumulated research does not show sufficient proof of a direct connection between television violence and aggressive behavior. Too much of the research that draws a correlation between television violence and aggressive behavior is conducted in an unrealistic laboratory setting."

According to Kaplan and Singer

> The lab setting doesn't seem to generalize to the real world. We're trying to argue that research should meet certain criteria before it is used to justify changes in public policy. When you look closely at the [past] research, television doesn't show potent effects on aggressive behavior.

---

[56]Gerbner, "Assessing Television's Try for a Non-Combat Hour."
[57]*Los Angeles Times,* January 7, 1972.

It is fascinating that so many hours of research and so much money has been spent and directed at the possible effect of TV violence on aggressive behavior, when it is most likely that television is not a significant cause of human aggression. Instead of castigating the networks it may be more useful to ask why the public is so fascinated by programs portraying violence.

The professors suggested researchers "could turn their attention to economic, developmental, social and cultural factors" in an attempt to find the major causes of violence. However, they add, further research into television would be useful, especially if it focused on the probability that television is a major influence in promoting aggression in a natural setting. A more natural setting, according to Kaplan and Singer, would include social sanctions against aggression which are lacking in a lab setting, and a broader sample of subjects and long-term viewing by subjects.

Other conclusions drawn by Professors Kaplan and Singer were:

1. Violent television programming has not been shown to have the effect of reducing aggressive behavior by allowing a person to "drain off" his aggressive tendencies while watching violence on television.

2. There still remains the possibility that violence on television may contribute to violent behavior by "disturbed" viewers. "Unfortunately, the literature and current methodology does not permit us to evaluate such possibilities," the professors said.

3. There is a difference in the influences of fantasy violence and real violence—as portrayed on news shows—on aggressive behavior.

They concluded, "As in so many other areas of juvenile delinquency, we have to conclude, based on many studies, that a clear causal connection between mass media violence and actual violent behavior is still inconclusive. Yet it is our observation that several studies indicate a degree of brutalization occurs from certain types of programs."

One approach the authors would recommend is psychodrama for young people to counteract some of the negative influence of violence seen in films and on television. The psychodrama approach would involve the dramatization of actual cases of violence, but instead of emphasizing the delinquent acts in a positive light as do the mass media, the sessions would emphasize the "causes" or reasons for the violent behavior. Such reasons would invariably turn out to indicate some weakness in the personality of the violent individual or in his social relationships.

In the psychodrama context violence would not be aggrandized; rather, violence would be explored with a group of youngsters to help them understand their own real feelings on the subject. The sessions might be filmed and distributed to a wider audience of youngsters. A greater understanding of the social dynamics and rationales for violence described here, combined with the actual participation of young people (live and on film), might produce some valuable force for counterattacking the growing problems of violence by juveniles in a society that seems to perpetuate a climate of violence.

Drug Use,
Delinquency,
and
Social Change

DRUG ABUSE has been a problem since the beginning of recorded history. The Bible cites cases of the use of substances that were no doubt antecedents of modern drugs. In the contemporary period, from around 1920 up to the present, Western civilization has had serious problems with the abuse of morphine, an alkaloid of opium, and heroin, a derivative of morphine, and, to a lesser extent, with the use of marijuana. There is little argument about the destructive impact of opiate addiction; however, a sizable segment of the population advocates the legalization of marijuana.

With the advent of what has been termed the hippie movement in the early 1960s, another configuration of drug use emerged: the psychedelic drug scene. It did not replace or supplement the use of opiates and marijuana but developed alongside the traditional pattern. Although it is hard to pin down actual numbers of drug users, there is reasonable evidence that the emergence of the psychedelic drug pattern has more than doubled the overall use of drugs in Western societies.

Traditionally, the opiate drugs, especially heroin, have been used to block out an onerous social environment, to attempt to resolve personal problems, and to escape into a state of reverie. Although heroin has been used to some extent by young people in the middle and upper segments of society, opiate addiction has been predominantly a lower class phenomenon. Heroin has been widely used by young people in urban ghettos to escape from the oppressive conditions of poverty and racial discrimination. For these youngsters, heroin provides a horrendous way to blank out a dim future of limited opportunity and little hope. A dramatic portrait of the meaning of heroin to a ghetto youth is almost poetically provided by Piri Thomas, a former addict himself, in his perceptive book on Spanish Harlem:

> Heroin does a lot for one—and it's all bad. It becomes your whole life once you allow it to sink its white teeth in your blood stream. . . . Yet there is something about dogie—heroin—it's a super-duper tranquilizer. All your troubles become a bunch of bleary blurred memories when you're in a nod of your own special dimension. And it was only when my messed-up system became a screaming want for the next fix did I really know just how short an escape from reality it really brought. The shivering, nose-running, crawling damp, ice-cold skin it produced were just the next worst step of—like my guts were gonna blow up and muscles in my body becoming so tight I could almost hear them snapping.[1]

Heroin abuse is cyclical and appears to be on the rise as we approach the 1980s. In the 1970s, in the United States we experienced some peaks and valleys in the use of heroin. Between 1969 and 1971, a virtual epidemic of heroin abuse hit the United States. Whether through the intervention of drug treatment centers or more effective law enforcement (including the disruption of the famous French-Corsican Connection), figures on heroin use declined sharply in major U. S. cities in 1972 and 1973. What appeared to be a decisive victory, however, was apparently no more than an extended time-out.

In Washington, D. C., and New York, for example, heroin use in 1977 is on the rise, judging from the increase in heroin-positive urine samples collected from arrestees and the growing number of people entering addiction programs. According to Mark H. Greene, M. D., formerly of the U. S. Public Health Service, the recent higher incidence coincided with an upward trend in the purity of street heroin, an increase in heroin overdose deaths and a rise in property crimes.[2] Many middle class youngsters who were introduced to drugs in the psychedelic scene of the sixties stayed on to become heroin addicts in the seventies. This route of drug abuse is exemplified in the following case history of a young man named Ed. Ed's story, cogently written by John Luce, is presented in detail because it reveals a complex drug path traveled by many youths in recent years:

---

[1] Piri Thomas, *Down These Mean Streets* (New York: Knopf, 1967), pp. 200–201. © 1967 by Alfred A. Knopf, Inc. Reprinted by permission.

[2] *Human Behavior* (July 1976).

Ed was raised in the Richmond district of San Francisco, but he visited the Haight-Ashbury often as a child. His mother was depressed and disoriented during those days. She also drank heavily after her husband, a plumbing contractor, left home. Yet she still had relatively lucid moments in which her bitterness was tempered by maternal feelings. So, when the weather matched her mental state, she would dress her son in short pants, shop with him on Haight Street, and take him to the Haight Theater for Saturday matinees.

Ed loved sitting in the ancient movie palace. He felt secured by the thought that life could be stable, relaxed by the celluloid sensations that enveloped him. But this ease was shattered shortly after his fourteenth birthday, when his mother died. Ed then moved in with his grandmother, a religious fundamentalist who resented having to take care of him. He went to high school, began dating, and grew to his present six-foot height. "But I always felt like some part of me was missing," he says. "I couldn't make it with the other kids. I was angry, guilty about my mother, full of these weird sexual feelings. I couldn't concentrate. I tried to keep myself together with booze."

... He sedated himself with marijuana and succumbed to the psychedelic messiahs in San Francisco who hoped to alter themselves and society with LSD.

"I really blossomed behind acid," Ed remembers: "Before I was just maintaining, but LSD turned life into a circus; suddenly it all made sense to me. I dug on peace and love, like we are all only one. So I started dropping acid pretty regular, man, and I knew there was just no point to school. . . ."

Ed survived the summer, but his dream of peace and love perished in July. The death occurred during an STP trip which unearthed frightening feelings. "Everything fell apart," Ed says about his experience. "Walking on the street, I freaked on all the tourists and gangsters there. . . . I wanted to kill myself. Some shrink at the clinic put me straight, but I was never the same after. . . ."

In 1968 amphetamines helped Ed endure the Haight-Ashbury. So did the clinic physicians, who tried to keep him eating and stitched his head after it was cracked open during a flurry with the police. But as he increased his speed intake, Ed started to pay the price for self-medication. His euphoric highs led to agonizing lows; his paranoia intensified; he lost three teeth to pyorrhea and, to malnutrition, forty pounds. After the July riots on Haight Street, he began injecting barbiturates to insulate himself from his environment and to ease his agitation. By September, when the clinic closed again for lack of medicine and money, he was strung out on barbs.

The clinic reopened in January 1969 and helped Ed get into Mendocino State Hospital for three months to heal his abcesses and curb his addiction. He then returned to the Haight, hoping to find something there to do. But the Straight Theater had closed by this point; the rock musicians had abandoned the district; and the new community had been overrun by a new population made up of desperate runaways, grizzled winos, burnt-out speed freaks, barbiturate and heroin addicts from New York and other cities, and blacks from the Flatlands and the Fillmore district nearby. Ed mingled with the street people. . . . When President Nixon's Operation Intercept cut the flow of marijuana across the Mexican border in September, 1969, he found heroin.

"Smack is the greatest," he says, ". . . the mellowest downer of all. You get none of the side effects of speed and barbs. After you fix, you feel the rush, like an orgasm if it's good dope. Then you float for about four hours; nothing positive, just a normal feeling, nowhere. It's like being half asleep, like watching a movie; nothing gets through to you; you're safe and warm. The big thing is, you don't hurt. You can walk around with rotting teeth and a busted appendix and not feel it. You don't need sex, you don't need food, you don't need people, you don't care. It's like death without permanence, life without pain.

"For me, the only hard part is keeping in H, paying my connection, man. I know these rich cats who can get good smack and shoot it for years and nothing happens, but me, you know, it's a hustle to stay alive. I run about a $100-, $150-a-day habit, so I have to cop twice that much to keep my fence happy. I was driving cabs in 1970; I'd stage these robberies and keep the receipts. Now, me and my partner are into burglary; no strongarm stuff—you feel quiet on dope—just boosting TV sets from houses where we know the people are away. And I do a skin flick once in a while. But it's a hassle, believe me. Everybody on the street wants to rip you off; you can get burned from pushers who try and sell you sugar or rat poison. Then there's always the threat of the law."

Ed found some help for his problem through the Haight-Ashbury Free Clinic and an understanding physician, Dr. George "Skip" Gay. Despite this aid, Ed maintains a gloomy perspective on life.

"I never really belonged in this world," Ed says today as he tries to talk himself unconscious. "I've seen lots of scenes, man, but I've never been part of one. People have treated me like an animal as long as I can remember. Dope meant hope once, and Skip and the kids at the Clinic treat me right; I think I can make it if they can find me a job there. But, you know, my head is really hurting. Sometimes I think it'd be better for everyone if I just overdosed and died."[3]

---

[3]John Luce, "End of the Road: A Case Study" in *"It's So Good, Don't Even Try It Once"—Heroin in Perspective,* ed., David E. Smith and George R. Gay. © 1972. Reprinted by permission of Prentice-Hall, Inc., Englewood Cliffs, N. J. pp. 144–77.

Ed's story is descriptive of one type of drug addict. In fact, there are a variety of types of adolescent drug users. The majority of users tend to be casual dilettantes who use occasionally—and seldom get heavily hooked on any drug. A study of heavier, more definitive drug abusers by Virginia Lewis and Daniel Glaser revealed five basic types of addicts.[4] Lewis and Glaser list five distinct lifestyles for the 150 addicts they studied passing from the Federal Correctional Institution at Terminal Island to an aftercare program in the Los Angeles area. For the most part, they observed that these groups seldom interacted—either inside or out of prison. The five lifestyles they delineated were:

1. *Expressive Students.* Representing the middle and upper classes were the *expressive students,* so-called not because they were necessarily students but because of their intellectual (or quasi-intellectual) approach to drug use. They frequently became the success stories of the aftercare program, which seemed to appeal to their intellectualism.

2. *Social World Alternators.* They came from every social class but were notably adept at adapting to any milieu. One thirty-nine-year-old black man the researchers interviewed was the son of a Texas minister and had been "a ghetto street hustler, a pimp, the area campaign manager of a prominent white political candidate, a dealer-addict and a paraprofessional in addiction therapy." Others succeeded in more legitimate enterprises, turning on to heroin or cocaine when their various activities brought them into contact with criminal groups such as street gangs, thieves, and prostitutes. They just flowed with whatever was happening.

3. *Low-Riders.* As with Expressive Students, these people were also counterculture adherents—only with a defiant, aggressive stance. These were the motorcycle and street gang members who cultivated their habits while hanging out at a favorite corner or bar. Most were white, and when rehabilitation worked, it was usually because of the lack of cohesiveness in their groups and the jobs available to them as compared to blacks and Chicanos. Since, however, most were the products of broken homes, had little education, sporadic jobs, and frequent run-ins with the authorities, rehabilitation meant introducing them to a whole new way of life.

4. *Barrio Addicts.* They were almost exclusively Mexican-Americans or others of Latin extraction, although they also included a handful of Spanish-speaking Anglos—all women. This group was rooted in chronic, abject poverty, working when they could at menial tasks and supporting their habits by stealing and smuggling dope across the border. Those who were able to stay clean, more than any other group, attributed their success to the weekly urine test. It served both as an incentive and as an excuse their friends would accept.

5. *Ghetto Hustlers.* Last on the list were the Ghetto Hustlers, who were

---

[4]*Human Behavior* (March 1975).

mostly black, except for some of their female companions. "Occupationally," note Lewis and Glaser, "the men in this group have been extremely disadvantaged in legitimate employment, so they turned to such illegal fund-raising activities as confidence games, theft and prostitution. The majority, however, resumed their addictive habit as well as their criminal activities when released from prison."

Drug Abuse: A National Problem

The five patterns delineate the most definitive drug user types, but in a sense we are a nation of drug users. Those of us who do not use drugs are repeatedly urged to do so by the advertisements of pharmaceutical companies on radio and television, in newspapers and magazines. Occasionally a federal or state agency will take action to prevent some company from pushing a drug proved to be harmful or dangerous or believed to have harmful effects. Many people, however, buy and use drugs without prescription on the assumption that they may relieve some annoying symptom or otherwise do some good. A recent study, for example, indicated that approximately two out of every ten people in California use or have used some form of barbiturate or tranquilizer and that one million Americans have become pill abusers.

While there are some regulations limiting the advertising of alcoholic beverages, the messages of the liquor companies manage to reach the public. People consume enormous quantities of alcohol, a drug that is insidiously addictive and often leads to physical and emotional destruction. An authority, Dr. Joel Fort, determined that one out of every ten drinkers has an alcoholic problem.

Many illegal drugs are widely and easily available. Barbiturates, amphetamines, and other drugs that might be harmful if misused are widely prescribed by physicians. Barbiturates are used in the treatment of epileptics, for instance. Amphetamines are frequently prescribed for dieters and the listless, tranquilizers for the agitated. Any adult with money enough to pay a physician's fee can lawfully obtain a quantity of these drugs appropriate to his needs. They are, however, classified as dangerous drugs in all fifty states and can be lawfully acquired *only* with the prescription of a physician.

The sale, purchase, or possession of specified dangerous drugs, narcotics, and marijuana is a criminal offense under both federal and state law. Forty-six states have in force versions of the Uniform Narcotic Law, providing severe punishment for offenders. In many states, the nonmedical use of opiates and the possession of paraphernalia to administer them (needles and syringes) constitute violations of public health laws. Other states have statutes making it an offense to associate with known addicts or to be present in a place where the illicit drugs or narcotics are used or found. The addict or habitual drug user is therefore in almost perpetual violation of one or more state or federal laws. This is a special status not shared by other offenders. New York State in 1973 introduced the toughest laws yet imposed on drug addicts.

Although many people use drugs, not all drug users are addicted. The behavior of the drug addict, according to Alfred Lindesmith, is distinguished by the following factors:

1. An intense *conscious* desire for the drug.

2. A tendency to *relapse*—to revert to the use of the drug even after physiological dependence has been removed.

3. Psychological dependence on the drug as a twenty-four-hour necessity. Heroin addicts require one to four "fixes" or shots per day.

4. The impulse to increase dosage far beyond bodily needs. The addict usually requires a progressively increased amount of his drug to satisfy his habit.

5. Identification of oneself as a drug addict. Authorities are agreed that there is a compulsion to continue taking the drug and a willingness to do whatever is necessary to obtain it, regardless of cost. The result is that most traditional addicts, members of the lower socioeconomic class, must concentrate all their efforts on obtaining their drugs and the money to pay for them. Moreover, there is some indication that the impulse to revert to the use of drugs is never eradicated.[5]

Dr. Joel Fort, an international authority and a pioneer in the field of controlling drug abuse, has summarized the effects of the most commonly used drugs of the seventies (see Table 10.1).

Heroin, morphine, and codeine are opium derivatives. Morphine is valuable in medicine because of its pain-relieving properties. It obliterates pain and relieves anxiety associated with pain. Nearly every human being in severe pain welcomes the effects of morphine. But its chronic use creates increased tolerance and psychological and physical dependence. It is therefore considered the prototype of all addictive drugs. When it is withheld from a physically dependent person, a well-defined withdrawal syndrome results: yawning, watering of the eyes, sweating, and dilation of the pupils of the eyes.

Heroin, the drug most commonly abused by traditional addicts, creates physical and psychological dependence, a compulsion to overuse the drug, and withdrawal symptoms. Barbiturates also create physical and psychological dependence and produce many of the same symptoms as alcohol when used in excess. These drugs are manufactured in most Western societies and have a legitimate medical use. Since they can be obtained legally by prescription, the extent of illegal use of barbiturates by drug addicts is unknown. The cost is not great enough to require criminal activity for gain.

---

[5] Alfred R. Lindesmith, *Opiate Addiction* 2d ed. (Evanston, Ill.: Principia Press, 1947), pp. 44–46.

Table 10.1

Major Drugs: Their Uses and Effects

	DRUG TYPE	NAME	ORIGIN	AVERAGE AMOUNT TAKEN	HOW TAKEN	SHORT-TERM EFFECTS OF AVERAGE AMOUNT DESCRIPTION
DEPRESSANTS	ALCOHOL □	Beer Distilled spirits Wine	Grain Grain Fruit	12 ounces 1½ ounces 3 ounces	Swallowed	Relaxation, breakdown of inhibitions, euphoria, depression, decreased alertness
	BARBITURATES □	Chloral hydrate Doriden Nembutal Phenobarbital Seconal	Synthetic	500 milligrams 400 milligrams 400 milligrams 50–100 milligrams 50–100 milligrams	Swallowed	Relaxation, euphoria, decreased alertness, drowsiness, impaired coordination, sleep
	INHALANTS ●	Aerosols (Freon) Airplane glue Amyl nitrite Nitrous oxide	Synthetic	Varies	Inhaled	Relaxation, euphoria, impaired coordination
	NARCOTICS ●	Codeine Demerol Heroin Methadone Morphine Opium Percodan	Opium poppy Synthetic Opium poppy Synthetic Opium poppy Opium poppy Synthetic	15–50 milligrams 50–150 milligrams Varies 5–15 milligrams 10 milligrams Varies 15–50 milligrams	Swallowed Injected Sniffed/injected Swallowed/injected Injected Inhaled/swallowed Swallowed	Relaxation, relief of pain & anxiety, decreased alertness, euphoria, hallucinations
	TRANQUILIZERS	Librium Miltown/Equanil Thorazine	Synthetic	5–25 milligrams 300–400 milligrams 5–25 milligrams	Swallowed	Relief of anxiety & tension, suppression of hallucinations & aggression, sleep
PSYCHEDELICS	CANNABIS □	Hashish Marijuana THC	Cannabis plant Cannabis plant Synthetic	Varies	Inhaled/swallowed Inhaled/swallowed Swallowed/injected	Relaxation, breakdown of inhibitions, alteration of perceptions, euphoria, increased appetite
	HALLUCINOGENS ●	DMT LSD Mescaline Nutmeg Psilocybin Scopolamine STP	Synthetic Synthetic Cactus Nutmeg tree Psilocybe mushroom Henbane plant/synthetic Synthetic	Varies 150–200 micrograms 350 milligrams 1/3 ounce 25 milligrams .5 milligram 5 milligrams	Inhaled Swallowed/injected Swallowed Swallowed/sniffed Swallowed Swallowed Swallowed	Perceptual changes—especially visual, increased energy, hallucinations, panic
STIMULANTS	AMPHETAMINES ●	Benzedrine Dexedrine Methedrine Preludin	Synthetic	2.5–5 milligrams	Swallowed/injected	Increased alertness, excitation, euphoria, decreased appetite
	ANTIDEPRESSANTS	Elavil Ritalin Tofranil	Synthetic	10–25 milligrams	Swallowed/injected	Relief of anxiety & depression, temporary impotence
	CAFFEINE	Coffee Cola No-Doz Tea	Coffee bean Kola nut Synthetic Tea leaves	1–2 cups 10 ounces 5 milligrams 1–2 cups	Swallowed	Increased alertness
	COCAINE ●□		Coca leaves	Varies	Sniffed/injected	Feeling of self-confidence & power, intense exhilaration
	NICOTINE □	Cigarettes Cigars Pipes Snuff	Tobacco leaves	Varies	Inhaled Inhaled Inhaled Sniffed	Relaxation, constriction of blood vessels

SOURCE: Joel Fort, "Major Drugs and Their Effects," *Playboy* Magazine, September 1972, pp. 143–45. Reproduced by special permission of PLAYBOY Magazine. Copyright © 1972 by Playboy.

NOTE: Drug types are listed alphabetically. Within each of the three major categories, symbols □ ● indicate danger to the health of the individual user (assuming short-term use of

| DURATION | SHORT-TERM EFFECTS OF LARGE AMOUNT | RISK OF DEPENDENCE | | TOLERANCE (increasing amounts needed for same effect) | LONG-TERM EFFECTS (continued excessive use) | MEDICAL USES |
		HABITUATION (psychological)	ADDICTION (physical)			
2-4 hrs.	Stupor, nausea, unconsciousness, hangover, death	High	Moderate	Yes	Obesity, impotence, psychosis, ulcers, malnutrition, liver & brain damage, delirium tremens, death	None
4-8 hrs.	Slurred speech, stupor, hangover, death	High	High	Yes	Excessive sleepiness, confusion, irritability, severe withdrawal sickness	For insomnia, tension & epileptic seizures
1-3 hrs.	Stupor, death	High	None	Possibly	Hallucinations; liver, kidney, bone-marrow & brain damage; death	None None Dilation of blood vessels Light anesthetic
4 hrs.	Stupor, death	High	High	Yes	Lethargy, constipation, weight loss, temporary sterility & impotence, withdrawal sickness	For cough Pain-killer None in U.S. Withdrawal from heroin Pain-killer For diarrhea Pain-killer
12-24 hrs.	Drowsiness, blurred vision, dizziness, slurred speech, allergic reaction, stupor	Moderate	Moderate Moderate None	No	Destruction of blood cells, jaundice, coma, death	For tension, anxiety, psychosis; alcoholism
2-4 hrs.	Panic, stupor	Moderate	None	No	Fatigue, psychosis	For tension, depression, headache, poor appetite
1/2 hr. 10-12 hrs. 12-14 hrs. Varies 6-8 hrs. Varies 12-14 hrs.	Anxiety, hallucinations, psychosis, exhaustion, tremors, vomiting, panic	Low	None	Yes	Increased delusions & panic, psychosis	(LSD and psilocybin have been tested for treatment of alcoholism, drug addiction, mental illness & migraine)
4-8 hrs.	Restlessness, rapid speech, irritability, insomnia, stomach disorders, convulsions	High	None	Yes	Insomnia, excitability, skin disorders, malnutrition, delusions, hallucinations, psychosis	For obesity, depression, excessive fatigue, narcolepsy, children's behavior disorders
12-24 hrs.	Nausea, hypertension, weight loss, insomnia	Low	None	No Yes No	Stupor, coma, convulsions, congestive heart failure, damage to liver & white blood cells, death	For anxiety or over-sedation, children's behavior disorders
2-4 hrs.	Restlessness, insomnia, upset stomach	High	None	Yes	Restlessness, irritability, insomnia, stomach disorders	For oversedation & headache
4 hrs.	Irritability, depression, psychosis	High	None	Yes	Damage to nasal septum & blood vessels, psychosis	Local anesthetic
1/4-2 hrs.	Headache, loss of appetite, nausea	High	None	Yes	Impaired breathing, heart & lung disease, cancer, death	None (used as insecticide)

average amounts and considering risk of addiction). The bullet ● signifies the greatest danger. Drug effects vary widely, depending on the amount consumed, its purity, the presence of other drugs in the user's system and—most important—his personality and the setting in which he takes the drug. Alcohol, caffeine, and nicotine are not legally considered drugs. Illegal drugs include opium, heroin, all hallucinogens except nutmeg, cocaine, and all Cannabis drugs.

Cocaine, like heroin, is a habit-forming drug, and its distribution is regulated by antinarcotics laws. While heroin is a depressant-tranquilizer, cocaine is a stimulant. It creates a psychological, but apparently no physical, dependence. Exhilaration stimulated by cocaine lasts only a few hours. Because of the short duration of the effect of the drug and its high cost, it is not commonly used to any great extent by street addicts. It has become a drug commonly used by affluent people and is widely used by rock musicians.

The amphetamines, particularly Benzedrine, are frequently prescribed by physicians as stimulants. The effect of these drugs is in many ways similar to that produced by cocaine. Since they can be lawfully obtained by prescription, the extent of their use by drug addicts is unknown, but on the basis of interviews with many addicts we can speculate that there is an extensive use pattern.

Marijuana is not a physically addictive drug like the opiates, but for some users it does tend to create psychological dependence. Dr. Joel Fort estimates that almost thirty million Americans have tried pot and ten million have become regular users. The plant from which it is obtained grows wild in many parts of the United States, but since the passage of the Marijuana Tax Act of 1937, which controls its production and distribution, most of the marijuana in the United States has been illegally imported from Mexico. Marijuana cigarettes in 1974 sold for twenty to forty cents each. The effect of marijuana is similar to that of alcohol, but the effects of withdrawal, if any, are far less serious for the marijuana smoker than for the alcoholic. Marijuana is used by juveniles essentially for pleasurable feelings. Nevertheless, as a result of enforcement-policy changes, arrests and prosecutions for its possession have greatly increased in recent years.

Another drug mention by Dr. Fort that is seldom discussed in treatises on delinquency and yet deserves attention is nicotine. As the evidence mounts that tobacco smoking is dangerous to a person's health, it becomes increasingly difficult to control its use by children. Although smoking is not viewed as "delinquent" as is the use of other substances by children, it remains a deviant pattern of drug use that deserves more attention. One study by T. L. Chen and William R. Rakip provides some insights into nicotine as a problem.[6]

Despite warnings that "cigarette smoking is hazardous to your health," which have scared a lot of adults out of their habit, the younger generation seems to be relatively immune to commonsense appeals. And if the trend continues, nearly one and one-half million children now in school can expect to live shorter lives because of that vice. According to Chen and Rakip it appears that the time has come to initiate smoking education into the regular school curriculum. But are teachers prepared to tackle the evils of tobacco? For the most part, the 162 elementary, junior high, and high school teachers

---

[6] *Human Behavior* (March 1975).

polled by Chen and Rakip perceived smoking as a health hazard serious enough to warrant a smoking education program, but not many felt qualified to deal with the issue.

Only about 10 percent of the teachers had any special training in the health hazards of smoking; the vast majority learned along with the rest of the public through mass media and professional reports or personal experience. Not surprisingly, then, they felt they would make ineffective instructors and suggested instead that a health education specialist or public health professional be called in to do the job. They seemed to feel that such efforts could be most successfully directed at elementary and junior high students and their parents rather than at high school and college students or teachers.

Chen and Rakip found that although a majority of the teachers claimed they didn't mind discussing the subject if the student brought it up, only 1 percent said they would offer any assistance. Still, 62 percent had reportedly tried to influence student smoking behavior. Most of those who had not were among the thirty-eight current smokers and did not feel comfortable preaching what they could not practice. The thirty-seven ex-smokers were the most active in trying to impress their young charges. Although most people do not consider children smokers as participating in real delinquent behavior, the health hazards remain present.

In conclusion, Chen and Rakip suggest that schools looking to promote a smoking education program might start by finding a zealous ex-smoker to lead the way. Furthermore, they add, a program that also aims "to reduce teacher smoking behavior will, in turn, put those teachers in a better position for reducing student smoking."

Many experts feel that the terms *drug* and *narcotic* should apply only to the opiates, not to marijuana or cocaine. Although both marijuana and cocaine have been included in the coverage of antinarcotic legislation (the most recent being the Comprehensive Drug Abuse, Prevention, and Control Act of 1970), they are not opiates, and their effects are not at all comparable to the effects of opiates. Barbiturates, amphetamines, and other synthetic tranquilizers and stimulants create psychological dependence and only in some instances physical dependence. Because of the increased use of synthetic drugs by addicts, the sale and distribution of these drugs have increasingly come under federal and state regulation. However, since they are prescribed by doctors for patients of all social classes to alleviate stress, their habitual use is not stigmatized as drug addiction.

Drug use by young people is definitely a growing problem. In 1975 the FBI's *Uniform Crime Reports* indicated that 79,449 city youths under eighteen years of age were arrested for violating "narcotic drug laws." In 1960 there were 1,583 youths arrested on narcotics charges, and in 1967 the total was 13,904. In slightly over a decade, therefore, the number of urban youth under eighteen who have been arrested for violating narcotic drug laws has increased from 1,583 offenses (1960) to 77,449 offenses (1975). Obviously the nation is confronted with a staggering drug problem among its youth. Since most juvenile drug use goes undetected by official agencies, the "hidden users" would swell these statistics.

The widespread and increasing use of drugs tends to affect the school situation of many young people. In this context a study by S. E. Lerner and R. L. Linden revealed something of the pattern of drug abuse in the elementary schools.[7]

The findings of a study carried out on a sample of 194 elementary school students (69 fourth graders, 63 fifth graders, and 62 sixth graders) to determine at what grade levels and to what extent upper elementary school students used psychoactive drugs was reported by Lerner and Linden. Inhalants had been used at least once in the previous year by 23.1 percent of fourth graders, 11.1 percent of fifth graders and 8.0 percent of sixth graders, while beer and wine had been used by 59.4 percent, 73.0 percent and 62.9 percent respectively. A general trend of greater use of tobacco, marijuana, beer/wine, hard liquor, amphetamines, barbiturates, codeine and methaqualone was evident as students advanced by grade. Data were also presented on drug availability and reasons for use. Since the findings evidence the extensive use of certain psychoactive drugs by elementary school students, Lerner and Linden recommended that drug education be initiated at the kindergarten or first grade level.

In another study N. Galli explored the extent and nature of drug use among elementary school students as well as students in the junior and senior high school.[8] Findings indicated that while drug usage began to increase in the seventh grade, substantial increases occurred after this grade level. For all substances drug use peaked in the ninth or tenth grade.

In response to the growing problem of drugs in the schools, various programs were developed to counterattack the situation. One study by R. L. Nail and E. K. E. Gunderson came to some dismal conclusions about the value of drug education in the schools.[9]

Increasing evidence supports the contention that most drug abuse education efforts are ineffective. Whether at an individual school or at the federal level, marked disappointment prevails concerning the accomplishments of the great majority of such programs. The Nail and Gunderson report briefly summarized the "state of the art" regarding drug abuse education in its broadest context, with frequent reference to authoritative figures in the field of drug abuse education. Personal decision making was discussed, and certain advantages and hazards were presented concerning reliance on youthful attempts to reach independent conclusions regarding drug use. According to

---

[7]S. E. Lerner and R. L. Linden, "Drugs in the Elementary School," *Juvenile Drug Education* 4 (April 1974):69–79.

[8]N. Galli, "Patterns of Student Drug Use," *Juvenile Drug Education* 4 (May 1974):83–93.

[9]R. L. Nail and E. K. E. Gunderson, "Drug Education Results," *Juvenile Drug Education* 5 (1975):65–75.

Nail and Gunderson, "the evidence appears to make a case for an unemotional, honest, and informative presentation of drug abuse topics, thus allowing rational youth to deal more effectively with drug abuse issues at an individual level."

Apart from education in the schools, in recent years police have injected undercover policemen into high schools in an effort to control the problem with a vigorous arrest policy. Apart from such arrests the law appears to have a limited effect on potential adolescent drug users. A study by Steven Burkett and Eric L. Jensen examined the relationship between belief in the certainty of apprehension and self-reported marijuana use.[10] The relative importance of this belief and ties to conventional others as sources of control were studied. An anonymous questionnaire was administered to 546 male and 510 female senior class students in three high schools located in an all-white suburb of Washington. Estimates of apprehension were measured by responses to the statement: "If I were to use marijuana, I would probably get caught." The students were asked about the number of their close friends using marijuana to determine the extent of involvement with others. Burkett and Jensen found that "marijuana use is unlikely, given the absence of group supports. This holds true for youth who maintain conventional ties and for those with weak ties. Involvement with nonusing peers is related to patterns of use and the belief that one will get caught if he tries. The effectiveness of the law as a deterrent is questionable given peer involvement and reinforcement for beliefs which discount or support the certainty of apprehension as a reason for nonuse."[11]

One reason for a greater concern with drug use among youths is that in most cases drug abuse is interrelated with more serious offenses that are required to support a habit. Not all juvenile drug users commit thefts and robberies to support their habit, but many do, especially those addicted to heroin. Most heroin addicts need anywhere from $25 to $100 or more a day to support their habit. A habit costing $75 a day is high but not unusual. It is estimated that the addict must steal between $3 and $5 in merchandise for each dollar he realizes in cash. Thus the average addict steals from $500 to over $2,000 worth of merchandise a week. Since estimates of the total number of addicts vary from sixty thousand to one million, the amount stolen may reach several billion dollars a year.

Statistics and research alone do not fully account for the growing problem of drug use and abuse in America among young people, nor do they convey the full impact of the problem on society. Because of the magnitude of drug use, law enforcement has stopped trying to arrest every user. For example, although it is illegal, marijuana use is a widespread practice in both the youth

---

[10]Steven Burkett and Eric L. Jensen, "Conventional Ties, Peer Influence, and the Fear of Apprehension: A Study of Adolescent Marijuana Use," *Sociological Quarterly* (Fall 1975):54–67.

[11]Burkett and Jensen, "Conventional Ties, Peer Influence, and Fear of Apprehension: A Study of Adolescent Marijuana Use," p. 57.

and adult population. If law enforcement was completely effective, based on recent surveys, one-third of the high school and half of the college population would be subject to arrest. Therefore, a considerable amount of drug use in the seventies is accepted by the general population, even though the behavior is illegal. This acceptance may be one of the reasons young people become addicted, since youths from all strata grow up in a drug-using society.

Becoming Addicted

The interplay of family factors, peer associations, and personality development all affect how youths become addicted to drugs. In a study by E. G. Moses into the sociopsychoanalytic characteristics of young suburban white heroin addicts, an attempt was made to identify their character traits, to determine what in society selects and develops these traits, and to find out what in their character facilitates drug addiction.[12] The method involved two instruments —an interpretive questionnaire to reveal a person's dynamic striving and the Rorschach. The findings indicated four types of heroin addicts on the basis of the character traits that emerged. They were: "identity seekers, born losers, the insatiably needy, and the exploitative."

In determining "how youths become addicted," there is always the paradox of two or more children who seem to come from the same social environment and yet turn out differently. Some become addicts and others do not. A control study by Starlet R. Craig and Barry S. Brown, analyzed this issue.[13] Among their sample were Angie and Lisa. Angie and Lisa were both sixteen-year-old black girls living in the inner city; they liked school and were fairly good students. Angie could hardly remember her father, who left home when she was five; Lisa's dad moved out a year ago when he and her mother decided to split up. Lisa and Angie would seem to have quite a bit in common, but on one point they differ sharply; Lisa has never touched drugs and Angie is a heroin addict.

According to Craig and Brown, "It's not all that easy to pick the drug-using teens from among the abstainers on background information alone." Comparing a group of sixty-five black teenagers in treatment at the National Treatment Administration with a similarly composed group of nonusers drawn from Washington, D. C.'s recreational and youth programs, Craig and Brown found little, other than drug use, that would distinguish the two groups of youths from each other.

Both groups seemed to share similar childhood experiences, including weekly church attendance (77 percent of the users, 82 percent of the nonusers)

---

[12]E. G. Moses, "Social Character and Heroin Addiction," *Proceedings of the Thirty-first Congress on Alcoholism and Drug Dependence* (January 1975):132.

[13]*Human Behavior* (September 1975).

and frequent sports activities, usually at a nearby city recreation center. Significantly more of the users, however, were living with or raised by only one parent when they were between the ages of six and twelve.

By adolescence, this point of difference had disappeared, with only 45 percent of the users and 46 percent of the nonusers still living with both biological parents. The researchers note: "family instability is considerable in both groups but is more intense for drug users at an earlier age." Church attendance had declined greatly for both groups and so had use of the community recreation centers, although nonusers were involved in sports activities and organized community programs to a greater extent than users.

In terms of education, around three-quarters of both groups said they liked school and rated themselves as at least average students. The drug users were nevertheless more likely to drop out, note Craig and Brown, and they also reported having fewer "close" friends. In their opinion, however, these differences may be "the consequences of drug use rather than its causes." Craig and Brown concluded that

> the most distinctive differences between users and nonusers seemed to be their attitude toward drugs. Nearly half the abstainers said that they avoided drugs because they had seen their effect on others or because the physical dangers concerned them; 70 percent of the users, on the other hand, reported succumbing to curiosity and peer pressure. Furthermore, 32 percent of the users had immediate family members who were also into drugs, while the same was true for only 2 percent of the nonusers.

This led Craig and Brown to speculate about a kind of "behavioral contagion" within drug-using families.

There is increasing evidence to support the conclusion that many people become addicted to drugs in order to escape from their problems. Some psychiatrists attribute drug abuse to the need to modify deep feelings of inadequacy and inferiority. The following five categories tend to account for most patterns of addiction:

1. *Normal people who have accidentally become addicted.* These include the person who is given a drug to alleviate severe physical trauma and finds this experience so satisfying that he continues to use it until he becomes physiologically dependent on it. Withdrawal proves painful and may be rejected. Once withdrawal is rejected and the use of the drug made continuous, we have addiction. Also included in this category are people who start using drugs because of social relationships. The girl friend of an addict, for example, may become addicted to keep pace with her boyfriend. One could speculate, of course, that she would not have related to an addict if she did not have a personality problem of her own.

2. *The person who has been introduced to drug use by "friends."* It has

been pointed out that unsuccessful gang members, and at times entire gangs, sometimes shift from either delinquent or conflict adaptations to retreatist (drug use) adaptations. These are referred to by Richard A. Cloward and Lloyd E. Ohlin as "double failures": failures in society and failures in the gang world. There is often strong peer-group pressure placed on a youth to use drugs.

3. *The sociopath.* We have discussed this personality type at considerable length. The sociopath's antisocial, compulsive, and hedonistic pleasures are the most important things in his life. The sociopath living in an impoverished socioeconomic area is likely to have access to drugs and to try them. If he finds them particularly satisfying, he may become addicted.

4. *The neurotic.* This group probably includes a large percentage of the addict population. Drugs are the neurotic's personal form of self-therapy. He takes drugs to feel better, to relieve anxiety. Drugs provide an escape from problems, and he tends to revert to drugs whenever a problem confronts him. Sociologists and psychiatrists have noted that a significant number of lower class addicts aspire beyond their means to achieve. Their families have inculcated unattainable levels of aspiration and expectation in them. Drugs help to solve the emotional pain of their sense of rejection and failure.

5. *The psychotic.* Many psychiatrists take the position that heroin addiction is a symptom of a severe emotional disorder and that heroin addiction may mask psychosis. A 1954 study by Donald L. Gerard and Conan Kornetsky reflects an opinion about heroin addiction that persists in the 1970s. Gerard and Kornetsky's conclusions parallel those of many psychiatric researchers and are summarized in the following points:

> The social and psychiatric characteristics of thirty-two minor male opiate addicts who were admitted to the United States Public Health Service Hospital at Lexington, Ky., were studied. All were genuinely addicted to opiate drugs.
>
> Although the majority of the patients studied were Negro and Puerto Rican adolescents coming from "deprived" communities in New York City or Chicago, they came from a variety of social backgrounds; and the majority were reared by economically comfortable families with middle-class educational and occupational status and goals.
>
> There was no common interpersonal family background except that the families of these patients were of the types which psychiatric experience suggests to be productive of serious difficulties in adjustment.
>
> All the subjects showed marked disturbances in their adjustment patterns independent of, and preceding their involvement with, opiate drug use. They were placed in four diagnostic categories: (1) overt schizophrenia; (2) incipient schizophrenia or "borderline" states; (3) delinquency-dominated character disorders; and (4) "inadequate" personalities. They displayed in common a patterned disturbance or syn-

drome of characteristics: (1) dysphoria; (2) problems of sexual identification; and (3) disturbances of interpersonal relations characterized by inability to enter prolonged, close, or friendly relationships with their peers or adults.

Several common adaptive functions of opiate drug addiction were noted: (a) The difficulties of living as a drug addict in our society facilitate the denial and avoidance of the patient's underlying problems. (b) Opiate drug use helped treat the overt psychiatric symptomatology of many of the cases. (c) Opiate drugs were helpful in controlling the anxiety and strain which these patients experienced in a variety of interpersonal situations. (d) Opiate drug use gave, to these patients, regressive and oral satisfactions which were accompanied by a feeling of comfortable separateness from, and a lack of involvement in, their current difficulties in living.

The writers' observations suggest that a successful treatment program for the adolescent addict requires a psychiatric facility prepared to undertake long-range treatment of delinquent emotionally disturbed boys.[14]

The Female Drug Addict

Females who become heroin users parallel the male addict in many ways; however, there are some variations worth noting. They more often than not begin as the consort of a male user; however, when thrown onto their own resources as a heroin user, women will generally resort to petty theft, selling drugs, and prostitution to support their habit.

The case of Paula, a New York drug addict, provides a fairly typical case history of the traditional process of heroin addiction acted out by females in urban areas. Here is her story as told to one of the authors:

I was born by mistake twenty-seven years ago. According to what I'm told, since I don't recall too much before I was nine or ten, I was a problem child. I was put into a problem child's institution at a very early age. I think I was a year or a year and a half old when I was placed. I progressed from there to different institutions until I was sixteen. The last reformatory I was in was a so-called treatment center. Here I got my final street education.

Most of the kids there, including myself, were considered incorrigible. Most of the guys had criminal records. Some of the girls had been whores from the age of ten or eleven, and a couple of the boys had

[14]Donald L. Gerard, and Conan Kornetsky, "A Social and Psychiatric Study of Adolescent Opiate Addicts," *The Psychiatric Quarterly* 28 (January 1954):12–13.

committed the act of rape (or what was called rape) and even murder. They were accomplished thieves and con men. I absorbed all of their teachings readily. I enjoyed it.

I think I always knew I was going to use drugs. I used my first form of drugs when I was twelve. There were two guys who lived in the same apartment house with my family. I admired and looked up to them. They were about seventeen or eighteen at the time. I was allowed home visits once or twice a year for a weekend (when my behavior, in the institution I was in at the time, was good enough).

Whenever I did manage a home visit, I looked forward to hanging out at night in front of the house with these guys. They seemed to know I was hurting inside and tolerated me. One summer night I saw them going to the roof of the house, and I followed them. They were smoking (I found out a few minutes later) some weed [marijuana]. It smelled good to me, and I asked for a drag. I turned on. I remember that I felt it was the most beautiful thing that had ever happened to me. I was very happy and started to imitate all the singers I liked. The guys gave me lots of approval for my singing. From then on, I was one of them and got all the pot I could use.

After that year, I was introduced to cocaine by the same two guys, and horned [sniffed] it whenever the opportunity arose. For fourteen years I enjoyed all the drugs I ever used. Heroin crept up on me. I normally weighed 125 pounds. There was a period when I was badly strung out [addicted] on heroin and weighed 90 pounds. I thought my clothes had stretched!

I had a six-year period of using every form of narcotic and everything that went with it. Maybe if I describe the average life of an addict in New York City, you will get an idea of what my life was like for the years before I got to Synanon.

My hours were from six to six. That is, six in the evening to six in the morning. (It took me a year to go to sleep before 2:00 A.M. at Synanon.) I'd get up as late as possible, because the sun hurt my eyes. I didn't want people to look at me.

You know something's terribly wrong. You're different. Squares are scurrying around, bumping up against each other. They look insane to you. Addicts talk a lot about how crazy squares are.

You get dressed, and if you happen to have some drugs you take your morning fix. From there on in, you begin to scramble for bread [money] and drugs, and anything goes. I would buy or sell drugs. Most pushers are addicts. They're not the big-time people you read about with beautiful apartments. The heavier pushers [those with large quantities of drugs] are usually addicts too. That's the reason they're pushing. It's a simple matter of economics. You buy a quantity. You cut the drugs yourself. You sell a little bit. You make a little money to buy more dope.

Most of the time you're broke, so you use your wiles. You'll use anything you've learned. You con, and being female you have a few tools that guys don't have. I did a few nasty things in my time. I turned out as a whore. I participated in many degrading acts. If you check Krafft-Ebing, you will find a pretty good catalog of what I had to do to make my money.

When I could, I worked with people who were experienced in different con games. I especially liked one con game called a Murphy. Someone fronts for you, acts as your pimp at a bar. The trick [customer for prostitution] gives your pimp some money on account. He thinks he's going to meet you in a nearby hotel. As soon as the money changes hands, you, of course, disappear. There's a lot of men like that who come into New York from out of town. They're dying to have their money taken away from them.

Then there's till-tapping. One person diverts the storekeeper's attention and the other one puts his hand in the cash register. Then there are vending machines you can always break into when you get desperate. And when all else fails, there is a gun. If you happen to have one and the weight to hold it and not shake too much.

You're constantly looking for a good connection. Yours is never there. If you spend a lot of money, you might have a good connection. One that lasts for three months or so. But there's always a shortage of drugs. Something always happens. Like there's a bust [arrest] in the neighborhood and everyone who's holding [has dope] gets off the street. On some days, you might travel on foot for miles with $50 in your pocket and not touch a penny of it because you don't want to go to the man [connection] short. You want to get to him with the full amount so you'll be sure to get as much drugs as you can buy. There are very few meals eaten or sleep involved.

If you get drugs that are pretty strong, you can go along on them for a few hours. But usually drugs are so weak and cut down, you have to fix [inject the drugs] six or eight times a day to feel normal. When you have a real habit going, you don't really get loaded like you see acted out in the movies or read about. You need the drug to feel normal.

After the first few months of addiction, the stuff takes over. The demand builds higher and higher and the supply is never enough. You need more and more drugs and money. I spent as much for myself as I did for my old man. (You would call him a pimp—I didn't think he was.) If I made $100 a day, it would be spent on drugs.

The first three years that I used drugs, I didn't try to kick it. At that time, the situation was ideal for a junkie. My old man was a connection. He had a lot of dope, and I stayed in our apartment most of the time. As a matter of fact, when I was taken care of, I stayed in once for nine solid months. I went out about once a week—at night.

Then, of course, the drugs ran out and a little reality crept in. My old man sent me to some people he knew in another part of town who were running a whorehouse. They had a large apartment and a telephone for appointments. The place was closed down a few months later, and I hit the street as a street whore uninitiated in street bargaining. But I had to take a chance, and that's when I got my first arrest for soliciting.

I almost died the first time I was arrested and put in the tank [cell for addicts only]. When I landed in the jail infirmary, I knew something was wrong. I got a suspended sentence the next Monday, and of course went right to a connection.

I don't think I really seriously thought about kicking for five years. I felt that dope was my fate, that I had to be an addict for the rest of my life.

In 1957 I went to Lexington [the federal hospital for addicts] to try to quit. I heard that it was a hospital. I found out it was also a lockup. I left in ten days, sicker than when I arrived. In Lex you're given a purer form of drugs to "help" your withdrawal pains. That year, methadone was given orally. You of course exaggerate the extent of your habit so you can get as much M and goofballs [sleeping pills] as possible. If you get any kind of habit from these drugs, they are a lot worse to kick than a heroin habit. I was pretty disillusioned with Lexington.

By the time I got back to New York, my old man had been busted and was sent to a federal prison. Most of the people I hung out with in New York were connected with jazz in one way or another. Most of the junkies and their wives were connected with the jazz-music business. One of these junkie musicians' wives got a letter from another musician's wife in California describing a bunch of addicts living on the beach in Ocean Park, California. They were supposedly trying to do something for each other and their drug problem. My family had moved out to California, and I thought I'd see what it was all about. I didn't believe Synanon really existed. But I'd see what it was all about; and anyway, I would find a Broadway in Los Angeles. I knew if there was one, I'd find some stuff. I didn't think I was taking a real chance by going to the Coast.

Earlier that year I made my first real effort to kick. I did this in different people's apartments. Every Saturday for months I wouldn't use any stuff. Of course, by Sunday morning I'd realize how stupid it was, especially if there was any money or dope around.

On one of these weekends, I almost killed myself, accidentally. The girl whose apartment I was kicking in that Saturday gave me a bottle of goofballs to help me. It was ridiculous, because all these pills do is leave you immobile. You may think you're moving, but you probably haven't budged an inch. I tried escaping from this fifth-floor apartment by climbing out of a window. It was separated by four feet from a fire escape. I somehow managed to get down one flight. I burst into someone's apartment through their window, to get out their front door!

I was really running scared and alone. I called a trick I knew who had liked me and who I thought would help me if he knew my problem. I guessed right. He said he'd come over. I decided to shoot all the drugs I had, together with some goofballs. By the time he arrived, I was in a coma. He got a chambermaid to open the door to my hotel room, threw me in the shower, and they did the best they could to revive me.

He contacted my sister (whom I'd seen twice in five years) and with her arranged for my plane fare to the Coast. He also gave my sister a check for a couple hundred dollars (to be mailed to my parents' home in thirty days). There was a stipulation that I promise to stay in Los Angeles at least six months. That's how long he thought it would take to straighten me out!

I was put on a nonstop flight to Los Angeles in May of 1959. When I landed in California I was a physical and emotional wreck.[15]

Paula was successfully treated for her addiction problem at Synanon.

Two psychologists, Frederic Suffet and Richard Brotman, draw a number of relevant conclusions about female narcotic addicts from their analysis of several studies.[16] When they reviewed the findings on female drug use, Suffet and Brotman found that whether the drug is marijuana or heroin, women are usually initiated into the scene by men. One study pointed out that marriage to a male addict is associated with a wife later getting hooked on heroin, while men who marry addicts are more likely to stay clean. In a study of needle sharing, it appeared that most men (68 percent) but few women (29 percent) "hit" themselves. The data imply, say Suffet and Brotman, that it is a man who puts the first needle in a woman's vein.

Most studies of drugs for "recreational and pleasure-oriented use" indicate that males tend to be the regular users, although among the very young and bohemian that sex gap narrows. While females are still more likely than males to spurn illicit drugs, they are the major consumers of "psychotherapeutics" (e.g., barbiturates and other sedatives, tranquilizers, antidepressants, and amphetamines). When persons were asked what they used to cope with life, more men reported they hit the bottle while women said they popped pills. When heroin addicts were asked why they first dabbled in the opiate, women were more likely than men to cite "relief of personal disturbance." It was found that female addicts held conventional values (more so than their college sisters

[15]Lewis Yablonsky, *The Tunnel Back: Synanon* (New York: Macmillan, 1965), pp. 16–17. Copyright 1965 by Lewis Yablonsky. Reprinted with permission of Macmillan Publishing Co., Inc.
[16]*Human Behavior* (August 1976).

who smoked pot), except that 47 percent of them turned to prostitution to support their habits.

Although Suffet and Brotman admit that "social forecasting is a notoriously risky business," they ventured some predictions about the future of female drug use. Since "recreational" drugs are linked with liberated lifestyles, more women will begin to try marijuana and "other such drugs." It follows, they say, that more women will be introducing women to drugs.

As women achieve equality and become more immune to sex-role stress, say the researchers, the degree of psychotherapeutic drug use may fall. On the other hand, "as they take their rightful place in the work world, they will be subject to the same pressures men experience. They may continue to pop pills or they may turn to booze to forget the strains of the office."

Suffet and Brotman are less certain about the future of female heroin addiction, although they do conclude that "some women, particularly those denied normal life chances, who enter the addict world will continue to run the risk of prostitution or other illegal activity."

Alcoholism and Delinquency

Alcoholism has been defined as "a chronic behavioral disorder manifested by repeated drinking of alcoholic beverages in excess of the dietary and social uses of the community and to an extent that *interferes with the drinker's health or his social or economic functioning.*"[17] According to one expert, Dr. Joel Fort, of the 70 million Americans who consume alcoholic beverages, approximately 5 million—some 4 percent of our total population—are said to be alcoholics, chronic excessive drinkers included in the above definition.[18] Alcoholism is considered the nation's fourth greatest health problem, and since it results in serious economic consequences to the alcoholic and his family, its prevalence contributes substantially to delinquency. And because of its deleterious impact on parents, alcoholism significantly affects the problems of juvenile delinquency.

In terms of direct impact, 95,831 "city youths" were arrested for liquor-law violations in 1972.[19] This figure undoubtedly reflects only a small percentage of all youths who use or abuse alcohol.

The National Council on Alcoholism reports that the proportion of high school students who drink has more than doubled from 1969 to 1976 and that

---

[17]Mark Keller, "Alcoholism: Nature and Extent of the Problem," *Annals of the American Academy of Political and Social Science* 315 (January 1958):2. Emphasis added.

[18]Personal communication.

[19]Federal Bureau of Investigation, *Uniform Crime Reports for the United States, 1972* (Washington, D. C.: U. S. Government Printing Office, 1973), p. 126.

in the same period the age of the youngest alcoholic has dropped from age fourteen to twelve.

According to Jack Wright and James Kitchens,

> The drinking patterns of children tend to model those of their parents and the immediate sociocultural milieu. . . . Like father, like son is true in many areas, and as a result boys are more likely to drink than girls. The children of Catholic and Jewish parents are more likely to drink than their Protestant or Mormon peers. Higher percentages of teenage drinkers are to be found in the North and East than in the South. While adult drinking tends to follow social class lines, no consistent relationship of teenage drinking to class or race has been found.[20]

Probably because drinking alcoholic beverages is a source of pleasure for about half the population, the person addicted to alcohol is not rejected by society to the same extent as is the drug addict. There is an increasing tendency to regard the alcoholic as a sick person who requires hospitalization and treatment. Evidence to support this position is based on physiological and psychological data.

Medical experts maintain that excessive use of alcohol results in such physical complications as malnutrition, cirrhosis of the liver, polyneuritis, and gastrointestinal bleeding. Psychologists and psychiatrists note the compulsive nature and self-harming characteristics of the alcoholic's drinking patterns. The actions of the alcoholic so closely approximate those of an emotionally sick individual that alcoholism is widely viewed as a disease, seldom as a crime.

Alcoholism is listed in the medical bible, *Standard Nomenclature of Diseases*, under the heading of addictions. The laws prohibiting the sale or possession of narcotics, marijuana, and dangerous drugs, however, do not currently apply to the sale or possession of alcoholic beverages. They once did in the United States. The Eighteenth Amendment to the Constitution, which provided the legal support for this prohibition, was repealed in 1933, after it had been in effect for thirteen years. It was the only amendment to the Constitution ever to be repealed.

Since 1933, the law has not treated the alcoholic as harshly as it does other addicts. In fact, in recent years, both the American Medical Association and the American Psychiatric Association have taken the position that alcoholism is an illness and is entitled to treatment by any means at our disposal.

In some states, the time, place, and manner of sale of alcoholic beverages are regulated by law. In virtually all states there are laws prohibiting the sale of alcoholic beverages to persons below a designated age, usually eighteen. There are also laws prohibiting certain types of advertising and limiting the

---

[20]Jack Wright and James Kitchens, *Social Problems in America* (Columbus, Ohio: Charles E. Merrill, 1976), p. 97.

use of mass media. Nevertheless, none of these laws makes it an offense to consume alcoholic drinks.

While many states have laws prohibiting public drunkenness, many of these laws apply only when public drunkenness is accompanied by a breach of the peace. In Georgia and Alabama, for example, drunkenness that is manifested by boisterous or indecent conduct or loud and profane discourse is a crime. In other jurisdictions, disorderly conduct statutes apply to those who are drunk in public. State and local laws provide for jail sentences ranging from five days to six months, the most common being thirty days. Habitual drunkenness may be punished by two years in prison.

Some of these laws are being seriously challenged in the courts. In one recent decision, the U. S. Fourth Circuit Court of Appeals ruled that a two-year sentence imposed for public drunkenness was "cruel and unusual punishment." The court ruled that the state could not stamp a chronic alcoholic as a criminal if his drunken display was involuntary and the result of disease. Detention for treatment was not precluded as long as the defendant was not marked a criminal. Another court held that proof of chronic alcoholism was a defense against a charge of drunkenness because the defendant had lost the power of self-control in the use of alcoholic beverages.

Every state has a law against drunken driving. Because of the belief that drunken drivers account for a disproportionate share of automobile accidents, efforts to punish drunken drivers are emphasized. In California, for example, the police may, if they believe a driver to be intoxicated, require him to submit to a blood test for sobriety. If he refuses to submit to the test, his driver's license is suspended. While the constitutionality of this law is doubtful, the law does reflect the increasing concern about drunken driving. But aside from these laws against drunken driving and public drunkenness, there are few statutes regulating the behavior of the alcohol user.

The use of alcohol is related to delinquency in two ways:

1. *Directly,* when the use of alcohol is an offense for a minor. Also drunken driving is forbidden by the statutes of every state. Public drunkenness that interferes with others is forbidden in most states. Where state laws do not provide penalties for such behavior, county, municipal, or other local laws usually do.

Over 40 percent of all arrests made by the police are for public drunkenness, drunken driving, and other violations of law regulating the consumption of liquor—offenses *directly* attributable to the use of alcoholic beverages. An additional 12 percent are for disorderly conduct and vagrancy, offenses usually associated with excessive use of alcohol. Persons arrested for these offenses, which account for over half of all arrests, are not necessarily alcoholics, although at the time of their arrests they had shown evidence of having been under the influence of alcohol.

2. *Indirectly,* when the excessive use of alcohol contributes to the commission of serious crimes. We have no way of knowing how many serious

offenders are alcoholics or how many offenses are committed by persons under the influence of alcoholic beverages. One study of felons in California indicated that 98 percent of them consumed alcoholic beverages and that 29 percent of these claimed that they were intoxicated at the time they committed the offense for which they were sent to prison. An equal percentage stated that the use of alcohol was a problem for them prior to imprisonment.[21] These findings are similar to results obtained in previous studies in other states. We have no way of knowing whether or not these persons would have committed felonies if they had not been problem drinkers. Although there is no evidence to indicate that the use of alcohol stimulates a desire to commit crimes, economic and social disadvantages suffered by the problem drinker may influence him in the direction of serious crime. Many juveniles indicate that they have committed serious delinquent acts under the influence of alcohol.

Alcohol is a drug that seems to be back in vogue with youths in the seventies, after being put down to some degree during the sixties. Despite the fact that alcohol remains illegal in most jurisdictions for young people under eighteen, drinking alcoholic beverages appears to be a growing pattern of accepted behavior in juvenile peer groups. Most youths appear to drink because of the positive immediate effects it has on their personality. Drinking tends to mask feelings of inadequacy, gives some youths a sense of power, and, simply, provides euphoric feelings.

A number of sociologists see adolescent drinking as a form of rebellion. Robert F. Bales reasons that abstinence norms may actually encourage the use of alcohol as a symbol of aggression against authority. He writes:

> The breaking of the taboo becomes an ideal way of expressing dissent and aggression, especially where the original solidarity of the group is weak and aggression is strong. Thus total prohibition sometimes overshoots the mark and encourages the very thing it is designed to prevent. This situation is frequently found among individual alcoholics whose parents were firm teetotalers and absolutely forbade their sons to drink.[22]

Based on a study of the drinking patterns of 1,410 high school students, C. Norman Alexander, Jr., affirmed Bales's observations:

> It has been shown that the likelihood of drinking and of legitimating the use of alcohol (in opposition to parental expectations) is inversely related to the closeness of the adolescent to an abstinent father. Further-

---

[21]Austin H. MacCormick, "Correctional Views on Alcohol, Alcoholism, and Crime," *Crime and Delinquency* 9 (January 1963):15–28.

[22]Robert F. Bales, "Cultural Differences in Rates of Alcoholism," in *Drinking and Intoxication,* ed. Raymond G. McCarthy (New York: Free Press of Glencoe, 1959), pp. 263–67.

more, among drinkers who lack peer support for alcohol use, rejection of father is associated with frequent disobedience of parental authority in order to "get even" with them. And, when positive peer influence to drink is lacking, the rejection of parental authority (negative affect and frequent disobedience) is associated with frequent drinking, excessive drinking leading to extreme intoxication, and drinking for psychological rather than social reasons—all of these early drinking patterns being common in histories of problem-drinkers. In anticipating these results it was reasoned that drinking, when not due to positive pressures to drink, is a negative response, an expression of rebellion against the paternal authority figure.

The present data support Bales' hypothesis that drinking in a normative setting of abstinence is largely antinormative. Drinking in this type of social situation tends to become rebellious behavior when drinkers lack social support. Thus the high rates of problem-drinking and alcoholism among religious and cultural groups who promulgate abstinence norms may well be due to similar, socially aggressive drinking patterns. Other observers have examined differential rates of alcoholism, interpreting abstinence-oriented drinking behaviors as nonnormative (lacking social regulation), pronormative (adoption of the "horrible example" role-model), and antinormative (rebellious). This analysis has specified the "rebellion" hypothesis in terms of a more general social psychological theory and has subjected it to test in a relatively homogeneous cultural milieu in the context of father-son relationships. Hence, it has been possible to demonstrate that *anti*normative aspects of drinking are important in abstinence-oriented social situations and that this is certainly a significant factor in the high incidence of problem behaviors among those who drink in these social environments.[23]

Hallucinatory Drug Use

Although the "hippie scene" of the late sixties seems to have diminished as a sociocultural phenomenon, it left in its wake a definitive pattern of drug use still prevalent in the seventies.

The hallucinatory drug scene emerged about 1969 and exists today alongside the narcotic drug culture. The problem peaked in 1968, dropped somewhat, then leveled off to an accepted use pattern in the seventies. Psychedelic drugs such as LSD and marijuana are illegal, yet their use is differentiated from the opiate narcotic use pattern in several ways:

1. Most participants in the heroin narcotic use pattern come from a

---

[23]C. Norman Alexander, "Alcohol and Adolescent Rebellion," *Social Forces* 45 (June 1967):548. Copyright © The University of North Carolina Press.

predominantly lower socioeconomic background. They generally have grown up in the urban ghettos. Most participants in the psychedelic drug scene, on the other hand, come mostly from the middle and upper classes.

2. Users in the narcotic drug subculture have a delinquent self-concept and for the most part are aware that their acts are illegal and deviant. Many try to kick the habit. In contrast, the psychedelic drug user tends to see himself as a seeker of a new religious-philosophical state of existence. He does not believe himself to be either addicted or delinquent. He is aware that the drugs he is using are illegal but does not believe he is really committing an illegal act.

3. Members of the heroin narcotic drug subculture are generally involved in a criminal way of life. Those making the psychedelic scene consider themselves part of a "new community" of liberation and openness.

4. Marijuana appears to have different effects on the two types of drug users. For the traditional heroin narcotic addict, marijuana is simply a way of getting high and having kicks. In psychedelia, smoking pot is considered simply part of a better lifestyle. For these users, marijuana's impact is closer to the effects of LSD—an experience usually unknown to the heroin addict.

Hallucinatory drug use has become a widespread activity of adolescents. The essential drugs used are pills and marijuana.

Marijuana

Marijuana is an intoxicant used daily by many young people in Western society. "Grass" is plentiful; usually the only questions raised about it concern its strength. It is used without question, without guilt, and with little self-examination.

A report by Dr. Robert L. DuPont, director of The National Institute on Drug Abuse, reveals that marijuana use has become more widespread and is being used by youths at an earlier age. The report states that:

> Youths, experimenting with marijuana at an earlier age, are contributing to an alarming upswing in the nation's drug abuse problem. . . . Dr. Robert L. DuPont, director of the National Institute on Drug Abuse, told reporters he was "quite alarmed" about the growing use of marijuana among young people.
>
> He speculated that use was increasing because marijuana is more readily available now and because of the "contagious phenomena" that challenges nonusers to follow their friends' examples.
>
> The Institute released four new surveys costing $2.2 million that indicated:
>
> —Marijuana use among 12- to 17-year-olds almost doubled between 1972 and 1974.
>
> —Fifty-five percent of the 3 million high school seniors in the class

of 1975 experimented with illegal drugs and two-thirds thought marijuana use should be legal or only a minor violation.

—About 300,000 of the 19 million young men aged 20 to 30 years used heroin within the last year, another 1 to 2 million used other illegal drugs and 7 million smoked marijuana.

One of the consultants on the reports, Ira Cisin of George Washington University, said, "The trend toward earlier introduction to drug use is definitely upward."

The findings showed that 6% of children from 12 to 13 years old had used marijuana in 1974, up from 4% in 1972.

Cisin also reported two other trends:

"Males have historically had more experience than females with illicit drug use, but the sex difference is disappearing among teenagers. Nonwhites have historically had more experience than whites with illicit drugs, but the race difference has disappeared—indeed it had reversed —among the teenagers. Persons in college represent the maximum risk group for illicit drug use.

"It is apparently inevitable that young people are going to experiment with cigarettes, alcohol and marijuana, and that this experience will lead too many young people to a regular pattern of undesirable use of these drugs."[24]

Marijuana has, over the years, been given a seal of approval, even by some of the staunchest advocates of stamping it out. A report issued by the mayor of New York in 1944 stated that the use of marijuana had no deleterious effects. On the basis of extensive investigation, research psychologist William H. McGlothlin concludes that while marijuana is not totally harmless, its possible harmful effects have been exaggerated.[25]

In contrast, another researcher in the field of marijuana use for over twenty years, Dr. Constandinos J. Miras of the University of Athens, asserts that he can recognize a chronic marijuana user by the way he walks, talks, and acts. He defines a chronic user as one who has smoked at least two marijuana cigarettes a day for two years. Dr. Miras alleges that chronic users have "slowed speech, lethargy, and lowered inhibitions." Some become "suddenly violent without any apparent provocation." Dr. Miras' most serious charge is that prolonged marijuana use produces brain damage. His studies with radioactive THC (a chemical known as tetrahydrocannibinol, found in all parts of the marijuana plant) have shown that the substance passes through the brain very quickly. Chronic users, according to Dr. Miras, are prone to anemia, eye inflammations, and respiratory infections, and there is also good evidence of

---

[24]*Los Angeles Times,* October 2, 1975.

[25]From a lecture by William H. McGlothlin given at UCLA, March 1966.

abnormal brain-wave readings.[26] (It is important to note that Dr. Miras' research is related to Greek marijuana users. There is evidence that the marijuana used in Greece is somewhat different in nature and strength from the type used in the United States and northern Europe.) A recent study by M. Duncan Stanton, James Mintz, and Randall M. Frankin, revealed "that heavy marijuana use can produce the flashback usually associated with the use of L.S.D."[27]

The researchers drew on data from a previous survey of army personnel who did time in Vietnam to see whether or not, among other considerations, those subjects who claimed drug flashbacks inhaled more pot than those who had no such afterivisions. They isolated a subsample of twelve marijuana smokers who reported flashbacks that they attributed to the weed. Five of the twelve were "habitual" users (at least 200 episodes), while the others were somewhat more moderate in their smoking habits. Interestingly, only three of the twelve also reported dropping acid; all of them were among the "habitual" puffers.

To see whether or not heavy marijuana use increased the likelihood of repeat performances, data on a group of thirty-one habitual smokers who used no other drug were examined. Only one of them reported a pot flashback. The researchers point out that "there is no indication that the amount of pot inhaled has anything to do with flashbacks. But when the acid users were examined separately, it was found that those who reported warmed-over experiences used a lot more pot than the nonflashbackers."

In sum, there did not seem to be any association between amount of acid use and the occurrence of flashbacks, while among the acid users, there was a slight relation between marijuana and flashbacks. No other drug use was a significant predictor of flashbacks.

Psychiatrist Joel Hochman concludes, on the basis of his extensive research at UCLA, that marijuana use has few deleterious effects.[28] In an interesting discussion of the pharmacologic effects of marijuana, noted pharmacologist Frederick H. Meyer concludes:

> Thus the effects of marijuana, both operationally and in its mechanism of action, correspond exactly to those of other sedatives and anesthetics, especially alcohol. The apparent distinctiveness of marijuana is due mostly to the use of a route of administration that permits the rapid development of an effect and to properties of the active components that lead to rapid decrease in the effects. One is driven to the conclusion that the differences between the dominant attitudes and consequent laws toward marijuana and alcohol are unrelated to the pharmacologic effects

---

[26]From a lecture by Constandinos J. Miras given at UCLA, March 1966.

[27] *Human Behavior* (August 1976).

[28]Joel Hochman, *Marijuana and Social Evolution* (Englewood Cliffs, N. J.: Prentice-Hall, 1972).

of the drugs but are due to a conflict between the mores of the dominant and one or more of the subcultures in this country.[29]

Dr. Norman Zinberg carried out an extensive survey of the several major areas of concern about marijuana, including allegations and counter-data on the emotional syndrome, possible psychosis, brain damage, chromosome damage, marijuana as a steppingstone to heroin, sex impairment, and as a general health hazard. On the basis of all the evidence on both sides of the controversy, Zinberg summarized his conclusions in this way:

> Obviously there are areas of concern. Drawing any hot substance into the lungs cannot be good for anyone, but we should remember that no marijuana smoker in this country uses as many cigarettes a day as tobacco smokers do. Also, marijuana is an intoxicant; and despite the research showing that someone high on marijuana does better on a driving simulator than someone high on alcohol, driving under the influence of any intoxicant must be considered a real danger. Finally, it is my absolute conviction that adolescents below the age of 18 should not use intoxicants of any kind, whether nicotine, alcohol, or marijuana. The 14-, 15-, or 16-year-old struggling to develop in this complex society needs as clear a head as possible. One argument made some years ago for the legalization of illicit substances was based on the possibility that parents and other authorities could more readily control above-ground use of licit substances than they could control the underground use of illicit substances. . . .
>
> In the end, after all this work and all these words, I still find myself echoing the remark made by Dr. Daniel X. Freedman of the University of Chicago, after a Drug Abuse Council conference on marijuana. "Nobody can tell you it's harmless. Each person must decide for himself what he wants to do." With each passing day, however, more people agree with Andrew T. Weil's remark that marijuana is "among the least toxic drugs known to modern medicine."[30]

Pills

The use of amphetamines, or "speed" (methedrine crystals and liquid, and amphetamine pills), is a destructive practice. Speed gets its name from the effect it produces: it accelerates the functioning of the central nervous system. The user does not become especially euphoric, but he does move more quickly,

---

[29]Frederick H. Meyer, "Pharmacologic Effects of Marijuana," in *The New Social Drug,* ed. David E. Smith (Englewood Cliffs, N. J.: Prentice-Hall, 1970), p. 39.

[30]Norman E. Zinberg, "The War Over Marijuana," *Psychology Today* (December 1976).

becomes more compulsive, and gets an intense feeling of being high. He is called a speed freak or meth freak.

As we have noted, most narcotics addicts try to kick the habit, not once but many times. Because many speed freaks have a feeble grasp on a psychedelic philosophy and consider themselves seekers, they are not readily inclined to admit to their addiction. The speed freak deludes himself into believing he is on a spiritual trip, and this tends to keep him in the drug trap.

Speed freaks may walk the streets for periods of up to several days without sleep. Their health and brain processes are often severely impaired by the drugs. Hepatitis is a common disease among meth freaks because several people often use the same needle to inject the drug intravenously without adequate sterilization.

Speed addicts reflect an unusual problem. Their thin veneer of pseudo-philosophy and their bizarre clothes mask a standard self-destructive pattern of old-fashioned drug addiction. Even though they may live in a psychedelic culture, they find it necessary to wheel and deal on the borderline of the illegal drug pusher's world to survive.

Speed freaks, unlike LSD and marijuana users, become both physically and emotionally dependent on the drug. Any normative values they hold will be sidestepped in their efforts to get the drug. And, like other drug addicts, they have great difficulty withdrawing from use of the drug. Severe emotional depression is a standard result of withdrawal, and the meth addict goes on another cycle of speed to escape from the depression. Some meth freaks, according to physicians, suffer permanent brain damage and irreparable damage to the nervous system.

LSD

Although the use of LSD (lysergic acid diethylamide) is much abused, the mental distortions produced by the chemical have an emotional impact that meshes with the user's search for emotional liberation. Despite its misuse for fun and highs, the LSD trip sometimes, under proper circumstances, seems a deep and meaningful spiritual experience.

Compared with the opium derivatives, LSD is a very recent discovery.[31] The ergot alkaloids are a group of drugs obtained from the fungus ergot, which grows on rye and gives rise to a great number of medically useful compounds, such as ergonovine and ergotamine. These latter compounds are used to contract the uterus after childbirth and to treat migraine headaches. LSD was first synthesized in 1938 as an intermediate stage leading to the synthesis of ergo-

---

[31]With the permission of David E. Smith, the following commentary is derived from his excellent article, "Lysergic Acid Diethylamide: An Historical Perspective," *Journal of Psychedelic Drugs* 1 (Summer 1967):2–7.

novine. Its profound psychological effects were completely unknown at that time.

In 1943, Dr. Albert Hoffman, who was one of the people involved in the original synthesis, began working with it again. This time he was seeking a stimulant using lysergic acid (the base of all the ergot alkaloids) in combination with a chemical similar in structure to nikethamide, a central nervous system stimulant.

One day when he was working with this drug, Dr. Hoffman began to experience some peculiar psychological effects, which he described:

> In the afternoon of April 16, 1943, when I was working on this problem, I was seized by a peculiar sensation of vertigo and restlessness. Objects, as well as the shape of my associates in the laboratory, appeared to undergo optical changes. I was unable to concentrate on my work. In a dreamlike state I left for home, where an irresistible urge to lie down overcame me. I drew the curtains and immediately fell into a peculiar state similar to drunkenness, characterized by an exaggerated imagination. With my eyes closed, fantastic pictures of extraordinary plasticity and intensive color seemed to surge toward me. After two hours this state gradually wore off.

When a person ingests an average dose of LSD (150–250 micrograms), nothing happens for the first thirty or forty-five minutes. The first thing the individual usually notices is a change in the way he perceives things. The walls and other objects may become a bit wavy or seem to move. Then he might notice that colors are much brighter than usual. As time goes on, colors can seem exquisitely more intense and beautiful than ever seen before. It is also common to see a halo or rainbow effect around white lights.

Hallucinations, or false sensory perceptions without any basis in external reality, are rather rare with LSD. More common are what may be called pseudohallucinations. The individual may see something out of the ordinary, but at the same time he usually knows his perception has no basis in external reality; if he sees dancing geometric forms or brilliantly colored pulsating shapes, he realizes that they don't really exist out there.

There is another kind of rather remarkable perceptual change referred to as synesthesia—a translation of one type of sensory experience into another. If the LSD user is listening to music, for example, he can sometimes feel the vibrations of the music surging through his body; or he may see the actual notes moving or colors beating in rhythm with the music.

A third kind of change comes in the area of cognitive functioning, or ordinary thinking. When someone is under the influence of LSD there is no loss of awareness. The tripper is fully conscious and usually remembers most of the experience. Thoughts move much more rapidly than usual. One doesn't necessarily think in a logical way or on the basis of causal relationships. Things that are ordinarily thought of as opposites can now exist together in harmony, and in fact become indistinguishable; black and white or good and bad are equal. A person can feel heavy and light at the same time. There is a kind of breakdown of logical thinking; but if the tripper is asked to perform some ordinary task—write his name or take a psychological test—he can usually do it, although he is likely to resent the interruption of his drug-induced experience.

The time sense is frequently affected. Past, present, and future get mixed up. Strange bodily sensations may occur. A tripper's body may seem to lose its solidity and distinctness, and to blend into the universe. Sometimes hands seem to flicker and become disconnected from the body. The LSD user may feel his neck elongate, and experience other Alice-in-Wonderland phenomena.

The adverse effects of LSD are largely psychological, and can be divided into acute immediate effects and chronic aftereffects.

When a person takes LSD, he may feel that he has lost control of himself —as indeed he may have done. Under this circumstance, some people panic. In their desperation to escape from this powerless state, they sometimes literally run away in blind terror. If they do not run away, they may become excessively fearful and suspicious of the people who are with them. Convinced that their companions are trying to harm them, they lash out at them first.

In other ways, too, people under the influence of LSD often show very poor judgment. More than one person on a trip has jumped out of a window under the impression that he could fly. There have been reports that LSD users have actually jumped out of windows or committed suicide by walking into the ocean, feeling they were "simply part of the universe." Many people have experienced feelings of invincibility and omnipotence. "It doesn't matter if my body dies; my spirit will live." This mind-body dissociation has led to a variety of disastrous results. Some people, feeling this omnipotence, have stepped confidently into the paths of cars and trains, and never stepped anywhere again.

Further adverse effects sometimes occur after the acute effects of the drug have apparently worn off. Some people have had prolonged psychotic reactions. These psychotic consequences do not appear to be totally irreversible, but in some cases the emotional disorders have lasted for many months.

Another type of adverse side effect is the recurrence of the acute effects of the drug many days and sometimes weeks or months after the individual has taken it. This recurrence of symptoms can have a frightening impact. The person may feel he is losing his mind. The recurrence of "flashback" phenomenon is relatively rare, but seems to occur more frequently to individuals who take the drug regularly.

One of the keenest observers of the hippie phenomenon is Dr. David E. Smith, who founded the Haight-Ashbury Free Medical Clinic in 1967. Since 1967, Dr. Smith has studied and lectured about the hippie movement in large cities around the country. In a recent interview (1977), one of the authors recorded Dr. Smith's views on the size and shape of the counterculture of the seventies and its concomitant drug use.

The hippie movement is now about ten times bigger than it was at its public peak in 1967. The media image, the flamboyant street scene and the Woodstock festivals are dead; yet the life-style continues. There are mini-type Haight-Ashbury's in cities all over the country. Our research reveals over 400 rural communes in Northern California alone (involving around 10,000 people) and there are similar communes in most states around the country. Also, almost every city has a form of urban commune.

There are now operating rules in effect in the seventies as compared to the sixties. Hip people now reject publicity. There is a greater awareness of social realities, so that many hip people have become political. They work for positive change in their community. Generally, drugs are not used as promiscuously as they were in the sixties, even though heroin has infiltrated the situation. In general, recruitment of people into the hippie life style seems to be growing because there are more open doors in every community. It is no longer necessary to go to New York, San Francisco, or Los Angeles to participate in the hippie life style.

The scene has opened up widespread social experimentation with cultural alternatives. For example, the Free Clinic idea for providing medical and social help has become an enormous development. There are now over 300 free clinics around the country handling over two million client visits a year. Communal experiments also now take a variety of new forms. Many are basically political or religious systems.

A large percentage of young people in the United States now go through some hippie phase, including experimentation with psychedelic drugs. And even though most return to a straight life, their experience invariably affects the way they live out their lives. So the hippie culture continues as strongly as ever and has enormously affected the dominant society.

This subtle infiltration of the hippie phenomenon into the straight world and the use of hallucinogenic drugs have produced a variety of impacts on American society. Not all of the results are completely new or different to the American way of life; however, in combination, the total gestalt of the counterculture has significantly affected the society.

Psychedelic drugs (especially marijuana) have introduced a vehicle for pleasure, new perceptions, and in some cases instant personality and social change. "I can't change anything around me. But I can change my perception of everything around me."

Communes, of various types, both urban and rural, have become permanent and compelling new lifestyles. "The work of life gets done without anyone laying a heavy power trip on anyone else—and we are all loving brothers and sisters."

A more natural, organic way of life has been emphasized and adopted by many people. "I've become supercareful about the food I am putting into my body. We grow things for ourselves."

Pollution and ecological self-destruction have become important causes for action as people have become increasingly aware of these problems. "We can see more clearly the ecocide being committed on our natural resources and it has to stop."

War of any kind is increasingly viewed as a horrendous absurdity. "I will not put my body in any position to be killed or to kill my brothers and sisters."

Anarchism, the absence of all government and rules, is increasingly considered a more natural and positive state of being. "Everyone should be free to do their own thing."

All of these issues and others have become significant credos of the new lifestyle that has been spontaneously developed by several million young people around the country. Freedom is the key principle acted upon, and a new pattern of life has emerged within the hardening shell of the traditional system.

Revolution and social change are usually laden with the fallout of unanticipated problems. Among these, for the counterculture movement, has been the replacement of the more benign psychedelic drugs and love by heroin and violence.

The "new junkie" paradox that emerged from the hippie movement is graphically described by Drs. George and Anne Gay. (Dr. George Gay is chief of the Heroin Section and Director of the Drug Detoxification, Rehabilitation, and Aftercare Project of the Haight-Ashbury Free Medical Clinic.)

> It is no longer buried in Black and Puerto Rican ghettos; no longer confined to the "ignorant" poor. Heroin is in the suburbs, and white parents are beginning to know the impotent range of fear and despair that black parents have lived with for decades; the call from school, from the police, from some hospital somewhere. The call that rips you from complacency and tells you the cold, neon, street-corner truth: your kid has been arrested; your kid is a junkie.
>
> Your daughter, the lovely, clear-eyed child who was going to marry a nice attractive, sensible, hard-working young man, who was going to give you grandchildren and comfort your old age—well . . . she ran off with a greasy slob on a motorcycle. When he got tired of fucking her, he split, so now she is turning tricks on the street, hustling for enough bread to cop a balloon [a bag of heroin actually sold in a rubber balloon].[32]

---

[32]Anne C. Gay and George R. Gay, "Evolution of a Drug Culture in a Decade of Mendacity," in *"It's So Good, Don't Even Try It Once"—Heroin in Perspective,* ed. David E. Smith and George R. Gay. © 1972. Reprinted by permission of Prentice-Hall, Inc., Englewood Cliffs, N. J.

Drugs and a group process are often used for the self-deception of social reality. One young man recently told one of the authors how in his commune they all got high one day and, as a group, concluded that the revolution for social justice and equality had been won. Unfortunately, the continued use of various types of soma pills or drugs alters nothing but the user's perception for a moderate period of time and often impairs the person's ability to concretely change the society in a more humanistic direction. Drug use, therefore, is not only a problem for the young user. Drug abuse has a variety of significant impacts on social change and the structure of the overall society.

There is increasing evidence that the "hippie" era was transitory for many young people. M. R. Ramos found that most of the hippies of the sixties and early seventies have gone straight.

In 1974 as a sociology student at Yale University I was given a grant to spend a year hitchhiking around the country to find, interview and determine the fate of my old street friends and acquaintances. I eventually talked to nearly 70 of them and found that 30 percent continue to remain outside the mainstream of society—as junkies, international narcotic dealers, prison inmates, rural mountain people, gay activists and religious proselytizers. But my most surprising finding was that for the other 70 percent jobs—not drugs or rebellion —have become the focus in life. They are teachers, truck drivers, waitresses, law students, musicians, servicemen, Playboy bunnies, nurses, artists, newspaper reporters, housewives, store managers, electricians, secretaries, construction workers, actresses, carpenters and parents. Few people, including myself, would have expected so many hardcore street people, half of whom (excluding myself) were using heroin, to have made such a positive adjustment to the straight world.

All the literature and all the experts suggested that drug use was a self-perpetuating malady to be combated at all costs; and few if any, disagreed—except the drug users themselves. After talking to my old street friends, I believe that the natural disintegration of adolescent peer groups combined with drug use becoming less appealing over time has done more to reform young people on drugs than incarceration or treatment centers could have hoped to accomplish.

The fact that hippies were predominantly young, white, middle-class drug users, unlike the predominantly older, black, lower class drug users of the past, meant they had greater opportunities to reintegrate into society when they tired of their youthful defiance.

After visiting my old street friends and acquaintances (whose names and identifying details have been changed in the following account) and trying to reconcile the memories I had of them during our days in Georgetown with their present lifestyles, I feel that America's fears of drugs and strange new lifestyles among its young people were highly exaggerated."[33]

Legal Drug Abuse: 1984 in the Seventies

The described patterns of drug use among young people do not emerge in a social vacuum. There is a legal, widespread use of drugs by many parents of young drug users. The American pattern of legal drug abuse by adults may be a vital force in influencing illegal drug use in children.

One study of the relationship between parents as "role models" for drug use was revealing. During a twelve-week period family court counselors evaluated the consecutive discharges of the juvenile courts covering a fourteen-county area (83 percent of the population) within South Carolina. Information from these evaluations was summarized in three major ways: (1) simple demographic description of the 268 juvenile offenders in the sample; (2) description of the substance use of juvenile offenders (alcohol, marijuana, and drug usage) and their parents (alcohol use); and (3) the relationships between juvenile substance use and other variables in the study. The results indicated that (1) there were major racial differences on most variables utilized; thus all further analyses were performed separately by race; (2) on all indicators of substance use (except mother's alcohol use) whites were heavier users than blacks; (3) there was a consistent positive interrelationship among juvenile substance use (alcohol, marijuana, and drugs) and between father's and mother's alcohol use; (4) father's alcohol use was consistently positively related to all juvenile substance use variables; (5) mother's alcohol use was consistently positively related to all juvenile substance use. In summary, the study rather conclusively found a relationship between parental substance abuse and the use and abuse of children.[34] If parents are the drug abuse models for their children, the following situation portends some dramatic increases in the abuse of drugs by juveniles in the 1980s.

In 1976 there were over 275 million legal prescriptions written by physicians for psychoactive drugs, such as amphetamines and barbiturates. These drugs were essentially used by "right-thinking," generally conservative, middle and upper class people who had no reason to have a criminal self-concept. This use, however, indirectly facilitates juvenile delinquency because it demon-

---

[33]M. R. Ramos, "Where Have All the Hippies Gone," *The Washington Post-Potomac,* January 4, 1976.

[34]D. E. Stenmark, J. H. Wachwitz, M. C. Pelfrey, and F. Dougherty, "Substance Use Among Juvenile Offenders Relationship to Parental Substance Use and Demographic Characteristics," *Addictive Diseases* 5 (January 1974):46–57.

strates to children that drug use is an acceptable way to cope with the stresses and strains of living. When, as an adolescent, the child turns to drugs to solve his problems, he may find himself labeled "juvenile delinquent."

In a penetrating article, Drs. Henry L. Lennard, Leon J. Epstein, Arnold Bernstein, and Donald C. Ransom make a devastating comment on this pattern of drug abuse.[35] They allege that the pharmaceutical companies are engaged in promoting drug use: "In order to extend the potential market for its product, the pharmaceutical industry, in its communications to physicians, all too often practices mystification in relabeling an increasing number of human and personal problems as medical problems."[36]

They continue by elucidating on their meaning of *mystification:*

It is apparent that the pharmaceutical industry is redefining and relabeling as medical problems calling for drug intervention a wide range of human behaviors which, in the past, have been viewed as falling within the bounds of the normal trials and tribulations of human existence. Much evidence for this position is to be found in the advertisements of drug companies, both in medical journals and in direct mailings to physicians.

A series of examples will be sufficient to illustrate this point. The first involves the potential personal conflict a young woman may experience when first going off to college.

On the inside front cover of one journal [*Journal of the American College Health Association*] an advertisement states: "A Whole New World ... of Anxiety" ... "to help free her of excessive anxiety ... adjunctive Librium." Accompanying the bold print is a full-page picture of an attractive, worried-looking young woman, standing with an armful of books. In captions surrounding her, the potential problems of a new college student are foretold: "Exposure to new friends and other influences may force her to reevaluate herself and her goals." ... "Her newly stimulated intellectual curiosity may make her more sensitive to and apprehensive about unstable national and world conditions." The text suggests that Librium (chlordiazepoxide HCl), together with counseling and reassurance "can help the anxious student to handle the primary problem and to 'get her back on her feet.' " Thus, the normal problems and conflicts associated with the status change and personal growth that accompany the college experience are relabeled medical-psychiatric problems, and as such are subject to amelioration through Librium.

---

[35]Henry L. Lennard et al., "Hazards Implicit in Prescribing Psychoactive Drugs," *Science* 169 (July 31, 1970):438–41. Copyright 1970 by the American Association for the Advancement of Science.

[36]Lennard et al., "Hazards Implicit in Prescribing Psychoactive Drugs," p. 438.

Another journal has an advertisement that advises a physician on how he can help deal with such everyday anxieties of childhood as school and dental visits. This advertisement, in the *American Journal of Diseases of Children,* portrays a tearful little girl, and in large type appear the words: "School, the dark, separation, dental visits, 'monsters.'" On the subsequent page the physician is told in bold print that "The everyday anxieties of childhood sometimes get out of hand." In small print below he reads that "A child can usually deal with his anxieties. But sometimes the anxieties overpower the child. Then, he needs your help.

"Your help may include Vistaril (hydroxyzine pamoate)."

The advertisement, in effect, presents an oversimplified conception of behavior and behavior change. Potential anxiety engendered by new and different situations is defined as undesirable, as constituting a medical and psychiatric problem which requires the intervention of a physician and, most particularly, intervention through the prescription of a psychoactive drug.

Physicians and parents with low tolerance for anxiety, or those with limited ability to meet the demands of even a temporarily troubled child, are more prone to believe that the child is disturbed and in need of drug treatment.

There is, however, no substantial evidence for the proposition that the prescribed drug does indeed facilitate children's participation in school situations. *What is especially disturbing about advertisements such as this is that they tend to enlist the help of physicians to introduce children to a pattern of psychoactive drug use. Paradoxically, such drug use, at a later date, without a physician's prescription, is deplored both by the medical profession and the community at large.* [37]

Psychoactive drugs, according to Lennard and his colleagues, play an important role in many parent-child relationships. The authors describe an ad on a box of physicians' samples of Tofranil (imipramine hydrochloride), a psychic energizer used to combat depression:

On the box is a picture of an adolescent girl. Above the picture in bold print is the legend, "Missing, Kathy Miller." Below the picture we read, "$500 reward for information concerning her whereabouts." Alongside in white print we read the plea, "Kathy, please come home!" Inside the box is a letter entitled, "Kathy, We love you. . . . Please come home." We quote: "Dear Doctor: For parents, inability to communicate with their children is a significant loss. The 'What did I do wrong?'

---

[37]Lennard et al., "Hazards Implicit in Prescribing Psychoactive Drugs," pp. 438–39. Emphasis added.

lament of the parent may be accompanied by feelings of incapacity, inferiority, guilt and unworthiness. Many may, in fact, be suffering from symptoms of pathological depression. What can Tofranil, imipramine hydrochloride, do for your depressed patient?"[38]

The advertisement than goes on to describe how Tofranil can relieve these symptoms.

The drug manufacturer thus suggests a fascinating method of handling a delinquent runaway: first, remove the delinquency problem from the realm of family dynamics, then convert it into a medical problem that can be "cured" by drugs. The parents, rather than dealing with the behavioral situation, are encouraged to allay their fears and anxieties with a drug. In this way, the authors point out, drug use is set up as a model for the false resolution of an intrafamily problem. The authors comment: "Thus, when a physician prescribes a drug for the control or solution (or both) of personal problems of living, he does more than merely relieve the discomfort caused by the problem. He simultaneously communicates a model for an acceptable and useful way of dealing with personal and interpersonal problems. The implications attached to this model and its long-term effects are what concern us."[39]

A gross error in rationality is also emphasized by these advertisements of the pharmaceutical establishment. Promotion pieces describe specific psychotropic drugs as altering specific emotional states and effecting specific psychological processes—this even though it has been clearly established that any agent produces not a single effect but a diffusion of effects. In other words, the manufacturer singles out the desired effects of a drug's impact and labels them "main effects"; all other changes are labeled "side effects," regardless of whether they are positive or negative, merely uncomfortable or highly dangerous. Using this philosophy, an advertisement for heroin could read: "Here is the solution to all your problems. Relief is just a fix away. Warning: may be addictive." Essentially this statement is true. But it is totally misleading because it fails to mention that the addictive "side effects" are so horrendous that they negate any positive benefits of the drug.

"Mystification" in legal drug use is a complex matter that undoubtedly influences the way people perceive their personal and interpersonal problems. Lennard and his colleagues conclude:

> Drug giving and drug taking represent all too brittle and undiscriminating responses, and ultimately, in our view, they will breed only more frustration and more alienation. Changing the human environment is a monumental undertaking. While seeking to change cognitive shapes

[38]Lennard et al., "Hazards Implicit in Prescribing Psychoactive Drugs," p. 438.
[39]Lennard et al., "Hazards Implicit in Prescribing Psychoactive Drugs," p. 439.

through chemical means is more convenient and economical, the drug solution has already become another technological Trojan horse.

The ultimate task is to alter the shapes of human relatedness and social arrangements that determine the context and the substance of our existence. To maintain, as do significant groups within the pharmaceutical industry, the medical profession, and the youth culture, that this can be accomplished merely through chemical means is indeed to have fallen victim to mystification.[40]

There is little doubt that this adult concept of the power of psychoactive drugs effects the patterns of drug use of youth. The concept of drug use to alter and resolve human problems has in the past decade been a central theme of youth movements. The tremendous growth of drug use among young people stems in part from the tremendous affirmation of its use by adults in "legal form." Allen Geller and Maxwell Boas describe succinctly the adult influence on juvenile drug use:

> Today's teenagers entered a world in which mood-changing substances were a fact of existence; sleeping pills, stimulants, tranquilizers, depressants and many other varieties of mind-altering chemical compounds had long been absorbed into the nation's pharmacopoeia, and copping pills, swallowing capsules and downing tablets were a national habit. Our youngsters' indulgence in drugs can hardly be blamed on some sinister outside influence; they witnessed firsthand the tranquilizer-amphetamine-barbiturate boom of the fifties as their own parents took eagerly to psychic delights. They grew up regarding chemicals as tools to be used to manipulate the inner mind. Some youngsters were even recipients of these drugs; until the dangers were clearly delineated, it was not uncommon for parents to dose their children with half of a barbiturate tablet so that they would be sure to go to sleep.[41]

On an even more profound and potentially deleterious level, the use of methadone as a cure for heroin addiction poses another future problem for youth. "Methadone maintenance," the legal substitution of methadone addiction for heroin addiction, may ultimately be used to "cure" adolescent drug addicts. Social policy related to this "cure" could have many more negative consequences than the original problem. At a 1972 conference of medical and other experts in the field of "methadone maintenance," the mode and implications of this new, perhaps dangerous, "cure" were detailed:

---

[40]Lennard et al., "Hazards Implicit in Prescribing Psychoactive Drugs," p. 441.

[41]From *The Drug Beat* by Allen Geller and Maxwell Boas, p. xvi. Copyright 1971 by McGraw-Hill Book Company. Used with permission of McGraw-Hill Book Company.

Methadone Called More Than Heroin Substitute

A thousand drug experts, both professional and paraprofessional, were told here yesterday that methadone may be more than a drug clinically administered as an alternative to heroin. It appears actually capable of modifying the mental anguish that creates craving for drugs.

This cautious assessment was advanced at the Fourth National Conference on Methadone Treatment at the Sheraton-Palace Hotel by Dr. Leon Wurmser, associate professor of psychiatry and clinical director of the University of Maryland's Drug Abuse Program.

Wurmser said that every narcotic addict with whom he has dealt over a period of years showed a massive character disorder, and in addition came from a family with equally massive disturbances.

In most cases, he said, the addict turned to drugs in the first place as an attempt at "self-treatment" to deal with overwhelming feelings of rage, depression or anxiety.

"In all of them, these feelings were reduced as soon as they were on methadone," he said. "In a few of them, the feelings disappeared altogether; in some they still occurred occasionally, but had a less overwhelming quality. Some of them stated simply the drug made them feel normal and relaxed." ...

"It is obvious that in none of these patients was the underlying inner problems resolved, but the dampening of the mood disorder brought about by methadone was experienced as a great relief."

Wurmser said it is not yet known how methadone, or other narcotics, work. Taken orally and at a stabilized level, methadone has been found to "blockade" the effects of injected heroin and eliminate the addict's "heroin hunger."

What has not been satisfactorily explained up to now, Wurmser said, is that the narcotics hunger, or craving, can be diminished or eliminated with methadone, even at doses far below the blockade level.

"Methadone seems to cope ... in such a specific way with these conditions that, at least in many instances, methadone maintenance may acquire a second rationale—besides that of blockade—namely, that of a bona fide psychotropic agent or one exerting an effect on the mind."

This effect on craving, he said, appears to be entirely independent from the "high—the euphoria—that attends narcotics use.

Dr. Stuart L. Nightingale of Johns Hopkins and chief of Maryland's Department of Health and Mental Hygiene Drug Abuse Administration, told a general session of the conference that methadone should be as available to treat addicted adolescents as it is adults, on an inpatient and ambulatory basis.

He said addiction is a "disease of adolescence," since most addiction begins in adolescence. "*If we wait to use methadone, we lose our chance to save them,*" Nightingale said. [Emphasis added.]

He acknowledged that treating the adolescent addict with methadone is at once "controversial and symbolic," noting:

"How successful long-term methadone detoxification or maintenance is for the treatment of an addict who has not yet failed himself and society in every way, has great implications for those who treat addicts and for society in general."[42]

The obvious implications of the medical position in this article is that "methadone maintenance" for adolescents would be beneficial, not only for drug addiction but for "exerting an effect on the mind" or personality of youths. This perspective is highly debatable, since the use of this potent drug by adolescents in a legal program might lead to the insidious consequence of enslaving more youths on drugs—albeit legal drugs.

An unusual chance to follow what happens to the young methadone user developed at the Boston City Hospital Drug Dependency Clinic. During the clinic's first nine months of operation, more than two-thirds of 1,400 people who applied for help were less than twenty-six years old. Whether they made it or not hinged on several key factors, according to researchers Dr. Chaim M. Rosenberg, Dr. Gerald E. Davidson and Vernon D. Patch, who teach psychiatry at Harvard Medical School.

The first hurdle was getting in. More than 95 percent of the applicants were admitted during the clinic's early weeks. Later, a waiting list became necessary. When the list began to put a few months' distance between the optimism of signing up and the reality of getting that methadone, nearly half the applicants "quit" before they started. As the lining-up time stretched nerves and months further, still smaller numbers of applicants returned for treatment.

The clinic used low doses of methadone aimed at withdrawal in its first two months. According to Drs. Rosenberg, Davidson and Patch, "This method was tough to take. The monthly dropout level hovered between 35 and 40 percent. When a switch was ordered to high-dose methadone maintenance, and a waiting list screened out many probable backsliders, the failure rate fell to 20 and then 15 percent. After about five months, intake of new patients had been sharply reduced. A majority of the stable group remaining were on dosages kept constant somewhere between 60 and 100 mg. Monthly dropouts then skidded to less than 10 percent."[43]

Compared to young addicts who left early, those fading out of the program after several months were more likely to be employed at the time of admission and living with family members. Ironically, they tended to have a greater drug habit than early dropouts and so were getting bigger initial methadone doses than the more marginal addicts. One might assume the less

---

[42] Carolyn Anspacher, "Methadone Called More Than Heroin Substitute," *San Francisco Chronicle,* January 10, 1972.

[43] *Human Behavior* (April 1973).

addicted would be easier to rehabilitate, but they actually departed before the heavily hooked.

While Boston Clinic's total dropout rate from the waiting list and treatment exceeded 60 percent during its first nine months, the researchers point out some striking progress in those who remained. "Well over half the urine samples examined during the clinic's first few months contained morphine and quinine. Some specimens were negative even for methadone, so the patients probably were pushing their intended medicine. By the end of the nine-month period, two-thirds of the urine samples contained only methadone."[44]

Getting young people to remain in treatment apparently is a major challenge, the same challenge handed to those who treat veteran addicts. Methadone is no panacea either for old-timers or addicted youth. But when they do stick with clinics, "it leads to a rapid reduction in heroin use and criminal behavior," according to the researchers. Stressing the enormous relapse rate under other programs, the psychiatrists conclude that methadone treatment for young people "can be justified only by its clear superiority over alternative treatment methods."

In many respects the tendency to dispense more and more psychoactive and tranquilizing drugs, including methadone, in a legal context constitutes a potentially serious problem that may enlarge an already existing serious juvenile drug problem. Just as juveniles turn to violence in a "violent society," so many youngsters become drug abusers in a drug-using social system.

---

[44] *Human Behavior* (April 1973).

Part Three

THE
CAUSAL
CONTEXT
OF CRIME
AND
DELINQUENCY

A FUNDAMENTAL PURSUIT of criminology and the study of delinquency is the search for causes. The endeavor to understand the causal context or background of crime and delinquency has historically challenged the best minds of all civilized societies. In examining the variety of causal explanations of crime and delinquency, we must keep in mind several concepts and issues as guides to their scientific validity:

    1. A relationship of factors is not necessarily a causal nexus. The fact that a preponderance of criminals and delinquents come from broken homes does not necessarily mean that a broken home must cause delinquency and crime.

    2. No single theory explains all crime and delinquency. Different patterns of crime and delinquency require different causal explanations. The sexual psychopath, the burglar, and the violent gang youth would not tend to emerge from the same causal context.

    3. Primary and secondary causes should not be confused. The lack of social workers or poor school facilities are not primary causes of delinquency; however, a broken home *may* be a primary causal factor.

    4. One cannot logically isolate one single cause of crime or delinquency. Causation is a multifactored condition. The relative weight of each factor is difficult to determine.

5. In examining causal explanations based on research with offenders, we have the problem of separating the causal force from the impacts of the administration of justice (arrest, jail, courts, prison).

These factors and others that will emerge in the discussion make the issue of causation a complex matter for analysis.

The following analysis makes it clear that a search for a theory inclusive enough to explain all criminality would be unproductive.

> A skid-row drunk lying in a gutter is a crime. So is the killing of an unfaithful wife. A Cosa Nostra conspiracy to bribe public officials is crime. So is a strong-arm robbery by a 15-year-old-boy. The embezzlement of a corporation's funds by an executive is crime. So is the possession of marihuana cigarettes by a student. These crimes can no more be lumped together for purposes of analysis than can measles and schizophrenia, or lung cancer and a broken ankle. As with disease, so with crime: if causes are to be understood, if risks are to be evaluated, and if preventive or remedial actions are to be taken, each kind must be looked at separately. Thinking of "crime" as a whole is futile.[1]

Although traditional crime, organized crime, white collar crime, and political crime may have some elements in common, the differences are so great that some theories explaining criminal behavior are likely to be more relevant to one than to another.

We have divided what we consider to be theoretical formulations into two broad categories:

1. Those theories that attempt to explain the criminal or delinquent behavior of people who are given the status of criminal or delinquent. An assumption basic to all of these theories is that the cause or causes of criminality can be attributed to some characteristic or characteristics of the offender or the subculture with which he is identified. Constitutional, psychological, and subcultural deviance theories, grouped into this broad category, will be considered in Chapter 11.

2. Those theories that seek to explain criminality or delinquency as a response to some societal attribute or policies. Some of the questions these theories deal with are: Why does a society have a high incidence of crime and delinquency? Why is there a high incidence of a particular type of crime? Why do some subgroups in the society have higher crime or delinquency rates than others? These theories, most of which may be regarded as macrosociological, will be considered in Chapter 12.

---

[1] *The Challenge of Crime in a Free Society: A Report by the President's Commission on Law Enforcement and Administration of Justice* (Washington, D.C.: U.S. Government Printing Office, 1967), p. 3.

Explanations of Crime and Delinquency: Emphasis on the Individual

THE DEMON THEORY, or some modification of it, has been an accepted explanation of crime for a long period of recorded history. Any person who failed to follow the accustomed ways of the group was assumed to be possessed by demons. There was little or no distinction between crime and sin. The offender was regarded as an antagonist to both the group and the gods. Criminal action was caused by evil spirits, who took possession of a man's soul and forced him to perform their evil will. During the Middle Ages, when Christianity dominated the life of Western man, the theory of possession by the devil tended to merge with the Christian concept of original sin.

The influence of the theories of demonology and natural depravity upon the legal codes and the practices of the courts is evidenced by the fact that as late as the nineteenth century a formal indictment in England accused the criminal of "being prompted and instigated by the devil." In the United States, as late as 1862 a state supreme court declared that "to know the right, and still the wrong pursue, proceeds from a perverse will brought about by the seduction of the evil one."[1] Even in contemporary society, people will remark, "He's full of the devil," or "I'm going to shake the devil out of you."

---

[1]John M. Gillette and James M. Reinhardt, *Current Social Problems* (New York: American Book Company, 1933), pp. 652–53.

In an address to six thousand people at his weekly public audience in Rome on November 29, 1972, Pope Paul VI said that the devil is dominating "communities and entire societies" through sex, narcotics, and doctrinal errors. His address included the following references to the devil:

"We are all under obscure domination. It is by Satan, the prince of this world, the No. 1 enemy." He said the devil was a "terrific reality—mysterious and awe inspiring." He criticized those who question the existence of the devil saying: "This obscure and disturbing being does exist."

The Rev. John Narvone, an American professor at the Gregorian University in Rome, has studied Satan and narcotics. He has a theory that drug addicts risk becoming outright "apprentices" of the devil.[2] The concept of demonology is generally believed to be nonsensical by most criminologists. However, the pronouncements of many clergymen and the popularity of films such as *The Exorcist* keep this concept of criminality alive in the public mind.

The Classical School of Criminology

A significant effort to explain crime in a philosophical manner was made by Cesare Beccaria, the founder of what is now known as the classical school of criminology. Beccaria's theory postulated that only conduct dangerous to the state or to other people should be prohibited and that punishment should be no more severe than deemed necessary to deter persons from committing such crimes. The importance of knowing in advance the amount of punishment to be administered led to the adoption of the fixed or "determinate" sentence.

Accepting the Christian doctrine of free will, the classical school postulated that man could choose between good and evil alternatives. The explanation of crime included the notion that man was essentially hedonistic, desiring a maximum of pleasure and the avoidance of pain. A man committed a crime because the pleasure anticipated from the criminal act was greater than the subsequent pain that might be expected.

A major proponent of the classical explanation was Jeremy Bentham. In 1825 he published a book called *An Introduction to the Principles of Morals and Legislation,* in which he proposed a "penal pharmacy" where definitely prescribed punishments were to be applied for specific crimes. The assumption was that men had free will and could decide whether or not it was personally profitable to commit a crime. It was assumed that if the punishment or pain was always more than the pleasure or benefit from a crime, the potential offender would be rational and be deterred from committing the offense.

The classical philosophical and judicial view of crime is still held by

---

[2]"Pope Blames Devil for Sex and Drug Evils," *Los Angeles Times* (AP), December 1, 1972.

many contemporary courts. The counterpoint position to the classical view is determinism. This position asserts almost no free will. It postulates that the socialization process and all the social factors that impinge on an individual determine his personality. In this framework an individual has no free will or individual choice. He is propelled by social forces and other conditions beyond his control. The controversy over the contradictory positions of free will and social determinism is still discussed in contemporary society.[3]

Physiological Explanations of Criminality

The Italian Positivist School

Cesare Lombroso, an Italian medical doctor, on the basis of research with military personnel and inmates of Italian military prisons, developed a theory that challenged Beccaria and the classical school. His chief investigative work was done between 1864 and 1878. Lombroso and his followers became known as the positive school of criminology, essentially because they attempted to base their conclusions on objective firsthand empirical data.

Lombroso's major early conclusions were that criminal tendencies were hereditary and that "born criminals" were characterized by physical stigmata. To Lombroso the born criminal was an *atavist,* a throwback to an earlier, more primitive species of man. Lombroso concluded that:

1. Criminals are at birth a distinct type.
2. They can be recognized by certain stigmata (e.g., "long lower jaw, scanty beard, low sensitivity to pain").
3. These stigmata or physical characteristics do not cause crime, but enable identification of criminal types.
4. Only through severe social intervention can born criminals be restrained from criminal behavior.

After his initial studies, Lombroso greatly modified his theories. A central error in his early studies was that he neglected to note that most of the criminals in the Italian army were Sicilians and thus were a distinct physical type. They did not, however, commit more crimes than the general population because of their *physical typology,* as Lombroso alleged, but because they came from a culture that was more criminally oriented. Lombroso and his followers in the Italian school, Ferri, Garofalo and others, later included more social factors in their analyses of criminality.

Although Lombroso was obviously wrong about his born-criminal the-

---

[3]The argument was recently revived in a probing analysis by David Matza. *Delinquency and Drift* (New York: Wiley, 1966).

sis, he did make significant contributions to the field of criminology. His research (*a*) caused a focus on the firsthand study of criminals and moved the field from a philosophical posture of analysis to empirical research; (*b*) broadened the discussion of crime causation; (*c*) produced a school of criminology that attracted many distinguished students to the field; and (*d*) produced a reform of the Beccaria-Bentham classical school.

Enrico Ferri described the impact of the new "positivist school" on the classical school:

> The general opinion of classic criminalists and of the people at large is that crime involves a moral guilt, because it is due to the free will of the individual who leaves the path of virtue and chooses the path of crime, and therefore it must be suppressed by meeting it with a proportionate quantity of punishment. This is to this day the current conception of crime. And the illusion of a free human will (the only miraculous factor in the eternal ocean of cause and effect) leads to the assumption that one can choose freely between virtue and vice. How can you still believe in the existence of a free will when modern psychology, armed with all the instruments of positive modern research, denies that there is any free will and demonstrates that every act of a human being is the result of an interaction between the personality and the environment of man?
>
> It has continued in the nineteenth century to look upon crime in the same way that the Middle Ages did: "Whoever commits murder or theft is alone the absolute arbiter to decide whether he wants to commit the crime or not." This remains the foundation of the classic school of criminology. This explains why it could travel on its way more rapidly than the positive school of criminology. And yet, it took half a century from the time of Beccaria before the penal codes showed signs of the reformatory influence of the classic school of criminology. So that it has also taken quite a long time to establish it so well that it became accepted by general consent, as it is today. The positive school of criminology was born in 1878, and although it does not stand for a mere reform of the methods of criminal justice, but for a complete and fundamental transformation of criminal justice itself, it has already gone quite a distance and made considerable conquests which begin to show in our country. It is a fact that the penal code now in force in this country represents a compromise, so far as the theory of personal responsibility is concerned, between the old theory of free will and the conclusions of the positive school which denies this free will.[4]

---

[4]Enrico Ferri, *Criminal Sociology* (Boston: Little, Brown, 1901).

Later Studies of Physical Types and Crime

In 1901 Dr. Charles B. Goring, an English prison official, tested Lombroso's theory by measuring three thousand criminals and comparing these measurements with those of one thousand students at Cambridge University. He found no significant differences in physical types between criminals and noncriminals.[5] Later studies by Hooton and Kretschmer on physical types and crime postulated a degree of support for Lombroso's original thesis.[6] A close appraisal of their research methods, however, tends to make their conclusions suspect.

In the 1940s William Sheldon also concluded that there was a relationship between certain physical characteristics and temperamental characteristics.[7] Sheldon divided human beings into four physical types, based upon body measurements: *endomorphs,* who tend to be fat; *mesomorphs,* who tend to be muscular with large bones and athletic build; *ectomorphs,* who are inclined to be thin and fragile; and *balanced types,* a "combination category," composed of people who showed no marked predominance of any single type.

Each body type, according to Sheldon, was characterized by a distinctive temperament. *Endomorphs* were described as viscerotonic, submissive, and little interested in physical activity or adventure. *Mesomorphs* were described as somatotonic, physically active, self-assertive, and daring. *Ectomorphs* were categorized as cerebrotonic, inhibited, and introverted.

Sheldon attributed the various body types and their characteristics to heredity, maintaining that they were genetically determined. In a study of two hundred juvenile delinquents, he found that about 60 percent were mesomorphs. Since most police officers, army officers, football players, and other energetic leaders of our society are also likely to be mesomorphic, this correlation between mesomorphy and delinquency was not considered to be a causal explanation of delinquency.

In a review of Sheldon's work in the *American Sociological Review,* Sutherland virtually demolished his conclusions. Here are some of Sutherland's criticisms:

> 1. Sheldon defines delinquency in terms of "disappointingness" and not in terms of violation of the law.
> 2. His method of scoring delinquents is subjective and unreliable. For example, he defines "first-order psychopathy" in terms of subjec-

---

[5]Charles Goring, *The English Convict* (London: His Majesty's Stationery Office, 1913).

[6]Earnest A. Hooton, *Crime and the Man* (Cambridge, Mass.: Harvard University Press, 1939); Ernest Kretschmer, *Physique and Character* (London: Kegan Paul, Trench, Trubner, 1936).

[7]William II. Sheldon, *The Varieties of Delinquent Youth* (New York: Harper, 1949).

tively determined interference with adjustment, apparently the same as "disappointingness."

3. The varieties of delinquent youth he presents are overlapping and inconsistent. They do not differ significantly from each other in their somatotypes or psychiatric indices.

4. The relationship of the psychiatric indices to social fitness is not made clear.[8]

Sheldon and Eleanor Glueck revived interest in William Sheldon's somatotypes in the 1950s. They found that 60.1 percent of the delinquents they studied were mesomorphs, as against 30.7 percent of the nondelinquents. They were cautious in their interpretation of these findings, concluding that "there is no 'delinquent personality' in the sense of a constant and stable combination of physique, character, and temperament which determines that a certain individual would become delinquent."[9]

Although no causal relationship has been established between any physical characteristic and criminal behavior, there is some evidence that the muscular mesomorphic child is more likely to become delinquent than children with other body types, *all other things being equal.* The mesomorph, who is by definition muscular, active, and relatively uninhibited, may be more likely than others to take action defined as delinquent by society when confronted with unfavorable social environment. Research exploring the possibility of using body types as a predictive device has been going on for many years. The conclusions so far have been inconclusive, if not outright specious.

Chromosomes and Criminality

Studies of chromosomal deviation have attempted to show a correlation between criminal behavior and males possessing an extra male chromosome, called the Y gonosome; that is, they are XYY, rather than the normal XY. In spite of the varied and conflicting results of the various studies, there are some suggestive consistencies of behavior and traits that appear to be evolved from the research. In general, they include the fact that, among criminals, the chance of possessing an extra Y gonosome is up to sixty times greater than it is among the general population; also, a higher frequency of aggressive and disturbed behavior and higher rates of violent crime were found among those having an extra Y gonosome.

One theory holds that the criminal act itself is biologically and hereditarily determined; that is, there is a direct relationship between the biological

---

[8]Edwin H. Sutherland, "Critique of Sheldon's *Varieties of Delinquent Youth,*" *American Sociological Review* 16 (February 1951):10–13.

[9]Sheldon Glueck and Eleanor Glueck, *Unraveling Juvenile Delinquency* (New York: Commonwealth Fund, 1950), p. 221.

structure and the behavior that is supposedly determined by it. A second theory is that what is genetically transmitted is a general tendency to maladjustment and that, given certain environmental pressures, this disposition leads to criminal behavior. Inherent in this theory is the supposition that crime is just one of many possible outcomes of a defective physiological structure.

If criminality is inherited, then noncriminality or conforming behavior must also be inherited. If we accept that the factors determining criminal behavior already exist at birth, then it follows that the influence of environment is not very important. If, however, criminal behavior is frequently found among persons lacking genetic defects, or if biological defects are found among a great many noncriminals, then the genetic theory of crime becomes questionable. Before we can reach any conclusions on the relationship between chromosomes and criminality, we would need to know what proportion of criminals do not have genetic or biological defects. If the number is large, the theory is defective.[10]

Modern Positivism

The classical and the positivistic conceptions of crime and delinquency continue as central subjects for discussion. Each view projects its own image of man and his motives. The classical school of criminology (Bentham, Beccaria) sketched man as essentially having free will, implying that a person who chooses to violate the law must and can be restrained from this impulse by a proper measure of punishment. In counterpoint, the positivists believed in what is today more often called determinism. They viewed the criminal as something of a billiard ball, propelled by conditions outside his control.

As early as 1906 Ferri stated these opposing views most succinctly:

> "Whoever commits murder or theft is alone the absolute arbiter to decide whether he wants to commit the crime or not." This remains the foundation of the classic school of criminology. . . . The positive school of criminology maintains, on the contrary, that it is not the criminal who wills; in order to be a criminal it is rather necessary that the individual should find himself permanently or transitorily in such personal, physical, and moral conditions, and live in such an environment, which become for him a chain of cause and effect, externally and internally, that disposes him toward crime. This is our conclusion, which I anticipate, and it constitutes the vastly different and opposite method, which the

[10]Menachim Amir and Yitzcham Berman, "Chromosomal Deviation and Crime," *Federal Probation* 34(June 1970):55–62. See also Robert W. Stock, "The XYY and the Criminal," *New York Times Magazine.* October 20, 1968, p. 30.

positive school of criminology employs as compared to the leading principle of the classic school of criminal science.[11]

Matza, after closely reviewing each of these conceptions in depth, presents a more middle-of-the-road viewpoint. He first points to the danger of being overdeterministic. Using the juvenile court concept as an example of overdeterminism, he comments:

> To philosophically attribute fault to underlying conditions, but to actually hold the immediate agent responsible is an invitation to distrust. And to refer to penal sanction as protective care is to compound the distrust. Thus, by its insistence on a philosophy of child welfare and its addiction to word magic, the juvenile court systematically interferes with its alleged program. By its own hypocrisy perceived and real, it prepares the way for the delinquent's withdrawal of legitimacy. Without the grant of legitimacy, the court's lofty aspirations cannot be effectively pursued.
>
> Thus, the ideology of child welfare supports the delinquent's viewpoint in two ways. It confirms his conception of irresponsibility, and it feeds his sense of injustice. Both support the processes by which the moral bind of law is neutralized. Both facilitate the drift into delinquency.[12]

Matza believes that contemporary theorists in the field of criminology have gone too far in the direction of positivism. Although he does not attempt fully to revive the classical viewpoint, he does attempt to incorporate "some modified versions of the classical viewpoint into the current framework of positive criminology." Matza posits what he refers to as "soft determinism" in discussing his basic concept of delinquency and drift. He contends that man is neither wholly free nor wholly constrained, but somewhere midway between the two. The delinquent is never totally a lawbreaker. He drifts into delinquency.

> The image of the delinquent I wish to convey is one of drift; an actor neither compelled nor committed to deeds nor freely choosing them; neither different in any simple or fundamental sense from the law abiding, nor the same; conforming to certain traditions in American life while partially unreceptive to other more conventional traditions; and finally, an actor whose motivational system may be explored along lines explicitly commended by classical criminology—his peculiar relation to

---

[11]Enrico Ferri, *The Positive School of Criminology* (Chicago: Kerr, 1906), p. 23.

[12]Matza, *Delinquency and Drift*, pp. 97–98.

legal institutions. . . . The delinquent transiently exists in a limbo between convention and crime, responding in turn to the demands of each, flirting now with one, now the other, but postponing commitment, evading decision. Thus, he drifts between criminal and conventional action.[13]

One argument against this theory of drift, almost of accident, was offered by Ferri back in 1906:

It is evident that the idea of accident, applied to physical nature, is unscientific. Every physical phenomenon is the necessary effect of the causes that determined it beforehand. If those causes are known to us, we have the conviction that the phenomenon is necessary, is fate, and, if we do not know them, we think it is accidental. The same is true of human phenomena. But since we do not know the internal and external causes in the majority of cases, we pretend that they are free phenomena, that is to say, that they are not determined necessarily by their causes.[14]

Matza believes that most delinquents are drifters: "The delinquent as drifter more approximates the substantial majority of juvenile delinquents who do not become adult criminals than the minority who do." To Matza, delinquency is seldom a youth's total career. Most delinquents, he believes, participate in juvenile delinquency as a part-time enterprise.

Sykes and Matza describe five ways in which delinquents deny that their behavior is bad. These techniques tend to neutralize their responsibility for delinquent activity:

1. *The denial of personal responsibility.* Here the delinquent uses a kind of social word play. "Of course I'm delinquent. Who wouldn't be, coming from my background?" He then can neutralize personal responsibility by detailing the background of a broken home, lack of love, and a host of other factors.
2. *The denial of harm to anyone.* In this pattern of neutralization, stealing a car is only borrowing it; truancy harms no one; and drug use "doesn't hurt anyone but me."
3. *The delinquent denies that the person injured or wronged is really a victim.* "The [assaulted] teacher was unfair"; the victim of a mugging "was only a queer"; and the gang youth assaulted was "out to get me."

---

[13]Matza, *Delinquency and Drift,* p. 28.

[14]Ferri, *Positive School of Criminology,* pp. 35–36.

4. *The delinquent condemns the condemners.* "Society is much more corrupt than I am."
5. *Delinquent group or gang loyalties supersede loyalty to the norms of an impersonal society.* "When I stabbed him I was only defending my turf." The youth places his gang or delinquent group and its values (even if delinquent) above the law, the school, and society.[15]

All of these factors tend to neutralize the delinquent's belief that he is delinquent or has done anything wrong. These rationalizations enable him to deny any real personal responsibility for delinquent behavior.

In any case, according to Matza, the delinquent is really not delinquent, but is acting out the "subterranean values" of the society. Who can deny that the mass public admires and respects a smart operator, even if his actions are illegal? The delinquent may in his own self-concept merely be acting out the norms he sees beneath the surface of the law. In some respects, the delinquent may see himself as a lower class white collar criminal. He feels there is really nothing wrong with his behavior. In fact, he feels he is being unfairly treated by being punished for what society does not really condemn.

By adapting concepts found in the larger society, the delinquent rationally negates his own offense. Since the law supports self-defense as a justification for violent action, it is easy for the delinquent to justify in his own mind the use of violence to defend his gang turf. The delinquent also uses the concept of insanity ("I went crazy") to negate his offense, and he widens the extenuating circumstance of "accident" to include recklessness. The sense of injustice found in the delinquent subculture is thus reinforced by the vagaries of many societal laws and norms. Many of society's irrational prescriptions weaken prohibitions of certain actions by the juvenile and facilitate the drift to juvenile delinquency, and in time into a criminal career.

The Psychoanalytic View of Crime and Delinquency

Psychoanalytic theory, as originally formulated by Sigmund Freud, has been offered as an explanation of delinquent and criminal behavior. According to psychoanalytic theory, the individual begins life with two basic instincts or urges: Eros, the life or love instinct, and Thanatos, the death or hate instinct. The personality of the normal adult is composed of the id, the ego, and the superego. At birth there is only the id, the reservoir of both the life and the death instincts. The id seeks immediate gratification and is concerned with striving after pleasure. It is governed by the *pleasure principle,* seeking the

---

[15]Gresham Sykes and David Matza, "Techniques of Neutralization: A Theory of Delinquency," *American Sociological Review* 22(December 1957):665–66.

maximization of pleasure and the avoidance of pain. It has no idea of time or reality.

In the first few years of life the individual develops an ego and a superego. The *ego* is the part of the self in closest contact with the social reality. It directs behavior toward the satisfaction of urges consistent with a knowledge of social and physical reality. In living out the *reality principle* through the ego, the individual may postpone immediate gratification; he does not abandon it.

Morality, remorse, and feelings of guilt arise with the development of the *superego,* the chief force in the socialization of the individual. The superego is sociologically or culturally conditioned. It includes the development of a *conscience* and an *ego ideal.* The ego ideal represents what we *should* do and the conscience gives us guilt feelings when we do "wrong."

The following oversimplified model serves to illustrate the operation of the Freudian id, ego, and superego: A child sees cookies on the table. His id demands immediate gratification, and he is governed by the pleasure principle. He grabs a cookie. His mother slaps his hand and takes the cookie away from him. When he has developed an ego, he waits for his mother to leave before taking a cookie, or he asks for one and coaxes if it is denied him. In either case he has applied the reality principle and postponed gratification. When he has developed a superego, he will not take the cookie if it is defined as wrong for him to do so. If he does take the cookie without being observed, he feels guilty.

Psychoanalytic theory tends to attribute delinquency or criminality to any of the following causes:

1. Inability to control criminal drives (id) because of a deficiency in ego or superego development. Because of faulty development, the delinquent or criminal is believed to possess little capacity for repressing instinctual (criminal) impulses. The individual who is dominated by his id is consequently criminal.
2. Antisocial character formation resulting from a disturbed ego development. This occurs during the first three years of life.
3. An overdeveloped superego, which makes no provision for the satisfaction of the demands of the id. Offenders of this type are considered neurotic.

Freudians, neo-Freudians, and other psychoanalytic schools attribute criminality to inner conflicts, emotional problems, unconscious feelings of insecurity, inadequacy, and inferiority. They regard criminal behavior and delinquencies as symptoms of underlying emotional problems. Psychoanalytic theory does not explain the criminal acts of the "normal" criminal, who simply learns to be criminal from differential association with criminal teachers. Psychoanalysis offers an explanation for the impulsive behavior of the psychotic, the neurotic, and the psychopath. This behavior, in psychoanalytic terms, would generally be id-dominated behavior evidencing ego deficiency, the inability to control criminal impulses.[16]

For criminologists the most important assertion of psychoanalytic theory is that in order to understand criminality we must understand unconscious motivation. In this context everyone is basically, in his id, a criminal. Freud further asserts that if this is true, we must condemn in others the criminal thrust that lurks in all of us. This accounts for the psychoanalytic assumption that *the public demands severe punishment for certain crimes because the offender has acted as the rest of us would like to act ourselves.* Another philosopher put it this way: "We stamp out in others the evil we dimly perceive in ourselves."

The classical Freudian view of the interplay of crime and punishment has been most comprehensively and cogently presented in Alexander and Staub's *The Criminal, the Judge, and the Public.* Several of its central themes are worth pondering for the light they cast on past and present attitudes toward offenders:

1. *Psychodynamically, all people are born criminals.* The human being enters the world as a criminal, i.e., socially not adjusted. During the first years of his life he preserves his criminality to the fullest degree, concerned only with achieving pleasure and avoiding pain. Between the ages of four and six the development of the criminal begins to differentiate itself from that of the normal. During this period (the latency period), which ends at puberty, the future normal individual partially succeeds in repressing his genuine criminal instinctive drives and stops their actual expression. He converts or transforms these criminal libidal drives into socially acceptable forms. The future criminal fails to accomplish this adjustment.

The criminal carries out in his actions his natural unbridled instinctual drives. He acts as the child would act if it only could. The repressed and therefore unconscious criminality of the normal man finds a few socially harmless outlets, such as dream and fantasy life, neurotic symptoms, and also some transitional forms of behavior that are less harmless, like dueling, boxing, bullfights, and occasionally the free expression of criminality in war. According to Alexander and Staub, "The universal criminality of the man of today demands violent, purely physical outlets."[17]

2. *The Oedipus complex is a fundamental psychodynamic fact that produces criminality unless it is successfully resolved.* The Freudian doctrine of the Oedipus complex asserts that all boys have a natural hostility toward

---

[16]For a detailed presentation of the psychoanalytic explanation of criminality and delinquency, see Kate Friedlander, *The Psychoanalytic Approach to Juvenile Delinquency* (New York: International Universities Press, 1947), and Walter Bromberg, *Crime and the Mind* (Philadelphia: Lippincott, 1948).

[17]Franz Alexander and Hugo Staub, *The Criminal, the Judge, and the Public* (Glencoe, Ill.: Free Press, 1956), p. 52.

their fathers and a love for their mothers that encompasses sexual desire. The guilt and anxiety aroused by these feelings must be resolved, according to Freud, if the youth is to grow up to become a psychologically healthy man. Alexander and Staub are extreme and dogmatic about the "fact" of the Oedipal condition:

> It took two decades of psychoanalytical research to prove conclusively that the Oedipus complex presented the chief unconscious psychological content of neurotic symptoms. It was found that all those psychological undercurrents which the adult person usually represses are affectively connected with the Oedipus situation of early childhood; these psychic currents, after they are repressed, continue in the unconscious, tied as with a navel cord to the infantile Oedipus complex.[18]

A major concomitant of the Oedipus complex is the assumption that a youth who represses his hostility toward his father will displace his aggression elsewhere. For the Freudian psychoanalyst, this accounts for much of the violent behavior (including homicide) of delinquent youths. The Freudian asserts that when the Oedipal situation is resolved through psychoanalysis, the analysand, now aware of the real object of his aggression, can curb his hostility.

3. *Uncovering unconscious motives is the fundamental task of criminology.*

> Theoretically speaking, every human being's responsibility is limited, because no human act is performed under the full control of the conscious ego. We must, therefore, always evaluate the quantitative distribution of conscious and unconscious motivations of every given act. Only such evaluation will provide us with definite criteria for purposes of diagnosis, or of sentencing or of any other measure which we might consider necessary to take in regard to a given act. The tast of the judge of the future will be the establishment of such a psychological diagnosis; the measures resulting from such a diagnosis will, therefore, be founded on the psychological understanding of the criminal.[19]

Among those who take the extreme psychoanalytic view, certain criminal patterns are symbolic reflections of unconscious motivation. For example, the use of a gun by an armed robber is considered a reaction formation to a sense of male impotence. The gun is considered a symbol of male potency, and without attempting to be facetious, some extremists of the psychoanalytic

---

[18]Alexander and Staub, *The Criminal, the Judge, and the Public,* p. 73.
[19]Alexander and Staub, *The Criminal, the Judge, and the Public,* p. 85.

school contend that when the armed robber says, "Stick 'em up," he is symbolically trying to adjust his unconscious sense of impotence. Similarly, the crime of breaking-entering and theft is considered to be displaced unconscious rape. These are the things the courts must understand, according to Alexander and Staub, before taking any "measures" against offenders.

4. *The first rebellious act or crime is committed in early childhood and is an important determinant of one's sense of justice.*

> The first crime which all humans, without exception, sooner or later commit is the violation of the prescription for cleanliness. Under the rule of this penal code of the nursery, man for the first time becomes acquainted with the punishment which the world metes out to the individual transgressors.[20]

Therefore, according to Alexander and Staub, Ferenczi is right when he speaks of "sphincter morality" as the beginning and the foundation of adult human morality.[21] A refractory criminal who persists in his spiteful rejection of social demands is like "a baby sitting on its little chamber pot persistently rejecting any demands coming from the outside; it sits in this sovereign position and feels superior to the grown-ups."[22]

Alexander and Staub allege that the moment when the child begins to impose inhibitions on the demands of his own sphincter, he makes the first decisive step toward adjustment to the outside world, because at that moment he creates an inhibitory agency within his own personality. In brief, the child begins to develop internal reference points for conduct and a sense of justice or injustice from his toilet training. The justice (or lack of it) of this training becomes a prototype of future restrictions on the child's instinctual life, and a disturbance during this phase of development may naturally serve as a cause of future disturbance in one's social adjustment.

Freudian psychoanalytic theory remains a prevalent construct among social workers and psychiatrists treating offenders, but criminologists today tend to a greater inclusion of social factors and the societal framework in their search for an understanding of the causes of crime and delinquency.

Reinforcement Theory and Criminality

A widely accepted psychological theory that explains the learning process is called reinforcement theory. Fundamental to this theoretical approach is the idea that learning does not take place unless there is some sort of reinforce-

---

[20]Alexander and Staub, *The Criminal, the Judge, and the Public,* p. 55.

[21]Sandor Ferenczi, "Psychoanalysis of Sexual Habits," in *Sex in Psychoanalysis,* trans. Ernest Jones (New York: Basic Books, 1950).

[22]Alexander and Staub, *The Criminal, the Judge, and the Public,* p. 55.

ment, some equivalent of reward or punishment. Trasler applied this theory in an effort to determine *how a person learns not to be a criminal or delinquent.* The basic assumption of the theory—still in the development stage—is that *the individual learns not to become a criminal by a training procedure.* He learns to inhibit certain kinds of behavior, some of which are defined as criminal. Trasler tested this assumption in an experiment with rats, using *passive avoidance conditioning.*

In this experiment, the rat first learned how to obtain food by depressing a lever. An electric shock was then substituted for the food. The rat learned to avoid depressing the lever, even though the original drive, hunger, remained. Even when the unpleasant stimulus was removed, the rat would not touch the lever. The researchers concluded that it was in this way that the rat acquired "anxiety." An individual's aversion to criminality is believed to develop in the same way. The individual is conditioned to feel anxiety in anticipation of punishment, even though the punishment originally used to condition him is no longer present.

According to this theory, the degree of anxiety is in direct proportion to the amount of punishment meted out during one's early conditioning or socialization process. The intensity of the anxiety is a function of the severity of fear stimulated at the time of conditioning. The theory alleges that persons predisposed to criminal behavior have not been adequately punished for criminal acts during childhood. No anxiety is aroused by contemplating a criminal act because there was little or no fear-producing punishment.

Trasler lists the following as points of importance in adequate social conditioning:

1. The effectiveness of social conditioning will depend upon the strength of the unconditioned reaction (anxiety) with which it is associated.

2. Where there is a strong dependent relationship between a child and his parents, the sanction of withdrawal of approval will evoke intense anxiety.

3. The relationship between a child and his parents is likely to be one of dependence if it is (*a*) exclusive, (*b*) affectionate, and (*c*) reliable.[23]

Differences in conditioning methods, differences in sensitivity and family attitudes toward crime, and differences in class attitudes toward crime determine whether or not an individual will be predisposed to criminal behavior.

---

[23]Gordon Trasler, *The Explanation of Criminality* (London: Routledge & Kegan Paul, 1962).

Differential Association and Crime

A noted French scholar, Gabriel Tarde, was among the first to contend that patterns of delinquency and crime are learned in much the same manner as any other occupation. Learning, according to Tarde, occurs by imitation and in association with others. Imitation, as Tarde conceived it, involves more than simply emulating the behavior of another. The process is similar to that of *identification*, as the term is used in modern psychology. The individual is assumed to have selected a role model and fashioned his behavior after that model. To Tarde, crime is not a characteristic that the individual inherits or a disease he contracts; it is an occupation that he learns from others. The only difference between crime and any lawful occupation is in the content of what is learned.[24]

A more systematic explanation of the way criminal behavior patterns are acquired was developed by Edwin Sutherland and later elaborated upon by Donald Cressey, his student and collaborator. The central thesis of the theory, known as differential association, is that "criminal behavior is learned through interaction with others in intimate personal groups. The learning includes techniques of committing criminal acts, plus the motives, drives, rationalizations, and attitudes favorable to the commission of crime."[25] The basic principles of differential association are stated as follows:

1. *Criminal behavior is learned.* Negatively, this means that criminal behavior is not inherited, as such; also, the person who is not already trained in crime does not invent criminal behavior, just as a person does not make mechanical inventions unless he has had training in mechanics.

2. *Criminal bejavior is learned in interaction with other persons in a process of communication.* This communication is verbal in many respects but includes "the communication of gestures."

3. The principal part of the learning of criminal behavior occurs within *intimate personal groups.* Negatively, this means that the impersonal agencies of communication, such as movies and newspapers, play a relatively unimportant part in the genesis of criminal behavior.

4. When criminal behavior is learned, the learning includes (*a*) *techniques of committing the crime,* which are sometimes very complicated, sometimes very simple; (*b*) *the specific direction of motives, drives, rationalizations, and attitudes.*

5. The specific direction of motives and drives is *learned from definitions of the legal codes as favorable or unfavorable.* In some societies an individual is surrounded by persons who invariably define the legal

---

[24]Gabriel Tarde, *Penal Philosophy* (Boston: Little, Brown, 1912).

[25]Edwin H. Sutherland and Donald R. Cressey, *Criminology,* 8th ed., 1970, p. 75. By permission of the publishers, J. B. Lippincott Company.

codes as rules to be observed, while in others he is surrounded by persons whose definitions are favorable to the violation of the legal codes. In our American society these definitions are almost always mixed, with the consequence that we have culture conflict in relation to the legal codes.

6. *A person becomes delinquent because of an excess of definitions favorable to violation of law over definitions unfavorable to violation of law.* This is the principle of differential association. It refers to both criminal and anti-criminal associations and has to do with counteracting forces. When persons become criminal, *they do so because of contacts with criminal patterns* and also because of isolation from anti-criminal patterns. Any person inevitably assimilates the surrounding culture unless other patterns are in conflict; a Southerner does not pronounce "r" because other Southerners do not pronounce "r". Negatively, this proposition of differential association means that associations which are neutral so far as crime is concerned have little or no effect on the genesis of criminal behavior. Much of the experience of a person is neutral in this sense, e.g., learning to brush one's teeth. This behavior has no negative or positive effect on criminal behavior except as it may be related to associations which are concerned with the legal codes. This neutral behavior is important especially as an occupier of the time of a child so that he is not in contact with criminal behavior during the time he is so engaged in the neutral behavior.

7. *Differential associations may vary in frequency, duration, priority, and intensity.* This means that associations with criminal behavior and also associations with anti-criminal behavior vary in those respects. "Frequency" and "duration" as modalities of associations are obvious and need no explanation. "Priority" is assumed to be important in the sense that lawful behavior developed in early childhood may persist throughout life, and also that delinquent behavior developed in early childhood may persist throughout life. This tendency, however, has not been adequately demonstrated, and priority seems to be important principally through its selective influence. "Intensity" is not precisely defined but it has to do with such things as the prestige of the source of a criminal or anti-criminal pattern and with emotional reactions related to the associations. In a precise description of the criminal behavior of a person these modalities would be stated in quantitative form and a mathematical ratio be reached. A formula in this sense has not been developed, and the development of such a formula would be extremely difficult.

8. The process of learning criminal behavior by association with criminal and anti-criminal patterns involves all of the mechanisms that are involved in any other learning. Negatively, this means that the learning of criminal behavior is not restricted to the process of imitation. A person who is seduced, for instance, *learns criminal behavior by association,* but this process would not ordinarily be described as imitation.

9. While criminal behavior is an expression of general needs and values, it is not explained by those general needs and values since non-criminal behavior is an expression of the same needs and values. Thieves generally steal in order to secure money, but likewise honest laborers work in order to secure money. The attempts by many scholars to explain criminal behavior by general drives and values, such as the happiness principle, striving for social status, the money motive, or frustration, have been and must continue to be futile since they explain lawful behavior as completely as they explain criminal behavior. They are similar to respiration, which is necessary for any behavior but which does not differentiate criminal from non-criminal behavior.[26]

This theory does not explain why some people associate with those who approve of violation of the law while others do not, nor does it explain why some individuals become intensely committed to definitions *favorable* to the law while others with similar associations do not. It remains significant, however, because most current theorists have adopted the emphasis that differential association places on social learning through interaction in intimate groups as the principal method of the transmission of criminal values.

The impact of Sutherland's theory on criminology was detailed by Cressey in an article in *Social Problems*. Sutherland's theory has had such a profound impact on the field of criminology in the United States that it is pertinent to present most of Cressey's remarks on the origin and development of the theory of differential association:

The first formal statement of Edwin H. Sutherland's theory of differential association appeared in the third edition of his *Principles of Criminology,* in 1939. Sutherland later pointed out that the idea of differential association was stated in an earlier edition of the text, and he confessed that he was unaware that this statement was a general theory of criminal behavior. At the insistence of his colleagues, he drew up a formal set of propositions based on this earlier notion and appended it to the 1939 edition of the textbook.

In one sense, this first formal statement of the theory of differential association was short lived. For reasons which never have been clear, the statement of the theory was qualified so that it pertained only to "systematic criminal behavior," rather than to the more general category, "criminal behavior." Further, the statement was redundant, for it proposed generally that individual criminality is learned in a process of differential association with criminal and anti-criminal behavior patterns, but then went on to use "consistency" of association with the two kinds of patterns as one of the conditions affecting the impact of differential associa-

---

[26]Sutherland and Cressey, *Criminology,* pp. 77–79.

tion on individuals. Thus, "consistency" of behavior patterns presented was used as a general explanation of criminality, but "consistency" also was used to describe the process by which differential association takes place. . . .

He also deleted the word "systematic," principally because it led to errors of interpretation. He believed that "systematic criminal behavior" included almost all criminal behavior, while his readers, colleagues, and students considered only a very small proportion of criminal behavior to be "systematic." The theory now refers to all criminal behavior.

The current statement of the theory of differential association holds, in essence, that "criminal behavior is learned in interaction with persons in a pattern of communication," and that the specific direction of motives, drives, rationalizations, and attitudes—whether in the direction of anti-criminality or criminality—is learned from persons who define the codes as rules to be observed and from persons whose attitudes are favorable to violation of legal codes. "A person becomes delinquent because of an excess of definitions favorable to violation of law over definitions unfavorable to violations of law." In any society, the two kinds of definitions of what is desirable in reference to legal codes exist side by side, and a person might present contradictory definitions to another person at different times and in different situations. Sutherland called the process of receiving these definitions "differential association," because the content of what is learned in association with criminal behavior patterns differs from the content of what is learned in association with anti-criminal behavior patterns. "When persons become criminals, they do so because of contacts with criminal behavior patterns and also because of isolation from anti-criminal patterns." These contacts, however, "may vary in frequency, duration, priority, and intensity."

When this idea is applied to a nation, a city, or a group, it becomes a sociological theory, rather than a social psychological theory, for it deals with differential rates of crime and delinquency. For example, a high crime rate in urban areas, as compared to rural areas, can be considered an end product of a situation in which a relatively large proportion of persons are presented with an excess of criminal behavior patterns. Similarly, the fact that the rate for all crimes is not higher in some urban areas than it is in some rural areas can be attributed to differences in probabilities of exposure to criminal behavior patterns. The important general point is that in a multi-group type of social organization, alternative and inconsistent standards of conduct are possessed by various groups, so that individuals who are members of one group have a higher probability of learning to use legal means for achieving success, or of learning to deny the importance of success, while individuals in other groups learn to accept the importance of success and to achieve it by illegal means. Stated in another way, there are alternative educational processes in operation, varying with groups, so that a person may be educated in either conventional or criminal means of achieving success. Sutherland called this situation "differential social organization" or "differential group organization," and he proposed that "differential group organization should explain the crime rate, while differential association should explain the criminal behavior of a person. The two explanations must be consistent with each other."

Sutherland's theory has had an important effect on sociological thought about criminality and crime, if only because it has become the center of controversy. Strangely, it seems to have received more discussion, comment, and research attention in the last five years than in the first fifteen years of its existence. Also, there rapidly is developing a situation in which probation, parole, and prison workers have at least heard of the theory, even if they are barely beginning to try using it for prevention of crime and rehabilitation of criminals. A social worker has recently written, "The hallmark of this new departure (in delinquency prevention) is the recognition that delinquency is not primarily a psychological problem of neuroses but a social problem of differential values. Essentially most delinquent behavior arises from the fact that core concepts of what is right and wrong, what is worth striving for and what is attainable, are not transmitted with equal force and clarity throughout the community."[27]

Social Alienation and Criminality

Clarence R. Jeffery proposes a theory of social alienation to explain criminality. He points out that the concept of crime must exist before the concept of the criminal is possible. Antisocial behavior is not criminal behavior until a system of criminal law emerges. He states that all of the theories of crime now put forth in criminology are theories of criminal behavior, attempting to explain the behavior of the criminal. Regardless of the adequacy of the theories of behavior, they do not explain why the behavior is regarded as criminal. This is why Jeffery feels that criminologists need a theory of crime that explains the origin and development of criminal law in terms of the institutional structure of society.

A Theory of the Development of Law

Law came into existence at a time when the tribal system was disintegrating and social cohesion was no longer available as a means of social con-

---

[27]Donald R. Cressey, "The Theory of Differential Association: An Introduction," *Social Problems* 8 (Summer 1960):2–6. Reprinted by permission of the Society for the Study of Social Problems.

trol. Primitive law is custom enforced by the kinship group and based on the cohesiveness of the group. It is private and personal in nature and in operation.

Law is a product of impersonalization and the decline in social cohesion. It is a product of urbanization. Law emerges in a society whenever intimate, personal relationships are no longer efficient as agents of social control.[28]

Jeffery groups explanations of criminal behavior into two schools: the psychological and the sociological.

The *psychological* school is based on the proposition that criminals differ from noncriminals in terms of personality traits that are expressed in some form of antisocial behavior. Criminal behavior is caused by emotional or mental conflict. The most damaging criticism raised against the psychological school is the observation that few neurotics are criminals and that most criminals are neither neurotic nor psychotic.

Jeffery chose Sutherland, with his theory of differential association, to represent the *sociological* school. Jeffery describes it as basically a theory of learning and states that criminal behavior is learned from contact with those who maintain criminal attitudes and practices. Criminal behavior is learned by association with criminal and antisocial patterns. He points out the following criticisms of the theory of differential association:

1. The theory does not explain the origin of criminality.
2. It does not explain crimes of passion or accident.
3. The theory does not explain crimes by those with no prior contact with criminal attitudes.
4. It does not explain the noncriminal living in a criminal environment.
5. The theory does not differentiate between criminal and noncriminal behavior.
6. It does not take into account motivation or "differential response patterns." People respond differently to similar situations.
7. The theory does not account for the differential rate of crime associated with age, sex, urban areas, and minority groups.[29]

Jeffery advanced a *theory of social alienation* in an attempt to integrate the psychological and sociological concepts of criminality. His theory states that crime rates are highest in groups where social inteaction is characterized by isolation, anonymity, impersonalization, and anomie.

According to this theory, the criminal is one who lacks interperson-

[28]Clarence R. Jeffery, "An Integrated Theory of Crime and Criminal Behavior," *Journal of Criminal Law, Criminology, and Police Science* 50 (March 1959):533–52. Summary on p. 536.
[29]Jeffery, "Integrated Theory of Crime and Criminal Behavior," p. 537.

al relationships and suffers from interpersonal failure. The typical criminal has failed to achieve satisfactory interpersonal relations with others; he is lonely and emotionally isolated; he lacks membership in lawful primary groups, is insecure, hostile, aggressive; he feels unloved and unwanted, and has an inadequate sense of belonging. He is the product of social impersonalization.

The theory of social alienation is in essential agreement with the psychological thinking that places emphasis on such concepts as feelings of rejection, emotional starvation, psychological isolation from others, and so forth.

Jeffery's theory is in agreement with Sutherland's theory in that both emphasize the importance of social interaction that occurs in the primary group. It differs from differential association in the following respects: (1) It explains sudden crimes of passion. (2) It explains why an individual can live in a delinquent subculture and yet isolate himself from delinquent patterns. (3) It explains why a person with no history of association with criminals can commit criminal acts. (4) It explains the origin of criminal behavior in the first place by suggesting that high crime rates exist in areas characterized by anonymous, impersonal relationships. The theory of social alienation represents an attempt to integrate the sociological and psychological schools. It retains emphasis on social interaction while emphasizing the emotional content of human interaction.

In support of his theory, Jeffery points to the fact that crime rates are high for young adult males who live in urban slum areas, who are from lower socioeconomic groups, and who are members of minority groups. In these areas one also finds social isolation, a preponderance of impersonal relationships, and anonymity.

Types of Alienation

Jeffery divided social alienation into three types. First there is *individual alienation.* The individual is alienated and isolated from interpersonal relations. This person is often characterized as a sociopath. He does not accept the values of the society.

The second type is *group alienation.* The group to which the person belongs is alienated and isolated from the larger community. The individual who identifies with such a group is often characterized as a cultural deviate or a dyssocial person. A lack of integration of the various segments of society produces alienation of the segments.

The third type is *legal alienation.* The differential treatment of Negroes and whites, and of lower class and upper class individuals, in courts of law illustrates the fact that different social groups have differential access to justice. In a large, complex society, government by representation replaces government by direct citizen participation. The function and processes of government are removed from the people and placed in the hands of a corps of professional politicians and lobbyists. A type of alienation exists between legal values and those expressed in other institutions of our society.[30]

The Dropout

Our observations of urban slum areas with high crime rates agree with those of Jeffery regarding to preponderance of impersonal relations and relative anonymity and, to some extent, social isolation. We do not agree, however, that the alienated individual is necessarily a sociopath.

The lower class dropout is a poor achiever at school and finds himself cast in the role of manual laborer or "unemployable." He, too, generally feels powerless to change his destiny. The lower class dropout (1) expresses hatred and envy of the more affluent and is ashamed of his poverty; (2) rejects manual labor and menial tasks as undesirable and wants high-status employment; (3) often identifies with a violent or delinquent gang; (4) expresses ideas favorable to the use of violence and often commits violent acts; (5) generally uses marijuana or opiates; (6) takes an extreme position on most issues (black involuntary dropouts express hostility toward "Whitey" and favor violent action against him); (7) feels powerless to effect any change in the system or to contribute significantly to change, and does not try.

The middle class and lower class dropouts have in common a hatred for the "establishment" or system and consider its leaders to be betrayers of the dream. Nevertheless, as we have seen, neither of them participates actively in formal social or political organizations, largely because of their feeling of powerlessness.

The middle class dropout appears to be cynical and passive, whereas the lower class dropout appears to be frustrated and angry. The middle class dropout may be characterized as an idealist without hope of effecting changes he considers essential. The lower class dropout generally resents the system in which he finds himself but has no alternative system to offer.

In contrast with the traditional (lower class) delinquent, the new deviants, the hippies, reject the means, the goals, and the values of the society.

The hippies' deviant behavior and posture reflect a much more devastating attack on the basic structure of American society than the traditional delinquent pattern. Traditional American delinquents accept the goals of the society even though they find it necessary to pursue them in a deviant way. The lower class American delinquent, therefore, is really affirming the validity of the goals of American society by striving

---

[30]Jeffery, "Integrated Theory of Crime and Criminal Behavior," pp. 550–51.

for them at any cost. Traditional crime and delinquency in this context is a tribute to the goals and values of American society.[31]

Violent conflict often emerges between middle class dropouts and minority group members residing in urban slum areas.

> The urban slum areas where hippies have moved pose some special and complicated violence problems for the movement. The conflict situations usually emanate from difficulties felt and acted upon by the older resident population.
>
> A common problem of hostility is the older residents' resentment of the seemingly blatant and looser sexual morality of the hippies. Their hang-loose ethics and more open sexual freedom produce an up-tight feeling and an envy that often produce aggression. The fun and games of the hippies without working also generate hostile feelings in many urban slum dwellers who are working hard toward success in an achievement-oriented society.
>
> Some subterranean conflicts also exist between the older urban-area minority residents and the new minority-group hippies. The violence that is generated may be related to the fact that the hippies have had and have rejected the very goals that the minority groups [and their children] are seeking. The middle- and upper-class hippies walked away from material affluence and available opportunity channels to American success in jobs and symbols. The anger of the minority-group urban dwellers, although perhaps unclear in their own minds, may stem from the frustration of seeing this wanton rejection of things they are taught daily to desire by the mass media. They have accepted the value system that validates the pursuit of materialism as the major way to achieve the "good life" in America.
>
> The crass rejection by the hippies of deified material objectives is a threat to the dreams of minority groups. They may have to question whether the goals they are working and battling for are really worth the struggle. If these people (the hippies), who had it all, can so easily walk away and enter conditions of poverty even more severe than their own, it raises the issue that perhaps their valued goals—such as the color TV, the new car, travel, and the house in the country—are not worth the struggle.
>
> In summary, the hippies present a challenge to the way in which minority groups rationalize their own suffering. To them the hippies are implicitly saying that the god material success is a false god. A partial result of this caldron of value confusion, frustration, and anger produced by the hippies is the acting out of violence.[32]

---

[31]Lewis Yablonsky, *The Hippie Trip* (Indianapolis: Pegasus, 1968), p. 318.
[32]Yablonsky, *The Hippie Trip,* pp. 308–9.

A considerable amount of this frustration and violent acting out takes place in the black urban ghettos. The National Advisory Commission on Civil Disorders concluded that in the summer riots of 1967, Negroes were acting against the symbols of white American society, authority, and property in Negro neighborhoods.[33] The lower class (involuntary) Negro dropout played a significant role in these disorders. According to the commission, the typical rioter was a high school dropout, underemployed or employed in a menial job, highly distrustful of the political system, frustrated by powerlessness, alienated from and hostile to the institutions of law and government.

The riots were undoubtedly precipitated by many complex forces and events, but it is clear that the presence of large numbers of dropouts contributed greatly to the availability of violent manpower. Despite the absence of formal organization or planning, a large number of dropouts demonstrated their ability to bring about considerable destruction and, perhaps as a side effect of their activity, a measure of social change.

Containment Theory

To explain the way in which criminal behavior is influenced by a variety of factors, Walter Reckless offers the containment theory:

1. At the top of a vertical arrangement impinging on an individual is a layer of *social pressures.* Pressure factors include adverse living conditions and economic conditions, minority group status, lack of opportunities, and family conflicts.

2. The pressures include what Reckless refers to as *pull factors.* These draw the individual away from the accepted norms. They include bad companions, delinquent or criminal subculture, and deviant groups.

3. In the situation immediately surrounding the individual is the structure of effective or ineffective *external containment.* This structure consists of effective family living and supportive groups.

4. The next layer is the *inner containment* within the individual. It is a product of good or poor internalization. When external containment is weak, inner containment must be additionally strong to withstand the pushes from within and the pulls and pressures from without.

5. The bottom layer consists of the *pushes.* These include inner tensions, hostility, aggressiveness, strong feelings of inadequacy and inferiority, and organic impairments.[34]

Reckless uses outer containment and inner containment as intervening variables. The individual may be pressured into criminality by unfavorable

---

[33] *Report of the National Advisory Commission on Civil Disorders* (Washington, D. C.: U.S. Government Printing Office, 1968), pp. 6–10.

[34] Walter C. Reckless, *The Crime Problem* (New York: Appleton-Century-Crofts, 1961), pp. 355–56.

economic conditions or pulled into it by association with a delinquent subculture if his outer containment is deficient. The lack of outer containment is evidenced by the lack of well-defined limits to behavior, the breakdown of rules, the absence of definite roles for adolescents to play, and the failure of family life to present adequate limits and roles to the youth.

Reckless contends that a boy in a high-delinquency area where outer containment is weak may remain nondelinquent if inner containment is good. Inner containment consists of good ego strength, self-control, good self-conceptualization, and strong resistance against diversions.

Containment theory does have the advantage of merging the psychological and the sociological viewpoints of crime causation. It facilitates an analysis of the inner personal forces that propel a person to commit a crime, and at the same time permits an examination of the sociocultural forces that shape his motivation and personality.

A Reference Group Theory of Delinquency

How does a youth become committed to a delinquent subculture? The relationship between the important forces that socialize a child and his participation in delinquent subcultures may be summed up in the following propositions:

1. *The family is the first personal reference group of the child.* A *psyche group* is one in which the individual as a person receives sustenance, recognition, approval, and appreciation for just being himself. It consists of those persons with whom the individual wants to associate in a person-to-person manner and with whom he values emotional relationships. A *sociogroup* is one in which the individual's efforts and ideals are focused toward objectives that are not his alone. Concerns must be shared and obligations held in common. The psyche group and the sociogroup are both face-to-face groups. It is the psyche group that is the *personal reference group* of the individual. The family is the first such group of which he is a member. How long it remains his personal reference group depends on its functional ability.

2. *The family is a normative reference group.* A reference group is a group in which the individual is motivated to gain or maintain membership. When a membership group becomes a reference group, it performs a normative function and may also perform a comparison function.

A normative reference group is a reference group whose norms conform to those of the larger society. The family is such a group. In it the parents function as agents of society in transmitting the culture to the child. Even in families with criminal parents, the child is likely to be encouraged by the parents to conform to the norms of the society and to be punished for deviation.

3. *Prior to a boy's participation in a delinquent act, a street group has become a personal reference group for him.* The term *street group* is used

instead of *gang* to indicate amorphous character, lack of structure, and the fact that the group need *not* be committed to a delinquent subculture.

4. *The street group that becomes the personal reference group of the lower class boy in a large city is likely to have a delinquent culture.*

5. *A boy for whom a street group is a personal reference group is likely, in the dynamic assessment preceding a delinquent act, to decide in favor of the delinquent act.* The street group, whether or not it has a delinquent culture, has no clearly defined objectives and engages in a considerable amount of experimental behavior, some of which is delinquent. Once the street group has become a youth's personal reference group, the youth desires the approval of the group. The boys in his personal reference group who are with him at the time of the act will exercise an important influence upon the outcome of his assessment. He cannot afford to have them regard him as "punking out" or "chicken." In all probability, he will participate in the delinquent act.

6. *As a member of a personal reference group, the individual tends to import into its context attitudes and ways of behaving to which he is currently adhering in sociogroup life.* Important studies of intergenerational conflict in families of immigrants illustrate the fact that children acquire attitudes and ways of behaving in school and in other sociogroups and bring these attitudes into the home. The result in immigrant families has been the rejection of parental norms and values. The same process appears to operate in lower class families. Applying the standards learned in school, the lower class boy will find his parents on the low end of the scale in education, occupation, and morals. Importing these attitudes into the home leads him to reject his parents and tends to neutralize the normative influence they might exercise.

A youth's parents are usually opposed to his affiliation in a street group. How, then, does a boy who is a member of a normative personal reference group, his family, become a member of a delinquent personal reference group, a street group with a delinquent subculture?

The process may be traced through the following steps:

1. The lower class boy, a few years after he enters the school system, usually before he is ten years of age, becomes aware of the fact that by the standards of the educational system, his parents are failures. Their occupations are rated low, their education is considered poor, their residence is depreciated, and their habits of dress, eating, and personal cleanliness are clearly below the standards held up to him at school. The boy's resentment toward his parents grows.

2. The lower class boy perceives himself as unlikely to succeed at school. This confirms his feelings of inferiority and inadequacy. He accepts the vague success goal imparted to him at school and correctly appraises the likelihood of his failure.

3. Other than the success goal, the lower class boy acquires no realistic goal of any kind. It is amazing how many will reply, "I don't know," to the question "What do you want to be?" Each boy knows that he is not likely to

become president, governor, an industrialist, or a member of any of the professions or occupations viewed with favor in his classroom or in his textbooks. He knows that he can become a worker of some sort, but this sort of endeavor is viewed as inferior by the middle class school system.

4. The boy in the lower class family perceives himself as viewed with disfavor at home because he consumes without contributing. Time and time again boys say that they are accused of eating too much, being too hard on clothes, and spending too much.

5. The boy, whether in a lower class or middle class family, is objectively inferior to the adults in the family, his parents, in earnings, skills, and prestige. As a result, he tends to see himself as generally inferior. He acquires feelings of social competence only as a result of experiences in which he has produced intended effects on other people: making them respond, obtaining expressions of affection, having expressions of affection accepted, and giving advice that is accepted. Failure to experience feelings of social competence in the family confirms feelings of inferiority and leads the individual to seek other groups in which he can succeed.

6. The boy, lower class or middle class, who fails to acquire feelings of social competence in the family, and does not derive satisfactions in normative sociogroups such as work or school groups, gravitates to the street for a great deal of his social life.

7. On the street he finds others who, like himself, have been unsuccessful in experiencing social competence in the family or anywhere else. These boys have few relationships in normative sociogroups. If a street group is already in existence, the boy tries to join it. If he is accepted: if he wins recognition, approval, and appreciation; if here he can make others respond and occasionally have his advice accepted, the group becomes his personal reference group. The group tends to have a delinquent culture; the boy thus becomes a member of a delinquent personal reference group.[35]

---

[35]Derived from Martin R. Haskell, "Toward a Reference Group Theory of Juvenile Delinquency," *Social Problems* 8(Winter 1961):220–30. Reprinted by permission of the Society for the Study of Social Problems.

Explanations of Crime and Delinquency: Emphasis on the Group and Society

THE NOTED FRENCH sociologist Emile Durkheim considered crime an integral part of all societies. Having defined crime as an act that is punished, he expressed the view that a society exempt from crime was utterly impossible. The dominant group in the society invariably defines certain behavior as undesirable and punishable. It is this societal definition that confers criminal character upon the act, and not the intrinsic quality of the act. According to Durkheim:

> Crime is present . . . in all societies of all types. Its form changes; the acts thus characterized are not the same everywhere; but, everywhere and always, there have been men who have behaved in such a way as to draw upon themselves penal repression. If, in proportion as societies pass from the lower to the higher types, the rate of criminality . . . tended to decline, it might be believed that crime, while still normal, is tending to lose this character of normality. [Actually] it has everywhere in-

creased. . . . There is, then, no phenomenon that presents more indisputably all the symptoms of normality, since it appears closely connected with the conditions of all collective life.[1]

Durkheim did recognize that some criminal behavior was pathological and was made punishable with the complete consensus of the society—murder, for example. With respect to other behavior classified as criminal there is less general agreement.

In a society that permits individuals to differ more or less from the collective type, it is inevitable that some acts are criminal. However, since nothing is "good" indefinitely and to an unlimited extent, people must be free to deviate; otherwise, social change would be impossible.

As Durkheim saw it, if progress is to be made, individual originality must be able to express itself. For the originality of the idealist to find expression it is necessary that the originality of the criminal also be expressible. It would never have been possible to establish the freedom of thought we now enjoy if the regulations prohibiting it had not been violated by people who were at one time classified as criminals. It should be remembered that the founding fathers of the United States were at first considered legally criminals in the context of the British Empire. Crime is thus a valuable force for social change.

Anomie, as first presented by Emile Durkheim in his search for the cause of suicide and later elaborated upon by Robert K. Merton and others, is characterized as a condition in which an individual feels a loss of orientation; he is without outside controls he can trust or believe in. For such an individual, little is real or meaningful; he cannot relate to society wholly, and its norms and values are without meaning to him. He is free of the restrictions imposed on those belonging to society and, free, he is lost.[2]

In his treatise on anomic suicide, Durkheim points out the dangers of such freedom from acceptable restraint. "Those who have only empty space above them are almost inevitably lost in it, if no force restrain them."[3]

Durkheim points out that "no living being can be happy or even exist unless his needs are sufficiently proportioned to his means."[4] Society limits the means available to him. Society also sets goals appropriate to each category of people in it. There may be some flexibility, but there are also limits. "To pursue a goal which is by definition unattainable is to condemn oneself to a

---

[1]Emile Durkheim, *The Rules of Sociological Method,* 8th ed., trans. Sarah A. Solvag and John H. Mueller (Glencoe, Ill.: Free Press, 1950), pp. 65–66.

[2]Emile Durkheim, *Suicide,* trans. John. A. Spaulding and George Simpson (Glencoe, Ill.: Free Press, 1951).

[3]Durkheim, *Suicide,* p. 257.

[4]Durkheim, *Suicide,* p. 246.

state of perpetual unhappiness."[5] Yet, in our society, as in the France of Durkheim's time, *all classes contend among themselves because no established classification any longer exists.* Society, according to Durkheim, is the only agency that is acceptable to people as a regulator of the desires of men. It is the only agency recognized as superior to the individual, with the acknowledged right to make demands and impose restrictions. Yet ". . . discipline can be useful only if considered just by the peoples subject to it. When it is maintained only by custom and force, peace and harmony are illusory; the spirit of unrest and discontent are latent; appetites superficially restrained are ready for revolt."[6]

Merton relates crime to anomie through the four following concepts:

1. Society, in the United States, places an emphasis on success as represented by possessions and their consumption, and at the same time, for some people, blocks legitimate paths to the achievement of that goal. Success is assumed to be achievable by all.

2. The access to legitimate means of achievement are effectively denied to many members of the lower classes and to members of minority groups.

3. The conflict thus established is often resolved by resorting to illegal means of achievement of acceptable goals.

4. On the other hand, an individual may deny the value of the goal and act out that denial in the destruction of property.

Resorting to either illegitimate means or destruction of the goal is anomie. It is an inability to correlate the ends of action and the action to the values of society. Since legitimate means and shared goals become contradictory, the individual must relieve his anxiety and frustration by denying the one or the other as meaningful. As distance grows between institutional means and cultural goals, anomie grows more prevalent.[7]

Some people, for whatever reason, come to reject the goals defined by the society as appropriate and the means defined as legitimate. If they seek to substitute other means and other goals for those dictated by the society, they may move toward rebellion. A solution does not come easily. It may require a reorganization of society. This seems to be the solution some are striving for on a national level by peaceful means. Effective civil rights legislation and the chance of equal opportunity for all in reality could reduce the disparity between goal and means for many of our people. The attempt to reduce the wide difference in income may be helpful to others. Unless these objectives are attained, we can, by applying this theoretical position, predict increased criminality and/or increased rebellion.

---

[5]Durkehim, *Suicide,* p. 248.

[6]Durkheim, *Suicide,* p. 251.

[7]Robert K. Merton, *Social Theory and Social Structure* (Glencoe, Ill.: Free Press, 1957), pp. 131–60.

Crime and Dislocations in the Social System

In the larger context of society, Robert K. Merton examined the way in which the social structure exerts definite pressure upon some persons to engage in nonconformist behavior. He asserts that deviant behavior results from discrepancies between culturally defined goals and the socially structured means of achieving them.

According to Merton, American society defines success as a goal for everyone. Some of the socially approved means of achieving success are hard work, education, and thrift. The emphasis in our society, he points out, is on the *goals*—winning the game—not on the *means*—how you do it. Since some people do not have equal access to approved means, they have a more limited chance to achieve the goals of the society unless they deviate.

Merton describes five basic modes of adaptation to the goals and means of the society:

Adaptation I: conformity to both culture goals and means. This is the most commonly used adaptation in every society.

Adaptation II: innovation, the acceptance of the cultural emphasis on success goals without equally internalizing the morally prescribed norms governing the means for their attainment. The individual accepts the goals of wealth and power, but does not accept work as means. The innovator may choose illegal means and become a criminal. This choice is particularly attractive to the person who concludes that he does not have access to approved means of achieving his goals.

Adpatation III: ritualism, the rejection of culturally defined goals with conformity to the mores defining the means. The ritualistic individual does not try to get ahead; he is overly involved with the ritualistic means of success.

Adaptation IV: retreatism, the rejection of both the culturally defined goals and the institutionalized means. The individual escapes by becoming a drug addict, an alcoholic, a psychotic, or by some other method.

Adaptation V: rebellion, the rejection of both the goals and the means of attaining them. The rebel attempts to introduce a "new social order."[8]

We would like to add another adaptation to those described by Merton.

---

[8]Merton, *Social Theory and Social Structure,* pp. 141–56.

Adaptation VI: dropping out, the rejection of both the culturally defined goals and the institutionalized means by taking no action to effectu-
ate change. The "dropout" simply waits for something to happen. While
waiting, to keep alive and to relieve boredom he engages in behavior
defined as criminal by the society whenever he finds such behavior appropriate.

In general Merton's fundamental explanation of the tendency to criminality is that the emphasis on goals rather than on the means of attaining them
causes many people who cannot achieve material success goals through legitimate means to resort to any means, including crime.

Merton's point of reference for accounting for criminality is found in the
analysis of social dislocations. This is the fundamental direction taken by many
recent sociological students of crime causation.

Economic Determinism

The Dutch criminologist William A. Bonger, a Marxist, was the principal
proponent of a theory of economic causation of crime. Bonger attributed
criminal acts, particularly crimes against property, directly to the poverty of
the proletariat in a competitive capitalistic system. Poverty, which resulted
from unsuccessful economic competition, led to personal disorganization and
was an inherent part of a capitalist society. The solution to crime, according
to this theory, could be achieved only through the reorganization of the means
of production and the development of a classless society. Bonger described this
viewpoint this way:

> The egoistic tendency does not by itself make a man criminal. For
> this something else is necessary. . . . For example, a man who is enriched
> by the exploitation of children may nevertheless remain all his life an
> honest man from the legal point of view. He does not think of stealing,
> because he has a surer and more lucrative means of getting wealth,
> although he lacks the moral sense which would prevent him from com-
> mitting a crime if the thought of it occurred to him. . . . As a consequence
> of the present environment, man has become very egoistic and hence
> more capable of crime, than if the environment had developed the germs
> of altruism.
>
> The present economic system is based upon exchange. . . . Such a
> mode of production cannot fail to have an egoistic character. A society
> based upon exchange isolates the individuals by weakening the bond that
> unites them. When it is a question of exchange the two parties interested
> think only of their own advantage even to the detriment of the other
> party.

... No commerce without trickery is a proverbial expression (among consumers), and with the ancients Mercury, the god of commerce, was also the god of thieves. This is true, that the merchant and the thief are alike in taking account exclusively of their own interest to the detriment of those with whom they have to do.[9]

There has been sufficient evidence since Bonger wrote to indicate that poverty alone does not cause crime and that most poor people are not criminals. Most Western societies, however, have assumed greater responsibility for care of the unemployed and the poor than they did in Bonger's time. A commentary of Bonger's that still appears to hold true is his observation that conspicuous consumption tends indirectly to set goals impossible of legitimate achievement by people in the lower strata of society.Bonger's postulate of the discrepancy between culturally approved goals and institutionalized means of achieving them as a cause of crime has been incorporated into the theoretical positions of many recent sociologists.

Economic determinism, as part of a contemporary radical criminology has been supported by the work of Gordon and others.[10] According to this view, capitalist societies depend on basically competitive forms of social and economic interaction and upon substantial inequalities in the allocation of social resources. Without competition and a competitive ideology workers might not be included to struggle to improve their relative income and status in society by working harder. Although property rights are protected, capitalist societies do not guarantee economic security to most individual members. *Driven by fear of economic insecurity and by a competitive desire to gain some of the goods unequally distributed throughout the society, many individuals will eventually become "criminals."*

The following three different kinds of crime in the United States provide examples of functionally similar rationality:

1. *Ghetto Crime.* The legitimate jobs open to many young ghetto residents typically pay low wages, offer relatively demeaning assignments, and carry constant risk of layoff. Many types of "crimes" available in the ghetto offer higher monetary return, higher status, and often low risk of arrest and punishment.

2. *Organized Crime.* Activities like gambling, prostitution, and drug distribution are illegal for various reasons, but there is a demand

---

[9]William A. Bonger, *Criminality and Economic Conditions* (Boston: Little, Brown, 1916), pp. 401–2.

[10]David M. Gordon, "Capitalism, Class and Crime in America," *Crime and Delinquency* (April 1973): 163–86.

for these activities. Opportunities for monetary rewards are great, and the risks of arrest and punishment low.

    3. *Corporate Crime.* Corporations exist to protect and augment the capital of their owners. If it becomes difficult to do this lawfully, corporate officials will try to do it another way.

Gordon also points out that current patterns of crime and punishment in the United States support the capitalist system in the following three ways:

    1. The pervasive patterns of selective law enforcement reinforce a prevalent ideology in the society that *individuals rather than institutions are to blame for social problems.*

    2. The patterns of crime and punishment manage "legitimately" to neutralize the potential opposition to the system of many oppressed citizens. The cycle of crime, imprisonment, parole, and recidivism denies to the poor, particularly the black poor, meaningful participation in a society and also denies them decent employment opportunities and keeps them on the run.

    3. By treating criminals as animals and misfits, as enemies of the state, we are permitted to continue to avoid some basic questions about the dehumanizing effects of our social institutions.

A critical theory of criminal law that generally supports Gordon's position is stated by Quinney in the following terms:

1. American society is based on an advanced capitalist economy.
2. The state is organized to serve the interests of the dominant economic class, the capitalist ruling class.
3. Criminal law is an instrument of the state and ruling class to maintain and perpetuate the existing social and economic order.
4. Crime control in capitalist society is accomplished through a variety of institutions and agencies established and administered by a governmental elite, representing ruling class interests, for the purpose of establishing domestic order.
5. The contradictions of advanced capitalism—the disjunction between existence and essence—require that the subordinate classes remain oppressed by whatever means necessary, especially through the coercion and violence of the legal system.
6. Only with the collapse of capitalist society and the creation of a new society, based on socialist principles, will there be a solution to the crime problem.

    As capitalist society is further threatened by its own contradictions, criminal law is increasingly used in the attempt to maintain domestic order. The underclass, the class that must remain oppressed for the triumph of the dominant economic class, will continue to be the object of criminal law as long as the dominant class seeks to perpetuate itself.[11]

Social Disorganization and Crime

Ecologists are largely involved in establishing relationships between residential areas and the natural groups that inhabit them. The urban industrial community may be described as consisting of five successive zones:

    I. The central business district tends in American cities to be at once the retail, financial, recreational, civic, and political centers. By day the skyscrapers and canyon-like streets of the downtown district are thronged with shoppers, clerks and office workers. . . . The central business district has few inhabitants. . . .

    II. The zone in transition . . . [is] an interstitial area in the throes of change from residence to business and industry. Here are to be found the slum or semi-slum districts. . . .

    III. The zone of workingmen's homes . . . [lies] beyond the factory belt surrounding the central business district, which is still accessible, often within walking distance to the workers. . . .

    IV. The better residential zone is inhabited chiefly by the families engaged in professional and clerical pursuits who have high school if not college education. . . . This is the home of the great middle class. . . .

    V. The commuter's zone comprises the suburban districts. . . .[12]

These descriptive categories were based on observations of Chicago. While many urban communities do not follow this explicit pattern, residential areas surrounding industrial centers in the great majority of our cities are comparable "zones in transition."

Burgess noted that Zone II, in transition from workingmen's homes to business and industry, was the area in which social disorganization was greatest. Clifford R. Shaw and other students of Burgess conducted extensive studies of Chicago and twenty-one other cities, dividing the urban population into mile-square areas and quantifying the deterioration, and found support for Burgess' viewpoint.

---

[11]Richard Quinney, *Criminal Justice in America* (Boston: Little, Brown & Co., 1974), p. 24.

[12]Robert E. Park, Ernest W. Burgess, and R. D. McKenzie, *The City* (Chicago: University of Chicago Press, 1925), p. 50.

Shaw concentrated upon an analysis of the distribution of juvenile delinquency. He found that the highest concentration of delinquency rates occurred
in Zone I and that there was a progressive slope in rates downward away from
Zone I. The results were the same for such other indicia of social disorganization as crime rates, rates of mental disorder, and truancy rates. (See Table 12.1)

Shaw found that the greatest concentration of delinquents occurred in
areas of marked social disorganization and described the process as follows:

> In the process of city growth, the neighborhood organizations,
> cultural institutions and social standards in practically all of the areas
> adjacent to the central business district and the major industrial centers
> are subject to rapid change and disorganization. The gradual invasion of
> these areas by industry and commerce, the continuous movement of the
> older residents out of the area and the influx of newer groups, the
> confusion of many divergent cultural standards, the economic insecurity
> of the families, all combine to render difficult the development of a stable
> and efficient neighborhood organization for the education and control of
> the child and the suppression of lawlessness.[13]

Table 12.1

Social Data by Zones

Community Problems	Zones				
	I	II	III	IV	V
Rates of delinquents, 1927–1933	9.8	6.7	4.5	2.5	1.8
Rates of truants, 1927–1933	4.4	3.1	1.7	1.0	0.7
Boys' court rates, 1938	6.3	5.9	3.9	2.6	1.6
Rates of infant mortality, 1923–1933	86.7	67.5	54.7	45.9	41.3
Rates of tuberculosis, 1931–1937	33.5	25.0	18.4	12.5	9.2
Rates of mental disorder, 1922–1934	32.0	18.8	13.2	110.1	8.4
Rates of adult criminals, 1920	2.2	1.6	0.8	0.6	0.4

SOURCE: Clifford R. Shaw and Henry McKay, *Juvenile Delinquency and Urban Areas*
(Chicago: University of Chicago Press, 1942), p. 158, Table 1. © 1942 by The University of
Chicago.

[13]National Commission on Law Observance and Enforcement, *Report on the Causes of Crime,* vol.
2, no. 13 (Washington, D.C.: U.S. Government Printing Office, 1931), p. 387.

In the slum area delinquent traditions were transmitted to the new arrival. There were adult criminal gangs engaged in theft and the sale of stolen goods. Children were exposed to a variety of contradictory standards and forms of behavior. They were often found guilty in the courts for behavior that was approved by the neighborhood in which they lived. High-delinquency areas developed social values and patterns of behavior that conflicted with the values of the larger society. Thus behavior that was considered "correct" by the norms of the slum neighborhood was considered delinquent and criminal by the norms and laws of the larger society. This condition of social disorganization is often referred to as "culture conflict."

Cultural Dimension of Criminality

Social Theory of Crime

Donald R. Taft and Ralph W. England, Jr., formulated a social theory that attempts to explain the high rate of crime in the United States and other Western societies. He sees criminality resulting from a combination of the following aspects of the culture:

1. *American culture is dynamic.* Our standards are constantly changing. "The wrong of yesterday is the right of today."

2. *American culture is complex.* According to Taft, crime is the product of culture conflict, and culture conflict is widespread as a result of immigration and internal migration.

3. *American culture is materialistic.* "Speaking generally, the underprivileged and unsuccessful accept the same values as the successful and aspire to imitate their success." It is apparent that the underprivileged have a more difficult time achieving success goals than the privileged.

4. *American social relations are increasingly impersonal.* Primary relationships in the family and neighborhood have declined. Anonymity breeds alienation and a greater impetus to crime and delinquency.

5. *American culture fosters restricted group loyalties.* "Preference for men, not wholly because of their personal qualities, but because they are natives, neighbors, Masons, or of our race, class, or creed, is widespread and not essentially different in quality from gang loyalty." This leaves people out, produces conflict, hostility, and crime.

6. *Survival of frontier values.* Among frontier values that have survived into the present are the tradition of extreme individualism and the tendency of some groups within our society to take the law into their own hands.[14]

---

[14]Donald R. Taft and Ralph W. England, Jr., *Criminology* (New York: Macmillan, 1964), pp. 27–31.

All of these factors in American culture, according to Taft and England, "normally" produce a high incidence of crime.

The Criminogenic Society

Barron presents a detailed analysis of the criminogenic aspects of the American society and culture.[15] He discusses several official and unofficial American values which are likely to encourage norm-violating and illegal behavior. These are:

1. *Success.* There is an emphasis in our culture on the importance of succeeding and asserting one's self. The well-known quotation of football coach Lombardi is cited. "Winning isn't everything, it is the only thing." Americans hate to admit failure. They feel frustrated if they do not achieve success. There is also a very high value placed on moving up, going higher on the scale toward ultimate success. When people realize that they are not going to succeed and are not moving up through hard work, thrift, study, etc., many turn to crime and delinquency as ways of achieving success.

2. *Status and Power Ascendance.* The answer to the question "How far can I get?" is found in terms of social status. Evidence of higher status is provided by high grades, expensive cars, expensive clothes, jewelry, etc. Dollars provide the power. Money and material goods have become values in themselves. People who cannot obtain them lawfully may violate laws in order to get them.

3. *Resistance to Authority.* Independence, individuality, and non-conformity are encouraged. All these involve resistance to authority. Americans tend to ridicule literal observance and strict conformity. This tendency applies to observance of laws. The Caspar Milquetoast is an object of ridicule.

4. *Toughness.* There are class differences in the emphasis on toughness. However, in every subculture people are encouraged to fight back. Violence is celebrated in crime and gangster programs, on TV, in films, in magazines, etc.

5. *Dupery.* People are rewarded for getting the better of others. The observation of P. T. Barnum that "there's a sucker born every minute" meets with general agreement if not approval. Official norms and laws are violated with the tacit acceptance of the society or group as long as violations are concealed. People are proud of getting the better of others.

6. *American culture is dynamic.* Changes in norms are so rapid that differences between right and wrong are weakened.

---

[15]Milton L. Barron, "The Criminogenic Society: Social Values and Deviance," in *Current Perspectives on Criminal Behavior,* ed. Abraham S. Blumberg (New York: Alfred A. Knopf, 1974), pp. 68–86.

7. *American culture offers alternative and conflicting values and norms.* Behavior that is defined as illegal in the American society may not necessarily be "wrong" in the subcultures of some groups.

8. *Social relations in the American society have become increasingly impersonal.* Urban living, in which one hardly knows his neighbor, does not provide the informal controls of rural society.

9. *A multigroup society fosters a duality of loyalty and ethics.* Many people apply one code of ethics in their relations with members of their ingroup and a different code with outgroup members.

Barron tempers the impact of criminogenic theory by acknowledging that widespread crime and corruption existed at other times in history and occur in other places than the United States. Nevertheless, although they are not peculiar to American society, they appear to be a part of it.

Subculture of Delinquency

Albert Cohen views delinquent youths as comprising a subculture with a value system different from the dominant one found in the inclusive American culture. Lower class children, according to Cohen, use the delinquent subculture as a mode of reaction and adjustment to a dominant middle class society that indirectly discriminates against them because of their lower class position. Lower class youths, trained in a different value system, are not adequately socialized to fulfill the status requirements of middle class society. Despite this differential socialization, they are unfairly exposed to the middle class aspirations and judgments they cannot fulfill. This conflict produces in the lower class youths what Cohen has termed "status frustration." In reaction, they manifest a delinquent adjustment, acting out their status frustrations in "non-utilitarian, malicious, negativistic" forms of delinquency.

In such settings as the school and community center, the lower class youth finds himself exposed to generally middle class agents of the society (teachers and social workers). Their efforts to impose on him their middle class values of orderliness, cleanliness, responsibility, and ambition are met with sharp negativism.

Cohen lists nine middle class values that are specifically rejected by the lower class child: (1) ambition; (2) responsibility; (3) the cultivation of skills and tangible achievement; (4) postponement of immediate satisfactions and self-indulgence in the interest of long-term goals; (5) rationality, in the sense of forethought, planning, and budgeting of time; (6) the rational cultivation of manners, courtesy, personality; (7) the need to control physical aggression and violence; (8) the need for wholesome recreation; and (9) respect for property and its proper care.

The lower class child, in reaction against these unfair impositions, substitutes norms that reverse those of the larger society: "The delinquent subculture takes its norms from the larger subculture, but turns them upside down. The delinquent's conduct is right by the standards of his subculture precisely because it is wrong by the norms of the larger culture."[16] The dominant theme of the delinquent subculture is the explicit and wholesale repudiation of middle class standards and the adoption of their very antitheses. In this negative polarity of "just for the hell of it." vandalism and violence, lower class youths attempt to adjust their status frustration and hostility toward the larger society's unfair imposition of middle class values upon them; and the gang is the vehicle for their delinquencies. The individual delinquent is "the exception rather than the rule."[17]

Cohen's position on the gang's relation to the community and the family parallels the conceptions of the early Chicago school.

> Relations with gang members tend to be intensely solidary and imperious. Relations with other groups tend to be indifferent, hostile or rebellious. Gang members are unusually resistant to the efforts of home, school and other agencies to regulate, not only their delinquent activities, but any activities carried on within the group, and to efforts to compete with the gang for the time and other resources of its members. It may be argued that the resistance of gang members to the authority of the home may not be a result of their membership in gangs but that membership in gangs, on the contrary, is a result of ineffective family supervision, the breakdown of parental authority and the hostility of the child toward the parents; in short, that the delinquent gang recruits members who have already achieved autonomy. Certainly a previous breakdown in family controls facilitates recruitment into delinquent gangs. But we are not speaking of the autonomy, the emancipation of *individuals*. It is not the individual delinquent but the gang that is autonomous. For many of our subcultural delinquents the claims of the home are very real and very compelling. The point is that the gang is a separate, distinct and often irresistible focus of attraction, loyalty, and solidarity.[18]

In summary, the delinquent subculture described by Cohen represents a collective effort on the part of the youths to resolve adjustment problems produced by dislocations in the larger society. In the gang the norms of the larger society are reversed so that nonutilitarian deviant behavior (especially violence) becomes a legitimized activity. The gang thus serves lower class boys as a legitimate opportunity structure for striking back at a larger society that produces their status-frustration problems.

---

[16]Reprinted with permission of The Macmillan Company from *Delinquent Boys* by Albert K. Cohen, p. 19. © The Free Press, a Corporation, 1955.

[17]Cohen, *Delinquent Boys*, p. 46.

[18]Cohen, *Delinquent Boys*, p. 31.

Delinquent Opportunity System

In their analysis of delinquency causation, Cloward and Ohlin "attempt to explore two questions: (1) Why do delinquent 'norms,' or rules of conduct, develop? (2) What are the conditions which account for the distinctive content of various systems of delinquent norms—such as those prescribing violence or theft or drug-use?"[19]

Cloward and Ohlin rely heavily on the concept of the delinquent subculture. In their view:

> A delinquent subculture is one in which certain forms of delinquent activity are essential requirements for the performance of the dominant roles supported by the subculture. It is the central position accorded to specifically delinquent activity that distinguishes the delinquent subculture from other deviant subcultures.[20]

They define three dominant kinds of delinquent subculture—the "criminal," the "conflict,' and the "retreatist." Cloward and Ohlin recognize that the extent to which the norms of the delinquent subculture control behavior will vary from one member to another. Their description of each subculture is therefore stated in terms of the fully doctrinated member rather than the average member:

> *The "criminal"*—devoted to theft, extortion, and other illegal means of securing an income; some of whose members may graduate into the ranks of organized or professional crime.
> *The "conflict"*—where the participation in acts of violence becomes an important means of securing status.
> *The "retreatist"*—the most enigmatic group, where the consumption of drugs is stressed, and addiction is prevalent.

Their central explanation for the emergence of delinquent subcultures is derived from the theories of Durkheim and Merton. Their basic view is "that pressures toward the formation of delinquent subcultures originate in marked discrepancies between culturally induced aspirations among lower class youth and the possibilities of achieving them by legitimate means."[21]

Cultural goals become an important aspect of Cloward and Ohlin's thesis. In describing two categories of need, physical and social, Durkheim makes the point that physical needs are satiable, whereas social gratification

---

[19]Reprinted with permission of The Macmillan Company from *Delinquency and Opportunity* by Richard A. Cloward and Lloyd E. Ohlin. © The Free Press, a Corporation, 1960.

[20]Cloward and Ohlin, *Delinquency and Opportunity,* p. 7.

[21]Cloward and Ohlin, *Delinquency and Opportunity,* p. 36.

is "an insatiable and bottomless abyss." Given this condition, Cloward and Ohlin state that when men's goals become unlimited, their actions can no longer be controlled by norms, and a state of normlessness or anomie exists.

Cloward and Ohlin turn to Merton's elaboration of Durkheim's basic postulate to account for the various patterns of deviant behavior. In Merton's view, anomie (normlessness) and the breakdown of social control emerge not because of insatiable goals alone but because of a lack of fit between the goals and the legitimate means for attaining them. As Merton specifies, "Aberrant behavior may be regarded sociologically as a symptom of dissociation between culturally prescribed aspirations and socially structured avenues of realizing these aspirations."[22]

Merton's formulation, according to Cloward and Ohlin, helps to explain the existence of a large proportion of law violators among lower class youths. Because they are denied equal access to normative social opportunity, they experience a greater pull toward deviance.

> The ideology of common success-goals and equal opportunity may become an empty myth for those who find themselves cut off from legitimate pathways upward. We may predict, then, that the pressure to engage in deviant behavior will be greatest in the lower levels of the society.
>
> Our hypothesis can be summarized as follows: The disparity between what lower class youth are led to want and what is actually available to them is the source of a major problem of adjustment. Adolescents who form delinquent subcultures, we suggest, have internalized an emphasis upon conventional goals. Faced with limitations on legitimate avenues of access to these goals, and unable to revise their aspirations downward, they experience intense frustrations; the exploration of nonconformist alternatives may be the result.[23]

Cloward and Ohlin view the gang as one of the "nonconformist alternatives" these boys may explore. Alienated youths band together in the collectivity of the gang in an effort to resolve their mutual problems. The same theme is used to explain the normative patterning of gangs: the conflict, criminal, and retreatist. A youth's selection of one type of subcultural adjustment over another is related to the degree of availability of these illegitimate "opportunity structures" in various sociocultural settings.

> We believe that the way in which these problems are resolved may depend upon the kind of support for one or another type of illegitimate activity that is given at different points in the social structure. If, in a

---

[22]Merton, *Social Theory and Social Structure,* p. 134.

[23]Cloward and Ohlin, *Delinquency and Opportunity,* p. 86.

given social location, illegal or criminal means are not readily available, then we should not expect a criminal subculture to develop among adolescents. By the same logic, we should expect the manipulation of violence to become a primary avenue to higher status only in areas where the means of violence are not denied to the young. To give a third example, drug addiction and participation in subcultures organized around the consumption of drugs presuppose that persons can secure access to drugs and knowledge about how to use them. In some parts of the social structure, this would be very difficult; in others, very easy. In short, there are marked differences from one part of the social structure to another in the types of illegitimate adaptation that are available to persons in search of solutions to problems of adjustment arising from the restricted availability of legitimate means. In this sense, then, we can think of individuals as being located in two opportunity structures—one legitimate, the other illegitimate. Given limited access to success-goals by legitimate means, the nature of the delinquent response that may result will vary according to the availability of various illegitimate means.[24]

Cloward and Ohlin tend to minimize the importance of individual personality factors and characteristics. "The social milieu affects the nature of the deviant response whatever the motivation and social position (i.e., age, sex, socioeconomic level) of the participants in the delinquent subculture."[25]

Criminal subcultures, according to Cloward and Ohlin, are most likely to occur in the somewhat stable slum neighborhoods that provide a hierarchy of criminal opportunity. In some conflict with Cohen's description of delinquency as "malicious, negativistic, and nonutilitarian," Cloward and Ohlin argue that for many youths in this type of neighborhood, the desire to move up in the neighborhood criminal hierarchy may cause them to overconform to delinquent values and behavior in order to show off their criminal ability. Such criminal overconformity, Cloward and Ohlin maintain, accounts for rash, nonutilitarian delinquent acts.

> The criminal subculture is likely to arise in a neighborhood milieu characterized by close bonds between different age-levels of offender, and between criminal and conventional elements. As a consequence of these integrative relationships, a new opportunity structure emerges which provides alternative avenues to success-goals. Hence the pressures generated by restrictions on legitimate access to success-goals are drained off. Social controls over the conduct of the young are effectively exercised,

---

[24]Cloward and Ohlin, *Delinquency and Crime,* pp. 151–52.
[25]Cloward and Ohlin, *Delinquency and Crime,* p. 160.

limiting expressive behavior and constraining the discontented to adopt instrumental, if criminalistic, styles of life.[26]

Conflict subcultures, according to Cloward and Ohlin, tend to arise in disorganized slums that provide no organized hierarchy for criminal development. These slums, with their high degree of disorganization and their orientation toward the present, offer both limited legitimate and illegitimate opportunity structures. The social disorganization of such slums contributes to the breakdown of social control.

> The young in such areas are also exposed to acute frustrations, arising from conditions in which access to success-goals is blocked by the absence of any institutionalized channels, legitimate or illegitimate. They are deprived not only of conventional opportunity but also of criminal routes to the "big money." In other words, precisely when frustrations are maximized, social controls are weakened. Social controls and channels to success-goals are generally related: where opportunities exist, patterns of control will be found; where opportunities are absent, patterns of social control are likely to be absent too. The association of these two features of social organization is a logical implication of our theory.[27]

The lack of opportunity in these areas causes such youths to seek it in other ways. "Adolescents turn to violence in search of status. Violence comes to be ascendant, in short, under conditions of relative detachment from all institutionalized systems of opportunity and social control."[28]

The retreatist subculture emerges, according to Cloward and Ohlin, as an adjustment pattern for those lower class youths who have failed to find a position in the criminal or conflict subculture and have also failed to use either legitimate or illegitimate opportunity structures. "Persons who experience this 'double failure' are likely to move into a retreatist pattern of behavior."[29]

Some youths who either drop out of other types of subcultures or find the conflict or criminal subculture no longer functional may also resort to the retreatist pattern. Cloward and Ohlin conclude that limitations on both legitimate and illegitimate opportunity structures produce intense pressures toward retreatist behavior. All three types of delinquent behavior are viewed by Cloward and Ohlin as adjustment patterns that utilize the most available opportunity structure provided by the anomic social system.

---

[26]Cloward and Ohlin, *Delinquency and Crime,* p. 171.

[27]Cloward and Ohlin, *Delinquency and Crime,* pp. 174–75.

[28]Cloward and Ohlin, *Delinquency and Crime,* p. 178.

[29]Cloward and Ohlin, *Delinquency and Crime,* p. 181.

Lower Class Culture and "Normal" Delinquency

Using cultural concepts in a somewhat different fashion, Walter Miller projects a lower class adolescent theory of gangs. He maintains (in a fashion somewhat similar to Cohen's position) that the values of lower class culture produce deviance because they are "naturally" in discord with middle class values. The youth who heavily conforms to lower class values is thus automatically delinquent. Miller lists a set of characteristics of lower class culture that tend to foster delinquent behavior. These include such focal concerns as trouble, toughness, "smartness" (ability to con), excitement (kicks).

According to Miller, gang activity is, in part, a striving to prove masculinity. Females are exploited by tough gang hoods in the "normal" process of relating. Girls are "conquest objects" utilized to prove and boost the masculinity of the street-corner male.

Miller further theorizes that the gap between levels of aspiration of lower class youths and their general ability to achieve produces distinct types of lower class categories, which reveal the degree of delinquency proneness of a youth:

1. *"Stable" lower class.* This group consists of youngsters who, for all practical purposes, do not aspire to higher status or who have no realistic possibility of achieving such aspiration.
2. *Aspiring but conflicted lower class.* This group represents those for whom family or other community influences have produced a desire to elevate their status, but who lack the necessary personal attributes or cultural "equipment" to make the grade, or for whom cultural pressures effectively inhibit aspirations.
3. *Successfully aspiring lower class.* This group, popularly assumed to be the most prevalent, includes those who have both the will and the capability to elevate their status. . . .[30]

Miller emphasizes the fact that lower class youths who are confronted with the largest gap between aspirations and possibilities for achievement are most delinquency prone. Such youths are apt to utilize heavily the normal range of lower class delinquent patterns in an effort to achieve prestige and status:

. . . toughness, physical prowess, skill, fearlessness, bravery, ability to con people, gaining money by wits, shrewdness, adroitness, smart repartee, seeking and finding thrills, risk, danger, freedom from external constraint, and freedom from superordinate authority. These are the explicit

---

[30]William C. Kvaraceus and Walter B. Miller, *Delinquent Behavior* (Washington, D.C.: National Education Association, 1959), vol. 1, *Culture and the Individual,* p. 72.

values of the most important and essential reference group of many delinquent youngsters. These are the things he respects and strives to attain. The lower class youngster who engages in a long and recurrent series of delinquent behaviors that are sanctioned by his peer group is acting so as to achieve prestige within his reference system.[31]

The Adolescent Striving for Manhood

Bloch and Niederhoffer, in a somewhat different interpretation, view delinquent behavior as a universal and normal adolescent striving for adult status. Their hypothesis is reached by the utilization of considerable cross-cultural material that attempts to reveal the differences and similarities of the adolescent condition in a variety of societies. Their basis position is presented in the following concise statement:

> The adolescent period in all cultures, visualized as a phase of striving for the attainment of adult status, produces experiences which are much the same for all youths, and certain common dynamisms for expressing reaction to such subjectively held experience. The intensity of the adolescent experience and the vehemence of external expression depend on a variety of factors, including the general societal attitudes toward adolescence, the duration of the adolescent period itself, and the degree to which the society tends to facilitate entrance into adulthood by virtue of institutionalized patterns, ceremonials, rites and rituals, and socially supported emotional and intellectual preparation. When a society does not make adequate preparation, formal or otherwise, for the induction of its adolescents to the adult status, equivalent forms of behavior arise spontaneously among adolescents themselves, reinforced by their own group structure, which seemingly provide the same psychological content and function as the more formalized rituals found in other societies. This the gang structure appears to do in American society, apparently satisfying deep-seated needs experienced by adolescents in all cultures. Such, very briefly, is our hypothesis.[32]

In their analysis they attempt to assess the effects of such cultural patterns as puberty rites, self-decoration, and circumcision on adolescent behavior. Gang behavior, with its symbolic evidence of the "urge for manhood," is seen as an American equivalent of the puberty rites of other cultures. The gang is thus viewed as a vehicle for accomplishing the assumed highly desired status of manhood.

---

[31]Kvaraceus and Miller, *Delinquent Behavior,* p. 69.

[32]Herbert A Bloch and Arthur Niederhoffer, *The Gang* (New York: Philosophical Library, 1958), p. 17.

According to Bloch and Niederhoffer, gang structure has a high degree of stability. In their criticism of those investigators who attribute characteristics of flux and "movement" to gang organization, they argue:

> Observations of gang behavior in various neighborhoods of New York City, for example, seem to reveal just the opposite to be true. In fact, one of the outstanding characteristics of numerous gangs which have been observed appears to be their highly non-mobile and stationary nature, a fact to which many exasperated shopkeepers and building custodians, as well as the police, can amply testify. Gangs, thus, might just as well be characterized by an absence of movement since, for the most part, they frequent the same corner or candy store for hours on end, every day of the week.[33]

Bloch and Niederhoffer strongly emphasize the highly controversial point that delinquency is a " characteristic of all adolescent groups" and that the organizational structures of all adolescent groups (delinquent or not) are similar:

> In respect to the type of organizational structure, there is little to distinguish, in one sense, between middle and lower class adolescent groups. Although middle class groups of teenagers are not as apt to have the formal, almost military, structure characteristic of certain lower class "war gangs" . . . they do have similar and well-defined informal patterns of leadership and control. Even here, however, the distinctions become blurred and, upon occasion, almost indistinguishable when one recalls the ceremonial designations and ritualistic roles performed by college functionaries.[34]

Using data about adolescents from such diverse groups as the Mundugumor of New Guinea, the Manus of the Admiralty Islands, the Kaffirs of South Africa, the Comanche and Plains Indians, and a tightly knit delinquent New York gang, Bloch and Niderhoffer attempt to draw the inference that the ganging process provides symbolic evidence of the urge to manhood. They conclude:

> 1. Adolescent gangs may be profitably studied by using as a frame of reference the theory of power.
> 2. The gang's attempt to gain status and power through the domination and manipulation of persons and events is a collective representation of the individual gang member's guiding fiction, which is "to prove

---

[33]Bloch and Niederhoffer, *The Gang,* pp. 6–7.
[34]Bloch and Niederhoffer, *The Gang,* p. 9.

he is a man." In passing it is worthy of note that Alfred Adler's system of psychology is "tailor made" for the analysis of the gang since it is principally concerned with the struggle for power and the "masculine protest."

3. The presence of the gang, real, constructive or symbolic, gives the individual member ego support and courage. He gains a psychological sense of power and manhood which he does not possess at all when he is on his own.

4. If single gangs can pose a threat to the peace and safety of the community—and they certainly do so—then the well-meaning efforts to organize several gangs into a confederation may be a very grave error. Without significant changes in behavior and values on the part of such gangs, this maneuver may only multiply to extremely dangerous proportions the looming menace which even now we find difficult to control.[35]

Labeling Theory

A person convicted of a crime is given the status of criminal. The term *criminal* may, therefore, be viewed as a stigmatizing label. Once given the stigmatizing label the individual may be subjected to isolation, segregation, degradation, incarceration, and chemical or psychological treatment. These things can happen to him if he is found guilty of a crime and labeled criminal *whether or not he actually committed the crime.* In a sense, we may view all of this punishment as the result of the labeling rather than of the behavior.

Becker, a leading exponent of labeling theory, put it this way:

Social groups create deviance by making the rules whose infraction consti-
tutes deviance, and by applying those rules to particular people and labeling them as outsiders. From this point of view, deviance is *not* a quality of the act the person commits, but rather a consequence of the application by others of rules and sanctions to an "offender." The deviant is one to whom that label has successfully been applied; deviant behavior is behavior that people so label.[36]

It is clear from the above that the labeling theorist does not consider criminality a property inherent in certain types of behavior, but rather a status conferred upon a person who is found to have engaged in the behavior.

Another implication of this theory is that the process of labeling is itself a critical determinant of the subsequent deviant or conforming career of the individual. For example, Tannenbaum says,

---

[35]Bloch and Niederhoffer, *The Gang,* p. 217.
[36]Howard S. Becker, *Outsiders* (New York: Free Press, 1963), p. 9.

The young delinquent becomes bad because he is defined as bad and because he is not believed if he is good. . . .

The person becomes the thing he is described as being. Nor does it seem to matter whether the valuation is made by those who would punish or those who would reform. . . . Their [police, courts, parents, etc.] very enthusiasm defeats their aim. The harder they work to reform the evil, the greater the evil grows under their hands.[37]

One of the institutions most often guilty of labeling juveniles is the school. The school is in a position to be the greatest influence upon the lives of juveniles—particularly toward career orientation. If the student is labeled negatively in the school, he will likely come to regard himself as inferior and unlikely to succeed at school or elsewhere. The student who is given failing grades seldom makes a comeback. He tends to view himself as a failure and drops out of school.

A third implication of this theoretical position is that one of the factors determining whether deviancy will be reduced, repeated, or even broadened to include a wider range of acts is the nature of the reactions of the group to the initial act.[38] The reactions may have several possible effects. On the one hand, if the reprimanding institution wisely and discreetly imposes firm sanctions on the individual and attempts to involve the individual in acceptable activities, the chances are good that the individual will conform to the acceptable ways of the society and will develop a good self-image. On the other hand, if the sanctions are harsh, degrading, public—particularly if the actor is forced to leave the acceptable mainstream of society—chances of future deviancy may be heightened. It is possible that institutions contribute highly to delinquency by reacting to misbehaving juveniles in such a way that they are pushed away, excluded, further alienated from more responsible persons and standards, rather than pulled back in and rescued. In other words, there seems to be a tendency to shut out rather than open up opportunities for a juvenile to become involved in a legitimate, acceptable, conforming-to-the-norm situation. The person labeled criminal is excluded even more.

Labeling theory raises serious questions about the advisability of recklessly stigmatizing people with labels like "criminal" and "delinquent" where the objective is principally to deter the behavior. When we attach the stigmatizing label we may actually contribute to an increase in the undesirable behavior by seriously handicapping the individual's efforts to secure employment, training, licenses, etc. Labeling theory does little to explain delinquent or criminal

---

[37]Frank Tannenbaum, *Crime and the Community* (New York: McGraw-Hill, 1951), p. 18.

[38]Albert K. Cohen, "The Sociology of the Deviant Act: Anomie Theory and Beyond," *American Sociological Review* 30 (February 1965):5–14. For the effect of sanctions, see John Delamater, "On the Nature of Deviance," *Social Forces* 46(June 1968):445–55.

behavior. It does a great deal, however, to emphasize the damage that can be done by attaching stigmatizing labels. The creation of the juvenile court and the introduction of specialized judicial detention and treatment services for children was intended to avoid giving them the stigmatizing label of criminal. Now that the term *juvenile delinquent* has become a stigmatizing label it may be time to reexamine the entire juvenile justice system.

All sorts of data acquired in the course of the delinquency and criminality-labeling process are now in computers. Niederhoffer points out that the arrest, which places the stigma of criminal on an individual, is the culmination of a systematic labeling process. The labeling process begins with suspicion with the suspect being known only to the police or some other investigatory agency. Eventually the courts certify the label of the defendant's criminality. The data is then computerized. The tremendous increase in the use of computers means that the label attached to a person as a result of his arrest and later on his conviction becomes a matter of permanent record available to law-enforcement agencies and others throughout the country. By 1971 there was hardly one of the hundred largest law-enforcement agencies without computer services. Stigmatizing data went to data banks of the Federal Bureau of Investigation and the National Crime Information Center. The availability of this data to persons who might misuse it constitutes a threat to our freedom and privacy. Regarding this, Niederhoffer has this to say:

> The other side of computer technology is that it constitutes a threat to democracy—to privacy and freedom to dissent. Inevitably computerized information systems will place everyone in America from the age of fourteen to seventy into the category of possible suspect. And there is no statute of limitations on tapes, disks, and memory banks; they can be held thirty, forty, and fifty years, or in perpetuity. Moreover, not only state and federal law enforcement agencies, but also the Pentagon, the Army, the Navy, and the Air Force, have gathered data on millions of citizens. They, too, are interested in "troublemakers." The C.I.A. and the State Department have their computerized card files. The Civil Service Commission has millions of names listed in its security files. And how many other governmental agencies are quietly amassing their own computer banks of data on "persons of interest"? In addition, the federal agencies intermesh with private agencies and organizations that collect information on credit risks, peace demonstrators, welfare recipients, radicals, liberals, intellectuals, and writers and speakers critical of the government's policies.
>
> It is disheartening to contemplate that every "person of interest" may now be shadowed from birth to grave by a web of computers. With computers as masters, we are a nation in which the citizens are under control and under suspicion. In fact, a campaign is under way to assign

a "universal identifier" code number to each person in America, so that any scrap of information collected anytime and anyplace can be easily assembled.[39]

The possibility of a future "Senator Joseph McCarthy" using stigmatizing data contained in computers is raised by Niederhoffer in the following terms:

> In a series of speeches in early 1950, McCarthy ominously waved a paper alleged to contain a list of 205 (then 81, and finally 57) Communists holding government positions. The source of the information was reputed to be files supplied by the State Department in testimony before the Tydings Committee in the Senate, McCarthy ranted:
>
>> *I am not making charges. I am giving the committee information of individuals who appear by all the rules of common sense as being very bad security risks.*
>
> Armed with a few incomplete dossiers, McCarthy terrorized the nation's leaders, demolished reputations, and devastated countless lives.
> What would happen today if someone like Senator McCarthy could produce, not a spurious piece of paper, but an awe-inspiring computer printout of thousands or perhaps millions of names of people singled out as security risks because they had taken part in a demonstration against the Vietnam War? What would result if he arbitrarily demanded that they be dismissed immediately from their jobs in government or universities? The computer and all its ramifications just discussed constitute an electronic straitjacket, constraining freedom of thought and restricting even politically neutral activity, let alone dissent.
> Furthermore, the typical victim of computer accusations is virtually helpless. He may never be able to pinpoint or prove the source of error in the computer record that damns him. And the very features of the computer that induce a paralysis of will in its victims generate in the minds of its masters a peculiar faith in its infallibility that nurtures bureaucratic arrogance.[40]

The following incident appears to justify Niederhoffer's fears:

> In October 1970 an assault charge against a defendant in a Washington, D.C. court was dropped by the prosecutor because the arrest was

---

[39]Arthur Niederhoffer, "Criminal Justice by Dossier: Law Enforcement, Labeling, and Liberty." in *Current Prospectives on Criminal Behavior,* ed. Abraham S. Blumberg (Alfred A. Knopf, 1974) pp. 47–67.

[40]Niederhoffer, "Criminal Justice by Dossier," p. 60.

obviously an error. Soon after, at the request of the defendant, the Washington, D.C., police department destroyed the arrest records, the mug shots, and the fingerprints. However, in accordance with standard operating procedure, it had already forwarded copies of the records and the fingerprints to the central office of the F. B. I. Following its usual procedures, the the F. B. I. refused outright to invalidate or destroy this criminal history, although the case was unfounded.[41]

Conflict Theory of Criminal Behavior

The explanation of criminality as a form of deviant behavior must deal with at least two problems:

1. The process by which individuals come to commit acts that are defined by society as crimes.

2. The kinds of groups and areas that produce certain kinds of criminality.

Those criminologists who seek to explain why certain behavior is defined as criminal tend toward a conflict theory explanation. What becomes defined as a crime is related to the power of some groups in the society to include in the criminal law their values and interests. The same power strucure, or one closely related to it, by its enforcement of the law imposes a variation of the same values and interests.

This point of view leads to the conclusion that the passage of virtually all criminal laws, the policies of nearly all law-enforcement agencies, and the operation of the criminal justice system is in some way influenced by political pressures of competing interest groups. Economic interest groups exercise a predominant influence on the governmental system, including the legislative, enforcement, and criminal justice systems.

Culture Conflict and Crime

The criminal law is a body of rules or norms of conduct that prohibit specific forms of conduct and provide for punishment for them. The type of conduct prohibited often depends upon the character and interests of the groups that influence legislation.[42] Everyone is required to obey the rules set forth by the state, as described in the penal code. Some people, however, belong to groups that have sets of rules or norms of conduct different from those required by the overall society's criminal law. Culture conflict arises when an individual is committed to rules that are contrary to those of the overall

---

[41]Niederhoffer, "Criminal Justice by Dossier," p. 63.

[42]Thorsten Sellin, *Culture Conflict and Crime* (New York: Social Science Research Council, 1938), p. 21.

society. Whether behavior is criminal or noncriminal depends upon which conduct norms are applied.

Culture conflict is a common experience among immigrants to the United States. They come with many customs and traditions that are not acceptable in this country. Prior to World War II, when American influence was less pervasive than it is now, the problem was even more acute. Consider the Oriental tradition of "family honor." Under this system, if a woman committed adultery, it was the duty of either her elder brother or her father to kill her. This was not something that he *might* do; he was *obligated* to do it. If a man were to kill his daughter for that or for any other reason in this country, he would be convicted of murder.

There are still many conduct norms of foreign countries that clash with those found in the United States and lead immigrants into trouble with the law. When culture conflict arises in this way, it is referred to as primary culture conflict.[43]

Another type of culture conflict arises when people are committed to a subculture within the country that differs in some respects from the norms of the overall society. This sort of conflict is experienced by a person migrating from a rural area to an urban center—the Puerto Rican migrating from the island to New York City or a Negro family moving from the rural south to the urban north.[44] When culture conflict arises as a result of conflicting conduct norms within the society, it is referred to as secondary culture conflict. The overall society has defined the "right ways" of doing things, and the subculture has defined other "right ways" of doing things. "The hallmark of the delinquent subculture is the explicit and wholesale repudiation of middle class standards and the adoption of their very antithesis."[45]

Whether we regard the delinquent subculture as a repudiation of middle class standards or simply a way of conforming to lower class standards, it contains rules of behavior at variance from those of the overall culture of our society, and often leads to behavior that is legally viewed as delinquent.

Group Conflict Theory as Explanation of Crime

In developing a group conflict theory, Vold began with assumptions long established in sociology: first, that man is always involved in groups and, second, that action within groups and between groups is influenced by opposing individual and group interests. Society is a collection of such groups in equilibrium; that is, opposing group interests are in some way balanced or reconciled. There is a continuous struggle within and between groups to im-

---

[43]Sellin, *Culture Conflict and Crime,* p. 6.

[44]Sellin, *Culture Conflict and Crime,* p. 70.

[45]Cohen, *Delinquent Boys,* p. 3.

prove relative status. Groups come into conflict when the interests and purposes they serve tend to overlap and become competitive. As conflict between groups intensifies, loyalties to groups intensify. The outcome of group conflict is either victory for one side and defeat for the other or some form of compromise. Politics is primarily a way of finding practical compromises between antagonistic groups.[46] In a democracy, a struggle between conflicting groups often culminates in legislation translating compromise into law. Those who produce legislative majorities dominate policies that decide who is likely to be involved in violation of the law. Crime, then, may be seen as minority group behavior.[47] Some of those whose actions have become illegal as a result of legislation violate the law as individuals. Many of those who belong to groups that oppose the law react as a group—a conflict group. The juvenile gang, in this sense, would be an example of a "minority group" in opposition to the rules of the dominant "majority."

In a group-centered conflict, "criminal" behavior occurs when action is based on the principle that *"the end justifies the means"* and *the end object is the maintenance of the group position.*[48] This principle is the rationalization offered to justify the actions of a juvenile gang, of organized crime running gambling operations, of the white collar criminals who fixed prices in the steel and electric conspiracies, and of the people involved in Watergate. Whenever there is genuine conflict between groups and interpretations, correctness is decided by the exercise of power and/or persuasion.

Richard Quinney has developed a comprehensive group conflict theory which he calls the *social reality of crime.* As he sees it, the legal order gives reality to the crime problem in the United States.

The theory of the social reality of crime, as formulated, contains six propositions and a number of statements within each. These may be summarized as follows:[49]

1. The Official Definition of Crime: *Crime as a legal definition of human conduct is created by agents of the dominant class in a politically organized society.*

Crime, as *officially* determined, is a *definition* of behavior that is conferred on some people by those in power. Legislators, police, prosecutors, judges, and other agents of the law are responsible for formulating and administering criminal law. Upon *formulation* and *application* of these definitions

---

[46]George B. Vold, "Group Conflict Theory as Explanation of Crime," in *Deviance, Conflict and Criminality,* ed. R. Serge Denisoff and Charles H. McCaghy (Chicago: Rand McNally, 1973), pp. 77–88.

[47]Vold, "Group Conflict Theory as Explanation of Crime," p. 81.

[48]Vold, "Group Conflict Theory as Explanation of Crime," p. 84.

[49]This revised version of the theory is contained in: Richard Quinney, *Criminology* (Boston: Little Brown & Co., 1975) pp. 37–41.

of crime, persons and behaviors become criminal. The greater the number of definitions of crime that are formulated and applied, the greater the amount of crime.

2. Formulating Definitions of Crime: *Definitions of crime are composed of behaviors that conflict with the interests of the dominant class.*

Definitions of crime are formulated, and ultimately incorporated into the criminal law, according to the interests of those who have the power to translate their interests into public policy. The definitions of crime change as the interests of the dominant class change. From the initial definitions of crime to the subsequent procedures, correctional and penal programs, and policies for controlling and preventing crime, those who have the power regulate the behavior of those without power.

3. Applying Definitions of Crime: *Definitions of crime are applied by the class that has the power to shape the enforcement and administration of criminal law.*

The dominant interests intervene in all the stages at which definitions of crime are created and also operate where the definitions of crime reach the *application* stage. Those whose interests conflict with the ones represented in the law must either change their behavior or possibly find it defined as criminal. Law-enforcement efforts and judicial activity are likely to increase when the interests of the dominant class are threatened. The criminal law is not applied directly by those in power; its enforcement and administration are delegated to authorized *legal agents.* As legal agents evaluate more behaviors and persons as worthy of being defined as crime, the probability that definitions of crime will be applied grows.

4. How Behavior Patterns Develop in Relation to Definitions of Crime: *Behavior patterns are structured in relation to definitions of crime, and within this context people engage in actions that have relative probabilities of being defined as criminal.*

The probability that persons will develop action patterns with a high potential for being defined as criminal depends on structured opportunities, learning experiences, interpersonal associations and identifications, and self-conceptions. Personal action patterns develop among those defined as criminal because they are so defined. Those who have been defined as criminal begin to conceive of themselves as criminal, adjust to the definitions imposed upon them, and learn to play the criminal role.

5. Constructing an Ideology of Crime: *An ideology of crime is constructed and diffused by the dominant class to secure its hegemony.*

An ideology which includes ideas about the nature of crime, the relevance of crime, offenders' characteristics, appropriate reactions to crime, and the relation of crime to the social order is diffused throughout the society in personal and mass communication. The President's Commission on Law Enforcement and Administration of Justice is the best contemporary example of the state's role in shaping an ideology of crime. Official policy on crime has been established in a crime bill, the Omnibus Crime Control and Safe Streets Act of 1968. This bill, a reaction to the growing fears of class conflict in American society, creates an image of a severe crime problem and, in so doing, threatens to negate some of our basic constitutional guarantees in the name of controlling crime. The conceptions that are most critical in actually formulating and applying the definitions of crime are those held by the dominant class. These conceptions are certain to be incorporated into the social reality of crime.

6. Constructing the Social Reality of Crime: *The social reality of crime is constructed by the formulation and application of definitions of crime, the development of behavior patterns in relation to these definitions, and the construction of an ideology of crime.*

Application of Theory to an Understanding of Crime and Criminality

An examination of the theories discussed in this and the preceding chapter clearly indicates that some theories contribute more than others to an understanding of particular types of crime and criminals. Psychoanalytic theory, reinforcement theory, and containment theory all contribute to an understanding of the drug addict, the sex offender, the violent offender, the sociopath, and the juvenile delinquent.

The activities of the career criminal, the professional criminal, the white collar criminal, and the trust violator may best be explained by such theories as differential association, anomie (Durkehim and Merton), social alienation, and reference group theory. The high incidence of such crimes in the United States may best be explained by such theories as modern positivism, the cultural dimension (Taft), economic determinism, social disorganization, culture conflict, and group conflict theories.

Such theoretical formulations as differential association, reference group theory, the subculture of delinquency (Cohen), the adolescent striving for manhood (Bloch and Niederhoffer), delinquency and opportunity (Cloward and Ohlin), and lower class culture (Miller and Kvaraceus) all contribute to an understanding of the normal delinquent.

Political crime is best explained by group conflict theorists. The social reality of crime (Quinney), by emphasizing the role of the power segment in influencing the content of the criminal law, law-enforcement policies, and the action of law-enforcement personnel, contributes a great deal to an understanding of political crime and the reaction to it. Social alienation theory (Jeffery) also contributes to an understanding of political crime.

Quinney's theory also goes a long way toward explaining the feeble reaction to organized crime and white collar crime. The important people in organized crime and white collar crime make large contributions to candidates of both major parties, and are able to influence legislation and law enforcement. The businessmen involved in white collar crime, in particular, are economically, socially, and politically so closely related to the power segment as to be virtually immune from prosecution and entirely immune from serious legal sanctions.

Part Four

TREATMENT
AND
CONTROL
OF
DELINQUENCY

ACCORDING TO DURKHEIM, crime is an inevitable consequence of social complexity and individual freedom. It is one of the prices paid for freedom. After noting that nothing is good indefinitely, he said, "To make progress, individual originality must be able to express itself. In order that the originality of the idealist whose dreams transcend his century may find expression, it is necessary that the originality of the criminal ... shall also be possible. One does not occur without the other."[1]

This does not mean that criminal or delinquent behavior should be condoned, but it does imply that if people were to be controlled to such an extent that no crime could exist, serious negative consequences would result for the whole society. We would be living in a police state in which Big Brother watched over every act. A society in which all people are compelled to conform to all the legal norms not only substantially reduces individual freedom but also tends to inhibit desirable social change.

Nevertheless, a society in which rules of behavior considered important by most of its members may be violated with impunity by some of them would be riven by serious cleavages. The failure of the political structure to inhibit

[1]Emile Durkheim, *The Rules of Sociological Method,* trans. Sarah A. Solvag and John H. Mueller (Glencoe, Ill.: Free Press, 1950), p. 71.

423

behavior regarded as undesirable by most people through the enactment and enforcement of laws could result in violent reaction on the part of the majority. Those strongly supporting such norms could become extremely hostile to those violating them and forcefully repress them. Kangaroo courts and arbitrary "order" might very well replace a legal system that protects the rights of the weak as well as the strong. The vigilante and posse would then replace the more civilized governmental enforcement agent.

For these reasons and others, all societies have institutionalized systems for responding to and attempting to control crime and delinquency. In Western societies these traditionally include the police, courts, custodial institutions, and various methods of supervising and treating offenders in the community (e.g., probation and parole). The avowed basic objective of most of these organized responses to crime and delinquency is the prevention of crime and delinquency and the ultimate resocialization of offenders. In the following six chapters we shall describe some of the ways in which the American society attempts to achieve these objectives by means of a correctional system.[2]

When a juvenile has been found to be delinquent and is turned over to a correctional system, society has decided that his behavior will be closely supervised for a period of time; that he is to be deprived of some or all of his liberty for a period of time; that some change in his values, attitudes, and behavior is desirable; and that this experience with the correctional system will result in less likelihood of his violating the law. Thus we see that the correctional system has been assigned four basic functions: (1) the protective, (2) the punitive, (3) the reformative, and (4) the rehabilitative.

The correctional system is charged with protecting society from the actions of those people whose behavior or potential behavior is believed to be dangerous to the persons or property of others. We do not screen our population in order to isolate such persons for treatment. Rather, many delinquents are confined in correctional institutions for long periods on the assumption that they are a menace to society when at liberty. The custodial institution, at least temporarily, serves the function of incapacitating the offender.

What is not generally recognized is that any form of supervision in the community also can perform a protective function. Probation or parole supervision helps to protect society by setting limits on the activity of an individual and by discouraging behavior that may be dangerous to the persons or property of others. To be sure, a person cannot be as strictly supervised in the

---

[2]As we have seen, the male offender comprises the basic crime problem in Western societies. Men in custodial institutions and in various correctional treatment programs outnumber women by a ratio of approximately fourteen to one. For these reasons this overall analysis will focus on the custodial impacts and conditions of the treatment of male offenders. For a comprehensive analysis of women's correction and treatment, see David A. Ward and Gene G. Kassebaum, *Women's Prison* (Chicago: Aldine, 1965).

community as he can in prison. The question that must be raised with respect to each person sentenced is, How much supervision is necessary if society is to be adequately protected? A corollary question would be, How dangerous is this person? Obviously, we need greater protection from the potential attacks of an aggressive sociopath than we do from a "normal" individual who commits burglaries, larcenies, or other property offenses to support his immediate needs or even as a career. While probation or parole may not be as effective in protecting society from some delinquents, it may be far more effective than the state training school in performing a rehabilitative function (by getting the probationer or parolee a job, additional training, etc.).

With respect to juveniles, we tend to deny that punishment is a legitimate goal of the correctional system. The rationale for punishment, when it is accepted as a goal, is that it will deter the person punished as well as others who will abstain from undesirable behavior to avoid punishment. The correctional system for juveniles has as its official goal the reform and rehabilitation of children entrusted to it by juvenile courts.

In Chapter 13, we shall deal with institutions for delinquents. It is in these institutions that the protective function is most emphasized, and the punitive function most experienced. In Chapter 14, we shall deal with community treatment and prevention programs. It is in these programs that the rehabilitative and reformative functions are most emphasized, and protective and punitive functions least emphasized. In Chapter 15, we shall discuss probation and parole, the two actions of a correctional system that leave the greatest autonomy to the person serving the sentence of a court. In Chapter 16, we shall describe various treatment strategies employed in institutional and community settings. Finally, in Chapter 17, we shall present recommendations for the treatment and control of juvenile delinquency, recommendations we consider most relevant supplemented by our own.

Chapter

13

Institutions for Delinquents

INSTITUTIONS FOR JUVENILES, known as "training schools" or "reformatories" when originally established, were patterned after adult prisons. The major difference over the years has been an increased emphasis on occupational training and rehabilitation. Therapeutic services were introduced during the 1930s and 1940s, and these were expanded considerably in the 1960s. This analysis will focus on the therapeutically oriented institutions, as well as the training schools, for juveniles.

On June 30, 1973, there were 794 publicly operated juvenile detention and correctional facilities in the United States holding 45,694 juveniles. Table 13.1 lists the type of facility, number of each, and number of children housed in each. More than half of the total were held in training schools.

Juvenile institutions have many of the same problems as prisons for adults. The juvenile institution, however, places greater emphasis on rehabilitation, less on custody. They have have populations varying from twenty to three hundred children offering a diversity of educational, vocational, and therapeutic programs, including individual casework, group therapy, guided group interaction, role training, and milieu therapy. After leaving these institutions, children are usually assisted in their adjustment to the community by aftercare personnel of the institution or by social work agencies in the communities in which they reside.

Table 13.1

Type of Institution, Number of Each, and
Number of Children Held

Type of Institution	Number of Institutions	Number of Children
Training Schools	187	26,427
Ranches, Forestry Camps, and Farms	103	4,959
Halfway Houses	59	713
Group Homes	90	889
Detention Centers	319	10,782
Shelters	19	190
Reception and Diagnostic Centers	17	1,734
	794	45,694

SOURCE: Children's Bureau, U.S. Department of Health, Education, and Welfare, *Institutions Serving Delinquent Children: Guides and Goals* (Washington, D.C.: U.S. Government Printing Office, 1974),

Some states have established publicly supported treatment schools with programs similar to those believed to have been successful in schools operated by private agencies. Because of budgetary limitations, however, publicly supported treatment schools are generally less adequately staffed than those supported by private agencies.

The State Training School for Juvenile Delinquents

The state training school is the "total institution" for juveniles. The security is not as complete as in the adult prison, and rehabilitation programs are more prevalent. Nevertheless, the social system of the state training school is very similar to that of the prison. What is even more important is that the effect on juveniles placed in such institutions is also similar. In the following pages, we shall present the observations of three people who have experienced life in a training school. The first report is by Claude Brown, a young man who on three separate occasions was a resident at the New York State Training School in Warwick. Later in life he achieved considerable literary success for his book *Manchild in the Promised Land,* in which he describes many of these experiences. The second is a description of the same institution by a research who was working on a doctoral dissertation. The third is by Alan Breed, a former superintendent of the Preston School, a state training school in California, who is now head of the California Youth Authority.

Warwick School for Boys: A State Training School

The Warwick School for Boys, a Division for Youth facility of the state of New York, is a total institution for juveniles, serving boys from thirteen to fifteen years of age committed by juvenile courts in New York City and the southeastern portion of New York State. Boys sent to the institution spend from eleven to thirteen months at Warwick.

The Warwick School, situated in a suburban area of Warwick, includes 740 acres of landscaped countryside. Boys are housed in cottages, each with its own dining area. Total capacity is 260. There is a school on the grounds, which offers an academic program with emphasis on remedial reading and advanced reading to a basic skill level. Twenty-one teachers conduct ungraded classes under the direction of an educational director assisted by a vocational supervisor and an academic supervisor. The vocational education program includes courses in barbering, printing, carpentry, electrical work, and drafting. Boys, in addition to attending classes, work in the vocational program and perform housekeeping services in their cottages.

Recreational programs include intramural sports, films, recreational trips, and other sociocultural experiences. Recreational facilities include a baseball diamond, football field, and gymnasium, which includes a basketball court. The treatment program includes group counseling and individual casework provided by seven social workers under the supervision of a director of social services. The two full-time chaplains, one Catholic and one Protestant, offer family counseling. A psychologist conducts psychological testing and aptitude testing. Diagnostic and therapeutic services and staff training are provided by the five part-time psychiatrists. Medical and dental services are available at infirmary facilities on the grounds, and full-time nurses are on duty at the infirmary. Visiting by parents is encouraged; boys are permitted home visits on a regular basis, and can earn incentive visits.[1]

A Boy's View: Claude Brown

I came out of the reception center on a Friday afternoon. They put me in cottage C2. There were mostly Puerto Rican fellows in there, a few

---

[1] *A Division for Youth Facility: Warwick School for Boys* (Albany: New York State Division for Youth, 1973).

Negroes, and a sprinkling of white cats. The cottage parents were Puerto Rican. I remember it well.

When they were bringing us all up the walk of the cottage area, a lot of cats started bowing their heads and saying, "Bye, Brown," in a whisper, as if they thought I was going to my funeral or something. . . .

Warwick was a funny kind of place. It was a jail in disguise. The windows in the cottage and in most of the buildings were divided into very small sections, and they had steel dividers that were painted to look like wood. The panes between the dividers were only about six square inches, and the windows were usually down from the top and up from the bottom. It would look like a normal house to anybody from the outside. But if any of the cats had tried to push a window up more from the bottom or pull it down more from the top, they would have found out that it had slats on the side, long wooden slats that wouldn't allow the window to go up or down any more than a couple of inches farther.

It was a pretty place. They had people walking around looking like they were free, but you had to have a pass to go anywhere and if you were gone too long, they had somebody out looking for you. They had what they called "area men," and the area men were like detectives up at Warwick. Anytime something happened—if something had been stolen or if someone had gotten stabbed—these were the cats who came around and investigated and found out who had done it. They were usually big cats, strong-arm boys. And they usually found out what it was they wanted to know.

The area men would come for you if you were gone from a place too long, and they would bring runners. Runners were like trusties. They would run after guys in the woods if they ran away, and they'd bring them back. The runners usually came from cottage A4 or one in the D group, where most of the big cats were. A4 was a crazy cottage. They had the nuts in there; they had the rapists, murderers, and perverts in there. These were the most brutal cats up there, and everybody knew it. A lot of times when people ran away, if they saw these cats behind them they would stop, because they knew they didn't have much chance of getting away. And if they gave the A4 guys a hard time, they'd catch hell when they were caught.

To someone passing by, Warwick looked just like a boys' camp. *But everybody was under guard, all the time,* and everybody had a job to do. You worked in the bakery or in an office or on the work gangs, and so on. Work gangs were a lot like chain gangs, minus the chains. In the summer, work gangs just busted rock and threw sledgehammers and picked onions and stuff like that. In the winter, the work gangs shoveled coal and shoveled snow. If you were a decent guy or if you could be trusted, you could get a job in one of the offices or in one of the buildings. That where most of the younger guys worked if they weren't hell raisers.

Most of the older guys were runners. They'd take people back from offices, take them around whenever they had to to go see their sponsors or social workers. That sort of business. Everybody had a place to fit into, so it seemed. . . .

One of the first guys I met up at Warwick was a guy I'd read about in the paper. Just about everybody had read about him, I suppose. He had been blamed for shooting somebody in the Polo Grounds in the summer of 1950. It was a jive tip, but there were a whole lot of cats up there on humbles. He was a damn nice guy, but they had him in A4, the crazy cottage. Just about all the guys under sixteen who were up there for murder were in A4.

This guy was on Mrs. Washington's gang with me, and he was telling me one day how they sent him up there on a humble. He said when this guy had gotten shot in the Polo Grounds, they started looking in all the houses on Edgecombe Avenue, and that's where he lived. They started looking for guns and stuff. They had a house-to-house search for guns. And they found a .22 rifle in his house. The man had been shot with a .45, but they blamed it on him.

He turned out to be a real nice cat. It was a funny thing, but all the cats I met up there and all the cats I knew on the streets who had been accused of murder or who had actually killed somebody always seemed to be the nicest cats. . . .

There were a lot of real hip young criminals at Warwick. It wasn't like Wiltwyck. For one thing, Wiltwyck only had about a hundred guys, and Warwick had five hundred. And Warwick had guys from all over New York City. They had cats from Brooklyn, the Bronx, Manhattan, Queens, and Richmond—everywhere. There were even cats from small towns upstate and from suburban areas of New York City. And Warwick had real criminals. Nobody at Wiltwyck was there for murder, and they didn't have any cats up there who knew how to steal a car without the keys. But it seemed like just about everybody at Warwick not only knew how to pick locks but knew how to cross wires in cars and get them started without keys. Just about everybody knew how to pick pockets and roll reefers, and a lot of cats knew how to cut drugs. They knew how much sugar to put with heroin to make a cap or a bag. There was so much to learn.

You learned something new from everybody you met. It seemed like just about all the Puerto Rican guys were up there for using drugs. They had a lot of colored cats up there for using drugs, but most of them were jive. Most of these guys were just using drugs to be down and to have a rep as a junkie. You could tell that these cats were jive by the way they went around saying, "Yeah, man, do you shoot stuff?" and all this sort of nonsense, as though they were bragging about it. They would start talking about how much stuff they used a day. I'd look at them and say, "Yeah, like, that's real nice," but they could never make me feel bad or anything, because all I had to do was say my name was Claude Brown. I didn't have to use drugs. I already had a reputation. I'd been other places. I knew people from here, I knew people from there.

Cats had heard about me when I was in Brooklyn gang fighting with K. B. and the Robins. And when I got shot, it was something that everybody seemed to respect me for. I'd only gotten shot with a .32, but the word was out that I'd gotten shot in the stomach with a .38. Cats didn't believe it. They'd come up to me and say, "Man, did you really git shot wit a .38?" and I'd either joke it off or act like they were being silly. I'd say, "Shit, people have gotten shot with .45's, so what?" They would go away marveling.

When we were in the dormitory getting ready to take a shower, the cool guys would say, "Hey, Brown, could I see your scar?" or they would just say, "Man, is that your scar?" I'd say, "Yeah, that's it." If they were hip cats, they might just say something like, "Yeah, man, those bullets can really fuck you up." And I'd say something like, "Yeah, but you can keep gittin' up behind 'em."

Cats used to come up and offer me ins or reefers or horse or anything I wanted. I had two or three flunkies after I'd been there for a month. It was no sweat for me; I was ready to stay there for a long time and live real good. I knew how to get along there. I'd had a place waiting for me long before I came. If I'd known that Warwick was going to be as good as it turned out to be, I would never have been so afraid. As a matter of fact, I might have gotten there a whole lot sooner.

At Warwick, it all depended on you when you went home for a visit. The first time, you had to stay there twelve weeks before you could go home. After that, you could go home for a three-day visit, from Friday to Monday, every eight weeks. That's if you didn't lose any days for fucking up or fighting. This was pretty good, because some people were always going home, and they would see your fellows and bring messages back, and your fellows were always coming up every Friday. A new batch of guys would come up and drugs would come up. When you came back from a weekend home visit, you were searched everywhere. They'd even search in the crack of your ass. You had to go to the doctor and let him look for a dose of clap. But cats would always manage to bring back at least a cap of horse or least one reefer. Everybody could always manage to smuggle in a little bit of something. . . .

We all came out of Warwick better criminals. Other guys were better for the things that I could teach them, and I was better for the things that they could teach me. Before I went to Warwick, I used to be real slow at rolling reefers and at dummying reefers, but when I came back from Warwick, I was a real pro at that, and I knew how to boost weak pot with embalming fluid. I even knew how to cut drugs, I had it told to me so many times, I learned a lot of things at Warwick. The good thing about Warwick was that when you went home on visits, you could do stuff, go back up to Warwick, and kind of hide out. If the cops were looking for you in the city, you'd be at Warwick....

After about eight months at Warwick, they told me that I'd be going home in about a month. When K. B. heard about it, he panicked. He said, "I want to go home too, man. These people better let me outta here."

"Look, K. B., I been tellin' you ever since I came here, if you want to git outta this place, you got to stop fuckin' up. It's, like, you gotta stop all that beboppin' and you gotta stop all that fuckin' up with the area men, like, just goin' around tryin' to be bad. You can do that shit with the cats around here, but if you start screamin' on the area men like that, you can't possibly win, man. Because these are the cats who can keep you up here all your life if they want to."

"Look, Claude, you don't understand. I'm from Brooklyn. There's a whole lotta stuff goin' on up here that I can't stay out of. You know, like, when my fellas, the Robins or the Stompers, go to war, it's, like, I've got to git into it too, because cats gon be lookin' for me to kick my ass or stab me or some kinda shit like that even if I don't come right out and declare war, because they know, like, I'm in this clique, man. Just about everybody who comes up here from Brooklyn, they know who's in what gang."

I said, "Yeah, man, but that's not the main thing. The main thing is to stop screamin' on the area men. You can go and have your rumbles and shit if you want, but you know if you stab anybody and they find out about it, you're through. The only way you gon make it outta here is to cool it. Didn't I tell you I wasn't gon stay up here a year when I came? And now I'm walkin', right? So it must be somethin' to it."

K. B. said, "Yeah, Claude, it's, like, yeah, man; I should-a listened to you, 'cause I know you usually know what you're talkin' about. I'm gon change my whole way-a actin' up here. And I'm gon be gittin' outta here soon. I'm gon be gittin' outta here in about three months now, just you watch."

I left Warwick after staying up there for about nine months and three weeks. I came home and went to the High School of Commerce, down around Broadway and Sixty-fifth Street.

I didn't go for school too much. The cats there were really dressing, and I didn't have any money. The only way I could make some money was by not going to school. If I told Dad I needed about four or five pair of pants and some nice shirts, he would start talking all that nonsense again about, "I didn't have my first pair-a long pants till I was out workin'." That shit didn't make any sense, not to me. He had been living down on a farm, and this was New York City. People looked crazy going around in New York City with one pair of pants, but this was the way he saw it, and this was the way he talked. I think the nigger used to talk this nonsense because he didn't want to get up off any money to buy me some clothes. So I just said, "Fuck it, I'll buy my own."

The only way I could buy my own was by selling pot when I went to school. And I'd take some loaded craps down there, some bones, and I would beat the paddy boys out of all their money. They were the only ones who were dumb enough to shoot craps with bones.

After a while, I just got tired. I never went to any of the classes, and if I did go to one, I didn't know anything. I felt kind of dumb, so I stopped going there. The only time I went to school was when I wanted to make some money. I'd go there and stay a couple of hours. Maybe I'd take Turk with me. Turk would sell some pot, and I'd shoot some craps, and when we got enough money, we'd go uptown. . . .[2]

A Researcher's View

The Cottage Experience.   When the time came to go to an assigned cottage, fear and anxiety replaced boredom. Exaggerated stories and rumors stressed the importance of saying "Yes, sir," and "No, sir," to the officer. The boys had heard of beatings, and of forced homosexual experiences. Although the weaker boys were the most apprehensive, even some of the older and stronger ones showed some anxiety. The grapevine advised that getting along in the cottage meant fighting back, learning the slang, and adhering to the group standards.

The society that had already formed in the reception center was certain to be cruel because the frustrating conditions of the reception experience reinforced the former gang experience of many of these boys. By virtue of its physical power and cohesion, the hardened delinquent group set the standards, values, and patterns for the general body of inmates in the cottages. The inexperienced, that is, the nongangster delinquent, found it difficult to reconcile the formal demands of the administration with those of his companions. In their conversations with the observer a few of the more hardened delinquents identified some of their fellow inmates as nice boys who were out of place at Ralston [pseudonym for Warwick].

---

[2]Reprinted with permission of Macmillan Publishing Co., Inc. from *Manchild in the Promised Land* by Claude Brown. Copyright © Claude Brown, 1965. Emphasis added.

Boys were rated by their fellow inmates according to their ability to protect themselves and to resist homosexual advances. It was important to be shrewd in social situations to avoid being tricked or "jived." At the bottom of the role and status hierarchy was the scapegoat, generally a physically weak boy. Isolated, nicknamed, and the butt of group ridicule, the scapegoat served to integrate the inmate group who displaced their aggressions and tensions on him.

For a new boy, entering a cottage was somewhat like coming into a class after it has been in existence for several sessions. In an institution for delinquents this disadvatage is magnified many times. Each new boy is a threat to the group already in the cottage. It is important therefore that the group test the new recruits to identify and exclude the types it rejects, i.e., the weaklings and the possible stool pigeons. Physical and mental coercion of the deviant was permitted. If it failed, isolation and exploitation were the alternatives. In the process of "johning" a new boy, the victim was lured or tricked into breaking institutional rules.

The formation of cliques and the development of positive and negative attractions among inmates was facilitated by the group's recognition of social types. In addition to the "john" (fool) these included: (1) the punk (homosexual), (2) the bulldozer or husko (bully), (3) the wolf or fiend (the highly sexed boy who may or may not indulge in homosexual relations), (4) the top lap (sycophant), (5) the rat (informer), (6) the bug (abnormal), (7) the fluter (miser).

The prized personal attributes were group loyalty, fighting ability, generosity up to a certain point, skill in debates, and familiarity with the techniques and lore of the underworld. The principal means of achieving status was through competition in either physical or verbal conflicts.

The antisocial mores of the majority of the boys were peculiarly adapted to an institutional setting which stressed dominant and subordinate relations. In its very set-up the administration appeared to the boys as the common enemy. As a result, if a boy was cooperative with the administration and established a reputation for "ratting," he would be isolated from his cottage group. If he tried to establish a closer relationship with the administration for his own protection or to obtain an earlier release, he became a greater threat to the solidarity and welfare of the cottage group and his position was even more untenable.

Relations Between Staff and Inmates.   Since the inmate code described above underscored social distance between the boy and the staff, there was little possibility of developing rapport between the two. In their unceasing fight against staff domination the boys presented a united front. This front was the chief weapon against the boy who cultivated the good graces of the officers. Though the common denominator was conflict, the attitude toward the various representatives of authority in the institutional set-up differed. Usually the boys conformed because they had to; but such conformity obviously represented no real change in their value systems—the goal of institutional treatment.

Director. The director of Ralston, who was rarely seen by the boys, was seldom the butt of their hostility. His direct, hearty, sympathetic way of speaking gained him a measure of popularity. They were, however, suspicious of the "wheel horse" personnel with whom they had daily contact.

Clinic Personnel. The clinic personnel faced severe obstacles in attempting to help most of these boys. The widespread distrust of the clinic was engendered by the fact that its personnel constantly strove to effect a closer liaison with the individual boy than the inmate mores sanctioned. In consequence the boys tried to manipulate the caseworkers' professional objectives for their own ends.

The clinic personnel faced another obstacle—their relation with the resident staff. As nonresidents, the clinic staff was able to avoid close contacts with the problems, responsibilities, and vexations of institutional life. The nonresident staff member, looking in from the outside, found it easy to be critical. At the same time the institutional workers had less opportunity to mingle with the normal community, and were thus handicapped in replenishing their emotional reserves. The result was friction.

The boys' hostility toward the clinic staff extended to the sponsor, the clinical staff member assigned to help each boy with his problems. Sometimes the sponsor was regarded as a stool pigeon. The boys spoke of "jiving" him. Because they realized that the impression they created on the members of the clinic staff would affect not only their work assignment but their length of stay at Ralston, they tried to make as favorable a case for themselves as possible. Instead of openly resisting, they usually conformed at least superficially.

The records, at the time of the survey, were accessible to the boys who worked in the offices. They told the participant observer that they looked up what was said about them in the case folders. These contained all the information that the institution had about the boy and his family, the results of the diagnostic tests, and the comments and recommendations of the various department members. Some said that the sponsors did not hold their remarks in confidence, but relayed them to the cottage masters. Others said that the sponsors appeared disinterested and neglectful. According to one: "Sponsors are no damn good. All they do is make you talk to them and then they write it down and try to frame you. They are all old men and old fogies." The boys would have liked to have someone young who could understand them. Most of them felt that the recreation worker more nearly filled this bill than any other staff member. As a matter of fact, the director of the athletic program had the least trouble with the boys, possibly because he had more in common with them than most of the other staff members.

The boys resented most the women sponsors. "How," one boy said, "can a guy talk about sex or jerking off or anything like that? A guy resents being under a woman." This remark is important for the insight it should convey into the role of the female in the lower socioeconomic groups that predominate in institutional population. The boys said that they came to the initial meeting with their sponsors forewarned about what to do, e.g., how to cope with their foibles and how to manipulate these to their own advantage. Often a boy would attempt to play off the sponsor against the rest of the staff. . . .

Evaluation of the Ralston Program.   Unfortunately most of these boys return to the surroundings which fostered their precommitment activities. By virtue of their time at Ralston, their status and prestige among their friends and acquaintances is not diminished but enhanced. The Ralston experience, according to the observer, has chiefly been an introduction to the occupational risk of the professional criminal.

Subsequent discussion of the effect of such institutional treatment will reveal that this statement is not an exaggeration. The best that can be said for the small minority of boys who are able to survive the experience without contamination is that it has had little effect. For the majority of the boys who fall between these two extremes an experience like Ralston is likely to have exposed them to much harm. For most of them, release to the community represents a delicately shifting and precarious equilibrium, which may be easily upset by incidents in the crucial postinstitutional period. Chance remarks of relatives or friends, the attitudes of neighbors upon their return home, or any one of count-less fortuitous circumstances may help to decide an individual's fate when contrary predisposing forces seem to cancel each other out.

Cures at Ralston could be claimed only for the very small minority able to assimilate the "ethos" of the greater society through a particularly meaningful relationship with an individual officer. The majority of the boys experienced no change in their values or philosophical orientation. They learned only to accommodate by withdrawal through fantasy, which protected their personal will against boredom or invasion by the institution.

The boys with whom the observer talked were unanimous in expressing strong feelings of hate. They said they had not learned anything good. One boy who broke parole and was returned to Ralston expressed the sentiments of many others in saying: "This damn place is no good. Look at these hands, all chapped. That's the only thing you get out of the place. It's no good. All it teaches is things that the boys shouldn't know about. They don't know about punking but when they come up here, they learn. It doesn't teach you nothing." He continued by commenting on the language which the little boys picked up so quickly.

One boy said that when he got out he was going to rob and steal. Maybe this was just talk, but he certainly wasn't talking about being honest. Another boy who was not a confirmed delinquent expressed his opinion of Ralston as follows:

"Ralston does teach a fellow to be careful about getting into trouble with the law but this isn't because it tries to teach that. It's only because in most cases, they don't want to come back to this place, and will try their best to stay out of trouble. I don't like the many months that must be spent here because I think only a few months are necessary to make the average boy realize the error of his ways.

"Thus far, I haven't seen any training of boys to be good citizens as long as I've been here. If that's what the school is supposed to be for then the most important part of our education here is most sadly neglected. So far, I haven't seen any part of the day set aside for training in any such thing as citizenship. It seems to me that most of this time is taken up to make a boy more respectful to the superiors at Ralston.

"Most of the boys think it's punishment to be here, and hardly any of them think of it as a training school. Some of the boys think that all they had to do is spend time for doing something wrong and getting into trouble with the police. Most of them resent the whole thing.

"My idea is that they don't try to send a boy home early here. They try to judge a boy by the way he acts up here, but the boy will act differently when he returns to the city. Some guys resent being here and act bad up here, but when they get back to the city, they act differently altogether. From my experience, this place don't seem to help the boys. Maybe a boy has been good while he is at home and comes up here for some minor reason and mixes with other boys who know all the different kinds of rackets in and out and learns new tricks. When he gets out, he may become ambitious and try some of those new tricks he's learned. Usually the result is that he ends up in a place just like this or worse after a small amount of time. The only thing to do is give the boys a better chance and give the ones who didn't do much wrong a better kind of place, if they must be sent away. . . . I don't think this place is worth the money; perhaps they could make it worthwhile if they do a little weeding out of some of the boys and some of the officers. Right now, it certainly teaches one thing. It teaches you not to get caught."[3]

---

[3]From *Juvenile Delinquency* By Sophia M. Robison, pp. 380–94. Copyright 1960 by Holt, Rinehart and Winston, Inc. Reprinted by permission of Holt, Rinehart and Winston, Inc.

A Superintendent's View

... Whether the age group be that of the Fricot Ranch School, or the other end of our training school continuum—Preston, Youth Training School—the same basic structure and method of operation exists. At Fricot the informal social organization of the boys is at a somewhat primitive level, but the basic structure which later crystalizes into a rigid pattern at Preston is already recognizable. There is one other difference at Fricot, also brought about by the extreme youth of the wards, and that is the almost total lack of any ethnic subgroupings. One can only wish that this refusal to judge one another on the basis of race or religion on the part of the Fricot boys could be a continuing pattern of their social structure. Unfortunately, they are soon contaminated by their elders during postinstitutional experiences and the results are already recognizable at the Nelles and Paso Robles age groupings.

In reviewing the literature covering the subject of inmate social organizations, I was impressed with the similarity of structure in institutions across the nation. Only the names—titles and other colloquialisms —vary whether we are talking about gangs, groups, cliques, firms, families, associations, crowd, straights, chipmunks, angels, devils, bloods, or the infamous LaRaza, we mean only one thing—an inmate social body organized for some purpose.

Each institution group has a hierarchy power structure which has five distinct subgroupings. Although the names or titles will vary from one institution to another, the structure and role identity are very similar.

1. *Leader—El Presidente—Duke.* In most cases, this is just one person, easily identified, except with Mexican groups where the leadership is seldom known to nonmembers. Under certain circumstances, a small clique of "strong boys" may operate in this capacity, but this condition will usually only arise for a short period of time after a leader has gone home, and a strong replacement is not readily available. The method by which a leader is selected or appointed varies greatly from one institution to another, but the qualifications for leadership appear to be quite similar. He will possess qualities inherent in all leaders—sensitivity to the group, magnetic personality, ease of verbalization, creativity, and he is generally daring. Although he will be able to fight well, the leader is able to use the power of the majority to force his will, rather than the strength of his own body. His position can be maintained only as long as he is able to manipulate the group to support him.

2. *Lieutenants—Vice Presidents—Tough Boys.* Normally, operating directly under the leader, this group will be the most influential social body within a living unit or institutionwide organization. It is the policy-

formulating, action-taking group, and from its ranks comes the new leader when the old one goes home. They are usually the strongest, toughest, and most verbal boys.

3. *Straights—Conformists.* These are the youngsters who stay quietly in the background, not attempting to act tough, but avoiding contact with lower status boys. Frequently, they are institutionalized boys who have learned to fade into the setting by keeping their emotional distance and cooperating with those on top.

4. *Mess-ups.* Youngsters falling into this group display childish behavior and constantly fight and argue among themselves. They feel that they get blamed for everything and are in constant conflict with staff. Within this general group you will find the "finks," or talebearers, who are not to be trusted and are thoroughly disliked. The "kissy" ingratiates himself with staff and is despised because of this by the group. The "mess-up" is scorned because his inappropriate behavior often brings about group punishment and because he arouses in the group feelings which must be repressed or denied.

5. *Scapegoats—Punks—Stone-outs.* They are at the bottom of the pecking order and are exploited by all above them. New boys fall into this category unless they have unusual physical strength, courage, or intelligence. Besides new boys, one will also find in this group the mental defectives, personality disorder cases that become too obnoxious or unpredictable to be accepted, homosexuals, boys who are being punished by their peer group for serious infractions of the code, and boys who are "chicken" and unwilling to fight or accept a challenge. Movement upwards from one subgrouping to another is generally determined by the leadership clique and is dependent upon an individual's success in fighting someone in a group higher in the social structure—willingness to cooperate over a period of time with the power hierarchy—or the more gradual process of upward mobility that comes during long institutional stays and the corresponding graduation of upper group members. The ultimate position one holds in the social structure, however, is always dependent upon the placement granted by the power clique.

The power accruing to the leader, or the strong clique, comes about most commonly and obviously through the use of physical aggression, a technique which occurs with greater frequency than most institution administrators are willing to admit.[4]

The participant-observers of the inmate culture in state training schools that we have quoted, although they viewed the institutions from entirely different levels, appear to agree that the power accruing to the leader or the

---

[4]Allen F. Breed, "Inmate Subcultures," *California Youth Authority Quarterly* 16(Spring 1963): 6–7.

strong clique in the institution comes about through the use of physical aggression. They also agree that the "tough" boys make up the most influential body in the institution and that institutionalized delinquents conform sufficiently to the norms set by the system so that they manage to get their own way.

In recent years intergang and interracial conflict has flared in juvenile reformatories. Some of these conflicts have been of such proportions as to be labeled "miniriots."

Juvenile Detention Camp: Anatomy of a Riot

Shortly before 11 P.M. May 2, the customary quiet of a walled camp in the San Dimas foothills was shattered by the sounds of boys screaming and glass breaking.

Youths rampaged through the camp's 94-bed open dorm, wielding table legs, forks, wooden stakes, ceramic ashtrays, belts, even beds, as weapons in a fever to do each other harm.

Some just ran—in fear for their lives.

In all, that night there were 80 youths—many of them street-sophisticated, muscular 17- and 18-year-olds described as "hard-core" by their probation officers—and five probation officers on duty in the dorm of the county-run maximum security camp for juvenile offenders.

After it was over and the sheriffs, the deputies, the ambulances, the doctors, the paramedics and the injured had gone, it was determined that 15 young wards of the county and the five probation officers had been injured in the melee.

Nine inmates had escaped. Today, three of them are still at large. . . .

"There are always racial overtones in a camp setting," according to one staff officer.

"The degree of racial overtones varies, depending on how hot the day is, how lax the staff is, and what they allow in terms of racial comments."

Question: "Was there any indication the blacks felt shortchanged at the camp?"

"Only after the situation (riot) had taken place," one black camp officer told an investigator. "After we started talking to the individuals, things came out."

Among the things that "came out" was the apparent existence of resentment among black inmates over the "privilege" extended Mexican-American inmates to hold La Raza meetings in camp.

There was nothing equivalent to La Raza for the blacks at Camp Rockey.

"There is no actual group or togetherness amongst the blacks as there is amongst the Chicanos," a white camp officer said. "Chicanos, when incarcerated or contained in institutions, have been known to band together."

"Even though they might be enemies in the community, when they come to camp, La Raza sticks together. They do their best to support one another and to hang together. Here at Camp Rockey the La Raza movement has been a positive one."

"Now the blacks have never, during the present camp programming, indicated a real desire to get together," he said. "They are much more fragmented and many are very much enemies with one another. . . ."

On the Saturday evening before the riot on Sunday, the camp's weight-lifting champion, a 5-foot-9, 185-pound, black 18-year-old, went out to the weight pit on the field to work out.

The pit was occupied by Chicano youths, holding a La Raza meeting.

The black left the field. The next morning at breakfast he punched two Mexican-Americans at a table that seats eight on each side. The punches followed an exchange of racial slurs.

On the witness stand in Juvenile Court, the black youth said he had "heard this Mexican-American at the end of the table say '(obscenity) niggers.' I said, 'Why you want to talk racial that way?' And then he said to '(obscenity) me.' "

Lawyer: "And what did you do then?"

"I said '(obscenity) all of you.' " After that, he was escorted out of the dining hall but reentered a few minutes later by another door.

"When I went by (a Chicano ward) he said, 'I'm gonna shank you'."

"What does that mean?"

"Cut me, stick me," he replied.

"What did you do then?"

"I hit him."

When that happened, "bedlam broke loose" in the dining hall, according to a probation officer who was there. The riot was yet to come that night. The breakfast disturbance was the prelude.

"Immediately all the wards stood up, picked up forks, spoons, started throwing pitchers of hot coffee, cups, trays," the officer said of the breakfast incident.

"The whole population of the dining hall polarized. The blacks came into one area, the Chicanos into another. I saw a young black standing up on a table swinging with both arms. The KPs came out of the kitchen. A lot of kids took off outside.

"They broke out, through the door, and, as it settled down, well it didn't settle down, but as it continued to develop, all the black kids went out of the dining hall and all the Chicanos stayed in.

"All the white kids—a few of them were kind of scattered around everywhere—most of them ran down to the administration building (for protection).

"The minority in Camp Rockey is the white youth so he didn't really know where to go."

Outside, "the black kids broke off some of the stakes holding up trees, they found pieces of pipe, pieces of chairs from the dining hall and they were trying to break windows and get into the dining hall. The Mexican-Americans were trying to get out. So a lot of windows were busted as a result."

It took "approximately two to four hours, I guess, before we finally got them all settled back down to where they could all actually be in the same building," he said.

A veteran of the rioting at Camp Rockey mused on the twofold nature of his role as a camp officer—part cop, part counselor.

"There's a difference if the staff member is acquainted with juveniles and knows how to work with juveniles ... to where you're not classed (by them) as a worker or 'the man,' " he said.

"We are the man as well as the friend of these guys. If he does something wrong, we're the ones that have to punish him, more or less. As well, we have to and try to show him a better way to do it.

"So when you have new staff members staffing a maximum security institution, I do not feel that it's fair to the other guys working here."

In the present open-door arrangement, the officers know the wards, know they [the boys] have the edge in numbers.

"In other words," another officer said, "it's a security camp, and it isn't secure at all. It's a very insecure situation as far as I'm concerned ... I've been in the county (employ) for seven years, and this is too much."

"In other words, you are pretty much at the mercy of the boys?" he was asked.

"Why, definitely, definitely. We've got nothing but the files, man. You know, we gotta play their game. They don't have to play our game.

"When the (trouble) comes down, we can't do anything about it. Just say 'No, don't do that, don't do this.' And if you give a man a zero you've got to write out a gram (report), have it approved by the supervisor and it's just not worth going through all the paper work. Administrators don't give a damn anyway, so why should we?"[5]

Conflicting Attitudes on Juvenile Treatment

A common problem in juvenile institutions is conflict and mutual hostility between treatment personnel and those concerned with custody and discipline. This problem of "parental value conflict" often emerges most sharply in an institution changing over from a "juvenile prison" emphasizing custody and discipline to a rehabilitation approach.

George H. Weber carried out a penetrating study that reveals the conflict that occurs in a training school where two divergent systems of resocialization exist.[6] He analyzed a state training school that was shifting from a generally custodial-punitive approach to a psychiatric-social work approach entailing diagnosis, group therapy, and individual attention. The institution housed 150 boys between the ages of twelve and sixteen in five cottages. The staff was composed of five social workers, two psychologists, one psychiatrist, and forty-six cottage parents.

Weber noted the following areas of organizational changes:

---

[5]Dorothy Townsend, "Juvenile Detention Camp: Anatomy of a Riot," *Los Angeles Times,* August 8, 1976. Copyright, 1976, *Los Angeles Times.* Reprinted by permission.

[6]George H. Weber, "Emotional and Defensive Reactions of Cottage Parents," in *The Prison,* ed. Donald R. Cressey (New York: Holt, Rinehart and Winston, 1961), pp. 189–228.

The approach generally shifted from tight control of behavior to permissiveness that allowed acting out. This pattern was more congenial to members of the treatment staff, as they considered it helped them to see the child "as he really was." Therapeutic or counseling functions were substantially removed from cottage parents and given to the regular therapeutic staff. Cottage parents were explicitly instructed not to attempt any counseling and to "make sure they did not interfere with the child treatment program."

Several noticeable effects resulted from these organizational changes:

1. A degree of disciplinary power was taken away from the cottage parents. Instead of controlling a boy through fear of punishment, the cottage parent was forced to establish a relationship based on friendship.

2. The cottage parents were given a subordinate and confusing role in the organization. Their frustrations and anger were often displaced onto the boys.

3. Often the boys would play one authority figure (the cottage parent) against another (the therapist).

After a time the institution began to move more smoothly and positively toward its rehabilitative goal. The research revealed, however, the inherent conflicts that exist between a custodial emphasis and a rehabilitative approach in the institutional treatment of juveniles.

New York's "Residential Treatment Centers"

New York State was one of the first to give financial support to private institutions for juveniles. Some six institutions established by private charitable organizations and operated under private auspices have been officially classified as "residential treatment centers" by the State of New York. The designation is made by the New York City Commission for the Foster Care of Children. Accreditation by this group leads to substantial financial benefits, and hence the evaluations are made with considerable care. The six institutions designated as residential treatment centers by the commission provide a combination of individual and milieu therapy based on a clinical study of each child.

A majority of the cases accepted by these institutions are referred by the children's court; others are referred by the New York City Department of Welfare, mental hospitals, child guidance clinics, social agencies, and private psychiatrists. Because of intake policies and limits of capacity, the number of referrals is four or five times the number actually accepted. All the children accepted in the institutions are considered to be emotionally disturbed and in need of psychotherapeutic treatment.

Before a child is accepted, the intake study must indicate that he is amenable to treatment by the facilities available at the institution. Children with IQs below 70 are not considered acceptable. The ratio of staff (including all types of service, treatment, custodial, and managerial) to inmates varies between one to one and four to five. Psychiatrists are available as consultants to the psychiatric social workers. Psychologists, in the main, administer tests. Social workers, in addition to providing individual casework and group therapy, are often assigned the task of coordinating all of the services. Each center has a school geared to the institutional approach. Insofar as practicable, the education of the child is coordinated with the activities of those directly involved in his therapy.

Most residential treatment centers of this type are located in country-side areas, a considerable distance from the cities from which virtually all of the inmates come. Although distances are not very great by modern stan-dards, transportation costs are prohibitive for most poor people. Contacts between children and their parents and relatives are therefore limited during the period of institutionalization. Contacts between staff members and the children and their families are likewise limited when the children are returned to their urban communities. Furthermore, the distances between the institu-tions and the family residences make it difficult for staff members to work with parents and institutionalized children in an effort to improve relationships between them. While no two residential treatment centers are identical, a description of one of them will serve to illustrate the ways in which these institutions function.

Wiltwyck School for Boys

Wiltwyck was established in 1937 by the New York Protestant Episcopal City Missions Society to house Negro Protestant boys. Boys between the ages of eight and twelve are referred to Wiltwyck by the children's court and the Welfare Department of New York City. It has become interracial and has a capacity of about one hundred boys. In 1958, according to reports sub-mitted to the city, there were seventy-seven Negroes, twenty-seven whites, and thirteen Puerto Ricans under the supervision of Wiltwyck, including the institution itself, its group home, and foster homes at which former residents were placed. There are a few boys fourteen years old or over at the institution.

The typical boy at Wiltwyck is considered to be suffering from serious emotional disturbance or maladjustment as a result of parental neglect or mistreatment. The intake committee rejects boys believed too psychotic or unmanageable to be fitted into the minimum-custody open setting of the institution. The average length of stay is about two years.

The boys are divided into eight "living groups" or cottage groups, with ten to fourteen boys in each. Two counselors live and work with each group, and there are four relief counselors. Counselors have complete responsibility for the boys except when they are assigned to an activity or treatment under the supervision of another staff member. In the past, "cottage parents," who lived in the cottages with the boys and were to fulfill the roles of father and mother, performed the duties now assigned to counselors. The change was made because it was believed that the counselors not only would provide guidance, leadership, and advice for the boys but also would serve as young male role models, believed necessary for fatherless children.

The philosophy of the institution is nonpunitive and permissive. Boys may freely express their feelings of antagonism and hostility but must bear the consequences of any misbehavior. "Consequences" may follow misbehavior, but they are not to be regarded as punishment. An effort is made to get the boy to distinguish between rejection of the misbehavior (harmful consequences follow) and rejection of himself. In this way the institution sets limits for the boy.

In addition to a therapeutic program, the institution provides indoor games, movies, television, arts and crafts, social dancing, hikes, camping, swimming, and other sports.

The professional treatment staff includes eleven caseworkers, two case-work supervisors, one assistant casework supervisor, three psychiatrists, a psychologist engaged in testing, two group therapists, an art therapist, a drama therapist, a dance therapist, and three remedial reading therapists. Every boy sees a caseworker every week or two. The same caseworker sees the parents of the boys under his charge at least once a month, in an effort to prepare the boy and his family for home visits and for the eventual return home.

The school facility at Wiltwyck is a "600" school (a school for problem children) of the City of New York. There are seven ungraded classes. Besides regular academic subjects such as reading, arithmetic, and social studies, there are classes in shopwork, including ceramics, metalwork, and mechanical drawing. The school places strong emphasis on achievement. There are ten teachers assigned to the school, seven of whom have been certified as competent to teach in a 600 school.

Aftercare services are provided for at least six months after the child is returned to the community. Children receive aftercare supervision whether they return to their own homes, go to a group home supported by the institution, or are placed in foster homes. The principal aftercare service is an interview by a social caseworker once or twice a month.

A study of sixty-five boys five years after they left Wiltwyck showed that 70.8 percent had made a good or reasonably good adjustment after release from the school; 43.2 percent had not had any court appearances; 27.6 percent had appeared in court for one of three reasons: a request to return to Wiltwyck, running away from home, or truancy; 29.2 percent were failures, having appeared in court on serious charges. A carefully controlled study comparing Wiltwyck with a New England training school whose program was based on strict discipline and formal education showed that Wiltwyck exceeded the training school in developing improved attitudes. The improved attitudes and the low percentage of recidivists were believed by the researchers to be the result of the Wiltwyck experience.[7]

Removing the child from the urban scene and placing him in a residential treatment center not readily accessible to his old habitat to some extent protects society from the offender's potential for delinquency. Because most residential treatment centers provide minimum security, many young people run away. They are then placed in state training schools or prisons when these steps are deemed necessary to control the child and protect society.

The Delinquent Subculture in a Residential Treatment Center

The Reckless study indicated that at least in the Boy's Industrial School at Lancaster, Ohio, there appeared to be limited conflict between the inmate system and the administration. In contrast to this finding, other evidence supports the view that even in a residential treatment center distinct delinquency-oriented subcultures develop within the overall social system. These subcultures often tend to be the primary reference groups of youths "doing time." The values and orientations of these institutional delinquent subcultures (like the inmate system of the adult prison) often sabotage the thrust of the treatment program.

Howard W. Polsky carried out several years of significant research into this issue in a cottage-type residential treatment center called Hawthorne-Cedar Knolls in New York.[8] Supported by the Jewish Board of Guardians, Hawthorne-Cedar Knolls School is essentially devoted to individual psychoanalytic treatment of emotionally disturbed delinquent children, as well as withdrawn, bizarrely acting, prepsychotic, and fragile children who are not able to live in the community. All treatment planning, implementation, and evaluation are done through four unit treatment teams, each under the guidance of a unit adminstrator. These units include:

1. *Girls' unit,* comprised of forty-eight girls from thirteen to eighteen years of age, housed in three cottages.
2. *Junior boys' unit,* comprised of seventy boys from eight to thirteen years of age, housed in one cottage and in three wings of another cottage.
3. *Intermediate boys' unit,* comprised of fifty boys from thirteen to fifteen years of age, housed in three cottages.

---

[7]William McCord and Joan McCord, "Two Approaches to the Cure of Delinquents," *Journal of Criminal Law, Criminology, and Police Science* 44(December 1953):442–67.

[8]Howard W. Polsky, *Cottage Six* (New York: Russell Sage Foundation, 1962).

4. *Senior boys' unit,* comprised of fifty boys from sixteen to eighteen years of age, housed in three cottages.

The school provides academic and vocational courses and intensive remedial programs. A full range of clinical services is provided by psychiatrists, psychologists, and social workers. Treatment includes individual psychotherapy, group therapy, family therapy, and other services provided in accordance with the child's individual needs as seen by the staff. Social workers provide continuing contacts with parents of residents. There is an elaborate recreational program, and facilities include two gymnasiums, an outdoor swimming pool, ball fields, and recreation rooms in each cottage. Recreational trips are made outside the institution. While approximately half the students are Jewish, about 25 percent are Negro or Puerto Rican, and the remainder from other ethnic groups.[9]

The focus of Polsky's study was on the cottage's subcultural values and the relationships between the socialization process in the cottage and the treatment program. He observed a definite hierarchy of status in the cottage he studied by participant observation. The stratification system was essentially based on power "toughness" and the ability to manipulate (precisely the behavioral patterns the institutions were supposed to change).

As far as group processes and structure were concerned, Polsky came to the following conclusions:

1. The boys were highly conscious of each other's position in the rigid social hierarchy. It was this preoccupation with each other's relative strength that dominated and framed much of the boys' interactions, even apparently the most simple kinds, such as the passing of food at the dining table. He observed that "there was very little opportunity for the group to work together to dilute these crystallized roles based on toughness."

2. Another great imbalance appeared to exist around the issue of sharing. He observed, for example, that food was used as a tool to exert pressure and control. There was an individualistic and inequitable distribution of power: the top clique controlled choice items such as butter, and all boys at other tables had to go to them for it. Standing in line for food often became a testing ground as boys tried to step in front of each other and show their superiority. It became natural for the tougher, older boys in the cottage to control those of lower status. In the cottage there was a formalistic organization around authority. This was not worked out in rules or as a constitution, but as the accretion of experience—implicit recognition by all the boys of exactly where they stood vis-à-vis the others. When a high-status boy was challenged by someone of lower status, a very dramatic outbreak occurred, and generally the upstart was "put in his place."

---

[9]"Some Facts About the Hawthorn-Cedar Knolls School," mimeographed. This material was furnished by Frank Modica, assistant director of the school, on September 19, 1973.

3. Within this cottage there was very little tendency to make status contingent upon service to the cottage. Nor did status within the cottage seem to depend in any way on skills developed outside it. Status seemed to be determined solely by toughness and ability to control others. The constant hazing of a scapegoat by the group could become so oppressive that the scapegoat would have either to "stand up" or to leave. The consolidation of the group against one or several of its members was established procedure in the cottage. The soil in which scapegoating flourished was the pervasive "ranking" (a pattern of insults) and shaming, dominant characteristics of the pecking order.

4. Finally, there seemed to be a tendency within the cottage for some solidarity to form within subgroups on the basis of close association; there was little or no tendency toward overall cottage solidarity. In the course of time these cliques became increasingly crystallized. Clique loyalties predominated. In time, the top clique became quite effective in exerting control over the others, and the top clique's attitude toward the staff, whether defiance or cooperation, was established as the basic pattern for the entire cottage.

The cottage, according to Polsky, was therefore culturally and organizationally "delinquent-bound." There was little opportunity for the boys to offset the constant, overwhelming malintegrative-expressive behavior by neutral or positive socioemotional interactions. Polsky found that the cottage was to a large extent a vacuum in which peer-group authoritarianism and toughness reigned supreme. The individuals tested their emotional problems upon each other and in fact moved very little together in meeting challenges placed before them as a cottage group. In the elaboration of their personality distortions, interpersonal cyclical movements were set up in which a predponderance of negative individual acting out resulted in a kind of group pathology. The negative delinquent cottage culture was thus a major source of resistance to treatment.

Polsky's research indicates the absolute necessity of extending individual and group therapy programs to encompass the entire pattern of living in juvenile institutions. The separation of treatment from the youth's day-to-day encounters and lifestyle in the cottage tends to sabotage the treatment program and render it relatively ineffectual.

In general, the programs of juvenile institutions are superior to adult correctional efforts; however, with some exceptions they suffer from similar problems. These include:

1. The existence of a criminogenic "crime school" atmosphere and value system.
2. An artificial "homosexual" environment.
3. A "doing time" atmosphere.
4. A schism between treatment program and delinquent subculture.

Lincoln Hall

Lincoln Hall is a private, residential treatment school located in a semirural area about fifty miles from New York City. Founded in 1863 as the New York Catholic Protectory, the school is owned by a lay board of managers and administered by a religious congregation, the Christian Brothers.

Eligible for placement at Lincoln Hall are boys, eleven to sixteen years of age, who are adjudged by the Family Court of New York State to be delinquent, in need of supervision, or neglected, or youngsters referred by the Bureau of Child Welfare of the New York City Department of Social Services who fall into the above categories or are otherwise in need of institutional care (by reason of homelessness, for example). No specified religious persuasion is requisite for admittance to Lincoln Hall. Length of stay is up to eighteen months.

The school grounds include a farm, six baseball diamonds, and other athletic and recreational facilities. The physical structure is modern and includes a gymnasium, shop buildings, a school building, a residence for the Brothers, and eleven cottages, each housing twenty-four boys.

Lincoln Hall is staffed by three hundred full- and part-time people, including teachers, remedial educators, social workers, cottage counselors, psychiatrists, dentists, nurses, and others. Two brothers are assigned to each cottage; one is in charge of the cottage and gives religious instruction, the other teaches in the school. Lay teachers are hired to augment the religious on the academic faculty.

The clinical and casework staffs are headed administratively by psychiatrists. Each person on the professional staff is an essential member of the therapeutic team, which endeavors to meet the needs of the boy. Casework, cottage living, academic education, vocational training, group work, psychiatry, psychology, medicine, nursing, recreation—all play an important role in the team approach to the treatment of the boy. Periodic case reviews, case conferences, and intercommunication between and among staff members are the principal means of developing the team approach.

Lincoln Hall differs somewhat from Hawthorne-Cedar Knolls, a Jewish agency, and Berkshire Farm for Boys, an interfaith residential treatment center, in its emphasis on discipline. Punishment in the form of control is part of the treatment. Corporal punishment is never tolerated. Punishment is administered in the form of deprivation of privileges, the performance of extra chores, and temporary isolation from the group when such measures appear to answer the needs of the particular individual at the time. Discipline, then, is seen as part of the treatment.

When a staff member finds it necessary to impose some sanction, the boy is given interpretation and support in this situation. Ideally, the boy should be made to recognize the need for punishment and be willing to accept it. As at Wiltwyck, the punishment, or its functional equivalent, is used to set limits for the boys and help them to set limits for themselves. One important objective is to get the boy to see the difference between rejection of what he has done and rejection of himself. As Brother Hynes notes, for discipline to be genuinely and lastingly effective it must be based on love, respect, and concern for the young people in question.[10]

Periodic weekend and holiday visits by the boy to his home are also a part of the treatment program. Visits are arranged for and approved jointly by the cottage supervisor, the social worker, and any other staff member working directly with the boy. A boy's progress in cottage conduct, achievement, and overall adjustment is recorded on weekly rating cards. These progress cards are coordinated with a program of counseling by the cottage supervisors. Casework service with the family as well as with the boy is an essential part of the treatment program of Lincoln Hall, since good family relationships are essential for the proper development of children and since problems in this area are common to boys entrusted to Lincoln Hall.

A crucial part of the treatment program is the period immediately following the boy's return to the community, the first stage of the Lincoln Hall continued-care program. An essential part of the work with the boy and his family during this crucial phase of treatment is the casework service given by the same social worker who has worked with them since the boy's admission to the institution. This service will take the form of energetic, concerted effort to see that each boy who leaves Lincoln Hall is immediately placed in school or in employment, thereby obviating the dangers of idleness and mischief. The practice of class supervision and friendly encouragement is accomplished by means of weekly or biweekly interviews.[11]

Highfields

The prototype for another type of treatment-oriented small residential group center is the Highfields program, originated in 1950 in New Jersey. The program was not designed for deeply disturbed or mentally deficient children. The Highfields approach limits the population to twenty boys, aged sixteen and seventeen, assigned directly from the juvenile court. They are youths who have not previously been committed to a correctional institution.

The boys who lived in the first experimental Highfields stayed there for an average of four months. During the day they worked at a nearby institution performing menial labor. There were few security measures and little or no

---

[10]Christian Hynes, "Discipline in a Treatment-Oriented School for Delinquent Boys," *Federal Probation* 33(December 1969):29.

[11]Hynes, "Discipline in a Treatment-Oriented School." More recent information about Lincoln Hall was taken from a 1973 pamphlet, "Principles of the Lincoln Hall Program," provided by Brother Christopher Foley, F.S.C., executive director of Lincoln Hall.

authoritarian leadership. Every evening the boys were divided into two groups of ten each for a meeting built around the technique of guided group interaction.

The guided group interaction sessions are at the heart of the Highfields approach. The method is cogently described as follows:

> Rehabilitation begins with changes in attitudes. But how can these be brought about? The boys entering Highfields have for years identified themselves as delinquents. Their close friends are deliquent. Group pressure has generally pushed and pulled them into delinquency and prevented their rehabilitation. Most delinquents feel rejected and discriminated against by their parents. They generally manifest strong emotional reactions, particularly against their fathers, but often aginst their mothers, brothers, and sisters. By the time they are confronted with law-enforcing agencies they have developed strong ego defenses. They do not take the responsibility for their delinquency. Instead, they tend to blame others—their parents, their associates, and society.
>
> The whole Highfields experience is directed toward piercing through these strong defenses against rehabilitation, toward undermining delinquent attitudes, and toward developing a self-conception favorable to reformation. The sessions on guided group interaction are especially directed to achieve this objective.
>
> Guided group interaction has the merit of combining the psychological and the sociological approaches to the control of human behavior. The psychological approach aims to change the self-conception of the boy from a delinquent to a nondelinquent. But this process involves changing the mood of the boy from impulses to law breaking to impulses to be law abiding.[12]

At Highfields, emphasis was placed on normal social activities and values. This was accomplished by four devices intended "to help the boys be like everybody else." (1) Family members and friends of boys were encouraged to visit them at Highfields, and see how they were getting along. (2) An effort was made to educate the surrounding community to accept the boys, rather than to show suspicion or reject them entirely. (3) Perhaps most important, the boys did useful work and were paid for it. (4) The stay at Highfields was limited to a maximum of four months. This time factor was considered an important device that contributed to successful rehabilitation.

Institutions modeled after the original Highfields have been developed around the country. Some are now located in central city areas. Much like the original, they house about twenty persons each, and custodial personnel is held

---

[12]Lloyd W. McCorkle, *The Highfields Story* (New York: Holt, Rinehart and Winston, 1958), p. v.

to a minimum. Residents are permitted to receive visitors frequently and to leave the premises with visitors. Residents usually work outside the institution and participate in group therapy sessions on a regular basis.

The philosophy, operation, effect, and potentialities of the Highfields program have been summarized as follows:

1. Its thoroughgoing use of the group as an instrument of rehabilitation is social-psychologically sound and has been verified by experience.

2. The method of guided interaction directs group influences toward rehabilitation rather than, as in the large reformatory, to the reinforcement of attitudes of delinquency and hostility to authority.

3. In the guided group interaction sessions the youth achieves an understanding of himself and his motivations which enables him to make constructive plans for his future.

4. Highfields greatly reduces the time of treatment from the usual one to five years in training schools or reformatories to three or four months.

5. It requires a minimum of staff as compared with other methods of treatment.

6. Highfields has far lower per capita costs than other institutions for the treatment of delinquents.

7. There is every reason to believe that Highfields can be successfully established elsewhere provided the new projects incorporate its philosophy, its design of operation, and a specially trained staff.[13]

The Highfields experiment has been considered generally successful by several research evaluations. With some variations, it was successfully replicated in Provo, Utah.[14] While Highfields was originally designed for adolescents, a similar type of institutional approach is now used for adult probationers and parolees.

Contributions of Residential Treatment Centers

It is apparent from the foregoing that at least some state training schools do not have as damaging an effect on juveniles as do prisons. Furthermore, even in the best sort of residential treatment center a delinquent subculture develops to challenge administration norms. The small Highfields-type residence pro-

---

[13]H. Ashley Weeks, *Youthful Offenders at Highfields* (Ann Arbor: University of Michigan Press, 1958), pp. xvii–xviii. See also McCorkle, *Highfields Story.*

[14]Lamar T. Empey and Jerome Rabow, "The Provo Experiment in Delinquency Rehabilitation," *American Sociological Review* 26 (October 1961):679–95.

vides the best opportunity for staff members to challenge the leadership of the delinquent subculture. Nevertheless, the failure rate at Wiltwyck, Lincoln Hall, and the other residential treatment centers mentioned is far lower than that of the state training schools. Scientific comparisons between the two types of institution are difficult if not impossible, however, because the populations are not really comparable. The admission committees of the residential treatment centers can refuse to take a boy if they feel their program does not suit his needs; the state training school must take every boy a court sends to it. This power to select gives the residential treatment center an advantage. The fact that residential treatment centers are privately operated and are able to spend more than state-run schools has enabled them to experiment with costly programs and make considerable progress in treatment.

Community Treatment and Prevention Programs

A VARIETY OF METHODS has evolved for treating the offender in the community. Dominant among these are probation and parole. Another strategy involves community crime- and delinquency-prevention programs in high-delinquency areas. And the federal government's large-scale programs for eliminating poverty have delinquency-prevention implications.

All of these varied approaches rest on the assumption that there are advantages to treating the offender or potential offender in the community. The general advantages of community-based programs are that they are less costly and have a better chance for success than institutional programs because the environment is more natural than the onerous and artificial milieu of the prison. The prime disadvantage of treating the offender in the community is the fact that the individual is apt to be living within the same environmental set of causal forces that originally produced his crime or delinquency. These negative forces must be vitiated or overcome if the individual is to function as a law-abiding citizen, whether or not he spends time in a correctional institution.

Community Crime and Delinquency Prevention

In addition to the standard approaches of probation and parole, a variety of other systems attempt to prevent crime. These include attacks on the problem at various levels in the social system.

Macrosociological programs, or efforts at large-scale social change, have been organized to provide opportunities for more people to achieve the culturally approved goals of the society without having to resort to illegal means. These include increased access to education, training, and employment for all members of the society, including those in the lowest socioeconomic categories. Examples of such societal efforts formerly included the federal Office of Economic Opportunity and its subsidiary poverty programs—programs that were substantially dismantled by the Nixon and Ford administrations. President Carter is attempting to redevelop these programs.

On another level, neighborhood and community programs have been designed to reduce the incidence of criminality and delinquency in problem areas. These programs are based on the assumption that certain urban areas with high delinquency rates tend to foster crime and delinquency and that the development of indigenous anticriminal leadership and services in these areas would reduce the incidence of criminal and delinquent behavior.

Clinical treatment programs, largely psychological in orientation, have been developed on the assumption that delinquent behavior results from personal pathology. The programs developed include psychiatric casework, social group work, and combinations of these with services to individuals and families. Professional people, usually social workers, attempt to modify attitudes and behavior patterns of persons deemed likely to engage in delinquent behavior.

Child Guidance Programs

Virtually every large city in the United States has one or more child guidance clinics offering treatment to adolescents. These services are not limited to children considered delinquent or diagnosed as predelinquent, but they have been considered useful in preventing delinquent behavior. Problem children are referred to these clinics by social work agencies, schools, police, and at times juvenile courts. The first clinic of this type directed at delinquency prevention was established by Dr. William Healy in Chicago in 1909 as an adjunct of the Chicago juvenile court.

In an attempt to evaluate the effect of child guidance on delinquency in Boston, the Cambridge-Somerville Youth Study was instituted in 1936.[1] The program continued for nine years, through 1945. On the basis of interviews

---

[1] Edwin Powers and Helen Witmer, *An Experiment in the Prevention of Delinquency: The Cambridge-Somerville Youth Study* (New York: Columbia University Press, 1951).

with teachers, psychiatric evaluations, and psychological tests, some 750 boys attending schools in Cambridge and Somerville, Massachusetts, were classified as to the likelihood of their becoming delinquent. By a random process 325 were assigned to an experimental group to receive preventive treatment and a matched group of 325 boys was studied as a control group. The experimental group was provided with family guidance, individual counseling, tutoring, camp and recreational facilities, correction of health defects, medical care, and when deemed necessary, financial assistance from community agencies. Services were provided for an average of five years. Surprisingly, followup studies made five, ten, and twenty-five years later revealed no statistically significant difference between the treated and the untreated group with respect to number of criminal convictions or age at conviction. The treatment program had been relatively ineffective as a preventive of delinquency or criminality.[2]

Area Projects in Delinquency Prevention

In contrast to the child guidance or clinical approach, which attempts to work on the child, area programs try to change the social environment in which the child grows up. Such programs coordinate the activities of existing facilities and agencies and establish additional facilities if this seems advisable. Community organization experts attempt to activate or organize councils representing as many social welfare agencies as will cooperate and sometimes seek to organize the people of the delinquency or problem area into neighborhood committees for action.

The Chicago Area Project. The first important program of this sort was initiated by Clifford R. Shaw in Chicago in 1933. The program was developed after the research of Shaw and his colleagues had clearly indicated that the slum areas of large cities were characterized by a disproportionately large number of delinquent children and criminals. The program was based on several assumptions that have become standard:

1. In high-delinquency areas, delinquency is symptomatic of deeper social ills. It is a product of the social milieu. The same blighted areas that have high delinquency rates also have high rates of economic dependency, illness, infant mortality, substandard housing, and poverty. (This is as true today as it was in the 1930s.)

2. Delinquency cannot be attributed to factors inherent in race or nationality groups.

3. Delinquency in deteriorated areas may frequently be regarded as conformity to the expectations, behavior patterns, and values of the groups of boys in the neighborhood.

---

[2]Joan McCord and William McCord, "A Follow-up Report on the Cambridge-Somerville Youth Study," *Annals of the American Academy of Political and Social Science* 322 (March 1959):89–98.

4. Most delinquents in deteriorated areas are not inferior to children in the more privileged communities in any fundamental way. Delinquency is a part of the social tradition of the neighborhood; a large segment of the population tolerates, reinforces, and even encourages delinquent behavior.

5. Current practices in dealing with delinquency have been ineffective. It is not possible to save a boy apart from his family or community. A community with a new morale and new leadership directed in socially constructive channels is essential.

6. *The local neighborhood can be organized to deal effectively with its own problems. There exists in the neighborhood sufficient indigenous leadership to bring about changes in attitudes, sentiments, ideals, and loyalties for the construction of a more acceptable community lifestyle.*

The Chicago Area Project organized community committees in six areas of Chicago: Hegewisch, Russell Square, South Side, Near North Side, Near West Side, and Near Northwest Side. Twenty-two neighborhood centers involving over 7,500 children developed in these areas. The community committees were organized with the aid of a staff member of the project, but the staff member did not exercise control. He was available to mobilize needed resources or as an adviser only if called upon by the committee. The neighborhood committee selected a qualified local resident as director, and that person was then employed as a staff member of the area project. Policy decisions were left to the neighborhood committee, whether the "experts" on the staff of the area project agreed or not. The residents of the neighborhood were in control.[3] Ten years after its inception, the Russell Square Community Committee, for example, had 125 active members and 700 contributing members. These included local businessmen and political leaders, bartenders, plumbers, carpenters, workers, and some former delinquents.

The projects encouraged the expansion of existing facilities for recreation and the construction of new ones. Efforts were made to improve school-community relations and particularly to encourage teachers to remain in the schools. Clubwork, discussion groups, and hobby groups were used as tools for developing community spirit.

One of the most important aspects of the area-project program has been the preparation of offenders for return to the community. Offenders soon to be released are visited in their institutions, encouraged to participate in committee activities upon their return, and helped to establish contacts with employers and other local groups. These legitimate activities furnish the framework within which the offender returning from an institution can become accepted and can come to think of himself as a full member of the community.

The social climate of a community can be expected to improve as the people in it assume greater responsibility for its direction. A community

---

[3]Solomon Kobrin, "The Chicago Area Project: A 25-Year Assessment," *Annals of the American Academy of Political and Social Science* 322 (March 1959):19–29.

administered by outsiders is less likely to develop esprit de corps. The Chicago Area Project demonstrated that people can be found in the deteriorated areas of our cities capable of supplying the leadership necessary to increase constructive action. While the effect of the Chicago Area Project on delinquency was not precisely measured, in all probability delinquency was substantially reduced as a consequence of the effort. The Chicago Area Project was the pioneer model for many comparable programs that have emerged in recent years.

The Mid-City Project: Boston.   The Mid-City Project was a delinquency-control program in a lower class district of Boston, in operation between 1954 and 1957. It was in many ways similar to the Cambridge-Somerville Youth Study and the Chicago Area Project. A major objective of the project was to reduce the amount of illegal activity engaged in by resident adolescents. On the assumption that delinquent behavior by lower class adolescents, whatever their personality characteristics, was to a significant extent influenced by characteristics of the community, the project initiated action programs directed at three of the societal units considered to exert important influence on delinquent behavior: the community, the family, and the gang.

The community program concentrated on developing and strengthening local citizens' groups so that they might deal with delinquency more effectively. An attempt was also made to secure the cooperation of professional agencies operating in the community, including settlement houses, churches, schools, the police, the court, and the probation department. One of the goals of the program was to increase cooperation among the assorted professional agencies and between those agencies and the citizens' groups. The long-range goal was to improve the processes of delinquency prevention and control.

The family program was based on the assumption that problem families contribute to delinquency. Families that had used public welfare services over a long period of time were located and subjected to an intensive program of psychiatrically oriented casework.

The gang program was modeled after the New York City Youth Board detached-worker program. Detached street workers were assigned to groups with instructions to contact, establish relationships with, and attempt to change the attitudes and behavior patterns of gangs in the area.

All workers were professionally trained, with degrees in groupwork, casework, or both. Each worker devoted primary attention to a single group, maintaining intensive contact with group members over an extended period. Psychiatric consulation was available on a regular basis.

Contact was maintained with 400 youngsters between the ages of twelve and twenty-one, comprising the membership of twenty-one corner gangs. Seven of these, totaling 205 members, were subjected to intensive attention. Workers contacted these groups on an average of three and a half times a week. Contact periods averaged five or six hours. The total duration of the services was from ten to thirty-four months. Four of the groups were white male,

Catholic, largely Irish, with some Italian and French-Canadian membership. One was Negro male, one white female, and one Negro female. The average size of the male groups was thirty; of the female, nine. The groups were indigenous, self-formed, and inheritors of a gang tradition that in some cases extended back almost fifty years.

In evaluating the results of the project, researchers concluded that there was no significant measurable inhibition of lawbreaking or morally disapproved behavior as a consequence of the project efforts. They found the program's impact was negligible in a counteracting the thrust toward delinquent behavior that was reinforced by the general values of the community.[4]

Coping with Gangs and Delinquency in the Community

The following discussion, although focused on resolving the gang problem, has broader implications. Many of the programs described have usefulness in preventing delinquency in general.

Levels of Attack

Whatever specific factors determine the emergence of a specific violent gang at a particular time and place, there is little reason to question the observation that the *existence* of violent gangs are *recurrent social phenomena in many places* and must ultimately be related to deeper, more general disruptions in the social fabric itself. If this consideration is relevant to a thorough assessment of the problem, it must be equally relevant to a thorough and effective attack upon it. Since the roots go deep, we cannot expect the problem to disappear without recourse to remedies that go to the roots. All of which is to make the commonplace observation that a society that fails to find remedies for its own disorganization and for its own institutionalized inequities is likely to continue to suffer from their consequences—those of violent gangs among them.

Nothing in this perhaps overrepeated observation provides a valid argument for inaction. What is implied, however, is a working discrimination between the necessary strategy for broad social change and the practical tactics of local control.[5] If we cannot "immediately" eradicate the roots, there may well be something immediate and effective we can do about the branches and tendrils as they emerge in the social soil of our particular communities. Ac-

---

[4]Walter B. Miller, "The Impact of a Total Community Delinquency Control Project," *Social Problems* 10 (Fall 1962):168–91.

[5]On the broader societal front, governmental and private programs aimed at reducing social and economic inequalities, equalizing opportunities, facilitating the integration of new populations— each of these would work to ameliorate the background conditions that foster the gang problem.

cordingly, the central emphasis of this discussion will be upon the treatment and control of the violent gang in its emergent form.

Reaching the Violent Gang

Community gang-prevention projects are usually subdivisions of larger delinquency-control programs. The only type of preventive project expressly designed for the violent gang is the detached-worker program. In this approach, a professional, usually a social worker, is assigned to a particular gang. The essential avowed goal of the youth worker is to redirect the gangs from destructive behavior patterns into "constructive" activities.

The most highly developed detached-worker program, which has served as a model for gang control in large urban areas nationally, is the approach designed and utilized by the New York City Youth Board. In the Youth Board manual, *Reaching the Unreached,* the board's diagnosis of the gang problem and principles for working with gangs are stated as follows:

1. Participation in a street gang or club, like participation in any natural group, is a part of the growing-up process of adolescence. Such primary group associations possess potentialities for positive growth and development. Through such a group, the individual can gain security and develop positive ways of living with other individuals. Within the structure of his group the individual can develop such characteristics as loyalty, leadership, and community responsibility.

2. Some street clubs or gangs, as a result of more fundamental factors such as family disorganization, economic insecurity, racial and religious discrimination, poor housing, lack of recreational and educational facilities, emotional maladjustments of their leaders and members, etc., have developed patterns of antisocial behavior, the most widely known of which is street fighting. This type of teen-age gang warfare over the past decade has produced an annual toll of innumerable injuries and several deaths.

3. While the protection of the community at times necessitates the use of repressive measures in dealing with the antisocial street clubs or gangs, these methods do not bring about basic changes in attitudes or behavior.

4. Street club members can be reached and will respond to sympathy, acceptance, affection, and understanding when approached by adults who possess those characteristics and reach out to them on their own level.

5. The positive relationship that is developed between an adult worker and a street club can serve as a catalytic agent for modifying antisocial attitudes and behavior. This relationship can also be used to

help the individual member meet his needs in some more positive way. . . .

6. To be effective, detached work must be coordinated, unified, and applied on a saturation basis.

7. Because of the close relationship that is necessary for workers to develop with club members, and because of such factors as group loyalty, distrust and fear of other clubs, it is imperative that detached workers be assigned to only one street club.[6]

On the basis of these assumptions, the Youth Board established seven goals for work with street gangs: (1) reduction of antisocial behavior, particularly street fighting; (2) friendly relationships with other street gangs; (3) increased democratic participation within the gangs; (4) broadened social horizons; (5) responsibility for self-direction; (6) improved personal and social adjustment of the individual; and (7) improved community relations.

Issues Involved in Detached-Worker Gang Work

Reaching the gang through detached youth workers utilizing the above-stated principles and goals often entails pitfalls not specified in policy or in the manuals. Foremost among these potential problems is the possibility of inaccurately diagnosing gang structure. Distinctly different treatment methods are required for treating the *social,* the *delinquent,* and the *violent gang.* The blurring of these differentiations produces ineffectual approaches, even with a sincere and dedicated worker.

With reference to the violent gang in particular, the fact that differential levels of involvement (i.e., core group and various marginal categories) and participation dictate different treatment prescriptions is of crucial significance.[7] The marginal gang member can generally be reached through the more conventional methods of recreation, providing a job, counseling, and so on, whereas the core violent gang leader and participants require a differential approach.

The diagnostic assumption that working through the violent gang leader will redirect the gang provides another problem. Often working through the leader of a violent gang solidifies its structure. Official sanction of the sociopathic leader by a worker may give status to an individual who was formerly considered a "character" by most of the marginal gang participants.

Merely gaining access to violent gang participants is frequently mistaken for acceptance and rapport. Contrary to popular belief, getting in touch with

---

[6]*Reaching the Unreached: Fundamental Aspects of the Program of the New York City Youth Board* (New York: New York City Youth Board, 1952), pp. 107–8.

[7]See Chapter 6, "Juvenile Gang Patterns."

the gang is not difficult for a detached worker. However, the meaning given to the relationship by gang members varies and is of major significance. If the gang worker appears as a "mark" to most members, a "do-gooder" who doesn't know the score, they will simply use him for money, cigarettes, or whatever favors they can obtain. The negative nature of this situation is not simply the gang worker's being duped, but his incorrect assumption of success. Many gang workers, rather than resocializing gang members, are themselves negatively affected by the gang. They may rationalize their personal motives toward "adventuresome" gang behavior as necessary to maintain their relationship. In fact, this behavior is not necessary. Becoming themselves a "gang member" neutralizes their impact as an adequate adult role model. The negative nature of the gang worker's mistaken assumptions is revealed by the following verbatim statement of a detached gang worker:

> Shortly afterward I got another break. One afternoon the boys were hanging around and a "crap" game started. I decided it would be strategic for me to participate so that I might get closer to them. During the course of the game one of the fellows turned to me and said, "Say man, you're supposed to be out here to change us and it seems like we're making you like us instead." Actually there was real significance in his words because the boys were beginning to understand that I accepted them as they were and in turn their acceptance of me was growing.[8]

When the detached gang worker is duped by the gang or misinterprets the meaning of a situation, he is reinforcing rather than modifying illegal behavior. In his capacity as gang worker he is, in effect, a carrier of the values and norms of the larger society. Initially the gang member resists the intrusion into the subculture he has created (to act out his problems). The gang will attempt to get what it can without changing and then seduce the detached worker into becoming part of the gang. The gang worker should be aware of the negative implication of compromising the relevant norms of the larger society in order to gain false acceptance and superficial approval. When he does this, he is fairly quickly eliminated as a force for changing the gang, since they begin to view him as a mark or sucker susceptible to manipulation. This defeats the objectives the worker is attempting to achieve.

The gang worker must have a realistic image of gang structure, or he is likely to be duped by the illusory conceptions of the gang described by its members. The worker's acceptance of the fantastic stories created by core gang participants produces a reinforcement of undesirable gang mythology.

The validity of such antisocial patterns as gang warfare, territory, and peace meetings should be challenged and discouraged rather than accepted

---

[8] *Reaching the Unreached,* pp. 113–14.

and, in some cases, aggrandized and given legitimacy. The enlightened detached gang worker can sometimes operate effectively through the use of ridicule, disbelief, and criticism.

The worker is often presented with wild stories of gang activity, some believed and some not believed by the gang participants themselves. If he "buys" their story, the worker becomes a dupe who loses his potential for positive influence. On the other hand, if the worker pushes the "gang stories" of divisions and warfare to their illogical conclusion by sensitive caricaturing, he makes treatment progress. First, he achieves stature with the boys as an adult person who can't be "conned" or manipulated. This the gang boys respect. Second, he turns the gang and its members back upon self-evaluation and assessment. This process causes them to begin to look at themselves and their gang as it exists in reality. The following is an actual report of a worker's handling of a problem.

A Case In Point.   Four marginal gang boys enter a gang worker's office; they are obviously nervous but attempting to give a "cool" appearance:

> FIRST GANG BOY: Well, that's it—we'll whip it on tonight at seven and then the whole city will rumble. I mean we're not going to sit still for that bullshit. The Dragons are through once and for all.
>
> WORKER: Now, really, what is all this bullshit anyway? Wait a minute, I have to make a call. (Makes an inconsequential phone call, emphasizing disinterest in the mass rumble that is supposed to engulf the city, then turns to the boys with a look of disgust.) Now, what's all this rumble stuff about?
>
> GANG BOY: Well, they're suppose to whip it on tonight. Duke says . . .
>
> WORKER: Wait a minute now. Duke told you this? (In disbelief) He told you this and you believe him?
>
> GANG BOY: Well, yeah—he and Pete met with Loco from the uptown Dragons, and he says that . . .
>
> WORKER (interrupting): Just a minute. You mean to tell me those nuts Duke, Loco, and Pete cook up some nonsense about a rumble and you guys jump right into the fire. (In disbelief) How stupid can you get?
>
> SECOND GANG BOY: I told them it was a lot of crap and . . .
>
> WORKER: Don't tell them. Why didn't you tell Duke—right there? Besides, you guys don't really have anyone to fight for you anyway. (Refers at length to a previous meeting with twelve of the "gang" where they finally agreed they were the only twelve they could count on in a fight.)
>
> THIRD GANG BOY: Well, Duke and Jerry say our ten divisions can . . .

FOURTH GANG BOY (interrupts): Oh, man, you guys still dig all that bullshit. (Turns) I didn't believe none of it—but they all got excited.

WORKER: Maybe one of these days you guys will wise up. Let's talk about something important. Are you all set up for the game at the Columbia gym Sunday?[9]

At the time the worker drops the gang-war subject but picks it up later with the police and another social agency in order to check it out further. If the worker had become involved and called a peace meeting with relevant gang leaders, he might have poured gasoline on the fire by reinforcing, joining, and helping develop a possible gang rumble. What occurred as a result of his not being drawn in was to destroy the potential support of many marginals for a rumble, discredit the gang leader's fantasy, cause the youths to examine some of the mythology of their near-group structure, and change over to a positive subject. Another main goal in this type of ridiculing approach is to encourage the marginal members to confront the fantasy of the gang and the gang-war plans on their own at the source—the leader. In some cases they effectively mimic the worker's sarcastic and caustic comments with the provocative gang leader, vitiating the leader's negative impact toward violence. Castrating his fantasy through sarcasm and ridicule helps to minimize his negative effect, rather than support and reinforce the gang leader's potential impact.

The "conned" detached worker tends unwittingly to reward what is in fact sociopathic behavior. The misguided worker not only legitimizes the gang and its core but also provides them with a type of "social director." In this role he aids the violent gang leader in his nefarious activities by providing attractive activities, dances, athletic events, and so on for marginal members.

He may be incorporated into and become part of the gang's structure. Having a gang worker attached to one's gang becomes a status symbol of being a real "down," "bad," or tough gang. As one violent gang leader expressed it: "We're a real down club. We got a president, a war counselor, and a Youth Board man."

The incorrectly oriented detached worker may indirectly help to produce and articulate violent gang culture.

Some Guidelines for More Effective Use of the Detached-Worker Approach

Reaching the gang in its own milieu through the detached gang worker is a significant approach to the violent gang problem. However, several issues

---

[9]Lewis Yablonsky, *The Violent Gang* (New York: Macmillan, 1962), pp. 242–43. Copyright 1962 by Lewis Yablonsky.

require revision and redefinition if this approach is to modify rather than solidify or reinforce violent gang structure and behavior. On the basis of the near-group conception of violent gang organization and other factors that have emerged in the analysis, the following guidelines are suggested for a more effective approach to the violent gang problem.

(*a*) It is necessary for the detached gang worker to be trained to diagnose accurately several types of gang structure. Different approaches are required for the social, delinquent, and violent gangs.

(*b*) The accurate diagnosis of the violent gang reveals different degrees of participation and involvement. Marginal members may be worked with through more conventional treatment approaches; core violent gang participants and leaders require a different and more intense form of treatment.

(*c*) A violent gang can be further integrated by working through the leaders. The detached gang worker should avoid giving the leader credence, since this may reinforce violent gang structure. Providing the sociopathic leader with "official" status and activity opportunities for his gang tends to defeat rather than achieve sound corrective goals.

(*d*) The detached gang worker, as an official representative of the more inclusive society, must avoid sanctioning or participating in deviance to gain what will turn out to be a false acceptance and rapport. He should serve as an adequate law-abiding adult role model. In this way, he may become a bridge or vehicle for bringing the larger society's constructive values and norms to the gang.

Violent gangs should not be treated by any official community program as a "legitimate" social structure. Giving credence to the violent gang by providing it with an official representative of society is giving tacit authorization to pathology and violence. For example, peace meetings that involve gang leaders and paid representatives of city government implicitly provide an illegal, pathological enterprise with official support.

These conclusions are not based upon moral or legal considerations but upon the nature of gang organization. An entity, such as the violent gang, cannot be treated as a unit. The type of detached-worker policies and the programs that have been employed in the past appear to solidify and legitimize the violent gang, reinforcing its pathological behavior rather than modifying its antisocial activity.

Rather than "redirecting" and implicitly reinforcing the violent gang as an institutionalized and legitimized pattern of illegal behavior, the focus should be upon eliminating it as an entity. This goal may be worked toward by a combination of modified detached gang work, police action, incarceration, group therapy, and a new "milieu-therapy" approach to sociopathic behavior. If these approaches are utilized, the violent gang may be dismembered, its participants resocialized and legally reconnected into the inclusive society.

The Halfway House and Community Treatment

Most inmates of prisons and training schools prior to their incarceration were members of delinquent groups with subcultures deviating materially from that of the dominant culture in our society. While in these institutions, inmates are subjected to a continuous acculturation and assimilation of the delinquent value system. They tend to develop a vocabulary that reflects attitudes, beliefs, opinions, and orientations different from and often opposing those of the conventional person, if they did not have such attitudes when they arrived at the institution. The roles played by the inmate and the roles he is required to play upon his release are vastly different in most important aspects. This is obviously true of the important family roles. The inmate is living apart from his parents, his brothers and sisters, or any other relatives with whom he normally resides. We often forget that he is also away from his community roles and normal occupational roles.

In spite of the fact that most inmates do some work while at an institution, the attitudes attached to the role of worker differ materially from the attitudes required for satisfactory achievement in a work situation on the outside. Workers in the correctional labor system are encouraged to be nonproductive, dilatory, and contentious. Institutionally developed attitudes affect the individual's concept of the role of the job seeker. In reform school or prison, the inmate does not have to seek a job. It is considered to be the duty of the officials to provide him with work and the inmate comes to feel that he has a right to a job. Foremen in prison are content with a limited amount of productivity, the standards being far lower than those set by foremen and employers outside the institution. Far more cooperation than the inmate is accustomed to give is expected of him by fellow workers, foremen, and employers when he works on the outside.[10]

As a result of his stay at a correctional institution, a man is disconnected from his ordinary occupational, family, and community roles. While inside, he adjusts to prison life, and upon his release he may be expected to have difficulty reestablishing occupational and family roles in the community. He needs time to adjust and to reconnect to society. Institutions organized to facilitate the necessary transition are called halfway houses, to symbolize their status as an establishment between a prison and the residence of a free citizen. The halfway house as now constituted is a temporary residence for released offenders, usually located in the community in which the inmates resided before they were incarcerated, or as near to that community as possible. At the halfway house, a building housing twenty to fifty people under the supervision of a correctional authority, the released prisoner can look for a job, work on a job,

---

[10]Martin R. Haskell, "An Alternative to More and Larger Prisons: A Role Training Program for Social Reconnection," *Group Psychotherapy* 14(March-June 1961):30–38.

meet with family and friends, and begin to assume the roles normally accept-able in his community.

Institutions of this type were set up by private charitable organizations as early as the nineteenth century. In 1896, the Volunteers of America opened Hope Hall, a residence in New York for men released from the New York State Prison at Ossining. Governmental agencies began to implement halfway-house programs in the late 1950s and early 1960s. Other private organizations fol-lowed suit in the next several years.

In the field of corrections, halfway houses exist for various types of offenders. Some are under the supervision of parole departments and house people released from prison to parole. Others are for people who have com-pleted their prison sentence and have no place to go. Still others are operated by probation departments and serve in lieu of confinement in a prison. They are sometimes referred to as partway houses and are viewed as halfway institu-tions that avoid the total disconnection of the prisoner from the community. In the late 1960s and early 1970s, some halfway houses were established for offenders still under sentence to confinement. Such facilities are called "prere-lease guidance centers" and house prisoners who are working in the commu-nity on "work-release programs." As of 1973, the total number of people in halfway houses was still relatively small.[11]

In a survey of community-based correctional programs, it was discov-ered that twenty-eight state departments of correction have such programs, with five more planned to go into effect by 1974. Without exception, each of the twenty-eight correction departments with community treatment programs featured work release or work furlough. Of these, twelve also included "school release" or study release. Most of the programs included one or more of the following: individual and group counseling, prerelease orientation, family counseling, accelerated release for those participating in the program, commu-nity involvement and use of volunteers, and maximum use of all community resources.[12]

The Bureau of Prisons, an agency of the federal government, operates eighteen community treatment centers, the first of which was established in Chicago in 1961. Most of these serve both male and female offenders and are operated out of hotels or apartment facilities. Prior to October 1970, these facilities were limited to persons scheduled for release from correctional insti-tutions. Since that date, persons on probation or parole could be required to reside in or participate in the program of a community treatment center as a condition of probation or parole. The actual and projected population of these centers is 10 percent persons on probation and parole and 90 percent inmates

[11]National Institute of Mental Health, *Graduated Release* (Washington, D.C.: U.S. Government Printing Office, 1971), chap. IV, "Halfway Houses," pp. 15–22.

[12]Bertram S. Griggs and Gary R. McCune, "Community-Based Correctional Programs: A Survey and Analysis," *Federal Probation* 36 (June 1972):7–13.

of correctional institutions scheduled for release. If the states follow suit, community-based treatment centers now used largely as halfway houses for people leaving prisons may become halfway-in houses aiding in the treatment of probationers.[13]   Such community treatment centers serve the following functions:

1. Provide some continuity with education and training programs begun in the correctional institutions
2. Assist the offender in obtaining adequate employment
3. Increase utilization of community resources
4. Provide needed support during this difficult initial period of adjustment.[14]

Thalheimer describes the present function of halfway houses in the following terms:

> The very name halfway house suggests its position in the corrections world: halfway-in, a more structured environment than probation and parole; halfway-out, a less structured environment than institutions. As halfway-in houses they represent a last stop before incarceration for probationers and parolees facing or having faced revocation; as halfway-out houses, they provide services to prereleasees and parolees leaving institutions. Halfway houses also provide a residential alternative to jail or outright release for accused offenders awaiting trial or convicted offenders awaiting sentencing.
>
> The role of halfway houses within corrections has increased significantly in the past decade. The 1974 *Directory of Halfway Houses* belonging to the International Halfway House Association includes houses from most of the 50 states, with a total of 1,370 houses listed; there are, in addition, a substantial number of halfway houses which do not belong to the association.[15]

Work-Release Programs

The terms *work release* and *work furlough* have been applied to programs designed to treat the offender in the community. The first work-release program in the United States began in Wisconsin in 1913. This program permitted

---

[13]Griggs and McCune, "Community-Based Correctional Programs," p. 11.

[14]Griggs and McCune, "Community-Based Correctional Programs," p. 12.

[15]Donald J. Thalheimer, *Cost Analysis of Correctional Standards: Halfway Houses,* Vol. II, (Washington, D.C.: U. S. Dept. of Justice, Law Enforcement Assistance Administration, October, 1975), p. 1.

persons assigned to it, ones convicted of misdemeanors, to work in the community during the day and spend the night in jail. In 1957, North Carolina established the first work-release program for persons convicted of felonies. Such programs were in existence in a majority of the states by 1972. The principal objective stated in the laws establishing work-release programs is the rehabilitation of the offender. Obviously, if he is permitted to work or go to school in the community, it should be easier to establish and maintain his connections with the community. This cannot be done well in a prison regardless of the level of its rehabilitation and treatment programs. To achieve this objective, all work-release programs permit education and vocational training as well as actual employment. Programs are generally a responsibility of the state corrections department. However, in some states, notably New York, the commissioner of corrections establishes the rules with the approval of the chairman of the board of parole. The warden of each prison decides which inmates may participate in work-release programs, however. The following criteria are used to determine whether an inmate is suitable for a work-release program:

1. He is not a high security risk.
2. He is not likely to commit crimes of violence.
3. He is likely to be rehabilitated.
4. He is trustworthy.[16]

Since most correctional institutions do not permit inmates to have money on their persons, wages of those on work release are turned over to the institution. In managing an inmate's money, priorities are given to paying for his room and board, travel expenses, support of dependents, and fines and debts; the balance, if any, is saved and given to him upon his release. In some jurisdictions the person on work release spends his nonworking hours in the county jail or other local correctional facility. In others, he goes back to the prison after his work-release time. In most instances, however, halfway houses or work-release centers are used.[17]

By 1965 there were twenty-four states with work-release programs. However, few states had a well-articulated program. In most states work release was restricted to the misdemeanant. Recidivist rates for work-release prisoners is low. North Carolina, for example, reported a recidivist rate of 6 percent. This may be attributed to the care exercised in selecting only good risks for work release. Escapes from such programs are also very low. Wisconsin reported 8 percent in 1960, and North Carolina reported 5 percent in 1964.

---

[16]Lawrence S. Root, "Work Release Legislation," *Federal Probation* 36 (March 1972):38–43.

[17]Root, "Work Release Legislation," pp. 40–41.

Apparently, the public is ready to accept work release as adequate punishment for misdemeanants.[18]

The Anticriminal Society: Synanon

Changes in the correctional system that are heralded as "new" are usually not fundamentally different from past practices. Correctional institutions are still essentially prisons, and community programs continue to be bureaucratically operated. A "new" correctional system tends to be a variation or modification of the old basic structure.

An organization that is truly fundamentally new and unique in its approach to crime and delinquency is Synanon, a social movement that has helped hundreds of people, young and old, to overcome severe past patterns of crime, delinquency, and drug addiction. Synanon is a prototype of hundreds of organizations around the country; consequently it will be discussed in detail here.[19]

The organization was founded in 1958 by a brilliant social planner, Charles E. Dederich. Dederich himself at first led a handful of addicts out of their formerly encapsulated lives of drug addiction, crime, and prison. With the help of this core group, he produced a unique social constellation that has benefited many more people caught in the morass of crime and delinquency.

The name Synanon originated with a newly arrived addict in the early days of the organization. In his attempt to say a word foreign to him, either "symposium" or "seminar"—he wasn't sure which he meant—he blurted out, "I want to get into another one of those sym ... sem ... synanons." In this way, a new word was introduced into the language to describe a new social phenomenon.

Synanon's program is composed of more than symposiums and seminars. It encompasses a new kind of group therapy; an approach to racial integration; a humane solution to some facets of bureaucratic organization; a different way of being religious; a new method of attack therapy; an unusual kind of communication; and an exciting, fresh approach to the cultural arts and philosophy. One side effect of intense participation in the diverse human experiences of Synanon is that people who were criminals and prisoners have found a new mode of existence and now lead constructive lives.

The organization has steadily moved beyond its original work of treating drug addiction and crime. The function of Synanon as a vehicle for construc-

---

[18]Stanley E. Grupp, "Work Release and the Misdemeanant," *Federal Probation* 29 (June 1965): 6–12.

[19]Parts of this section are derived from Lewis Yablonsky, *The Tunnel Back: Synanon* (New York: Macmillan, 1965; Baltimore: Penguin Books, 1967).

tive personal and social change has become clearer as the theory and method are increasingly utilized by people who were never addicts or criminals and who had no history of serious character disorder.

This integration of "squares," ex-addicts, and former criminals of all ages and from all walks of life is a significant reason why Synanon works. Perhaps for the first time in their lives, offenders have the opportunity for intimate associations with law-abiding persons in the unusual community of Synanon.

Synanon Compared with Prisons

The offender has a close familiarity with the traditional "correctional" systems. Reformatories, prisons, jails, mental hospitals, addict hospitals—he knows them all. Even at his first arrest, he is already equipped with a set of attitudes for handling encounters with society's law enforcers. He learns the proper set of attitudes and responses on the streets, and these are reinforced in jail.

The bad guys are the cops, squares (nonaddicts), judges, jailers, and prison administrators; on the right side of the fence are "righteous dope fiends" and "stand-up guys." The criminal-addict learns quickly to trust the right guys and to hate and distrust all squares. He can "smell a cop a mile away," and he can pick a dope fiend out of a crowd.

In prison, if he's a right guy, he lives according to inmate rules. He believes "Thou shalt not squeal," he engages in petty larceny, and he gets some homosexual kicks from the prison punks. If he is a solid member of the in-group, he cons the staff members whenever he can. They are the enemy inside the walls, who represent the enemy (square society) outside the walls.

Almost all members of hospital and prison officialdom are stereotyped by the inmate code—at best as inept, at worst as proper targets of extreme rebellious hatred. For most inmates they are objects to be manipulated for quick release, or they are tricks to beat for small scores to relieve the boredom and monotony of custody. In the chess game of manipulation, the institution's officials are pawns. This inmate code tends to confirm and reinforce criminal-addict ethics and behavior.

By contrast, the offender entering Synanon is usually baffled by what he finds. Everyone is a right guy, including the administrators. If he tries to play his usual prison games, he is laughed at. He can't hate the officials in Synanon because they are people like himself. He cannot even hate squares because they are the people who support the organization.

If he wants to break out (a common subject of conversation in prison), he is invited to get lost by the Synanon staff. At every turn he discovers new responses to old situations and, most important, other people who know how he feels. Instead of receiving a callous reaction, he is told, "I remember how

I felt when I first got here," and this is followed by a detailed description of the feeling he is experiencing at the time. This is often disconcerting and frightening because it is a new and strange situation. Yet, at the same time, the sight of others like himself who have "made it" gives him confidence.

In Synanon he finds a new society. He encounters understanding and affection from people who have had life experiences similar to his own. He finds a community with which he can identify, people toward whom he can express the best human emotions that are in him, rather than the worst. He finds friends who will pull him up when he begins to slip or fall short of what he has set out to do: to develop and mature. In the new society, he finds a vehicle for expressing his best human qualities and potentialities.

Caste and Stratification

As has been indicated, an inmate subculture usually develops within any institution, producing a "we-they" attitude between the professional administration and the inmates. The underground inmate society has norms, patterns of behavior, and goals different from and usually in conflict with those of the overall institution.

The inmates and officialdom are divided into two segregated strata, or camps. The inmates may in one context be viewed as a caste of untouchables. They are restricted to an inferior position in the hierarchy, and in prison there is no possibility of their moving up. It is conceded by most correctional administrators that this inmate-administration conflict situation contradicts and impedes therapeutic progress for the inmate.

The inmate subsystem helps the patient or inmate cope with the new set of problems that he finds in most institutions. He feels rejected by the larger society and tries to compensate for this rejection. One way he does this is to reject and rebel against the administrators of society's rejection—the prison staff.

Synanon does not have a "we-they" caste system. It provides an openended stratification situation. Upward mobility is distinctly possible in the organization. (As Jack Hurst put it to one Synanon "prospect" during an indoctrination session, "In a couple of years . . . you just might be a big shot around here.") Not only is upward social mobility possible in Synanon, but healthy status-seeking is encouraged.

Synanon assumes, with some supportive evidence, that a person's position in its hierarchy is a correlate of social maturity, "mental health," increased work ability, and a clear understanding of the Synanon organization. Another assumption is that the social skills learned in Synanon are useful within the larger society. (The reverse appears to be true of the "skills" learned in prison society.) The "we-they" problem is nonexistent in Synanon, since administration and inmates are one and the same.

Tough Guys and Synanon Status

Synanon attempts to discourage the tough-guy criminal attitude. There is no symptom reinforcement of tough-guy behavior at Synanon, as there often is in jails and hospitals. In other settings, the offender receives approval from his fellow inmates and to some extent from professionals for being a tough guy.

In what is known as a "verbal haircut," Reid Kimball, an ex-criminal executive at Synanon, partially reveals the way Synanon attacks this tough-guy syndrome. The following comments made by Reid are taken from a more extended attack approach used on a group of tough-guy newcomers:

> Some of you guys in here will make it, whatever that means. I guess on some level, you want to quit being real nuts, lunatics, and locked up. It seems quite obvious that before that happens, you will have to quit doing what you've been doing. If this place was San Quentin or Sing Sing, I might agree with your tough-guy act. In prison, I suppose you have to let it be known that you were a hotshot on the streets and that you're a bad guy inside the walls. This is what you do to get status in prison. But think of how ludicrous it is when you come here to this place and you try to be tough guys or gangsters. In this place, if you make progress, you act like an adult.

Attacking the Criminal Mask: A "Haircut"

The criminal addict's self-concept makes him inept and keeps him on the wrong side of the law. A postulate at Synanon is that this face to the world must be changed and a new one developed. At Synanon this involves a 180-degree turn from the offender's past patterns of behavior. As the newcomer learns, criminal language, jargon, and values are viewed with disdain and extreme disapproval. The newcomer is permitted to hang on to his past destructive mold for a brief time. In short order, however, new words and behavior patterns are ruthlessly demanded.

Dederich has described part of Synanon's resocialization process in this area as follows:

> First you remove the chemical. You stop him from using drugs, and you do this by telling him to do it. He doesn't know he can do it himself, so you tell him to do it. We tell him he can stay and he can have a little job. We tell him we have a lot of fun and he might get his name in the newspapers. We say, "People come down and you can show off and have a fine time as long as you don't shoot dope. You want to shoot dope, fine, but someplace else, not here." He stops using drugs. Then you start working on secondary aspects of the syndrome. Addicts live by the discipline of narcotics; therefore, they talk about this all the time. They

discuss petty theft and short con; none of them is well enough for big con. Addicts never pull any big scores; they can't—they're sick people. They talk about this.

The next thing you do is attack the language. Eliminating their criminal language is very important. We get them off drugs by telling them, "Live here without using drugs and you can have all this." We get them off the negative language by initially giving them another. Since there is some vague connection between their personality problem and the social sciences, we encourage them to use this language. The language of psychology and sociology is great stuff. Whether or not the recovering addict knows what he's talking about is exquisitely unimportant at this time.

Very quickly, in a matter of about ninety days, they turn into junior psychiatrists and sociologists. They become familiar with the use of a dozen or twenty words and misuse them. Who cares! It doesn't make any difference. Now they're talking about "hidden superego," "transferences," "displacement," "primary and secondary groups." This is all coming out, and they're not saying "fix, fix, fix" all the time. "I used twenty dollars a day." "I used thirty dollars a day." "Joe went to jail." "I went to jail behind this broad." "Where did you do time?" and all that. They get off that, and they talk about ids, superegos, and group structure. They make another set of noises.

First, they substitute this sociological-psychological language wholesale. Eventually, when they come to learn something of the meanings of the words, they stop using them. Of course, like any intelligent adult, you don't lard your social conversation with technical terms. No one does this if he's in his right mind.

Language is, of course, the vehicle of culture and behavior; and at Synanon, it is instrumental in shifting the behavior patterns that the addict has used in the past. He begins to use a new, still undeveloped set of social-emotional muscles. This shift is not accomplished by loving and affectionate cajoling or by discussion of the criminal's symptoms of addiction and crime. There is minimal symptom reinforcement of criminal patterns. Behavior and thinking are modified by verbal-sledgehammer attacks. The attack is modulated and tuned by the expert synanist. The individual is blasted, then supported, and he seems to learn to change his behavior as a result of this positive traumatic verbal experience.

Group and Personal Identity

Dederich was once asked what he called Synanon inmates, and he replied, "We call them people."

Synanon members are not identified as wards, prisoners, or patients, and this makes a big difference in their self-identity and outlook. The person can identify himself with the constructive goals of the organization for which he works. After he kicks the habit, he automatically becomes an employee in the organization. In this capacity he is encouraged to take part in Synanon's management and development.

In the traditional institution, the inmate feels helpless and hopeless about his destiny. He has limited control over the institution, since it is run by administrators who are usually indifferent to his opinions about its management. Moreover, as we have noted, prison administrators are seen as representatives of society's rejection of the inmate, and this sets up additional blocks to correction. Inmates have a clear authority object for their frustrations and hatreds: the prison staff. At Synanon there is no such split, since the administration consists of coworkers and colleagues. There is no "they" to hate within the organization.

Involvement in Synanon may help to foster empathy in a person whose problem is alienation. Identification with Synanon involves feelings of concern for the other members and for the destiny of the totality of Synanon. The development of these empathic qualities reverses the inmate's past sociopathic lack of social concern.

The work assigned at Synanon is real work, unlike the often contrived jobs in prisons and mental hospitals. There is no basket weaving at Synanon. All work serves the real needs of the organization. This includes the functions of the "hustlers" of food, the office staff, the maintenance and service crews, the automotive crew, the operations crew, a sales crew, and the coordinating staff. Since its inception Synanon has always had fewer hands than it needs to carry out the many dimensions of its necessary work. Therefore, everyone in Synanon has meaningful work to do.

Cultural activities are in accord with the wishes and desires of the residents. There are no special rewards for participating other than those that the individual gets from the activity. He voluntarily attends lectures and seminars, takes part in theatrical groups and semantics classes. He doesn't participate, as he might in prison, for the sake of early parole.

There have been attempts at self-government in prisons and hospitals. In these settings, however, the inmates recognize that final decisions on important policy matters remain with the administration. In Synanon, perhaps for the first time in his life, the member assumes a significant role in controlling his future. Leadership in a constructive situation is a new experience for him, and it appears to develop responsibility. The residents of Synanon, unlike patients and inmates, are involved with the growth and development of their own organizations. Because there is a generally held belief by the residents that "Synanon saved our lives," the esprit de corps in the organization is quite powerful. Few inmates would give three cheers for dear old San Quentin, but Synanon people seem to enjoy praising their alma mater at every opportunity and work hard for its growth and development.

Group Psychotherapy in Prison and at Synanon

One significant major difference between the Synanon game and the usual institutional forms of group psychotherapy is that the Synanon sessions are not directed by professional therapists. There is some evidence that prison inmates participate in group psychotherapy with an eye on the gate leading out. Consciously and unconsciously, the prisoner may verbalize "insights," seemingly indicating therapeutic progress, in an effort to convince the therapist and prison officials that he has changed and is ready for release. At a group therapy session observed by one of the authors in a California prison, several inmates made a great show of getting wonderful insights, and as one fellow put it, "This program really makes me see life more clearly." But several inmates admitted in private, "Of course, I want to look good to get out of this dump."

Synanon sessions are more closely related to the real-life problems that confront the members. Given the lack of caste division, lines of communication are open throughout the organization. This, plus a goldfish-bowl atmosphere, is conducive to a more extensive reevaluation of underlying problems. ("We tell all our dirty little secrets.") The Synanon sessions make intense efforts to surface all possible data, since they are vital to the protection and growth of both the person and the organization. There is a strong belief at Synanon that a person who has been a criminal and a pathological liar cannot be allowed to lie at all, not even a little bit. The Synanon sessions are, in part, emotional first-aid stations where members must be completely candid and truthful. Unlike the usual prison or institutional group therapy situation, the Synanon member has nothing to lose and everything to gain from telling the truth.

Synanon in the Community

Synanon members have a qualitatively different relationship with the overall community than prisoners or inmates. The almost total isolation of the prisoner from the outside world is a major impediment to correction. The institutional setting isolates the confined offender and prevents the formation of relationships that might help him make the necessary transition to life outside the walls.

Synanon is in the community, and its members interact with outsiders on equal terms. Synanon's various homes receive hundreds of visits each week from both professionals and laymen. Unlike prisoners, Synanon people are not set apart and put on display for curious observers. They are not visited involuntarily, as in a prison, where approval for a visit is given by an administrator and the inmates have no control over the situation. People who live in Synanon can be selective about their guests, and they sometimes exercise this right. On rare occasions, visitors who do not behave properly are asked to leave.

All Synanon residents have significant experience in closely interacting with a variety of people from all walks of life. This type of experience seems to socialize Synanon people to function more effectively in the larger society, and thus fulfills a significant correctional goal.

In summary, the following elements reflect the significant difference found between Synanon and traditional correctional institutions:

1. There is a qualitative difference between indoctrination at Synanon and in other settings. The contractual arrangements for therapy and the prospect's expectation of success in Synanon are different. The indoctrination of the prospect by people who have themselves been in his shoes and succeeded appears to be a significant element, providing the newcomer with a role model of what he can become.

2. Synanon provides the possibility of upward mobility, whereas prisons and reformatories have caste systems. Becoming a Synanist provides incentive for changing one's criminal motivation to anticriminal motivation. The Synanon resident can actually achieve any role in the organization. In contrast, in the institution an inmate or patient is locked into the inmate position.

3. There is a qualitative difference between the Synanon and the form of group therapy carried on in prisons and hospitals. This is partly a function of differences in the overall social-system context. The Synanon resident, as a voluntary participant, has little to gain from faking progress, whereas in prison the appearance of being "rehabilitated" may be rewarded by an earlier release from custody. The Synanon person is encouraged to reveal and deal with his problems honestly by others who have traveled the established Synanon route to recovery.

4. The Synanon subculture is allied with the larger societal structure as traditional institutions never are. The flow of members of the community through Synanon and the participation of Synanon members in the larger society place it closer to the real-life situations of the outer world than the artificial communities of traditional institutions. In addition, Synanon residents have an involvement with and a commitment to their organization, whereas traditional institutions usually engender hostility and rebellion.

The Principal Social Forces at Work in Synanon

The following elements comprise the essential forces at work in the Synanon process:

Involvement.   Initially the Synanon society is able to involve and control the newcomer by providing an interesting social setting comprised of understanding associates who will not be outmaneuvered by manipulative behavior.

Achievable Success Goals.   Within the context of this system, the newcomer can (perhaps for the first time) see a realistic possibility for legitimate achievement and prestige. Synanon provides a rational opportunity structure for the success-oriented individual. He is no longer restricted to inmate status, since there is no inmate-staff division and all residents are staff members.

New Social Role.   Being a Synanist is a new social role. It can be temporarily or indefinitely occupied in the process of social growth and development. (Many residents have made the decision to make Synanon their lifework.) This new role is a legitimate one, supported by the former offender's community as well as by the inclusive society. With the opening of new Synanon houses and development of new projects, Synanon-trained staff is increasingly in demand. Since the Synanon organization is not a hospital or an institution, there is no compulsion to move out of this satisfying community.

Social Growth.   In the process of acquiring legitimate social status in Synanon, the offender necessarily, as a side effect, develops the ability to relate, communicate, and work with others. The values of truth, honesty, and industry become necessary means to this goal of status achievement. With enough practice and time, the individual socialized in this way reacts according to these values naturally.

Social Control.   The control of deviance is a by-product of the individual's status seeking. Conformity to the norms is necessary for achievement. Anomie, the dislocation of goals and means, is minimal. The norms are valid and adhered to within the social system, since the means are available for legitimate goal attainment.

Another form of control is embodied in the threat of ostracism. This, too, becomes a binding force. The relative newcomer in Synanon usually does not feel adequate for participation in the larger society. After a sufficient period of Synanon social living the resident no longer fears banishment and is adequately prepared for life on the outside (if this is his choice). However, he may remain voluntarily because he feels that Synanon is a valid way of life for him. In Synanon, he has learned and acquired a gratifying social role that enables him to help others who can benefit from the Synanon approach.

Another form of social control is the Synanon game. Here the individual is required to tell the truth. This helps to regulate his behavior. Transgressions are often prevented by the knowledge that his deviance will rapidly and necessarily be brought to the attention of the Synanon community in a Synanon session. He is living in a community where others know about and, perhaps more important, care about his behavior.

Empathy and Self-Identity.   The constant self-assessment required in daily life and in the Synanon sessions fosters the consolidation of self-identity and empathy. The individual's self-estimation is under constant assessment by relevant others, who become sensitive to and concerned about him. The process provides the opportunity for the individual almost literally to see himself as others see him. He is also compelled, as part of this process, to develop the ability to identify with and understand others. A side effect is personal growth and the development of social awareness, the ability to communicate, and empathic effectiveness.

When these socialization processes take hold, the individual becomes reconnected with the larger society and personally develops within the constructive framework of both Synanon and the larger society. The total combination of Synanon processes provide what Charles Dederich has aptly called "a tunnel back into the human race."

The Delancey Street Foundation

The Synanon program was not intended by its founder necessarily to prepare people for independent living in the community. Synanon residents were expected to live in Synanon indefinitely, and even those who came to reside outside of Synanon were expected to maintain their "lifeline" to the family. Some of the ex-addicts did break with Synanon and may have succeeded on their own. Currently there are no reliable data on the success or failure of people who have left Synanon.

John Maher, a former addict and ex-Synanon member, formed the Delancey Street Foundation in 1971.[20] Maher, with a team of associates, leased a large building in San Francisco. By 1975 the organization had a resident population of 300 addicts. The underlying philosophy of the Delancey Street Foundation was not too different from that of Synanon, except for the effort to prepare people to live as nonaddicts in the community and to discourage people from staying more than two years. While at Delancey, the residents are expected to acquire vocational, business, or professional skills that they will need if they are to succeed in the outside community.

Maher chose the name *Delancey Street* because it was supposed to symbolize the self-reliant spirit of immigrants from Europe who had come to Delancey Street, New York, in the nineteenth century.

Like Synanon, Delancey Street Foundation emphasizes its role as a family and does not receive government support or subsidy. It relies on voluntary contributions of friends and sympathizers; family-run enterprises; outside earnings of its residents; and donations of food, clothing, equipment, and money from business people. The cost of maintaining a person in Delancey is approximately four dollars a day compared to a cost of eighteen dollars a day to maintain a person in prison.

Enterprises include a restaurant that the family bought in downtown San Francisco, a moving company, and a flower business. From maintenance and food service through administration, everyone at Delancey Street has some kind of job. Obviously, many of these jobs involve work within the residence

---

[20]The information contained in this section was obtained during a visit by the authors to the Delancey Street Foundation house in San Francisco. In the course of the visit the authors had an opportunity to look over the premises, talk to some of the residents, and interview John Maher, the leader and moving force behind the "family" and the foundation.

—cleaning, food service, repairs, and other maintenance work. The organization also sends maintenance crews to do painting, gardening, and cleaning for pay in the community. They also have a work-training program to prepare people to assume outside jobs when they leave Delancey Street.

Formal education is encouraged through counseling, tutoring, and the use of community resources such as night schools and university extension courses. The most important educational and therapeutic service rendered, however, is the therapeutic milieu, an environment that rejects use of drugs and violence and gives acceptance and a family type of protection from outsiders.

The principal therapy offered, one in which all residents must participate, is the "circus," a version of the Synanon games. Each session lasts about three hours. The emphasis at these encounter sessions is mutual criticism and the development of self-awareness.

Nonresidents participate in the games by contributing monthly dues and thus becoming game club members. Students, teachers, doctors, mechanics, housewives, and others are included as game club members. Some come to learn something about the process, others to learn something about people who have been in trouble, and others come to learn something about themselves.

Summary

Detached-worker programs have been developed in all of our big cities in an effort to encourage the gang boy to move from delinquent to nondelinquent activities and values. The increased use of halfway houses and partway houses in the 1970s represents what is probably the most significant trend in the community treatment of delinquents. The use of the halfway house, once limited to providing a less structured environment for the youth coming out of a state training school, has come to be used as a last stop before removal from the community to a state training school. Synanon, and institutions modeled on it, all permit even greater interaction between the delinquent and others in the community.

Community treatment centers, halfway houses, and partway houses make it possible for the individual to maintain relatively normal relationships in the community. Probation and parole go even further toward encouraging an individual to live a normal life in the community. Modern correctional methods, then, focus on "normal" relationships in the community and do not deprive the delinquent of all of his connections to society.

Chapter
15

Probation
and
Parole

THE TWO ACTIONS of a correctional system that leave the greatest autonomy to the person serving a sentence of a court are probation and parole. The first, probation, represents the sentence imposed by a court in lieu of confinement. The person sentenced spends no time at all in a correctional institution with the exception of time he may have spent in detention prior to his trial. Once he is sentenced to probation by a judge, the offender is relatively free as long as he conforms to the conditions imposed by the judge. He is placed under the supervision of a probation officer, who is a peace officer charged with seeing that these conditions are met. The probation officer has many other duties and problems, some of which will be discussed in this chapter.

Parole is similar to probation in that the parolee is also relatively free in the community. He, too, is supervised by a peace officer, usually called a parole agent. The major difference between probation and parole is that the parolee has served at least part of his sentence in a correctional institution. He is released from the correctional institution prior to the expiration of his sentence and allowed to serve the remainder of his sentence in the community, provided he lives up to the conditions imposed by the releasing authority.

Probation

Probation is a treatment program in which the final action in an adjudicated offender's case is suspended, so that he remains at liberty, subject to conditions imposed by or for a court under the supervision and guidance of a probation officer. The correctional system provides for the treatment and supervision of offenders in the community by placing them on probation in lieu of confinement in a custodial insitution. In most states, probationers serve the sentence of a court under the supervision of a probation officer assigned by the court. The judge has broad powers in this situation and sets the conditions of probation and the length of the supervision period. He maintains the power to order revocation of probation, usually for a violation of one of the conditions set by him or his agent or for the commission of another offense. The effect of revocation is to send a probationer to a custodial institution.[1]

A few states have centralized probation systems, but most of the 3,068 counties in the United States exercise autonomy within limits set by state statutes. For example, the probation system in California is a centralized system that authorizes each county to provide facilities, services, and regulations. In many states, probation is an activity of the court—criminal, juvenile, or other—with the probation officer serving as an appointee of the judge. There is therefore considerable variation in the use of probation and the manner in which it is administered.[2]

In general, adult probation services are state functions and juvenile probation services tend to be local functions. In thirty-two states, juvenile courts administer probation services. In thirty states, adult probation is combined with parole services.[3] In terms of the number of persons served and of total operating costs, the juvenile probation system has approximately twice as many resources per capita as the adult system.[4]

More than half the offenders sentenced to correctional treatment in 1965 (684,088 individuals) were placed on probation. By 1975 the number was over a million. The average case load assigned to a probation officer is usually around seventy-five. The typical probation case load is usually a random mixture of cases requiring varying amounts of service and surveillance.

The probation officer sees that the probationer lives up to the conditions of the probation. He assists the probationer with problems at work or school, or with members of his family, and provides guidance. Dressler notes four central techniques used by the probation officer:

---

[1]David Dressler, *Practice and Theory of Probation and Parole* (New York: Columbia University Press, 1969), pp. 16–36.

[2]Dressler, *Practice and Theory of Probation and Parole,* p. 27.

[3]President's Commission on Law Enforcement and Administration of Justice, *Task Force Report: Corrections* (Washington, D.C.: U.S. Government Printing Office, 1967), p. 35.

[4]*Task Force Report: Corrections,* p. 27.

1. *Manipulative techniques.* The environment may be manipulated in the interests of the person seeking help. The end product is usually something material and tangible received by the individual under care; for example, financial aid rendered by the agency or an employer persuaded to rehire a discharged worker.

2. *Executive techniques.* The probation officer may refer the individual to other resources in the community for help that the correctional agency cannot render. For example, the probation officer may refer the individual to a legal aid society or secure public assistance for him.

3. *Guidance techniques.* The probation officer may give personal advice and guidance on problems not requiring complex psychological techniques. The advice is likely to be fairly direct and the guidance comparatively superficial. The end product is intangible, although it may facilitate the achievement of tangible goals. For example, the individual is advised how to budget his income or helped to explore the possibilities of training in a trade.

4. *Counseling techniques.* These are based largely upon pyschological orientations and require considerable skill. The services are intangible, concerned with deep-seated problems in the emotional area; for example, aid in adjusting a marital situation or help in overcoming specific emotional conflicts.[5]

It is obvious that a probation officer cannot possibly perform all of these services for seventy-five people, the average case load. Authorities are agreed that there are far too few probation officers and that not all of them are adequately trained. Contacts are infrequent and services inadequate. Nevertheless, the success of probation, as measured by those who complete probation without revocation, has been surprisingly high. A review of several probation studies indicates an average success rate of about 75 percent.[6]

Conditions of Probation

Because probation has always been regarded as a form of leniency through which the judge permits a convicted man to remain in the community instead of being sent to prison, the power of the judge to impose conditions is seldom challenged. The courts have even upheld conditions of probation that restrict the constitutional rights of a probationer, where the restrictions have a clear-cut relationship to his rehabilitation. However, the limitations imposed on a probationer must not be capricious or impossible.

In an analysis of standards relating to probation, Carl H. Imlay and Charles R. Glasheen list the following questionable conditions of probation imposed by some courts across the country:

---

[5]Dressler, *Practice and Theory of Probation and Parole,* pp. 151-52.

[6]*Task Force Report: Corrections,* p. 28.

1. Must attend church.
2. Cannot marry without permission of the supervising officer.
3. Cannot smoke.
4. Total abstention from alcohol.
5. Cannot frequent places where liquor is served or sold.
6. Must not grow a beard or long hair or wear clothing not in conformance with the customs of the community.
7. Require the wife to report when the probationer is unable to.
8. Submit to search and seizure at the discretion of the probation officer, including home as well as person.
9. Pursue medical or psychiatric treatment.
10. Unrealistic fines and restitution.
11. Refrain from driving a car, especially where a car is needed in work or in the home.
12. Requirement as to how earnings are to be spent.
13. Refrain from associating with *any* person who has been convicted at one time or another.
14. Requirement to pursue employment that is contrary to probationer's interests.
15. Requirement to contribute to a charitable cause.
16. Requirement to do charitable work.
17. Cannot become pregnant during probation.
18. Unrealistic restrictions on travel (e.g., a weekend trip from Chicago to Milwaukee to visit family members).
19. Restrictions on dates.
20. Be at home at unrealistic evening hours.
21. Unrealistic reporting requirements (e.g., an invalid, a person living a considerable distance from the office or during hours of probationer's employment).
22. Requirement to attend school when past the compulsory attendance age.
23. Requirement to live in a special place of noninstitutional residence.[7]

Some of the conditions imposed violate the constitutional rights of probationers. For example, requiring a probationer to attend church violates freedom of religion. Conditions attempting to regulate hair style, clothing style, or appearance violate the probationer's right to expression. Middle class and middle-aged people in our society tend to regard long hair and certain styles of dress as symptomatic of antisocial conduct. Some deduce from certain lifestyles such behavior as rioting, pot-smoking, drug abuse, and sexual deviance. Judges who feel this way at times order probationers to cut their hair

[7]Carl H. Imlay and Charles R. Glasheen, "See What Condition Your Conditions Are In," *Federal Probation* 35(June 1971):3–11.

and dress in a clean-cut manner. Not only are such conditions vague, they violate the constitutional rights of a person to determine his own hair style and dress. Probation officers given the power to enforce such a condition may interpret it in various ways, thus further placing the probationer at the mercy of the whims of others. Imlay and Glasheen cite several cases in which courts have upheld the right of an individual to present himself to the world in the manner of his choice. While these dicisions do not specifically apply to probationers, they could be made to apply to probationers; they could be made to apply by courts unless there is some relationship between the required physical appearance and the probationer's rehabilitation.

While a person convicted of a crime no longer has a privilege against self-incrimination regarding that particular crime, he may not be required to give evidence against himself regarding some other possible violation of law. If a condition of probation requires that an offender answer all questions about himself and he accepts the condition, he may be regarded as having waived the privilege against self-incrimination, although this question has not yet been decided by the courts. Conditions restricting the rights of association of probationers and those requiring them to submit to search have been upheld by the courts.

The probation officer is now given greater discretion than heretofore in interpreting the conditions imposed by the court in favor of greater freedom for the probationer. For example, one condition imposed on a probationer is that he not associate with known criminals. For many years this provision has interfered with the application of group therapy to offenders on probation. The first efforts to break this barrier were made by Drs. Alexander B. Smith and Alexander Bassin, probation officers of the New York State Supreme Court in Brooklyn. They initiated group therapy sessions for probationers at the clinic of the Brooklyn Association for the Rehabilitation of Offenders (BARO) despite the fact that association with known criminals violated a condition of probation. The judges and the probation department accepted the activities of the BARO clinic as a permissible exception to probation conditions.

When Synanon was first established in California in 1958, probationers and parolees going to Synanon were considered to be in violation of probation or parole. However, by the late 1960s the policies of the probation and parole agencies had changed, making it possible for probationers and parolees to participate in Synanon activities.

With respect to standard conditions, Imlay and Glasheen say:

> The American Bar Association Standards refer to probation as "an affirmative correction tool." In this spirit we would expect that each of the conditions of probation would be of benefit to the probationer and relevant to his rehabilitation program; consequently, each condition should be tested to see whether it performs that function. There are several conditions which are routinely applied, as it is believed that they

are helpful to the defendant's rehabilitation. Perhaps the most fundamental of these conditions is that the probationer shall not violate any law. (Although failure to support one's legal dependents would be a violation of the law in most jurisdictions and thus implicit in this condition, it is often set out expressly.) The idea that the probationer shall not ieave the jurisdiction without permission is also considered fundamental. In most instances the probationer is required to be employed and in some cases the type of his employment is restricted. Of necessity the probation order usually contains a condition relating to the probationer's reporting to a probation officer. In the hope of preventing further offenses of the same type, other conditions are often imposed. For example, some courts have restricted those with whom the probationer may associate, prohibited a telephone in a defendant's home, restricted the use of an automobile, prohibited the defendant from employing women, and have ordered the probationer to stay away from a particular woman. While these special restrictions might not be relevant in preventing recidivism in probationers generally, they may be helpful in an individual case. For example, a restriction against having a telephone in his home may be highly relevant to the rehabilitation program of a bookmaker. It may have no discernible relationship to the program for a tax-evading businessman.

It is for this reason that the ABA Standards recommend that the sentencing court be authorized to prescribe conditions to fit the circumstances of each case.[8]

The objectives of a probation program have been listed as follows:

1. To determine, after careful investigation and analysis, whether probation is the most appropriate treatment plan.
2. To help the individual, juvenile or adult, accept the reality of community rules and legal sanctions, and to work on such personality factors and environmental conditions as interfere with his acceptance of such limitations.
3. To help the probationer (an individual who according to a decision by society can be rehabilitated while continuing to live in the community) change his behavior to meet society's demands and to make a different use of himself—a use that is positive, constructive, and in conformance with the standards imposed by society. This process is referred to as probation casework.
4. To provide children who cannot be cared for in their own homes with foster homes or institutional care; to continuously evaluate the use of

---

[8]Imlay and Glasheen, "See What Condition Your Conditions Are In," pp. 3–4.

the placement with a view toward eventual return home; to work with the child's parents, as well as the child, toward termination of the separation from home.

5. To recommend termination of probation whenever it is recognized that this service is no longer needed or appropriate.[9]

Probation Supervision in the Community

Contact is generally established when, having been placed on probation by a court, a juvenile or adult appears for his first appointment. The probation officer to whom the person is assigned has usually received an advanced report from the probation officer who investigated the case.

During the initial interview, the ward's attitude is of primary concern and often determines the treatment program arranged for him. The resistant person is generally seen more frequently than one who relates easily. Priority for treatment is usually given to (1) those probationers the probation officers feel they can definitely aid, and (2) those probationers against whom the most complaints have been made.

There is considerable difference in case loads between juvenile and adult probation. The juvenile probation officer typically has about 15 probationers. The adult probation officer may have between 200 and 250 probationers. Juvenile probation officers do considerably more work on each case than do adult probation officers.

The probation officer makes an effort to influence the parents as well as the probationer. The probation officer has the power to remove the probationer from the home and place him in a foster home or remove him from the community and place him in an institution. When dealing with adults, the probation officer places most of the responsibility on the individual. Most adults are placed on probation at the request of the probation officer and as a result of court determinations.

Probation officers have two major problems: the amount of their paperwork and the size of their case loads. The vast amount of paperwork that is requried is responsible for much of the ineffectiveness of the program, since it takes valuable time away from the vital human association between the probation officer and his client. (One probation officer indicated, for example, that he often found himself looking for ways to cut his interviews short to allow himself enough time to finish his paperwork.)

Nearly all probation officers are dissatisfied with the size of their case loads. One probation officer who had 226 individuals under his supervision met with approximately 90 wards a month. He obviously had little time to attempt rehabilitation or therapy of any kind. Even with the smaller case loads of

---

[9]The program described is that of the Los Angeles County Probation Department.

juvenile probation officers, an individual is seldom seen more than twice a month.

According to one officer, for every eighty-five cases on probation, about fifteen are placed in camps or special schools. About thirty-five clients are dismissed within six months, and the other thirty-five are visited rather informally in their homes to see how they are doing. When handled in this way, the actual case load is not too large. A juvenile probation officer with a case load of seventy-five may place his clients in three categories: (1) minimum services (seen once a month or less); (2) medium services (seen once a month); (3) maximum services (seen frequently). Normally, only about ten would fall into the third category and be seen once or possibly two to three times a week. Obviously, youths seen once a month or less do not receive the attention they require.

Probation Detention Facilities: Los Padrinos

Los Padrinos is one of the several detention facilities operated by the Los Angeles County Probation Department where children are detained pending court hearing, disposition, and placement. The facilities are separate from the detention facilities for nondelinquent juveniles. These, the "dependent" or "neglected" children, are usually housed at MacClaren Hall. The primary function of Los Padrinos is detention. The intent of the program at Los Padrinos is to help prepare children for their next destination, a camp, foster home, probation, or reception center of the California Youth Authority.

The juvenile arrives at Los Padrinos as a result of certain legal procedures. Any minor taken into custody under age eighteen must be released within forty-eight hours after having been taken into custody unless a petition to declare him a ward or dependent child of the juvenile court has been filed. Within seventy-two hours, the youth must appear before juvenile court if a petition has been filed against him. If no petition is filed, he must be released. At this hearing, known as the detention hearing, the court decides whether to put the child in detention. A child is kept in detention for one of the following reasons:

1. The juvenile concerned is destitute, without supervision, and is in the need of protective custody.
2. The release of the juvenile would endanger his person or morals.
3. The juvenile has a record as a runaway and if released could be expected to leave the jurisdiction of the court.
4. The record of the juvenile and the gravity of the offense are such that his release would prove dangerous to public welfare.
5. The juvenile is in need of medical care and is not receiving it.

Los Padrinos' facilities include a large gymnasium, a swimming pool, a library, schoolrooms, and extensive play areas. The institution houses both boys and girls. There are ten boys' units and four girls' units housing a total of approximately three hundred children. Each unit usually houses twenty children, with four staff members on duty at all times. The age range is eight to eighteen. A special complex for younger boys has one unit for eight-to-twelve-year-olds and another unit for twelve-to-fifteen-year-olds.

Upon entering Los Padrinos, the child is first given a complete medical checkup. Many of the children come directly from the scene of apprehension, sometimes badly beaten, in poor health, and generally poorly clothed. Upon completion of the checkup, the child is stripped of his possessions, and clothing is issued for the remainder of his stay. Each child has a separate room.

Security at Los Padrinos is provided by the control staff. This team is on call twenty-four hours a day and can get to any unit in about thirty seconds if it has to. The control staff is in charge of all movement of children in and out of the institution. In the area where the control staff is based, a control monitor pipes music to all units and can also monitor all rooms and outside areas in order to hear what is going on. At night the monitor automatically makes a complete scan of the entire institution every three minutes. This monitor is never turned off.

When entering Los Padrinos, one goes through one of four main security doors at the entrance. These doors have no locks on the inside, so even if a staff member were attacked, his keys would be of no use. The doors must be released by the person on duty at the control desk inside the cage.

Los Padrinos is not a treatment facility. The average length of stay is twenty-eight days for boys and thirty-one days for girls. There is, however, no maximum time limit on length of stay. The court decides how long a ward will be at Los Padrinos.

A special unit called the Intensive Care Unit houses wards who are unable to control their behavior or cannot adjust to group living. The Intensive Care Unit has twenty single rooms and two maximum-security cells, which are completely bare; these two rooms are very seldom used. A child is usually kept in this unit for only twenty-four hours and then only as a last resort. Children who are extremely violent or who attempt suicide are sent to downtown Juvenile Hall, which has a staff of psychiatrists and psychologists and is close to General Hospital.

Parole

Parole is a treatment program in which the offender, after serving part of a term in a correctional institution, is conditionally released under the supervision and treatment of a parole officer.

Several requirements define the minimum time to be served before eligibility for parole occurs:

1. It might be the minimum of the sentence less good-time allowance. For example, if the sentence is five to ten years, the prisoner is eligible for parole in five years, less time off for good behavior.

2. It might be a specified part of the maximum of the sentence. If the law specifies that one-third the maximum sentence be served and the sentence is five to ten years, the prisoner is eligible for release on parole in three years and four months, less time off for good behavior.

3. There are other formulas applied fixing minimum time to be served before one can be released on parole. For example, when a life sentence is imposed by a federal court, the earliest possible release is in fifteen years. When a life sentence is imposed by a California court, the earliest possible release is in seven years.

There are basically three types of agencies that are empowered to grant parole: a board set up for the correctional institution; a central parole board for a state; and a group of officials, usually called a parole commission, whose principal functions are other than granting parole. The institutional board is composed mainly of personnel from the specific prison in which the candidate for parole is confined. It usually includes the warden. This means that conformity to the rules of the prison may be the principal criterion applied. However, even where representatives of a central parole board come to the prison to conduct parole hearings, they are greatly influenced by the recommendations of the warden and other custodial people. The prisoner who does not conform to prison rules is not likely to be released on parole. The advantage of the central parole board is that it provides uniform standards throughout the state. This type of releasing authority predominates in adult parole. Institutional boards are the releasing authority for juveniles in thirty-three states.[10]

The national average of time spent in correctional institutions before first release on parole was twenty-eight months. States with the lowest average of confinement before first release were Vermont, twelve months; Wyoming, sixteen months; South Dakota, seventeen months; Montana, eighteen months; Maine, nineteen months; Idaho, twenty months; and Oregon, twenty-two months. All of these are relatively small states. Some our largest states keep prisoners in confinement for longer periods of time; for example, the average time spent in confinement before first release was thirty months in California and thirty-seven months in New York and Pennsylvania.[11]

Parole is not a right of every individual in prison. It is viewed as a privilege granted to a prisoner for good behavior and progress while in prison and is considered useful in his rehabilitation outside the prison. In practice it

---

[10]Dressler, *Practice and Theory of Probation and Parole,* pp. 86–87.

[11]Daniel Glaser, Fred Cohen, and Vincent O'Leary, *The Sentencing and Parole Process* (Washington, D.C.: U.S. Government Printing Office, 1966), p. 12.

is a system of conditional release that permits a prisoner to leave the prison before the completion of his maximum sentence and live in the community under supervision of a parole officer.

Parole is beneficial to society in that, to some extent, it protects society from the individual while he is on parole. It is also beneficial to the parolee because he may serve part of his sentence in relative freedom, outside the prison; he may assume most of his community roles and possibly get some assistance in obtaining employment. If a parolee violates the conditions of his parole, the parole may be revoked and he may be taken back to prison. The parolee may have an extremely hard time obtaining employment and otherwise adapting in the community. A parole officer may help him with his personal problems so he will be able to reassume his normal community roles.

Before a prisoner is placed on parole, he must receive a determination of readiness by the parole authority. After he has received this determination he has a parole hearing. This is an interview with a representative of the parole authority to determine his willingness and ability to obey the law and the conditions of the parole agreement. Once all of the necessary hearings have been held, the final decision rests with the parole board. The board reviews all of the pertinent reports and records on the individual, such as a complete social history revealing the nature of the offense, a family history, and statements of teachers, clergymen, employers, or others who may furnish information relative to the prisoner's readiness for parole. Also considered is a complete record of past and present offenses. The reports of prison officials regarding the prisoner's behavior in prison and his efforts at rehabilitation are given great weight. The individual is given medical and psychological tests to help determine his ability to function once again in society. The parole officer must draw up a plan for the parolee to follow outside the prison. This must include plans for employment, housing, and the resolution of other anticipated problems.[12]

It is expected that while in prison, the prisoner will be provided with job training or some vocational skills that will better prepare him for life in the community. Recreational, educational, and vocational-training facilities in prison are intended to help in rehabilitation. Medical, psychological, and counseling programs, group therapy sessions, and other therapeutic processes are supposed to prepare the individual to reenter society.

A counseling program is one important aspect of a prerelease preparation program. The prisoner may be deemed ready for release when he appears before a parole hearing officer. However, he may suffer anxieties and fears

---

[12]See Dressler, *Practice and Theory of Probation and Parole,* Chap. 7, for a detailed discussion of the process of selection for parole. See also Reed K. Clegg, *Probation and Parole* (Springfield, Ill.: Charles C Thomas, 1964).

about the outside world. Whether or not the parolee leaves the prison with hostile attitudes will depend in part on the way the parole hearings are held and the way he has been treated in prison.

Parole is in every sense a continuation of the correctional process. The goal is to help reestablish the parolee in the community as a law-abiding citizen. Parole supervision includes efforts to discover the strengths in the parolee's personality and his ways of dealing with emotional problems. The parole officer cannot permit the parolee to become dependent on him for all decisions and solutions to his problems. The individual on parole must learn to handle successfully difficult situations that may arise. However, the parole officer should be able to obtain help for the parolee when required.

The parole officer has three main functions in his relationship with the parolee. The first is to use his knowledge of community resources to help the parolee and his family adjust to society. The second is to provide or obtain treatment for the parolee when required. This includes dealing with psychological problems. The third function is supervision. The parole officer is supposed to do what he can to keep the parolee from violating the conditions of his parole. He may visit the parolee's home or work location to determine his progress. He may also interview family members and other important persons who can help the parole officer in determining the parolee's progress. The necessity of field visits depends on each individual case. Visits may occur as often as once a week or as seldom as once a month, depending on the parolee's adjustment.[13]

The parolee is required to accept and sign the parole agreement. He is told that if he breaks any conditions his parole will be revoked and he will have to go back to prison.

The period of parole varies from state to state and among individuals as well. It largely depends on the progress made by the parolee in the community. In most cases, parole lasts from two to five years.

Parole officers do not receive specific training in the role of a parole officer. At school they may have taken courses in one or more of the social sciences such as psychology, sociology, social welfare, or criminology. However, probation and parole authorities have consistently failed to agree upon a program of academic training and therefore have not set up specific academic requirements for appointment. The social science fields do teach things about parole but do not provide adequate training. Educators in schools of social work are in general agreement that a master's degree in social work is an excellent form of academic preparation for work in the parole and probations fields. However, few parole officers have such degrees.[14]

Weller and Flood have presented an excellent analysis of the parole

---

[13]National Conference on Parole, *Parole in Principle and Practice* (New York: National Probation and Parole Association, 1957), pp. 65–129.

[14]Clegg, *Probation and Parole,* p. 121.

agent's job at the Colorado State Parole Department, one which can serve as a model for parole.[15]

The Parole Agent's Tasks

Examination of the parole agent's job at the Colarado State Parole Department reveals the following analysis of tasks and subtasks. Although different officers specialize in different tasks and different subtasks, there are *three general tasks* that are performed:

1. *Investigation*
   This general task consists of all the activities that a parole officer may perform in connection with the collection of information and the preparation of reports which are required by the parole board, the parole administrator, or the institution from which the offender is being paroled, both prior to and after parole is granted.
2. *Supervision and Counseling*
   This general task concerns all activities related to general supervision, counseling, and guidance that a parole officer may perform for a parolee during his adjudicated term of parole.
3. *Enforcement*
   This general task concerns all activities that a parole agent may perform in connection with investigation of suspected parole violations and those activities related to the revocation of parole as well as the collection of information regarding general parole adjustment by the parolee.

The general task of *Investigation* has two major subtasks as its components:

1. Preparole Institutional Interview—those activities connected with the interviewing of the inmate immediately after his arrival at the institution for the purpose of collecting data relevant to formulation of an acceptable parole plan.
2. Field Agent Investigation—those activities centering on the collection of information and interviewing of residential and employment contacts in the community in which the parolee wishes to be paroled. This is compiled into a report entitled "Preparole Investigation."

The general task of *Supervision and Counseling* has four major subtasks identified with it:

1. Initial Interview and Routine Contacts—a subtask concerned with the initial interview of the parolee by the parole agent at the

[15]Charles D. Weller and John L. Flood, *An Operational Analysis of the Parole Task* (Boulder, Colo.: Western Interstate Commission for Higher Education, 1969).

institution prior to release and at the District Office immediately following parole release, as well as the periodic procedures of reporting of the parolee to the parole agent.

2. Personal Counseling—a subtask that includes all the activities connected with securing and maintaining employment opportunities for the parolee; the provision of guidance related to family relationships; financial guidance and/or supervision related to a satisfactory financial condition for the parolee and his family; provision of necessary treatment or therapy for sustaining the mental health of the parolee.

3. Narcotics—a subtask involving a range of activities related to the investigation, supervision, and guidance of parolees who have been known narcotics users or who are currently suspected of using narcotics.

4. Alcoholism—a subtask related to the elements of work associated with the guidance, supervision, and assistance necessary to support a known alcoholic in a manner which will deter his use of alcoholic beverages.

The general task of *Enforcement* has one major subtask as its primary component:

Parole Violation—a subtask including the activities of the supervising field parole agent related to the surveillance and arrest, if necessary, of parolees suspected of a violation of the terms and conditions of parole and a determination of the facts related thereto. It also includes the Special Services Investigation, which is a part of the subtask oriented toward law-enforcement activities. These include the investigation, arrest, and interrogation of suspected parole violators and preparation of reports describing the violation of the terms and conditions of parole. This subtask includes the extradition and transportation of parole absconders and parole violators inter- and intrastate.[16]

Table 15.1 illustrates the connection between each task and the three objectives of parole: protection of the community, rehabilitation of the parolee, and furthering justice.

The services performed by parole divisions are essentially the same as those performed by probation departments. The principal difference is that probation occurs in lieu of confinement while parole follows confinement. Another important difference is that probation services are generally rendered within the confines of a court complex and under the jurisdiction of a court,

---

[16]Weller and Flood, *Operational Analysis of the Parole Task,* pp. 16–18.

Table 15.1

A Parole Agent's Tasks Related to Objectives

General Tasks	Subtasks	Objectives
A. Investigation	1. Preparole institutional interview	Protection
	2. Field agent investigation	Rehabilitation
		Justice
B. Supervision and Counseling	1. Initial interview and routine contacts	Protection
	2. Personal guidance	Rehabilitation
	3. Narcotic supervision	Justice
	4. Alcoholism supervision	
C. Enforcement	1. Field agent investigation	Protection
	2. Special services investigation	Rehabilitation
	and enforcement	Justice
	3. Extradition—transportation of violators	

SOURCE: Charles D. Weller and John L. Flood, *An Operational Analysis of the Parole Task* (Boulder, Colo.: Western Interstate Commission for Higher Education, 1969), p. 6.

NOTE: *A general task* is defined as a function of a job that can be performed independently of any other function comprising a job. *A subtask* is defined as one of several functions that support the performance of a task. The general task cannot be performed without completion of the several subtasks on which it is based.

while parole services are generally under the jurisdiction of a correctional authority.

There has been a tendency in recent years to combine probation and parole operations under one organization, and this is always done for those convicted in federal courts. Both probation and parole deal with adjudged criminals and delinquents outside of institutions, and since the services they render are similar, it is logical that they should be placed under one administrative agency. If that agency also controls the confinement facilities, coordination and integration of the various correctional services and institutions are facilitated.

Although many offenders are not returned to the community until the completion of their sentences, more than 60 percent of adult felons are released on parole prior to the expiration of the maximum terms of their sentences. Parole is generally granted by an administrative board or agency, which bases its decision on the applicant's prior history, his readiness for release, and his need for supervision and assistance in the community prior to the expiration of his sentence. The average number of persons on parole from state and federal prisons during 1965 was 112,142. State and federal training schools for youthful offenders accounted for 60,483 cases.[17]

It is estimated that 35 to 45 percent of adult offenders released on parole are returned to prison. The majority are returned for violations of parole regulations. About a third are returned after being convicted of new felonies. Violation rates are higher for juveniles.[18]

Of the approximately 103,000 prisoners released from custody in 1974 to resume life in the community, 75 percent, over 77,000, were given conditional release, virtually all of which was to parole supervision.[19] According to the FBI, of those persons released on parole in 1972, 71 percent repeated (were convicted of other offenses) within four years, and 57 percent of those placed on probation repeated within the same four years.[20] These data indicate a far higher failure rate on parole and probation than in previous years. One possible explanation that is often ignored is that a far greater number of persons released from prisons were placed on parole with no corresponding increase in parole personnel or services. For example, in 1965, according to the *Task Force Report,* about 60 percent were released on parole. In 1975, the percentage was about 75 percent.

Whatever the explanation, there is no doubt that the media and many experts were charging that the parole system had failed. California newspapers, for example, were headlining the fact that state statistics indicated that 25 percent of the persons arrested for robbery in the first three months of 1976 were parolees.[21] They did not bother to explain that less than 5 percent of the total of felony arrests were of parolees. Nor did they explain that using computerized files our police are more likely to "suspect" parolees. There were no data on how many of these people were found guilty of the offense.

In New York State a Citizen's Inquiry on Parole and Criminal Justice, after noting deficiencies in the state parole system, concluded that "Discretionary release and compulsory community supervision which rely on the rehabilitation theory should therefore be discontinued."[22]

Smith and Berlin, commenting on this report, had this to say:

---

[17] *Task Force Report: Corrections,* p. 60.

[18] *Task Force Report: Corrections* p. 62.

[19] U.S. Department of Justice, *National Prisoner Statistics Bulletin, Prisoners in State and Federal Institutions, 1974* (Washington, D.C.: U.S. Government Printing Office, 1975), p. 4.

[20] Federal Bureau of Investigation, *Uniform Crime Reports, 1975* (Washington, D.C.: U.S. Government Printing Office, 1976), p. 44.

[21] *Los Angeles Times,* December 28, 1976.

[22] *Report on Parole* (New York City: Citizens' Inquiry on Parole and Criminal Justice, 1974), p. 17.

It emphasized the high rate of recidivism of parolees, the inadequacy of parole's employment program, the difficulties in assisting parolees in obtaining needed money, unreasonable difficulties caused parolees in obtaining motor vehicle driving licenses and the fact that parolees are returned to prison at only a slightly better rate than those who serve out their terms. The report is particularly critical of the "enormous amount of unstructured and invisible discretion exercised by the parole board and the parole service." Specifically, the paper criticizes the parole board's release interviews and parole eligibility decisions which are "rule of thumb," not based on rational criteria for determining at what point an inmate is sufficiently "rehabilitated" to merit release on parole. Moreover, the report indicates the contradictory role of the parole officer as social worker and law enforcer and notes the enormous power he wields in deciding whom and when to charge with violations of parole so that revocation proceedings may be initiated. While there is truth in some of the criticisms, and a kernel of truth in others, overall the report was based on poor research methodology and aimed at creating a small sensation: . . . It is quite conceivable that another group of researchers using the above methodology, interviewing other officials and perusing the material mentioned might have arrived at other conclusions.[23]

Governor Walker of Illinois announced on February 18, 1975, at a National Governor's Conference, that he would scrap parole on the same basis that the Citizens' Inquiry on Parole and Criminal Justice in New York State advocated.[24]

The high failure rates may be attributed in part to deficiencies in the correctional system. The custodial institution fails to prepare the inmate adequately for release to the community, or the parole system fails to plan properly for the offender's release. Ideally, the parole process should begin when an offender is first received in an institution. An institutional program of training and treatment should be projected from a study of his background and an assessment of his potential. Simultaneously, trained staff members, institutional or parole, should be working with the offender's family and employer or potential employer to develop a release plan.

There are, however, wide discrepancies between what parole should be and what it actually is in most jurisdictions.[25] According to a national survey in 1965, adults released on parole were supervised in case loads averaging sixty-eight. The average case load for juveniles was about sixty-four. These

---

[23]Alexander B. Smith and Louis Berlin, *Introduction to Probation and Parole*, (St. Paul, Minn.: West Publishing Co., 1976), pp. 67–68.

[24]Smith and Berlin, *Introduction to Probation and Parole*, pp. 195–96.

[25]Smith and Berlin, *Introduction to Probation and Parole*, pp. 201–2.

case-load averages do not include the heavy time commitment that aftercare workers must make in contacting parents and others in the community in connection with the release of juveniles. The best estimates available from current research indicate that case loads should average thirty-five or fewer per officer.[26]

By 1977, parole services had not been significantly improved, and critics had become more vocal in their demands for the dismantling of the parole system. One alternative offered involves longer sentences and release without supervision. Another alternative is diversion from the criminal justice system. A third possibility, one which does not have much support in 1977, is close supervision parole in lieu of confinement. This latter course of action would require case loads of fifteen to twenty and a doubling of parole resources. The expansion of parole services would not be nearly as costly as keeping people in prison for longer periods. Studies indicate that the cost of keeping an adult offender in a state institution is about six times as great as that required to supervise him on probation. The cost of keeping a married man is prison is $11,000 compared to an annual average of less than $365 on parole and/or probation.[27] One wonders why political figures and law-enforcement personnel appear more willing to expand the very costly prison system than they are to provide adequate funds and personnel to parole and probation services, a far less costly way of dealing with the problem.

Procedural Rights at Revocation Hearings: Probation and Parole

The United States Supreme Court, in an unanimous decision rendered the case of *Morrissey* v. *Brewer,* on June 29, 1972, decided that a parolee accused of violating the conditions of parole was entitled to due process before a decision could be made to send him back to confinement. While each state had the right to set up its own code of procedure, the Court held that the following minimum requirements of due process must be afforded the parolees:

1. Written notice of the alleged parole violations.
2. Disclosure of the evidence against him.
3. The opportunity to appear and speak on his own behalf and present witnesses and documentary evidence.
4. The right to confront and cross-examine adverse witnesses (unless the hearing officer specifically finds good cause for not allowing confrontation).

---

[26]Smith and Berlin, *Introduction to Probation and Parole,* p. 70.

[27]Chamber of Commerce of the United States, "Marshaling Citizen Power to Modernize Corrections," in *Penology* ed. George G. Killinger and Paul F. Cromwell, Jr. (St. Paul, Minn.: West Publishing, 1973), p. 384.

5. A "neutral and detached" hearing body such as a traditional parole board, members of which need not be judicial officers or lawyers; and (finally) a written statement by the factfinders as to the evidence relied on and reasons for revoking parole.

The Court did not equate a parole-revocation proceeding to a criminal prosecution. For example, it permitted the consideration of *hearsay evidence,* including letters, affidavits, and other material that would not be admissible in a criminal trial.[28]

In the case of *Gagnon* v. *Scarpelli,* the Supreme Court extended the minimum requirements provided by the *Morrissey* case to probation-revocation proceedings. The Court found no difference between the due-process rights required in parole and probation-revocation proceedings.[29] In the *Gagnon* case, the Court also established the right to counsel for indigent prisoners in both parole- and probation-revocation proceedings.

While the United States Supreme Court has provided the same minimum requirements to satisfy due process, parole agencies have considerable more difficulty in providing them. Probation is imposed directly by a court as part of the sentencing process after a finding of guilty. The court sets the conditions, determines the period of probation (normally up to five years), modifies probation during its continuance, transfers probation jurisdiction to another judicial district when necessary, issues a warrant for the probationer's arrest on an alleged probation violation, and conducts the probation-revocation hearing. The probation officer acts directly for the court in supervising persons on probation. The judge may conduct a preliminary hearing immediately after a violation of probation is alleged. He may appoint counsel, and he can subpoena witnesses and conduct a hearing as required in the *Gagnon* v. *Scarpelli* case.

Parole, on the other hand, is a form of conditional release with the parolee under control of a parole board, an administrative agency. The parole officer is acting for the parole board, not the courts. The actual parole-revocation hearing is before a representative of the parole board. In a sense, then, the parole hearing officer represents the same agency that is charging the parolee with the violation. If the revocation of all forms of conditional liberty, parole as well as probation, were turned over to the judicial process of the courts, the decision of guilt would be made by a judge, not by an administrative officer. If we do this, we will come closer to granting the parolee due process of law before depriving him of his liberty.[30]

Prior to the decisions in the *Morrissey* and *Gagnon* cases, parolees or probationers were given hearings at which they could argue their cases and present statements of witnesses. They did not have the right to call witnesses,

---

[28]*Morrissey* v. *Brewer,* 408 U.S. 471 (1972), pp. 486–89.

[29]*Gagnon* v. *Scarpelli,* 411 U.S. 778 (1973), pp. 786–87.

[30]H. Richmond Fisher, "Probation and Parole Revocation: The Anomaly of Divergent Procedures," *Federal Probation* 36 (September 1974):23–29.

nor did they have access to police records or parole officers' reports. The requirements of the *Morrissey* and *Gagnon* cases also established the right to counsel and have turned a revocation proceeding into what correctional people regard as a trial. They are, therefore, opposed to this sort of proceeding. In California, the result has been an approximately 50 percent decrease in the number of paroled male felons who are returned to prison for technical violations (infractions other than a felony) of parole. In the early 1970s before the impact of the court decisions, about two thousand parolees were returned to California prisons each year for technical violations. By 1975, the rate of return had been cut by roughly 50 percent.

An attorney experienced in parole-revocation proceedings stated that the old hearings were nothing more than "jokes." He is quoted as saying: "A parolee would be in prison six to eight months *before a hearing* and would be violated [parole revoked] 99 times out of 100." Wilmer Leon, a former parole agent who is now an administrative officer of the California Adult Authority, is quoted as saying: "In the old days I could say a man was deteriorating . . . if I found a bottle in his room, and that he wrote bad checks when he drank. Ninety-five percent of the time I made a recommendation, the guy went back."[31]

The Volunteer in Probation and Parole

Most of the duties of probation and parole in Sweden are performed by volunteers under the supervision of 150 paid professionals. As a matter of fact, probation in the United States began as a voluntary activity of interested citizens. For some years, however, the role of the probation officer has been professionalized and institutionalized. People occupying the position of probation officer have acquired skills and expertise and are generally performing a valuable service in an effective manner. It is understandable, therefore, that the addition of volunteers to the staffs of probation departments is viewed as a threat to the security of the probation officer. Despite this fact, many probation departments throughout the country use volunteers to supplement the activities of probation officers. Considering the large case loads of the probation officers, the utilization of volunteers appears to be an excellent idea. The use of volunteers by the probation department of Royal Oak, Michigan, for example, appears to fulfill this need for extra manpower and to utilize the services of the volunteer in an effective manner.

The need for more staff, more resources, and greater community understanding paved the way for the use of the volunteer in Royal Oak. As with most program innovations, the involvement of the community in improving the

---

[31]Michael A. Levett, "Parole Revocation: Released Prisoners Getting a Better Break," *Los Angeles Times,* August 5, 1976.

correctional process generated much anxiety. The most important problem centered around the need to define the role of the volunteer while, at the same time, preserving the role and importance of the paid professional. If probation duties could be performed by an unpaid volunteer, this would constitute a threat to the security of the probation officer. A related problem is the traditional skepticism and suspicion toward any new concept or program on the part of correctional agencies.[32]

Because of these problems the role of the corrections volunteer had to be narrowly defined. Corrections literature clearly shows that no volunteers are seen as providing "professional" services. The role of the volunteer is limited to that of complementing or supplementing the work of the professional staff. The volunteer, therefore, has been looked upon as one who simply relieves the professional of routine, nonprofessional tasks so that the professional's time can be freed to allow him to devote his attention to where it is needed most. This implies that the services that volunteers offer to offenders are different from those that are made available by the probation officer.

The distinction between many of the services provided by probation officers, who in most instances lack advanced academic training themselves, is more imagined than real. The work of the volunteer must be directed to the advantage of the probationers, and the probation officer has an important supervisory role. The role of the paid professional becomes even more important because it is he who must harness this valuable resource, provide adequate training and supervision, and assign responsibilities in ways that will yield the greatest benefits.

The typical volunteer is a sensitive and concerned person who has demonstrated maturity in his ability to solve his own problems and in adjusting to society. He is able to relate well to others and, primarily in an intuitive way, to implement basic social work principles and values that are important in the establishment of any helping relationship. Many volunteers would rather be referred to as "unpaid staff" because they have the credentials and experience that would qualify them for employment. Also, the average volunteer appears to be aware of society's ills (particularly in the area of juvenile delinquency and adult crime), desires to become involved in implementing change, and seeks the opportunity to participate and contribute.[33]

Court service volunteers are told during their screening interview that they will be expected to serve for at least a twelve-month period and that they will be expected to see a probationer at least once a week. The professional staff runs the program, not the volunteer. A member of the staff observes the volunteer-probationer relationship through the eyes of the volunteer by way

[32]Ira M. Schwartz, "Volunteers and Professionals: A Team in the Correctional Process," *Federal Probation* 35 (September 1971): 46–50.
[33]Schwartz, "Volunteers and Professionals," p. 47.

of the volunteer's written or oral reports. Thus, the staff knows where more intensive supervision is necessary.

Less than 5 percent of all court service volunteers have dropped out during their first year, and over 85 percent of those who have completed a full year of service have continued in the program.[34]

It is estimated that over five hundred courts and nearly an equal number of parole and detention locales use volunteers. In addition, other social service agencies are thought to use a combined total of sixty million volunteers. These people are motivated by altruism, humanitarianism, the desire to continue personal growth and development, the need to form more meaningful interpersonal relationships, the need for a change of pace in their usual routine of activities, or a combination of any of the above.[35] In general, middle class people, who are in a position to pay their own expenses, volunteer for programs in greater numbers than minority groups, ex-offenders, offenders themselves, youth, and older people who needed their expenses defrayed.[36] Frequently, it is difficult to establish relationships between middle class volunteers and minority group members on parole and probation. One of the authors headed an aftercare program in New York City for several years. As part of that program, he established a "Big Brother Project" using volunteers. The volunteers, without exception, were middle class Caucasians. The boys who asked for Big Brothers were, with one exception, black or Puerto Rican. While a few useful Big Brother relationships were established, for the most part, the needs of the boys were not met. The Big Brother project was abandoned, and two minority group persons were hired to assist in the aftercare program, performing the functions previously assigned to the volunteers. Such persons are now called paraprofessionals.[37]

Paraprofessionals in Probation and Parole

In 1965 the President's Commission on Law Enforcement and Administration of Justice reported an immediate need to increase the correctional work force eightfold. In actual numbers, probation and parole services could have absorbed 20,000 additional workers in 1965. To alleviate this manpower shortage there has been an expansion in the use of nonprofessionals as assistants to probation officers and parole agents. This is a practical solution to the problem because there exists a large pool of untrained, unemployed nonprofessionals

---

[34]Schwartz, "Volunteers and Professionals," p. 47.

[35]Ivan H. Scheier and Judith Lake Berry, *Guidelines and Standards for the Use of Volunteers in Correctional Programs* (Washington, D.C.: U.S. Government Printing Office, 1972).

[36]Smith and Berlin, *Introduction to Probation and Parole,* pp. 225–26.

[37]Martin R. Haskell, "The Berkshire Farm Aftercare Program," *Group Psychotherapy* (September 1959):183.

who can be trained to perform signficant services under professional guidance. The use of nonprofessionals in correction work goes back at least to 1841, when volunteers began the first probation service. By 1972 there were 200 courts in the United States using part- or full-time volunteers to provide correctional services. The volunteers have been useful because they are usually well-educated, middle class people who are aware of community resources and can assist in the task of rehabilitation.[38]

In the 1970s indigenous, paraprofessionals, people of the same social class as the population served, have been hired to work as assistants to parole agents and probation officers. The service performed by the indigenous para-professional differs from that of the volunteer not only because he is paid for his work but because he is better able to communicate with the parolee or probationer. Persons hired are usually of the same social class and ethnic group as the parolees. Furthermore, ex-convicts, former addicts, and others with histories in crime and delinquency similar to those of parolees are frequently hired as indigenous paraprofessionals.[39]

In April 1973, one of the authors of this book directed a training seminar in psychodrama and role-training for the probation department of Riverside County, California. For two full days he was in close contact with some thirty-five persons employed by that department, attempting to train them in difficult action skills. A number of the persons sent for this training were indigenous paraprofessionals. Some were members of minority groups. The paraprofessionals, all of whom had been released from correctional institutions for violations of law, including possession and use of narcotics, participated actively in the training, displayed an active interest in helping others, and appeared to be effective. The directors of the training program were impressed with the ability of the paraprofessionals and the cooperative spirit both they and the probation officers displayed. Certainly the paraprofessionals we saw in Riverside County probation work should be helpful in reaching un-motiviated, mistrustful, and hard-to-reach probationers of their social class and ethnic group. It would be far more difficult for the middle class probation officer to bridge the gap himself. The paraprofessionals, under supervision of trained probation officers, make excellent teammates. The experience of Syna-non, Alcoholics Anonymous, and similar organizations indicates that people who have succeeded in overcoming problems can effectively contribute to the solution of similar problems in others. Furthermore, employing paraprofes-sionals in such roles does a great deal to reinforce their commitment to nondelinquent roles. Not only does the job provide income but also a sense of self-worth that comes with the knowledge that one is able to help others.

The Chicago-based probation officer–case aide (POCA) action research

---

[38]Donald W. Beless, William S. Pilcher, and Ellen Jo Ryan, "Use of Indigenous Nonprofessionals in Probation and Parole," *Federal Probation* 36(March 1972):10–18.

[39]Beless, Pilcher, and Ryan, "Indigenous Paraprofessionals in Probation and Parole, p. 12.

project experimented with the use of part-time indigenous paraprofessionals, some of whom were former offenders, as assistants to probation officers. Each of 161 probationers was assigned to a probation officer assistant (POA). Altogether 53 POAs were employed by the project. Two professionally trained probation staff officers each supervised 20 POAs. While POAs provided direct correctional services, the supervisors retained legal responsibility for all subjects assigned to POAs. All POAs worked part-time, each supervising up to 3 probationers.

The project staff members found that a sizable number of POAs were able to establish a positive working relationship with their clients. Their ability to empathize and simply listen provided an obvious benefit to the clients. For the most part, the project staff was pleased with the performance of the POAs. A number of the POAs found solutions to some of their own problems while working with the problems of others. To the probationer, the indigenous paraprofessional provides a role model, a person like himself who is succeeding at something. To the indigenous paraprofessional, the relationship raises his self-concept—he is helping someone.[40]

Some Bureaucratic Problems of Probation and Parole

The foregoing description of probation and parole is an assessment of these formal practices in the community. In collaboration with a probation officer with long experience in the field, we will attempt to set forth here some of the underlying problems of probation and parole. While the criticisms may be more applicable to some programs than others, it is our feeling that a realistic assessment of practices is vital to an understanding of the dynamics of probation and parole.

Most probation officers have two major problems: too much paper work and too many probationers. The average supervising probation officer has a voluminous amount of paperwork, including maintaining a casework file, writing up all client and family contacts, dictating violation reports, writing up "work determination" plans, and other tasks. Many probation officers complain that they hardly have time to see their probationers because of paperwork demands. Because of other tasks, a probation officer may actually utilize only about 10 percent of his total time in face-to-face meetings with his clients. It is not unusual for a client to go many months without seeing his probation officer because he may "report" by mail.

Probation departments tend to place a very high priority on paperwork. It is a "measurable" way of evaluating the job the probation officer (and thus the probation department) is doing. "Good casework management" usually

---

[40]Beless, Pilcher, and Ryan, "Indigenous Paraprofessionals in Probation and Parole," pp. 13–15.

means that all of the casework planning and recording is up to date and that all "reports" have been filed on time; everything "looks good," and there is an obvious "product" that can be evaluated and converted into charts and graphs and statistics. However, these paper results tell very little if anything about the probation officer's interpersonal skills or professional knowledge; they reveal very little about his effectiveness in dealing with problems of clients or in modifying delinquent behavior.

A case load of over one hundred is more than any probation officer can effectively handle. A new probation officer may require six months just to match the many names with the correct faces. Because he cannot respond to the needs of this many people, the probation officer can handle only the "emergencies" and those clients who require some sort of "official report" because of a new arrest. A high percentage of the probation officer's direct contact with probationers is stimulated by new arrests and violations of probation. The "quiet" case is apt to get little if any meaningful attention. As is true with public agency case loads, only the clients who literally "scream" are ever heard.

Part of the paperwork problem is that probation departments operate in a civil service, bureaucratic framework. In bureaucracies, people get promoted for a variety of reasons, most of which have little to do with skill, attitudes, and effectiveness in dealing with clients. The necessary prerequisite, and in many cases the most important element in most probation offices, is "time in service." Extra points are awarded for seniority. This factor is optimistically referred to as *experience,* the assumption being that time is a positive thing.

A critical probation officer made the following statement on this issue: "Too often, an intellectually limited, authoritarian, racially prejudiced probation officer with twenty-years service is still an intellectually limited, authoritarian, racially prejudiced probation officer." "Experience," he pointed out, can reinforce bigotry and ineptitude just as readily as it can know-how. Yet "experience"—which really means time on the job—is the most important consideration in promotions. Many of the most sensitive jobs in the probation department, those requiring the most knowledge and skill, are open only to those officers who have achieved a certain level of promotion because of "time on the job." Every high-level probation officer knows that, regardless of the level of his incompetence, all he has to do is "hang in there" and the mere passage of time will move him up the ladder. Of course, an organization that does not stress ability and competence will promote many people who do not have these qualities and will adjust to operating without these qualities. Such an agency will manage to define its goals so that either they are achievable without these qualities, or they are so general and incomprehensible that no one will be able to determine whether they have been achieved or not.

According to our informant, "The probation department expects very little casework out of its officers and overtly and covertly communicates this."

It is difficult to talk about rehabilitation where the officers may have case loads of from 175 to as high as 250 offenders. The very best that a probation officer can do with a case load of over 100 is make some attempt to keep tabs on the probationers and report new arrests and other violations of probation to the court. It is a common joke in probation departments that when a probationer walks into the probation office on "reporting night," he is immediately told, "Don't sit down, you won't be here that long." This exaggeration makes the point regarding the limited time a probation officer actually has to devote to each of 175 probationers.

Chapter
16

Treatment
Strategies

FOR MANY YEARS correctional institutions have experimented with treatment programs, some of which included individual or group therapy for offenders. A number of institutions now include some form of counseling or therapy as a part of their treatment programs. Probation officers and parole agents are expected to provide counseling to their probationers. Some officers even work with families of probationers or parolees.

In the communities we find social agencies that provide counseling and psychotherapeutic services for delinquents. When a court or a probation officer refers a juvenile to such an agency, it is assumed that the treatment will do the juvenile some good. An examination of the professional literature in psychology, psychiatry, social work, and corrections reveals a large number of articles, each describing the application of one form of therapy or another to delinquents. The authors of these articles usually claim success. The tendency of persons in the fields of corrections and mental health has been to match one claim against another and choose among them. The people associated with the Community Treatment Project of the California Youth Authority made a very important contribution to the establishment of goals in treatment by emphasizing the personality differences among juveniles and seeking to develop treatment strategies most effective for each type. In Chapter 3 we discussed their classification system, which places juveniles into three major categories and nine subcategories based on "interpersonal (I) maturity levels." Work on this system was begun in the 1950s and has continued into the 1970s. The I-level system that the Community Treatment Project has developed is compatible with the categorization employed by psychiatrists Lester E. Hewitt and Richard L. Jenkins at the Michigan Child Guidance Institute. The Community Treatment Project's I_2 level closely resembles Hewitt and Jenkins' *unsocialized aggressive child* category, the I_3 level is similar to their *socialized delinquent child* category, and the I_4 level to their *overinhibited child* category.

The California Community Treatment Project has for many years worked extensively to develop treatment strategies appropriate to each category. Don C. Gibbons, in evaluating the application of interpersonal maturity levels theory, notes that there have been no studies to determine whether delinquents are more or less mature than nondelinquents. He does, however, acknowledge the value of differential treatment being applied in a selective manner to deal with suggested deficiencies.[1] We concur with those who recognize the need for differential treatment. The task ahead for those interested in differential treatment is to develop a typology that can be effectively employed in determining the needs of juveniles and then develop a treatment strategy to provide the treatment appropriate to each category.

In this chapter we shall describe several treatment strategies that have been and are being employed in the treatment of delinquents and others. We would hypothesize that a particular approach may be more effective with some categories of delinquents than with others. Unfortunately, only limited research is available to establish their relative effectiveness.

Individual Counseling and Therapy

In individual or therapy counseling, there are two persons present—the therapist or counselor and the patient or counselee. What occurs in the course of the counseling depends largely on the philosophy, training, and ability of the therapist. If the therapist or counselor is a psychiatric social worker with a psychoanalytic orientation, therapy is likely to involve the use of psychoanalytic interpretations to understand the juvenile's behavior. If the therapist or counselor is a psychologist, probation officer, or other person trained in transactional analysis, the session will include an analysis of the "games" the delinquent is playing. Similarly, the psychodramatist, the reality therapist, and the gestalt therapist impose their systems in an effort to gain understanding of the juvenile and to increase his understanding of himself and of reality. Dr. Richard R. Korn, in describing an individual counseling session, points up some of the problems posed by this therapeutic approach:

---

[1]Don C. Gibbons, "Differential Treatment of Delinquents and Interpersonal Maturity Levels Theory: A Critique," *Social Service Review* 44(March 1970):22–33.

The problems and methods [of individual counseling] may be concretely illustrated by the record of a fairly typical first counseling session with a nonneurotic delinquent of average intelligence who was transferred, as a disciplinary case, to an adult institution.

The counselor opened the session by asking why the inmate had come to see him.

INMATE: Well, I've been talking to a few of the guys. . . . They said it might be a good idea.

COUNSELOR: Why?

INMATE (in a fairly convincing attempt to appear reticent): Well—they said it did them good. . . . They said a guy needs somebody he can talk to around here . . . somebody he can trust. A . . . a friend.

COUNSELOR: And the reason you asked to see me was that you felt that I might be a friend? Why did you feel this?

INMATE (a little defensively): Because they told me, I guess. Aren't you supposed to be a friend to the guys?

COUNSELOR: Well, let's see now. What is a friend supposed to do? (Inmate looks puzzled.) Let's take your best buddy, for example. Why do you consider him a friend?

INMATE (puzzled and a little more aggressive): I dunno . . . we help each other, I guess. We do things for each other.

COUNSELOR: And friends are people who do things for each other?

INMATE: Yes.

COUNSELOR: Fine. Now, as my friend, what is it you feel you'd like to do for me?

INMATE (visibly upset): I don't get it. Aren't you supposed to help? Isn't that your job?

COUNSELOR: Wait a minute—I'm getting lost. A little while ago you were talking about friends and you said that friends help each other. Now you're talking about my job.

INMATE (increasingly annoyed): Maybe I'm crazy, but I thought you people are supposed to help us.

COUNSELOR: I think I get it now. When you said "friends" you weren't talking about the kind of friendship that works both ways. The kind you meant was where I help you, not where you do anything for me.

INMATE: Well . . . I guess so. If you put it that way.

COUNSELOR: Okay. (Relaxing noticeably from his previous tone of persistence.) Now, how do you feel I can help you?

INMATE: Well, you're supposed to help people get rehabilitated, aren't you?

COUNSELOR: Wait. I'm lost again. You say I'm supposed to do something for people. I thought you wanted me to do something for you. So you want me to help you get rehabilitated?

INMATE: Sure.

COUNSELOR: Fine. Rehabilitated from what?

INMATE: Well, so I won't get in trouble anymore.

COUNSELOR: What trouble?

At this point the inmate launched into a vehement recital of the abuses to which he had been subjected from his first contact with the juvenile authorities to his most recent difficulties with his probation officer immediately prior to the offense (stealing a car) leading to his present sentence. During the entire recital he never referred to any offense he had committed but, instead, laid exclusive emphasis on his mistreatment.

The counselor heard this account out with an expression of growing puzzlement which was not lost on the inmate, who continued with increasing vehemence as his listener appeared increasingly puzzled. At length the counselor, with a final gesture of bewilderment, broke in:

COUNSELOR: Wait. . . . I don't understand. When you said you wanted me to help you stop getting into trouble I thought you meant the kind of trouble that got you in here. Your difficulties with the law, for example. You've talked about your troubles with different people and how they get you angry but you haven't talked about what got you into jail.

INMATE (visibly trying to control himself): But I am talking about that! I'm talking about those bastards responsible for me being here.

COUNSELOR: How do you mean?

The inmate again repeated his tirade, interspersing it with frequent remarks addressed to the counselor. ("What about this? Do you think that was right? Is that the way to treat a young guy?" etc.) The counselor once more looked puzzled, and broke in again.

COUNSELOR: I still don't see it. We'd better get more specific. Now take your last trouble—the one that got you into the reformatory. This car you stole . . .

INMATE (excitedly): It was that —— P.O. [probation officer]. I asked him if I could get a job in New York. He said no.

COUNSELOR: What job?

(The inmate admitted that it wasn't a specific job.)

COUNSELOR: But I still don't follow. The probation officer wouldn't let you work in New York. By the way—don't the regulations forbid probationers from leaving the state?

INMATE: Well, he could've given me a break.

COUNSELOR: That may be—but I still don't follow you. He wouldn't let you work in New York, so you and a few other guys stole a car. How does that figure?

(Here the inmate "blew up" and started to denounce "bug doctors who don't help a guy but only cross-examine him.")

COUNSELOR: Wait a bit, now. You said before that you wanted me to help you. We've been trying to find out how. But so far you haven't been talking about anything the matter with you at all. All you've talked about are these other people and things wrong with them. Now are we supposed to rehabilitate you or rehabilitate them?

INMATE: I don't give a —— who you rehabilitate. I've had about enough of this. If you don't mind, let's call the whole thing off.

COUNSELOR: But I do mind. Here you've been telling me that my job is to rehabilitate you and we haven't talked five minutes and now you want to call the whole thing off. Don't you want to be rehabilitated?

(Inmate is silent.)

COUNSELOR: Let's see if we can review this thing and put it in the right perspective. You said you wanted to be rehabilitated. I asked you from what and you said from getting into trouble. Then I asked you to talk about your troubles and you told me about this probation officer. He didn't give you what you wanted so you stole a car. Now as near as I can understand it, the way to keep you out of trouble is to get people to give you what you want.

INMATE: That's not true, dammit!

COUNSELOR: Well, let's see now. Have I given you what you wanted?

INMATE: Hell, no!

COUNSELOR: You're pretty mad at me right now, aren't you?

(Counselor smiles. Inmate is silent, looks away.)

COUNSELOR (in a half-chiding, half-kidding tone): Here, not ten minutes ago you were talking about what good friends we could be and now you're acting like I'm your worst enemy.

INMATE (very halfheartedly, trying not to look at the counselor's face): It's true, isn't it?

COUNSELOR: C'mon now. Now you're just trying to get mad. You won't even look at me because you're afraid you'll smile.

(Inmate cannot repress a smile. Counselor drops his kidding tone and gets businesslike again.)

COUNSELOR: Okay. Now that we've agreed to stop kidding, let's get down to cases. Why did you come to see me today?

(Inmate halfheartedly starts to talk about rehabilitation again, but the counselor cuts in.)

COUNSELOR: Come on, now. I thought we agreed to stop conning. Why did you come?

INMATE: Well . . . I heard you sometimes see guys . . . and . . .

COUNSELOR: And what?

INMATE: Help them.

COUNSELOR: How?

INMATE: Well, I tell you my story . . . and . . .

COUNSELOR: And then? What happens then?

(Inmate is silent.)

INMATE (finally): You tell them about it.

COUNSELOR: Who do I tell?

INMATE: You know—people who read them.

COUNSELOR: Should I write a report on this session?

INMATE: Hell, no!

COUNSELOR: What do you think we should do?

INMATE (looking away): Maybe I could . . . (Falls silent.)

COUNSELOR (quietly): Maybe you could come and talk to me when we really have something to talk about?

INMATE: Yeah. . . . Aw, hell. . . : (Laughs.)

This interview illustrates the problems and possibilities inherent in the crucial first counseling session with an adaptive offender of average intelligence who attempted to conceal his true feelings and his motive to manipulate under the disguise of a request for friendly help. . . .

The special character of the adaptive delinquent's motivations concerning treatment requires a special counseling technique. The usual methods of permissiveness, nondirection, and acceptance require modification. To have permitted the delinquent to "define the relationship" would have been disastrous, since that definition would have left the counselor no alternative to the roles of dupe or oppressor ("sucker" or "s-o-b"). Similarly, to have encouraged this adaptive delinquent to "solve his problems in his own way" would have been merely to collaborate with him in the continuation of his antisocial pattern: the manipulation of personal relationships for the purposes of self-aggrandizement and exploitation.[2]

---

[2]From *Criminology and Penology* by Richard R. Korn and Lloyd W. McCorkle, pp. 562–66. Copyright 1959 by Holt, Rinehart and Winston, Inc. Reprinted by permission of Holt, Rinehart and Winston, Inc.

Reality Therapy

Dr. William Glasser, a psychiatrist who has worked with delinquent girls at the Ventura School in California, has developed a treatment strategy that he calls reality therapy. Dr. Glasser maintains that from a treatment standpoint both the theory and practice of reality therapy are incompatible with the prevalent concept of mental illness. He describes the task of the therapist as one of becoming *involved* with the patient and then inducing the patient to face reality. A major objective is to get the patient to decide to take the *responsible* path. Dr. Glasser feels that reality therapy differs from conventional therapy on six points related to involvement:

     1. Because we do not accept the concept of mental illness, the patient cannot become involved with us as a mentally ill person who has no responsibility for his behavior.

     2. Working in the present and toward the future, we do not get involved with the patient's history because we can neither change what happened to him nor accept that he is limited by his past.

     3. We relate to patients as ourselves, not as transference figures.

     4. We do not look for unconscious conflicts or the reasons for them. A patient cannot become involved with us by excusing his behavior on the basis of unconscious motivations.

     5. We emphasize the morality of behavior. We face the issue of right and wrong which we believe solidifies the involvement, in contrast to conventional psychiatrists who do not make the distinction between right and wrong, feeling it would be detrimental to attaining the transference relationship they seek.

     6. We teach patients better ways to fulfill their needs. The proper involvement will not be maintained unless the patient is helped to find more satisfactory patterns of behavior. Conventional therapists do not feel that teaching better behavior is a part of therapy.[3]

The case of Maria illustrates Dr. Glasser's application of reality therapy:

     Apathetic and despondent, Maria, a seventeen-and-a-half-year-old girl, was a far different problem from Jeri. Jeri was at least capable of taking care of herself fairly well, albeit illegally. She had good intelligence and some sort of warped self-reliance. Maria, on the other hand, had almost nothing. In institutions since she was about twelve, before then in foster homes, with no family, few friends, not too much intelligence (although test results are misleadingly low on these deprived girls), she came to my attention after she was involved in a serious fight in her

---

[3]From pp. 44–45 and 80–81 in *Reality Therapy* by William Glasser. Copyright © 1965 by William Glasser, M.D. By permission of Harper & Row, Publisher, Inc.

cottage. I was asked to see her in the discipline cottage because she seemed so hopeless. She had been sitting in her room, eating little, and making no effort to contact any of the cottage staff. There seemed to be little we could do for her because she had given up herself. The fight that brought her into discipline was the result of a building frustration caused by an older, smarter girl, Sonia, who, recognizing Maria's desperate need for affection, pretended to like her in order to get Maria to be a virtual slave. Maria had attacked another girl whom Sonia had openly preferred to her and who joined with Sonia in making fun of Maria.

When I sat with her in the day room of the discipline unit, she refused to speak, just sitting apathetically and staring at the floor. I asked her my routine getting-acquainted questions, such as, How long have you been at the school? What are you here for? What are your plans? Do you want to return to your cottage? Maria just sat and stared. Finally she asked me to leave her alone. She had seen plenty of psyches (as our girls call psychiatrists) before, but she never talked to them. It was a discouraging interview, if it could be called an interview at all. We were worlds apart. After about twenty very long minutes I said, "I will see you next week." Saying nothing, she walked quietly back to her room. I felt that I had made no impression whatsoever. None!

Each week for seven weeks the same scene was repeated, except for different questions, and few enough of them because I could not think of what to ask. My most frequent question was, "Don't you want to get out of here?" Her reply, on occasions when she did reply, was, "What for?" My attempts to answer were met with silence. I did not have a good answer because she was obviously involved with no one and had no way to fulfill her needs—her isolated room was probably the most comfortable place for her. At least in a room by herself she did not have to see others doing and feeling what was not possible for her.

At the eighth visit I detected the first glimmer of hope. She said "Hi" in answer to my "Hi" and looked at me occasionally during the interview. I decided on a whim to ask her about her tattoos. Tattoos are the rule with our girls, nine girls out of ten have some. On her legs and arms Maria had twenty or thirty self-inflicted tattoos—dots, crosses, words, initials, and various marks, all common with our girls. I asked her if she would like a large, particularly ugly tattoo removed. Unexpectedly, she said she would; she would like them all out. Her request surprised me because girls like Maria are more apt to add tattoos rather than want them out. Lonely, isolated girls, particularly in juvenile halls, derive some sense of existence through the pain of pushing ink or dirt into their skin and by the mark produced by the act. It is a way they have, they tell me, of making sure they are still there. On the next visit we talked further about her tattoos and her feelings of hopelessness. In addition, she brought up her fear that her housemother, toward whom she had some warm feeling, would not take her back into the cottage because of what she had done. Although a housemother can refuse to take a girl back into the cottage when there are serious fights between girls, she rarely does so. I said I did not know whether or not her housemother would take her back, but that I would have her housemother stop by and see her if Maria wished it. She said she would appreciate seeing her housemother very much.

Maria now started to make progress. Her housemother, who liked her and recognized the loneliness in her quiet, uncomplaining ways, visited her and told her she was welcome back in the cottage. Her housemother also said how much she missed Maria's help with the cottage housework. Maria had been a tireless worker in the cottage. I told Maria that I had discussed her problems with the girls in my therapy group and that they wanted her to join the group. My few interviews, together with the powerful effect of the housemother's visit, had already caused some change in Maria when she left discipline. The girls in my group therapy took a special interest in her, something which might have been resented by a more sophisticated girl, but was deeply appreciated by Maria. The technique of getting girls who are more responsible to become particularly interested in someone like Maria is strongly therapeutic for them because it directly leads to fulfilling their needs and helps them to identify with the staff, thereby helping to sever ties with their own delinquent group.

Taking more interest in school, Maria began to learn to read for the first time. In the group we talked at length about what she might do, and it was decided that a work home with small children, whom she could love and who might love her in return, would be best. Older girls who have no families do well in carefully selected homes where they are paid to do housework and child care. Although by then she was no problem, we kept her a few extra months so that some of her worst tattoos could be removed and to allow her to become more accustomed to relating to people.

The case of Maria illustrates that the key to involvement is neither to give up nor to push too hard. No matter how lonely and isolated a girl may be, if the therapist adheres to the present and points to a hopeful future and, in cases like Maria's, expands her initial involvement into a series of involvements as soon as possible, great changes can take place. Here the need for group therapy was critical for there she could gain strength from relating to more responsible girls and could see how she might emulate their more responsible behavior. Through our persistence Maria, perhaps for the first time in her life, was able to fulfill her needs.

From her good relationship with her housemother, Maria was able to go to a work home where her hard work and love for children were deeply appreciated. Later she married and our assistant superintendent has several pictures of Maria's growing and successful family in her "grandchildren" picture gallery.[4]

Group Therapy with Offenders

Dr. J. L. Moreno, a psychiatrist, first introduced group therapy and group psychotherapy into the correctional process in 1931. Before this innovation, the only form of therapy employed in the corrections and mental health fields was individual therapy, that is, a therapist-patient relationship. The group therapy methodology was described by Dr. Moreno in an article published in 1932 by the National Committee on Prisons and Prison Labor. The historic article was based on his work at Sing Sing Prison in New York. Dr. Moreno's later research and action methods used at the Hudson Training School for Girls provided valuable material for his now classic work, *Who Shall Survive?*[5]

Virtually every correctional institution for delinquents now has some form of group therapy included in its program. Some programs are therapist centered; that is, the therapist attempts to treat each member of the group individually or together but does not intentionally use the members of the group to help one another. Other programs are group centered. In such groups, the therapist considers every member of the group to be a therapeutic agent of every other member. Guided group interaction, which will be discussed below, is a group-centered method. Here the group is treated as an interactional unit. Some groups are psychoanalytically oriented, with the therapist seeking to give individual members of the group insight into their problems from a psychoanalytic point of view. Others are spontaneous and free and encourage members of the group to develop spontaneity. Psychodrama and role training are action methods designed to develop spontaneity and to modify illegal behavior.

In individual therapy sessions, an offender can rationalize, distort, or simply lie about what is taking place. However, in group therapy he must necessarily be aware that his description of the group process is subject to a wider commentary and audience. Group methods, therefore, usually have broader impact than individual methods. An interesting anecdote that partially illustrates this point, with special reference to social control, is described by Korn in an article on a group therapy program that he directed in Vermont. Two youths, both members of the same therapy group, found some money on the grounds of the institution. Both knew that if they kept the money, one or

---

[4]Glasser, *Reality Therapy,* pp. 80–82.

[5]J. L. Moreno, *Who Shall Survive?* Nervous and Mental Disease Monograph Series, no. 58 (New York, 1934). Reprinted by Beacon House.

the other, or both, might discuss the find in the group session. If they accepted the need to tell the truth in their therapy, they were confronted with a role conflict, and one or both might "cop out," tell the truth on the other. The group process produces an open situation that tends to merge the prison underworld with its more formal structure.

In addition to blending the subculture of the institution with its upper world, group therapy also opens up the therapist's activity to wider inspection and more critical analysis, not only by his peers, but by his clients. What he does as a group therapist is much more open to discussion than what he does in the individual therapy situation. The process of group therapy, therefore, presents the possibility for much greater impact than individual therapy, not only upon offenders, but also upon staff and the total social system of the institution.

In dyadic therapeutic interaction (single therapist–single patient), two personalities who may be far apart in intellectual abilities attempt to communicate about one of the individuals' problems (usually the offender's). Generally speaking, therapists tend to come from a different sociocultural milieu than criminals. Therapeutic communication may therefore be significantly impaired. This is not necessarily the case in group therapy. Delinquents in group therapy are (by definition) in interaction with others who have comparable levels of understanding and usually a similar set of difficulties.

In group therapy delinquents become co-therapists with each other, and this seems to increase the potentiality of group understanding. Often in group psychotherapy, offenders who have difficulty interpreting and diagnosing their own problems are experts vis-à-vis their fellows. In fact, many sociopaths, generally considered the most difficult type of delinquent to treat, are excellent diagnosticians and interpreters of the problems of other delinquents. Sociopaths can thus be enlisted as effective co-therapists, and this sometimes has a positive fallout effect on their own behavior.

In comparing group therapy with individual therapy (formal psychoanalysis in particular), one finds that the average offender's educational background and intellectual abilities are more adaptively geared to the group process. In psychoanalysis with offenders, for example, the therapist may develop excellent and appropriate formulations about the offender's problem. However, the analyst may have considerable difficulty inducing the offender to understand himself in the same way that the psychoanalyst thinks he understands the criminal. In group psychotherapy, which tends to operate on a less sophisticated intellectual level, the offender, with other offenders as co-therapists, is more likely to develop insights and understanding of his behavior beneficial to his treatment. The offender can thus relearn behavior patterns upon an emotional and action level in group process, rather than being required to attempt an intellectual analysis that may be foreign to his thought processes.

Guided Group Interaction

Guided group interaction is a form of group treatment developed by Dr. Lloyd McCorkle during World War II while on duty with the army at Fort Knox, Kentucky. The treatment gained prominence in the area of delinquency when it was successfully applied by Dr. McCorkle at Highfields, a partway house for delinquent boys in New Jersey. Little emphasis is placed on academic training as a prerequisite for group leadership of guided group interaction sessions, and for that reason it is widely used in halfway houses throughout the country.[6] Guided group interaction is based on the view that delinquent adolescents can realistically appraise their life situations and make decisions based on that appraisal. The leader encourages free discussion of the events of the day and of relationships within the group. It is a "here and now" approach to behavior and concentrates on developing concern for others and mutual concerns with others. Each individual is encouraged to recognize his shortcomings and deal with them. The following is a description of a guided group interaction session:

> A guided group interaction meeting usually runs for ninety minutes. Typically, ten or twelve boys file into the room promptly at the scheduled hour, dragging in their own chairs. The director may introduce a new boy to the others, explaining that he was there to help them with their problems, as the experienced members were to help him with his.
>
> Immediately after such an introduction, Harvey, one of the group members who has been at the center for some months now, becomes the focus of attention, describing, in a somewhat belligerent tone, a clash he has had that morning with his work supervisor. The latter had taken offense at a comment he had meant to be humorous, and had yelled at him. Harvey, in turn, had grabbed the employee's arm. The employee had then shouted, "Get your —— hands off of me." Although the narrator was giving a version of the incident favorable to his point of view, the other boys were hesitant to credit it, one after another criticizing him for having deliberately aggravated the employee: "What's wrong with you, Harvey? The man was simply doing his job." Harvey replies that he felt he had been humiliated, or "put down" by the employee, to which the others retort: "You put yourself down." Harvey, now aroused, states that he would not have grabbed the employee's arm if he had not "hollered and cussed at me," at which, he said, he himself had become excited and scared.

---

[6]Oliver J. Keller, Jr., and Benedict S. Alper, *Halfway Houses: Community Centered Correction* (Lexington, Mass.: Lexington Books, D. C. Heath and Company, 1970), pp. 69–72.

At this point, the leader intervenes, for the first time in fifteen minutes, quietly asking the group why they thought Harvey had acted as he did. The boys are quick to reply that, although he had been at the center for five months, Harvey could still be expected to make "smart" remarks and wisecracks. Almost half the group now hurl questions at Harvey, many of them simultaneously, all accusing him of being a troublemaker, a faker, and a "bad mouth." [These are euphemisms for more profane language.] Harvey at this point admits that the employee with whom he had argued probably agreed with the group's opinion of himself.

One boy then asks, "What will it take to get you interested in people?" When all he gets back is a muttered reply, another boy comments, "It would be easy to talk Harvey into committing a crime if he was 'on the outside.' " Here again (ten minutes having elapsed since his last question), the leader quietly asks, "Why?" The boy replies: "It doesn't matter much to him. Harvey seems like a weak person." The comments that follow are not all so negative, the boys admitting that, "Harvey does not enjoy hurting people like he used to."

The significance of this remark can better be judged by the fact that Harvey had had a long history of violent assault. In his most recent act, the one resulting in his arrest and conviction, he had forced a grown man, at the point of a gun, to crawl, bare-chested, on a gravel road. After several hundred feet of such humiliation and torture, when the victim, his chest torn and bleeding, attempted to lift himself up from the road, he had been met with threats that his head would be blown off.

Harvey now voices his concern that he might get sent to the state training school. "Why do you enjoy wising off?" The leader asks this question, to which Harvey admits that he didn't think of the feelings of others. Then one of the group comments, "If Harvey doesn't like someone, he just messes over him. He doesn't care."

"Does Harvey intend to hurt people here, at this time?" the leader asks, to which one boy replies, "No, he didn't mean to. His smart remarks were more off the cuff."

The counselor cuts in: "Harvey is not really sorry about the employee. He is simply sorry because he knows the man will be riding him from here on. He's sorry for himself, not for what he did."

The conversation had now gone on for an hour, and Harvey was permitted to step down from the "hot seat." In his place came Stanley, a black boy who had hit another boy with a mop because, "He told me I was lying. I didn't want him lying on me."

"How did this affect you?" the group asked. "Why did it make you mad when the boy said you were lying?"

Stanley began to get angry. "I thought it was like a team here. I got attached to you guys, and then, when I tell you what I've done, you give me hell even though I said I was sorry."

The boys, thoroughly aroused, all reject his statements. "How come no one in the group can talk to you, Stan? What are you going to do about it, Stan?"

Incensed, Stanley remarks that he is "a cool gent," who does not have to justify himself to anybody. The others better not "mess" with him.

Harvey, now a discussant rather than the target of the group's concern, comments, "You're not near as cool as you think you are, Stan."

Another asks, "What does this 'cool' mean, Stan? Suppose you tell us just what this 'being cool' means."

Stanley becomes thoroughly belligerent at this point: "Anything I feel like doing, I'll do it. Besides, Harvey'd better watch himself, 'cause I don't like him messing with me."

The intensity of the attacks now increases: "What is this threatening stuff, Stan? Let's face it, Stan, you do threaten people."

Above the loud and angry attacks Stanley is heard defending himself: "That still stands. Ain't no one going to mess over me."

Another member of the group, stung but undaunted by his threats, asks, "What are you, Stan, a giant superman?"

Stanley fights back, "You just —— with me and you'll find out. I won't let little boys like you —— over me. I can handle myself pretty well. I ain't been —— up like I have been. I been trying."

Suddenly he seems to change his tactics and, although still furious, pretends complete agreement though in a low monotone, "I'll go by what the group says. If you say I don't know what I'm doing, I guess I don't."

The others are not so easily placated. One comments, "Now you're playing games, Stan. You're acting like a baby. Your threats aren't bothering anybody."

Quite subdued, now, Stanley: "I don't mean it as a threat. I've been saying that kind of stuff all my life." As if he suddenly realizes that he himself has let drop his guard, Stanley shouts back angrily, "But nobody better tangle with Stan!"

Suddenly the air is thick with obscenities. A third boy, Frank, as angry as Stanley, now remarks, "You don't scare me none. Go ahead and make your move."

A fight appearing imminent, the leader, who has been silent during all the foregoing, quietly asks, "What's the group doing now? Aren't you trying to force a challenge?"

The tension eases and one of the group says quietly, "We just want him to stop that kind of ——."

Stanley rejoins, "I ain't going to like these boys, if they keep messing with me."

For the remaining quarter hour the leader now took over, giving a summary of what had taken place. He referred to Harvey's clash with the employee and his belief that progress had been made, because this was the first time that Harvey had admitted being afraid. He was confident of Harvey's ability to control himself even when other people shout at him. He pointed out that Harvey had acted belligerently because of his fear of being "put down" before the group. The leader then emphasized the boys' concern for one another by relating how, when Harvey had recently got himself into an embarrassing situation, it had been Stanley who had stepped forward and permitted Harvey to "save face."

He then referred to Stanley's attack with a mop on another boy, pointing out that Stanley had told the other boy he was sorry. "Stan says he's trying to change, and he complains that the group won't recognize this. The group, on the other hand, says it does care for Stan, but it's not afraid of him either. The group feels that Stan is trying to 'put them down' by making them afraid of Stan. But," he continued, "Stan is showing us some of his true feelings in contrast to Frank who has been playing it real 'cool' in keeping his feelings hidden."

Here Frank admitted that, "I've had these feelings for a long, long time," that he often felt angry, and that he tried to conceal it by "playing it cool."

The leader then criticized the group for not having stopped Frank at the point when he had challenged Stanley to "make his move."

"The group should have asked what was going on because Frank left the issue of helping Stan and simply got mad."

Frank, his head low, in an undertone: "I might as well let my anger out here, or I'll never get out of this place."

The leader assured him, "Don't worry about letting it out."

The meeting ended with Stanley, still appearing angry, remarking, "I don't know what to say."

With the other boys looking concerned, the director closed the meeting: "You boys recognize you've got problems, and you're doing something about them."[7]

Transactional Analysis

Eric Berne, the psychiatrist who developed the treatment strategy called transactional analysis, based it on the assumption that every person has available a limited repertoire of three ego states.[8] These are:

---

[7]Keller and Alper, *Halfway Houses,* pp. 69–72. Reprinted by permission of the publisher.
[8]Eric Berne, *Transactional Analysis in Psychotherapy* (New York: Grove Press, 1961). See also, Eric Berne, *Games People Play* (New York: Grove Press, 1964).

1. PARENT: ego states that resemble those of parental figures. Tells us how to do things and what we should and should not be doing.

2. ADULT: ego states that are autonomously directed toward objective appraisal of reality. Examines and evaluates. Bases decisions on facts.

3. CHILD: still active ego states that were fixated in childhood. The "I want to" feelings and emotions.

The treatment in transactional analysis consists of efforts to get PARENT, ADULT, and CHILD to work together, to allow ADULT to solve problems.

In transactional analysis terms, a *stroke* is a fundamental unit of social action. *An exchange of strokes is a transaction.* When interacting with others, transactions take the form of (1) rituals, (2) pastimes, (3) games, (4) intimacy, and (5) activity. Each person in interaction with others seeks as many satisfactions as possible from his transactions with others. The most gratifying social contacts are games and intimacy. Most games are ways of avoiding intimacy. In transactional analysis, the focus is on finding out which ego states (PARENT, ADULT, or CHILD) implement the stimulus and which the response. To attain autonomy, the individual must become game-free. He must overcome the programming of the past. The transactional analysis group is considered effective in analyzing transactions. When applied to delinquents, it has been found helpful in improving life positions, vocations, recreations, and interpersonal relationships. It is said to help people become responsible for their future.

The following account illustrates how quickly members of a group learn to analyze transactions:

> The following transactions occurred at one of our earlier meetings and are offered as a good example of how quickly the members learn how to analyze them.
>
> Jerry, an alcoholic, comes into the meeting room, already partially occupied, before the meeting commenced. He is obviously under the influence of alcohol. Upon being introduced to Larry who wears his hair long, and adorns himself with beads, Jerry slurs out something about a "hair do" and "hippie." The group leader is smoking a cigar. Jerry asks him, "Aren't you afraid that cigar will make you sick or something?" The group leader offers Jerry a cigar. After the meeting has commenced Jerry first tells how he wrestles with his sons, how they are going to become real "he-men." He then turns to Larry:
>
> JERRY: If my kids wore their hair long, I'd kick the s— out of them.
>
> LARRY: Well, OK. You'd kick the s— out of 'em. What I'm concerned about is getting a job. . . .
>
> JERRY (interrupting): Wanta job—cut your goddamn hair! Let me ask you, do you think you're cute with your long hair and beads?

LARRY: No, I just wear it this way (clears throat). . . .

JERRY (winking at other group members, apparently to let them in on the "sport"): Tell me, bud, why do you wear your hair long?

LARRY: Why do you drink?

JERRY: Why do *I* drink . . . hmm.

LARRY: I'm not listening to you, anyway.

JERRY (eyes narrowing, pitch of voice raising): Why aren't you listening to me?

LARRY (tilting his head, strengthening his voice): Because you've been drinking. My mother was a lush. I don't like lushes.

JERRY (voice higher yet): You calling me a lush?

LARRY: If you want it that way. . . .

DOUG (probably our sincerest and best-motivated client): Boy, Jerry! He sure hooked your Child! You started out being the big, bullying Parent, trying to hook Larry's Child, but instead you hooked his Parent.

BARBARA (Jerry's spouse, pointing her index finger to the ceiling): That's right, Doug he *is* a bully when he's drunk—an *Irish* bully!

DOUG: OK, Barbara, but now you're being a punishing Parent.

BARBARA (voice raising, eyes moistening): OK, so I'm a Parent, but if *you* had to—Well, I am working at being an Adult. Anyhow, Larry, if you want to wear your hair long, do it. You're still OK.

The meeting ended on a friendly note, with the group giving Larry some "strokes." Jerry remained subdued and depressed.

The following transactions, occurring at a later meeting involving the same group, illustrate how the group leader may receive the "hot seat" technique. The meeting commences with a brief discussion by the group leader on the four life positions. The desirability of striving for the position, "I'm OK; you're OK" was stressed. Billy, a check-writer, recently reparoled, attempted to maneuver the group into playing a game:

BILLY: I can't buy this I'm OK, you're OK, because it's just brainwashing stuff, because *nobody's OK*. I just read where a probation officer was convicted of taking a bribe.

GROUP LEADER (interrupting): Of embezzlement.

BILLY: So what! He's a crook! They're *all* crooks! A guy comes up on a check rap in front of a crooked judge and gets 5 years. . . .

JUDY (interrupting): Are you saying you're OK and the rest of us are not? You're perfect?

BILLY: You're damn right.

DON: Well, these federal probation officers haven't done *me* a bit of good. And those stupid bastards in the employment agencies! They're drawing their paychecks, and when you ask for help . . . what a run-around. . . .

JERRY (referring to group leader): Mr. Nick's a probation officer and I think he's OK. He always played it straight with me. . . . (I'm a good boy, aren't I, papa?)

BILLY: Oh yeh? What *goodies* are you *getting* out of this, Mr. Nick?

GROUP LEADER: My Adult gets a salary. My Parent is trying to do something about helping people free up the Adult and making it the boss —and protecting society; and my Child is curious about what comes out of TA.

JERRY: Don't you *resent* what Billy's saying? *I* would!

GROUP LEADER: What's important for us to do is to analyze what part of us—Parent, Adult, Child—is doing the talking.

JUDY: I think it was Billy's Parent talking just now—and, well I guess it was my Parent telling him *he* thinks *he's* perfect (laughter).

DOUG: Well, Billy, you're *acting* like a Parent, but I picked up a lot of Child in what you *and* Don said.

DON: Child!

DOUG: Yeh, a not OK Child and a scared Child.

The discussion went on with Billy protesting that he isn't afraid of anything. The noteworthy things coming out of this session is Billy's confirmation of his life position of "I'm OK, you're not OK" which actually represents his reversal of the position, "I'm not OK, you're OK." His unloved and frightened Child sought group support for his need to rehearse his defenses. An attempt was made to entice the group leader into playing games, but Billy's maneuver was diverted into the more productive activity of analyzing group transactions. Billy never returned.

Summary.   Transactional analysis does not have all the answers and many of our group members do not profit by their participation, but those who do use it profitably have demonstrated remarkable improvement in their life positions and in their vocations, recreations, and interpersonal relationships. A former nomadic and depressive parole violator is studying to become an IBM computer analyst; an alcoholic probationer has voluntarily committed himself for treatment in a state hospital; another probationer without trade skills is studying to become an automobile mechanic. And there are others making similar attempts at improving themselves. Transactional Analysis helps a person to become responsible for his future; to feel "OK."[9]

Psychodrama and Role Training

Psychodrama was first created by Dr. J. L. Moreno in Vienna in 1910. He introduced the technique into the field of corrections in the United States in 1931, and it has been used continuously since that time. Psychodrama has never been widely applied in correctional settings because extensive training is required before one can be an effective psychodrama director. Role-training direction does not require as much training and is therefore widely used.

The authors of this book have conducted seminar workshops in psychodrama and role training in a variety of correctional settings in California since 1963. For example, over six hundred probation officers and parole agents have received training in these workshops. The following passage describes some of the techniques and objectives of psychodrama therapy.

Psychodrama

Psychodrama is an exploration by dramatic methods of the relationships a person has to others and the problems he encounters in his relationships. It may be viewed as an experimental procedure in which the individual may observe his relationship with others and manipulate them for any socioanalytic purpose. He may in the course of a psychodrama recognize the existence of problems; he may also become aware of alternative solutions to problems and experiment with possible choices between alternatives. In the course of these experiments he may examine several possible responses of others to each course of action upon which he embarks.

The director begins the session by a "warming up" process in which he helps the group to select a protagonist, the person around whose problems the session will revolve. The protagonist is asked to be himself on the stage and to enact situations in which he was involved in the past, is involved at present, or anticipates for the future. He is urged to choose scenes involving his relationships to others. The choice of enactment is left to him. Some forms of enactment commonly selected are:

1. The reenactment of a past scene or situation.
2. The enactment of a problem that presently involves the individual with someone else in the group or with the director.

---

[9]Richard C. Nicholson, "Transactional Analysis: A New Method for Helping Offenders," *Federal Probation* 34(September 1970):38–39.

3. The enactment of a situation which one anticipates for the future. This is called a future projection.

The objective of psychodrama, and the techniques employed, is not to train the individual for theatrical excellence but to provide him with an opportunity to play himself in all sorts of relationships, particularly those in which he has experienced difficulties, and to experiment with different forms of behavior. Unsatisfying relationships may be explored in the laboratory situation provided by the psychodramatic stage, a director, his assistants (called auxiliary egos), and a psychodramatic group. The individual examines his social relationships in the *here and now*. He presents his view of them on the stage in the presence of and with the help of other members of his psychodrama group. His enactments are then discussed by members of the group led by the director. Members of the group are encouraged to refer to their experiences in dealing with similar problems and the difficulties they encountered.

Role perception and skill in role enactment develop hand in hand. Because our culture does not define roles with sufficient precision to provide all the answers for satisfactory performance in them, some degree of spontaneity or creativity is necessary to meet situations which had not been anticipated in the culture. As the individual becomes more secure in action he becomes more spontaneous. Thus, participation in psychodrama should result in an increase in spontaneity.[10]

The following is excerpted from a psychodrama with a psychopathic delinquent reported by Dr. Raymond J. Corsini. Don, the protagonist, was fifteen years of age, the third of four children. At the age of six, he was maliciously breaking windows; at fourteen he was sent to a state institution after having been in trouble at least one hundred times for stealing, truancy, and other offenses. Don was sent to the institution for car theft. He is described by Dr. Corsini as being rather attractive, of average height, well nourished, and athletic. At the institution Don was in trouble on numerous occasions for running away, using bad language, and other misbehaviors. His attitude was defiant and openly contemptuous. The psychiatrist who had interviewed him upon his admission diagnosed him as a "primary psychopath with no apparent conception of right or wrong."

The psychodramatic group consisted of eleven boys, aged thirteen to sixteen; four were black, the others white. About the fourth week, Don escaped from the institution, stole a car, was followed by police, shot at, and apprehended. The session started with a replication of his escape and apprehension. Then a psychodrama was produced that exaggerated the *possible* destructive consequences of the same act.

---

[10]Martin R. Haskell, *An Introduction to Socioanalysis* (Long Beach, Calif.: California Institute of Socioanalysis, 1967), pp. 11–12.

SCENE I

Don is seated in a chair, driving the car. Immediately behind him are two policemen; the driver is sounding a siren and the other is shooting, "bang, bang, bang." A therapist touches Don and whispers, "You're shot, fall down." Don obediently falls to the ground and lies on his face. The therapist whispers to the police, "Go to him. You'll find that he is dead." The police come over, turn Don on his back.

"Well, he is dead."

"God, he is a mess. My bullet got him in the back of the head. It must have mushroomed and come out of his eyes. Practically his whole face is gone."

"We'd better call the ambulance."

SCENE II

An ambulance arrives, and the doctor looks over Don.

"He was killed instantly. Looks like a kid. What happened?"

"We didn't know his age. We blew our siren. It was a stolen car. He wouldn't stop so we shot at him."

"Well, it was probably a good thing. He is probably a no-good punk. Your bullet entered the back of his head, tore his brains up, and came out of his eyes. Let us put him in the ambulance and bring him to the morgue."

Don is picked up and placed on a table.

SCENE III

A morgue.

Morgue attendant: "Now, Mr. and Mrs. Jemm, I don't know if you want to see him. He doesn't look good. He is on a marble slab. He is naked, and he's full of blood. He practically has no face."

Father: "I want to see my boy. Now, don't cry mother. Maybe it is best." (Mother cries throughout the scene.)

Mother: "My poor boy. Look at him. My little Donnie. Oh, why did they have to kill him?"

Attendant: "Maybe it is all for the best. As I understand it, he may have killed others the way he was speeding. I only hope his soul is not in Hell."

SCENE IV

A church.

Priest: "Oh, almighty God, we commit into your hands the body and the soul of this poor little boy, Don Jemm. We hope that you will have pity on him. He was so young and he did not know how much grief, how much unhappiness he caused his parents and his brothers and sister.

We trust that he is not suffering in the pains of Hell. Dust to Dust, Ashes to Ashes."

SCENE V

A graveyard.

Don's body is placed into a coffin and then lowered into the grave. Mother cries throughout the scene.

Gravedigger: "Well, he is in the grave now. I guess that is all. The story of Don Jemm is over. Let me fill up the grave."

SEQUEL

After the session, the two therapists analyzed it, and discussed principally the ethics of what had been done. It was agreed that the scene probably had a considerable effect on Don. On leaving, he appeared pale and distraught. However, it was decided not to discuss the scene unless it was brought up spontaneously by Don or some of the members.

At the following session, no mention was made of the scene, either by Don or by any of the others. Don, it was observed, in contrast to his usual lively behavior was overly calm, and did not speak at all. Several sessions later, we noticed Don telling one of the boys to "quiet down, and not make a fool of himself." The group disbanded after about the twelfth session.

Several months later, a follow-up was made of the boys in the group. The behavior of Don had apparently changed greatly from that of his prior-to-therapy type. In the four months prior to the scene described, Don had been cited and reprimanded a total of thirty-four times. In the four months subsequent, he was cited only two times. Various personnel were interviewed, and the following remarks were obtained.

HOUSEFATHER: He's a changed boy. Before I could never trust him. Now, I can put implicit faith in him. He is a good influence on the others. I have seen him reading sections of the rule book to new kids. He stops fights between the others. He is quiet and reasonable. He is my best boy. This place has made a man out of him.

TEACHER: His work is much better, and his behavior is greatly improved. He is quiet and orderly. You would never believe it is the same boy.

SOCIAL WORKER: I am amazed at the change in this boy. Formerly, he was always in trouble. Now, he gets along well with everyone. I have rarely seen such a tremendous change. I have talks with him routinely every two weeks. At first he was sly and defiant, now he is respectful and very reasonable.

DISCIPLINARIAN: I was sure we would have to send him to the reformatory. If there was any serious trouble here, it was usually Don at the bottom of it. I noticed he started to change some time ago. I think it must have been that auto incident that did it. Made him wake up and realize what he was doing. Sometimes one incident can make a boy into a man.[11]

Role Training

Role training is a form of role playing in which emphasis is placed on the reenactment of performances in real life. In the course of a role-training session the individual is prepared to behave in a socially approved manner in social situations in which he is required to function.

The goals of role training are:

1. To differentiate in action those patterns of behavior which may have been inadequate, bringing inadequacies to the attention of the director, the individual and the role-training group.

2. To encourage the presentation of alternative patterns of behavior and to help the members of the group to explore alternatives, and each to expand his role repertoire. Each member of the group has an opportunity of objectively evaluating inadequate patterns of behavior which he observes in others. It is anticipated that he will thus learn to become critical of inadequacies and become better able to recognize these inadequacies in his own performances.

3. As each member of the role-training group learns (a) alternative patterns of behavior and (b) to become critical of inadequate patterns, it is anticipated that he will learn to distinguish between rejection of a pattern of behavior and rejection of himself as an individual. Once this distinction is internalized, the individual should tend less to experience failure in an enterprise as rejection of himself as a person. He should come to attribute the failure of inadequate performance in a role to lack of skill in the role.

4. Role training involves the transmission and the acquisition of social skill. With increased social skill the individual may be expected to experience increased success in occupational, family, and community roles in natural groups. His social relationships should, therefore, become more rewarding.[12]

The following is a report of a role-training session conducted at a federal prison by Rochelle J. Haskell.

Place: Federal Prison, Terminal Island, California

---

[11]Raymond J. Corsini, "Psychodrama with a Psychopath," *Group Psychotherapy, Psychodrama, and Sociometry,* J. L. Moreno, M.D., Editor, 11(March 1958):35–38.

[12]M. R. Haskell, *Introduction to Socioanalysis,* pp. 16–17.

Date: January 22, 1973 (4th session of 10)

Time: 6:30–8:30 P.M.

Attending: Bill, Bob, George, James, Jim, Lewis, Mike, Sam, Tommy

Director: Rochelle J. Haskell

Warm-Up.   As you know, we use role training as a way of preparing ourselves for any situation we expect to face in the future. At our last session, Bob and Sam raised the question of preparing to face a parole board. Since many of the people here may have to appear before such a board in the near future, it might be a good idea to work on this. Although we cannot predict exactly what questions will be raised at a particular hearing, we can, if we role train for it, consider a great many possibilities and prepare to deal with them. This should have the effect of preparing us to deal better with whatever comes up.

I must confess that I have never directed a session designed to prepare people to appear before a parole board but, strange as it may seem, about a year ago I ran a session preparing parole agents to appear before a promotion board of the California Youth Authority. It would seem to me that the approach should be similar. After all, in both cases we have a few people meeting to make a decision that will, in each instance, affect the life of another person. We have also used role training to prepare graduate students to take oral examinations before a faculty committee. I will have to make that sort of appearance. That, too, is not too different from facing a parole board, although the stakes are different. There are two basic similarities:

1. We are, in all of these cases, out to impress the board or committee to act in our favor.

2. The better we are prepared to cope with questions raised, the better impression we will make.

Role Playing.   Let us begin with Sam who says he is about to face a parole board, or parole commissioner.

DIRECTOR: Sam, you are about to appear before a parole commissioner. How about coming up here to prepare for it.

(Sam moves into the action area.)

DIRECTOR: Have you ever appeared before a parole commissioner before?

SAM: Yes, and I was always very nervous. I'm nervous now.

DIRECTOR: What is it that worries you most?

SAM: Well, I am in for two bank robberies. I shot two people and even though they weren't hurt seriously it will be held against me.

DIRECTOR: You are now in the anteroom waiting to face the parole commissioner. What are you thinking about?

SAM (in soliloquy in which he thinks out loud): I want to go straight now. I've got to convince them.

GEORGE (doubling with Sam): They'll never believe me.

SAM: I've done all right in the joint. I know I don't want to go back again.

GEORGE (doubling): I've said that before. Why should they believe me now?

SAM: My dad believes me now. He never did before. He said he'll send me to college and I'll go.

DIRECTOR: Are you ready to go in?

SAM: As ready as I'll ever be.

DIRECTOR: Who can play the part of parole commissioner?

JIM: I've appeared before parole commissioners many times. I can really give him a hard time.

(Jim moves to action area.)

JIM (as commissioner): Your record shows that you failed on parole twice. Why do you feel that you will make it this time?

SAM: I feel I am a different person now. I've read a lot and studied, and counseling has helped me.

JIM: What have you been doing in the institution?

SAM: I've been participating in group therapy sessions and reading a lot.

JIM: Have you done any work here?

SAM: I have worked in the office of the chief psychologist.

JIM: That sounds like an easy job. What did you do?

SAM: I filed records and typed information.

JIM: You almost killed innocent people when you were out. Why should I believe you won't do it again?

SAM: I was nearly killed in that robbery. I learned my lesson. I'll never risk that again.

JIM: How can we be sure that you won't kill someone next time?

SAM: Sir, the only thing I can say is that I've learned my lesson.

Discussion. There was an animated discussion in which everyone participated. The question that several members of the group raised was how could the parole commissioner tell if a man was conning him or not. Mike and Lewis said they would give a man a chance if he had a job to go to. Tommy and Lewis felt that what the man was doing in the institution would influence them. James said he would try to find out whether a man had changed in the institution. He saw little change in Bob, but some change in Sam.

The most important thing a parole commissioner would be looking for was employment possibilities, if parole was granted. Another important consideration would be what a candidate for parole was doing in prison. It was important to be in some program that would prepare a man for release. Mike, Bill, and Sam said they would move into training programs to prepare them for work outside the institution. They would then emphasize this to the parole commissioner. The discussion was active; everyone participated.[13]

John G. Hill, a correctional counselor in a Los Angeles County probation camp for juveniles, describes the rationale for and the methodology of using psychodrama to reduce aggressive behavior in a juvenile institution.

One of the major problems faced by correctional counselors in the care and treatment of juvenile offenders in the institutional setting is that of the aggressive, assaultive ward. He presents unique difficulties in terms of control and adaptability especially in the group living situation, and as his behavior directly affects the behavior of his peers, his negative acting out exerts undue pressures upon the group as a whole. . . .

With these thoughts in mind the possibility of utilizing psychodrama as a treatment tool in dealing with the aggressive ward became readily apparent based on four major assumptions.

1. Aggressive and assaultive impulses could be channeled in a controlled monitored setting allowing full expression without the danger of physical injury.

2. Motives behind these impulses could be explored in a manner readily visible to the wards involved.

3. Immediate catharsis could be achieved, reducing the probability of uncontrolled aggression and pressure in the group living situation.

4. Precipitating problems could be alleviated, examined, and explored as they occurred by a restaging of the problem in a psychodramatic setting. . . .

An examination of the case of David M. will serve as an example of the process in action. David M. is a Mexican-American youth of seventeen years, committed to Camp Fenner for murder. He is a large heavyset boy, intensively gang oriented. His case file reveals a record of seventeen arrests ranging from assaults and robberies to the committing offense.

---

[13]Rochelle J. Haskell, "Will a Role-Training Program Administered to Stutterers Achieve a Reduction in the Severity of Disfluencies?" (M.A. thesis, California State University at Long Beach, July 1973).

David entered "A" dormitory reluctantly. His initial reaction to camp was negative in the extreme. Within three hours of entering the program he had managed to alienate virtually everyone in the dormitory, staff and peers alike. His answer to every reasonable request was a resounding obscenity. The consensus of opinion by staff was that David should be removed to a security or "lock up" facility as soon as possible. This would probably have been initiated in short order had he not become involved in an incident with the reigning *chicano* in the dorm, Leon, a member of a rival gang. Staff intervened before blows were struck and David and six other wards were taken to the office for counseling. . . .

It was felt that the psychodramatic approach might prove effective in this case and the transition from encounter group to psychodrama was made by setting the stage for a reenactment of the confrontation between David and Leon. Initially an *auxiliary ego* staff member played the part of Leon to alleviate the bad emotional climate.

David was seated in a chair facing staff who assumed the *role* of the *other,* Leon.

DAVID: You bastards (indicating the group as a whole) are always messin' with me.

STAFF: Man, you come walking in here like some *vato loco* trying to prove how tough you are, what do you expect?

David does a double take and demands to know who staff is. Is he to be a staff or is he supposed to be Leon? The ground rules are repeated, indicating that what we are trying to accomplish is to relive the incident so that we can see what the problem is.

DAVID: How come that punk (indicating Leon) don't do it himself?

Leon becomes visibly agitated and starts to get out of his chair. He is waved back. Staff explains that because of the charged atmosphere and raw feelings a substitute for Leon is being used. David is to regard staff as Leon for purposes of the psychodrama and respond to him accordingly. The initial confrontation is reviewed with the wards explaining that David had challenged Leon and that Leon had reacted by questioning David's right to enter the dormitory as a new boy and throw his weight around. Staff, assuming the *role* of Leon, picked it up from there.

STAFF: How come you think you're such a bad ass? You can't come walking in here talking all that crap and shoving people around. You better get your act together.

DAVID: Screw you man! You don't tell Mad Dog what to do or not to do!

STAFF: Mad Dog? Mad Dog? They usually put mad dogs to sleep. What does that mean Mad Dog? Everyone here knows where dogs come from.

Leon laughs from the sidelines as David balls up his fists and glares about him.

DAVID: I'm going to waste you *puto*! (This is directed toward the vacant space halfway between staff and Leon.)

The interchange continues for some minutes and is evidently a source of some satisfaction to David who begins to relax as he realizes that he can express himself verbally without fear of physical retaliation. Another ward, James, a black who has been in obvious delight over the exchange, is moved into position next to David to act as his *double.*

STAFF: (Continuing) I don't know how a punk like you stayed alive on the outs. If I'd seen you out there I would have brought back your *cojones* in a paper bag.

DAVID: (Reddening at this reflection on his manhood struggles with himself for a moment before answering) At least I got *cojones.* You ain't nothing but a *vieja.* You ain't nothing at all unless you got your home-boys around.

At this point James who has obviously been anxious to participate interjects as David's *double*—helping David to present himself more effectively.

JAMES (as David): Yeah, you think you runnin' this dorm, tellin' every-body what to do all the time. You think you cool but you ain't crap!

David is somewhat taken aback at the unexpected support he has found and warms to his role. He begins to reflect on his statements picking up cues from James.

DAVID: Yeah, how come when I come in here you all of a sudden start giving orders? You ain't no better than me even if you been here longer. . .

Leon now enters the session to play himself. The interchange be-tween the two boys was now taking place in fairly normal tones as Leon, having vented his personal feelings from the group begins dealing with David on the level of a person of authority trying to reason with a recalcitrant underling. David was resisting this process by pointedly ignoring Leon's arguments and discussing his own feelings of right and justice. While he played the *role* of wronged party with obvious relish it was apparent that he had little or no insight at this point into his role in the problem.

Staff suggested that the wards physically exchange places and Leon play the *role* of David while David assume the *part* of Leon. Both boys initially balked at the idea of role reversal but at the urging of others in the group reluctantly exchanged seats. Leon was the first to begin the dialogue. He assumed an exaggerated stance of braggadocio, fists clenched and lips drawn back. He stared defiantly at David.

LEON: (As David) You *puto,* you ain't gonna tell me what to do!

David was obviously struggling at this point, not sure of how he should react. Then, apparently remembering Leon's tirade against him, launched into a vituperative monologue which continued for some minutes despite Leon's attempts to interrupt. The other members of the group seemed to be enjoying the performance immensely.

When David finally ran out of words staff asked him what he was feeling at that moment.

DAVID: I don't know man, but I really got pissed off when he called me a *puto* and started staring at me like that. It made me feel like just kicking him and going off on him.

STAFF: Do you want to go off on him now?

DAVID: Yeh, yeh I do!

STAFF: (Handing David a towel) Okay, hit the desk with this. Hit the desk like it was Leon.

David takes the towel and tentatively hits the desk; once, twice, three times. Then he knots the end and brings it crashing down a half a dozen times.

STAFF: Who are you hitting, David?

DAVID: Him, Leon, the Flores.

STAFF: (Turning to the *audience*) What's happening here?

JERRY: It seem to me that he's getting pissed off at Leon for doing the same thing to him that he did to Leon.

MIKE: I think he's pissed off at himself.

STAFF: (To David) What do you think about that?

DAVID: I don't know what you're talking about.

LEON: Look man, I was doing the same thing you were doing from the first minute you walked in here. So maybe you can see how you was coming off.

David struggles with this concept for a moment then crashes the towel violently against the desk.

DAVID: You guys don't know crap!

David does not say this too convincingly, however. The rest of the group have had a glimpse of the truth and immediately begin to belabor the point.

STEVE: Hey man, maybe you got angry because you know the way it really is. Maybe you better face it instead of copping out.

JERRY: (Changing allegiance) Yeah, don't seem like you can take what you was giving out.

CARLOS: That's the trouble with you man, you don't know what's coming down even when everyone else can see it! . . .

Suddenly David lashes out with the towel striking Leon across the face, then screams at the group.

DAVID: Damn it! Why don't you *putos* get off my back?

Leon has reacted by pulling the towel out of David's hands and is about to hit him with the knotted end when staff intervenes and pushes both boys back into their chairs. The other boys have leaped up anticipating a fight.

STAFF: Okay, okay, now just sit down and calm down.

Leon is rubbing his face, looking daggers at David who is sitting slumped in his chair breathing heavily. The other members of the group settle back as staff asks them to explain what has just happened.

JAMES: I think David knows what's happening and is afraid to face it. He can't admit he's wrong so he has to take it out on somebody.

MIKE: Yeh, he acts just like my little brother when he doesn't get his way or what he wants. He has a tantrum.

JERRY: Yeah, he acting like a kid.

The others all echo Jerry's sentiments as David sits in his chair fighting back tears. Leon, sensing that David has just passed through an emotional crisis, relaxes and begins to talk. He becomes quite reflective and adult.

LEON: I don't know, sometimes it's hard to be real. I mean to really see yourself. (He reflects for a moment.) When I was on the outs . . . when I was a kid, I got into fights all the time. I guess I was a real *vato loco,* everybody thought I was crazy, even my parents. I was in the hospital maybe five or six times. When I was fifteen I got shot and everybody thought I was going to die. When I got back on the streets I was a big man. I was tough. Then I started thinking how weird it was that it took almost getting killed and having a hole in my side to make me a person of respect. Anyway, now I had my rep and didn't have to go around personally going off on people. Sure, I done some gang banging but most of the time since then I kept laid back out of sight. I got things I want to do. I got a *vieja* and a kid. I guess I know what David feels like. I guess he still got to make his rep. He's just not going about it the right way. Going off on *vatos* in camp ain't gonna make it. That way somebody going to do him when he gets back on the street. We all got to get along here and do our time the best way we can. We got to stick together. When I was sitting here doing his trip I was getting next to how he was feeling. I guess because I been there myself.

Leon has appeared to have lost all his animosity and during the course of his soliloquy David listened intently. David seemed surprised that Leon expressed empathy with his feeling, especially in view of the towel incident. He was having difficulty in controlling his tears.

STAFF: (To David) Okay, how are you feeling now?

DAVID: I don't know man. I don't know how I'm feeling. I feel all washed out. I feel like I don't give a damn about anything. I'm tired.

LEON: You got to get with it. You were talking that everyone was down on you without giving you a chance. Well it seems to me that you were down on everybody without giving us a chance.

DAVID: I don't know. With the *putos* on the street you got to get them before they get you, you know that, otherwise they walk all over you. I know you got homeboys here but no one is going to walk over me.

LEON: Okay, no one is going to walk over you here as long as you take care of business. There's too many dudes out there that want to see us firing on each other. You're just going to make it harder on yourself and the rest of us unless you're cool.

DAVID: (Shaking his head to indicate doubt reflects for a moment then tentatively holds out his hand. He finds it hard to meet Leon's eye.) Okay, okay. I'm sorry about the towel, huh? I guess I was pretty pissed off.

Leon takes David's hand and shakes it firmly making the comment that he can clearly see why they call him Mad Dog. At this point David has some recognition of responsibility to the group.

For David the psychodrama was both a catharsis and an initiation into the group living setting of "A" dormitory. While the session could not be considered a panacea for David's problems it did provide the initial step which allowed him to remain in the program instead of being transferred to a maximum security prison. Perhaps most important, for the first time, it allowed him to see himself as others saw him; the beginnings of insight.[14]

The foregoing examples are cases handled in an institutional setting. One of the authors, in his work with gangs, often used role playing in crisis situations. Gang life moves so fast that it is not possible to wait until gang members are apprehended and placed in an institution. To prevent crime, one must respond to emergencies. In the following account, the underlying theory and elements of a psychodramatic session (warmup, action, and postdiscussion) are applied to (1) an immediate "live" problem, (2) of an "emergency" nature, (3) in the "open community," and (4) often emerging unexpectedly.

---

[14]John G. Hill, "Reducing Aggressive Behavior in the Institutional Setting through Psychodrama," *Group Psychotherapy, Psychodrama, and Sociometry,* Zerka T. Moreno, Editor, 48(June 1977), p. 83.

A disturbed gang leader, accompanied by two friends, accosted me as I was walking down the street, pulled out a switchblade knife, and announced that he was on his way to kill a youth who lived in a nearby neighborhood on the upper west side of Manhattan. I moved into action armed with a psychodramatic approach.

First, I was prepared for this emergency-possibility, since on a continuing basis I had made sociometric tests which revealed the relationships of various gangs and gang networks in the area. I knew the gangs that were feuding and the leadership patterns of each group. More than that, the youth facing me already had had previous exposure to psychodrama; this was helpful, as we could move right into action. In short, the groundwork was set for this emergency use of psychodrama.

I asked myself: why did the youth stop me before he went to stab the other youth? I suspected the chances were good that he really did not want to commit this violence and wanted me to help him find a way out.

The "Ape," as this boy was called by the gang, was openly defiant and upset. His opening remark was:

> "Man, I'm packin'; I got my blade (switch-blade knife) right here. I'm going to cut the s— out of those m— f— Dragons. I'm going up and get them now . . . once and for all."

In short, he had a knife and was going to stab any Dragon gang boys he met that day. It was also reasonable to assume that he would stab any youth who, in his hysterical judgment, was a Dragon.

The boys followed me to my nearby office and the session began with the use of another gang boy as an auxiliary ego in the role of the potential victim. A paper ruler replaced the knife (for obvious reasons), and the "killing" was acted out in my office under controlled psychodramatic conditions.

The psychodrama, in brief, had all of the elements of a real gang killing. The Ape (the subject) cursed, fumed, threatened, and shouted at the victim, who hurled threats and insults in return. Ape worked himself into a frenzy and then stabbed the auxiliary ego (the gang boy playing the part) with the paper knife. The psychodramatic victim fell dead on the floor.

The Ape was then confronted with the consequences of his act in all of its dimensions, including the effect on his family. He began to regret what he had done and was particularly remorseful when (psychodramatically) an auxiliary ego playing the role of a court judge sentenced him "to death in the electric chair."

The psychodrama accomplished at least two things for this very potential killer: (1) He no longer was motivated to kill, since he had already accomplished this psychodramatically. (2) He was confronted with the consequences of this rash act; this was an added dimension of consideration. Many gang boys are unable to think ahead in a situation to the outcome. These factors possibly served as a deterrent to the actual commission of a murder. Of course, this boy required and received further therapy, which sought to deal with his more basic personality problems. Moreover, considerably more work was attempted on the gang networks, so as to minimize their potential for violence. However, the emergency psychodrama, *in situ,* the immediate situation, did deter the possibility of Ape's committing a homicide, at least on that particular day.[15]

Group psychotherapy and psychodrama provide the opportunity for actual direct role training. Here offenders can view themselves and others through presenting their problems for group discussion and analysis. More than that, they are in a position to correct (or edit) their illegal actions in the presented situations. The offender can try out or practice legally conforming roles in the presence of criminal "experts," who quickly detect whether he is conning the group or playing it straight. In a role-playing session in which offenders were being trained for future employment, for example, one offender (who was soon to be released from prison) went through the motions of getting a job with apparent disinterest. This fact was quickly and forcefully brought out in the open by other members of the group, producing a valuable discussion on the basic need of employment for going straight. In another session one of the authors observed a violent offender learn to control his assaultive impulse by talking about, rather than acting out, his wish to assault a member of the group. He learned to talk about violent impulses rather than assault first and discuss later.

A characteristic of group treatment, therefore, is that it provides an opportunity for violent offenders to talk or act out their illegal motivations in a controlled setting. After acting out their destructive impulses in the session, they may no longer have the need to carry them out in reality. The group also gives offenders and their peer co-therapists an opportunity to assess the meaning of violence through discussion. An empathic group can help the violent offender understand his compulsive emotions. Among other things, he learns he is not alone in his feelings.

Many offenders have difficulty controlling immediate compulsions for future goals. They tend to live in the moment and often lack the ability to relate the past to the present, the present to the future. The thought of future punishment of past experience doesn't usually enter their conscious delibera-

---

[15]Lewis Yablonsky, "Sociopathology of the Violent Gang and Its Treatment," in *Progress in Psychotherapy,* ed. Jules H. Masserman and J. L. Moreno (New York: Grune & Stratton, 1956–60), vol. 5, *Reviews and Integrations* (1960), pp. 167–68. Reprinted by permission.

tions to serve as a deterrent to illegal action. Training in understanding time dimensions is therefore often useful in crime prevention.

Psychodrama as a group process provides such time flexibility. The offender can act out the past, immediate, or expected problem situations that are disturbing him. The process is useful in working with criminals who manifest impulsive behavior. Psychodrama, in particular the "future-projection technique," by means of which a person propels himself into a future situation, provides an opportunity for the offender to plan for a legally conforming future. This technique has been used with offenders about to be released into the open community in order to project them into relevant future social situations in which they will find themselves. These role-test situations include potential problems in the community, on the job, with the family, with supervising probation officers, and others.

The role-training process tends to build up the offender's resistance to efforts on the part of his criminal friends to seduce him back into criminal activity. Psychodrama provides an opportunity for the immediate-situation-oriented criminal to review some of his past and future behavior with its many implications for resisting criminal activity. To the offender with con-man or sociopathic characteristics, words are cheap. Considerable research indicates that it is very difficult to lie in action during psychodrama. Because group pressures make distortion so difficult, the offender is forced to assess his behavior and its rationale closely. This, combined with opportunities to try out legally conforming behavior patterns before such severe judges as his peers, helps the offender to reexamine and reject his illegal behavior patterns and learn socially conforming practices. The total array of such group processes as group therapy, psychodrama, role playing, future projection, and role training constitute a significant body of treatment methods.

Chapter
17

Recommendations for Prevention, Control, and Treatment of Crime and Delinquency

IN THE PRECEDING CHAPTERS, we have described various types of delinquency and categories of offenders. We have also presented explanations for the high incidence of delinquency as well as explanations for various types of delinquent behavior. Various treatment techniques were also described. In addition, we have discussed the juvenile court system and the ways in which it operates and the correctional system, including modernization programs. All of these together represent society's efforts to protect people from harm, to punish those who harm others or society in general, and to rehabilitate offenders so they may be deterred from further violation of the law.

Sociologists are often reluctant to make recommendations for changes in the law, in the administration of the criminal justice system, or in correctional policies. The prevailing attitude in sociological circles is that sociologists should maintain scientific objectivity in their studies, report the results of their research, and leave the conclusions to be drawn by others. When they testify before legislative committees, their answers to questions are often so heavily qualified and so larded with professional jargon that it is exceedingly difficult to determine what policy changes they favor, if any. Books and articles also attempt to maintain this sort of professional detachment. The result is that our legislators tend to rely heavily on the expertise of law-enforcement people and correctional administrators in deciding what legislation should be enacted to prevent crime and control criminal behavior. In our opinion, sociologists with years of experience in the field of delinquency should freely present their opinions and recommendations, even though many of their assertions are not based on firm empirical evidence.

Given this prelude, we shall offer in this chapter some recommendations for, we hope, reducing the amount of delinquency in our society . These recommendations involve changes in the law, the juvenile justice system, the police structure, and the correctional system. While we assume full responsibility for every suggestion made, we believe that the vast majority of psychologists and sociologists active in the study or treatment of delinquency would support our recommendations.

In general, we concur with the following principles offered by the Youth Development and Delinquency Prevention Administration as a set of guides in devising programs of youth development and delinquency prevention.

1. *Delinquent behavior in the young has as its most general cause their exclusion from socially acceptable, responsible, and therefore personally gratifying roles.* While there may be wide variation in individual capacity to withstand the strain and frustration of such exclusion, failure to provide access to socially meaningful roles represents the fundamental conditions underlying waywardness in the youth group.

2. *Roles are made available to the young by the institutions in which they participate.* Institution is here defined in the generic sense of established arrangements for conducting valued societal functions. Each such institution is constituted by a pattern of differentiated roles having a specifiable design. These designs may vary with respect to their capacity to allocate to their membership roles eliciting strong identification with the goals and values of the institution.

3. *With respect to the problem of delinquency, the critical matter in institutional role allocation is the acquisition of roles imparting to the individual a legitimate identity.* The latter type of role has the effect of creating in the person a firm attachment to the aims, values, and norms (rules and regulations) of the institutions, and of sharply reducing the probability of his involvement in delinquent activity.

4. *Since roles are a product of institutional design and procedure, and since obstruction to a favorable course of youth development arises from failure to provide roles creating legitimate identity, a rational strategy of delinquency reduction and control must address the task of institutional change.* It is clearly implied that the changes sought should be those capable of expanding the range of roles generating legitimate identity in young persons.

5. *Among the institutions significant in the lives of young persons during the period of maximum vulnerability to delinquency and/or withdrawal, the school is of central importance.* Delinquency is distinctively

a problem of the adolescent period. Deficits in socialization attributable to faulty family experience may produce any of a wide variety of personal or social problems. Whether these deficits result in delinquent behavior depends on the course of adolescent experience. As the school, specifically the secondary school, is the "institutional home" of the adolescent in the structure of modern society, it constitutes the primary locus of adolescent experience. Consequently, in its focus on institutional change, the proposed strategy specifies the educational institution as its primary target.

6. *The process through which illegitimate identities are formed and a commitment to delinquent activity arises among adolescents is best understood by contrast with the formation and maintenance of legitimate identity by adults.* Rates of crime for adults are substantially lower than those for adolescents. Adult status is characterized by opportunity for relatively meaningful participation in the economic and political activities of society. Utilization of such opportunity imparts a sense of competence and power and reduces alienation from the values and norms of basic societal institutions. Cut off from opportunity for similar participation by radical confinement to the milieu of the school, adolescents are significantly less likely to develop feelings of competence, of power, of usefulness. The presence of these elements of experience fosters the formation of legitimate identity; their absence creates alienation and fosters the formation of illegitimate identity.

7. *The tie of the young person to the school as his "institutional home" is maintained and reinforced by (a) the direct rewards of approval for valued academic and social performance; and (b) by the indirect rewards of a credible promise of a desirable occupational future.* Those adolescents whose interests, capacities, and talents are not engaged by the standard curriculum format are denied the rewards of current approval and of future promise, are thereby placed into a situation of drift with respect to the values and norms of the school, undergo loss of a sense of their legitimacy as persons, and become vulnerable to deviant and delinquent conduct expressive of discontent and rebellion.

8. *Young persons whose controlling ties to the school have been weakened, who thereby acquire a history of misbehavior, becoming subject to the repeated intervention of the juvenile justice system, are rendered increasingly vulnerable to delinquency through a process of building up of stigmatizing labels.* Repeated exposure to official treatment with its imposition of restrictions on normal activity tends to promote the development of an illegitimate identity, which in turn forms the basis for repeated infraction. The resulting escalation of stigma entangles the person in a web of self-fulfilling prophecy which becomes increasingly difficult to escape.

9. *To cope with this problem it is necessary to develop mechanisms*

to divert troublesome youth from the juvenile justice system. To be effective, these mechanisms should be designed to increase youth participation in activities that forge legitimate identities by (*a*) avoiding their segregation into groups made up solely of stigmatized and troubled individuals, and (*b*) enlarging their opportunities, as members of "mixed" groups, for involvement in school, work, community projects, political activity, and family life. Such activities, lying outside the correctional system, build a commitment to conformity.

10. *An important secondary target of institutional change is the juvenile corrections system itself, whose bureaucratic insulation from the communities of its clients impairs its effectiveness.* Because of their insulation, agents of juvenile justice are perceived as an alien, external, and hostile force without legitimating support from community leaders and other sources of local influence. The remedy lies in (*a*) creating a role for local community leadership in the administration of juvenile justice; and (*b*) inducing the agents of juvenile corrections to engage in "system advocacy," whereby they exert pressure on a variety of community institutions, notably the school system, to so alter their procedures as to enhance opportunities for their clients to develop a commitment to conformity.[1]

Removing Blocks to Adult Status

An important goal of the male adolescent is the status of manhood. Many young men are frustrated in their drive to adulthood by dislocations in the social system. For example, there are legal obstacles to employment that discriminate against young people. Most states have laws either barring or limiting employment possibilities of adolescents. Even where no legal obstacles exist, young people are sometimes denied employment as a result of union membership policies and management hiring policies. Young people see themselves discriminated against by laws and regulations controlling the use of alcoholic beverages, drugs, gathering in groups, school attendance, hours on the street, and even dress. The fact that adults impose on young people regulations that they do not make applicable to themselves is often viewed as unjust and hypocritical and produces hostility that can express itself in delinquent patterns.

Another felt area of discrimination is the relatively powerless role of the student. Most students have a limited role in determining the schools' curricula and policies. Yet school is an aspect of their lives that exerts a powerful

[1]*Delinquency Prevention Through Youth Development,* Youth Development and Delinquency Administration Publication no. (SRS)73–26013 (Washington, D.C.: U.S. Government Printing Office, May 1972), pp. 28–30.

control over their futures. The demand for student power has produced violence, clashes with police, and judicial action.

Except for the recently granted—and little used—right to vote in federal elections, political power, too, is denied them. The adult world makes the decisions that affect the lives of the young, often without giving the young any relevant voice in the decision-making process. And so young people find themselves drafted into the army to fight wars they consider unjust, with no lawful means of influencing the decisions that sent them there.

This sort of discrimination has always been with us, but young people today, because of an increased exposure to data provided by mass media, particularly television, are more keenly aware of these issues than ever before. This complex of status frustrations and resentments leads many youngsters into delinquent behavior.

One significant step toward the reduction of juvenile delinquency would be to define the social roles of the adolescent clearly, to give him greater status and power in the social system.

Improving the Educational System

The model of the school as a factory, with the students as raw material and the curriculum providing information he must somehow absorb, should be modified. A more appropriate model might be the school as department store, with the student as a customer and the curriculum a product that must be made attractive enough for him to want to buy it. This would require the school to provide material that adolescents are willing, even eager, to accept. The role of student would then be defined in such a way as to be appropriate for all persons under the age of eighteen.

As we have seen, delinquency often results from the tendencies of adolescents to accept gangs or other delinquent groups as their reference groups. Steps need to be taken either to counteract these tendencies or to redirect the values of the delinquent groups. The educational system can encourage adherence to nondelinquent reference groups in the following ways:

1. By providing classes organized around the problem of developing realistic goals prior to age eleven. Qualifications, opportunities, salaries, and training requirements applicable to all occupations would be stressed.
2. By providing counseling services to boys and girls before their eleventh year to assist them in deciding upon appropriate occupational and social goals. In a society in which upward social mobility for members of the lower class depends on educational achievement, compulsion is not the only means of encouraging scholastic effort. Too many lower class youths do not develop any realistic goals,

attend school because they are compelled to do so, put forth a minimum of effort, and drop out at the first opportunity. Relating education to attainable and relevant goals makes it more acceptable to most young people.
3. By encouraging greater respect for skilled and semiskilled workers and their crafts and occupations. Field trips to watch such persons at work and films and lectures emphasizing their contributions to society might produce a greater motivation for such occupations. Many lower class adolescents tend to display contempt for the occupations of their parents, view their parents as failures, and perceive most occupational opportunities that are easily available to them as undesirable. This kind of dissatisfaction often leads to delinquency.
4. By stimulating the organization of normative social groups on school property on the basis of occupational choice, recreational choice, or educational interest. For example, carpentry clubs, future teachers clubs, mechanical clubs, gardening clubs, art clubs, music clubs, or clubs devoted to sporting activities might productively be developed.[2]

School properties should be made more generally available to young people after school is out. In the afternoon or evening, when such use will not interfere with classroom instruction, the rooms and grounds may be made available for athletic events, intellectual pursuits, social activities, and other interests that attract young people into constructive patterns of behavior.

Whether one accepts differential association or reference group theory as an explanation for the way in which young people become involved in or committed to delinquent behavior, one must conclude that membership in special interest groups could reduce activity in gangs with delinquent value systems.

Minimizing the Negative Impacts of the Courts

Wherever feasible, we recommend *diversion* from the juvenile court. The jurisdiction of the juvenile courts should be limited to children under the age of eighteen who commit acts that would be classified as criminal if committed by adults. Children now classified as "dependent" and "neglected" should be handled separately under the jurisdiction of a family court. They would thus not be defendants in court proceedings pursuant to the petitions of others. Rather the entire family would be brought before a family court on a petition alleging that a family requires the attention of that court. Such a court could not stigmatize the children, nor could it order dependent and neglected chil-

---

[2]Martin R. Haskell, "Toward a Reference Group Theory of Juvenile Delinquency," *Social Problems* 8(Winter 1960–61):220–30.

dren to be placed in institutions in close proximity with young people who are committed to a criminal or delinquent value system.

Outside of the courts, neighborhood councils consisting of representatives of the school, social welfare organizations, and parent-teacher associations could deal with all children who present disciplinary problems or who commit minor offenses. The model presented by the British white paper discussed in Chapter 2 could be used. A policeman who apprehended a child for a minor disciplinary problem—running away, incorrigible behavior, vandalism—could deliver him to such a neighborhood committee or authority.

The advantages of this approach would be:

1. The youth would not be stigmatized as a result of action by such a group.

2. The fact that an individual would appear before a committee drawn from his own neighborhood and social class could be an important factor in reducing insidious class differences.

3. Relatives, neighbors, and friends of the youth brought before such a tribunal would be more likely to be convinced of the fairness of the proceeding and the desirability of the action taken.

4. Action deemed necessary to maintain discipline would not be confused with the punishment of criminal behavior.

5. Children who present discipline problems would not be forced into close association with children who are committed to criminal or delinquent values.

6. Action taken by a neighborhood authority would be more likely to reinforce the authority of the family.

A neighborhood authority of this type would not and should not be concerned with the problem of guilt or innocence but, in the tradition of educators and social workers, would be concerned primarily with the course of action most likely to redirect the activities and attitudes of the young person toward nondelinquent behavior.

Expanding Community Treatment Facilities

There is considerable evidence that placing people in custody often serves to reinforce patterns of criminal behavior. If people are not yet committed to criminal or delinquent attitudes and values when they enter a correctional institution, they are likely to learn them there. Those who arrive with few criminal skills often acquire them before they leave.

Correctional institutions cannot be entirely abolished. They serve two very important functions: (1) they protect society from those persons who are dangerous to others, and (2) they serve as a deterrent for those who are not yet committed to a criminal way of life. However, those offenders who do not absolutely require custody should be treated in the community.

Experiments with halfway houses, work furlough programs, and close-supervision parole services indicate that persons are most amenable to treatment before they have been shut up in institutions. There already are halfway houses in which people spend their days in constructive activities and are permitted to return to their homes at night. There are others where people live and receive therapy at night but engage in their normal activities in the community during the day. In these facilities treatment can be effectively administered without completely separating the individual from his natural community and family roles: the final test of successful rehabilitation.

Close-supervision parole, with case loads limited to approximately fifteen persons, has proved successful in maintaining people in the community who might otherwise serve sentences in total institutions. The advantage of close-supervision parole is that the individual has an opportunity to maintain his occupational or educational role while being aided to develop more constructive relationships with members of his family, fellow workers, employers, and other noncriminal people. If a person is not likely to harm others, close-supervision parole provides a form of supervision most likely to result in rehabilitation.

Another advantage of close-supervision parole is that it can take advantage of all the available resources of the community. The individual may be referred for psychiatric or social work treatment if this is indicated. He may avail himself of the training facilities and services of state departments of employment, youth opportunity centers, and other agencies serving the people in his community. Once he is in a custodial institution, his range of resources is greatly limited.

In this context of community programs, governmental agencies might subsidize noncriminal organizations like Synanon without compromising or interfering with their development or approach. People who went to Synanon would not be stigmatized by the criminal label and would thus have an opportunity to correct their criminal or delinquent behavior voluntarily.

In brief, we recommend increased support and establishment of community-based programs in lieu of confinement in custodial institutions. Confinement in a total institution would be ordered only in those instances where it was clearly necessary to protect society or where all other treatment efforts had failed.

We would keep young people out of correctional institutions by expanding probation, community treatment centers, and other community treatment programs. In this connection we recommend following the action of Massachusetts, which ordered all its correctional institutions for juveniles closed by April 1973. The rationale for closing these institutions, the way Massachusetts accomplished the closing, and the alternative treatment programs that were developed are described in the following report.

Rationale for Closing Institutions

The change from institutional to community care for youth in Massachusetts came about because this state, although well intentioned, was failing to effectively rehabilitate the juveniles adjudged legally delinquent and committed to its care by the courts. This failure to cure took the form of isolated institutions, apart from the rest of society, wherein antiquated methods of "therapy" and "education" were practiced. Youths who underwent institutional care in the state reform schools showed a predictable and alarming tendency to *reappear* in the judicial and penal system.

The high concentration of low-income children—about 90 percent of the children committed to the department each year come from families receiving some form of welfare—demonstrated that many treatment alternatives were not available to the disadvantaged. Since about 60 percent of the families from which the children come have histories of parental alcoholism, drug use, mental instability, or child abuse, it was further obvious that the children's problems were complex and required individualized attention. Recidivism studies in the state that revealed more than a 70 percent return rate for reform school graduates confirmed that the "reform" schools failed to treat the underlying problems created in the child through poverty or family neglect.

Institutions failed for reasons inherent in their aims and operation. *Their primary role was custodial.* Society wanted the children kept out of sight and out of trouble, and the staffs of the institutions obliged. The expenditure of energy to keep the children confined, orderly, and obedient left practically no time for the requisite amount of individual attention, and ensured that the children's problems would *not* be resolved. This built in futility engendered frustration in staff and bitterness in the youth, and created new problems. This "treatment" became for many children the first step in criminal careers. Youth who suffered violent treatment at the hands of their peers, as well as beatings from staff, solitary confinement, loneliness, boredom, were expected by society to return from these experiences the same social conditions which produced their "delinquency" and lead well-ordered lives.

The expense of Massachusetts' juvenile institutions was insupportable, given their failure to achieve their avowed goals—reduce criminal behavior, rehabilitate, divert children from criminal lives. It was in the light of these failures, and based on the humane premise that children *from all backgrounds* should have equal access to effective treatment, that the Massachusetts training schools were closed. *The needed social services could be more inexpensively purchased and better provided through regionalized purchase of care.* With this in mind, Commissioner

Jerome Miller set out in 1969, under a legislative mandate for reform, to change the Massachusetts system.

Closing the Institutions.   The Industrial School at Shirley was closed on January 3, 1972. The population of 62 boys, reduced from its onetime level of 150–200, underwent thorough medical, dental, and psychological evaluations prior to placements in group homes, on parole home, into intensive parole with private casework services, and into other DYS (Department of Youth Services) facilities.

The Lyman School in Westboro, which had held nearly 300 boys in the 1960s, was closed in mid-January. The population of 74 boys went to the J.O.E. (Juvenile Opportunities Extension) conference at the University of Masschusetts, as did 25 girls from the Lancaster School for Girls. The conference, specifically designed to facilitate the closings, lasted for a month, during which time each youth worked with his own advocate, who provided housing, counseling, and preplacement research. At the end of the conference the youth went to their respective placements.

The Lancaster School for Girls, with the exception of one cottage used for a residential program, was closed August 1972. Several residential programs run by independent groups use cottages on the grounds.

John Augustus Hall, in Oakdale, once populated by 100 boys from age seven to twelve, was closed in January 1972, and was temporarily used as a reception unit for testing before reception services were established regionally. The 19 youth in residence when the institution closed were placed in a variety of home and group settings.

The Institute for Juvenile Guidance at Bridgwater, a 100-year-old Bastille-like maximum security facility for the "most vicious" youth committed to the department, was closed in January 1970, and was placed by purchased care in public and private institutions, both in this state and other parts of the country. During the 1960s, 120 children or more occupied this facility, which had the most primitive conditions of any institutions in the state.

Three detention centers across the state have seen their populations reduced from over 100 to less than 50, and now take court-detained youths only on an emergency basis. Nonmaximum security detention alternatives have been developed regionally.

The summary closing of institutions forced the expansion of residential and nonresidential programs and encouraged the improvement of regional mechanisms to serve DYS youth. Each regional office must identify, develop, and support the services needed for the youth within the region. The office concentrates on diverting youth away from the adjudication process, casework services, developing treatment alternatives, and involving community leaders in prevention programs.

A regional court liaison program, originally designed to inform the courts of new department programs, evolved into a key placement organ, closely linked to the regional offices. Department employees attend juvenile courts and act, during preliminary hearings and trials, as youth advocates. They also work with the probation departments and judges, as well as the children, to establish the optimum treatment plan for the child before adjudication. In this manner, by establishing treatment plans before commitment to the department, detention periods are often eliminated entirely and the children are spared "dead time" waiting for placement. Beyond this placement function, court liaison officers encourage the courts to *refer* the children in place of commitment. The child thus receives services through the department without the stigmatization of a commitment record.

Staff formerly employed in institutions were freed for reassignment alternatives, a procedure required by civil service law. For workers accustomed to custodial treatment, regionalization offered the first chance at diversified work with youth. Some staff felt threatened by the change and uncomfortable with new methods. Some staff from institutional days remain hostile and resistant to the reform.

The shift to purchase of care in a regional structure can greatly reduce the number of direct employees for the department's successful operation. Present plans call for a reduction in departmental employees of fifty workers, or 50 percent, which would represent a savings of about $4 million. This money would be available for purchase of service care directly beneficial to the youth under the department's authority.

The New Alternatives.   Approximately 1,200 youths are committed each year to the care of the department. This figure fluctuates, and is declining in the face of increased court referrals (referrals put the child in the temporary care of the court, but do not result in the stigmatizing "criminal record" attached to commitment). Presently, department committed and referred youth occupy the following placements: 500 are in group homes; 190 are in foster homes; 150 are in specialized residential placements (private schools, private psychiatric hospitals, etc); 600 participate in some day-care program, which may be educational, recreational, or involve individual or family counseling.

The department contends that no more than 5 percent of the youth placed in its care required secure surroundings. For those youth who do require high security, the department purchases services from a private organization that occupies one of the old detention buildings owned by the state. This program treats approximately thirty-five to forty youth at any one time.

In detention (youth awaiting trial), the department has greatly reduced populations within closed facilities, and aims to eliminate closed detention for all but the most severely disturbed. Historically, within this state and others, the detention period within large institutions has provided a dangerous "crime school" period in which children mildly charged have been confined with the severely disturbed. Moreover, children have been confined away from their families and home communities for lengthy periods.

The department has developed shelter-care detention facilities, structured much like small group homes, which support detained youth pending trial and assist in pretrial casework investigations. Neighborhood YMCA facilities have donated their physical resources jointly with department personnel to establish local detention programs. And foster homes have been contracted to provide spaces for a certain percentage of detention youth. All these services have been established regionally according to need, and many face expansion in the future. As of January 1973, the department operates ten shelter-care detention facilities, cooperates with five local "Y" programs, and uses twenty-one foster placements for detention. It should be noted that with the cooperation of the courts and court liaison personnel, some youth are sent home as an alternative to what in the past would have been closed detention.

For those youth who need residential care, possibilities include short-term group homes (three to four months), long-term group homes (one to two years), drug halfway houses, foster homes, private boarding schools, and intensive private psychiatric hospitals. Many youth do not need residential programs but can function successfully with the day-care counseling and support. Others need only jobs or job training, or special educational help.

Group homes provide the largest share of residential treatment. With few exceptions, they offer group and individual therapy, and a limited number supply family and casework therapy. All group homes offer an educational program in some form. A large portion operate their own on-grounds schools with private tutorial assistance. The remainder utilize existing schools in the community with or without providing private tutorial assistance. Vocational training and employment is emphasized in some.

The thirteen LEAA (Law Enforcement Assistance Administration) funded group homes comprise a separate category of short-term care. All have some form of group, individual, or family therapy. All emphasize education and provide individualized tutorial assistance. While some operate schools on their own grounds, other use local schools. All provide some form of recreational program.

Group homes often specialize in particular problems, and are contracted for particular children. Twenty-seven group facilities specialize in emotionally disturbed youth across a wide range, from mild disturbances to severe emotional disturbances and character disorders. Seven group homes specialize in mentally retarded youngsters, and fourteen specialize in drug rehabilitation. In the latter category, treatment modalities range from the Synanon treatment model to "primal scream" therapy. Nearly all the drug therapy programs provide either individual, group, or family therapy. Fourteen residential schools and academies are used for the specially academically talented youth in the department. Three homes provide services for girls whose needs may include support during pregnancy, and placements are arranged with the American School for the Deaf and The Devereaux School for the handicapped and multihandicapped.

From May 1972, the number of foster home placements used by the department more than doubled, from 85 to 189 homes. This increase reflected not only the department's overall intention to expand foster placements, but was partly a function of several new uses of foster care treatment. Under the Equal Employment Act (federal funding), the department hired eighteen persons to make their homes available with foster care for both committed and detained youth; 21 foster homes have been developed for youth awaiting trial, as an alternative to closed detention.

Nonresidential placements, as of October 1972, served 616 youth across the state. These services vary from community college educational programs to intensive counseling, and may occupy from a few hours to an entire day, one or more days per week. Some of the programs are intensive summer programs that provide follow-up work once the children are back in the regular public school session. Examples of the programs utilized include Neighborhood Youth Corps, Catholic Charities, local drug councils, and others. One of the most successful programs purchased by the department is the Community Aftercare Program, a private nonprofit corporation that provides counseling and activities directed by university student volunteers. This program is particularly active in the metropolitan areas where there is a large resource of university students, and many needy urban children.

Future Directions.   The department, in eliminating training schools in Massachusetts, deliberately *eliminated* its own function as a "correction" agency. Central now to the department's function is the concept that *"delinquent" children are children in need of services.*

The department's planning unit anticipates that the number of youth committed to the department in 1973 will remain at about the same level—approximately one thousand youth—primarily as a result of our efforts to divert youth through court liaison officers, using LEAA funds to implement court-based diversion and referral. The department projects that the number of youth referred to DYS will increase from about 350 in 1972 to 900 in 1973.

The number of youth discharged from DYS is projected to remain about the same as in 1972, reflecting the new department policy to keep youth on an inactive list, rather than discharging them. (This retains departmental jurisdiction over the youth to age twenty-one.)

The current "mix" of placement resources faces expansion in the area of intensive, foster and day-care programs: secure detention and group care resources are expected to be decreased; and forestry, shelter care, and foster care detention will remain at their current levels. The program mix will broaden the types of services available but stay within the fiscal constraints imposed by the state. (Department's projected 1973 budget for purchased services totals $8,347,000.)[3]

Recommended Treatment of the Sociopath

The aggressive sociopath is dangerous, and society requires protection from his violent behavior. No successful method has been developed for treating him in the community. Including the sociopath in the programs of community treatment centers weakens the effectiveness of such programs with other persons. The sociopath does not usually succeed on probation or parole, and placing such a person under supervision takes up valuable time of the probation officers and parole agents that could be better spent with children who need guidance and help and who can benefit by treatment. The sociopath presents similar problems in other correctional institutions.

For correctional institutions to become therapeutic communities, the sociopaths must be removed. The conclusion arrived at by most correctional people and professionals, based on years of experience, is that the sociopath is untreatable in a correctional facility. Furthermore, his presence in the correctional institution interferes with the treatment of other prisoners. We concur with these conclusions. There is evidence that a specialized hospital for sociopaths has been moderately successful in Wales. Changes in behavior of sociopaths have also been reported as having occurred in the therapeutic milieu provided by Wiltwyck and Synanon. We therefore recommend that the sociopath be referred to:

1. Synanon or a Synanon-type institution, providing the sociopath volunteers to go to such an institution and the institution agrees to accept him. The facilities at Synanon could be greatly expanded and others established in large population centers at relatively little cost. Persons with years of experience at Synanon would be available to establish and administer such facilities. Persons who are considered too dan-

---

[3]Yitzhak Bakal, "The Massachusetts Experience," *Delinquency Prevention Reporter* 3(April 1973):1–5.

gerous to go to Synanon or are not acceptable to Synanon would be directed to a hospital for sociopaths.

2. For the very young sociopath, a milieu therapy setting such as Wilt-wyck.

3. Hospitals specifically designed to treat the sociopath. The Welsh hospital previously mentioned might be used as a model, with modifications introduced and researched.

The removal of the sociopath from the correctional facility would make it more feasible to emphasize either (*a*) work-release programs with prisoners employed for reasonable wages in the community, or (*b*) educational release programs with prisoners attending vocational schools, colleges, or on-the-job training programs in the community. The modern correctional institution would then become a residence for delinquents to which they would return at night for treatment under the supervision of highly trained correctional personnel. Reformatories and state training schools would be phased out of existence, as they were in Massachusetts.

Amnesty upon Completion of Sentence

When an offender—adolescent or adult—has successfully completed his "sentence," whether in an institution or on probation or parole, he should be considered to have "paid his debt to society." Arrest records, conviction records, court records, and prison records handicap an individual when he seeks legitimate employment. Arrest and conviction records often stigmatize people for the rest of their lives, hamper efforts at rehabilitation, and reinforce criminality.

If a youth sentenced to probation were assured at the outset that upon satisfactory completion of his sentence all records of his arrest and conviction would be unavailable to anyone outside of law-enforcement agencies, and that he would then be free of any stigma, many individuals would be greatly encouraged to cooperate fully in their programs of rehabilitation. For the individual who has served a sentence at a state prison and is released on parole, the prospect of complete clearance upon satisfactory completion of parole would seem to be a tremendous incentive. It might also tend to reduce conflict in the institution.

The sentence imposed by a court is not the only punishment an individual suffers upon conviction of a felony. There are all sorts of subtle and not so subtle sanctions imposed, some by law, and some resulting from the application of informal sanctions. Those later convicted may be denied licenses to drive automobiles, trucks, or taxicabs, licenses needed by many to earn their livelihood. They may be denied local licenses required by some cities for those who wish to engage in business. They may be denied passports and security clearances required for certain types of employment. All of the above-mentioned formal sanctions are imposed by federal, state, or local laws *in addition to the sentence to confinement.*

Added to these are a number of informal sanctions, "unwritten penalites" imposed by society on the person convicted. He may be charged higher premiums on automobile insurance as an "assigned risk" and, in some instances, be denied insurance entirely. Bonding companies may refuse to bond him. Credit bureaus, listing his conviction, seriously injure his chances of getting credit. What is even more disastrous, potential employers may refuse to hire him because of his record of delinquency.

Persons who are arrested and not convicted also suffer as a result of the maintenance of arrest records by the FBI and by local police agencies. These records are often available to prospective employers and provide the basis for denial of jobs, credit, and other privileges. To maintain such records and to release them under any conditions is a serious infringement on the rights of an individual to the presumption of innocence.

Law-enforcement officials logically maintain that a record of previous offenders is useful for tracking down criminals. The legitimate law-enforcement objectives of the police could be served by permitting the maintenance of a classified file that would not be available to anyone under any circumstances except to a police agency for use in investigating criminal activity. No one could be required to state whether he had a record of arrest when applying for a job, and the police would be forbidden by law from supplying any record of arrest or conviction.

Approximately half the people in lower socioeconomic groups who live in ghettos have arrest records, and a considerable number have records of conviction. If the police continue to make arrests at the present rate and if the criminal codes continue to be used as they are at the present time, we may soon find that a majority of people, particularly poor people, have arrest records. When this happens, the deterrent effect of the criminal law will become even less than it is now. We must remove these records from public availability and give people a new start. It is with this in mind that we recommend amnesty for all offenders upon completion of their legal sentences.

All of these recommendations are directed at reducing the punitive emphasis in the administration of justice and allowing us to advance toward the goal of real rehabilitation. Increasingly repressive measures have not been successful. Reintegrating and properly socializing potential and apparent offenders into the community seems to constitute the most logical direction for an effective correctional approach. Increasing the involvement of people in the larger society and strengthening their commitment to its normative patterns appear to be the most valid ways of ultimately minimizing crime and delinquency.

Name Index

Subject Index